A Source Book
for the Study of
Personality
and Politics

DATE DUE

ILL#2230893	5/27/98

A Source Book for the Study of Personality and Politics

edited by

FRED I. GREENSTEIN
Wesleyan University

MICHAEL LERNER
Yale University

Markham Publishing Company / Chicago

MARKHAM POLITICAL SCIENCE SERIES
Aaron Wildavsky, Editor

Copyright © 1971 by Markham Publishing Company
All Rights Reserved
Printed in U.S.A.
Library of Congress Catalog Card Number: 79-136623
Standard Book Number: 8410-3014-6

To Harold D. Lasswell

Contributors

James David Barber
Yale University
Reinhard Bendix
University of California, Berkeley
Rufus P. Browning
Michigan State University
Robert Coles, M.D.
Cambridge, Massachusetts
Philip E. Converse
University of Michigan
Giuseppe Di Palma
University of California, Berkeley
Georges Dupeux
University of Bordeaux
Erik H. Erikson
Harvard University
Richard Flacks
University of California,
Santa Barbara
Alexander L. George
Stanford University
Fred I. Greenstein
Wesleyan University
Alex Inkeles
Stanford University
Herbert Jacob
Northwestern University
Irving Janis
Yale University
Daniel Katz
University of Michigan
Robert E. Lane
Yale University

Harold D. Lasswell
Yale University, Emeritus
City University of New York
Robert S. Liebert, M.D.
New York, New York
Daniel J. Levinson
Yale University
Herbert McClosky
University of California, Berkeley
Stanley Milgram
City University of New York
Robert E. Osgood
Johns Hopkins University
Talcott Parsons
Harvard University
Brent M. Rutherford
University of Oregon
Nevitt Sanford
The Wright Institute
Berkeley, California
Edward A. Shils
University of Chicago
Peterhouse, Cambridge
University
M. Brewster Smith
University of California, Santa Cruz
Robert C. Tucker
Princeton University
Edwin A. Weinstein
Albert Einstein Medical School
Yeshiva University
Frederick Wyatt
University of Michigan

Introductory Remarks

Four decades have passed since Harold Lasswell set forth the first systematic discussion of the importance of learning how political life is affected by the personal lives and psyches of political actors. Lasswell asked the following rhetorical questions:

Can we conceive the development of the human personality as a functioning whole, and discern the turning-points in the typical subjective histories of typical public characters? Can we place this subjective history in relation to the physical and cultural factors which were developmentally significant? [Finally, can we employ such knowledge of personality and politics to] deepen our understanding of the whole social and political order?[1]

This volume contains answers to Lasswell's questions. We have assembled a collection of what we consider to have been among the most seminal—or potentially seminal—writings in the literature on personality and politics. In doing so, we hope to provide the small but persistent band of political personality investigators (in several disciplines) with the first available source book of basic writings in their field and to show that there is a "critical mass" in the making in political personality studies.

In spite of the notorious difficulties of building a solid base of knowledge in this theoretically and methodologically bedeviled realm, the prima facie importance of the connections between personal psychology and political life has encouraged at least a few members of each new scholarly generation to pursue the issues Lasswell felt were so deserving of attention. Slowly, imperfectly, and certainly not in the precise form Lasswell would have envisaged in 1930, a cumulative personality-and-politics literature has begun to emerge. And, while social science has never found its Newton (and probably never will), personality-and-politics studies have profited from the gradual increase in appreciation of the complex requirements involved in producing work that is adequately conceived, intelligently grounded in theory, and methodologically sound.

There is a paradoxical reason for believing that political personality inquiry is at the threshold of becoming a progressively developing field of inquiry. Several of the more promising findings and formulations that have been reported were worked out more or less in isolation from each other. When diverse investigators converge spontaneously with complementary approaches and conclusions, one is led to suspect (although not to conclude on this basis alone) that they are "on to something." There is no special virtue in continuing the lack of communication, however. Another of our purposes in compiling this volume is to contribute to the rise of a more explicitly integrated community of intellectual interest.

Part One of this source book consists of general theoretical and methodological statements about personality-and-politics research. The methodological papers are mainly methodological at the conceptual level. The admittedly crucial "nuts and bolts" psychometric problems of testing and measurement receive little emphasis, either in Part One or in the three parts that follow. There are several reasons why we have chosen not to focus on measurement mechanics. First, our assumption is that satisfactory operationalization, measurement, and hypothesis testing must flow from satisfactory conceptualization: from knowing what should or should not *in principle* be expected from empirical analyses of specific sets of personality-and-politics problems. Given clear conceptualization and interesting, theoretically based substantive questions, the measurement technology will follow readily, if not easily. Second, the existing measurements literature is too complex and varied to represent adequately in the space at our disposal here. Moreover, an emphasis on the measurement questions that have actually arisen in research on personality and politics—for example, the seemingly endlessly drawn-out exchanges over artifacts in psychometric tests for "authoritarianism"—would lead to an imbalance in our selections. There is little or no measurements literature on some important questions and a great deal of inconclusive work on other less important questions. The problems of measurement call for a sustained independent discussion—and possibly another compendium.[2]

Following the contributions on general theoretical and methodological considerations assembled in Part One are three parts dealing, respectively, with: (1) *analysis of individual political actors;* (2) *typological analysis* of classes of political actors; and (3) analysis of how individuals and types *aggregate* into the complex social processes that comprise politics. We are, of course, aware that any single selection may, in fact, include two or all three of these general analytic issues; the principle of organization is a rough sorting device, not a bed of Procusteous.

Since our trinitarian division is the principle of organization used in Greenstein's *Personality and Politics: Problems of Evidence, Inference, and Conceptualization,*[3] a note on the relationship between that work and the present source book is in order. The two are intended to stand independently, but to be complementary. Most of the articles discussed in some detail at turning points in the argument of *Personality and Politics* are reprinted here, but some of the concerns of that work do not arise in the source book and some of the issues that will emerge in the pages to follow were not considered or were only alluded to in *Personality and Politics.* In short, depending upon his needs and interests, the reader may find it useful to draw on either or both work, in whole or in part. Considered together, the two works provide a foundation for a course in personality and politics. They do not, however, provide the raw materials for a comprehensive course on *all* aspects of political psychology. Indeed, a curriculum, rather than a course, would be needed for that task since political behavior is inevitably influenced, if only indirectly, by the entire range of issues that concern the complex discipline of psychology and the cognate fields of psychiatry, psychoanalysis, psychological anthropology, etc. The point where "personality psychology" leaves off and developmental psychology, the study of attitudes, perception, motivation, cognition, and all the other issues of the psychology curriculum, begins is by no means clear. Nevertheless, the selections chosen for this anthology do not, by and large, suffer from excessive boundary diffuseness, as a glance at the Table of Contents should demonstrate.

A note on criteria for inclusion and exclusion of contributions: our overriding concern has been to assemble a reasonably self-contained work, emphasizing contributions that are *basic,* not in the sense of being definitive, but rather in the sense of raising fundamental issues. The field of personality-and-politics study, even though it is beginning to take on substantial form, is emphatically not one to which a few, simple rules of investigative procedure can be applied. The human stuff of politics manifests itself in indirect, often complex ways. Considerable theoretical sophistication is necessary for conducting satisfactory inquiry. We believe that the selections contained in this source book can help provide that sophistication. We have sought to assemble writings that can be read and reread—that are likely to continue to be provocative over the years. In doing so we have in mind not only the instructor attempting to find materials for a personality-and-politics seminar, but also the graduate student or advanced scholar embarked on a program of self-education in preparation of conducting his own personality-and-politics research.

The final selection in this volume, a chapter from Lasswell's *Psychopathology and Politics* which happens to serve our purposes especially well, is the only contribution which is a passage from a larger discussion rather than a self-contained writing. We have chosen to use articles and other short writings because they are more likely to stand independently than are chapters taken out of context from book-length presentations and because they often are less readily accessible to the reader who does not have a major library at his disposal. Nothing is deleted from the text or notes of the works reprinted, although we have taken advantage of authors' second thought expansions and modifications of their writings, indicating where we have done so. We are indebted to Professor Alexander George for permission to publish a hitherto unpublished essay on psychological biography which, in its unpublished published form has long been recognized as one of the clearest statements on the topic.

The selections are introduced with prefatory remarks by the editors. These range from a few words to a short essay. Our purpose is to suggest relationships among the various writings and to signal to the reader implications that might otherwise not have occurred to him. Where we have reprinted a work that is complex and not easily followed by the lay reader—for example, Lasswell's essay on typologies and Smith's report on the use of "authoritarianism" measures in a study of Peace Corps workers—we actually present a précis of the selection, on the assumption that the redundancy would enhance understanding. Naturally, the authors are not to be held responsible for our interpretations of their work.

We are indebted to the authors and their publishers for their permission to bring these works together. Above all, we are indebted to the student of personality and politics whose words we quoted at the beginning of this introduction. We trust that another forty years will not have to pass before the challenge he posed begins to be adequately met.

Notes

[1] Harold D. Lasswell, *Psychopathology and Politics* (Chicago: University of Chicago Press, 1930); reprinted in *Political Writings of Harold D. Lasswell* (Glencoe, Ill.: Free Press, 1951) and in paperback with "Afterthoughts Thirty Years Later" (New York: Viking Press, 1960), pp. 9–10.

[2] For a valuable introduction to personality measurement, see Allen L. Edwards, *The Measurement of Personality Traits by Scales and Inventories* (New York: Holt, Rinehart and Winston, 1970).

[3] Fred I. Greenstein, *Personality and Politics: Problems of Evidence, Inference and Conceptualization* (Chicago: Markham, 1969).

Contents

PART ONE

Theoretical and Methodological Considerations

1

An Initial Overview

This is the first and most overarching of the four essays on theoretical and methodological aspects of the study of personality and politics that introduce this reader. The essay begins with remarks on the connections among the intellectual disciplines of psychology, sociology, and political science, then narrows its focus to the subdiscipline of personality-and-politics inquiry. After a discussion of the need for systematic study of personality and politics (Section I) and of the reasons why a satisfactorily systematic literature has failed to develop (Section II), the essay sets forth a brief inventory of key conceptual distinctions that appear to be necessary for conducting inquiries in a manner that takes account of the complex relationships that often exist between aspects of personality and political behavior (Section III). The conceptual distinctions summarized in this essay are further elaborated in M. Brewster Smith's "A Map for the Analysis of Personality and Politics," an analytic discussion that appears as the second of the introductory essays on theory and methodology (p. 34); thus, this essay also serves as an introduction to the selection that follows it.

Section IV deals with whether and under what circumstances different kinds of personality variables ought *in principle* to be expected to influence political behavior. A penultimate section (V) preceding the summary and conclusions states some of the issues and problems hedging the three kinds of personality-and-politics investigations that are assembled in the second, third, and final parts of the reader: analyses of individual actors, typological analyses, and analyses of the aggregate effect of individuals and types of individuals on the functioning of political institutions.

THE STUDY OF PERSONALITY AND POLITICS: OVERALL CONSIDERATIONS

Fred I. Greenstein

From a perspective of Olympian abstraction it is possible, if somewhat empty, to set forth the following account of the relationship between psychology and political science. Let us think not in terms of the extremely varied activities that scholars with different guild memberships actually engage in, but rather in terms of what the general purposes and preoccupations of the disciplines seem to be.

Psychology, like sociology, evidently aspires to advance general propositions about human behavior. There seem to be two axes along which these basic disciplines divide Gaul: (1) Psychology, as Inkeles puts it, deals with the personal system, sociology with the social system.[1] (2) Psychology is concerned with those determinants of behavior that arise from within individuals, sociology with the effects of the environment, especially the human environment, on individuals' behavior. By this showing, the interests of psychology and sociology are mutually exclusive and exhaustive. Political science (like economics) then proves to be a subdivision of the two basic disciplines, specializing in behavior occurring in the polity, an institution of such great substantive importance and interest that it calls forth the intensive attention of a large community of investigators. It follows that all valid propositions from psychology and sociology may prove to be relevant to political science and other institution-specific social sciences, and that, as Simon says of economics, any "verified generalizations about human" political "behavior must have a place in the more general theories of human behavior to which psychology and sociology aspire."[2]

Suppose, however, that we shift from analytical ideal types to actual disciplines. We promptly discover, of course, that there are few if any "pure" sociologists or psychologists who meet our abstract disciplinary definitional criteria, even though the criteria *do* suggest the centers of gravity of interests in these fields. Real-world sociologists often study individuals and intrapsychic variables (e.g. attitudes). Real-world psychologists are interested in groups and (as the ubiquity of the term "stimulus" makes clear) the environment.

The abstract conception of political science's relation to the two general disciplines also fails to withstand contact with reality. We all know of the lack of integration of political science with psychology and sociology, as well as the heterogeneity of approach within all three fields. Therefore, although from the Olympian vantage point we can see the possibility for integrating a large number of the major concerns of psychology with those of political science (learning, perception, cognition, motivation, to name a few standard problem areas of psychology—all have im-

This essay is a much-condensed version of the argument in Greenstein's *Personality and Politics: Problems of Evidence, Inference, and Conceptualization* (Chicago: Markham, 1969). The essay, which was published in *American Behavioral Scientist,* 11 (November, 1967), 38–53, is here retitled for the purposes of introducing this reader. The original title was the same as that of the later book. A final point of bibliographical minutia: the essay was later somewhat revised and it is the revised version (with a few additional changes) that appears here. The revision was published in Seymour M. Lipset ed., *Politics and the Social Sciences* (New York: Oxford University Press, 1969), 163–206.

portant manifestations in politics), at the terrestrial level the bridges between the two fields are few and difficult to build. In fact, for reasons I shall suggest below, as political science has begun to reach out to other disciplines, the connections with sociology have been much richer and more rewarding than those with psychology (whether the academic psychologies, the various clinical psychologies, or the various psychological approaches to anthropology).

For the remainder of this essay, I shall consider ways in which the study of politics can draw upon simply one of the concerns of psychology—personality. "Personality and politics" is perhaps the area in which the greatest number of self-conscious efforts have been made to connect the two disciplines. And, interestingly, it is an area of inquiry that is notoriously vexed and controversial in its methodological and conceptual status. Although personality and politics writings have appeared with some persistence for several decades, the work in this area has not gained the confidence of the great bulk of practitioners in the parent disciplines, and has been limited in its influence.

This then is a highly selective and rather idiosyncratic traveler's report on the "personality and politics" literature, drawing on, synthesizing, and reconstructing various portions of it, on the basis of my reading of many such studies and a variety of cognate literature.[3] I shall make a number of conceptual distinctions and observations about research strategy. My purpose is to help place this controversial, methodologically gnarled literature on a firmer evidential and inferential basis.

An initial indicator of the messy state of affairs is the difficulty psychologists have had in defining the key term "personality." A standard discussion by Allport lists a full 50 *types* of definitions. For the present purposes, rather than offering still another detailed stipulative definition of "personality," it will be better simply to note typical research and theorizing that falls under the "personality and politics" rubric, and then make a few general remarks about the different meanings this term has had in the literature I am discussing.[4]

Much of the personality and politics literature can be grouped into three rough categories: psychological *case histories of single political* actors, psychological studies of *types of political actors,* and *aggregative* accounts of the collective effects of the distribution of individual political actors and types of actors on the functioning of political institutions (ranging from face-to-face groups through interaction among nations).

The case study literature includes "in-depth" studies of members of the general population by investigators such as Lane[5] and Smith, Bruner, and White.[6] It also includes psychological biographies of public figures.[7] I am using "typological" to refer to all classifications of political actors in psychological terms—ranging from the mere classification of an aggregate population in terms of the categories of some variable, through complex typologies identifying syndromes of interrelated attributes.

The best known and best developed (and possibly most controversial) of the typological literatures is that on "authoritarianism." [8] Other politically relevant categorizations are in terms of "dogmatism" (Rokeach),[9] "misanthropy" (Rosenberg),[10] "Machiavellianism" (Christie),[11] "tradition-inner-other directedness" (Riesman),[12] as well as the various psychological classifications of actual political role incumbents, such as Lasswell's agitator-administrator-theorist classification[13] and Barber's spectator-advertiser-reluctant-lawmaker.[14] Finally, aggregative accounts of personality and politics are the most vexed and controversial of all: here, for example, we find the very extensive corpus of writings on "national character" and the numerous speculations connecting intrapersonal emotional "tension" with conflict among nations.[15]

It is, as my reluctance to offer a formal definition suggests, difficult to pin down with any precision what the term "personality" means when it is used to summarize these various enterprises. And, in fact, later when we consider the various objections to personality explanations of politics, we shall see that the term has had a number of quite different referents. Very generally, it is clear that students of "personality and politics" are interested in discovering how the human "stuff" of politics affects the conduct of politics—the political consequences of what we are like and how we function as human beings, of individual similarities and differences. This suggests an interest in psychology that goes deeper than the usual rather "thin" use of psychological categories and evidence to characterize the goals of political actors and their cognitive maps. However, a large number of the issues that arise in attempting to clarify the tasks of students of personality and politics relate more generally to the use of any kind of psychological evidence in political analysis. Therefore, I shall by and large use such phrases as "personality and politics" and "political psychology" interchangeably, except at those points (for example in Section III) where there is a specific reason to make distinctions.

To a considerable extent, what makes the personality and politics literature controversial is precisely what makes it intriguing. Much of the extant work has direct or indirect roots in the still empirically problematic theories of psychoanalysis. Psychoanalytic hypotheses, especially those drawing upon the central notions of repression and ego defense, have the merit of offering nonobvious explanations of behavior that otherwise seems obscure and inexplicable, and especially of much of the "irrationality" and emotionalism that abounds in politics. The disadvantages of these explanations are suggested by the large volume of polemical and clarificatory literature on psychoanalysis that pours out.[16] Given the substantial continuing skepticism toward the basic theories and concepts of psychoanalysis, "applied" literatures taking these notions for granted are bound also to be skeptically received.

As a consequence, anyone interested in helping to organize and reconstruct the problems raised in the personality and politics literature is bound to find himself discussing problems that fall under the heading of ego defense. In suggesting methodological standards for this literature, we encounter questions about (for example) how to distinguish political behavior which has ego-defensive sources from the large quantity of political behavior (including "irrational" political behavior) that is plainly *not* ego-defensive in its sources, and how to make it possible for assertions about ego defensiveness to be consensually validated even in the absence of general agreement on theories and vocabularies such as those of psychoanalysis.

Section I of this essay deals with the need for a systematic personality and politics literature. Section II discusses the reasons why such a literature has not developed, elaborating further on the empirical and methodological difficulties that have bedeviled existing research, and noting a series of formal objections that sometimes have been advanced, denying the usefulness *in principle* of personality and politics research. Section III summarizes a rudimentary conceptual framework providing various distinctions relevant for analyzing personality and politics. Section IV employs the framework to show that the formal objections to personality and politics study, while lacking force as general objections, prove on analysis to point to a variety of useful substantive and methodological observations about political psychology and how it may be fruitfully studied.

In Section V, I offer a very brief and selective series of procedural suggestions about psychological case studies of single actors, typological studies, and aggregative research. For the single-case observations, I take my examples from what is generally recognized to be one of the most satisfactory of the psychological biographies, Alexander and Juliette George's *Woodrow Wilson and Colonel House: A Personality Study*. For the typological discussion, I shall draw mainly on the authoritarianism literature. My remarks on aggregation will be mainly schematic and monitory.

I. THE NEED FOR SYSTEMATIC STUDY OF POLITICAL PSYCHOLOGY [17]

Fifty-some years ago, Walter Lippmann observed that "to talk about politics without reference to human beings . . . is just the deepest error in our political thinking." [18] That it would be unfortunate to attempt political explanation without attention to the personal psychology of political actors seems on the face of it an unassailable, even a platitudinous, assertion. Such an assertion seems to hold no matter which of the two standard approaches to defining politics we use. We can treat as "political" all of the activities that go on within the formal structures of government, plus the informal, extragovernmental activities impinging upon government, such as political parties, interest groups, political socialization, and political communication. Or we can, in Lasswell's term, define politics "functionally" [19] to refer to some distinctive pattern of behavior that may manifest itself in any of the conventionally designated institutional settings (ranging from families and other face-to-face groups to international interaction). This pattern of behavior might, for example, be the exercise of power and influence, or it might be the processes of negotiation, accommodation, and bargaining that accompany conflict resolution, or it might be "the authoritative allocation of values."

"Politics," by both of these definitional tacks, is a matter of human behavior, and behavior—in the familiar formulation of Lewin and others—is a function of both the environmental situations in which actors find themselves and the personal psychological predispositions they bring to those situations. As Lazarus puts it:

The sources of man's behavior (his observable action) and his subjective experience (such as thoughts, feelings, and wishes) are twofold: the external stimuli that impinge on him and the internal dispositions that result from the interaction between inherited physiological characteristics and experience with the world. When we focus on the former, we note that a person acts in such-and-such a way because of certain qualities in a situation. For example, he attacks a friend because the friend insulted him, or he loses interest in a lecture because the teacher is dull or uninformed, or he fails in his program of study because the necessity of supporting himself through school leaves insufficient time for studying. It is evident that a man's behavior varies greatly from moment to moment, from circumstance to circumstance, changing with the changing conditions to which he is exposed.

Still, even as we recognize the dependency of behavior on outside stimuli, we are also aware that it cannot be accounted for on the basis of the external situation alone, but that in fact it must arise partly from personal characteristics.[20]

It would not be difficult to proliferate examples of political events that were critically dependent upon the personal characteristics of key actors, or of actors in the aggregate. Take Republican politics in 1964. An account of the main determinants of the Republican nomination that year, and of the nature of the subsequent election campaign, would have to include much more than descriptions of the personal characteristics of the party leaders and members. But any account would be incomplete that did not acknowledge the impact of such factors as the willingness of one of the strongest contenders for the nomination to divorce his wife and marry a divorced woman; the indecision of one of the party's elder statesmen; a politically damaging outburst of temper in a news conference (two years earlier) by the man who had been the party's 1960 presidential candidate; the self-defeating political style of the man who received the 1964 nomination (his unwillingness to placate his opponents within the party, his propensity to remind voters of the issues on which he was most vulnerable). Not to mention aggregate psychological phenomena bearing, for example, on the behavior of voters in the Republican primaries of that year and the actions of delegates to the national conventions.

Attempts to explain the outcomes of adversary relationships often place in particularly clear relief the need for psychological data. For example, the overwhelming defeat in 1967 of numerically superior, better equipped Arab armies by Israel quite obviously was a function of gross discrepancies between the levels of skill and motivation of the two sides, both among leaders and subordinates. A further example, which lays out with a rather grim clarity the possible life-or-death policy relevance of reliable knowledge of the inner tendencies of political actors, is provided by the 1962 Cuban missile crisis.

Clearly each phase of the Kennedy Administration's (and the Soviet Union's) strategic decision-making during that confrontation was intimately dependent upon assumptions about the psychological dispositions of the adversary, as can be seen from an exchange of correspondence by several scholars in the *New York Times* shortly after the initial success of Kennedy's blockade in reversing the Soviet missile-bearing ships, but before the withdrawal of the additional missiles that had already been installed in Cuba.[21] One group of correspondents argued that it was of the utmost importance for the Administration not to assert its demands on the Soviet Union in aggressively uncompromising terms. The Russians, their letter suggested, must be provided with face-saving means of acceding to American demands, lest they conclude that they had no recourse but to fight. In reply, another writer (Bernard Brodie, a RAND Corporation strategic theorist) drew on the special theory of the psychology of Communist leadership developed by Nathan Leites in his controversial *A Study of Bolshevism*. For the Communist leader, Leites suggests, it is an imperative that any sign of capitalist weakness be exploited for maximum advantage. But if the Communist advance meets determined resistance by an opponent capable of inflicting serious damage, retreat is not only possible but *necessary*. And to allow oneself to be influenced by considerations of prestige and provocativeness would be the worst kind of sentimentality. Thus the second correspondent, drawing upon diametrically opposed assumptions about the psychology of Soviet leadership, contended that an uncompromising American stance would make it *easier* rather than more difficult for the Russians to give in, and would decrease rather than increase the likelihood that miscalculations would lead to war.[22]

My concern at the moment, of course, is not to offer substantive hypotheses about the psychological questions raised by the foregoing examples, but rather to point out that there is a pressing need for what we presently have very little of:

systematic attention to questions that lie in the overlapping territories of psychology and political science. And the last of my examples should suggest why this need exists in the arena of politics as well as in the literatures of the social sciences.

II. WHY HAS POLITICAL PSYCHOLOGY BEEN SLOW TO DEVELOP?

An answer to why political psychology is not a well-developed field, but rather is in questionable repute, may be found partly in the sociology of inquiry and partly in its vicissitudes. A full account would draw upon the following points:

1. Systematic empirical study of politics has had a rather brief history.

2. For much of this history, political analysis has seemed to proceed in a quite acceptable fashion without making its psychological assumptions explicit. If one is studying "normal" actors in a familiar culture, it is often convenient simply to look at variations in the setting of politics, or merely to deal with the portion of the actor's psychological characteristics that relate to his social position (socioeconomic status, age, and sex, for example).

3. Implicit, common-sense psychological assumptions become less satisfactory when one attempts to explain (a) actors in one's own culture whose behavior deviates from expectations, or (b) actors from a different culture. (An example of the first is Woodrow Wilson's determined unwillingness, under certain circumstances, to follow the American politician's practice of compromising with one's adversaries, as described by George and George;[23] an example of the second is the possible applicability of Leites's theory of Bolshevik leadership to the Cuban missile crisis.) But when the political scientist does sense the importance of making explicit his assumptions about psychological aspects of politics, he is put off by the state of psychology. Rather than finding *a* psychological science on which to draw for insight, he finds a congeries of more or less competing models and frames of reference, with imperfect agreement on the nature of man's inner dispositions, the appropriate terms for characterizing them, and the methodologies for observation.

4. If the political scientist persists in his determination to make systematic use of psychology, he is likely to experience further discouragement. Much of the research and theory he encounters will seem singularly irrelevant to explaining the kind of complex behavior which interests him. And where psychological writers do address themselves to his subject matter, their political observations often seem naive and uninformed. Psychologists' insights seem irrelevant to political scientists, for the good reason that many psychologists do not conceive of their science as one which *should* attempt to explain concrete instances of social behavior, but rather as a means of understanding general principles underlying that behavior. A deliberate attempt is made, as one psychologist puts it, to treat psychology as "socially indifferent"—to strip away the elements that are specific, say, to behavior on a congressional committee, or at a political party convention.

When colleagues in other disciplines (mainly sociology, anthropology, political science, and economics) turn to psychology for help they are disappointed, and, indeed, often aggrieved. What they begin to read with enthusiasm they put down with depression. What seemed promising turns out to be sterile, palpably trivial, or false and, in any case, a waste of time. . . . Psychologists do study and must study things and activities possessing social content. There is no other way. . . . It is only that psychology has been a science that abstracts out of all these content-characterized behaviors the concepts which form the jargons of its subdisciplines. . . .

The writer goes on to suggest why it is that when psychologists *do* pronounce on problems of politics and society, their observations so often strike politically knowledgeable readers as dubious.

I am impressed with how naive and conventional my colleagues [in psychology] and I are when confronted with most social phenomena. We are ignorant of the historical dimensions of most social activity, we do not see the complex interweaving of institutions and arrangements. . . . In general, psychologists tend to be like laymen when they confront social phenomena, particularly those that involve large scale patterns. And the reason for all of this is that the main areas of social activity are only the *place* where psychologists study interesting sorts of things, rather than being the *focus of inquiry*.[24]

5. A final, and perhaps the most important, deterrent to a systematic political psychology has paradoxically been that a literature already existed—namely, the confused, confusing tangle of research, theory, and controversy on "personality and politics." Objections have been raised to this literature on empirical, on methodological, and on what might be called formal grounds.

Empirically, critics have pointed to the weakness and instability of the correlations that have been reported between various measures of personality and politics, for example, in the "trait correlation" studies of the 1930s, which sought to relate personality scales to attitude scales.[25] The failure to find relationships has suggested to many observers that the relationships are not there to be found, even under more favorable observational conditions.

In the instance of single-case psychological analysis, the empirical and the methodological difficulties are inseparable. For example, it has been pointed out that psychological biographies of political figures and, in general, case histories of single individuals, often seem to be arbitrary in their interpretations, incapable of replication, and more disposed to catalogue personal pathology than to illuminate adaptation. Quantitative, typological studies based on questionnaire data have encountered formidable difficulties in developing reliable and valid measures of personality and its political correlates, an example being the problems of response-set artifact which plagued the authoritarian personality studies of the 1950s.[26] And attempts at psychological explanation of aggregate phenomena—"national character," "international tensions," the functioning of various political institutions—have been most controversial of all. The standard label for the fallacy of explaining (say) Germany in terms of the typical German is "reductionism." [27] All three types of studies have seemed insensitive to historical and social determinants of political behavior.

In addition to the various empirical and methodological objections to personality and politics studies, there have been a number of suggestions that such investigation is *in principle* not promising. These formal objections are of great interest, because on careful examination they do not seem to provide valid reasons for avoiding the study of personality and politics, yet, nevertheless, they point to important insights for investigators in this area. The objections are susceptible of being rephrased positively in ways that help clarify the tasks that can be usefully performed by students of personality (in several senses of the term) and politics. These objections are most conveniently listed in detail after introducing a rudimentary frame of reference consisting of a schematic statement of the types of variables that are likely to be relevant to personality and politics research, and the ways these variables interact. They are formal objections to the study of personality and politics based on the allegedly greater explanatory power of "social characteristics" over "personality characteristics," the relative impact of "situation" and personality, the significance of ego-defensiveness in everyday action, and the impact of individual actors on events.

III. CONCEPTUAL DISTINCTIONS RELEVANT TO ANALYZING PERSONALITY AND POLITICS: A "MAP"

The frame of reference I want now briefly to present is more fully developed in M. Brewster Smith's lucid essay, "A Map for the Analysis of Personality and Politics," which is reprinted as the second chapter of this reader.[28] Smith's map is summarized in his Figure 4 (p. 42). His essay and the figure summarizing serve essentially as a heuristic device for reminding us of the complex interdependency of different classes of social and psychological determinants of political (and other) behavior. While Smith's statement introduces little that is new, it economically lays out a number of familiar distinctions that are of great importance, with due attention to the complexity of their contextual connections.

The summary figure graphically reminds us that political behavior (panel V of Figure 4) results, directly or indirectly, from the interaction of psychological variables with three classes of social variables: (1) the immediate situation (panel IV) within which the behavior occurs, (2) the immediate social environment (panel II) extending from birth through adult life, within which the actor's personality develops and his attitudes form, and (3) the "distal" social environment (panel I) which the individual does not experience directly, but which shapes his immediate environment (the distal environment includes the overarching features of the contemporary social and political system, and the historical antecedents of these features). And the map indicates the reciprocal effect of behavior on its psychological and social determinants.

Within the central psychological portion of his map (panel III), Smith outlines a conceptualization of personality expanded from his work with Bruner and White on the "functions" of opinions.[29] He makes the analytic distinction between attitudes and the ordinarily more enduring and deeply-rooted personality processes in which attitudes have their bases. It is the interaction of attitudes and situational stimuli that one looks at first, in order to explain behavior. But to understand the conditions of attitude formation, arousal, stability, and change, one must turn to the underlying personality processes.

One fundamental personality process (or structure) which may be more or less well-developed in any individual is specialized toward screening reality and assessing and adapting to the environment. To the degree that an attitude, say an importer's belief in the desirability of low tariffs, has its basis in the need to establish such means-ends relationships, it is said to serve the function of *object appraisal*.

A second fundamental personality process (again, one which varies in its importance from individual to individual) serves to cope with and respond to internal conflict, especially the deeper, anxiety-producing conflicts that have their source in the repression of unacceptable primitive desires and impulses. When an attitude[30] is influenced by the need to accommodate to inner conflict—when it "externalizes" these internal tensions—it is said to serve the function of ego defense. The relationships between inner needs and such attitudes may run the gamut of mechanisms of defense—projections, displacement, splitting, etc.

A third set of processes that may influence political attitudes consists of the various and ubiquitous psychological tendencies toward identification with others and toward orientation of the self to reference groups and examplars. To the degree that attitudes and behavior result from needs to be like or unlike significant others in one's immediate or distant environment, the function of *mediation of self-other relations* (referred to less aptly in *Opinions and Personality* as "social adjustment") is being performed.[31] Any single attitude or item of behavior might, in psycho-analytic jargon, be "over-determined," having its basis in more than one of these processes. But frequently it is possible to say that a particular attitude serves one or another predominant function for an individual. And if the same attitude has a different functional basis for different individuals, the same technique will not be appropriate to arouse, reinforce, or change the attitude.[32]

As partial as this summary is, it helps clarify a number of the formal objections to the study of personality and politics, some of which result from the slipperiness of the basic vocabulary for discussing these problems, and others from the complexity of the phenomena themselves—the kinds of variables that need to be observed, the difficulty of measuring them, and the intricacy of their interconnections.

IV. THE POSITIVE IMPLICATIONS OF CERTAIN OBJECTIONS TO THE STUDY OF PERSONALITY AND POLITICS

I begin with an objection that is clarified by the sharp distinction Smith makes between personality and its social antecedents (panels III and II of Figure 4), move on to an objection that bears on the interconnections among personality processes and dispositions (panel III), situations (panel IV), and behavior (panel V); then consider an objection to which the distinctions among types of personality processes (panel III) is relevant; and conclude with two objections that prove on examination not to be addressed to psychological issues at all.

"Social Characteristics" Versus "Personality Characteristics"

One standard objection to the study of personality and politics which we can clarify by referring to Smith's map runs as follows:

> Personality characteristics of individuals are less important than their social characteristics in influencing behavior. This makes it unpromising to concentrate research energies on studying the impact of personality.[33]

This appears to be an objection posing a pseudo-problem that needs to be dissolved conceptually, rather than resolved empirically. Consider the referents of "social characteristics" and "personality characteristics." By the latter we refer to inner dispositions of the individual (panel III). The term "characteristic" indicates a state of the organism. By the former, however, we usually have in mind ways of characterizing the individual in terms of his social setting, past and present (panel II). The term "characteristics," in other words, refers in this instance not to states of the organism, but to states of its environment. (This is made particularly clear by the common usage "*objective* social characteristics.") It follows that social and personality characteristics are in no way mutually exclusive. They do not compete as candidates for explanations of social behavior, but rather are complementary. Social "characteristics" can *cause* psychological "characteristics." They are not substitutes that can in some way be more important than personality characteristics.

The confusion resulting from failing to take account of the complementarity of "personality processes and dispositions" and the social "context for the development of personality and acquisition of attitudes" is one that easily arises under certain research conditions. Ideally, personality and attitude ought to be measured by various psychological instruments designed to observe the individual's current mental functioning. And the social determinants of personality and attitude ought also to be more or less directly observed—longitudinally and by procedures independent of the respondent's report of his environmental circumstances, past and present. But frequently our only option is to gather evidence both of current personality and attitudes and of social background by interviewing the respondent and by interpreting some of the things he tells us as measures of his environment, and others as measures of the traces that environment (and genetic constitution) have left upon him.

In relating the various measures of respondents' "characteristics" that we have at our disposal to some dependent variable, it is important that we make explicit which of the independent variables have social referents and which have psychological referents. Otherwise the standard research procedures employing partial correlations and other control devices for detecting spurious relationships encourage us to fall into the fallacy of simply *reducing* an association between personality and behavior to its social determinants—of failing, in Herbert Hyman's phrase, to distinguish between "developmental sequences" and "problems of spuriousness."

For an example of how this problem arises, we can consider the very interesting research report by Urie Bronfenbrenner entitled "Personality and Participation: The Case of the Vanishing Variable." Bronfenbrenner reports a study in which it was found that measures of personality were associated with participation in community affairs. However, as he notes, "it is a well-established fact that extent of participation varies with social class, with the lower classes participating the least." Therefore he proceeds to establish the relationship between personality and participation, controlling for social class (and certain other factors). The result: "Most of the earlier . . . significant relationships between personality measures now disappear, leaving only two significant correlations, both of them quite low." [34]

One common interpretation of such a finding would be that Bronfenbrenner had shown the irrelevance of personality to participation. Hyman suggests why this interpretation would be unsatisfactory, when he points out that "the concept of spuriousness cannot logically be intended to apply to antecedent conditions which are associated with . . . [an] independent variable as part of a developmental sequence. . . . [A]n explanatory factor that is *psychological* and a control factor that is *sociological* can be conceived as two different levels of description, i.e., one might regard . . . an objective position in society as leading to psychological processes. . . ." [35]

In the Bronfenbrenner example, then, an individual's "objective" socioeconomic background (as opposed to such subjective concomitants as his sense of class consciousness) needs to be analyzed as a possible social determinant of the psychological concomitants of participation.

The general import of our consideration of this objection, in the light of Smith's map, is to point to the desirability of distinguishing personality processes from their social antecedents and, so far as possible, obtaining independent observations of both personality and social background. As we shall see in discussing single-case and typological analyses, it is feasible to study personality determinants of political behavior without raising developmental questions about social background, but in fact questions about personality functioning lead logically and empirically to questions about background experience.

Situational Determinants Versus Personality Determinants

A second standard objection, also one that is illustrated by Smith's formulation, takes this form:

> Personality is not an important determinant of political behavior, because individuals with varying personality characteristics will tend to behave similarly when placed in common situations. And it is not useful to study personal variation, if the ways in which people vary do not affect their behavior.

Easton illustrates this objection with the example of political party leaders who differ in their personality characteristics and who are "confronted with the existence of powerful groups making demands upon their parties." Their "decisions and actions," he points out, will tend "to converge." [36]

But, as Easton's use of tendency language brings out, their decisions are still likely to reflect *some* personal variability.[37] Furthermore, under certain circumstances the personal characteristics of the leaders would be more likely to have an impact than under others. This suggests that the second objection can be rephrased in the following conditional form and that we can (as various commentators have) advance propositions about the circumstances under which it obtains.

> Under what circumstances do actors with differing personal characteristics (placed in common situations) vary in their behavior and under what circumstaces is their behavior uniform?

The portion of Smith's map that encompasses the familiar equation of "situation (IV)→personality and predisposition (III)→behavior (V)" helps us to isolate the contingencies that make it more or less likely that behavior will be a function of personality variations.[38] Each of the three elements in this equation can vary in ways that enhance or dampen the effects of personal variability.

Since the objection emphasizes the tendency of situations (including norms, roles, etc.) to reduce the effects of personal variability, it seems logical to begin by pointing to types of situations that actually *encourage* the expression of personal differences in behavior. As is often pointed out, *ambiguous* situations tend to leave room for personal variability to have an impact. Ambiguity is to be found in *new* situations, in *complex* situations, and in *contradictory* situations, among others. Another class of situation in which the expression of personal variations is fostered is that in which there are *no sanctions* attached to the alternative courses of behavior.

Paralleling the situational determinants of the expression of personal variability are psychological determinants. For example, if political actors lack *mental sets* which might lead them to structure their perceptions and resolve situational ambiguities, their inner dispositions are more likely to be reflected in their behavior.

If political actors have *intense* dispositions (other than the disposition to conform!), they are more likely to ignore environmental sanctions and to behave consistently with their varying dispositions.

Turning finally to behavior itself, the kind of behavior we choose to observe as our dependent variable will affect the likelihood of observing personal variations. For example, variation may be greater in peripheral than in central aspects of action. (That is, there may be personal differences, for example, in the *zealousness* of performance of actions and the *style* of performance even though there is not much variability in the specific *content* of the actions performed—e.g., in whether the individual votes, or writes a Congressman, or whom he votes for or writes to.) And to the degree that an act is *demanding* and not just a conventionally expected performance, it is more likely to exhibit personal variability.

Thus a general upshot of rephrasing the objection and considering it in the contextual perspective provided by the map is to sensitize us to circumstances under which situational and other considerations are more or less likely to bring out or suppress the expression of personal variability. This provides clues to where and when it is especially desirable to engage in analyses of the personal dispositions of individual political actors, and of types of actors.

We have seen that although situational determinants of behavior are sometimes discussed as if they invariably served to weaken the effects of personality on behavior, certain types of situations *enhance* the effects of personality. In fact, careful, theoretically sensitive attention to the situations within which behavior occurs often may be the key to discovering strong personality effects, as can be seen from the important and ingenious research of Browning and Jacob.[39]

Browning and Jacob administered McClelland TATs (measuring levels of need for achievement, power, and affiliation) to matched samples of politicians and nonpoliticians in the northern city of "Eastport" and to samples of politicians in two Louisiana parishes, "Casino" and "Christian." The most striking impression left by their findings, when considered independently of situational factors, was the lack of aggregate motivational difference between the politicians and nonpoliticians, and the extreme heterogeneity of the politicians on the McClelland measures. However, once controls were introduced for situational factors, particularly the actual (as opposed to the formal) norms and expectations connected with various political offices in the three communities, distinct motivational profiles began to emerge. Politicians fitting into a syndrome, which Browning has identified operationally in terms of high scores in the needs for achievement and power and low scores in the need for affiliation, were found in some political contexts and not in others.

In the Eastport political system, Browning and Jacob find that on the one hand "expectations are prevalent that it is possible to go to state legislative office or higher" and, on the other, alternative nonpolitical options for achievement in business are limited. In Louisiana "there is no consensus that the important decisions are to be made in the political process" and "opportunities for power and achievement abound in the commercial and industrial life of the area." The Eastport politicians are generally higher on the high-power-and-achievement, low-affiliation syndrome than those in Louisiana. Secondly, the same pattern of differences is systematically exhibited *within* each of the communities between the occupants of offices which provide possibilities for power and achievement and offices which do not (for example, sinecures). Browning and Jacob show special attention to the subtleties of situational variables in their classification of offices in terms of actual community expectations rather than their formal requirements: thus the office of Justice of the Peace is coded as high on power potential in Casino Parish, Louisiana, where this official plays an important role in the relations between gamblers and parish authorities; in Christian Parish, which has no gambling, Justice of the Peace is coded as low in power.

In the course of locating actor motivations in situational contexts, Browning and Jacob are in effect characterizing situations (community contexts and roles) in terms both of actual practices ("Does a particular local political office lead to higher office in community?") and of what Smith (panel II) calls "situational norms" ("What is the consensual expectation in community X of the consequences of running for a particular office?"). Clearly an actor's *own* expectations (which may not be consistent with community expectations assuming that there *is* a community consensus) also will be a key intervening variable mediating between his motivational processes and the situation. Browning shows this in his report elsewhere[40] of certain Eastport findings not alluded to in the paper with Jacob: a group of active, striving businessmen who took a leading part in redevelopment in Eastport were found to have the same motivational pattern as the high-power-and-achievement, low-affiliation politicians. But the businessmen came from apolitical families and evidently did not acquire a set of expectations and values that would legitimize partisan politics as a motivational outlet.[41]

The Importance of Ego-Defensive Determinants of Behavior

The objection we have just considered—that situations leave little room for personal variability to have an effect on behavior—implies a content-free definition of "personality." "Personality" equals the ways that persons vary. To the degree that one's definition of "personality" refers to some subset of the package of psychological dispositions, it is possible to advance the objection that "personality" as so defined is not sufficiently relevant to political behavior for personality and politics research to be of interest. Many commentators have in mind a conception of personality that places special emphasis on ego defense when they deprecate the importance of personality for politics. As I have pointed out, the deep motivational variables which are identified through the lenses of psychoanalytic theory and its descendents play a prominent role in the existing personality and politics literature. Depth psychology is central to such benchmark works as Lasswell's *Psychopathology and Politics,* Fromm's *Escape from Freedom,* and *The Authoritarian Personality.*[42]

Thus it is sometimes said that "personality" does not have an important impact on politics because mechanisms of ego defense, while they may be important in the pathological behavior of disturbed individuals, do not come significantly into play in the daily behavior of normal people. Here again is an assertion that can be rephrased conditionally:

> Under what circumstances are ego-defensive needs likely to manifest themselves in behavior?

In general, all of the circumstances that permit personal variability to be exhibited also leave room for particular aspects of personal variability, such as degrees and types of ego defensiveness. However, certain circumstances probably make the expression of ego-defensive needs likely and not merely possible, and these can be located in terms of the "situation→predispositions→behavior" formula.

(1) Certain types of situational stimuli undoubtedly have a greater "resonance" with the deeper layers of the personality than do others. These are stimuli which politicians learn to be wary of—for example, such issues as capital punishment, cruelty to animals, and, in recent years, fluoridation of drinking water. One element in these sensitive issues, Lane and Sears suggest, is that they touch upon "topics dealing with material commonly repressed by individuals. . . ." [43]

(2) The likelihood that ego-defensive needs will affect political behavior is also related to the degree to which actors "have" ego-defensive needs.

(3) Finally, certain types of response undoubtedly provide greater occasion for deep personality needs to find outlet than do others—for example, such responses as affirmations of loyalty in connection with the rallying activities of mass movements led by charismatic leaders, and the various other types of response deliberately designed to channel affect into politics.

Again, by rephrasing the objection in contingent form, and stating the circumstances under which it holds, we can mark off certain portions of the political landscape as promising hunting grounds for the political psychologist, and suggest where he might make most effective use of certain kinds of hypotheses and concepts—in this case, those of depth psychology.

Smith's formulation of personality (panel III) distinguishes three kinds of motivational processes. In addition to the defensive processes, he stresses the ego's constructive coping with the environment and the processes through which self-other relations are mediated. This formulation suggests the importance of developing techniques for classifying individuals in terms of the relative importance of these processes in their psychic economies. We begin to sense certain of the necessary theoretical and methodological refinements appropriate for distinguishing the often elusive but nevertheless important connections between personality and politics. Just as certain relationships are revealed only by virtue of a very careful characterization of the situations within which actors of diverse personal characteristics are to be found, there are relationships which seem to be detectable only if the appropriate personality categorizations are employed as intervening constructs.

A standard problem is the failure to distinguish behavior and orientations rooted in ego defense from object-appraisal-based behavior. These difficulties arise frequently in the political literature because hypotheses drawing upon ego-defense mechanisms often seem well suited to deal with the kinds of irrationality that political psychologists frequently seek to explain. But irrationality (choice of means that are inappropriate for the ends-in-view) also—perhaps most often—may have nonpathological roots; for example, in imperfect information.

The authors of *The Authoritarian Personality* interpreted certain responses to the F-scale and to various projective tests as indicators of unconscious needs—for example, acceptance of pessimistic statements about human nature, and the belief that "wild and dangerous things go on in the world." These needs, according to the theory presented in *The Authoritarian Personality,* are part of a personality pattern in which repressed hostility is displaced to the weak and subordinate; and repression has a variety of further indirect consequences for the personality, such as the tendency to project one's aggressive and sexual impulses onto others. Hyman and Sheatsley, however, were able to point out that some of the responses used to indicate ego-defensive authoritarianism were in fact the "normal" responses and stereotypes prevalent in lower class subcultures, and that socioeconomic rather than psychodynamic differences were probably being tapped in some of the research on authoritarianism.[44]

Hence the importance of obviating such confusions by using appropriate techniques for assessing ego defensiveness, and by observing the differential behavior of individuals who vary in their degree of ego-defensive need. Quite relevant to students of personality and politics is the work along these lines of Daniel Katz and his associates, reported in papers such as "The Measurement of Ego-Defense as Related to Attitude Change." [45] Katz, McClintock, and Sarnoff used devices such as the paranoia scale of the Minnesota Multiphasic Personality Inventory in order to classify subjects by level of ego defensiveness. Using attitude change techniques that are especially designed to penetrate moderate ego defenses, but are inappropriate for individuals who do not have strong ego defensive needs and too weak for strong ego defenders, they were able correctly to predict that attitude change would occur in the middle ego-defense category. As in the Browning and Jacob research, the finding of a personality effect was possible only when the appropriate categories of respondents were considered, and this in turn was dependent upon sensitivity to distinctions of the sort made in Smith's "map." [46]

The Impact of Actors on Outcomes

Finally, we may note two instructive objections to the study of the impact of "personality" on politics which raise questions about social processes rather than intrapersonal processes. These objections are located by the dotted feedback arrow lettered (I) on Smith's map, which indicates the impact of individual political behavior on "distal social antecedents" of behavior (panel I), including the political system itself. They thus point to the various issues I have summarized under the heading of "aggregation."

1. Sometimes, especially in certain kinds of sociological writings that take a strict Durkheimian approach to analyzing social phenomena "at the social level," one encounters the objection that:

> Personality characteristics tend to be randomly distributed in institutional roles. Personality therefore "cancels out" and can be ignored by analysts of political and other social phenomena.

The assumption underlying this objective seems, as Alex Inkeles points out, to be that "in 'real' groups and situations, the accidents of life history and factors other than personality which are responsible for recruitment [into institutional roles] will 'randomize' personality distribution in the major social statuses sufficiently so that taking systematic account of the influence of personality composition is unnecessary." But, as Inkeles easily shows, this assumption is false on two grounds.

First, "even if the personality composition of any group is randomly determined, random assortment would not in fact guarantee the same personality composition in the membership of all institutions of a given type. On the contrary, the very fact of randomness implies that the outcome would approximate a normal distribution. Consequently, some of the groups would by chance have a personality composition profoundly different from others, with possibly marked effects on the functioning of the institutions involved." Secondly,

There is no convincing evidence that randomness does consistently describe the assignment of personality types to major social statuses. On the contrary, there is a great deal of evidence to indicate that particular statuses often attract, or recruit preponderantly for, one or another personality characteristic, and that fact has a substantial effect on individual adjustment to roles and the general quality of institutional functioning.[47]

The objection turns out therefore to be based on unwarranted empirical assumptions. It proves not to be an obstacle to research, but rather—once it is examined —an opening gambit for identifying a crucial topic of investigation for the political psychologist: How are personality types distributed in social roles and with what consequences?

2. Sometimes, on grounds smacking of the nineteenth-century debates over social determinism, it is argued that:

> Personality is not of interest to political and other social analysts, because individual actors (personalities) are severely limited in the impact they can have on events.

Here again we have an assertion that can be reworded contingently, since the degree to which individuals' actions can have significant impact is clearly variable. The reworded formulation becomes: Under what circumstances are the actions of single individuals likely to have a greater or lesser effect on the course of events?

One determinant of the degree to which individual actors can have an impact on events (for example, political outcomes such as the output of a legislature or the advent of a war) is the degree to which the environment admits of restructuring. Technically speaking, we might describe situations or sequences of events in which modest interventions can produce disproportionately large results as "unstable." They are in precarious equilibrium. Some physical analogies are: massive rock formations at the side of a mountain which can be dislodged by the motion of a single keystone, or highly explosive compounds such as nitroglycerine. The situation (or chain of events) which does not admit of restructuring is usually one in which a variety of factors conspire to produce the same outcome. Hook, in *The Hero and History*,[48] offers the outbreak of World War I and of the February Revolution as instances of historical sequences which, if not "inevitable," probably could not have been averted by the actions of any single individual. On the other hand, Hook attempts to show in detail that, without the specific actions of Lenin, the October Revolution might well not have occurred.

Secondly, the likelihood of personal impact varies with the actor's location in the environment. Normally, of course, it is the positions of formal leadership that provide the greatest leverage for affecting events, but Crozier[49] describes examples of French organizations in which certain insulated roles at lower hierarchical levels offer greater decision-making potentialities than higher roles.

Thirdly, the likelihood of personal impact varies with the personal strengths and weaknesses of the actor.

Earlier we saw certain of the contingencies surrounding the degree to which variations in personality characteristics are likely to affect individual behavior, a phenomenon which I have elsewhere called "actor dispensability." [50] Now we see that the degree to which the actions of individuals affect larger outcomes—what might be called "action dispensability"—is also contingent on various preconditions.

Actor dispensability and action dispensability are logically independent. Actors can behave in highly idiosyncratic ways, but their behavior may be of little significance for whatever phenomenon the political analyst happens to be interested in. And actors may behave in ways that are crucial (necessary, or even sufficient) for political outcomes that interest us, but the acts they perform may be ones that any similarly placed actor might be expected to perform. However, as a matter of investigative strategy, the greater the degree that the action is crucial (say, a presidential order releasing intercontinental ballistic missiles), the greater is the likelihood that we will be interested in the actor's idiosyncrasies, even if their effect on his behavior is only peripheral rather than central.

In politics there are frequent examples of individual actions which have macroconsequences. I have already alluded to the well-known potency of American Presidents. Tucker has discussed at some length the probably even greater potential impact on outcomes of totalitarian leaders.[51] Because individual actors can have such great political consequences, psychological case histories of their personalities and behavior—if these can be conducted in an appropriately disciplined fashion—ought to have an important place in political studies. The possibly substantial impact of the individual under certain circumstances is also one of the factors that needs to be considered in our discussion of aggregative political accounts.

V. THREE VARIETIES OF PERSONALITY AND POLITICS RESEARCH: INDIVIDUAL CASE STUDIES, TYPOLOGICAL STUDIES, AGGREGATIVE ACCOUNTS

Even though any single contribution to the literature may contain more than one of the three kinds of analysis, there is a rough, unfolding logic making it reasonable to organize the issues that arise in personality and politics research in a sequence running from single-case analysis, through typological analysis, to aggregate analysis. Each of the three kinds of investigation poses its own problems, but one tends to lead to another. Frequently, for example, it is our inability to explain why some single political actor—such as Woodrow Wilson—has behaved in a fashion that does not seem consistent with our normal expectations for behavior in comparable situations that initially turns our attention to political personality. In the course of inferring the personality structures that account for the idiosyncrasies of our subject's behavior, we then may come to suspect that in important respects *our* actor resembles certain other political actors, and if we pursue the resemblances, we find ourselves moving inductively in the direction of creating a typology.

There is, however, a two-way trade between analyses of individuals and of types: it also is possible that the actor will in some respects fit an already existing typology, perhaps one with which there is associated a body of theory and empirical evidence relevant to making predictions about our biographical subject and identifying ways in which his behavior is patterned. Thus, for example, George and George were able to make use of the clinical literature on compulsive types in their treatment of Woodrow Wilson.[52]

And there is a three-way linking of individual, typological, and aggregative analyses. There are numerous theories about the relevance for systems—for example, Weimar Germany—of the distribution of individual types in the system.[53] And we have seen that it is possible—and perhaps more so in the political than in other spheres of life—that especially well-placed individuals, such as Presidents of the United States and totalitarian leaders, can have drastic effects on the aggregate system. On George and George's showing, Woodrow Wilson's key role in the failure of the United States to ratify the Paris Treaty and enter the League of Nations is a case in point. We have a long, if checkered, tradition of culture-and-personality (and social structure-and-personality) inquiry to remind us that the causal arrow also points in the opposite direction—that systems have impacts on the individuals and types of individuals that compose them.

Psychological Case Studies of Individual Political Actors

If a case study of a single actor is presented mainly as an illustrative exercise or an occasion for theoretical speculation, and these seem to be the purposes behind many of the case studies of actors from the general population that have been reported, there is likely to be little felt need to perfect standards of evidence and inference for characterizing the actor. Consequently questions of accuracy of diagnosis arise mainly in biographies of public figures. Biographers often are interested in demonstrating that some action of their protagonist has been responsible for a particular outcome (i.e. that his actions have not been dispensable), and under these circumstances it is important to know if any of the variance is a function of the actor's personal idiosyncracies. The analysis of the actor's personality becomes a crucial linchpin in a larger argument.

We cannot expect psychological case studies to achieve the degree of standardization and precision that is appropriate for quantitative studies in which "objective" instruments designed to classify individuals into types are used, and in which it is possible to characterize the reliability of the instrument statistically and to perfect its validity through correlational study. But it *should* be possible to work toward more adequate, more explicit standards for single-case analysis than presently obtain—in other words, to reduce the degree to which psychological biographies are arbitrary literary exercises, wholly dependent upon the whims of the biographer and subject to no consensual standards of evaluation.

There are a number of reasons why it presently is difficult to assess biographical reports, apart from the more mundane problems with sources and their use that inhere in any historical research: First, in most biographies it is unclear what the basis was for the necessary acts of selection through which certain portions of the biographical record are discussed and emphasized, and others are not. Secondly, it often is not clear what interpretive inferences are being made, what if any hypotheses about the subject of the biography have been rejected, and on what grounds. Interpretation is often implicit rather than explicit, and when it is explicit, it often seems "imposed" rather than to flow logically from general principles and specific evidence. Finally, as a particularly important instance of the previous point, the psychoanalytically inspired biographies in the personality and politics literature often seem (especially to the psychoanalytically uninitiated) to impose peculiarly unverifiable kinds of interpretations on the actor's behavior—interpretations in terms of ego-defensive motivation. Sometimes these interpretations seem to reduce the protagonist to his ego defenses and to be insensitive to the possibility that he may be reacting to the situations he encounters, in terms of the goals and cognitive assumptions he has acquired from his environment, in a more or less straightforward manner.

In asking what makes one single-actor psychological case study more convincing than another, I have found it convenient to reflect on the explicit and implicit practices employed by Alexander and Juliette George in their *Woodrow Wilson and Colonel House,* particularly their treatment of Wilson. Since a number of commentators[54] view this as one of the more satisfactory psychological biographies of political actors, we can turn to it for examples of appropriate technique (as well as assuming that whatever difficulties this work exhibits are likely to be fundamental difficulties with the methodology of such biographies, rather than examples of imperfect craftsmanship). Further, although George and George adopted the strategy of narrative exposition, addressing themselves only to a necessary minimum of methodological issues in the text of the book, the work clearly is guided by a very high degree of methodological (and theoretical) self-consciousness, and many of its methodological premises have been discussed in the appendix to the book and in a number of papers by one or both of the authors.[55]

Very generally, there seem to be two broad classes of reasons for the success of the Georges' study. The first set of reasons involves aspects of the logic of discovery—for example, their long-standing immersion in the details of Wilson's life, including extensive examination of the abundant and often highly revealing primary source material on Wilson; the depth and subtlety of the authors' familiarity with psychoanalytic theory; the long period of time they allowed themselves to develop, test, and reframe their hypothesis about Wilson. These factors, although vital, are not my present concern.[56] The other set of factors relates to the logic of demonstration. Even though George and George refer only briefly to such matters in their explicit remarks in the text of the study, it is evident that they paid far more than the customary amount of attention to developing assertions that were sound, from the standpoint of demonstration. Self-conscious attention to demonstration in psychological case studies seems to involve such elements as:

(1) Being explicit in formulating provisional hypotheses about the subject's personality (these may only be hypotheses about the adult phenomenology of the subject's personality, but analysis of an individual's "presenting characteristics" usually leads to developmental hypotheses about how he came to acquire these characteristics: at any rate, the explicit statement of the hypothesis serves to provide criteria for what to include in the biographical account).

(2) Distinguishing, as far as possible, between the observational data (on current functioning and past development) upon which the hypotheses are based and the interpretive hypotheses themselves.

(3) Establishing specific operational criteria for distinguishing observations that will be accepted in support of the hypothetical statements and those that will lead to rejection or modification of the hypotheses.

(4) At a minimum, ascertaining the reliability of the observational data, including the observations that serve as indicators of the terms used in the hypotheses.

(5) As far as possible, attempting to establish validity by assessing the standing in the relevant clinical literature of the "covering laws" upon which the inferential steps are based.

Space does not permit a detailed discussion of how all of these elements figure in the George and George account of Wilson. We may conclude these schematic remarks on the psychological case study simply by illustrating how several of them appear in the more complex and controversial of the authors' interpretations, those that deal with ego defensiveness.

The Georges employ psychodynamic notions in the hypotheses they advance about a number of aspects of Wilson's personal and political style and of his development. Among them are the hypotheses addressed to Wilson's stubborn, unyielding intractability and unwillingness to compromise under certain circumstances, which the Georges interpret as evidence of the compensatory needs that were fulfilled for Wilson by refusing to share power in areas with which he felt he was particularly competent to deal. Wilson's refusal to compromise was especially evident in the graduate school controversy that marked the final period of his presidency of Princeton, and in the closely parallel controversy during his unsuccessful effort to obtain Senate approval of the Paris Treaty, as well as in his dealings as Governor of New Jersey with the 1912 session of the state legislature (an episode the Georges deal with only briefly) and his conduct of peace negotiations in Paris.

For each of the circumstances in which Wilson showed extreme unwillingness to compromise, it is possible that an interpretation not suggesting that his behavior was a function of ego defense might be in order. A non-ego-defensive interpretation would be furthered if it could be shown that his responses to these situations (including those of his actions that molded the situations themselves) were responses that could normally be expected of political actors placed in comparable circumstances (with similar opportunities, restraints, and provocations), or if it could be shown that Wilson's consciously held attitudes were consistent with avoiding compromises under any circumstances. In fact, George and George, by analyzing these political encounters in very great detail, make it clear that Wilson had in each instance very great opportunities to attain his ostensible ends. He had only to admit other actors into the decision-making process and to make relatively slight accommodations and compromises. In other words, his actions did *not* seem to have been constrained mainly by the requirements of the situation.

Nor did they seem constrained by the requirements of Wilson's own values. George and George are able to present examples of explicit statements by Wilson[57] extolling precisely the kinds of compromises he adamantly resisted during the graduate school and League of Nations controversies. The Georges also point to Wilson's extraordinary flexibility and adaptability under certain other circumstances—namely, those of seeking power, as opposed to exercising power. This provides a further indication that his behavior was not mainly a function of his ideological precepts.

In addition, the authors were able to point to the *recurrent pattern* of Wilson's experience. If an actor is found repeatedly to thrust himself into quite similar encounters, it becomes increasingly appropriate to assume that it is his own more or less deep-seated personality dispositions, rather than environmental factors, that are accounting for the regularities.

Finally, George and George make explicit use of the clinical literature on compulsive personalities in order to help explain the juxtaposition of a variety of traits and behavior patterns in Wilson, and drawing on that literature they specify operational indicators of such terms as "low self-estimates" and "compensation," terms which appear in the hypothesis that Wilson's pursuit of power served compensatory functions. For example, they were able to predict circumstances under which—if their basic diagnosis is correct—Wilson should be expected to experience "euphoric" feelings in connection with the pursuit and exercise of power, and they were fortunate enough to have a sufficiently detailed body of historical data to detect evidence of such feelings.[58]

The foregoing—and other—self-conscious efforts at building up a rigorously probative argument are woven into the text of the Georges' narrative. It is therefore not surprising that the argument has "rung true" to readers in ways that other psychological biographies have not.

Analyses of Types of Political Actors

By far the largest single cluster of political or politically relevant inquiry by psychologists is the massive body of literature on "authoritarianism." *Woodrow*

Wilson and Colonel House displays exemplary methodological rigor and theoretical sophistication in an investigative mode that admits of a rather low degree of exactness. The authoritarianism studies, on the other hand, are executed in a research tradition that is highly developed methodologically. But authoritarianism inquiries—both the monumental original "Berkeley study"[59] and the countless subsequent studies—have been plagued with formidable problems of evidence, inference, and conceptualization. Within four years after the publication of *The Authoritarian Personality,* an entire volume of critical essays on that work and its immediate progeny had appeared.[60] Within eight years, a review article summarized 260 research reports on authoritarianism, many of them concerned with unraveling the controversial issues pointed up in the volume of critical essays.[61] And all of this preceded the elaborate methodological snarl that developed in the later 1950s over the finding that "response set" (the automatic tendency to respond positively or negatively to questionnaire items, independent of their content) seemed to have contributed to certain of the initial findings in the literature.

One of the more conspicuous difficulties with the original authoritarianism research was the failure to anticipate the complexity of the linkages between political attitudes and underlying personality processes: there was a tendency to equate authoritarian personality structure with right-wing political attitudes, and a failure to appreciate the possibility that the same personality needs could find alternative outlets, or that (because of the low cathexis of politics for many individuals) personality might not be expressed at all in political attitudes.[62]

A second difficulty bore on the problem of distinguishing ego-defensive from non-ego-defensive personality processes. The original theory guiding the Berkeley research was heavily psychodynamic. Subsequent reinterpretations of the findings suggested that high scores on the standard measure of authoritarianism might in some cases simply reflect the typical subcultural orientations toward topics referred to on the F-scale, by individuals of low educational attainment. Hyman and Sheatsley suggested this possibility in their contribution to the volume of critical essays on *The Authoritarian Personality*[63] by analyzing the content of the questionnaire items. The work several years later on response set pointed to the same possibility.[64]

In addition, it was pointed out that the inferences and assumptions in the original work about the relationship of psychological dispositions (personality and attitudes) to behavior were deficient, as were the sociological assumptions about the likely aggregate consequences of differing distributions of "authoritarians" in populations.[65]

In general, the issues raised by the literature had been inadequately conceptualized, and far too much theoretically vacuous data-gathering had been stimulated by the easy availability of the F-scale. The remedy, which in its general strategy is much the same as the prescriptions noted above for single-case analyses, is suggested by the diagnosis. There needs to be more extensive attention to explicit formulation of theories and hypotheses; greater clarity in distinguishing evidence from inference; more in the way of self-conscious attention both to distinguishing among the types of variables summarized in Figure 1 (Smith) and possible interactions among such variables. Here in skeletal form is a sketch of an approach to reconstructing this literature, in order to isolate important research issues.[66]

1. PHENOMENOLOGY.   Under this heading, it is possible to summarize all of the psychological characteristics composing a type that are readily observable with a minimum of interpretation; these are, in effect, the "presenting symptoms" of the type. For the purpose of political studies, the crucial presenting characteristic re-

ferred to in the authoritarianism literature is the pair of traits that in the original volume were labeled "authoritarian aggression" and "authoritarian submission"— the tendency of the authoritarian to abase himself before those who stand above him hierarchically, and to dominate whomever he senses to be weak, subordinate, or inferior. Other more or less directly politically relevant traits that seem to be present in this syndrome are the authoritarian's tendency to think in power terms (to be acutely sensitive to questions of who rules whom); his preference for order; his perceptual rigidity ("intolerance of ambiguity"); his use of stereotypes; and his dependence upon "external agencies" for guidance.

The above-mentioned traits "hang together" in a fairly intuitively convincing manner. In addition, the literature suggests that a whole series of less obvious traits are a part of this syndrome: superstitiousness, "exaggerated assertion of strength and toughness," pessimism about human nature, "concern with sexual 'goings-on,' " "impatience with and opposition to the subjective and the tender-minded." It is these rather exotic additional concomitants that lead us beyond phenomenology to the psychoanalytically based theory of the dynamics of "ego-defensive authoritarianism."

The basic research implication of explicitly stating the phenomenological aspects of authoritarian personality theory, however, is to lay out a first-order set of research questions that are potentially more answerable than the knotty issues that arise in explaining why personality traits cluster as they do and what life experiences are responsible for the clustering. At the phenomenological level, one can identify a set of research tasks that can be performed in ways that should elicit agreement about the findings by investigators of quite different theoretical persuasions.[67]

2. DYNAMICS.   Under this heading we can summarize our hypotheses about the processes underlying the observable. How are the observable features related to each other? What ties them together? As we have seen, the theory of dynamics on which the original research was based emphasizes ego defense.

The authoritarian, it is argued, is an individual with strong, but ambivalent, dispositions toward figures of authority. Denial of the negative side of these feelings is central to such an individual's functioning. The authoritarian is able to conceal from himself his rage toward those in authority only by the massive defense procedure of reaction formation, involving a total repression of critical and other unacceptable impulses toward authority and a bending over backwards in excessive praise of it. But repression has its costs and side-effects, and repressed impulses seek alternative outlets. Hostility not only is rechannelled toward whoever is perceived as weak and unauthoritative, but also has a more diffuse effect on the authoritarian's generally negative views of man and his works, as well as contributing to his need to scan his environment for signs of authority relationships, his tendency (via projection) to see the world as full of dangerous things and people, and his desire to punish others, for example, sex offenders, who have surrendered to their impulses. Feelings of personal weakness are covered by a facade of toughness. A side-effect of channeling enormous energy into repression and reaction formation is that the authoritarian's emotional capacities and even certain of his cognitive capacities are stunted. He is unable to face the prospect of canvassing his own psyche—for fear of what such introspection may yield—and therefore becomes highly dependent upon external sources of guidance.[68]

As we have also seen, other investigators and findings suggest that the phenomenology of authoritarianism can arise without having psychodynamic roots. In the language of Smith's Figure 4, authoritarianism may have its basis in needs for object appraisal as well as in externalization and ego defense. At the dynamic level, the research task becomes one of measuring and classifying different patterns of personality needs. Such investigations point in two directions: back to phenomenology (it seems likely that various phenomenological subtypes can be identified, some of which are related to ego-defensive needs and some of which are not), and on to developmental analysis.

3. DEVELOPMENT.   Questions of dynamics lead logically to questions of development. From asking how individuals with different "presenting symptoms" function, it is logical to proceed to questions about how they came to be the way they are. To the degree that research on dynamics points to two general types of authoritarianism (we can loosely refer to them as ego-defensive and cognitive authoritarianism), we would expect to find two quite different typical patterns of genesis.

4. DISTINGUISHING DEEPER PERSONALITY PROCESSES FROM ATTITUDES.   Figure 4 of Smith's essay setting forth his map indicates the analytical distinction that can be made between attitudes and the personality processes in which they may have their sources. At some points in this essay it has been sufficient to treat "personality" and "psychological" as synonymous, implying that all of what is entailed by the latter, including attitudes and beliefs, is summarized by the term "personality." For the kinds of tasks that concerned the authors of *The Authoritarian Personality,* the analytic distinction between underlying personality organization and attitudes needs to be sharply maintained. This contributes to avoiding difficulties such as the automatic equating of authoritarianism with political conservatism and ethnic prejudice, and encourages investigators to anticipate and observe the rather complex contingent associations that seem to exist between beliefs and inner needs.

5. ANALYZING THE INTERPLAY OF PERSONALITY AND ATTITUDES WITH SITUATIONS.   It is often pointed out that psychological dispositions may be imperfectly correlated with action, because due to situational restraints and opportunities, people may fail to act upon their impulses. It is well appreciated that situational stimuli may even produce behavior that is quite *in*consistent with underlying dispositions, making it utterly inappropriate to attempt to anticipate behavior from psychological data alone. For example, Katz and Benjamin found in research on the behavior of northern white college undergraduates toward Negro co-workers that authoritarians were actually more deferential toward Negroes than nonauthoritarians, a finding which they felt was "due to the authoritarian's fear of revealing anti-Negro attitudes in a potentially punitive environment." [69]

Analyses of Aggregation[70]

Political scientists are typically interested in those ancient preoccupations of Plato and Aristotle—political *systems*. What are their forms? Under what conditions are different forms found? How do they differ in performance? What leads them to be stable or to change? Studies of individual behavior and, pushing back in the causal chain, studies of the motivational bases of behavior, are undertaken by students of politics to a considerable extent not for their intrinsic interest but out of a concern with the collective effects of individual actors.

As Singer[71] points out, problems of moving from parts to wholes are endemic in a variety of fields. And as Smelser[72] points out, "We do not at present have the methodological capacity to argue causally from a mixture of aggregated states of individual members of a system to a global characteristic of a system." The simple extrapolation from impressionistic accounts of "national character" to equally impressionistic observations on system functioning, which characterized the literature of two decades ago, is justifiably passé.[73] There appear to be a variety of possible approaches, depending upon the data at one's disposal and one's theoretical concerns, to treating problems of aggregation in a disciplined fashion.

1. The prescription, stated at various points above, that actors be observed in their social situations, in effect means that studies of individual political actors tend automatically to shade into aggregate accounts of institutional functioning, at least at the small group level. And in the case of elite actors, as we have seen, the analysis of individuals may clarify the control mechanisms of large systems. The George and George treatment of Wilson's dealings with Lloyd George and Clemenceau at Paris, and with Lodge during the confirmation fight, takes into account both the dispositions of actors and the relationships among their roles. In effect we are provided with the beginnings of general accounts of some of the possible states of the social system of the international conference and of executive-legislative relations. The recent work on "compositional" or "structural" effects suggests ways that individual and group data can be combined in quantitative inquiries.[74]

2. Modern survey techniques now make it possible to obtain systematic "censuses" of the psychological disposition of populations of very large social systems. Thus it becomes possible to avoid the circularities that frequently have been noted in personality and culture research—the tendencies to infer individual characteristics from system properties or cultural products and then to explain the latter in terms of the former. In recent voting literature, very sophisticated individual data-based theories of a non-obvious sort have been advanced to explain such phenomena as the regular loss of congressional seats by the presidential party in the off-year elections, and the far greater stability of party voting from election to election in the United States than in France.[75]

3. But often it will not do simply to aggregate individual characteristics additively, in order to explain the aggregate. To use Singer's analogy: "We can pour pellets of steel into a container until it is full, with little qualitative change in the aggregate; it merely becomes larger. But if we do the same thing with pellets of enriched uranium under appropriate conditions, we will eventually arrive at the 'critical mass' threshold, with important qualitative changes in the aggregate as a result." [76] Thus the consequences of the difference between a 50 versus a 60 percent authoritarian-personality composition of a population may be disproportionately greater than the consequences of a 40 versus a 50 percent difference. Very little is presently known about such matters.[77]

In addition, as Ackley[78] puts it, "aggregation is a legitimate procedure when behavior of the individual units subject to aggregation is basically similar." This is certainly not the case with political actors. Rather than simple addition we need, in a figure of speech of Hyman's, ways of "weighting the sums" to account for the greater impact of the dispositions of actors in key roles.[79]

4. A way of approaching the problem of weighting for role incumbency is to make explicit our models of political systems and subsystems, stipulating the roles and their requirements in order to observe the fit between role and the personal dispositions of role incumbents. Lasswell in his essay on "Democratic Character" [80] followed the strategy of making explicit the behavioral requirements of an ideal-typical "democratic community" and theorizing about the personality types necessary (and permissible) for its functioning. Browning's efforts at modeling and simulation of community political recruitment processes can be interpreted as serving the same purposes—with a commendable degree of precision.[81]

VI. SUMMARY AND CONCLUSIONS

There is need for systematic inquiry into the ways political actors' personal psychological characteristics affect their behavior. But a satisfactory personality and politics literature has been slow to develop. The reasons for this are, I have suggested, partly in the sociology of knowledge and partly in the vexed methodological and conceptual state of the existing literature on personality and politics. To this a further answer might be added: the phenomena that need to be explained by political psychologists are enormously complicated and not easily observed.

What has preceded is a far too condensed sketch of a discussion designed to suggest ways of placing the study of personality and politics on a sounder methodological basis. My remarks have largely, in Smelser's phrase, been "methodological in a theoretical rather than an empirical sense." [82] Drawing upon the careful formulation put forth by Smith, I have suggested conceptual distinctions appropriate for reasoning about personality and politics, and attempted to use the distinctions to suggest how a variety of the formal objections to personality explanations of political behavior can be reconstructed in ways that point to the tasks and tacks appropriate for building up a more convincing literature in this area. Finally, I have attempted to suggest how three standard kinds of tasks for the personality and politics analyst—the psychological case study, typological inquiry, and aggregative analysis—relate to one another, and how each of these tasks can be pursued in a more satisfactory manner.

Riesman and Glazer once wryly commented that the field of culture-and-personality research (within which much of the personality and politics literature falls) has "more critics than practitioners." [83] Unfortunately, much of the critical activity has not contributed creatively to placing personality and politics investigations on a sounder evidential basis. Undoubtedly the progress that can be made in this direction is limited, and certainly "personality" is not the magic key to explaining all that hitherto has been puzzling about political behavior. Nevertheless, the need to know more about how the peculiar strengths and weaknesses of our species contribute to political outcomes seems sufficiently great to justify somewhat larger colonies of investigators than presently occupy the boundary territory between political science and the various branches of psychology, including personality psychology.

NOTES

[1] Alex Inkeles, "Sociology and Psychology," in Sigmund Koch, ed., *Psychology: A Study of a Science*, VI (New York: McGraw-Hill, 1963), pp. 318–19.

[2] Herbert A. Simon, "Theories of Decision-Making in Economics and Behavioral Science," *American Economic Review*, IL (1959): 253. Also his "Economics and Psychology," in Koch, *Psychology*, p. 686.

[3] Typical examples of work falling specifically under the "personality and politics" heading are cited below. Among the great many cognate literatures that address themselves to related issues are: philosophy of science (e.g. discussions of "reduction" of theories); research technology (e.g. the recent work on causal inference); and theory of history ("methodological individualism").

[4] Allport's famous list of types of definitions of the term "personality" appears in Gordon Allport, *Personality* (New York: Holt, 1937), pp. 24–57. For a further discussion of how the

term "personality" is used in this essay and of different uses of the term by political scientists and psychologists, see Fred I. Greenstein, *Personality and Politics: Problems of Evidence, Inference, and Conceptualization* (Chicago: Markham, 1969), pp. 2–5.

⁵ Robert E. Lane, *Political Ideology* (New York: Free Press, 1962).

⁶ M. Brewster Smith, Jerome Bruner, and Robert White, *Opinions and Personality* (New York: Wiley, 1956).

⁷ For example, Alexander L. George and Juliette L. George, *Woodrow Wilson and Colonel House: A Personality Study* (New York: John Day, 1956; paperback edition with new preface, New York: Dover, 1964); Lewis J. Edinger, *Kurt Schumacher: A Study in Personality and Political Behavior* (Stanford: Stanford University Press, 1965); Arnold Rogow, *James Forrestal: A Study of Personality, Politics, and Policy* (New York: Macmillan, 1963); E. Victor Wolfenstein, *The Revolutionary Personality: Lenin, Trotsky, Gandhi* (Princeton, N.J.: Princeton University Press, 1967).

⁸ Theodor W. Adorno, Else Frenkel-Brunswik, Daniel J. Levinson, and R. Nevitt Sanford, *The Authoritarian Personality* (New York: Harper, 1950); Richard Christie and Marie Jahoda, eds., *Studies in the Scope and Method of "The Authoritarian Personality"* (Glencoe, Ill.: Free Press, 1954).

⁹ Milton Rokeach, *The Open and Closed Mind* (New York: Basic Books, 1960).

¹⁰ Morris Rosenberg, "Misanthropy and Political Ideology," *American Sociological Review* 21 (1956): 690–95.

¹¹ See the forthcoming volume by Richard Christie and F. Geis, *Studies in Machiavellianism* (New York: Academic Press).

¹² David Riesman, with Nathan Glazer and Reuel Denney, *The Lonely Crowd* (New Haven, Conn.: Yale University Press, 1950).

¹³ Harold D. Lasswell, *Psychopathology and Politics* (Chicago, University of Chicago Press, 1930; paperback with afterthoughts by the author, 1960).

¹⁴ James D. Barber, *The Lawmakers* (New Haven, Conn.: Yale University Press, 1965).

¹⁵ For example, Geoffrey Gorer, "Burmese Personality," (New York: Institute of Intercultural Studies [mimeo], 1943); Ruth Benedict, *The Chrysanthemum and the Sword* (Boston: Houghton Mifflin, 1946); Geoffry Gorer, *The American People* (New York: Norton, 1948); Otto Klineberg, *Tensions Affecting International Understanding* (New York: Social Science Research Council Bulletin 62, 1950); Leon Bramson and George W. Goethals, *War: Studies from Psychology, Sociology, Anthropology* (New York: Basic Books, 1964).

¹⁶ For a representative slice of the polemical issues, see the symposium edited by Sidney Hook entitled *Psychoanalysis: Scientific Method and Philosophy* (New York: New York University Press, 1959). Among the more interesting clarificatory efforts are B. A. Farrell, "The Status of Psychoanalytic Theory," *Inquiry* 7 (1964): 104–23; Peter Madison, *Freud's Concept of Repression and Defense: Its Theoretical and Observational Language* (Minneapolis: University of Minnesota Press, 1961).

¹⁷ Substantial portions of Sections I–III draw on my "The Need for Systematic Inquiry into Personality and Politics: Introductory and Overview," *Journal of Social Issues* 24 (1968): 1–14. That article introduces and summarizes a symposium on "Personality and Politics: Methodological and Theoretical Issues."

¹⁸ Walter Lippmann, *Preface to Politics* (New York: Mitchell Kennerly, 1913), p. 2.

¹⁹ Lasswell seems first to have introduced the distinction between functional and conventional definitions of politics in Lasswell, *Psychopathology and Politics*, Chap. 4.

²⁰ Richard S. Lazarus, *Personality and Adjustment* (Englewood Cliffs, N.J.: Prentice-Hall, 1963), pp. 27–28.

²¹ *New York Times*, Oct. 28 and Nov. 13, 1962.

²² Nathan Leites, *The Operational Code of the Politburo* (New York: McGraw-Hill, 1951) and *A Study of Bolshevism* (Glencoe, Ill.: Free Press, 1953). For a later formulation by Leites, taking account of the missile crisis, see his "Kremlin Thoughts: Yielding, Rebuffing, Provoking, Retreating," RAND Corporation Memorandum RM–31618–ISA, May, 1963. These alternative theories of the psychological assumptions underlying policy options in the missile crisis are presented for illustrative purposes, and do not purport to deal adequately with the psychological and strategic issues raised by that sequence of events. Cf. Alexander L. George, "Presidential Control of Force: The Korean War and the Cuban Missile Crisis," paper presented at the 1967 Annual Meeting of the American Sociological Association.

²³ George and George, *Woodrow Wilson*, pp. 290–91.

²⁴ Richard A. Littman, "Psychology: The Socially Indifferent Science," *American Psychologist* 16 (1961): 232–36.

²⁵ The phrase "trait-correlational" is used by Smith, Bruner, and White in *Opinions and Personality*. For a discussion of the relevant literature, see Chap. 2 of that work.

²⁶ For representative examples of research in the aftermath of the response-set controversy, see Martha T. Mednick and Sarnoff A. Mednick, *Research in Personality* (New York: Holt, Rinehart and Winston, 1963). The work of Herbert McClosky is exemplary in its sophis-

ticated attention to instrument validation. See, for example, his "Conservatism and Personality," *American Political Science Review* 52 (1958): 27–45, and "Psychological Dimensions of Anomie" (with John H. Schaar), *American Sociological Review* (1965): 14–40.

[27] Theodore Abel, "Is a Psychiatric Interpretation of the German Enigma Necessary?" *American Sociological Review* 10 (1945): 457–64; Reinhard Bendix, "Compliant Behavior and Individual Personality," *American Journal of Sociology* 58 (1962): 292–303.

[28] Originally published in *Journal of Social Issues* 24 (1968): 15–28.

[29] Smith, Bruner, and White, *Opinions and Personality*.

[30] Or, for that matter, an action that is not mediated by much attitudinal activity.

[31] A more or less residual category of less dynamic determinants of attitudes is "relevant stylistic traits," such as cognitive style. For example, Smith, Bruner, and White found that one of their case-study subjects—Charles Lanlin—perceived political objects in a highly fragmented manner that seemed mainly to be a simple extension of a basic cognitive style which showed little capacity for abstraction.

[32] The classical example is race prejudice, which may be held for any of the foregoing reasons. The provision of new information may be appropriate to eliminate prejudices that have their origin in object appraisal, but the same technique may actually stiffen the attitudes of ego-defenders for whom prejudice may be a vital prop against intrapsychic perils. For the latter, some more or less psychotherapeutic technique is appropriate. But neither technique will reach the individual whose prejudice mainly performs the function of relating himself to others in his environment.

[33] The remainder of this section draws very heavily upon (and in a few instances directly incorporates the text of) my "The Impact of Personality on Politics: An Attempt to Clear Away Underbrush," *American Political Science Review* 61 (1967): 629–41. Most of the assertions made here are substantially expanded in that essay. Also see chapter two of my *Personality and Politics, op cit*.

[34] Urie Bronfenbrenner, "Personality and Participation: The Case of the Vanishing Variables," *Journal of Social Issues* 16 (1960): 54–63. For an alternative, and I think, more useful, approach to analyzing the determinants of participation, see David Horton Smith, "A Psychological Model of Individual Participation in Formal Voluntary Organizations: Applications to Some Chilean Data," *American Journal of Sociology* 72 (1966): 249–66.

[35] Herbert Hyman, *Survey Design and Analysis* (Glencoe: Free Press, 1955), pp 254–57.

[36] David Easton, *The Political System* (New York: Knopf, 1953), p. 196.

[37] In this objection, the implicit meaning of the term "personality" is "personal variability."

[38] The importance of considering the interaction of psychological and situational determinants of political behavior is emphasized in James Davies, *Human Nature in Politics* (New York: Wiley, 1963).

[39] Rufus P. Browning and Herbert Jacob, "Power Motivation and the Political Personality," *Public Opinion Quarterly* 28 (1964): 75–90.

[40] Rufus P. Browning, "The Interaction of Personality and Political System in Decisions to Run for Office: Some Data and a Simulation Technique," *Journal of Social Issues* 24, (1968): 93–110.

[41] The observations on the interplay of personality and situation in Browning and Jacob's work more than vindicate a strategy first proposed by Lasswell in *Psychopathology and Politics,* of isolating "functionally comparable" processes and phenomena for study in order to eliminate the high degree of "noise" and heterogeneity one finds when one examines personality concomitants of roles that are formally but not actually similar (such as in the Justice of Peace office in the two Louisiana parishes). Browning and Jacob's careful isolation of comparable situational opportunities for the exercise of power is a counterpart of Lasswell's strategy in devising his "political type" construct: individuals fitting into Lasswell's "political" (or power-centered) type seek out situations that are comparable in that they permit the exercise of power. These situations may or may not be a part of the formal political process. As Lasswell puts it, "the simple fact that a role is performed that is conventionally perceived as political . . . does not warrant classifying a person among the political personalities nor, conversely, does failure to play a conventionally recognized political role necessarily imply that the person is not power-oriented. Obviously the comprehensive appraisal of any social context must sample *all* value shaping and sharing processes, as they are *conventionally* understood, if the political personalities in the functional sense are to be identified. The point is implied, when, as is sometimes the case, it is said that during the rapid growth phase of a private capitalist economy the most power-centered persons engage in 'business'." Harold D. Lasswell, "A Note on 'Types' of Political Personality: Nuclear, Co-Relational, Developmental," *Journal of Social Issues* 24 (1968): 81–92.

[42] Lasswell, *Psychopathology and Politics*; Erich Fromm, *Escape from Freedom* (New York: Holt, Rinehart and Winston, 1941); Adorno et al., *The Authoritarian Personality*.

[43] Robert E. Lane and David O. Sears, *Public Opinion* (Englewood Cliffs, N.J.: Prentice-Hall, 1964), p. 76.

[44] Herbert Hyman and Paul B. Sheatsley, " 'The Authoritarian Personality'—A Methodological Critique," in Richard Christie and Marie Jahoda, eds., *Studies in the Scope and Method of "The Authoritarian Personality,"* pp. 50–122.

[45] Daniel Katz, Charles McClintock, and Irving Sarnoff, "The Measurement of Ego-Defense as Related to Attitude Change," *Journal of Personality* 25 (1957): 465–74.

[46] The attitude change procedure used by Katz and his associates was an "insight" technique, designed to introduce awareness of the role of defense mechanisms in producing one's attitudes. For the present purposes, which are largely illustrative, I shall ignore a number of thorny questions about whether Katz *et al.* were actually successful in measuring ego-defensiveness and reducing defensive barriers to attitude change.

[47] Alex Inkeles, "Sociology and Psychology," p. 354.

[48] Sidney Hook, *The Hero in History* (New York: John Day, 1943).

[49] Michel Crozier, *The Bureaucratic Phenomenon* (Chicago: University of Chicago Press, 1964), p. 192.

[50] This distinction is discussed at much greater length in my "The Impact of Personality on Politics: An Attempt to Clear Away Underbrush."

[51] Robert C. Tucker, "The Dictator and Totalitarianism," *World Politics* 17 (1965): 555–84.

[52] Alexander L. George, "Some Uses of Dynamic Psychology in Political Biography," unpublished paper, 1960.

[53] See Fromm's well-known account in *Escape from Freedom*. For an attempt to deal more systematically with aggregate effects of individual psychological characteristics, see Harry Eckstein, *A Theory of Stable Democracy*, Princeton University Center of International Studies, Research Monograph No. 10 (April, 1961).

[54] The most extended appreciation of the George and George volume is by Bernard Brodie: "A psychoanalytical Interpretation of Woodrow Wilson," Bruce Mazlish, ed., *Psychoanalysis and History* (Englewood Cliffs, N.J.: Prentice-Hall, 1963), pp. 115–23. For a brief set of critical remarks that are, I think, poorly taken, but illustrative of the lack of general awareness of the possibilities for rigorous reasoning in single-case psychological analysis, see Page Smith, *The Historian and History* (New York: Knopf, 1964), pp. 125–26.

[55] George and George, *Woodrow Wilson*, "Research Note," pp. 217–21; Alexander L. George and Juliette L. George, "Woodrow Wilson: Personality and Political Behavior," paper presented at the 1956 Annual Meeting of the American Political Science Association; Alexander George, see note 52; Alexander George, "Power as a Compensatory Value for Political Leaders," *Journal of Social Issues* 24 (1968): 29–50.

[56] Cf. the Preface to the Dover edition of *Woodrow Wilson and Colonel House.*

[57] *Woodrow Wilson and Colonel House*, pp. 290–91.

[58] See in particular George's paper cited in note 52, and his "Power as a Compensatory Value for Political Leaders."

[59] Adorno et al., *The Authoritarian Personality.*

[60] Christie and Jahoda, *Studies in the Scope and Method of "The Authoritarian Personality."*

[61] Richard Christie and Peggy Cook, "A Guide to Published Literature Relating to the Authoritarian Personality through 1956," *Journal of Psychology* 45 (1958): 171–99. For a recent literature review, see John P. Kirscht and Ronald C. Dillehay, *Dimensions of Authoritarianism* (Lexington: University of Kentucky Press, 1967).

[62] Edward Shils, "Authoritarianism: 'Right' and 'Left,' " in Christie and Jahoda, pp. 24–49.

[63] H. H. Hyman and P. B. Sheatsley, "Authoritarianism Re-examined," in Christie and Jahoda, *Studies in the Scope and Method of "The Authoritarian Personality,"* pp. 123–96.

[64] see the articles reprinted in Chap. 6 of Mednick and Mednick, *Research in Personality.*

[65] See Note 61.

[66] These remarks are substantially expanded upon in my "Personality and Political Socialization: The Theories of Authoritarian and Democratic Character," *Annals of the American Academy of Political and Social Science* 361 (1965): 81–95. The statements in quotation marks are from *The Authoritarian Personality*, unless otherwise indicated; for further documentation see "Personality and Political Socialization." In addition, portions of the passages that follow are adapted from my "The Need for Systematic Study of Personality and Politics."

[67] M. Brewster Smith has reported a technique that does not rely upon the overused F-scale for identifying individuals exhibiting the characteristics of the authoritarian type. See the description of Q-Sort analyses of psychiatric interview data in his "An Analysis of Two Measures of 'Authoritarianism' Among Peace Corps Teachers," *Journal of Personality* 33 (1965): 513–35.

[68] Greenstein, "Personality and Political Socialization," p. 87.

[69] Irwin Katz and Lawrence Benjamin, "Effects of White Authoritarianism in Biracial Work Groups," *Journal of Abnormal and Social Psychology* 61 (1960): 448–56.

[70] What follows is based on my "The Need for Systematic Study of Personality and Politics."

[71] J. David Singer, "Man and World Politics: The Psychological Interface," *Journal of Social Issues* 24 (1968): 127–56.

[72] Neil J. Smelser, "Personality and the Explanation of Political Phenomena at the Social-System Level: A Methodological Statement," *Journal of Social Issues* 24 (1968): 111–26.

[73] Alex Inkeles and Daniel J. Levinson, "National Character: The Study of Modal Personality and Sociocultural Systems," in Gardner Lindzey, ed., *Handbook of Social Psychology, II* (Cambridge, Mass.: Addison-Wesley, 1954), pp. 977–1020.

[74] Peter M. Blau, "Structural Effects," *American Sociological Review* 25 (1960): 178–93; James A. Davis, Joe L. Spaeth, and Carolyn Huson, "A Technique for Analyzing the Effects of Group Composition," *American Sociological Review* 26 (1961): 215–25.

[75] Angus Campbell, Phillip E. Converse, Warren E. Miller, and Donald E. Stokes, *Elections and the Political Order* (New York: Wiley, 1966). See especially Campell's chapter on "surge and decline" (pp. 400–62) and the discussion by Converse and Dupeux of "politicization" in France and the United States (pp. 269–91).

[76] J. David Singer, "Man and World Politics," p. 143.

[77] For methodological suggestions, see Hayward R. Alker, Jr., "The Long Road to International Relations Theory: Problems of Statistical Nonadditivity," *World Politics* 18 (1966): 623–55.

[78] Gardner Ackley, *Macroeconomic Theory* (New York: Macmillan, 1961), p. 573.

[79] Herbert Hyman, "The Modification of a Personality-Centered Conceptual System when the Project is Translated from a National to a Cross-National Study," in Bjorn Christiansen, Herbert Hyman, and Ragnar Rommetveit, *Cross-National Social Research* (Oslo: International Seminar, Institute for Social Research, 1951, mimeograph).

[80] Harold D. Lasswell, "Democratic Character," in *Political Writings of Harold D. Lasswell* (Glencoe: Free Press, 1951), pp. 465–525. See also the gloss on this essay in my "Harold D. Lasswell's Concept of Democratic Character," *Journal of Politics* 30 (1968): 696–709.

[81] Rufus Browning, "The Interaction of Personality and Political System."

[82] Neil J. Smelser, "Personality and the Explanation of Political Phenomena."

[83] David Riesman and Nathan Glazer, "The Lonely Crowd: A Reconsideration in 1960," in Seymour M. Lipset and Leo Lowenthal, eds., *Culture and Social Character* (New York: Free Press, 1961), p. 437.

2

Types of Variables and Their Interconnections

With exceptional expository elegance, Smith systematically builds up in this essay a visual representation of the principal types of variables that are likely to be present in analyses of the impact of personality on politics: situational, social background, and larger social system variables, plus a range of psychological predispositional variables—attitudes, self-other orientations, ego defenses, object appraisal (that is, cognitive) orientations, and aspects of personal style. Section III of the preceding selection summarizes Smith's map discussion in several paragraphs. A briefer summary, composed by Smith, appeared as an abstract published in the same periodical as the original article:[1] "A scheme is presented for the analysis of relationships in the sphere of personality and politics. The scheme places psychological determinants of political action in the context of other classes of determinants. It further exemplifies a 'functional' approach to the roots of political action in personality. The contributions of psychological, sociological, political-economic and historical perspectives to the explanation of political behavior are seen as complementary, not competitive."

NOTE

[1] *Journal of Social Issues,* 24 (July, 1968), 159.

A MAP FOR THE ANALYSIS
OF PERSONALITY AND POLITICS

M. Brewster Smith

Progress in the social and behavioral sciences has in general not been marked by major theoretical "breakthroughs." As those of us who profess one or another of these disciplines look upon the succession of research and theoretical interests that capture the center of the stage, we may sometimes wonder if there is indeed any progress at all. Particularly if we fixated on the physical sciences as models of what a good science should be,[1] we can easily become discouraged. As therapy for this depressive mood, however, one has only to scan the textbooks of former generations and some of the earlier landmark contributions to our fields: the fact of progress, of the cumulativeness of understanding that is the hallmark of science, is immediately apparent.

The progress that we see, however, is not on the pattern according to which Einstein included and supplanted Newton, or even on that by which the modern theory of the chemical valence bond makes sense of Mendeleyev's descriptive table of elements. In addition to the development and refinement of research methods and the accretion of facts, our kind of progress has involved developing some more or less satisfactory "theories of the middle range" (Merton, 1957), and, especially, a steady increase in the sophistication of the questions that we ask and in our sensitivity to the variables that are likely to be relevant to them.

To codify this kind of progress, and to make our gains readily accessible as we face new problems of research and application, we need something other than grand theory in the old literary style: we are not ready for genuinely theoretical integration, and to pretend that we are is to hamper rather than to aid us in attacking new problems with an open mind. Rather, it often seems most useful for particular purposes to attempt to link the islands of knowledge turned up in the pursuit of middle-range theories and to sort out the kinds of variables that appear likely to be relevant, by means of mapping operations that have only modest theoretical pretensions. When the variables are drawn from the home territory of different academic disciplines, as is bound to be the case in the study of any concrete social problem and is also true of many facets of a context-defined field like political science, ventures in mapping become particularly important. They are the best we can do toward interdisciplinary integration, which in these instances is required of us by the nature of the task.

This essay sketches such a map for the analysis of personality and politics, an outgrowth of my attempts to apply the approach developed in *Opinions and Personality* (Smith, Bruner and White, 1956; Smith, 1958) to the analysis of various social problems involving social attitudes and behavior, particularly McCarthyism, civil liberties and anti-Semitism.[2] While it obviously bears the marks of its origins, I have had to go considerably beyond the range of variables, mainly psychological ones, that Bruner, White and I were dealing with.

Originally published in the *Journal of Social Issues*, 24 (July, 1968), 15–28.

A map like this is *not* a theory that can be confirmed or falsified by testing deductions against evidence; it is rather a heuristic device, a declaration of intellectual strategy, that is to be judged as profitable or sterile rather than as true or false. I have found it personally useful in coming to grips with topics that were new to me, and in organizing what I think we know for my students in teaching. Placing particular variables and relationships as it does in larger context, it may have the further virtue of counteracting one's natural tendency to stress the exclusive importance of the variables or theories that one happens to be momentarily interested in. Many persisting disputes in the social sciences are like the story of the blind men and the elephant. A good map helps us to keep the whole elephant in view.

THE SCHEMATIC MAP

Schematic as it is, the map is too complicated to take in at a glance. Figure 1 presents the gross outlines—the continents in their asserted relationships. In

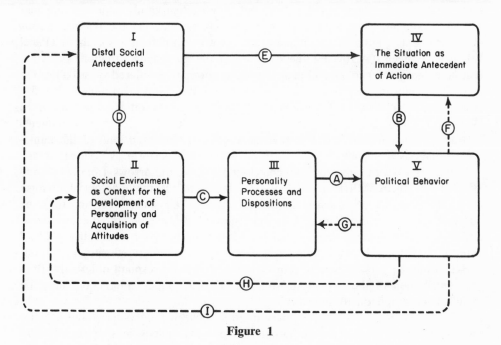

Figure 1

Figures 2 and 3, we will look in more detail at particular segments of the terrain. The full map, given in Figure 4, should then become intelligible. Certain intentional omissions and simplifications must finally be noted by way of qualification. Illustrations will be provided casually en route, for the most part without documentation from the literature.

The Map in Its Simplest Form

Figure 1 diagrams the major components of a framework for the analysis of personality and politics in terms of five major panels. In keeping with the psychological focus of the map, Panel III (which indicates types of variables relating to the processes and dispositions of personality) occupies the center of the stage. Causal relationships are indicated by arrows. Because we are used to reading from left to right, I have put the payoff in actual behavior (Panel V) at the extreme right. This panel is concerned with personal political decisions as carried into action: voting, information-seeking, policy formation or implementation, influence attempts or—the source of much of our psychological data—question answering. The data that come from our observations of people, what they say as well as what they do, belong here; only by reconstruction and inference do we arrive at the contents of the central personality panel.

Panel IV represents the person's behavioral situation as an immediate antecedent of action; Panel II includes features of the person's more enduring social environment to which we turn to explain how he has happened to become the sort of political actor that we find him to be; and Panel I represents the more remote or distal facts of politics, economics, history, etc., that contribute to the distinctive features of the environment in which he was socialized and of the immediate situations in which he acts. From the standpoint of the behaving individual, the contents of Panel I are conceptually distal but may be temporally contemporaneous: a political system, for example (Panel I), affects (Arrow D) the political norms about democracy, authority, legitimacy, etc., to which a person is socialized (Panel II); it also affects (Arrow E) the structure of the immediate situations of action that he is likely to encounter (Panel IV)—the alternatives offered on a ballot, the procedural rules in a legislative body, etc. Temporally distal determinants are also assigned to Panel I: thus the history of slavery, the plantation economy, the Civil War and Reconstruction as determinants of the politically relevant environments in which participants in southern politics have been socialized, and of the immediate situations that comprise the stage on which they perform as political actors.

If we start with behavioral outcomes in Panel V, the arrows (marked A and B) that link them with Panels III and IV represent the methodological premise emphasized by the great psychologist Kurt Lewin: all social behavior is to be analyzed as a joint resultant of characteristics of the *person,* on the one hand, and of his psychological *situation,* on the other. The behavior of a single political actor may differ substantially as he faces differently structured situations; conversely, different persons who face the same situation will respond differently. Both the contribution of the person and that of his situation, in interaction, must be included in any adequate analysis.

For long, there was a disciplinary quarrel between psychologists and sociologists about the relevance and importance of personal dispositions (primarily *attitudes*) versus situations in determining social behavior. To take this feature of our map seriously is to regard the argument as silly and outmoded: both classes of determinants are jointly indispensable. The study of "personality and politics" cannot afford to neglect situational factors, which must in principle be taken into account if we are to isolate the distinctive contributions of personality. In concrete cases in which analysis along these lines is undertaken so as to guide social action, one may ask, of course, whether the personal or the situational component is more *strategic* in terms of accessibility to major influence. It may be more feasible, for example, to influence the normative structure that pertains to interracial relations than to carry through the program of mass psychoanalysis that might be required in order to reverse authoritarian personality trends that predispose people toward prejudice and discriminatory behavior. The practical question of strategic importance and accessibility does not seem to be as charged with disciplinary *amour-propre* as are the theoretical issues that still tend to divide the proponents of personality-oriented and of situational approaches.

The dotted arrows of relationship that leave the behavioral panel require special mention. Political behavior has consequences as well as causes, and for the sake of formal completeness some of these are suggested by the dotted "feedback loops" in the map. As Leon Festinger has argued on the basis of considerable evidence, self-committing behavior may have effects in turn upon a person's attitudes (Arrow G) (Festinger, 1957; Brehm and Cohen, 1962). A political actor who adopts a position for expedient reasons may be convinced by his own rhetoric, or—similar in result though different in the process that is assumed—he may shift his attitudes to accord with his actions in order to reduce feelings of "dissonance." The dotted Arrows F, H and I merely recognize that individual behavior also has effects in the social world. What the person does in a situation may immediately change it (Arrow F); as we integrate across the behavior of many individuals, the joint consequences of the behavior of the many eventually alter the social environments that shape and support the attitudes of each (Arrow H). In the longer run (Arrow I), the behaviors of individuals constitute a society and its history.

To be sure, this is a psychologist's map that focuses on the attitudes and behavior of individual persons. A political sociologist would have to give explicit attention to matters that remain implicit in the feedback arrows—to the social structures according to which individual behaviors are integrated to have political effects. His map would necessarily be differently centered and elaborated than the present one.

Panels III and IV

With the broad framework laid out, we can now look at the details of Panels III and IV, still working from the proximal to the distal determinants of behavior (see Figure 2). The contents of Panel IV (The Situation as Immediate Antecedent of Action) remind us that an important component of any behavioral situation is the set of norms or prescriptions for behavior that are consensually held to apply in it. Students of political behavior at the various levels of governmental organization are concerned with recurring types of situations that confront the citizen as constituent, voter or petitioner: the legislator, the executive, the administrative functionary, the party leader. Much of the variation in personal behavior, not only across types of situations but within the same type in different political structures and different historical periods, will be attributable to differences and changes in the norms that prevail. Apart from the norms, there are of course many other situational features that are also important as codeterminants of action—among them, the competitive or cooperative relations that hold with other actors who participate in the situation, the degree of urgency with which decision or action is required, the contingencies of cost and benefit that obtain (see Thibaut and Kelley, 1959). Lore about the relevant features of political situations is a principal currency of political science.

Turn now to Panel III, Personality Processes and Dispositions. We are concerned here with inferred dispositions of the person that he brings to any situation he encounters, and with their basis in his experience and motivational processes. Social psychologists have come to use the term *attitudes* to refer to such dispositions, when they represent integrations of cognitive, emotional and conative tendencies around a psychological object such as a political figure or issue. Our problem is a dual one: to formulate how a person's attitudes come to bear on his political behavior and how these attitudes arise and are sustained in relation to their part in the ongoing operations of the person's psychological economy.

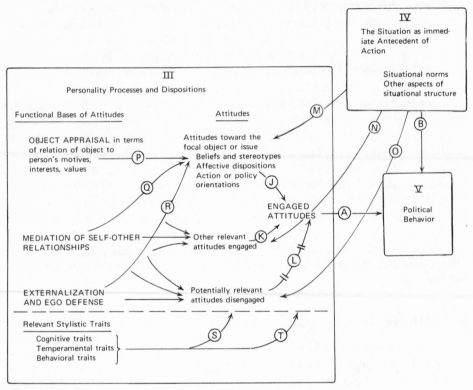

Figure 2

A first point suggested in Figure 2 is that we cannot take for granted just which of a person's attitudes will become engaged as a codeterminant of his behavior in a political situation. Political scientists are probably less naive than psychologists about this. A citizen's presidential vote for one or another candidate depends, as we know (Campbell, Converse, Miller, and Stokes, 1960), not only on his focal attitude toward that candidate, but also on attitudes toward the alternative candidates, toward party and toward issues. A legislator's vote on a bill will depend not only on situational factors (including whether or not a roll call is involved) and on his attitudes toward the focal issue but also on other relevant attitudes that become engaged—toward tangential issues, toward the party leadership, toward political survival or whatever. The situation plays a dual role here: both as a codeterminant, together with his engaged attitudes, of what he does (B) (the legislator may want to vote for a bill but not dare to), and as differentially activating certain of the actor's attitudes (M and N) while allowing or encouraging other potentially relevant attitudes to remain in abeyance (O). In recent years, issues concerning Negro civil rights have come to be posed in the Congress and elsewhere in such pointed terms that political actors probably find it less feasible than formerly to isolate their attitudes of democratic fair play from engagement—attitudes embodied in the American creed (Myrdal, 1962) to which most citizens have been socialized to some degree.

Social psychological research may elect to measure and manipulate one attitude at a time for good analytic reasons, but people rarely behave in such a piecemeal fashion. What gets into the mix of a person's engaged attitudes, and with what weighting, makes a big difference. Given the complexity of these relationships, there is no reason to suppose that people's political behavior should uniformly correspond to their attitudes on the focal issue. It is surprising that some psychologists and sociologists have been surprised at the lack of one-to-one correspondence between single attitudes and behavior and have questioned the validity of attitude measurement on these irrelevant grounds.

Moving toward the left of Panel III, we turn from the problem of how attitudes are differentially aroused to that of how they are formed and sustained. The approach taken here is the functional one which posits that a person acquires and maintains attitudes and other learned psychological structures to the extent that they are in some way useful to him in his inner economy of adjustment and his outer economy of adaptation. The scheme for classifying the functional basis of attitudes is one that I have discussed in greater detail elsewhere (Smith, Bruner and White, 1956; Smith, 1968). It answers the question, "Of what use to a man are his opinions?", under three rubrics: *object appraisal, mediation of self-other relationships* and *externalization and ego defense.*

Object Appraisal

Under object appraisal, we recognize the ways in which a person's attitudes serve him by "sizing up" significant aspects of the world in terms of their relevance to his motives, interests and values. As Walter Lippmann long ago (1922) made clear, all attitudes, not just "prejudice," involve an element of "prejudgment"; they are useful to the person in part because they prepare him for his encounters with reality enabling him to avoid the confusion and inefficiency of appraising each new situation afresh in all its complexity. In the most general way, holding *any* attitude brings a bit of order into the flux of a person's psychological world; the specific content of a person's attitudes reflects to varying degrees his appraisal of how the attitudinal object bears upon his interests and enterprises. This function involves reality testing and is likely to be involved to some minimal degree in even the least rational of attitudes—which on closer examination may turn out to be relatively reasonable within the person's own limited framework of appraisal.

Mediation of Self-Other Relationships

A person's attitudes not only embody a provisional appraisal of what for him is significant reality; they also serve to mediate the kind of relationships with others and the kind of conception of self that he is motivated to maintain. Is it important to the decision maker to think of himself as a liberal Democrat? Then his adopting a liberal stand on any of a variety of issues may contribute to his self regard. Does he rather set much stock in being right in the light of history? Such motivation, by orienting him toward an ideal reference group, may make him relatively independent of immediate social pressures. To the extent that by self-selective recruitment politicians are disproportionately likely to be "other directed" in Riesman's sense (1950), however, they may be predisposed by personality to be especially vulnerable to such pressures.

Externalization and Ego Defense

Finally comes the class of functions to which psychoanalytic depth psychology has given the closest attention, here labelled externalization and ego defense. This is the functional basis to which Lasswell (1930) gave exclusive emphasis in his classic formula for the political man: private motives displaced onto public objects, rationalized in terms of the public interest. It also underlies the conception of the "authoritarian personality" (Adorno, Frenkel-Brunswik, Levinson, and Sanford, 1950)—a posture in which an essentially weak ego puts up a facade of strength that requires bolstering through identification with the strong, the conventional and the in-group, and rejection of the weak, the immoral, the out-group. Given the appeal of depth interpretation in the study of personality and politics, there is little need to expand on these themes; it is more necessary to insist that externalization and ego defense are only part of the story.

The arrows P, Q and R raise the functional question about the motivational sources of any attitude that a person holds. Arrows S and T, near the bottom of the panel, reflect on their part a different kind of relationship. A person's attitudes and the way they engage with particular political situations bear the mark of his stylistic traits of personality as well as of the purposes that they serve for him. Intelligence or stupidity, Kennedy incisiveness or Eisenhower vagueness, zest or apathy, optimism or pessimism, decisiveness or hesitation—cognitive, temperamental and behavioral traits like these may have their own history in the residues of the person's previous motivational conflicts, but their immediate relevance for his political attitudes and behavior is hardly motivational. His attitudes and actions in the sphere of politics, as in other realms, inevitably reflect such pervasive personal qualities, which can have momentous behavioral consequences. A purely functional account is likely to neglect them.

Panel II

The foregoing analysis provides us with leverage for identifying aspects of the person's social environment that are relevant to the development, maintenance and change of his political attitudes and his stylistic personality traits, as we turn to Panel II at the left of our map (Figure 3). To the extent that a person's attitudes in a particular political context reflect processes of object appraisal, he should be responsive to the information that his environment provides about the attitudinal object or issue (Arrow U). The actual facts about it will be important in this connection only as they affect the information that is socially available to him, and as we know, the quality and quantity of this information vary widely from issue to issue and across the various niches that people occupy in society.

The information on a topic that reaches a person through the channels of communication has a dual relevance, as the internal arrows in Panel II are intended to suggest: not only does it feed into his processes of object appraisal, but it carries further information—a second-order message, so to speak—about the social norms that prevail. When discussions of birth control begin to percolate through

Catholic channels, or debates about the pros and cons of China policy through American ones, not only is new grist provided for object appraisal; the important news is conveyed that these previously taboo topics have become moot and discussable. As Arrow V indicates, the second motivational basis of attitudes—the mediation of self-other relations—then may lead to attitudinal consequences that point to a different resultant in behavior. It becomes safe to think in new ways.

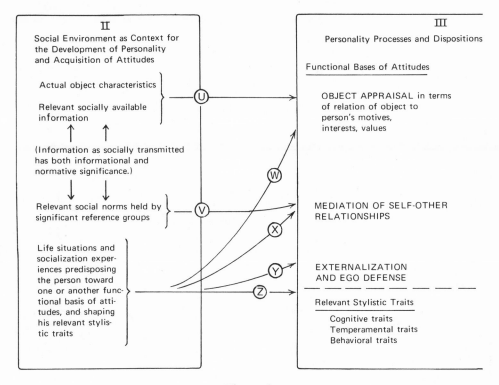

Figure 3

Besides providing the environmental data that the first two attitudinal functions can work with to generate new attitudes or to sustain or change established ones,[3] the person's life situation and socialization experiences may predispose him—in general, or in a particular topical domain—toward one or another of the functional bases of attitudes (Arrows W, X and Y). What makes the rational man, in whom the first function predominates? The Utopia has not yet arrived in which we know the answer, but recent studies of socialization are beginning to become relevant to the question, and it is a good guess that part of the story is rearing by loving and confident parents who give reasons for their discipline. In the shorter run, environments that augment one's self esteem and allay one's anxiety should also favor object appraisal. Research in the wake of Riesman (1950), including the Witkin group's studies of field dependence-independence (Witkin et al., 1962) and Miller and Swanson's (1958, 1960) work on child rearing and personality in entrepreneurial and bureaucratic families, contains suggestions about the sources of primary orientation to the second function, mediation of self-other relationships. As for externalization and ego defense, again the picture is not clear, but conditions that subject the developing person to arbitrary authority, that deflate self esteem, that arouse vague

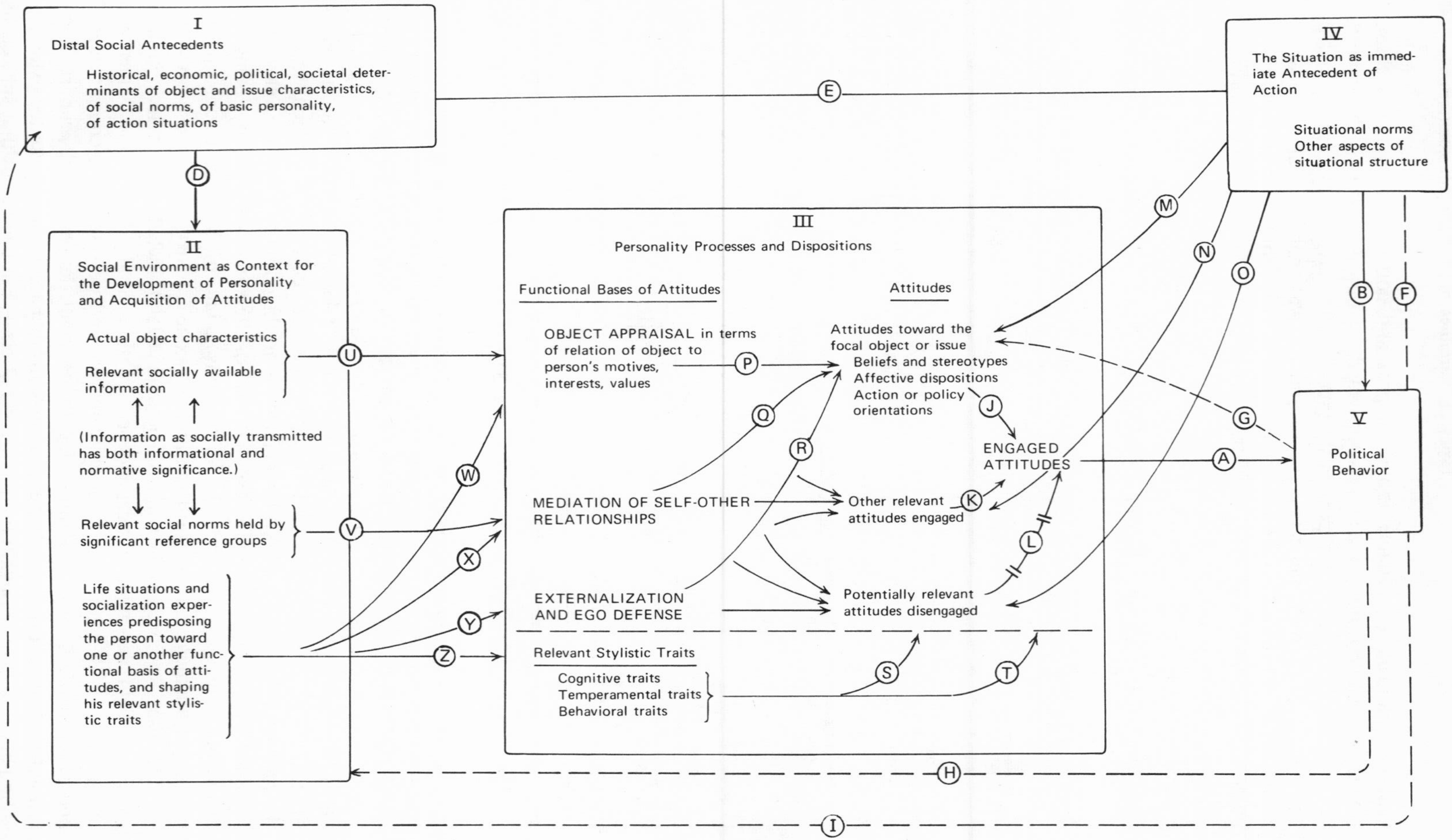

I — Distal Social Antecedents

Historical, economic, political, societal determinants of object and issue characteristics, of social norms, of basic personality, of action situations

II — Social Environment as Context for the Development of Personality and Acquisition of Attitudes

- Actual object characteristics
- Relevant socially available information

(Information as socially transmitted has both informational and normative significance.)

- Relevant social norms held by significant reference groups
- Life situations and socialization experiences predisposing the person toward one or another functional basis of attitudes, and shaping his relevant stylistic traits

III — Personality Processes and Dispositions

Functional Bases of Attitudes

- OBJECT APPRAISAL in terms of relation of object to person's motives, interests, values
- MEDIATION OF SELF-OTHER RELATIONSHIPS
- EXTERNALIZATION AND EGO DEFENSE

Relevant Stylistic Traits
- Cognitive traits
- Temperamental traits
- Behavioral traits

Attitudes

- Attitudes toward the focal object or issue
- Beliefs and stereotypes
- Affective dispositions
- Action or policy orientations

ENGAGED ATTITUDES

- Other relevant attitudes engaged
- Potentially relevant attitudes disengaged

IV — The Situation as immediate Antecedent of Action

- Situational norms
- Other aspects of situational structure

V — Political Behavior

Connecting labels: A, B, D, E, F, G, H, I, J, K, L, M, N, O, P, Q, R, S, T, U, V, W, X, Y, Z

Figure 4

anxiety, that provoke hostility but block its relatively direct expression toward the source of the frustration, seem likely sources.

The final arrow Z is drawn not to complete the alphabet but to make place for the findings of personality research, as they emerge, concerning the determinants in socialization of personal stylistic traits.

The entire map can now be reassembled in Figure 4. Arrows U to Z, taken together, replace Arrow C in Figure 1.

SOME OMISSIONS AND SIMPLIFICATIONS

The usefulness of a map and its inherent limitations are two sides of the same coin: its status as a simplification and schematization of reality. There are many complexities that the present map does not attempt to handle. Some of the major omissions, which I note briefly here, arise from the fact that the role of the basic psychological apparatuses and processes of motivation, perception and learning is assumed implicitly rather than explicitly delineated.

The triadic functional classification attempts to sort out the ways in which a person's attitudes are rooted in his underlying motives and their fusions and transformations, whatever they may be. It assumes but does not spell out a conception of human motivation.

As for perception, it would elaborate the map to an incomprehensible tangle to give due recognition to what we know about perceptual selectivity, the ways in which a person's existing expectations, motives and attitudes affect what he will attend to and how he will register and categorize it. A perceptual screening process intervenes between the environmental facts (Panel II) and what the person makes of them (Panel III); likewise between the immediate behavioral situation as it might appear to an objective observer (Panel IV) and how the person defines it for himself, which in the last analysis is the guise in which it affects his behavior.

In regard to learning, the present formulation makes the broad functionalist assumption that people in general acquire attitudes that are useful, that is, rewarding to them. But it ignores the details of the learning process, and such consequences of learning as the persistence of learned structures beyond their original point of usefulness. Much of the content of political attitudes, moreover, may be acquired by an individual quite incidentally, in his unfocused, only mildly attentive effort to make sense of his world. The culture says, in effect, "This is how things are with (Russia) (China) (Republicans) (Southerners) (Negroes) (socialized medicine)," and in the absence of better information, he takes note. Such incidentally learned, psychologically marginal "information" may at the time have little real payoff in object appraisal or social adjustment (the person may have no occasion for dealing with the object or issue, and it may not matter enough to his significant reference groups to become part of the currency of his self-other relationships), yet, should the occasion arise, the basis for resonance to certain political positions rather than others has been laid.

NOTES

¹ Other than meteorology, which in some respects offers such an appropriate model that I am puzzled that social scientists have not picked it up.

² In the area of McCarthyism and civil liberties, I prepared an unpublished memorandum for Samuel A. Stouffer in connection with planning for the studies leading to his book on the subject (Stouffer, 1955). The application to anti-Semitism is embodied in a pamphlet (Smith, 1965) on which I draw heavily in the present essay, with gratitude to the Anti-Defamation League of B'nai B'rith for support in the project of which it was a by-product.

³ Environment data play a much more incidental and erratic role in relation to the function of externalization and ego defense.

REFERENCES

Adorno, T. W., Frenkel-Brunswik, Else, Levinson, Daniel J. and Sanford, R. Nevitt. *The authoritarian personality*. New York: Harper, 1950.

Brehm, Jack W. and Cohen, Arthur R. *Explorations in cognitive dissonance*. New York: Wiley, 1962.

Campbell, Angus, Converse, Philip E., Miller, Warren E. and Stokes, Donald E. *The American voter*. New York: Wiley, 1960.

Festinger, Leon. *A theory of cognitive dissonance*. Chicago: Row, Peterson, 1957.

Lasswell, Harold D. *Psychopathology and politics*. Chicago: University of Chicago Press, 1930.

Lippmann, Walter. *Public opinion*. New York and London: Macmillan, 1922.

Merton, Robert K. *Social theory and social structure* (rev. ed.). Glencoe, Illinois: The Free Press, 1957.

Miller, Daniel R. and Swanson, Guy E. *The changing American parent*. New York: Wiley, 1958.

Miller, Daniel R. and Swanson, Guy E. *Inner conflict and defense*. New York: Holt, 1960.

Myrdal, Gunnar. *An American dilemma* (rev. ed.). New York: Harper, 1962.

Riesman, David. *The lonely crowd*. New Haven, Conn.: Yale University Press, 1950.

Smith, M. Brewster. Opinions, personality, and political behavior. *American Political Science Review*, 52, 1958: 1–17.

Smith, M. Brewster. *Determinants of anti-Semitism: a social-psychological map*. New York: Anti-defamation League of B'nai B'rith. N.D. (1965).

Smith, M. Brewster. Attitude change. *International encyclopedia of the social sciences*. New York: Macmillan and Free Press, 1968.

Smith, M. Brewster, Bruner, Jerome S., and White, Robert W. *Opinions and personality*. New York: Wiley, 1956.

Stouffer, Samuel A. *Communism, conformity, and civil liberties*. Garden City, N.Y.: Doubleday, 1955.

Thibaut, John W. and Kelley, Harold H. *The social psychology of groups*. New York: Wiley, 1959.

Witkin, Herman A., Dyk, R. B., Faterson, Hanna F., Goodenough, Donald R. and Karp, Stephen A. *Psychological differentiation. Studies of development*. New York: Wiley, 1962.

3

A Critique of Psychological Reductionism

This essay, by a well-known sociologist, is one of the most carefully thought out —and most often cited—of the various writings that criticize psychological (and especially psychiatric) explanations of complex sociopolitical phenomena. In particular, Bendix is replying to attempts to adduce psychiatric explanations of the explosion of brutal irrationality evidenced in German National Socialism. Thus, many of his examples are designed to refute or qualify the assertions of writers such as Erich Fromm that German "authoritarian character structure" (see selections 15–17, below) was in some way responsible for Nazism.

Bendix's essay is cast in broader terms than the specifics of explaining Nazism, however. His own summary of his argument, as stated in the abstract preceding the original publication is: "Propositions in sociology focus on what is true of large numbers of individuals, considered as social groups. Propositions in psychiatry focus on what is true of all men, while the underlying therapeutic evidence always deals with what is true of the individual. Psychiatric interpretations of collective behavior presuppose a nonexistent integration between the individual and conventional behavior patterns. But the experience of the Nazi regime suggests that people submit to social pressures regardless of their character structure. The mores and folkways of a society are the challenge with which people cope emotionally in a variety of ways." Thus the title of Bendix's essay, spun out into a declarative sentence, suggests that explanations of sociopolitical behavior in terms of the personality predispositions of political actors are of doubtful value because in fact individuals of diverse *individual personality* characteristics behave in identical (or at least similar) ways in the course of *complying* with the requirements of the social situations in which they are placed—for example, the severe sanctions for deviant behavior in Germany under the Nazis.

To the editors' way of thinking (see pp. 14–16 of selection one), this formulation overstates the lack of fit between underlying psychological predispositions and behavior in social and political situations. At a minimum, there appears to be room for individual psychological orientations to have an impact on the behavior of leaders, since leaders' roles may sometimes present few restraints on them. To continue the example of Nazi Germany, it has been argued that the totalitarian leader is especially unrestrained and that his personality is likely to have rather undiluted effects on his behavior, with great consequences for his political system.[1] By extension, personality characteristics are likely to affect the behavior of any political actor under circumstances that are lacking in sanctions imposing particular courses of action and in other ambiguous circumstances. Furthermore, as Bendix himself argues, there probably are individual differences in the *way* that sanctioned conformity occurs—the individual who believes in what he is doing and finds it emotionally satisfying is more likely to behave effectively, loyally and

45

expeditiously than his counterpart who conforms out of necessity. Furthermore, he is less likely to experience inner tension and its symptomatic concomitants. This is not to speak of the likelihood that some individuals will simply refuse to comply with characterologically repugnant injunctions.

On close reading, Bendix's essay allows for just such possible personality-and-politics connections. At base, his argument appears to be against *simplistic* nuts and bolts analyses of psychology and sociopolitical structure—for example, reductionist analyses that treat political behavior as if it were a simple extension of personal psychological dispositions.[2]

NOTES

[1] See Robert C. Tucker, "The Dictator and Totalitarianism," reprinted as selection 22 of this work.

[2] Bendix's remarks also are addressed to sociology as a discipline. He suggests that the tasks of sociology as an analytic enterprise are fundamentally different from those of psychiatry (and by extension, presumably, those of psychology more generally). This is a venerable argument that was classically stated in Durkheim's arguments for the explanation of "social facts" at a "social level." The present authors, as political scientists, choose not to enter into a recurrent and probably insoluable intramural debate among sociologists about the epistemological foundations of their discipline. It seems to us quite reasonable that both psychology and sociology can be seen as exercises in abstracting certain classes of phenomena from the multifaceted complexity of individual behavior in social settings. However, it also appears unlikely that attempts to analyze the *actual* social and political processes of the everyday world could proceed very far without reference to *both* psychological *and* social variables (see Smith's discussion in selection two). Bendix is systematically ambiguous about the degree to which his remarks are addressed to sociology as a discipline and the degree to which they relate to the explanation (no holds barred) of actual social phenomena (for example, why *did* Germany succumb to the Nazis?). His empirical examples of Germany clearly extend to the second set of considerations and it is instructive to see that, in discussing Germany, he is unable to escape advancing psychological hypotheses. He simply advances hypotheses of a good bit greater subtlety and complexity than those in the psychiatric literature of the 1940s and early 1950s on Nazism.

COMPLIANT BEHAVIOR AND INDIVIDUAL PERSONALITY

Reinhard Bendix

During the last two decades there have been increasing efforts to integrate the various fields of study in the social sciences and related disciplines. A case in point is the study of society and the study of the individual. Many promising areas of research have been opened up, because sociology and psychiatry[1] have been related one to the other. On the other hand, there are many pitfalls in applying the concepts and theories of one discipline to another field. Hence, work designed to integrate the social sciences not only calls for an understanding of the indivisibility of the subject matter but also for an acute awareness of the differences which exist between the disciplines. How, then, does the study of society and culture relate to the problems with which psychiatry deals? And how does the study of psychiatry relate to the problems with which sociology deals? I shall attempt to answer these questions under five headings: (1) the orientation of propositions in sociology; (2) the orientation of propositions in psychiatry; (3) culture patterns and the response of the individual; (4) the psychological insignificance of compliant behavior; and (5) culture and personality reconsidered.

I. THE ORIENTATION OF SOCIOLOGICAL PROPOSITIONS

Sociology aims at general propositions which are true of large numbers of people, considered as social groups. From the viewpoint of psychiatry such propositions are necessarily "superficial" and largely beside the point.

For example, it is well established that income and size of family are inversely related in the countries of the Western world. Sociologists have attempted to account for this relationship in a fairly consistent manner. Some years ago Alva Myrdal pointed out that modern civilization had fostered individualistic beliefs which prompted many families to restrict the number of their children. Family limitations seemed best suited to satisfy the desire of every family member for the development of each individual's personality. Child-bearing involved pain and discomfort for the mother; her desire for a career of her own would be frustrated for a longer or shorter period of time. Both parents would have other reasons for family limitation: children cause the interruption of sexual life, they reduce their parents' mobility, they interfere with social and cultural interests, they cause an increase in the family's expenses and a decrease in its standard of living,

Reprinted from "Compliant Behavior and Individual Personality," by Reinhard Bendix, by permission of the University of Chicago Press. Copyright © 1952 by the University of Chicago Press.

Originally published in *American Journal of Sociology,* 58 (1952), 292–303 with the following acknowledgement: "For the last year and a half the author has attended the staff meetings of the Psychiatric Annex to Cowell Hospital on the University of California campus. During this period he has also served as a psychotherapist, working under the supervision of a staff psychiatrist. His debt to Dr. Saxton Pope, the director of the clinic, is acknowledged." The acknowledgement constituted footnote one of the article; in reprinting the article, footnotes have been renumbered.

and they consequently expose the family as a whole to greater economic insecurities. Finally, there is the unwillingness of parents to have more children than they can properly care for, and the costs of what is thought of as "proper care" increase with each increase in income.[2]

Mrs. Myrdal's keen insights have been made the basis of several extensive research projects. In the studies of the Milbank Memorial Fund these basic ideas were elaborated into twenty-three formally stated hypotheses.[3] These hypotheses are of interest here as illustrations of the type of question a sociologist might ask. For example, the greater the adherence to tradition, the lower the proportion of families practicing contraception. At one level of analysis this is a useful abstraction. Yet a psychiatrist examining the same families would think that "adherence to tradition" is a phrase emptied of psychological meaning. Such significant questions as those pertaining to the history of the parent-child relation in each case are obviously left unanswered. Or, again, the dominant member of a family tends to be dominant also in determining the use of contraceptives and the size of the family. Yet the psychiatrist would think such a finding "superficial," since the fact of dominance suggests further questions, concerning the genesis of such dominance and its relation to the corresponding submissiveness of the other partner.

It may be objected that this statement is true as far as it goes but that there are certain propositions in sociology which are of great significance to psychiatry, nevertheless. I choose an example from the work of Georg Simmel to illustrate this point. Simmel states that adornment "singles out its wearer whose self-feeling it embodies and increases at the cost of others . . . while (at the same time) its pleasure is designed for others, since its owner can enjoy it only insofar as he mirrors himself in others." [4] Now, this juxtaposition of egoistic and altruistic elements in the use of adornments is certainly familiar in psychiatry. Yet, even here the proposition of the sociologist is "superficial" from the standpoint of psychiatry, in that it necessarily omits the biographical dimension. The interplay of egoistic and altruistic elements is of interest to the psychiatrist in terms of the meaning which it has for the individual as a result of his personal history. The same interplay is of interest to the sociologist in terms of the way in which adornment may aid a group of individuals to strengthen its internal cohesion as well as deepen the cleavage between itself and others. My point is that the sociologist, in focusing his attention on this latter aspect, must necessarily ignore the psychological meaning of adornment to the individual.

II. THE ORIENTATION OF PSYCHIATRIC PROPOSITIONS

Propositions advanced in the field of psychiatry may be examined also from the viewpoint of the sociologist. Take the example of maternal overprotection. Psychiatrically speaking, there is a clear syndrome of character traits which *may* arise from this source. Among these are unsolved conflicts with regard to the individual's tendencies toward dependence, weak superego formation, ambivalence with regard to the masculine or feminine components of the personality, and so on. That is to say, these and other traits have been repeatedly observed in persons whose mothers were overprotective. There is very little that the sociologist can infer from these observations. Schematically put, he could utilize this insight only in so far as he could be sure of two conditions: (*a*) that maternal overprotection is a phenomenon universally present (in varying degrees) in some sociologically defined groups and (*b*) that it elicits, whenever it is present, the same syndrome of responses in the male child. Yet, neither of these conditions can be verified. On the first point the sociologist does observe that the daily absence of the father from the home is a characteristic feature of urban family life and leads to a predominance of mother-child (as compared with father-child) contacts. But he *cannot* observe that the predominance of mother-child contacts leads in fact to maternal overprotection, nor can he be sure that the physical absence of the father is synonymous with the absence of psychologically effective father-figures. From the psychiatric viewpoint another uncertainty is added on the second point, since maternal overprotection need not lead to the syndromes described above; it only makes them possible to an indeterminate degree.

It is apparently difficult to arrive at sociological propositions when we utilize psychiatric theories. Part of this difficulty arises from the nature of therapy, whose aim is to cure not to establish valid generalizations. But since the theories of psychiatry are based on the empirical evidence derived from therapy, they run the danger of retrospective determinism, and this for two reasons. First, the personal history of every patient is determined by his cumulative experiences, and these account for the formation of specific symptoms. But it is deceptive to believe that the same experiences will lead to similar symptoms in other cases. Second, the therapist sees a sample of people who are distinguished from the population by the fact that they have decided to seek his help. He has little opportunity to compare his patients with a "control group" of persons who decide that they can manage their problems without such help. Both factors, the biographical determinability of neurotic symptoms in the individual case and the exclusion of "negative" cases by the very nature of therapy, lead to a systematic bias in favor of determinism and against a recognition of the important role which choices and accidents play in the development of the human personality.[5]

The difficulty of arriving at sociological propositions on the basis of psychiatric theories cannot be attributed solely to the nature of therapy, to the way in which the evidence for these theories is gathered. It may be attributed rather to the indeterminacy of each individual's development, which Erikson has formulated in the following terms: "While it is quite clear what *must* happen to keep the baby alive (the minimum supply necessary) and what *must not* happen, lest he die or be severely stunted (the maximum frustration tolerable), there is increasing [understanding of the] leeway in regard to what *may* happen." [6] In accordance with this model Erikson has constructed eight stages of the individual's development, each of which constitutes a phase of physiological and social maturation.[7] Thus the child is confronted at each stage with the task of resolving a developmental problem. His resolution will fall somewhere between the extremes if he is to be free to proceed to the next phase. It will be *his* resolution, and the therapist can only infer what this resolution has been from a knowledge of its consequences and of the familial setting.

This conceptualization of an individual's development clarifies the way in which social forces may affect his personality. In so far as these forces can be shown to have a widespread and relatively uniform effect on family life they pose for the child the perennial problems of psychological development in a special way. If, for example, the child is repeatedly shamed in his first efforts at independence, or autonomy, and if the same is true for a large number of children, then we may say that these children have "to come to terms" with this problem or challenge of their familial environment. Some children will fail in their efforts to develop autonomy in such an environment, others will succeed. But it should be apparent that we cannot infer the response of the whole group from a knowledge of the challenge or from a knowledge of these who failed.[8] Yet the propositions of psychiatry concentrate on those that fail;[9] they deal with the origin of neurotic symptoms. These symptoms are an individual's way of expressing and disguising his failure to solve successfully the problems of shame, guilt, doubt, and so on which are posed for him at different stages of his development. They are evidence of an impairment in a person's ability to relate himself to others.

It is apparent that this characterization of propositions in psychiatry is evaluative. It implies that a person's full ability to relate himself to others is normal and good, while his failure to do so is neurotic and bad.[10] My point is not to criticize this value judgment but to stress that it is indispensable in therapy and psychiatric theory. Every theory is based on some judgment of relevance. It is such a judgment which prompts the psychiatrist to analyze the psychodynamic factors which have led to the impairment of a person's relatedness to others. Other disciplines have other value orientations which also emerge out of the order of facts with which they are concerned. Thus, the sociologist's approach to the value orientation of the psychiatrist would be to question the distinction between normal and neurotic. He would question it, because he denies its sociological, though not its psychiatric, relevance. That is to say, the psychiatrist could easily persuade his sociological colleague that the impairment or distortion of an individual's ability to relate himself to others is evidence of his neurosis. But the sociologist would consider that the neurotic symptoms which may drive a person to see a therapist are also evidence of his creative or destructive effect on the society of which he is a member.[11] The sociologist would view a person's inability to relate himself to others as of interest only if it were a group phenomenon. And, if it is a group phenomenon, then the question arises whether psychodynamic factors can be cited to account for it.

III. CULTURAL PATTERNS AND THE RESPONSE OF THE INDIVIDUAL

This analysis raises important questions for the psychological interpretation of cultural patterns. Retrospective interpretations of *individual* case histories are probably quite reliable. But generalizations based on them imply that the difficulties which have created neurotic symptoms in the one case will do the same in most cases. In fact we know that they will not. Nevertheless, these generalizations of psychiatry are often applied to large numbers of people in an attempt to explain cultural phenomena in psychodynamic terms. Nazi propaganda, for example, placed a decided emphasis on such traits as will power, endurance, hardness, discipline, devotion, hard work, sacrifice, and many others. Kecskemeti and Leites have shown that these traits correspond to the "compulsive character" type of the psychoanalytic literature.[12] But how are we to interpret such a correspondence? The authors of the article here examined state the following reservations: One cannot say (1) that psychological causes (especially infantile experiences) alone or even primarily have caused the widespread development of compulsive traits among Germans; (2) how propaganda themes are related to psychological traits which are "fully ascertainable only in the psychoanalytic interview situation";[13] (3) that the compulsive themes of Nazi propaganda and the inferred frequency of compulsive personality traits in the German population are valid for the periods before or after the Nazi regime; (4) that "major transformations of the political structure of Germany are incompatible with present (and frequently compulsive) character structures";[14] (5) that there were no other (than the compulsive) types of character structure among the adherents or the opponents of the Nazis.[15] Considering these reservations, we can only say that Nazi propaganda will have a special appeal to people whose personalities predispose them to accept its slogans. The authors make several educated guesses concerning those segments of the German people most likely to exhibit the syndrome of the compulsive personality.

It may be safely said that it was more widely diffused among *lower middle class* persons than among persons higher up or lower down in the class system; among *males* than among females; among those who had been adolescents *before or around* 1933 than among those who were so afterwards; in *Northern Germany* than in Southern Germany; among Protestants than among Catholics; among city people than among country people; among *political followers* than among political leaders.[16]

Yet, despite these careful reservations, the authors attribute a character structure to a group of people who adhere to a set of cultural symbols. This character structure *would* correspond to these symbols *only if* all the personal histories of these people had actually led to the development of compulsive traits. That is to say, the authors substitute psychological traits for cultural symbols because it is *logically* possible to specify an analogous psychological syndrome for this, as for every other, set of cultural symbols which we could name.[17]

On the surface, this is a purely logical point. Yet, to attribute to psychological disposition what is in fact the result of economic pressure, political power, or historical tradition has a number of unexpected results. If we say that a cultural complex, e.g., the Nazi propaganda of the "strenuous life," attracts certain social groups whose members have compulsive personalities, we imply that people respond to cultural symbols because of their character structure. For instance, people with compulsive character traits will respond favorably to propaganda praising such traits. This statement implies that specific neurotic symptoms of individuals are widespread and therefore both cause and consequence of certain cultural symbols. Hence neurotic symptoms are here treated as an attribute of a culture. Certain symbols of a culture (e.g., Nazi propaganda) are the basis on which the character structure of particular groups in German society is inferred, and this inference is then used to show why the symbols had such wide appeal.

This circular reasoning rests on the assumption that people act as they do because their personality traits predispose them to do so. Indeed, if this could be proved, it would follow that a person's participation in a culture by itself reveals his character structure. Yet, people may respond favorably to such cultural symbols as propaganda slogans because of fear, apathy, acquiescence, greed, and many other reasons *in spite of,* as well as *because of,* their psychological disposition.[18] This assertion may appear as a logical contradiction at first glance. How can it be said that people respond favorably to a slogan despite, rather than because of, their psychological disposition? Of necessity every response reflects that disposition, including responses to cultural symbols. But their meanings for the individual is not revealed in the responses themselves. Both persons of compulsive disposition and those of permissive disposition may respond favorably to the slogans of the "strenuous life," the one because he agrees with them, the other because he has to. Now the second person, who feels forced to respond as he does, will be affected by his action; it is certainly revealing that he complies rather than revolts or emigrates. *But for our purposes it is sufficient to state that he has responded favorably, al-*

though his psychological disposition would prompt him to respond unfavorably. If cultural symbols are analyzed in terms of psychological analogies, then we obscure this characteristic disjunction between the symbol pattern of a culture and the ordinary lives of the people who are only partially involved with the historic traditions, the institutions, and the creative activities that give rise to these symbol patterns. If the symbols of a culture are taken as a clue to the characteristic personality types of its participants, then we underestimate the incongruity between institutions, culture patterns, and the psychological habitus of a people and we ignore an important source of social change.

IV. THE PSYCHOLOGICAL INSIGNIFICANCE OF COMPLIANT BEHAVIOR

Modern psychiatry in all its various schools asserts that the personality of an individual reveals an internally consistent pattern of responses to the most varied stimuli and that this pattern is in large part an outgrowth of early experience. This statement is intended to be true of all men. If it is to be utilized in sociology we would have to know: (*a*) what cultural or social conditions existed at a given time; (*b*) that these conditions have had a pervasive effect on the early familial environment of children; (*c*) that it is reasonable to attribute certain widespread personality syndromes in a culture to this configuration of the familial enivornment. Now psychiatric theory supports the view that a configuration of the familial environment tends to perpetuate itself from generation to generation; that is, parents treat their children in response to their own childhood experience, and so on for successive generations.[19] But before we can accept this view of the relation between society and personality formation, a number of questions need to be answered.

It is obviously difficult to understand the effect which given social conditions have on family life and, especially, on the way in which parents treat their children. The impact of specific social events always comes "too late" really to affect family life, at any rate from a psychiatric point of view. Schematically put, an overwhelming event occurs in year *x* which affects all families. But those people whose personalities are already formed (i.e., the parents) will not be changed profoundly, because their response to the event is predetermined by the familial environment of their own childhood. And the children will not be changed profoundly either, because they will take their cue from their parents' response to the event.[20]

These considerations make it appear doubtful that changes in family life occur as a direct response to catastrophic social experiences.[21] And recent historical experience demonstrates, I think, that this view is mistaken. Take, for example, the authoritarian pattern of German family life, which was mentioned previously. Several attempts have been made to "explain" the rise of nazism in Germany by reference to the German national character.[22] Because nazism was authoritarian, it was related to other authoritarian aspects of German society such as the so-called "authoritarian" family. Yet this entire literature makes no mention of the fact that the Nazis took a very dim view of the political reliability of the authoritarian family pattern. They organized children into paramilitary formations. They subjected them (or they encouraged their submission) to authority figures which were outside the family and could be controlled politically. And they used the children systematically to spy on their parents in order to control children and parents alike. It may well be that the Nazis effected a culmination of that generational conflict which had been in the making in Germany since before the first World War. But if that is the fact, the result has been to undermine the authoritarian family pattern, not to strengthen it or to rely upon it.[23] This evidence suggests that the authoritarian family stood opposed to a major social and political change and that it cannot be cited as a reason for that change. Far from explaining the rise of fascism in Germany, the authoritarian family pattern stands out as a bulwark against it.[24]

The fact is that this authoritarian family pattern has been undermined as a result of the experiences of parents and children under the Nazi regime. And once the traditional pattern of family life is seriously disrupted—as a result of major historical changes—one may expect the emergence not of one but of *many* new patterns.[25] The preceding discussion of the relation between society and the pattern of family life leads to the rather traditional view that the family is a conservative element which tends to stand opposed to major changes in the society.[26] People will accommodate themselves to these changes as best they can, but they will resist as long as possible any transformation of their familial way of life. If such transformation is forced upon the family, nevertheless, then its members will respond in a variety of ways which will depend on local conditions, on the development of fashions, on individual idiosyncrasies, and so on. Hence there is no reason to expect that the Nazi regime, for example, has had a clearly discernible effect on German family life other than the destruction of its traditional patterns.

This view is clearly not in keeping with some of the most widely accepted theories of "social psychiatry." The most clear-cut statement of these theories may be found in the work of Erich Fromm.

> In studying the psychological reactions of a social group we deal with the character structure of the members of the group, that is, of individual persons; we are interested, however, not in the peculiarities by which these persons differ from each other, but in that part of their character structure that is common to most members of the group. We can call this character the *social character*.[27]

This formulation makes it apparent that "social character" is a scientific fiction. Is it a useful fiction? The ideas and actions which a group of people have in common are described in the terminology of psychiatry and are thereby made to appear as the traits of an individual person. The conventional patterns of behavior which people share are necessarily "superficial," from the standpoint of psychiatry. Therefore, the theory of "social character" must maintain, if it is to be consistent, that the shared conventions of a culture are in fact indicative of the character structure of a people. This is indeed what Fromm asserts:

> If we look at social character from the standpoint of its function in the social process, we have to start with the statement that has been made with regard to its function for the individual: that by adapting himself to social conditions man develops those traits that make him *desire* to act as he *has* to act. . . . In other words, *the social character internalizes external necessities and thus harnesses human energy for the taks of a given economic and social system.*[28]

I believe this view to be erroneous. The evidence of friction between the individual and the external necessities to which he is continually subjected does not make it appear probable that people desire to act as they have to act. Fromm is, in fact, aware of this friction, but he merely suggests that people "internalize external necessities" *in the long run,* even if they fail to do so in the short run.[29]

But the friction between the social environment and the prevailing pattern of family life cannot be dismissed so easily. People do *not* always or even eventually desire to act as they have to act. It is quite possible that external necessities are *not* internalized but are endured, even in the long run. Instead, I submit the view that the external necessities of a country may acquire distinctive traits and may impose distinctive psychological burdens on the people. I believe it is to these burdens that we refer, somewhat vaguely, when we talk about a "social" or a "national" character. The concluding section of this essay is devoted to a discussion of this approach.

V. CULTURE AND PERSONALITY RECONSIDERED

It may be useful to recapitulate the preceding discussion. Psychiatric theory has emphasized the importance of childhood for the formation of the adult personality. It has emphasized also the tendency of familial patterns to perpetuate themselves from generation to generation. It is probable (*a*) that catastrophic events as such will not have fundamental psychological effects and (*b*) that historical changes which transform the prevailing patterns of family life are likely to destroy them rather than to establish new patterns.[30] People tend to resist major changes of their character structure and of their familial way of life. Many social and cultural changes are possible without major psychological transformations.

But, although it will not do to attribute a character structure to a cultural pattern, it is still possible to investigate the relation between these patterns and the psychological responses of large numbers of people. The traditions of a country, its institutions and ideologies, the experiences of its people with war and peace, with depression and prosperity, *have* significant psychological repercussions. How shall we interpret these if we do not resort to analogies from the psychodynamics of the individual?

The specific example chosen previously may serve as an illustration. It is probably true that Germans are more authoritarian than Americans are. But this statement refers to the whole complex of traditions and institutions in the two countries. There is no evidence to date that the *proportion* of people with compulsive traits is significantly larger among Germans than among Americans. People may be compulsive in their adherence to various forms of conduct, whether the prevailing culture pattern is authoritarian or otherwise.[31] But in each society people confront very distinct problems with which they have to cope, e.g., it is certain that questions of authority present different problems in Germany and the United States. It is merely a sophisticated ethnocentrism, which ignores this situational difference and which applies to the people of one society standards of mental health pertaining to the people of another society. Hence we must guard carefully against the fallacy of attributing to character structure what may be a part of the social environment. And we must resist the temptation of attributing to the people of another culture a psychological uniformity which we are unable to discover in our own.[32]

In terms of the preceding discussion I believe it to be more in keeping with the observed incongruity between institutions and psychological habitus to assume that all cultures of Western civilization have the same range of personality types. The differences between these cultures must then be accounted for at a level of abstraction with which the psychiatrist is not equipped to deal. In his study of a Mexican community Oscar Lewis has suggested recently that we might call this psychological dimension the "public personality" which is characteristic of a society.[33] When we study different societies or the same society over time, we notice differences in conventional conduct and in the expectations with which people in a society regard one another. For example, it is probable that in the United States among middle-class circles intensive, lifelong friendships are relatively rare compared with some European countries. Now this fact, *if* it is a fact, *could* be related to many aspects of American middle-class culture. Great mobility, a large number of relatively casual personal contacts, the degree to which the expression of personal feelings is restrained, the relative absence of social distance between people in different walks of life—these and many other aspects of the culture discourage intensive friendships between people of the same sex.[34] This fact and the conventional optimism and friendliness of interpersonal relations which is its related opposite are aspects of the "public personality" in the United States which differ from the character structure of the individual. They refer to a "public personality" in the sense that conventional behavior patterns (the type of conduct which we engage in because others expect it of us) make demands upon the emotions of the individual. I believe that two conclusions follow from this analysis.

The first is that we must avoid the idea, which Fromm has suggested, that men "desire to act as they have to act." It does not follow, for example, that Americans could not form intensive friendships under other circumstances; and the relative absence of such relations probably exacts its emotional toll. Nor is it convincing to argue, as Fromm seems to do, that Americans have "adjusted" to this situation and now do not want the kind of friendship which the circumstances of American life seem to have discouraged. Nor does it follow, finally, that the absence of friendship and the prevalence of friendliness are total liabilities, since this pattern makes for considerable ease in interpersonal relations, though it may give rise to a feeling of emptiness among a minority of especially sensitive people.[35] All this need not mean that men never desire to act as they have to act. It implies, rather, that men accommodate themselves to their circumstances and to social change as best they can. The conflicts which frequently arise between their desires and their conduct are reflected in the psychological tensions of everyday living. Different individuals will show greater or less tolerance for them, depending on their character structure as this is related to childhood experience. Hence, particular social changes will not lead to a determinable psychological response among masses of people. Rather, such changes will impose particular emotional burdens which some people can tolerate more easily than others, and those who can will have a greater opportunity for action.[36]

This interpretation leads to a second conclusion. We can infer the emotional problems with which masses of people were faced as a result of specific historical experiences; we cannot infer the emotional meaning of their response. An example from the preceding discussion may make this point clearer. The superficial friendliness of interpersonal relations was discussed as a characteristic of American middle-class culture. This conventional behavior pattern which makes superficial contacts between people easy and pleasant, while it makes deeply personal relationships appear difficult and full of risk, does not reveal what meaning it has for the individual. There will be those who take it seriously and make it a way of life, for example, the "typical" salesman or public relations man. There will be others who respond to this friendliness with cynicism. Others yet will enjoy being friendly but will not take it seriously. People who despair of its superficiality will seek intensive friendship, while others really enjoy the ease in casual personal contacts. Indeed, it would be rewarding to analyze the variety of responses which this behavior pattern elicits. But, for our purposes, it is sufficient to remark that large numbers of people have certain problems and certain conventional behavior patterns in common; they *do not* make a common response to these problems or conventions.

When we analyze the "social character" of a society, we are in fact characterizing the emotional problems with which the people are typically faced and which arise out of the institutions and historical traditions of that society. These institutions and traditions always elicit certain conventions, but they also elicit a wide range of responses to the conventions themselves, roughly corresponding to the range of personality types. We should therefore be properly sensitized to the emotional burdens *and* opportunities, to the psychological liabilities *and* assets, which every culture pattern entails. And we should learn to recognize that the traditions and institutions of every society present each of its members with peculiar emotional problems which he must resolve for himself in keeping with his psychological disposition. Hence, when we contrast one culture with another we refer to the typical psychological burdens which the demand for conformity imposes on the people. And if we attribute to these people a "social character" or a "national character" or a "basic personality type," we simply confuse the response with the stimulus and attribute to the people a uniformity of response which is contrary to all observed facts.

NOTES

[1] The following essay makes only reference to the body of theories which is sometimes designated as "depth psychology" and which has grown out of the pioneering work of Sigmund Freud. The terms "psychiatry" or "psychiatric theory" will be used in this general sense. The term "therapy" will be used for the empirical base on which psychiatry rests. The term "psychodynamic" is commonly used to single out those emotional processes, often unconscious, which can be traced to childhood experience and which in their entirety constitute the character structure or personality of an individual.

[2] See the extended discussion of these problems in Alva Myrdal, *Nation and Family* (New York: Harper & Bros., 1941), chap. iv; cf. also Guy Chapman, *Culture and Survival* (London: Jonathon Cape, 1940), pp. 160–79, and the excellent overall discussion by Frank Notestein, "Population—the Long View," in Theodore W. Schultz, ed., *Food for the World* (Chicago: University of Chicago Press, 1945), pp. 36–69.

[3] P. K. Whelpton and Clyde V. Kiser, "Social and Psychological Factors Affecting Fertility," *Milbank Memorial Fund Quarterly* 23 (October 1945): 147–49.

[4] Kurt H. Wolff, *The Sociology of Georg Simmel* (Glencoe, Ill.: Free Press, 1950), p. 339.

[5] The danger of retrospective determinism is not unique to psychiatric theory; cf. Reinhard Bendix, "Social Stratification and Political Power," *American Political Science Review* 46 (June 1952): 357–75.

[6] Erik H. Erikson, *Childhood and Society* (New York: W. W. Norton, 1950), p. 68. The author adds to this that "culture" largely determines the actual methods of child-rearing, which the members of the society "consider workable and insist on calling necessary." The later discussion will show why I do not share this view.

[7] *Ibid.,* chap. vii. The stages are called: trust vs. basic mistrust, autonomy vs. shame and doubt, initiative vs. guilt, industry vs. inferiority, identity vs. role diffusion, intimacy vs. isolation, generativity vs. stagnation, ego integrity vs. despair.

[8] It is often easier to anticipate the pathological rather than the nonpathological resolutions, and because of this "pathological" bias the theories of psychiatry have frequently underestimated the uncertainty or indeterminacy of the individual's development. For an interesting attempt to incorporate this perspective in the "psychiatric image of man" see Alexander Mitscherlich, *Freiheit und Unfreiheit in der Krankheit* (Hamburg: Classen & Goverts, 1946).

[9] Cf. the critical evaluation of modern psychiatry by Jean MacFarlane in "Looking Ahead in the Fields of Orthopsychiatric Research," *American Journal of Orthopsychiatry* 20 (January 1950): 85–91.

[10] These judgments can be stated in a factual manner, and they have a specific empirical content. A person's ability to relate himself to others and his manner of doing so are observable facts. The value element enters in when a given action is judged in terms of its meaning for, and its effect on, a person's relations to others. And such judgments are made as a result of the patient's decision to request therapy in order to improve his relations to others.

[11] I am not suggesting that therapy necessarily kills a person's creative ability in the effort of making him "normal," though the problem is frequently discussed in professional circles. It is interesting, however, that this discussion often ends with the assertion that a person's creative ability which is adversely affected by his therapy was probably not worth preserving. At any rate, psychiatrists are certainly troubled by this problem.

[12] Paul Kecskemeti and Nathan Leites, "Some Psychological Hypotheses on Nazi Germany," *Journal of Social Psychology* 26 (1947): 141–83; 27 (February 1948): 91–117; (May 1948): 241–70; (August 1948): 141–64.

[13] *Ibid.,* 26 (1947): 142.

[14] *Ibid.,* p. 143.

[15] These reservations are listed in the introductory section of the article by Kecskemeti and Leites, and others are added which concern the provisional character of psychoanalytic findings in the field of compulsion neurosis. I should add that this article differs strikingly from most other writings in this field in terms of the care with which these reservations are stipulated.

[16] Kecskemeti and Leites, *op. cit.,* p. 143.

[17] This has incidentally the added fascination of personalizing cultural abstractions, which makes these abstractions much more plausible in an intuitive way; cf. the typology of cultures in Ruth Benedict, *Patterns of Culture* (New York: Penguin Books, 1946), chap. iii, which goes back to the work of Nietzsche and Spengler.

[18] And those who do respond to these symbols in accordance with a compulsive disposition do not necessarily respond in the same way. There are significant differences, for example, between the responses of a Prussian Junker, a Nazi functionary, a Bavarian separatist, and a German Communist, yet all may have compulsive personalities. And, even if we take only Nazi functionaries, their differences in rank within the party would probably account for significant differences in their response to the Nazi slogans of the "strenuous life." Hannah Arendt has pointed out that cynicism with regard to the professed ideals of a totalitarian movement is great among persons who hold high rank in such a movement, while these ideals are believed most fervently by the average members or sympathizers. See Arendt, *The Origins of Totalitarianism* (New York: Harcourt, Brace, 1951), pp. 369–71.

[19] This assertion is not without ambiguity. Parents treat their children in response to their own childhood experience, but it does not follow that this response is one of simple imitation. Parents might also try to raise their children contrary to the way they were raised themselves. However, psychiatrists would contend that the overt treatment of children, whatever it may be, would always reveal the unresolved conflicts of the parents' own childhood experience. In this sense the psychodynamic significance of both imitation and opposition would be the same.

[20] Cf. the instructive studies of Anna Freud, who has shown that separation from the parents had a more traumatic effect on the children during the London blitz than the direct experience with death and destruction and that the effect of the latter depended on the response of the parents to the same experiences. See Anna Freud and Dorothy T. Buelingham, *War and Children and Infants without Families* (New York: International Universities Press, 1944). A similar point concerning the lack of effect of political catastrophe is made in G. W. Allport et al., "Personality under Social Catastrophe: Ninety Life Histories of the Nazi Revolution," in C. Kluckhohn and H. A. Murray, eds., *Personality in Nature, Society and Culture* (New York: A. A. Knopf, 1948), pp. 347–66. See also the earlier monographs of the Social Science Research Council on the superficial effects of the depression on family life.

[21] The origin of observed characteristics of present-day family life has sometimes been inferred from certain social conditions which are known historically. See, e.g., Erikson, *op. cit.,* pp. 244–65, where the author imputes the American mother's encouragement of a competitive spirit in her son to the conditions of the frontier, when self-reliance was an essential condition. This imputation is mistaken, and a number of other historical explanations would do equally well. After all, there are a large number of factors other than the frontier which have contributed to the competitiveness of American life.

[22] A survey of these and similar studies is contained in Otto Klineberg, *Tensions Affecting International Understanding* (New York: Social Science Research Council, 1950), pp. 36–46.

[23] The leaders of totaliarian movements apparently regard the family as a seedbed of resistance, even if it is of an authoritarian pattern, and we cannot suppose that millions of German parents suddenly decided to abdicate their authority over their children. There is evidence, on the other hand, to indicate that the Nazi movement was in part an outgrowth of the many youth movements, which had developed since the beginning of the twentieth century, and which were inspired by an antibourgeois, antiauthoritarian ideology. Of course, the

psychiatrist would regard this antiauthoritarianism as evidence of the authoritarian personality, which illustrates once more that his level of abstraction differs from that of the sociologist. It illustrates also that the psychiatrist can "prove anything" when he deals with groups rather than individuals, because his generalizations are not checked by negative cases.

[24] The organization of German youth under Communist leadership in East Germany is a continuation of the Nazi pattern under different auspices. The political *Gleichschaltung* of a reluctant adult population is being accomplished by making their children enthusiastic supporters of the regime. The regime offers these young people occupational opportunities by depriving their elders of their jobs through the imputation of political unreliability. In view of these methods of the Nazis and the Communists it is not illuminating to suggest that the "authoritarian family pattern" made Germans yield readily to totalitarian rule, even though this pattern by itself may not have contributed to the rise of totalitarianism. We do not know that "permissive family patterns" enable people to resist a dictatorial rule effectively, at least for a time; we do know that it would be easy to exploit the conflict between the young and the old generation for political purposes in a society in which age does not carry much prestige anyway.

[25] The recent history of child-rearing practices illustrates the rapid change in fashions which may occur once traditional methods are abandoned. (See Clark E. Vincent, "Trends in Infant Care Ideas," *Child Development* 22 [September 1951]: 199–209.)

[26] Social reformers for the last 3,000 years have held the view that marriage and the family are antisocial in that they prevent a man from doing his duty. It is characteristic of Plato and the ascetic tradition beginning with Jesus and the Apostle Paul and reflected in the views of the socialists of the nineteenth century. Fourier, for example, held that each man considered himself justified in any swindle because he was working for his wife and children. Cf. Alexander Gray, *The Socialist Tradition: Moses to Lenin* (London: Longmans, Green, 1947 ed.), pp. 191–92. A similar view is expressed, though on different grounds, in Sigmund Freud, *Civilization and Its Discontents* (London: Hogarth Press, 1937), 65–77.

[27] Erich Fromm, *Escape from Freedom* (New York: Farrar & Rinehart, 1942), p. 277.

[28] *Ibid.,* pp. 283, 284.

[29] *Ibid.,* pp. 284–85.

[30] As applied to the German case this would mean that the destructive effect of the Nazi experience on German family life is of much greater interest and relevance (for theoretical reasons) than is the supposed contribution of German family life to the rise of fascism.

[31] The literature which deals with these matters is noticeably ambiguous when it treats the conventionality of American life, which is so strongly anti-authoritarian, since conventionality is quite compatible with compulsive personality traits. By the same token, writers have often ignored the strong individualism of German life, which is combined with being "authoritarian." This confusion is rather marked in Fromm, *op. cit.,* pp. 240–56, but absent from Adolf Lowe, *The Price of Liberty* (London: Hogarth Press, 1937).

[32] Because of this we should attempt to discover in each society the diversity of responses which is hidden beneath the uniformity of conventional behavior that is "apparent" to the outside observer. A case in point are two recent books on Germany: Bertram Schaffner's *Father Land* (New York: Columbia University Press, 1948) and David Rodnick's *Postwar Germans* (New Haven, Conn.: Yale University Press, 1948). One author finds that the father is dominant, the child insecure and starved for affection; the other finds that the mother is dominant, the child secure and much loved. It is notable that both authors find it easy to relate their conflicting data to the "authoritarian pattern." Further research along these lines might be improved methodologically, but I doubt whether it would reveal a more consistent pattern of family life than these two studies taken together.

[33] Oscar Lewis, *Life in a Mexican Village: Tepoztlán Restudied* (Urbana: University of Illinois Press, 1951), pp. 422–26.

[34] The external factors which might account for the absence of friendship, such as distance and the infrequency of seeing the same friend often enough in a country of great geographic mobility, do not really explain much. My father, who was a lawyer in Germany, maintained a friendship with a fellow student over a period of over sixty years, with an occasional exchange of letters, although this friend was a medieval historian, although they did not meet more than six times during this whole period, although they lived at a considerable distance most of their lives, and despite the interruption caused by an official (Nazi) prohibition of their correspondence.

[35] Much impressionistic evidence seems to point to a reversal of this pattern in the "public personality" that characterizes German life, namely, intense friendships but an absence of friendliness and a considerable distance in the casual contacts of everyday life. See, e.g., David Rodnick, *op. cit.,* pp. 1–8. See also the striking discussion of Kurt Lewin, *Resolving Social Conflicts* (New York: Harper & Bros., 1948), pp. 3–33, where the author contrasts these conventional patterns (in the United States and Germany) in terms of the different degrees to which the individual's privacy is accessible to another person.

[36] As an example of this type of analysis, though it is not consistently carried through, I cite Norbert Elias, *Ueber den Prozess der Zivilisation* (Basel: Haus zum Falken, 1942) in which the author shows strikingly the emotional burdens which frequent exposure to physical aggression imposed on the nobility in early medieval France. The implication of this analysis is that only those were successful in this struggle who were equal to it emotionally. Elias shows that the concentration of power in the hands of the king forced the nobility, if it wanted favors from the court, to adopt the manners of polite society. But it does not follow, as Elias seems to imply, that the people who developed these polite manners at court were somehow the same people who had, not long before, excelled in physical aggression. Rather, the new circumstances of the court favored those who excelled at the subtleties of courtly behavior, while those who excelled in aggression were kept away from the court, or did not attend, and were unsuccessful in the supercilious maneuvers of a court society when they did attend. In this sense it is possible to speak of psychological aptitudes which given historical conditions probably favored without implying that those who were ill-adapted emotionally disappeared because they now desired to act as they had to act. It is more probable that they tried to act as they had to act, without desiring it and without being too good at it either.

4

How Personality Analysis Relates to Role Analysis

Personality analyses of political figures are sometimes deprecated on the grounds that role analysis would better explain the behavior. But, under scrutiny, the actual empirical referents to role explanations of, for example, Presidential activities turn out to be difficult to define. "Role," Levinson suggests, is often used to refer to several crucially different phenomena: it is not uncommon for theorists to slide back and forth between different meanings of "role" in the course of an explanation, obscuring whether they are analyzing *role demands* (a social datum), *role conceptions* (a psychological datum), *role performance* (a behavioral datum), or some, or all, of these.

Levinson suggests that, for most analytic purposes, we drop a unitary conception of role. He distinguishes sharply between role demands, conceptions, and performance. His analysis of these distinctions is a substantial contribution to careful conceptualization of personality-and-politics issues. Levinson insists on the importance of both the internal and external—the psychic and the social—aspects of roles on actual role performance. He warns against psychological "mirage" theories (which see "ideologies, role conceptions, and behavior" as "mere epiphenomena or by-products of unconscious fantasies and defenses") and sociological "sponge" theories ("in which man is merely a passive, mechanical absorber of the prevailing structural demands").

Levinson makes it clear that research is needed on role *and* personality, rather than on role *versus* personality. Such research would draw on a number of the distinctions Levinson makes: that is, the likelihood of overlap between role conceptions, demands, and performances; the likelihood that role demands may be "multiple and disunified"; and the utility of specifying the degree of coherence of role requirements, the consensus with which they are held, and the degree of individual choice they allow.

Levinson's discussion makes clear to the political scientist and sociologist that analysis of role conceptions and role performance often requires reference to the significance of inner reality; it warns the clinical psychologist—and others who have adopted clinical approaches—of the complex appraisal of the outer reality necessary for adequate explanation. Levinson's distinctions are particularly useful to those who propose to use Erikson's psychosocial schema (see selection seven below): this provides a conceptual basis for following Erikson's suggestions for exploring the interplay between psyche and society.

ROLE, PERSONALITY, AND SOCIAL STRUCTURE IN THE ORGANIZATIONAL SETTING

Daniel J. Levinson

During the past twenty years the concept of role has achieved wide currency in social psychology, sociology, and anthropology. From a sociopsychological point of view, one of its most alluring qualities is its double reference to the individual and to the collective matrix. The concept of role concerns the thoughts and actions of individuals, and, at the same time, it points up the influence upon the individual of socially patterned demands and standardizing forces. Partly for this reason, "role" has been seen by numerous writers (e.g., Gerth and Mills, 1953; Gross, Mason, and McEachern, 1958; Hartley and Hartley, 1952; Linton, 1945; Mead, 1934; Merton, 1957; Parsons, 1951; Sarbin, 1954) as a crucial concept for the linking of psychology, sociology, and anthropology. However, while the promise has seemed great, the fulfillment has thus far been relatively small. The concept of role remains one of the most overworked and underdeveloped in the social sciences.

My purpose here is to examine role theory primarily as it is used in the analysis of organizations (such as the hospital, business firm, prison, school). The organization provides a singularly useful arena for the development and application of role theory. It is small enough to be amenable to empirical study. Its structure is complex enough to provide a wide variety of social positions and role-standardizing forces. It offers an almost limitless opportunity to observe the individual personality *in vivo* (rather than in the psychologist's usual *vitro* of laboratory, survey questionnaire, or clinical office), selectively utilizing and modifying the demands and opportunities given in the social environment. The study of personality can, I submit, find no setting in which the reciprocal impact of psyche and situation is more clearly or more dramatically evidenced.

Organizational theory and research has traditionally been the province of sociology and related disciplines that focus most directly upon the collective unit. Chief emphasis has accordingly been given to such aspects of the organization as formal and informal structure, administrative policy, allocation of resources, level of output, and the like. Little interest has been shown in the individual member as such or in the relevance of personality for organizational functioning. The prevailing image of the organization has been that of a mechanical apparatus operating impersonally once it is set in motion by administrative edict. The prevailing conception of social role is consonant with this image: the individual member is regarded as a cog in the apparatus, what he thinks and does being determined by requirements in the organizational structure.

This paper has the following aims: (1) To examine the traditional conception of organizational structure and role and to assess its limitations from a sociopsychological point of view. (2) To examine the conception of social role that derives from this approach to social structure and that tends, by definition, to exclude consideration of personality. (3) To provide a formulation of several, analytically dis-

Reprinted from *Journal of Abnormal and Social Psychology* 58 (1959), 170–80. Copyright 1958 by the American Psychological Association, and reproduced by permission.

tinct, role concepts to be used in place of the global term "role." (4) To suggest a theoretical approach to the analysis of relationships among role, personality, and social structure.

TRADITIONAL VIEWS OF BUREAUCRATIC STRUCTURE AND ROLE

Human personality has been virtually excluded from traditional organization theory. Its absence is perhaps most clearly reflected in Weber's (1946, 1947) theory of bureaucracy, which has become a major source of current thought regarding social organization and social role. I shall examine this theory briefly here, in order to point up some of its psychological limitations but without doing justice to its many virtues. In Weber's writings, the bureaucratic organization is portrayed as a mono-lithic edifice. Norms are clearly defined and consistently applied, the agencies of role socialization succeed in inducing acceptance of organizational requirements, and the sanctions system provides the constraints and incentives needed to maintain behavioral conformity. Every individual is given a clearly defined role and readily "fills" it. There is little room in this tightly bound universe for more complex choice, for individual creativity, or for social change. As Gouldner (1954) has said of the studies carried out in this tradition: "Indeed, the social scene described has some-times been so completely stripped of people that the impression is unintentionally rendered that there are disembodied social forces afoot, able to realize their ambi-tions apart from human action" (p. 16).

For Weber, bureaucracy as an ideal type is administered by "experts" in a spirit of impersonal rationality and is operated on a principle of discipline according to which each member performs his required duties as efficiently as possible. Ration-ality in decision-making and obedience in performance are the pivots on which the entire system operates. In this scheme of things, emotion is regarded merely as a hindrance to efficiency, as something to be excluded from the bureaucratic process.

The antipathy to emotion and motivation in Weber's thinking is reflected as well in his formulation of three types of authority: traditional, charismatic, and rational-legal. The rational-legal administrator is the pillar of bureaucracy. He receives his legitimation impersonally, from "the system," by virtue of his *tech-nical* competence. His personal characteristics, his conception of the organization and its component groupings, his modes of relating to other persons (except that he be fair and impartial)—these and other psychological characteristics are not taken into theoretical consideration. There is no place in Weber's ideal type for the ties of affection, the competitive strivings, the subtle forms of support or of intimidation, so commonly found in even the most "rationalized" organizations. It is only the "charismatic" leader who becomes emotionally important to his fol-lowers and who must personally validate his right to lead.

While Weber has little to say about the problem of motivation, two motives implicitly become universal instincts in his conception of "bureaucratic man." These are *conformity* (the motive for automatic acceptance of structural norms), and *status-seeking* (the desire to advance oneself by the acquisition and exercise of technical competence). More complex motivations and feelings are ignored.

There has been widespread acknowledgment of both the merits and the limitations of Weber's protean thought. However, the relevance of personality for organizational structure and role definition remains a largely neglected problem in contemporary theory and research.[1] Our inadequacies are exemplified in the excellent *Reader in Bureaucracy,* edited by Merton, Gray, Hockey, and Selvin (1952). Although this book contains some of the most distinguished contributions to the field, it has almost nothing on the relation between organizational structure and personality. The editors suggest two lines of interrelation: first, that personality may be one determinant of occupational choice; and second, that a given type of structure may in time modify the personalities of its members. These are valuable hypotheses. However, they do not acknowledge the possibility that personality may have an impact on social structure. "The organization" is projected as an organism that either selects congenial personalities or makes over the recalcitrant ones to suit its own needs. This image is reflected in the editors' remark: "It would seem, therefore, that officials not initially suited to the demands of a bureaucratic position, progressively undergo modifications of personality" (p. 352). In other words, when social structure and personality fail to mesh, it is assumed to be personality alone that gives. Structure is the prime, uncaused, cause.

The impact of organizational structure on personality is indeed a significant problem for study. There is, however, a converse to this. When a member is critical of the organizational structure, he *may* maintain his personal values and traits, and work toward structural change. The manifold impact of personality on organizational structure and role remains to be investigated. To provide a theoretical basis for this type of investigation we need, I believe, to reexamine the concept of role.

"SOCIAL ROLE" AS A UNITARY CONCEPT

The concept of role is related to, and must be distinguished from, the concept of social position. A position is an element of organizational autonomy, a location in social space, a category of organizational membership. A role is, so to say, an aspect of organizational physiology; it involves function, adaptation, process. It is meaningful to say that a person "occupies" a social position; but it is inappropriate to say, as many do, that one occupies a role.

There are at least three specific senses in which the term "role" has been used, explicitly or implicitly, by different writers or by the same writer on different occasions.

a. Role may be defined as the *structurally given demands* (norms, expectations, taboos, responsibilities, and the like) associated with a given social position. Role is, in this sense, something outside the given individual, a set of pressures and facilitations that channel, guide, impede, support his functioning in the organization.

b. Role may be defined as the member's *orientation* or *conception* of the part he is to play in the organization. It is, so to say, his inner definition of what someone in his social position is supposed to think and do about it. Mead (1934) is probably the main source of this view of social role as an aspect of the person, and it is commonly used in analyses of occupational roles.

c. Role is commonly defined as the *actions* of the individual members— actions seen in terms of their relevance for the social structure (that is, seen in relation to the prevailing norms). In this sense, role refers to the ways in which members of a position act (with or without conscious intention) *in accord with or in violation of a given set of organizational norms.* Here, as in (b), role is defined as a characteristic of the actor rather than of his normative environment.

Many writers use a definition that embraces all of the above meanings without systematic distinction, and then shift, explicitly or implicitly, from one meaning to another. The following are but a few of many possible examples.[2]

Each of the above three meanings of "role" is to be found in the writings of Parsons: (a) "From the point of view of the actor, his role is defined by the normative expectations of the members of the group as formulated in its social traditions" (Parsons, 1945, p. 230). (b) "The role is that organized sector of an actor's orientation which constitutes and defines his participation in an interactive process" (Parsons and Shils, 1951, p. 23). (c) "The status-role (is) the organized subsystem of acts of the actor or actors" (Parsons, 1951, p. 26).

More often, the term is used in a way that includes all three meanings at once. In this *unitary,* all-embracing conception of role, there is, by assumption, a close fit between behavior and disposition (attitude, value), between societal prescription and individual adaptation. This point of view has its primary source in the writings of Linton, whose formulations of culture, status, and role have had enormous influence. According to Linton (1945), a role "includes the attitudes, values and behavior ascribed by the society to any and all persons occupying this status." In other words, society provides for each status or position a single mold that shapes the beliefs and actions of all its occupants.

Perhaps the most extensive formulation of this approach along sociopsychological lines is given by Newcomb (1950). Following Linton, Newcomb asserts, "Roles thus represent ways of carrying out the functions for which positions exist—ways which are generally agreed upon within (the) group" (p. 281). And, "Role is strictly a sociological concept; it purposely ignores individual, psychological facts" (p. 329). Having made this initial commitment to the "sociological" view that individual role-activity is a simple mirroring of group norms, Newcomb later attempts to find room for his "psychological" concerns with motivation, meaning, and individual differences. He does this by partially giving up the "unitary" concept of role, and introducing a distinction between "prescribed role" and "role behavior." He avers that prescribed role is a sociological concept, "referring to common factors in the behaviors required" (p. 459), whereas role behavior is a psychological concept that refers to the activities of a single individual. The implications of this distinction for his earlier general definition of role are left unstated.

Whatever the merits or faults of Newcomb's reformulation, it at least gives conceptual recognition to the possibility that social prescription and individual adaptation may not match. This possibility is virtually excluded in the definition of social role forwarded by Linton and used by so many social scientists. In this respect, though certainly not in all respects, Linton's view is like Weber's: both see individual behavior as predominantly determined by the collective matrix. The matrix is, in the former case, culture, and in the latter, bureaucracy.

In short, the "unitary" conception of role assumes that there is a 1:1 relationship, or at least a *high degree of congruence,* among the three role aspects noted above. In the theory of bureaucratic organization, the rationale for this assumption is somewhat as follows. The organizationally given requirements will be internalized by the members and will thus be mirrored in their role conceptions. People will know, and will want to do, what is expected of them. The agencies of role socialization will succeed except with a deviant minority—who constitute a separate problem for study. Individual action will in turn reflect the structural norms, since the appropriate role-conceptions will have been internalized and since the sanctions system rewards normative behavior and punishes deviant behavior. Thus, it is assumed that structural norms, individual role conceptions and individual role performance are three isomorphic reflections of a single entity: "the" role appropriate to a given organizational position.

It is, no doubt, reasonable to expect some degree of congruence among these aspects of a social role. Certainly, every organization contains numerous mechanisms designed to further such congruence. At the same time, it is a matter of common observation that organizations vary in the degree of their integration; structural demands are often contradictory, lines of authority may be defective, disagreements occur and reverberate at and below the surface of daily operations. To assume that what the organization requires, and what its members actually think and do, comprise a single, unified whole is severely to restrict our comprehension of organizational dynamics and change.

It is my thesis, then, that the unitary conception of social role is unrealistic and theoretically constricting. We should, I believe, eliminate the single term "role" except in the most general sense, i.e., of "role theory" as an overall frame of analysis. Let us, rather, give independent conceptual and empirical status to the above three concepts and others. Let us investigate the relationships of each concept with the others, making no assumptions about the degree of congruence among them. Further, let us investigate their relationships with various other characteristics of the organization and of its individual members. I would suggest that the role concepts be named and defined as follows.

ORGANIZATIONALLY GIVEN ROLE DEMANDS

The role demands are external to the individual whose role is being examined. They are the situational pressures that confront him as the occupant of a given structural position. They have manifold sources: in the official charter and policies of the organization; in the traditions and ideology, explicit as well as implicit, that help to define the organization's purposes and modes of operation; in the views about this position which are held by members of the position (who influence any single member) and by members of the various positions impinging upon this one; and so on.

It is a common assumption that the structural requirements for any position are as a rule defined with a *high degree of explicitness, clarity, and consensus* among all the parties involved. To take the position of hospital nurse as an example: it is assumed that her role requirements will be understood and agreed upon by the hospital administration, the nursing authorities, the physicians, etc. Yet one of the striking research findings in all manner of hospitals is the failure of consensus regarding the proper role of nurse (e.g., Burling, Lentz, and Wilson, 1956; Argyris, 1957). Similar findings have been obtained in school systems, business firms, and the like (e.g., Gross et al., 1958; Kornhauser, Dubin, and Ross, 1954).

In attempting to characterize the role requirements for a given position, one must therefore guard against the assumption that they are unified and logically coherent. There may be major differences and even contradictions between official norms, as defined by charter or by administrative authority, and the "informal" norms held by various groupings within the organization. Moreover, within a given status group, such as the top administrators, there may be several conflicting viewpoints concerning long range goals, current policies, and specific role requirements. In short, the structural demands themselves are often multiple and disunified. Few are the attempts to investigate the sources of such disunity, to acknowledge its frequency, or to take it into conceptual account in general structural theory.

It is important also to consider the specificity or *narrowness* with which the normative requirements are defined. Norms have an "ought" quality; they confer legitimacy and reward-value upon certain modes of action, thought and emotion, while condemning others. But there are degrees here. Normative evaluations cover a spectrum from "strongly required," through various degrees of qualitative kinds of "acceptable," to more or less stringently tabooed. Organizations differ in the width of the intermediate range on this spectrum. That is, they differ in the number and kinds of adaptation that are normatively acceptable. The wider this range—the less specific the norms—the greater is the area of personal choice for the individual. While the existence of such an intermediate range is generally acknowledged, structural analyses often proceed as though practically all norms were absolute prescriptions or proscriptions allowing few alternatives for individual action.

There are various other normative complexities to be reckoned with. A single set of role norms may be internally contradictory. In the case of the mental hospital nurse, for example, the norm of maintaining an "orderly ward" often conflicts with the norm of encouraging self-expression in patients. The individual nurse then has a range of choice, which may be narrow or wide, in balancing these conflicting requirements. There are also ambiguities in norms, and discrepancies between those held explicitly and those that are less verbalized and perhaps less conscious. These normative complexities permit, and may even induce, significant variations in individual role performance.

The degree of *coherence* among the structurally defined role requirements, the degree of *consensus* with which they are held, and the degree of *individual choice* they allow (the range of acceptable alternatives) are among the most significant properties of any organization. In some organizations, there is very great coherence of role requirements and a minimum of individual choice. In most cases, however, the degree of integration within roles and among sets of roles appears to be more moderate.[3] This structural pattern is of especial interest from a sociopsychological point of view. To the extent that the requirements for a given position are ambiguous, contradictory, or otherwise "open," the individual members have greater opportunity for selection among existing norms and for creation of new norms. In this process, personality plays an important part. I shall return to this issue shortly.

While the normative requirements (assigned tasks, rules governing authority-subordinate relationships, demands for work output, and the like) are of great importance, there are other aspects of the organization that have an impact on the individual member. I shall mention two that are sometimes neglected.

Role Facilities

In addition to the demands and obligations imposed upon the individual, we must also take into account the techniques, resources, and conditions of work—the means made available to him for fulfilling his organizational functions. The introduction of tranquillizing drugs in the mental hospital, or of automation in industry, has provided tremendous leverage for change in organizational structure and role-definition. The teacher-student ratio, an ecological characteristic of every school, grossly affects the probability that a given teacher will work creatively with individual students. In other words, technological and ecological facilities are not merely "tools" by which norms are met; they are often a crucial basis for the maintenance or change of an organizational form.

Role Dilemmas or Problematic Issues

In describing the tasks and rules governing a given organizational position, and the facilities provided for their realization, we are, as it were, looking at that position from the viewpoint of a higher administrative authority whose chief concern is "getting the job done." Bureaucracy is often analyzed from this (usually implicit) viewpoint. What is equally necessary, though less often done, is to look at the situation of the position-members from their own point of view: the meaning it has for them, the feelings it evokes, the ways in which it is stressful or supporting. From this sociopsychological perspective, new dimensions of role analysis emerge. The concept of role dilemma is an example. The usefulness of this concept stems from the fact that every human situation has its contradictions and its problematic features. Where such dilemmas exist, there is no "optimal" mode of adaptation; each mode has its advantages and its costs. Parsons (1951), in his discussion of "the situation of the patient," explores some of the dilemmas confronting the ill person in our society. Erikson (1957) and Pine and Levinson (1958) have written about the dilemmas of the mental hospital patient; for example, the conflicting pressures (from without and from within) toward cure through self-awareness and toward cure through repressive self-control. Role dilemmas of the psychiatric resident have been studied by Sharaf and Levinson (1957). Various studies have described the problems of the factory foreman caught in the conflicting cross-pressures between the workers he must supervise and the managers to whom he is responsible. The foreman's situation tends to evoke feelings of social marginality, mixed identifications, and conflicting tendencies to be a good "older brother" with subordinates and an "obedient son" with higher authority.

Role dilemmas have their sources both in organizational structure and in individual personality. Similarly, both structure and personality influence the varied forms of adaptation that are achieved. The point to be emphasized here is that every social structure confronts its members with adaptive dilemmas. If we are to comprehend this aspect of organizational life, we must conceive of social structure as having intrinsically *psychological* properties, as making complex psychological demands that affect, and are affected by, the personalities of its members.

PERSONAL ROLE DEFINITION

In the foregoing we have considered the patterning of the environment for an organizational position—the kind of sociopsychological world with which members of the position must deal. Let us turn now to the individual members themselves. Confronted with a complex system of requirements, facilities, and conditions of work, the individual effects his modes of adaptation. I shall use the term "personal role definition" to encompass the individual's adaptation within the organization. This may involve passive "adjustment," active furthering of current role demands, apparent conformity combined with indirect "sabotage," attempts at constructive innovation (revision of own role or of broader structural arrangements), and the like. The personal role definition may thus have varying degrees of fit with the role requirements. It may serve in various ways to maintain or to change the social structure. It may involve a high or a low degree of self-commitment and personal involvement on the part of the individual (Selznick, 1957).

For certain purposes, it is helpful to make a sharp distinction between two levels of adaptation: at a more *ideational* level, we may speak of a role conception; at a more *behavioral* level, there is a pattern of role performance. Each of these has an affective component. Role conception and role performance are independent though related variables; let us consider them in turn.

Individual (and Modal) Role Conceptions

The nature of a role conception may perhaps be clarified by placing it in relation to an ideology. The boundary between the two is certainly not a sharp one. However, ideology refers most directly to an orientation regarding the entire organizational (or other) structure—its puposes, its modes of operation, the prevailing forms of individual and group relationships, and so on. A role conception offers a definition and rationale for one position within the structure. If ideology portrays and rationalizes the organizational world, then role conception delineates the specific functions, values, and manner of functioning appropriate to one position within it.

The degree of uniformity or variability in individual role conceptions within a given position will presumably vary from one organization to another. When one or more types of role conception are commonly held (consensual), we may speak of modal types. The maintenance of structural stability requires that there be at least moderate consensus and that modal role conceptions be reasonably congruent with role requirements. At the same time, the presence of incongruent modal role conceptions may, under certain conditions, provide an ideational basis for major organizational change.

Starting with the primary assumption that each member "takes over" a structurally defined role, many social scientists tend to assume that there is great uniformity in role conception among the members of a given social position. They hold, in other words, that for every position there is a *dominant, modal role conception corresponding to the structural demands,* and that there is relatively little individual deviation from the modal pattern. Although this state of affairs may at times obtain, we know that the members of a given social position often have quite diverse conceptions of their proper roles (Greenblatt, Levinson, and Williams, 1957; Gross, Mason, and McEachern, 1958; Reissman and Rohrer, 1957; Bendix, 1956). After all, individual role conceptions are formed only partially within the present organizational setting. The individual's ideas about his occupational role are influenced by childhood experiences, by his values and other personality characteristics, by formal education and apprenticeship, and the like. The ideas of various potential reference groups within and outside of the organization are available through reading, informal contacts, etc. There is reason to expect, then, that the role conceptions of individuals in a given organizational position will vary and will not always conform to official role requirements. Both the diversities and the modal patterns must be considered in organizational analysis.

Individual (and Modal) Role Performance

This term refers to the overt behavioral aspect of role definition—to the more or less characteristic ways in which the individual acts as the occupant of a social position. Because role performance involves immediately observable behavior, its description would seem to present few systematic problems. However, the formulation of adequate variables for the analysis of role performance is in fact a major theoretical problem and one of the great stumbling blocks in empirical research.

Everyone would agree, I suppose, that role performance concerns only those aspects of the total stream of behavior that are structurally relevant. But which aspects of behavior are the important ones? And where shall the boundary be drawn between that which is structurally relevant and that which is incidental or idiosyncratic?

One's answer to these questions probably depends, above all, upon his conception of social structure. Those who conceive of social structure rather narrowly in terms of concrete work tasks and normative requirements, are inclined to take a similarly narrow view of role. In this view, role performance is simply the fulfillment of formal role norms, and anything else the person does is extraneous to role performance as such. Its proponents acknowledge that there are variations in "style" of performance but regard these as incidental. What is essential to *role* performance is the degree to which norms are met.

A more complex and inclusive conception of social structure requires correspondingly multidimensional delineation of role performance. An organization has, from this viewpoint, "latent" as well as "manifest" structure; it has a many faceted emotional climate; it tends to "demand" varied forms of interpersonal allegiance, friendship, deference, intimidation, ingratiation, rivalry, and the like. If characteristics such as these are considered intrinsic properties of social structure, then they must be included in the characterization of role performance. My own preference is for the more inclusive view. I regard social structure as having psychological as well as other properties, and I regard as intrinsic to role performance the varied meanings and feelings which the actor communicates to those about him. Ultimately, we must learn to characterize organizational behavior in a way that takes into account, and helps to illuminate, its functions for the individual, for the others with whom he interacts, and for the organization.

It is commonly assumed that there is great uniformity in role performance among the members of a given position. Or, in other words, that there is *a dominant, modal pattern of role performance corresponding to the structural requirements*. The rationale here parallels that given above for role conceptions. However, where individual variations in patterns of role performance have been investigated, several modal types rather than a single dominant pattern were found (Argyris, 1957; Greenblatt et al., 1957).

Nor is this variability surprising, except to those who have the most simplistic conception of social life. Role performance, like any form of human behavior, is the resultant of many forces. Some of these forces derive from the organizational matrix; for example, from role demands and the pressures of authority, from informal group influences, and from impending sanctions. Other determinants lie within the person, as for example his role conceptions and role relevant personality characteristics. Except in unusual cases where all forces operate to channel behavior in the same direction, role performance will reflect the individual's attempts at choice and compromise among diverse external and internal forces.

The relative contributions of various forms of influence to individual or modal role performance can be determined only *if each set of variables is defined and measured independently of the others.* That is, indeed, one of the major reasons for emphasizing and sharpening the distinctions among role performance, role conception, and role demands. Where these distinctions are not sharply drawn, there is a tendency to study one element and to assume that the others are in close fit. For example, we may learn from the official charter and the administrative authorities how the organization is supposed to work—the formal requirements —and then assume that it in fact operates in this way. Or, conversely, one may observe various regularities in role performance and then assume that these are structurally determined, without independently assessing the structural requirements. To do this is to make structural explanations purely tautologous.

More careful distinction among these aspects of social structure and role will also, I believe, permit greater use of personality theory in organizational analysis. Let us turn briefly to this question.

ROLE DEFINITION, PERSONALITY, AND SOCIAL STRUCTURE

Just as social structure presents massive forces which influence the individual from without toward certain forms of adaptation, so does personality present massive forces from within which lead him to select, create, and synthesize certain forms of adaptation rather than others. Role definition may be seen from one perspective as an aspect of personality. It represents the individual's attempt to structure his social reality, to define his place within it, and to guide his search for meaning and gratification. Role definition is, in this sense, an *ego achievement*—a reflection of the person's capacity to resolve conflicting demands, to utilize existing opportunities and create new ones, to find some balance between stability and change, conformity and autonomy, the ideal and the feasible, in a complex environment.

The formation of a role definition is, from a dynamic psychological point of view, an "external function" of the ego. Like the other external (reality-oriented) ego functions, it is influenced by the ways in which the ego carries out its "internal functions" of coping with, and attempting to synthesize, the demands of id, superego, and ego. These internal activities—the "psychodynamics" of personality— include among other things: unconscious fantasies; unconscious moral conceptions and the wishes against which they are directed; the characteristic ways in which unconscious processes are transformed or deflected in more conscious thought, feeling, and behavioral striving; conceptions of self and ways of maintaining or changing these conceptions in the face of changing pressures from within and from the external world.

In viewing role definition as an aspect of personality, I am suggesting that it is, *to varying degrees,* related to and imbedded within other aspects of personality. An individual's conception of his role in a particular organization is to be seen within a series of wider psychological contexts: his conception of his occupational role generally (occupational identity), his basic values, life-goals, and conception of self (ego identity), and so on. Thus, one's way of relating to authorities in the organization depends in part upon his relation to authority in general, and upon his fantasies, conscious as well as unconscious, about the "good" and the "bad" parental authority. His ways of dealing with the stressful aspects of organizational life are influenced by the impulses, anxieties, and modes of defense that these stresses activate in him (Argyris, 1957; Erikson, 1950; Henry, 1949; Blum, 1933; Pine and Levinson, 1957).

There are variations in the degree to which personal role definition is imbedded in, and influenced by, deeper-lying personality characteristics. The importance of individual or modal personality for role definition is a matter for empirical study and cannot be settled by casual assumption. Traditional sociological theory can be criticized for assuming that individual role definition is determined almost entirely by social structure. Similarly, dynamic personality theory will not take its rightful place as a crucial element of social psychology until it views the individual within his sociocultural environment. Lacking an adequate recognition and *conceptualization* of the individual's external reality—including the "reality" of social structure—personality researchers tend to assume that individual adaptation is primarily personality determined and that reality is, for the most part, an amorphous blob structured by the individual to suit his inner needs.

Clearly, individual role conception and role performance do not emanate, fully formed, from the depths of personality. Nor are they simply mirror images of a mold established by social structure. Elsewhere (Levinson, 1954), I have used the term "mirage" theory for the view, frequently held or implied in the psychoanalytic literature, that ideologies, role conceptions, and behavior are mere epiphenomena or by-products of unconscious fantasies and defenses. Similarly, the term "sponge" theory characterizes the view, commonly forwarded in the sociological literature, in which man is merely a passive, mechanical absorber of the prevailing structural demands.

Our understanding of personal role definition will remain seriously impaired as long as we fail to place it, analytically, in *both intrapersonal and structural-environmental contexts.* That is to say, we must be concerned with the meaning of role definition both for the individual personality and for the social system. A given role definition is influenced by, and has an influence upon, the *psyche* as well as the *socius.* If we are adequately to understand the nature, the determinants, and the consequences of role definition, we need the double perspective of personality and social structure. The use of these two reference points is, like the use of our two eyes in seeing, necessary for the achievement of depth in our social vision.

Theory and research on organizational roles must consider relationships among at least the following sets of characteristics: structurally given role demands and opportunities, personal role definition (including conceptions and performance), and personality in its role-related aspects. Many forms of relationship may exist among them. I shall mention only a few hypothetical possibilities.

In one type case, the role requirements are so narrowly defined, and the mechanisms of social control so powerful, that only one form of role performance can be sustained for any given position. An organization of this type may be able selectively to recruit and retain only individuals who, by virtue of personality, find this system meaningful and gratifying. If a congruent modal personality is achieved, a highly integrated and stable structure may well emerge. I would hypothesize that a structurally congruent modal personality is one condition, though by no means the only one, for the stability of a rigidly integrated system. (In modern times, of course, the rapidity of technological change prevents long-term stability in any organizational structure.)

However, an organization of this kind may acquire members who are not initially receptive to the structural order, that is, who are *incongruent* in role conception or in personality. Here, several alternative developments are possible.

1. The "incongruent" members may change so that their role conceptions and personalities come better to fit the structural requirements.

2. The incongruent ones may leave the organization, by choice or by expulsion. The high turnover in most of our organizations is due less to technical incompetence than to rejection of the "conditions of life" in the organization.

3. The incongruent ones may remain, but in a state of apathetic conformity. In this case, the person meets at least the minimal requirements of role performance but his role conceptions continue relatively unchanged, he gets little satisfaction from work, and he engages in repeated "sabotage" of organizational aims. This is an uncomfortably frequent occurrence in our society. In the Soviet Union as well, even after 40 years of enveloping social controls, there exist structurally incongruent forms of political ideology, occupational role definition, and personality (Inkeles, Hanfmann, and Beier, 1958).

4. The incongruent members may gain sufficient social power to change the organizational structure. This phenomenon is well known, though not well enough understood. For example, in certain of our mental hospitals, schools and prisons over the past 20–30 years, individuals with new ideas and personal characteristics have entered in large enough numbers, and in sufficiently strategic positions, to effect major structural changes. Similar ideological and structural transitions are evident in other types of organization, such as corporate business.

The foregoing are a few of many possible developments in a relatively monolithic structure. A somewhat looser organizational pattern is perhaps more commonly found. In this setting, structural change becomes a valued aim and innovation is seen as a legitimate function of members at various levels in the organization. To the extent that diversity and innovation are valued (rather than merely given lip-service), variations in individual role definition are tolerated or even encouraged within relatively wide limits. The role definitions that develop will reflect various degrees of synthesis and compromise between personal preference and structural demand.

In summary, I have suggested that a primary distinction be made between the structurally given role demands and the forms of role definition achieved by the individual members of an organization. Personal role definition then becomes a linking concept between personality and social structure. It can be seen as a reflection of those aspects of individual personality that are activated and sustained in a given structural-ecological environment. This view is opposed both to the "sociologizing" of individual behavior and to the "psychologizing" of organizational structure. At the same time, it is concerned with both the psychological properties of social structure and the structural properties of individual adaptation.

Finally, we should keep in mind that both personality structure and social structure inevitably have their internal contradictions. No individual is sufficiently all of a piece that he will for long find any form of adaptation, occupational or otherwise, totally satisfying. Whatever the psychic gains stemming from a particular role definition and social structure, there will also be losses: wishes that must be renounced or made unconscious, values that must be compromised, anxieties to be handled, personal goals that will at best be incompletely met. The organization has equivalent limitations. Its multiple purposes cannot all be optimally achieved. It faces recurrent dilemmas over conflicting requirements: control and freedom; centralization and decentralization of authority; security as against the risk of failure; specialization and diffusion of work function; stability and change; collective unity and diversity. Dilemmas such as these arise anew in different forms at each new step of organizational development, without permanent solution. And perpetual changes in technology, in scientific understanding, in material resources, in the demands and capacities of its members and the surrounding community, present new issues and require continuing organizational readjustment.

In short, every individual and every sociocultural form contains within itself the seeds of its own destruction—or its own reconstruction. To grasp both the sources of stability and the seeds of change in human affairs is one of the great challenges to contemporary social science.

NOTES

[1] Contemporary organization theory has benefited from criticisms and reformulations of Weber's theory by such writers as Barnard (1938), Friedrich (1950), Gerth and Mills (1953), Gouldner (1954), Merton (1957), and Parsons (in his introduction to Weber, 1947). Selznick (1957) has recently presented a conception of the administrative-managerial role that allows more room for psychological influences, but these are not explicitly conceptualized. There is growing though still inconclusive evidence from research on "culture and personality" work (Inkeles and Levinson, 1954) that social structures of various types both "require" and are influenced by modal personality, but this approach has received little application in research on organizations. An attempt at a distinctively sociopsychological approach, and a comprehensive view of the relevant literature, is presented by Argyris (1957).

[2] An argument very similar to the one made here is presented by Gross, Mason, and McEachern (1958) in a comprehensive overview and critique of role theory. They point up the assumption of high consensus regarding role demands and role conceptions in traditional role theory, and present empirical evidence contradicting this assumption. Their analysis is, however, less concerned than the present one with the converging of role theory and personality theory.

[3] The reduced integration reflects in part the tremendous rate of technological change, the geographical and occupational mobility, and the diversity in personality that characterize modern society. On the other hand, diversity is opposed by the standardization of culture on a mass basis and by the growth of large-scale organization itself. Trends toward increased standardization and uniformity are highlighted in Whyte's (1956) analysis.

REFERENCES

Argyris, C. *Human relations in a hospital.* New Haven, Conn.: Labor and Management Center, 1955.

Argyris, C. *Personality and organization.* New York: Harper, 1957.

Barnard, C. I. *The functions of the executive.* Cambridge, Mass.: Harvard University Press, 1938.

Bendix, R. *Work and authority in industry.* New York: Wiley, 1956.

Blum, F. H. *Toward a democratic work process.* New York: Harper, 1933.

Burling, T., Edith Lentz, and R. N. Wilson. *The give and take in hospitals.* New York: Putnam, 1956.

Erikson, E. H. *Childhood and society.* New York: Norton, 1950.

Erikson, K. T. Patient role and social uncertainty: A dilemma of the mentally ill. *Psychiatry* 20, 1957, 263–274.

Friedrich, C. J. *Constitutional government and democracy.* Boston: Little, Brown, 1950.

Gerth, H. H. and C. W. Mills. *Character and social structure.* New York: Harcourt, Brace, 1953.

Gouldner, A. W. *Patterns of industrial bureaucracy.* Glencoe, Ill.: Free Press, 1954.

Greenblatt, M., D. J. Levinson, and R. H. Williams (eds.). *The patient and the mental hospital.* Glencoe, Ill.: Free Press, 1957.

Gross, N., W. S. Mason, and A. W. McEachern. *Explorations in role analysis.* New York: Wiley, 1958.

Hartley, E. L., and Ruth E. Hartley. *Fundamentals of social psychology.* New York: Knopf, 1952.

Henry, W. E. The business executive: the psychodynamics of a social role. *American Journal of Sociology,* 54, 1949, 286–291.

Inkeles, A., Eugenia Hanfmann, and Helen Beier. Modal personality and adjustment to the Soviet political system. *Human Relations* 11, 1958, 3–22.

Inkeles, A., and D. J. Levinson. National character: The study of modal personality and socio-cultural systems. In G. Lindzey (ed.), *Handbook of social psychology.* Cambridge, Mass.: Addison-Wesley, 1954.

Kornhauser, A., R. Dublin, and A. M. Ross. *Industrial conflict.* New York: McGraw-Hill, 1954.

Levinson, D. J. *Idea systems in the individual and society.* Paper presented at Boston University, Founder's Day Institute, 1954. Mimeographed: Center for Sociopsychological Research, Massachusetts Mental Health Center.

Linton, R. *The cultural background of personality.* New York: Appleton-Century, 1945.

Mead, G. H. *Mind, self and society.* Chicago: University of Chicago Press, 1934.

Merton, R. K. *Social theory and social structure.* (Rev. ed.) Glencoe, Ill.: Free Press, 1957.

Merton, R. K., A. P. Gray, Barbara Hockey, and H. C. Selvin. *Reader in bureaucracy.* Glencoe, Ill.: Free Press, 1957.

Newcomb, T. M. *Social psychology.* New York: Dryden, 1950.

Parsons, T. *Essays in sociological theory.* (Rev. ed.) Glencoe, Ill.: Free Press, 1945.

Parsons, T. *The social system.* Glencoe, Ill.: Free Press, 1951.

Parsons, T., and E. A. Shils (eds.). *Toward a general theory of action.* Cambridge, Mass.: Harvard University Press, 1951.

Pine, F., and D. J. Levinson. Two patterns of ideology, role conception, and personality among mental hospital aides. In M. Greenblatt, D. J. Levinson, and R. H. Williams (eds.), *The patient and the mental hospital.* Glencoe, Ill.: Free Press, 1957.

Pine, F., and D. J. Levinson. *Problematic issues in the role of mental hospital patient.* Mimeographed: Center for Sociopsychological Research, Massachusetts Mental Health Center, 1958.

Reissman, L., and J. J. Rohrer (eds.). *Change and dilemma in the nursing profession.* New York: Putnam, 1957.

Sarbin, T. R. Role theory. In G. Lindzey (ed.), *Handbook of social psychology.* Cambridge, Mass.: Addison-Wesley, 1954.

Selznick, P. *Leadership in administration.* Evanston, Ill.: Row, Peterson, 1957.

Sharaf, M. R., and D. J. Levinson. Patterns of ideology and role definition among psychiatric residents. In M. Greenblatt, D. J. Levinson, and R. H. Williams (eds.), *The patient and the mental hospital.* Glencoe Ill.: Free Press, 1957.

Weber, M. *Essays in sociology.* Ed. by H. H. Gerth and C. W. Mills. New York: Oxford University Press, 1946.

Weber, M. *The theory of social and economic organization.* Ed. by T. Parsons. New York: Oxford University Press, 1947.

Whyte, W. F. *The organization man.* New York: Simon and Schuster, 1956.

PART TWO

Personality Analysis of Individual
Political Actors

5

A General Introduction to Psychobiography

This hitherto unpublished paper was written by Professor George in 1960. For over a decade, it has been well known among scholars, many of whom have drawn on and cited it. Professor George chose not to publish the paper at the time since he was in the process of refining portions of the argument and developing the technical implications of a number of points the paper raises. For some of these developments, see Alexander L. George, "Power as a Compensatory Value for Political Leaders," *Journal of Social Issues,* 25 (July 1968), 29–50. The editors have prevailed on Professor George to allow the belated publication of an analysis that, in many respects, he considers to be dated and that partially duplicates his *Journal of Social Issues* article. We publish this early paper of George's not only because of its recognized standing among students of personality and politics (which makes it appropriate for a source book), but also because it continues to be the simplest and most fluent general introduction essay available on the use of depth-psychological categories and procedures in analyses of individual political actors. In illustrating his methodological discussion with case materials on Woodrow Wilson, George draws on his and Juliette L. George's *Woodrow Wilson and Colonel House: A Personality Study,* one of the most rigorous and convincing of the psychobiographies of political figures.

SOME USES OF DYNAMIC PSYCHOLOGY IN POLITICAL BIOGRAPHY: CASE MATERIALS ON WOODROW WILSON

Alexander L. George

More so than historical writing at large, biography is selective. By choosing a single individual as his concern, the biographer can focus on those aspects of the historical process which interacted most directly with his subject. The nature of this interaction and, particularly, the extent to which it is reciprocal, is one of the central problems of biography. To what extent was the behavior of the subject culturally and situationally determined? To what extent did it reflect the individuality of his personality? Though variously worded by different writers, this twofold task of the biographer is a familiar and perplexing one.

In a brief but acute statement of the problem, the Committee on Historiography emphasized that the writing of biography requires both a systematic field theory of personality and hypotheses as to social roles.[1] While agreeing with this twofold emphasis, we have chosen for several reasons to focus attention in the present article upon the need for a systematic approach to personality factors. First, it would appear that historians generally are already more favorably disposed to the cultural approach, and better prepared to employ it, than to a systematic handling of personality components in biography. Second, we wish to show by introducing concrete case materials that a systematic personality approach may be necessary and particularly rewarding in the biographical study of innovating leaders, those who attempt to reinterpret and expand the functions of existing roles or to create new roles. We are particularly interested, that is, in "role-determining" as against "role-determined" leadership. At the same time, we agree that the creation or reinterpretation of leadership roles can only be understood in the context of social-historical dynamics and the institutional setting. The "great leader," as Gerth and Mills observe, has often been a man who has successfully managed such institutional dynamics and created new roles of leadership.[2]

We shall draw upon our previously reported study of Woodrow Wilson[3] in order to demonstrate how the personality component in a biography may be handled in a systematic fashion. And we shall attempt to show that dynamic psychology provides a number of hypotheses which can supplement a cultural or role analysis of Wilson's interest in constitution-writing and which permit the biographer to view the relationship between his "Presbyterian conscience" and his political stubbornness in a new light.

For a discussion of evidence and inference in the Georges' account of Wilson, see Fred I. Greenstein, *Personality and Politics: Problems of Evidence, Inference, and Conceptualization* (Chicago: Markham, 1969), Chapter 3. The author's acknowledgement in George's 1960 essay: In preparing this paper I benefited from opportunities for study and discussion as a fellow of the Center for Advanced Study in the Behavioral Sciences, 1956–57, and more recently from a research grant from the Foundations Fund for Research in Psychiatry.

SOME DEFICIENCIES OF PSYCHOLOGICAL BIOGRAPHIES

In the past three or four decades historians have occasionally turned to the new field of dynamic psychology for assistance in this task. At the same time, specialists in psychology, especially psychoanalysts, have themselves occasionally attempted to apply the insights and theories of their practice to historical figures.[4] The results of such efforts, from both sides, to merge history and psychology in the writing of political biography have not been encouraging. Even when their purpose was not to debunk a historical figure, most psychoanalytical biographies suffered from pronounced and basic deficiencies.

Three major deficiencies in this type of biography may be briefly mentioned. In the first place, in varying degrees such biographies exaggerate the purely psychological determinants of the political behavior of their subjects. In the cruder of these studies, the subject is represented as if in the grip of powerful unconscious and irrational drives which dictate his every thought and action. Even in more discriminating analyses, the revelation of human motive resulting from incisive insights into the subject's personality can easily oversimplify the complexity of motivation and political action.

Secondly, in viewing adult character and behavior as the legacy of certain early childhood experiences, psychological biographies often oversimplify the process of personality formation and the intricacy of personality structure and functioning. Such a psychological approach is by today's standards inadequate for it overlooks the relevance of important developments in "ego psychology" in the past few decades.[5] Contemporary students of personality emphasize that in the course of his development the individual develops a variety of defenses against underlying anxieties and hostilities. He may learn ways of curbing and controlling tendencies which handicap him in various situations; and he may even devise *constructive* strategies for harnessing personal needs and motivations and directing them into fruitful channels. In other words, the individual attempts to cope simultaneously with the demands of impulse, conscience and reality in developing a philosophy of life, a system of values, a set of attitudes and interests, and in choosing in various situations from among alternative courses of action.[6]

And, finally, to conclude this brief review of the major deficiencies encountered in psychological biographies, one is struck by the fact that the actions of the subject are often interpreted in ways which seem highly speculative and arbitrary. Few investigators in this field have come to grips with the admittedly difficult problem of making rigorous reconstructions of personality factors and plausible interpretations of their role in behavior from the types of historical materials usually available to the biographer. The result is that the use which the biographer makes of dynamic psychology often appears to consist in little more than borrowing certain terms and hypotheses, and superimposing them, more or less arbitrarily upon a smattering of the available historical materials concerning the subject.

PERSONALITY TYPES: THE PROBLEM OF DIAGNOSIS AND CLASSIFICATION

Typologies of personality or character are provided by most of the various schools of psychoanalysis and dynamic psychology. The depiction of a type is usually on the basis of one or more traits, or behavioral tendencies. Often, the characterization of types also includes some indication of the origins and underlying psychodynamics of that type of behavior, which enhances the usefulness of the typology to the biographer. We do not propose to review these typologies here or to attempt to assess their relative worth to the biographer.[7] Rather we wish to consider the status or nature of these personality types and some of the problems which arise in efforts to utilize them in biography.

Most of the types in question are to be understood as being general constructs, or *ideal types*. Though derived from empirical observation, they abstract and deliberately oversimplify reality.[8] Accordingly, their value to the biographer is necessarily limited, since his task is to describe and explain a particular individual in all his concreteness and complexity.

The biographer cannot be satisfied merely to label his subject as constituting an instance of, or bearing a certain resemblance to, a certain personality or character type. To do so oversimplifies the task of making fruitful use of the theories and findings of dynamic psychology and yields results of a limited and disappointing character. Many investigators whose initial attempt to use a personality approach in biography is of this character become disillusioned and abandon the task. They sense that to type their subject, as a "compulsive" for example, tends to caricature him rather than to explain very much of the richness, complexity and variety of his behavior throughout his career.

We are concerned here with a problem not always clearly recognized in the writing of psychological biographies. *Classification* is often confused with *diagnosis.* To tag the subject of the biography with a label or to pigeonhole him in one of a number of existing categories does not in itself provide what the biographer will need most: namely, a discriminating "theory," i.e., a set of assumptions or hypotheses, as to the structure and dynamics of his subject's personality system.

The "diagnosis *vs.* classification" problem also exists in clinical psychiatry where a distinction is sometimes made between the "sponge" and the "file-drawer" clinician.[9] The "sponge"-type clinician attempts to approach his patient with a relatively open mind, trying to derive a theory about that particular patient from an intensive analysis of his behavior and case history. In contrast, the "file-drawer"-type of clinician is more inclined to orient himself to the patient on the basis of general theories and past experience. The one attempts to construct a theory about the patient *de nouveau,* a theory that, as a result, may be highly particularistic; the other stresses gaining insight into the patient by making an astute classification of him on the basis of accumulated theory and experience.

The difference between these clinical approaches is mentioned here in order to point up alternative approaches available to the biographer. As will become clear, we are suggesting that though the biographer should indeed be familiar with available personality theories, he should nonetheless approach his subject as does the "sponge"-type clinician and undertake to develop as discriminating and refined a theory as possible of that particular personality.

In attempting to account for the subject's actions throughout his career, the biographer will have to make specific diagnoses of the operative state of his personality system in numerous situations. To this end, the biographer starts with as good a theory of the subject's personality as he can derive from secondary accounts and from a preliminary inspection of historical materials. Then he reviews chronologically, or developmentally, the history of his subject's behavior, attempting to assess the role that situational and personality factors played in specific instances.[10]

In utilizing a preliminary theory of the subject's personality to make specific diagnoses the biographer in a real sense also "tests" that theory. Detailed analysis of the subject's actions in a variety of individual situations provides new insights into the motivational dynamics of the subject's behavior; these insights, in turn, enable the biographer to progressively refine and improve the theory of the subject's personality with which he started. What the biographer hopes to achieve eventually is an account of the subject's personality that gives coherence and depth to the explanation of his behavior in a variety of situations and that illuminates the more subtle patterns that underlie whatever seeming "inconsistencies" of character and behavior he has displayed.

TWO USES OF PERSONALITY TYPES IN BIOGRAPHY

Despite the general nature of personality and character types, they may be of substantial use to the biographer in several ways. First, knowledge of these types assists the biographer in developing the kind of *preliminary* theory about the personality of his subject to which reference has already been made. Second, familiarity with the psychodynamics of behavior associated with a particular personality or character type provides the biographer with hypotheses for consideration in attempting to account for the actions of his subject, especially those that cannot be easily explained as adequate responses to the situation which confronted him. Let us consider these two general uses in somewhat greater detail.

A major shortcoming in many conventional biographies, including those of Wilson, is that they lack a systematic theory about the subject's personality and motivations. The biographer is usually satisfied to catalogue individual traits exhibited by the subject without exploring their possible interrelationship and their functional significance within the personality as a whole.[11] Various of Wilson's biographers,[12] for example, have called attention to his marked "conscientiousness," stubbornness," "single-track mind," and various other traits. They have done so, however, without indicating awareness that, according to Freudian theory, these traits are commonly exhibited by "compulsive" persons.

The term "compulsive" today is commonly applied to persons whose lives are regulated by a strict super-ego, or conscience, which dominates their personalities. Perhaps not generally known, however, is the fact that this type of behavior has been carefully studied over a period of many years by many clinicians; as a result, there are a number of detailed analyses and theories of compulsiveness and the compulsive type that attempt to account for the genesis and underlying dynamics of this type of behavior. Later in this paper we shall attempt to show how this rich body of observation and theory can be used by the biographer. It suffices here to observe that biographers of Wilson, being generally unfamiliar with such materials, have not been in a position to assess the significance of individual traits displayed by Wilson in terms of their underlying dynamics.[13]

Occasionally biographers of Wilson have been able, on the basis of an intensive analysis of a particularly well-documented episode in Wilson's career, to infer or to suggest that his choice of action in a particular situation was apparently governed by personal motives other than the aims and values which he was publicly espousing.[14] But generally they have hesitated to make diagnoses of the operative state of Wilson's personality system in specific situations, to explore in any systematic fashion the complexity and deeper levels of his motivation, or to postulate in detail the role of his personality in his political behavior. Therefore, while these biographers have sensed Wilson's personal involvement in politics and called attention to his many contradictions, their portraits of Wilson's personality are inevitably somewhat flat, even though accurately depicting behavioral tendencies at a surface level.

A familiarity with personality and character types identified in the literature of dynamic psychology will assist the biographer to construct a *preliminary* theory, or model, as to the structure and functioning of his subject's personality. For this purpose there are available to the biographer a variety of typologies of personality and character. Some of these are predominantly sociopsychological rather than clinical in their conception and orientation. Not all typologies of personality are comparable, since they have been constructed from different theoretical standpoints, for different purposes and applications. An overlapping can be noted, however, particularly among some of the typologies provided by various schools of psychoanalysis. Thus, for example, the "aggressive" person in Karen Horney's system bears a substantial resemblance to the Freudian concept of the compulsive type. Similarly, Alfred Adler's central emphasis upon the drive to power and superiority as a means of compensation for real or imagined defects finds a place in many other personality theories as well.

Given the variety of alternative typologies available, the biographer must obviously consider a number of them before choosing the type or types that seem most appropriate to his subject and most useful for the specific questions about the subject's motivations and behavior he is trying to clarify.

Personality theorists, Freudian and non-Freudian, have emphasized that the type-constructs formulated by them are not pure types. Rather, they view the personality functioning of an individual as a mixture of several trends, or types, in a more or less dynamic relationship to each other. This observation applies with particular force to Wilson, in whom several diverse trends can be detected.[15] Nonetheless, the present account is limited to discussing the applicability of the compulsive type to Wilson, partly because of limitations of space and partly because we feel that the compulsive component of his personality is particularly important for illuminating the self-defeating aspects of his behavior.

In any case, having found much evidence of compulsiveness and of the compulsive syndrome in the historical accounts of his life and career, we felt justified in adopting as a tentative working theory that Wilson had a compulsive personality.

We then considered his development and behavior in detail from this standpoint, examining the voluminous documentation of his career that is available to the biographer. In doing so, we encountered increasing evidence of behavior on his part that could not easily be subsumed under the simple model of the compulsive type. This forced us to refine and elaborate the theory as to his compulsiveness, and to attempt to state the *conditions* and to characterize the *situations* in which he did and did not behave in a way (for example, stubbornly) that was in accord with the expectations explicit or implicit in the personality model with which we were working.[16]

Gradually, then, the general construct of the compulsive type (which, as already mentioned, is to be taken as an abstraction and deliberate oversimplification of reality) was modified and brought into consonance with the complexities encountered in the individual case at hand. The point was reached when the picture of Wilson's personality that was emerging became too complex to be retained within the bounds of the compulsive model with which we had started. What remained of that model or theory was the notion of an important compulsive component in his personality and functioning. This component, we shall attempt to show, remained of considerable value as an explanatory principle for some of Wilson's political behavior that has puzzled and distressed many of his contemporaries and biographers.

Another major use of typologies and theories of personality to the biographer is that of providing alternative hypotheses for consideration in attempting to account for the actions and behavioral patterns of his subject. Such general hypotheses are not ready-made explanations to be employed arbitrarily or to be superimposed upon the data. Rather, as a statement of the dynamics of behavior and motivation often or typically associated with a certain personality type, they may serve to orient the biographer's effort to explain the actions of his subject.[17] A familiarity with such hypotheses broadens and deepens the biographer's assessment of the aims and values that the subject pursues in a given situation or in a series of situations. Furthermore, it sensitizes him to historical evidence of the possible operation of unconscious or unstated motives he might otherwise overlook.

During the preparation of our study of Wilson we combed the technical literature for hypotheses about the dynamics of motivation and behavior associated with compulsiveness that might illuminate the nature of Wilson's personal involvement in political activities.[18] We hoped to find clues to certain inept and apparently irrational actions on his part and to discover, if possible, a consistent pattern or thread in the various inconsistencies of behavior and character he displayed.

If Wilson is not the simple clinical stereotype of a compulsive, neither can he be regarded as a full-blown neurotic. True, one cannot read, for example, Karen Horney's insightful and penetrating descriptions of neurotic drives and of the neurotic character structure without being struck by the applicability of much of what she says to Wilson. But these descriptions are applicable only to a certain point and, upon reflection, one is on balance equally or more impressed with the extent to which Wilson's behavior and career *diverge* from those of her patients. This divergence from the clinical picture concerns precisely the critical question whether the neurotically disposed individual is able to deal adequately with his conflicts and hence retains the ability to function effectively.

For Wilson was, after all, a highly successful person. He was able to overcome a severe disturbance in childhood development; thereafter, not only did he keep fairly well in check the compulsive and neurotic components of his personality but he succeeded in large measure in harnessing them constructively to the achievement of socially productive purposes.[19] To the clinical psychologist, therefore, Wilson is interesting as much because he was able to overcome childhood difficulties and to perform as successfully as he did in public life, as he is because of the pathological pattern of self-defeating behavior he tended to repeat on several occasions during his public career.[20]

COMPULSIVENESS AND THE COMPULSIVE TYPE

To indicate briefly what is meant by compulsiveness and the compulsive type of personality is not an easy task since these concepts are employed somewhat differently within the various theoretical schools which comprise dynamic psychology.

The point to be made here is that the existence of different theoretical orientations and, particularly, of important lacunae in knowledge and theory within the field of dynamic psychology need not prevent the biographer from making fruitful use of systematic personality theory as a source of hypotheses that serve to orient and give direction to his own research.[21]

In any case, the usefulness of the technical literature to the biographer will be enhanced if the distinction is kept in mind between the question of the *origins* of compulsiveness and compulsive traits, about which there are various views, and the *dynamics* of such behavior, about which there is less disagreement. Similarly, the biographer will observe that specialists seem able to agree more readily on a characterization of the quality of compulsive behavior than on a list of specific traits common to all compulsive persons.

In Freudian theory various correlations are predicted between disturbances of different stages in libido development and the emergence of certain adult character traits. Disturbances in one of these stages of development leads, according to the theory, to the presence of orderliness, stinginess, and stubbornness in adult behavior.[22] These are general traits, or broad tendencies, that manifest themselves more specifically in a variety of ways. By combing the technical literature one can easily construct a richer, more elaborate list of traits which together comprise the syndrome or constellation.[23]

Thus, for example, the general trait "orderliness" may manifest itself in (a) "cleanliness" (corporeal, symbolic); (b) "conscientiousness" (single-track mind, concentration, drive, pedantism, reliability, punctuality, punctiliousness and thoroughness); (c) "regularity" (according to spatial and temporal aspects); (d) "plannedness"; (e) "norm conformity." [24]

Most personality and character types are usually described, at least in the first instance, in terms of certain manifest behavioral traits such as those that have been listed. If the description of a type does not link the traits in question with a theory of personality structure and motivational dynamics, the type-construct will obviously be of little value for motivational and situational analysis of an individual's behavior. At the same time, however, it is overly sanguine to expect that relationships between most manifest behavior traits and their inner, subjective functions for the personality will be of a simple one-to-one character. For, as clinical psychologists have particularly emphasized, the same item of manifest behavior may fulfill different functions for different personalities or, at different times, for the same individual. Particularly the political and social behavior of an individual, in which the biographer is most interested, is not likely to reflect single motives; it is more likely to be the outcome of a complex interplay of several motives and of efforts on the part of the person to adjust inner needs and strivings to one another as well as to external reality considerations.

A personality type construct is potentially more useful, therefore, if it is associated with a more or less distinctive type of motivational dynamics, whether or not this be invariably accompanied by a set of distinctive behavioral traits. From this standpoint, leaving aside for the present the question of its validity, the Freudian concept of the compulsive type is a particularly rich one in that it includes, in addition to the syndrome of traits already noted, a rather explicit and detailed set of structural-dynamic hypotheses of this kind.

We shall not attempt to recapitulate the rather involved and technical set of structural-dynamic hypotheses associated with the compulsive type in Freudian theory. Of immediate interest here is the fact that orderliness and stubbornness in persons of this type are said to derive in part from a desire for power or domination, which in turn is said to be related to a more basic need for self-esteem, or security.[25] Thus, according to the technical literature compulsives often show a marked interest in imposing orderly systems upon others, an activity from which they derive a sense of power. They also hold fast obstinately to their own way of doing things. They dislike to accommodate themselves to arrangements imposed from without, but expect immediate compliance from other people as soon as they have worked out a definite arrangement, plan or proposal of their own.

In the spheres of activity in which they seek power gratifications, compulsives are sensitive to interference. They may take advice badly (or only under special circumstances). Often they exhibit difficulties in deputing work to others, being convinced at bottom that they can do everything (in this sphere) better than others. This conviction is sometimes exaggerated to the point that they believe they are unique. Negativeness, secretiveness and vindictiveness are traits often displayed by compulsives. (Considerable evidence of most of these traits and tendencies, too, can be found in the historical materials on Wilson, many of them being noted by contemporaries and biographers.)[26]

While particularly that aspect of Freudian theory that regards interferences with libido development as the genesis of adult character traits has been criticized, the existence of certain constellations of adult traits, as in this instance, is less controversial and, in fact, appears to enjoy some empirical support.[27]

In revisions and elaborations of Freudian theory somewhat less emphasis is often placed upon specifying a distinctive content of compulsive behavior. Karen Horney, for example, regards compulsiveness as a characteristic quality of all neurotic needs. Thus, the craving for affection, power and prestige, and the ambition, submissiveness and withdrawal which different neurotics manifest all have a desperate, rigid, indiscriminate and insatiable quality, i.e., the quality of compulsiveness.[28]

Much of common to various of these formulations has been summarized in Harold D. Lasswell's account of the functional role of the compulsive dynamism in the personality system and of the general character of the circumstances in which it is adopted.[29] Thus, the compulsive dynamism is one of several possible defensive measures a child may adopt as a way out of an acute tension-producing situation that may arise during the course of socialization and learning. Tension is produced when a relatively elaborate set of requirements are imposed upon the child and reinforced by a system of rewards and punishments of a special intensity and applied in such manner so that deprivations and indulgences are balanced. One possible defensive measure against the ensuing tension is the adoption of a blind urge to act with intensity and rigidity, i.e., the dynamism of compulsiveness.

The reasons and conditions for the emergence of compulsiveness are, as has been suggested, somewhat difficult to formulate precisely. However, in making use of available knowledge of the compulsive personality for purposes of political biography, an answer to the causal question is not essential. Whatever creates a given personality dynamism, the dynamism itself—which is what interests the biographer the most—can be fairly readily identified in accounts of the subject's behavior.

In Wilson's case, even the circumstances under which the compulsive dynamism was adopted are richly suggested in materials collected by the official biographer.[30] Thus, accounts of early efforts at the boy's education, in which the father played a leading role, strongly suggest the sort of acute tension-producing situation that, we have already noted, is considered by specialists as predisposing to the adoption of the compulsive dynamism. This, however, evidently was not Wilson's initial method of coping with the tension-inducing situation; rather, for quite a while his method of defense took the form of a tendency to withdraw from the situation. For the time being the boy was unable, perhaps out of fear of failure, or unwilling, perhaps out of resentment, to cooperate with his father's efforts to advance his intellectual development. Wilson's early "slowness" (which specialists today might well consider a case of reading retardation based on emotional factors) was a matter of considerable concern to his family; it manifested itself most strikingly in his not learning his letters until he was nine and not learning to read readily until the age of eleven.[31]

At about this time the boy showed signs of beginning to cooperate actively with his father's efforts to tutor him and to make prodigious efforts to satisfy the perfectionist demands that the Presbyterian minister levied upon his son.[32] One can only speculate at the reasons for the change at this time; possibly it was connected with the birth of a younger brother when Wilson was ten. (Wilson had two older sisters but no younger brothers or sisters until this time; he himself recalled that he had clung to his mother and was laughed at as a "mama's boy" until he was a great big fellow.)

In any case, it is easy thereafter to find evidence of a compulsive bent to the young adolescent's personality. It requires no great familiarity with the technical literature on such matters to detect indications of compulsiveness in the youth's extreme conscientiousness, the manner in which he drove himself repeatedly to physical breakdowns, and the singleness of purpose he displayed in applying himself to the task of achieving knowledge and skill in the sphere of competence—politics and oratory—with which he quickly identified his ambitions.[33]

WILSON'S INTEREST IN CONSTITUTIONS

In the remainder of this paper we should like to develop the case, mainly by way of illustrative materials from the study of Wilson, for supplementing cultural and historical components in biography by an intensive and relatively systematic appraisal of personality.

A number of Wilson's biographers, including the official biographer,[34] have been struck by the interest in constitutions he displayed from early youth. Beginning in his fourteenth year he wrote or revised a half dozen constitutions, an activity that culminated in the Covenant of the League of Nations. It is our thesis that this activity on his part reflects the type of interest in order and power that compulsive persons often display. (See above, p. 85.) In other words, he was motivated in part (though not exclusively) by a desire to impose orderly systems upon others, deriving therefrom a sense of power or domination.

The historian will quickly object, and rightly so, offering a more obvious counter-hypothesis, which is certainly plausible; namely that Wilson's interest in writing constitutions was culturally determined. After all, it was part of the belief system of the age that progress in human affairs was to be achieved by such instrumentalities as better constitutions, institutional reform, etc. The fact that Wilson wrote or revised many constitutions, therefore, does not necessarily attest to a personal interest in order and power.

Is it possible to demonstrate that Wilson's motivation in the matter did not stem exclusively from identification with a role that was socially approved? Or is such a question entirely out of the reach of the historian? In the following remarks we shall attempt to show that such questions are capable of being dealt with on the basis of the materials and method of the historian.

First, why Wilson and not someone else? Why, in other words, did the belief system in question impress itself particularly on Wilson? Is it not more than a coincidence that in every club he joined as a youth he seized the earliest opportunity, often making it the first order of business, to revise its constitution in order to transform the club into a miniature House of Commons? Granted that constitution-making was part of the existing cultural and political ethos and that admiration for the British system was already widespread among American students of government, why should the task of revising the constitution and political structure of these groups always fall to Wilson? Why were none of these constitutions revised along desirable lines by others, before Wilson joined these clubs? It would seem that among his contemporaries it was Wilson who found constitution-making a particularly attractive occupation. The readiness with which he accepted for himself a role that was, to be sure, culturally sanctioned makes the inference plausible that personal motives were strongly engaged by the possibility that constitution writing afforded of ordering the relations of his fellow-beings.[35]

Secondly, what evidence can be found of an unconscious motive or need to impose orderly systems upon others? If such a motive exists, we may expect appropriate pleasurable feelings to ensue from its gratification. However, we cannot reasonably expect that the pleasure experienced by the individual in such instances will be fully articulated under ordinary circumstances. Hence, in the type of historical materials on the subject's inner life usually available to the biographer we can expect only episodic and fragmentary evidence of the fact that an activity on his part has satisfied deeply felt personality needs. This is in fact what we find in this case. For example, after rewriting the constitution of the Johns Hopkins debating society and transforming it into a "House of Commons," Wilson reported to his fiancee the great pleasure he had derived from the project: "It is characteristic of my whole self that I take so much pleasure in these proceedings of this society. . . . I have a sense of power in dealing with men collectively that I do not feel always in dealing with them singly." [36]

That constitution-writing had a deep personal meaning for Wilson is further suggested by the fact that such activities were always instrumental to his desire to exercise strong leadership. It is rather obvious even from historical accounts that rewriting constitutions was for Wilson a means of restructuring those institutional environments in which *he* wanted to exercise strong leadership. He wished to restructure the political arena in these instances in order to enhance the possibility of influencing and controlling others by means of oratory. This was a skill in which he was already adept as an adolescent and to the perfection of which he assiduously labored for years. In the model House of Commons which Wilson created, and in which as the outstanding debater he usually became "Prime Minister," independent leadership was possible and, as Wilson had foreseen, the skillful, inspirational orator could make his will prevail.[37]

From an early age, then, Wilson's scholarly interest in the workings of American political institutions was an adjunct of his ambition to become a great statesman. He wished to exercise power with great initiative and freedom from crippling controls or interference. The relationship between Wilson's theories of leadership and his own ambitions and changing life situation, which we cannot recapitulate here, is revealing in this respect.[38] Suffice it to say that when Wilson's career development is studied from this standpoint considerable light is thrown on the intriguing question of the role of personal motivations in political inventiveness and creativity. Political psychologists have hypothesized that a compulsive interest in order and power is often to be found in strong political leaders who were great institution-builders and who made it their task to transform society. The case study of Wilson lends support to this general hypothesis.

To posit such personal, unconscious components in the political motivation of some leaders by no means excludes the simultaneous operation of cultural determinants There is no doubt in Wilson's case that his personal interest in order and power was defined and channelized by the cultural and political matrix of the times. Moreover, concrete opportunities to rewrite constitutions and to exercise and perfect his talents as orator-leader were provided by existing situations in which he found himself or that he actively sought out.

Thus, the external situation in which the individual exists necessarily defines and delimits the field in which personality develops and in which personality needs and traits find expression. On the other hand, the interaction between the personality of a political leader and the milieu in which he operates may be, in an important sense, a reciprocal one. A leader's basic needs and values, his motives and dispositions, shape his perception of the situations that confront him and influence his definition and evaluation of the choices of action open to him.[39]

What is gained by attributing motivations of this character to a political leader? In this case, what difference does it make whether Wilson's interest in writing constitutions had the type of personal motivation in question? The postulate of a deep-seated, unconscious interest in imposing orderly systems upon others as a means of achieving a sense of power, we believe, accounts in part (but only in part) for Wilson's peculiar involvement in the League Covenant and in the making of the peace, the many strands of which we have attempted to document in our book. The biographer who is sensitive to the possible role of unconscious motivation is struck, for example, by the fact that it was Wilson's constant concern to reserve to himself final authorship of the Covenant, even though none of the ideas that entered into it were original with him, and that he appeared to derive peculiar pleasure from giving his own stamp to the phraseology of the document.[40]

Similarly, the postulate that Wilson derived from constitution-writing gratification of unconscious personal needs for power and domination may account in part (again only in part) for the tenacity with which he resisted efforts by various Senators to rewrite parts of the Covenant, which in some cases amounted merely to an alteration of its wording. Wilson appears to have subconsciously experienced all such efforts as attempts to "interfere" with or "dominate" him in a sphere of competence that he regarded as his own preserve.

Such an interpretation, taken alone, will seem highly speculative. The reader, we hope, will find it more plausible in the context of the theory of Wilson's personality that we have worked out and utilized in detail for purposes of analyzing Wilson's entire development and career. Briefly paraphrased here, the theory is that political leadership was a sphere of competence Wilson carved out for himself (from early adolescence on!) in order to derive therefrom compensation for the damaged self-esteem branded into his spirit as a child. Particularly when performing in his favored role as interpreter and instrument of the moral aspirations of the people, he considered himself as uniquely endowed and virtually infallible.

His personality needs were such that in the sphere of competence, which he regarded as peculiarly his own, he had to function "independently" and without "interference" in order to gain the compensatory gratification he sought from the political arena. These we believe to have been the underlying dynamics of his somewhat autocratic style of leadership to which many contemporaries and biographers have called attention.[41]

THE RELATIONSHIP BETWEEN WILSON'S MORALITY AND HIS STUBBORNNESS

The extraordinary role of "conscience" and "stubbornness" in Wilson's political behavior has been noted by numerous of his contemporaries and biographers. It has often been said that Wilson's refusal to compromise on certain notable occasions, particularly as President of Princeton and as President of the United States, was a reflection of his "Presbyterian conscience." When great principles were at stake, as on these occasions, he could not bring himself to compromise. In such situations Wilson characteristically portrayed himself as confronted by a choice between dishonorable compromise of principles and an uncompromising struggle for moral political goals. Accordingly, for him, there could be no alternative but to fight for truth and morality against all opposition, whatever the consequences.

No matter that others (including careful historians such as Arthur S. Link)[42] find his characterization of the situation in these terms unconvincing; that in fact Wilson was not really confronted by such an unpleasant either-or choice. The fact remains that *Wilson* saw it thus. However much one may deplore the political consequences of his refusal to compromise, so the argument goes, surely the only valid conclusion that can be drawn is that Wilson was possessed by an unusually strong sense of morality and rectitude that exercised a determining influence upon his political behavior.

It has seemed plausible, therefore, to attribute great importance to the Presbyterian culture in which Wilson was reared and from which, to condense this familiar thesis, he derived his unusual conscience and sense of morality.

Such a thesis must cope with various questions that can be legitimately raised. For example: If Wilson's refusal to compromise in certain instances is simply a matter of his Presbyterian conscience, then what of the numerous instances in which that same conscience was no bar to highly expedient, if not opportunistic political behavior on his part? [43] Clearly, at the very least a more refined theory as to the nature of the Presbyterian conscience and of its influence on political behavior is needed.

This general question is merely posed here. Instead of pursuing it further on this occasion let us consider, rather, the usefulness of looking at the relationship between Wilson's morality and his political stubbornness in terms of what is known about the dynamics of the compulsive type. To examine the problem of Wilson in these terms is not to deny the importance of his Presbyterian upbringing or related cultural factors. Nor does it thereby ignore the possibility, which need not be explored here, that compulsive personalities are or were frequently to be found among members of the Presbyterian subculture. Indeed, the Presbyterian ethos no doubt provided reinforcement and rationalization for Wilson's stubbornness. We have elsewhere observed that such a creed produces men of conviction who find it possible to cling to their principles no matter what the opposition. The feeling that they are responsible, through their conscience, only to God, gives them a sense of freedom from temporal authority and the opinions of their fellow men.[44]

The problem of Wilson's convictions that he was "right" in refusing to compromise, and was acting in conformity with moral standards, however, is more complex than it appears at first glance, as we will try to show.

The analysis of "stubborn" behavior in compulsive personalities indicates that it is often a form of aggression. Thus aggressive tendencies, usually repressed, find expression in situations that actually comprise, or can be represented by the individual to himself as comprising, struggles on behalf of goals that receive strong endorsement by the conscience. The operative mechanism is referred to as "idealization" and has been described in the following terms: "The realization that an ideal requirement is going to be fulfilled brings to the ego an increase in self-esteem. This may delude it into ignoring the fact that through the idealized actions There is an expression of instincts that ordinarily would have been repressed. . . . the ego relaxes its ordinary testing of reality and of impulses so that instinctual [in this case, aggressive] impulses may emerge relatively uncensored."[45] One is reminded in this connection of Wilson's repeated expressions of his "pleasure" and "delight" at an opportunity for a good fight, on behalf of a good cause, and his highly aggressive outbursts against opponents who blocked his high moral purposes. The instinctual nature of these eruptions is suggested by their extreme and intemperate quality; they were often personally unbecoming as well as politically inexpedient, and on occasion left Wilson shortly thereafter much chagrined at his loss of self-control.

Whatever the satisfactions of an uncompromising fight for what is "right," it may lead the compulsive person into essentially immoral behavior, behavior which strongly conflicts with role requirements and expectations. Given a culture in which political power is shared and in which the rules of the game enjoin compromise among those who participate in making political decisions for the community, to insist stubbornly that others submit to your own conception of what is truth and morality may in fact contravene political morality. The "right" thing for Wilson to do in the critical phases of his struggles at Princeton and with the Senate in the League matter, in terms of the prevailing political mores, was to have worked together with others who legitimately held power in order to advance as far as possible towards desirable political goals.

Wilson was well aware of this requirement. As a historian and astute student of American political institutions, he knew very well that the "right" thing for a statesman to do is to be practical and accomplish what he can. And he had expressed himself often on this very problem. In an address before the McCormick Theological Seminary, in the fall of 1909, for example, he had said: "I have often preached in my political utterances the doctrine of expediency, and I am an unabashed disciple of that doctrine. What I mean to say is, you cannot carry the world forward as fast as a few select individuals think. The individuals who have the vigor to lead must content themselves with a slackened pace and go only so fast as they can be followed. They must not be impractical. They must not be impossible. They must not insist upon getting at once what they know they cannot get."[46]

However, at several critical junctures in his public career, when he found his righteous purposes blocked by opponents who would not bend to his will, Wilson did not do the "right" thing; he did not compromise or accommodate, even when friends and political associates enjoined him to do so. Rather, he stubbornly persisted in his course and helped bring about his own personal defeat and the defeat of worthwhile measures which he was championing.

It seems, then, that we are confronted here by a form of self-defeating behavior in which the role of "conscience" in political stubbornness is perhaps much more complex than is implied in the familiar thesis of Wilson's "Presbyterian conscience" and his stiff-necked "morality."

But why must stubborn refusal to compromise be pushed to the point of self-defeat and the frustration of desirable legislation if not for Wilson's stated reason that he would have found it immoral to compromise great principles? Once again the literature on compulsiveness provides an alternative set of hypotheses with which to assess the available historical data. It is our thesis, which we have tried to document elsewhere,[47] that Wilson's stubborn refusals to compromise in situations where true morality and the requirements of his role demanded accommodation created feelings of guilt within him. He was vaguely disturbed by what he subconsciously sensed to be his own personal involvement in the fights with his opponents. The greater the stubbornness (a form of aggression against his opponents), the greater the inner anxiety at violating the moral injunction to compromise, which was a very real requirement of his political conscience.

This predicament was worked out in the following manner: stubborn refusal to compromise was maintained to the point where Wilson could demonstrate his "moral superiority" over his opponents. This could be achieved by manipulating the situation so that his opponents were also involved in "immoral" behavior, for example, by permitting their dislike of Wilson to warp their political good sense, by conspiring to defeat Wilson despite the merits of the issue at stake, by refusing to support desirable proposals just because he was championing them, etc. Thus, stubbornness was maintained so that, should it not succeed in forcing the capitulation of his opponents, it would provoke his defeat by selfish and immoral opponents. Thereby, he could at least assuage his anxiety and guilt for, whatever his "crime," it was outweighed by the demonstration in defeat of his "moral superiority" over his opponents.

These, we believe, were the underlying dynamics of the search for martyrdom which other writers[48] as well have seen in Wilson's ill-fated Western speaking tour on behalf of the League of Nations. Whether the available historical materials which we have cited in support of this thesis render it sufficiently plausible and convincing must be left to individual judgment. Instead of rephrasing the evidence and reasoning already presented on its behalf in our book, we shall confine ourselves here to noting that the mechanisms described above, as underlying the possible quest for martyrdom, are very well described in the literature on compulsive stubbornness.

". . . What is usually called stubbornness in the behavior of adult persons is an attempt to use other persons as instruments in the struggle with the super-ego. By provoking people to be unjust, they strive for a feeling of moral superiority which is needed to increase their self-esteem as a counter-balance against the pressure of the super-ego." [49]

". . . The stubborn behavior is maintained the more obstinately, the more an inner feeling exists that it is impossible to prove what needs to be proven, and that one is actually in the wrong. . . . The feeling, 'Whatever I do is still less wicked than what has been done to me,' is needed as a weapon against the super-ego and, if successful, may bring relief from feelings of guilt." [50]

In brief, therefore, the very "morality" in terms of which Wilson could initially legitimize the open expression of pent-up aggression and hostility ensnared him in profoundly immoral political behavior. His repeated protestations as the struggle with his opponents wore on that he had to do what was "right" and what conscience demanded were, in fact, a cloak for activity that was contrary to the requirements of his leadership role and some of the demands of his own conscience. The repeated protestations that he was acting merely as an instrument of the people's will and had no personal stakes in the battle were the external manifestation of desperate efforts to still inner doubts of the purity of his motivation in refusing compromise and to controvert the knowledge that gnawed from within that he was obstructing his own cause.[51] We have here an instance not of stern morality but of a type of rationalization which has been labelled the "moralization" mechanism, i.e., a tendency to interpret things as if they were in accord with ethical standards when they are actually (and subconsciously known to be) in striking contrast to them.[52]

Thus did Wilson go down to tragic defeat. A subtle personal involvement in political struggle prevented him from anchoring his actions in the profound wisdom of the maxim: "There comes a time in the life of every man when he must give up his principles and do what he thinks is right." [53]

THE SELF-DEFEATING PATTERN IN WILSON'S CAREER

The thesis of a self-defeating dynamism in Wilson's personality gains in plausibility from evidence that it was part of a pattern which tended to repeat itself under similar conditions during his career.[54] A number of Wilson's biographers have noted that Wilson's defeat in the fight for the League fits into a pattern of behavior he had displayed earlier in public life. Thus, after a painstaking analysis of the bitter and unsuccessful struggle Wilson waged with his opponents at Princeton, Professor Link was led to remark that "a political observer, had he studied carefully Wilson's career as president of Princeton University, might have forecast accurately the shape of things to come during the period when Wilson was president of the United States." Calling the former period a microcosm of the latter, Link ascribed to Wilson's uncompromising battles both in the graduate college controversy and in the League of Nations battle with the Senate "the character and proportions of a Greek tragedy." [55]

Similarly, writing many years before, Edmund Wilson, the distinguished man of letters, saw in the same events of Wilson's career evidence of a curious cyclical pattern that can be detected in the lives of other historical figures as well:

"It is possible to observe in certain lives, where conspicuously superior abilities are united with serious deficiencies, not the progress in a career or vocation that carries the talented man to a solid position or a definite goal, but a curve plotted over and over again and always dropping from some flight of achievement to a steep descent into failure." [56]

The type of enigmatic personality described here by a humanist is one which has been of long-standing interest to the clinician as well. Influenced by Freud's earlier description and analysis of neurotic careers, Franz Alexander in 1930 presented what has become a classical psychoanalytical account of this general character type.[57] In many cases, driven by unconscious motives, persons of this type alternate between committing a transgression and then seeking punishment.

Thereby, their careers may exhibit "alternating phases of rise and abrupt collapse," a pattern indicating that "aggressive and self-destructive tendencies" run along together. "The neurotic character," Alexander continues, "has fired the literary imagination since time immemorial. They are nearly all strong individualities who struggle in vain to hold the anti-social tendencies of their nature in check. They are born heroes who are predestined to a tragic fate."

Let us examine more closely the repetitive pattern of behavior that observers working from different standpoints have detected in his career.[58] As President of Princeton, Governor of New Jersey, and President of the United States, Wilson gained impressive early successes only to encounter equally impressive political deadlocks or set-backs later on. He entered each of these offices at a time when reform was the order of the day, and with a substantial fund of goodwill to draw upon. In each case there was an initial period during which the type of strong leadership he exercised in response to his inner needs coincided sufficiently with the type of leadership the external situation required for impressive accomplishment. He drove the faculty and trustees at Princeton to accomplish an unprecedented series of reforms. The New Jersey legislature of 1911 was a triumph of productivity in his hands. Later, he exacted a brilliant performance from the Sixty-Third Congress of the United States.

We are forced to recognize, therefore, that Wilson's personal involvements contributed importantly to the measure of political accomplishment he attained. In each position, however, his compulsive ambition and imperious methods helped in time to generate the type of bitter opposition that blocked further successes and threatened him with serious defeats. Wilson was skillful in the tactics of leadership only so long as it was possible to get exactly what he wanted from the trustees or the legislature. He could be adept and inventive in finding ways of mobilizing potential support. He could be, as in the first year of the Governorship and in the "honeymoon" period of the Presidency, extremely cordial, if firm; gracious, if determined; and generally willing to go through the motions of consulting and granting deference to legislators whose support he needed. It is this phase of his party leadership that excited the admiration of contemporaries, historians, and political scientists alike. It is essential to note, however, that Wilson's skillfulness in these situations always rested somewhat insecurely upon the expectation that he would be able to push through his proposed legislation in essentially unadulterated form. (As Wilson often put it, he was willing to accept alterations of "detail," but not of the "principles" of his legislative proposals.)

Once opposition crystalized in sufficient force to threaten the defeat or marked alteration of his proposed legislation, however, Wilson was faced with a different type of situation. Skillful political behavior—the logic of the situation— now demanded genuine consultation to explore the basis of disagreement and to arrive at mutual concessions, bargains, and formulas that would ensure passage of necessary legislation. In this type of situation Wilson found it difficult to operate on the basis of expediential considerations and at times proved singularly gauche as a politician. Once faced with genuine and effective opposition to a legislative proposal *to which he had committed his leadership aspirations,* Wilson became rigidly stubborn and tried to force through his measure without compromising it.[59] The greater the opposition, the greater his determination not to yield. He must win on his own terms or not at all!

Personally involved in these struggles, Wilson was incapable of realistically assessing the situation and of contriving skillful strategies for dividing the opposition and winning over a sufficient number to his side. Both at Princeton and later in the battle with the Senate over ratification of the treaty, Wilson was incapable of dealing effectively in his own interest with the more moderate of his opponents. In the heat of the battle, he could tolerate no ambiguity and could recognize no legitimate intermediate position. He tended to lump together all of his opponents. In such crises, therefore, his leadership was strongly divisive rather than unifying. He alienated the potential support of moderate elements who strongly sympathized with his general aims but felt some modification of his proposals to be necessary. Instead of modest concessions to win a sufficient number of moderates over, he stubbornly insisted upon his own position and rudely rebuffed their overtures, thus driving them into the arms of his most bitter and extreme opponents.[60] It was his singular ineptness in the art of political accommodation, once the battle was joined, which was at bottom responsible for some of Wilson's major political defeats at Princeton and in the Presidency.

In these situations—when opposition crystalized and threatened to block Wilson's plan—the desire to succeed in achieving a worthwhile goal, in essence if not in exact form, became of less importance than to maintain equilibrium of the personality system. He seems to have experienced opposition to his will in such situations as an unbearable threat to his self-esteem. To compromise in these circumstances was to submit to domination in the very sphere of power and political leadership in which he sought to repair his damaged self-esteem. Opposition to his will, therefore, set into motion disruptive anxieties and brought to the surface long-smouldering aggressive feelings that, as a child, he had not dared to express. The ensuing struggle for his self-esteem led, on the political level, to the type of stuborn, self-defeating behavior and the search for moral superiority over his opponents that we have already described.

NOTES

[1] *The Social Sciences in Historical Study: A Report of the Committee on Historiography,* Social Science Research Council, Bulletin 64, 1954, pp. 153–54. By "field theory of personality" the Committee had in mind one which takes into account the fact that " 'external factor,' not just childhood training, set norms and incentives and influence motivation and codes of conduct." (See also *Ibid.,* p. 61.)

[2] Hans Gerth and C. Wright Mills, *Character and Social Structure* (New York, 1953), chapter xiv, "The Sociology of Leadership." See also fn. 35, pp. 87, 88.

[3] A. L. George and J. L. George, *Woodrow Wilson and Colonel House: A Personality Study* (New York, 1956). (Hereafter referred to as *WW & CH.*)

[4] For a recent review of such studies see John A. Garraty, "The Interrelations of Psychology and Biography," *Psychological Bulletin* 51, No. 6 (1954): 569–82. See also Gordon W. Allport, *The Use of Personal Documents in Psychological Science,* Social Science Research Council Bulletin 49, 1942.

[5] For a brief review of this development see Calvin S. Hall and Gardner Lindzey, *Theories of Personality* (New York, 1957), pp. 64–65, 271–72.

[6] For a useful statement of major trends in social psychology and personality theory see Chapter 2, "Converging Approaches," in Smith, Bruner and White, *Opinions and Personality* (New York, 1956).

For a useful summary and synthesis of the ways in which unconscious needs find expression in political behavior see Robert E. Lane, *Political Life* (Glencoe, Illinois, 1959), chapter 9.

[7] Useful accounts of some of these typologies, and others drawn partly from social-psy-

chological standpoints, are available in Ruth L. Monroe, *Schools of Psychoanalytic Thought* (New York, 1955); Harold D. Lasswell, *Power and Personality* (New York, 1948); Robert E. Lane, "Political Character and Political Analysis," *Psychiatry* 16 (1953): 387–98. On trends in the study of political leadership, see Lester G. Seligman, "The Study of Political Leadership," *American Political Science Review* 44 (December 1950): 904–15.

[8] On this general point, see Gardner Murphy, *Personality: A Biosocial Approach to Origins and Structure* (New York and London, 1947), pp. 749–52.

[9] I am indebted to Dr. David Hamburg, Chairman, Psychiatry Department, Stanford University, for bringing this to my attention.

[10] The need for developmental analysis of personality that starts with some preliminary theory, or set of hypotheses, has been frequently emphasized by those writing on the problems of biography. See for example the following statement by the historian, Thomas C. Cochran: "Faced with the task of constructing an interpretive biography, the investigator trained in psychological methods would formulate hypotheses as he started work on the early life of his subject—hypotheses as to what sort of person the man would prove to be when he later became involved in different types of situations. A systematic testing of these hypotheses against the evidence provided at different stages in the life history would not only provide clues to the understanding of motives but would also focus the biography sharply on the processes of personality development." (In *The Social Sciences in Historical Study: A Report of the Committee on Historiography,* Social Science Research Council, Bulletin 64, 1954, p. 67.)

[11] Much dissatisfaction has been expressed in recent times with the conventional "trait" approach to the study of personality and leadership. See, for example, Cecil A Gibb, "The Principles and Traits of Leadership," *Journal of Abnormal and Social Psychology* 42 (1947): 267–84; Alvin Gouldner, *Studies in Leadership* (New York, 1950).

[12] Among the many useful personality sketches and interpretations of Wilson see particularly those recently provided by Arthur S. Link, *Wilson: The New Freedom* (Princeton, 1956), pp. 61 ff., 93–144; John A. Garraty, "Woodrow Wilson: A Study in Personality," *The South Atlantic Quarterly* 56, No. 2 (April, 1957): 176–85; John Morton Blum, *Woodrow Wilson and the Politics of Morality* (Boston, 1956).

The importance of personality is emphasized particularly in Garraty's account, which runs parallel to our own at many points.

[13] Thus Blum refers only parenthetically to Wilson's "compulsiveness" and his "obsessive sense of unrest" (*op. cit.,* pp. 5, 11, 75). Though he has explored the technical literature on compulsive behavior, Blum did not attempt a methodical exploitation of it in preparing his study of Wilson. (Personal communication to the author.)

The compulsive nature of Wilson's ambition and political style, his inability to pace his demands for reform more expediently, was earlier grasped by the official biographer (Ray Stannard Baker, *Woodrow Wilson: Life and Letters* (New York, 1927), II, pp. 153, 244–45; V, p. 119); by Link (see for example *Wilson: The Road to the White House* (Princeton, 1947), pp. viii–ix, 45, 90); by Edmund Wilson, "Woodrow Wilson at Princeton," *Shores of Light* (New York, 1952), pp. 312–13; and by Edward S. Corwin, in *Woodrow Wilson: Some Princeton Memories,* ed. William Starr Myers, pp. 34–35.

[14] See, for example, Arthur S. Link's perceptive account of Wilson's highly revealing reaction when his opponents at Princeton unexpectedly offered to accept a compromise proposal to which he had earlier committed himself. (*Op. cit.,* pp. 69–71, 75–76; see also *WW & CH,* pp. 42–43.)

[15] Thus, a fuller statement of the personality trends or types that can be detected in Wilson's personality would, in Freudian terms, probably have to include reference to the "oral character" and the "neurotic character" (see pp. 92, 93), as well as to the compulsive type. Similarly, if Karen Horney's typology is employed, Wilson would probably have to be described as an amalgam of her "compliant," "aggressive" and "detached" personality types. See K. Horney, *Our Inner Conflicts* (New York, 1945).

It should be noted that some of the "contradictions" in Wilson's character, often noted be contemporaries and biographers, can be understood in terms of the combination of trends, or types, of which his personality was composed.

[16] See *WW & CH,* pp. 115–22.

[17] I have omitted from this paper a discussion of the historian's method for explaining the "subjective" side of action (the "logic-of-the-situation" approach), and of the prospects for merging it with that of the clinician's. These prospects are not unfavorable, though the task is admittedly difficult. Both the historian and the clinician (as well as the political scientist!) are interested in intensive causal analysis of the single case and employ for this purpose a variant of the same type of interpretive procedure.

[18] A useful, detailed summary of theories about the dynamics of behavior in compulsives is provided in Otto Fenichel, *The Psychoanalytic Theory of Neurosis* (New York, 1945), pp. 268–310, 487–88, 530–31.

[19] On this point see also *WW & CH,* p. 320.

[20] We must reserve for another occasion an effort to account for Wilson's development of a viable personality organization and the ability to function as successfully as he did.

[21] The fact that there are various specialized terminologies within the field of dynamic psychology and that members of the various schools at times state their differences polemically tends to obscure the wide area of fundamental agreement among them and the fact that an important body of knowledge and insight into human behavior has been gradually developed around a common dynamic point of view. Moreover, dynamic psychology has based itself more recently upon a core of assumptions common to a number of approaches to the study of behavior: psychoanalysis, social anthropology, social psychology and learning theory. (See, for example, O. H. Mowrer and C. Kluckhohn, "Dynamic Theory of Personality," In J. McV. Hunt, ed., *Personality and the Behavior Disorders,* I (New York, 1944), pp. 69–135.)

[22] These traits, comprising the so-called "anal" or "anal compulsive" character, are sometimes formulated in different terms as instances of sublimations or reaction formations. Freud's statement of the type appears in his "Character and Anal Erotism," *Collected Works,* II (London, 1950), pp. 45–50. For more recent formulations, see Fenichel, *loc. cit.,* especially pp. 278–84.

An important restatement and interpretation of Freud's libido theory is provided by Erik H. Erikson in his *Childhood and Society* (New York, 1950). See also the attempt to clarify and elaborate operationally the Freudian character types in Henry A. Murray, *Explorations in Personality* (New York, 1938), pp. 361–85.

[23] For this purpose, in addition to the sources cited in the preceding footnote, see for example, William Healy and Augusta F. Bronner, *The Structure and Meaning of Psychoanalysis as Related to Personality and Behavior* (New York, 1930); William C. Menninger, "Characterologic and Symptomatic Expressions Related to the Anal Phase of Psychosexual Development," *Pyschoanalytic Quarterly* 12, 1943: 161–93.

[24] In the initial phase of our research we collected a large amount of evidence of the presence of most of these orderly traits in Wilson. Contemporaries and biographers have been impressed by various orderly traits in Wilson. For example, Wilson was "a stickler for accuracy" (David Lawrence, *The True Story of Woodrow Wilson,* p. 342); he had an extraordinary ability to concentrate and compartmentalize (Baker, *op. cit.,* II, p. 44) and himself often referred to his "single-track" mind (Alfred Maurice Low, *Woodrow Wilson—An Interpretation,* p. 282); he attempted to rigidly separate thinking and emotions and leaned over backwards to prevent private and personal considerations from interfering with public duties (Baker, *op. cit.,* II, p. 2; III, pp. 160–61; Edith Bolling Wilson, *My Memoir,* p. 162; Joseph Tumulty, *Woodrow Wilson As I Know Him,* pp. 473–74); he was pedantic, dogmatic and fastidious as a teacher (C. W. Mosher, Jr., "Woodrow Wilson's Methods in the Classroom," *Current History* 32 (June 1930): 502–03; Baker, *op. cit.,* II, p. 13); he was reliable and scrupulous in keeping his word, no matter what the inconvenience (E. B. Wilson, *op. cit.,* p. 171; Tumulty, *op. cit.,* p. 469); his punctuality was well-known and it was said that one could set one's watch from his comings and goings (Eleanor Wilson McAdoo, *The Woodrow Wilsons,* pp. 22, 60, 213; Lawrence, *op. cit.,* p. 126); he was punctilious, thorough and methodical (Baker, *op. cit.,* I, pp. 86–87, 182; E. W. McAdoo, *op. cit.,* pp. 24, 188; E. B. Wilson, *op. cit.,* pp. 90, 307, 347; A. S. Link, *Wilson: The Road to the White House,* p. 94); he was strikingly neat, orderly and regular in personal working habits (Baker, *op. cit.,* II, p. 46; V, p. 138; E. W. McAdoo, *op. cit.,* p. 20; E. B. Wilson, *op. cit.,* p. 79).

[25] The hypothesis that certain types of (compulsive or neurotic) personalities pursue power as a means of obtaining compensation for low self-esteem can be and has been divorced from the distinctive structural-dynamic framework and terminology of the Freudian school. Various versions of a similar hypothesis are provided by other schools of dynamic psychology. (See fn. 25.)

[26] In his personality profile of Wilson, Arthur S. Link, for example, identifies the following traits: a demand for unquestioning loyalty, egotism and a belief in the infallibility of his own judgment, vanity and a belief in his own superior wisdom and virtue, inability to rely upon others, indulgence in narrow prejudices and vindictiveness, intolerance of advice and resentment of criticism, a tendency to equate political opposition with personal antagonism, susceptibility to flattery. (*Wilson: The New Freedom,* pp. 67–68.) In his *Wilson: The Road to the White House,* the same biographer referred to his subject as possessing an "imperious will and intense conviction," a "headstrong and determined man who was usually able to rationalize his actions in terms of the moral law and to identify his position with the divine will" (p. ix).

In compulsives, too, an overevaluation and high development of the intellect is often found. At the same time, however, intellectualization is curiously combined with archaic features (superstitiousness and magical beliefs). It is noteworthy, therefore, that many writers (e.g., *ibid.,* p. 94) have been struck by the curious streak of superstitiousness in Wilson, a man otherwise noted for his emphasis on the intellect and on being guided by reason.

[27] See, for example, Robert R. Sears, *Survey of Objective Studies of Psychoanalytic Concepts,* Social Science Research Council Bulletin 51, 1943, pp. 67–70.

[28] Karen Horney, *The Neurotic Personality of Our Time* (New York, 1937); *Our Inner Conflicts* (New York, 1945).

[29] H. D. Lasswell, *Power and Personality* (New York, 1948), pp. 44–49.

[30] Some of these materials are presented in volume I (pp. 36 ff.) of Ray Stannard Baker, *Woodrow Wilson: Life and Letters* (New York, 1927). However, other relevant materials on Wilson's childhood, and, especially, on his relationship with his father were not included in the official biography and are to be found in the Baker Papers, Library of Congress. A fuller summary and interpretation of this material than is possible here is given in *WW & CH,* Chapter I.

[31] The significance of this childhood developmental problem has been overlooked in the otherwise authoritative biography by Arthur S. Link. There is no reference to it in Link's account of Wilson's formative years. On the contrary, Link asserts that "Wilson's boyhood was notable, if for nothing else, because of his normal development." (Wilson: *The Road to the White House,* p. 2.) The fact of Wilson's "slowness" is also omitted in the biographies by Garraty and Blum, though it is mentioned (and glossed over) by Baker, *op. cit.,* I, pp. 36–37. The stern, domineering and caustic manner of Wilson's father, a source of acute tension and discomfort for Wilson, is also muted in Baker's published account, though not in the materials which Baker collected for his biography. (See the preceding footnote.)

[32] A belated identification with his father appears to have accompanied Wilson's adoption of the compulsive dynamism at this time. The identification with the father was extremely strong on the manifest level and was rigidly maintained throughout Wilson's lifetime. At the same time, however, feelings of inferiority vis-à-vis the father, who had been the chief instrument of Wilson's damaged self-esteem, persisted throughout Wilson's life. For this and other reasons, accordingly, we have felt it necessary to postulate that the father-son conflict persisted in Wilson at an unconscious level. (Readers familiar with the technical literature will be reminded of the Freudian theory of the Oedipal basis of the inferiority complex.)

We have also postulated that aspects of Wilson's behavior in the struggles with Dean West and Senator Lodge constituted a displacement, or "acting out," of the unconscious hostility that he had experienced towards his father as a child but had not dared to express. (For a fuller statement of the thesis concerning the father-son relationship, see *WW & CH,* Chapter I, also pp. 46, 114–15, 270–73.) On the conditions under which Wilson's latent aggressive impulses could find overt expression against political opponents, see the discussion of "idealization," p. 90.

[33] Baker, *op. cit.,* I.

[34] Baker, *op. cit.,* I, pp. 45, 75–76, 94, 123–24, 148, 198–200, 302–03.

[35] In more general terms we are asserting the possibility that personality needs and motives of an unconscious character may govern an individual's selection of social and political roles and that these needs and motives may infuse themselves into the individual's performance of those roles. The fact that a person's behavior *can* be interpreted in terms of role theory, therefore, does not relieve the investigator from considering the possibility that aspects of basic personality are also expressing themselves in such behavior. It is incorrect, therefore, to define the problem as some proponents of role theory tend to do in terms of "role *vs.* personality." Rather, the interplay of role and personality needs to be considered.

[36] Baker, *op. cit.,* I, p. 199; *WW & CH,* p. 22.

[37] *Ibid.*

[38] See *WW & CH,* pp. 144–48, 321–22.

[39] *WW & CH,* p. xvii.

[40] See *WW & CH,* pp. 208–10, 223, 226–28.

[41] This theory is a special application of a general hypothesis concerning the pursuit of power as a means of compensation for low self-estimates, which Harold D. Lasswell has extracted from the findings and theories of various schools of dynamic psychology. (See his *Power and Personality,* p. 39 ff.) The hypothesis is evidently of wide, though not universal application in the study of political leaders.

We have discussed some of the problems of applying this general hypothesis to someone like Wilson, who pursued other values as well as power, in *WW & CH,* pp. 319–22, and in the paper, "Woodrow Wilson: Personality and Political Behavior," presented before a panel of the American Political Science Association, Washington, D.C., September, 1956.

As already noted, the pervasiveness of power strivings as compensation for organic or imagined defects was given early emphasis by Alfred Adler. The fruitfulness of Adler's theories for subsequent social psychological approaches to personality is now widely recognized. See, for example, Gardner Murphy, *op. cit.,* Chapter 24, "Compensation for Inferiority."

[42] *Wilson: The Road to the White House,* p. 76.

[43] See particularly Arthur S. Link, *Wilson: The Road to the White House,* and *WW & CH,* Chapters III and IV.

[44] *WW & CH*, pp. 4–5.

[45] Otto Fenichel, *Psychoanalytic Theory of Neurosis*, pp. 485–86.

[46] Baker, *op. cit.*, II, p. 307.

[47] *WW & CH*, pp. 290–98.

[48] See, for example, Richard Hofstadter, *The American Political Tradition*, 2nd ed. (New York, 1954), pp. 281–82; Thomas A. Bailey, *Woodrow Wilson and the Great Betrayal* (New York, 1945).

[49] Fenichel, *op. cit.*, p. 279.

[50] *Ibid.*, p. 497. See also Christine Olden, "The Psychology of Obstinacy," *Psychoanalytic Quarterly* 12 (1943): 240–55.

[51] *WW & CH*, pp. 297–98.

[52] See, for example, Fenichel, *op. cit.*, p. 486.

[53] It might be added that we have encountered no evidence that Wilson subsequently ever expressed or experienced any self-doubts as to the wisdom or correctness of his refusal to compromise in the struggle to ratify the peace treaty. On the contrary, his defeat and physical breakdown seem to have provided relief from the feelings of uneasiness experienced at the time.

[54] It should be emphasized that whether, to what extent, and how often the self-defeating dynamism referred to here finds expression depends upon the character of the situations encountered by the subject during his lifetime. Similarly, we have postulated that this destructive tendency was held in check to some extent by the development in Wilson's personality system of a constructive strategy whereby he generally committed his need for domination and achievement only to political projects which were about ready for realization. (On this point, not discussed further in this paper, see *WW & CH*, pp. 118, 320–22.)

[55] Arthur S. Link, *Wilson: The Road to the White House*, pp. 90–91. A similar observation is made by Blum, *op. cit.*, p. 36.

[56] Edmund Wilson, "Woodrow Wilson at Princeton," reprinted in his *Shores of Light* (New York, 1952), p. 322.

[57] "The Neurotic Character," *International Journal of Psychoanalysis* 11 (1930): 292–311. In contrast to true neurotics who squander their energy in futile inactivity, Alexander noted, persons of this character type live active and eventful lives; they "act out" repressed unconscious motives that are unacceptable to their ego. The neurotic element in such persons appears, that is, not so much in the form of circumscribed symptoms but permeates the personality and influences their entire behavior.

[58] The following paragraphs are a brief paraphrase of materials presented in *WW & CH*, pp. 116–21, 320–22, and in a paper at the meetings of the American Political Science Association, Washington, D.C., September, 1956.

[59] The italicized phrase is an important qualification to the general proposition. In the case of legislative proposals which were not "his" or to which he had not committed his aspirations for high achievement, for example the military "preparedness" legislation of 1915–16, Wilson was more flexible when confronted by effective Congressional opposition. (*WW & CH*, pp. 116, 121.)

[60] *WW & CH*, pp. 38, 45; chapter XIV, especially 286–89.

6

Medical Diagnosis and Political Explanation

The fascinating account that follows is a medical analysis of Woodrow Wilson's symptomatology and behavior following the stroke that incapacitated him in the midst of his unsuccessful campaign for Senate ratification of the Versailles Treaty. Dr. Weinstein, in the course of arguing that Wilson appeared to have exhibited the clinical syndrome of "anosognosia" (the incapacity to recognize aspects of one's disease) as well as other symptoms of brain damage, contends that it is inappropriate to diagnose behavior such as Wilson's in terms that assume the behavior must have *either* an organic *or* a psychological etiology. The exceedingly close connections that can exist between "physical" and "mental" states are well illustrated in Weinstein's case study, which also provides an instructive complement (but not contradiction) to Alexander George's summary of his and Juliette George's work on Wilson in Selection 5.

Conceptually inclined readers will find it instructive to return to M. Brewster Smith's mapping discussion (Selection 2) and ask themselves where physiological variables of the sort that Weinstein discusses ought to be located. The editors' assumption is that in Smith's graphic summary of his formulation (Figure 4, page 42) the appropriate location for organic processes would be at the far left of Panel III, which summarizes types of variables relating to personality processes and dispositions: the various physical capacities and propensities of the individual serve as partial underpinnings of the underlying personality processes Smith summarizes under the heading "functional bases of attitudes." Physiological, like sociological, variables are sometimes seen as contending with psychological variables as explanations of behavior. It is, however, more promising to think of these three types of variables as complementary, by conceiving of them in terms of sequential relationships—*social background* works on *physiological raw materials* to engender *psychological orientations* that mediate the specific *situational stimuli* that lead to political behavior.[1]

NOTES

[1] On the fallacy of seeing "sociological" explanations as competitive with "psychological" explanations, see the brief discussion in Fred I. Greenstein, *Personality and Politics: Problems of Evidence, Inference, and Conceptualization* (Chicago: Markham, 1969), pp. 36–40.

DENIAL OF PRESIDENTIAL DISABILITY:
A CASE STUDY OF WOODROW WILSON

Edwin A. Weinstein

On September 26, 1919, Woodrow Wilson, 28th President of the United States, sustained a cerebral vascular accident, which resulted in an enduring, severe left hemiparesis and changes in behavior. For reasons connected with the unique public office of the patient, he was not hospitalized, case records were not kept, no workup was done to define further the brain lesion, and no tests were performed to evaluate mental function. Because Wilson was the President of the United States, however, there is a vast amount of recorded data which are relevant to such issues as the relationship between "organic" and "psychological" factors in behavior associated with brain damage, the role of premorbid personality, and the way the behavior is shaped by the social milieu. A review of the published material is also germane to the understanding of the way "private" disturbances of behavior may be manifested in the world of public affairs. This paper is an attempt to correlate these aspects in an interpretation of the President's behavior in terms of the changes in symbolic organization which occur after damage to the nondominant cerebral hemisphere, with particular reference to the syndromes of anosognosia, or denial of illness.[1] A chronology of Wilson's life is provided in the Appendix.

THE CLINICAL HISTORY

The stroke occurred while the President was on a speechmaking tour through the Western states to win popular support for the Treaty of Versailles. The trip was undertaken against the advice of his physician, Rear-Admiral Cary Grayson. The President had had a severe attack of influenza in the spring from which a number of observers felt he had not completely recovered, and he had been under a great deal of emotional strain over the summer in connection with his fight for the League of Nations. The President had suffered from headaches and these became progressively worse throughout twenty-two days in which he gave forty major addresses plus rear platform speeches, and participated in parades and other ceremonies. He also experienced double vision and in his speeches stumbled over words, both symptoms being attributed to headaches and fatigue. During the journey the President also had episodes of "asthmatic" coughing, which occurred at night and forced him to sleep in a sitting position.

At 4:00 A.M. on the morning of September 26, the President's secretary, Joseph Tumulty, found him dressed and sitting in a chair. He had difficulty in

Reprinted by special permission of the William Alanson White Psychiatric Foundation, from *Psychiatry,* 30, No. 4 (November, 1967), 376–391. Dr. Weinstein, who, at the time of publication of this article, was a Research Associate, Washington School of Psychiatry, Attending Neurologist, Mount Sinai Hospital, New York, and Consulting Neurologist, National Naval Medical Center, Bethesda, Md., noted in connection with the original publication of this article the financial support of the U.S. Army Medical Research and Development Command, Office of the Surgeon General and the criticism and help of Professor Arthur S. Link, Editor of the Papers of Woodrow Wilson.

articulating and one side of his face was fallen. With tears the President said, "My dear boy, this has never happened to me before. I felt it coming on yesterday. I do not know what to do." He then pleaded with Tumulty not to cut the trip short as the President's friends and Senator Lodge would say he was a quitter, and the Treaty would be lost. When the President moved closer to continue the discussion, Tumulty noted that his entire left side was paralyzed. He then said, "I want to show them I can still fight and that I am not afraid. Just postpone the trip for twenty-four hours and I will be all right." [2]

By the time the party reached Washington, two days later, some power had returned and Wilson was able to walk from the train. On the morning of October 2, however, the President's wife found him unable to use his left arm, and he complained of numbness in it. When she returned from calling Dr. Grayson, she found her husband unconscious on the floor. According to Mrs. Wilson, he recovered consciousness within a few minutes. His illness was complicated by a urinary obstruction which became acute on October 17, with a threat of uremia, but which relieved itself spontaneously. On November 17 he sat up in a wheel chair for the first time. By December he could walk a short distance, but his leg remained markedly paretic and there is no evidence that he ever recovered any power in his left arm. He had great difficulty in sitting upright and a specially braced wheel chair was provided. There was also marked left facial and jaw weakness. Disturbed vision was present. The President had had reduced visual acuity in his left eye since a sudden episode of loss of vision in 1906, and a left homonymous hemianopia may have been superimposed as a consequence of the stroke. At his first Cabinet meeting after the stroke, in April, 1920, the officers, all known to Wilson for years, were announced by name individually as they entered, causing Josephus Daniels, Secretary of the Navy, to wonder if the President were blind.[3] Another suggestion of impaired vision came in May, when, in conversation with a visiting Minister, the President commented on having "smiled across the table" at a colleague of the Minister's in Paris, whereas Wilson had actually spoken to the man himself.[4]

The President was not aphasic but his voice was reported as weak and strained, and, after he had been speaking for some time, his speech would become indistinct. During November, 1919, he received a few visitors. By January, 1920, he had become more active, but did not go to the Executive Office and carried out his duties in a very limited way. Messages were screened by Mrs. Wilson or Dr. Grayson, and the President was seen for only brief periods by such colleagues as Tumulty, Cabinet members, and Democratic leaders. Usually, Mrs. Wilson received them in her sitting room and repeated to them what the President had told her should be done about a particular problem. Memoranda were answered by a short note in Mrs. Wilson's handwriting, quoting the President, or were not acknowledged. Cabinet members did what they could on their own and otherwise waited for the President to make appointments and reach decisions. On the single occasion when Vice President Marshall visited the White House, he was seen for a few minutes by the First Lady, who told him that she would send for him if there was anything she could think for him to do. The speech read to Congress on December 2, 1919, was composed by the President's stenographer on the basis of reports submitted by Cabinet members. In January, 1920, he sent a proposal for a speech for Secretary of the Treasury Houston's opinion. The statement contained so many factual errors as to make Houston doubt that the President had been the author.

Some observers noted that the President was clear and alert, and that at times he could be bright and witty. One such occasion was a visit early in December from Senator Fall, one of his bitterest Republican opponents, and Senator Hitchcock, the Democratic leader. The call was ostensibly to discuss the Mexican situation but actually the men had been sent by the Foreign Relations Committee to report on the clarity of the President's mind. When Fall unctuously told Wilson, "Well, Mr. President, we have all been praying for you." Wilson responded promptly with "Which way, Senator?"[5] In contrast to his highly controlled premorbid self, the President showed a good deal of emotional instability. Unfavorable news, sad stories, or even apparently innocuous events might provoke tears or temper. Mrs. Wilson has written that she rarely left the President for more than an hour as he would become nervous when alone. She or Dr. Grayson would be present during any interview, ready to intervene should the President become upset or fatigued.

Secretary Houson has left a report of the first Cabinet meeting after the stroke, held in April, 1920. Houston, a Cabinet member through both administrations, comments on his surprise at hearing his name and those of the other Cabinet officers announced as they entered. The President was bright and cheerful and began the session by cracking a joke about the Chicago aldermen who got their heads together to form a solid surface, but after that there was a silence as Wilson did not take the initiative. The critical railroad situation was brought up and the President seemed to have difficulty at first in fixing his mind on the discussion. Dr. Grayson looked in the door several times as if to warn the men not to weary the President, and at the end of an hour Mrs. Wilson suggested that the men leave.[6]

The President continued to hold Cabinet meetings intermittently throughout the remainder of his term. Statements to the press indicated steady improvement. On February 19, 1920, it was announced that he had recovered sufficiently to go to work in his study every morning at 9:30 A.M.; on April 26 it was announced that he was strong enough to resume full duties; and by the end of the month he had taken automobile rides unaccompanied by his physician. Privately, Dr. Grayson commented that the President, by sheer grit, would pull himself together and keep in good spirits for a week or ten days, during which time he dictated. He would then go into a slump and become depressed and irritable.

DENIAL OF ILLNESS

An outstanding feature of the President's behavior was his denial of his incapacity. According to his wife, when he regained consciousness and was able to talk, he requested that she and Dr. Grayson not reveal the nature of his illness should it prove serious. Two days later, on October 4, he called for his stenographer, but was dissuaded by Mrs. Wilson on the grounds that it was the Sabbath. On October 7 he dictated a diplomatic note and communicated his displeasure that a Cabinet meeting had been held in his absence. Immediately after recovering from his urethral obstruction, he began to work, sending letters and signing bills, including a veto of the Volstead Act on October 27. The President did not deny that he could not move his limbs but referred to himself as "lame," and neither he nor Mrs. Wilson would recognize that his paralysis was due to brain damage. Grayson states that Wilson would not accept the idea that he would never recover and asked repeatedly when he would be able to walk again. Visitors noted that he would cover himself in such a way as to conceal the paretic side.

Despite his disability, the President refused all suggestions that he resign. Moreover, he actively sought a nomination for a third term.[7] He declined to support any other Democratic candidate and criticized Governor Cox, the eventual candidate, as "weak," saying that Cox's nomination would be a joke. He expressly instructed Lansing's successor as Secretary of State, Bainbridge Colby, to place his name before the Convention should a deadlock or other suitable opportunity develop. He angrily threatened to fire his Postmaster General when Burleson asked his support for McAdoo. On hearing the news that Cox had been selected, the President became agitated,[8] despite the fact that Cox was a backer of the League of Nations. Even after his retirement, he still expressed thoughts of running again for the Presidency. According to Wimer, two weeks before his death Wilson was still of the opinion that he could have been elected for a third term.[9]

While such denial is commonly associated with brain damage, the deficit in brain function is not the only factor in the appearance and maintenance of the behavior. The conditions of brain function determine the pattern in which the denial occurs, and, to a great degree, its consistency, duration, and circumstances of appearance. Another important factor is the way the denial is reinforced by the attitudes of other persons. In the President's case, these attitudes were determined by their relationships to the President in personal, professional, and political contexts.

The initial statements of his condition issued to the press described the illness as a collapse due to overwork. The announcement calling off the trip, made on September 27, said that the President was suffering from exhaustion and a nervous breakdown. A dispatch published on September 29 quoted Dr. Grayson as satisfied that the President did not have any organic trouble. The first newspaper reference to the hemiparesis came in an interview on February 10, 1920, with Dr. Hugh Young.[10] Dr. Young said that there had been some impairment of function in the left limbs but that it had improved to the point where only the inclement weather prevented the President from leaving the White House. The physician regarded the President as organically sound, with, all organs functioning in a perfectly healthy manner. Dr. Young further maintained that the vigor and lucidity of his mental processes had not been affected in the slightest degree.

In her memoir, the President's wife reports asking another of the President's physicians, the neuropsychiatrist F. X. Dercum, whether the President should resign.[11] She states that he advised against resignation as this would remove the patient's greatest incentive to get well. He told her that Louis Pasteur had recovered from the same condition and had gone on to do his most brilliant work. Mrs. Wilson saw her task as following doctors' orders and shielding the President from any event that might upset him, and this included barring visits and communications that might pose problems. She was concerned with him as her husband rather than as the President of the United States. Moreover, Mrs. Wilson was afraid of hospitals and operations[12] and had rejected the recommendation of Dr. Young for surgical relief of the urinary obstruction.

The attitudes of Dr. Grayson and the President's secretary, Tumulty, were similarly determined by their personal relationship to the President. Grayson was not only the President's physician but also a close friend and companion, and had been regarded by Wilson and his wife as a member of the family. When, on October

6, the Cabinet met to get information about the President's condition, Grayson refused not only to declare the President disabled but also to tell the Cabinet anything beyond the fact that Wilson was suffering from a "nervous breakdown, indigestion and a depleted condition," adding the warning that any excitement might kill him. Moreover, as a Naval officer, Grayson was technically under the orders of the President as his Commander-in-Chief. Tumulty similarly declared that he could not be a party to ousting a chief who had been so kind, loyal, and wonderful to him, especially when the President was "lying on the small of his back."

Grayson reports a conversation with the President on April 13, 1920, when Wilson asked his opinion on resignation in view of the time it would take for him to recover his health and strength. The doctor replied by assuring the President of how well he was keeping in touch with and conducting the affairs of the Government. He then persuaded Wilson to hold his first Cabinet meeting, which took place on the following day.[13] Yet Carter Glass, a close friend of Wilson's and his first Secretary of the Treasury, reports that Tumulty and Grayson repeatedly approached him to talk the President out of seeking a third term.[14]

Politicians perceived the President's incapacity largely in terms of their party affiliations and professional roles. Out of lack of information about what was happening and deference to their leader, the Democrats hesitated to question his capacity and many saw the illness as brought on by the frustrations of dealing with Senator Lodge and the Republican opposition. In his keynote speech to the 1920 Democratic convention, Homer Cummings compared Wilson to the other martyred Presidents, Lincoln, Garfield, and McKinley. In a very real sense, the illness had become a political issue and denial a badge of party loyalty. While Senator Moses said openly that the President had brain damage and was incapable of carrying on his office, most Republicans, out of considerations of taste and political strategy, refrained from comment on the illness. It even entered into the protocol of foreign relationships. When the visiting Minister whom Wilson had failed to recognize was escorted away, he was told that the State Department expected that he would be generous in talking of the President's condition. This yielded a statement to the press that the Minister had ". . . found the President doing well, bright of mind and very gracious!"[15]

PREMORBID PERSONALITY

The content and degree of denial have a correlation with premorbid personality in respect to previous attitudes toward illness and incapacity and to the way in which characteristic modes of organizing and relating in the social environment serve in adaptation to stress.[16]

Wilson had a long medical history dating from the age of 17, when he withdrew from Davidson College after an attack of measles. At Princeton he was well except for recurrent gastrointestinal symptoms. In his second year at law school he became depressed, had indigestion and symptoms attributed to a cold, and left at the end of December, 1880, without his degree. During his unsuccessful law practice in Atlanta there were symptoms ascribed to his liver. Headaches in a sustained way began after he had gone to Johns Hopkins for graduate study.

The first signs of cerebral vascular involvement probably came in 1896, when Wilson, then a professor at Princeton, developed "writer's cramp." For a year he had difficulty using his right hand and, characteristically, he learned to write with his left hand. He recovered but in May, 1906, he suddenly lost the sight of his left eye and was again unable to work with his right hand. The symptoms improved over the summer but he was left with permanently impaired vision, and for some time after his return to Princeton in October, 1906, had discomfort writing with his right hand.[17] While complete medical records are not yet available, the history is strongly suggestive of occlusion of the left internal carotid artery.

Wilson showed many of the features of the so-called anosognosic personality in which the physical manifestations and consequences of illness and incapacity are somehow separated from the real self and given meaning in the context of principles and values. Such patients regard the incapacity of illness as a kind of moral weakness and loss of integrity which, like laziness, must be overcome through force of character. Wilson was apt either to joke about his numerous ailments or to neglect them. Once he had entered upon his career as teacher and statesman, his illnesses never interfered with what he regarded as his mission and duty. His first professional encounter with Dr. Grayson was typical. He was in bed with a digestive disturbance to which he referred as "turmoil in Central America." When Grayson suggested that he remain in bed, the President rejected the advice, as it would keep him from attending church.[18] His response to incapacity was to work harder. During his enforced vacation for his blindness he laid out the ill-fated plan for the reorganization of Princeton. His insistence on carrying on at the Peace Conference in April, 1919, while still in bed with an acute illness, his rejection of Dr. Grayson's advice not to undertake the Western trip, and his persistence in going through with it despite his suffering were entirely in character. While intolerant of physical weakness or limitation in himself, he was solicitous of others. On the last Western trip, he took the time to seek out and console a newspaper reporter who had been injured. None of the reporters on the trip knew that he was ill. When he found it difficult to breathe at night, out of consideration for his physician's comfort he would not call Dr. Grayson but would prop himself up in a chair, unaided.[19] Mrs. Wilson writes that during his long illness she never heard the President complain or express self-pity.

The ascetic attitude toward the physical self and the subordination of the flesh to the spirit were expressed in other areas of living. Wilson was thrifty and abstemious. He would not take more food on his plate than he could consume and faithfully observed the wartime meatless, wheatless, and gasless days. He drank wine and whisky on occasion, but discontinued the traditional White House gift shipment of Scotch whisky from Andrew Carnegie on principle. Wilson was perhaps overmodest about his looks, which were the subject of one of his favorite limericks. He was attentive to his clothes only when courting the second Mrs. Wilson. His belief that principle transcended the physical aspects of a situation was shown in his explanation of an occasion on which he reviewed a regiment, mounted on a horse, dressed in a high hat and cutaway. He told Mrs. Wilson that he did this to establish the precedence of civil authority over the military.

Wilson was punctual, methodical, and precise in both work and recreation. According to "Ike" Hoover, the White House usher, he would dictate a letter once, without later drafts or corrections.[20] Secretary Houston comments that in and out of Cabinet meetings he never detected a word or phrase out of place or heard the President use a bungling sentence. Comparing Wilson with other Presidents under whom he served over a period of forty-two years, Hoover considered Wilson the most efficient by far. Prior to the war, he would complete his daily work in three or four hours. He had a good memory for details and could spot inaccuracies quickly. Houston was especially impressed by his ability to make a pithy summary of complex subjects about which he had had little or no practical experience. Usually, the President made decisions promptly and communications were answered within twenty-four hours. With his Cabinet he did not express doubts or uncertainties and did not discuss or argue. Rather, he would request a memorandum with the "facts," on which he would make a decision, preferring written communications to personal interviews. He was, incidentally, the first President to make much use of the telephone. Houston, who had Wilson's confidence, felt that the President had a one-track mind in that he found it difficult to turn his thoughts and attention from one problem to another. In areas in which he was not absorbed at the time, he was apt to show little interest and would rely on subordinates. Even in his recreation the President was orderly and methodical. He played golf conscientiously and was particularly fond of motoring. Each trip was numbered, with no deviation permitted from a set route.

The President had a reserved, courteous manner and generally avoided shows of emotion. He was on formal terms with almost all of his associates, and Secretary Houston remarks that, prior to Wilson's illness, he never received a gesture of affection from him. His social life was largely limited to his devoted family and old Princeton friends. James Kerney, a journalist who knew Wilson throughout his political career, comments that he was "completely lacking in the gregarious instinct." [21] This is perhaps too broad a statement, but Wilson was distinctly not a hail fellow and was uncomfortable meeting new people outside of his official capacity. This attitude contrasts with the warm sentiments expressed in letters to friends and acquaintances. Although Wilson referred to himself as a man of strong emotions and his letters to his first wife were often very passionate, he was seen by others as controlled and detached. He would not acknowledge feelings of fear, and on an occasion when his Secret Service detail persuaded him to take a back seat in a theater box, he said that he felt guilty hiding behind women's skirts. He believed that his political decisions should not be swayed by sympathy, and strove to avoid any suspicion that he might be motivated by considerations of sentiment, friendship, or family. To this there were a few notable exceptions, such as forcing through the promotion of Dr. Grayson to Rear Admiral and attempting to secure the appointment of an old Princeton friend to the Federal Reserve Board. More frequently he was able to resolve the situation in terms of principle. Tumulty tells the story of how the President was personally approached by the two Missouri senators to appoint as postmaster an intimate friend of one of them. He had received an unfavorable report on the man and refused the request, offering to appoint anyone else. When the issue was finally put in terms of fighting for the character and reputation of the man, the President yielded.

For Wilson, the significance of events depended on the principles involved. These included belief in God, Christian duty and morality, democracy and the people, and what was right. In his idea of "right," he seemed to combine the meanings of correctness, rectitude, and privilege. These themes provided a guide to reality and a plan of action. Once the President felt that he was right and that a policy fitted in with God's design for mankind, he pressed ahead stubbornly. Yet, as Link states, he was not an inflexible dogmatist when it came to the methods and details that implemented the principles.[22] He was a versatile political strategist who, in attaining the Presidency could shift between conservatism and radicalism and could adjust his views to accord with popular sentiment. As he thought the Democratic party offered the only hope for constructive change, he believed that the party's most important task was to stay in power, and a Democratic Congress, under his leadership, put through the most progressive legislation in the country's history up to that time. Although he was an idealist, Wilson was not pushed into decisions by moral fervor but made them on practical grounds. Although he stated that America fought the first World War to uphold the right and make the world safe for democracy, the President was reluctantly pushed into it by the German commitment to an all-out victory, which included unrestricted submarine warfare. No war President has been more efficient.

In his personal relationships, Wilson showed a great need for affection and total approval. In a number of areas he did not bear criticism well; he demanded undivided loyalty and it was difficult for him to reconcile political opposition with personal friendship. He found it hard to accept failure in a cause to which he was committed and could maintain a vindictiveness to erstwhile opponents. Another characteristic pointed out by the Georges in their important psychological study is that when Wilson changed his course on some issue, he was apt to be highly critical of those holding the same ideas that he formerly held, such as pacifism during the first World War.[23] Under stress, as in the Princeton controversy over the location of the graduate school, he was apt to place personal and political quarrels in the context of moral and social issues.

Wilson had great faith in the people, a faith that appears in his theory that only the President represented all the people, in his political and economic philosophy of protecting the people against the political bosses and trusts, and in his statements of foreign policy. He gave as his reason for intervening in Mexico the aim of teaching the Mexican people to choose good rulers. Similarly, the concept provided a justification for entering the World War when Wilson differentiated the German people from their brutal, militaristic masters. His faith in "the people" was also expressed in his favorite political tactic of appealing to the people over the heads of their rulers and elected representatives. Yet, he did not enjoy contact with actual people and sometimes seemed ill at ease when meeting them in other than a pedagogical or Presidential role. However, a career of uninterrupted political success up to 1918 made the concept of "the people" a reality and reinforced his belief that he was close to the people and understood them.

The President's use of language was an important component of his prestige system and relationships. He was, as someone said, born halfway between the Bible and the dictionary. He was fond of telling how his father had taught him to regard bad grammar as a disgrace, and how his own clear, precise speech was the result of Dr. Wilson's insistence that one be able to say exactly what one meant. Another influence was that of his uncle, Dr. James Woodrow, a Presbyterian scholar and linguist. Relatively early in life, Wilson determined to become a statesman and he found in eloquent speech and writing the path to political power. He wrote the greater part of his speeches, and many of his most notable addresses were extemporaneous, given from a brief outline. He was the first President to address Congress in over a century. Wilson was an inspiring speaker who had a way of making everything he said sound important. As a teacher, he had the warm quality of imparting knowledge without seeming to be lecturing the student.[24] He used few gestures but he could sway audiences by putting complex political, social, and economic problems in terms of personal morality, elevating ideals, and homely illustrations. He himself wrote of his passion for interpreting the great thoughts of others to the world, and Kerney comments that once these ideas were dressed up in Wilson's marvelous language their original source was soon forgotten. A one-time associate and later harsh critic, William Bayard Hale, in a content analysis of Wilson's books and speeches, claimed that his fascination with images and other figures of speech was a substitute for rational thought.[25] The President's verbal skills were also demonstrated in his private life. He was a witty conversationalist with a large stock of jokes and anecdotes. With his family he liked to read aloud and delighted in recitations, imitations, and mock declamations.

SYMBOLIC REORGANIZATION AND THE POLITICS OF DENIAL

The major thesis of this paper is that the changes in symbolic organization associated with brain injury were a significant factor in what has been regarded as Wilson's irrational and ineffective political behavior. In this view, his major political mistakes arose in some degree from impairment of brain function and his attempt to deny and compensate for his incapacity. In the following section, a number of political events will be considered from the standpoint of symbolic reorganization.

Unlike the aphasic patient, who has difficulty in expressing himself in symbols, the patient with certain types of damage to the nondominant hemisphere uses language of symbolic complexity. Changes do occur in the relationship of the patient's language to his perception of his environment, so that his designations of places, persons, and events are, in large degree, metaphorical representations of his own experiences and problems, particularly those connected with incapacity and its anticipated consequences. The use of metaphors of place, for example, is shown in the phenomenon of disorientation for place. The patient misnames the hospital, usually designating some place close to his home or connected with his occupation. Or he falsifies or forgets events in selective fashion, and misidentifies objects like a crutch or plastic drinking straw. He may use humor, as in referring to the hospital as a repair shop for old vehicles. Such euphemisms are, in themselves, not pathognomonic of brain damage; moreover, in some contexts the patient may use the proper designation. What is characteristic of altered brain function is the person's consistent use of the same group of erroneous designations despite corrections and available cues, and his lack of differentiation of the social situations in which the language is relevant. While the patient has some knowledge of his disability, he is unaware of the extent to which he is denying or otherwise referring to it in his figures of speech. Rather, the metaphor is taken literally. When the President referred to Governor Cox as the "weakest" candidate, he may have been personifying his own paralysis; he did, in an apparently paradoxical fashion, refer favorably to Cox in some other context, not germane to incapacity.

The choice of the metaphor in which a patient represents his disability is determined by the concepts in which he has habitually classified his environment, related to other people, and established a "social" reality. For some persons, these symbolic themes are those of sex and violence, so that the incapacity may be described in a sexual idiom or attributed to physical violence. For President Wilson, the significant concepts were those of morality, God, duty, democracy, the people, and what was "right." These had formed the bases of his sense of identity and had made up the categories to which new experiences were assimilated and given form and meaning. Under the conditions of altered brain function, the patient continues to use the same organizing principles and the same "problem solving" language. However, the symbols are more highly condensed and the categories contain many more diverse referents. Thus, under the categories of what was moral and immoral and right and wrong, Wilson, after his stroke, included his illness and many facts of political life that he would not have so characterized previously. Under these conditions the meaning of experience depended less on the actual situation in which it occurred and more on the way it fitted into a personal identity system. Whereas previously Wilson had used language to accomplish his aims and shape the behavior of others, now his behavior had come under control of his language.

These changes in language occur not only after structural brain damage but also in transitory fashion with the changes in brain function associated with severe emotional stress. After brain injury, they are more marked and enduring and less susceptible to change and correction. The effects of brain damage always involve environmental stress, and it is impossible to separate the manifestations of the neural deficit per se from those of the adaptation. Accordingly, one cannot designate the point in time when the President's behavior became "organic" rather than "psychological." Moreover, it is extremely difficult to set a norm for political behavior and it is impossible to equate any act of political misjudgment with some mental deficit or maladaptive drive. The variables are much more numerous and complex and, in a retrospective study, one can only make a before and after comparison.

Historians consider that Wilson's first great political mistake in the Presidency was his issuing of an appeal to the people in October, 1918, to show their confidence in his leadership by electing a Democratic Congress.[26] Wilson made the appeal against the advice of colleagues and even contrary to the opinion of his wife, who usually differed with him only on matters of personal likes and dislikes. The war had been conducted on a nonpartisan basis and the message implied that the Republicans were not to be trusted to make the peace. The President's advisers were dismayed not only by the appeal, but also by the language, which Livermore describes as " . . . splenetic in temper and petulant in tone." Even Mrs. Wilson called it undignified. Though the President changed the language, he insisted on issuing the statement. It contained bitter references to the Republicans, such as the charge that " . . . the return of a Republican majority to either house of Congress would . . . certainly be interpreted on the other side of the water as a repudiation of my leadership." Despite the imminence of an Allied victory, the election was lost; according to Link, this was not because of repudiation, but because of the resentment of Western wheat farmers over a price ceiling while Southern cotton was uncontrolled.[27] In the references to the Republicans and to foreign opinion, the President may have been expressing a sense of inadequacy and frustration in dealing with the problems of the peace. Wilson never would admit in public that he had made a mistake but blamed the defeat on the insufficient loyalty to him of Democratic Congressmen. He also claimed, prior to attending the Peace Conference, that the French and British Prime Ministers did not truly represent their people.

Early in April, 1919, at the Peace Conference in Paris, the President was taken acutely ill with high fever, cough, vomiting, diarrhea, and insomnia. After initially suspecting that he had been poisoned, Grayson made a diagnosis of influenza. Throughout several days of acute discomfort, Wilson insisted on trying to work, then is reported as sleeping fitfully for three days. According to "Ike" Hoover,[28] the President showed peculiarities of behavior while he was still in bed, such as issuing an order forbidding members of the delegation to use cars for recreation. This was remarkable because motoring was the President's favorite diversion and previously he had solicitously suggested that the staff take as much recreation as possible. After getting back on his feet, the President expressed the idea that the French servants were spies who spoke perfect English and who overheard everything he said.[29] Wilson also claimed that he was personally responsible for the furniture in the palace and became disturbed because some of it had been moved. Hoover reports that the President and Admiral Grayson personally replaced couches and tables in their proper place.

There is a good deal of question as to the nature of the illness. During the preceding month, the President had developed a tic of the left facial muscles, a not uncommon manifestation of impaired cerebral circulation, and he may have sustained another stroke. He may have had a virus encephalopathy caused by influenza virus, and the production of such severe disturbances in behavior may have been enhanced by the effects of prior brain damage. Or, the fall in cerebral blood flow produced by the persistent paroxysms of coughing may have been the additional factor causing cerebral decompensation. The illness came on during a period of great tension at the Peace Conference and the President's state of physical exhaustion may have increased his susceptibility. His response to any incapacity was to work harder and assume more responsibility and this had the effect of further impairing his effectiveness.

The delusion that all of the French servants were spies, who spoke perfect English and overheard everything that Wilson said, can be interpreted as a condensed metaphorical representation of the events involved in the President's having to compromise with Clemenceau on the Saar and other matters of French security. "Perfect English" had long been a mainstay of Wilson's identity system, and the metaphor now provided an exquisitely meaningful validation and justification of experiences that otherwise would have resulted in profound feelings of guilt and failure. Under conditions of less stress and more normal conditions of brain function, the President might have attributed his failure to not having been eloquent enough, to not having presented his ideas more concisely, and to the many real political obstacles to agreement. One may contrast his behavior in Paris with his calm acceptance of his apparent defeat in the 1916 election when it seemed that Hughes was the winner. On that Election Eve Wilson retired early, with the observation that he had not made himself clearly understood by the voters.

The President's strange action in prohibiting the use of cars by the staff suggests the use of another favorite symbolic theme to resolve a sense of guilt and failure. When his passion for motoring and his previous generosity with his staff are recalled, it seems as if he were punishing himself. Much later, after the stroke, the President, while out motoring, would become upset when his car was passed by another vehicle. He would demand that the offending motorists be arrested and tried for speeding, and wrote to his Attorney General to ask whether as President he could act as a justice of the peace.[30] One wonders at the significance for him at the time of the words "justice" and "peace."

Much of the controversy over the Treaty had to do with changes in the language. Most Democrats saw the alterations in wording that moderate reservations would have required as inconsequential if the Treaty could only be ratified, particularly when it was evident that it would not pass the Senate in its original form. For Wilson, however, the words had a different order of significance because they were such highly condensed symbols of intense personal experience. This preoccupation with language contributed to the unfavorable result of his meeting with the Senate Foreign Relations Committee in August, 1919. The President was asked whether the United States would be obligated to go to war to punish an aggressor should a commercial boycott fail. He replied that while there was no legal obligation, there was a moral one. Wilson agreed that each country would determine for itself what was aggression, but he rejected the suggestion that it be explicitly stated that Congress use its own judgment, insisting that a moral obligation was superior to a legal one and in itself carried the force of truth and righteousness. He maintained that if the United States lived up to its moral obligation, then its judgment would of necessity be right. While a person might escape legal technicalities, he could not escape his own conscience.

It was such language which produced the Republican charge that the President had been evasive, although the Democrats considered his performance eloquent and high-minded. It is likely that Wilson was using the word "moral" in an idiosyncratic, personalized context. He had asked for a declaration of war only after a period of great reluctance and had sought justification for the war on moral grounds. His insistence on the specific language appears to have been his defense against feelings of guilt and inadequacy, especially after the compromises that he had been forced to make in Paris. When he said that moral obligations were superior to legal ones and that one could not escape one's conscience, he may well have meant his own conscience and the feeling that while he was legally justified in declaring war, he had not absolved himself of the moral guilt.

It was at this meeting that the President denied having had knowledge of the Secret Treaties prior to going to Europe. These were the arrangements that the Allies had made among themselves to divide up the territory of the defeated Central Powers, and they proved to be the greatest obstacle in the way of the President's aim of a just peace. Despite his denial, the Treaties were known to him and the provision in the Fourteen Points about open covenants was deliberately designed to offset the effect of the revealing of the Treaties by the Soviets after the Russian Revolution. It is likely that for a long time the President had wished to deny their existence and consequently acted as though they did not exist, but it was only under the conditions of altered brain function that he could deny them in the form of a selective amnesia. This explanation seems more plausible than the charges that the President was lying or had become grossly incompetent. Bailey points out that during the questioning Wilson freely and accurately gave intimate details of subjects that were no less important.

The symptom of diplopia on the Western tour in September, 1919, is evidence of brain involvement. Whether the President's language in his speeches shows any indications of impairment of brain function is difficult to determine. Wilson spoke extemporaneously to large groups of people under very difficult physical conditions and while subjected to political harassment. The speeches are of interest from the standpoint of symbolic representation of his ill-health and sense of failure. He seems to have equated the Treaty with his existence. Just prior to leaving on the trip he told H. H. Kohlsaat, a journalist, that he did not care if he died the minute after the Treaty was ratified.[31] His speeches contained progressively more and more references to death and suffering, talking of the American boys who had died in France for the redemption of the world. The President repeatedly mislocated the site of the assassination that had precipitated the war, putting Sarajevo in Serbia.[32]

In one sense the slip was a trivial one and Wilson may have simply forgotten his geography. Yet the mistake was not corrected and may have been perpetuated by preoccupation with his own death. His visual symptoms may have been expressed in statements such as the one that ". . . our soldiers had no curtain in front of the retinas of their eyes" to keep them from a vision of their cause.[33] He talked of truth gaining revenge ". . . even though its eyes were blinded by blood." [34] The President had difficulty in breathing at night and his cardiorespiratory problems may have been represented in ". . . you hear politics until you wish that both parties might be smothered in their own gas," [35] hardly a tactful reference to his own Democratic supporters. Wilson spoke of not being a quitter and charged that members of the Senate would be ". . . absolute contemptible quitters if they did not see the game through." Needless to say, such statements were not interpreted as self-referential, rhetorical devices but as *ad hominem* attacks.

Why, after his stroke, did the President not resign rather than remain in office for seventeen months, and why did he seek a third term? First, no one made him resign. While the Constitution stated that the Vice President should assume the Presidency if the President was unable to carry out his duties, there was, at the time, no provision as to how this should be done. Vice-President Marshall was not ambitious to succeed. The roles of the President's doctors, Mrs. Wilson, and the Cabinet and Congress in reinforcing the President's denial have been indicated. The question is an even more interesting one when the President's attitude is compared with his previously expressed ideas about resignation. He had long believed that the President should hold office only as long as he had the support of the people. Shortly after his first Inaugural, he considered resignation when it appeared as if Congress might not fulfill his pledge to end preferential treatment of American vessels passing through the Panama Canal, a practice which Wilson felt violated our treaty with Great Britain. In the 1916 Presidential campaign, he planned to resign if Hughes were elected rather than carry on for four months as a lame duck.

In his state of incapacity, however, the status and powers of the Presidency were necessary to avoid a total dissolution of identity. He had long relied on moral and intellectual superiority to feel loved and respected by most people. The denial of the loss was made possible by the altered state of brain function and the retention of the facility with metaphorical speech which had long enabled him to subordinate the physical reality to the organizing principle. Under these conditions it was his political opponents who were seen as immoral, incapable, and irresponsible. The statement by Mrs. Wilson that the President would become upset in her absense suggests that he even may have feared that she would abandon him.

Even with his supporters, the role of the Presidency had to be maintained in a highly doctrinaire fashion. He refused to permit his Secretary of State to send out routine congratulatory messages to foreign rulers. In January of 1920, Senator Hitchcock, who followed Wilson faithfully on the Treaty, wrote a personal note asking Wilson's help in obtaining the leadership of the Democratic caucus. The refusal, in Mrs. Wilson's handwriting, reads:

The President is so profoundly convinced that he ought not to give the slightest ground for the accusation that he has acceeded [*sic*] the proper boundaries of Executive authority and influence that he feels he is bound in conscience not to play any part in the choice to which you refer in your letter. At the same time he wanted me to express his profound gratitude for the leadership you have exorcised [*sic*] in the great matter of the Treaty.[36]

This definition of the Executive role is remarkable because in the past, to a far greater extent than most previous Presidents, Wilson had intervened forcefully in the affairs of the Congress and the Democratic party.

On February 5, 1920, the President wrote Secretary of State Lansing to ask if it were true that he had been calling Cabinet meetings. This was a surprising question as it was well known that they had occurred, and Cabinet meetings had been habitually held in the President's absences. When the President went to Paris, he had specifically requested that they be carried on. In reply to Lansing's letter of explanation, Wilson accused him of usurping Presidential authority and requested his resignation. In a narrow sense, the President was justified, as Lansing had not been sympathetic to him on vital parts of the Treaty, but the timing of the act hurt chances of ratification because it publicized the dissensions among the Democrats. For Wilson to admit that the meetings had been held properly was to acknowledge that he had been incompetent, and the firing of Lansing symbolized his Executive vigor and authority. The President was not only undisturbed by the criticism of his action but, when Tumulty showed him the newspaper accounts, he delightedly swung himself around in his wheel chair, exclaiming, "See how strong I am." [37]

Wilson clung to this view of the Presidential role even in retirement and continued to use it in the service of denial of incapacity. He is reported as refusing to buy a house because the property might be needed by the Government. He would not endorse old colleagues running for political office as such partisan conduct would be unseemly for a President. Wilson and his ex-Secretary of State, Colby, at Wilson's suggestion, opened a law office, but every potential client was turned away because, as a former President, Wilson could not be a party to any action involving the United States Government. After this "sublime position" had turned away thousands of dollars from prospective clients, the firm was dissolved in 1922 at Colby's request.[38]

The President retained his faith in the people, but, in his isolation from them, the "people" were largely the figure of speech through which he infused a feeling of validity into his denial. For example, when Secretary Houston tried to prepare the President for the shock of Harding's election, Wilson assured him that the people could not elect Harding. In January of 1920, the President drafted a remarkable proposal suggesting that his Republican opponents, whom he listed by name, resign and seek reelection on the issue of the League. If a majority were returned, then Wilson, with his Vice President, would resign after appointing as Secretary of State a Republican, who, according to the order of succession, would assume the Presidency. To assume that the Republicans would resign was, of course, unrealistic, and the President was persuaded to pigeonhole his proposal. What the President was also indicating, however, was that he might resign not because he was disabled but because he might not be carrying out the will of the people.

The President's humor, his bitter, paranoid references to people, and many of his sentimental gestures and statements were highly self-referential. He refused to pardon the pacifist Eugene Debs, because he had been a traitor to his country. In Cabinet meetings he is reported as repeating seemingly inappropriate jokes, including sardonic references to the death of the League.[39] When asked about his retirement plans, he made the comment that he would find it hard to "stand Mr. Harding's English." [40] The theme of language persisted in retirement—for example, in his plans to form a "Pure English Society." He also maintained a correspondence with many people on many subjects, and with visitors lightened the conversation with anecdotes, jokes, and limericks. Most of those which have been quoted seem to be metaphorical representations of his difficulties in speech and locomotion, including a story about a Scotsman who let his wife fall out of an airplane to win a wager dependent on his not speaking. He invariably referred to his cane as his "third leg," and recited the following original limerick to his friend Kerney:

> There was a young girl from Missouri,
> Who took her case to the jury,
> She said "Car ninety-three ran over my knee"
> But the jury said "We're from Missouri." [41]

He showed great sympathy for crippled soldiers and on automobile outings would stop to talk with any he might meet. His sight failed badly in the last years of his life and in his last published article, "The Road Away from Revolution," the use of metaphors of vision is striking.[42]

To the Democratic platform committee at the 1920 convention, the President submitted a recommendation urging an American mandate for Armenia in words that are poignantly significant. He stated that ". . . it is our Christian duty to assume guardianship over Armenia . . . to give to her distracted people the opportunities for peaceful happiness which they have vainly longed for through so many dark years of hopeless suffering and hideous distress." Wilson's life was a tragedy in that, under the conditions of his brain injury, the very qualities which had been the sources of his greatness became the agents of his political disaster.

NOTES

[1] In anosognosia, literally lack of knowledge of disease, the patient denies, ignores, or otherwise appears unaware of the existence of such deficits as hemiplegia, blindness, aphasia, the fact of an operation, and many other aspects of illness. He may completely deny or disown them, displace the symptoms to someone else, admit the manifestations but attribute them to some trivial or benign cause, or rationalize or explain them in delusional or confabulatory fashion. In the early stages following acute brain injury, patients are commonly bland, apathetic, or euphoric but, as brain function improves and complete denial cannot be sustained, patients show irritability and emotional instability. The denial serves as a defense against the catastrophic reaction so frequent after brain injuries. Under the necessary conditions of brain dysfunction, the content of the denial depends, in considerable degree, on features of the premorbid personality. In areas that do not concern their disabilities and the consequences of incapacity, anosognosic patients are generally quite rational and casual conversation may show no disturbance. Routine tests of memory and intelligence, similarly, may yield no significant deficit. See: Edwin A. Weinstein and Robert L. Kahn, *Denial of Illness: Symbolic and Physiological Aspects* (Springfield, Ill.: Thomas, 1955); Macdonald Critchley, *The Parietal Lobes* (London, Edward Arnold, 1953).

[2] Joseph Tumulty, *Woodrow Wilson as I Know Him* (Garden City, N. Y.: Doubleday, Page, 1921), pp. 446–48.

[3] Josephus Daniels, *The Wilson Era: Years of War and After, 1917–23* (Chapel Hill: University of North Carolina Press, 1946), p. 545.

[4] From the Long papers, quoted by Gene Smith in *When the Cheering Stopped: The Last Years of Woodrow Wilson* (New York: Morrow, 1964), p. 158. This episode may have been a reduplicative phenomenon. The false belief that an experience almost identical with a current one has occurred in the past is common in anosognosia.

[5] Edith B. Wilson, *My Memoir* (Indianapolis: Bobbs-Merrill, 1938), pp. 298–99.

[6] David F. Houston, *Eight Years with Wilson's Cabinet, 1913–1920,* 2 (Garden City, N.Y.: Doubleday, 1926), pp. 69–70).

[7] Kurt Wimer, "Woodrow Wilson and a Third Term Nomination," *Pennsylvania History* 29, 2, (1962): 193–211.

[8] Edmund W. Starling and Thomas Sugrue, *Starling of the White House* (New York: Simon & Schuster, 1946), p. 157.

[9] See footnote 7.

[10] *Baltimore Sun,* Feb. 10, 1920; p. 1.

[11] See footnote 5.

[12] Alden Hatch, *Edith Bolling Wilson: First Lady Extraordinary* (New York: Dodd Mead, 1961), p. 53.

[13] Cary T. Grayson, *Woodrow Wilson* (New York: Holt, Rinehart and Winston, 1960), p. 112.

[14] Rixey Smith and Norman Beasley, *Carter Glass: A Biography* (New York: Longmans Green, 1939), pp. 205–06.

[15] See footnote 4.

[16] This paper was written before the publication of the psychological study of Wilson by Freud and Bullitt (Sigmund Freud and William C. Bullitt, *Thomas Woodrow Wilson: A Psychological Study* (Boston: Houghton Mifflin, 1967).) Reference to it will be made in another communication.

[17] Ray S. Baker, *Woodrow Wilson, Life and Letters: Youth, Princeton, 1856–1910* (New York: Scribner's, 1927).

[18] See footnote 13, p. 2.

[19] See footnote 13, p. 97.

[20] Irwin H. Hoover, *Forty-two Years in the White House* (Boston: Houghton Mifflin, 1934).

[21] James Kerney, *The Political Education of Woodrow Wilson* (New York: Century, 1926).

[22] Arthur S. Link, *Woodrow Wilson and the Progressive Era, 1910–1917* (New York: Harper, 1954).

[23] Alexander L. George and Juliette L. George, *Woodrow Wilson and Colonel House: A Personality Study* (New York: Dover, 1964), p. 120.

[24] Allen W. Dulles, "A Foreign Affairs Scholar Views the Real Woodrow Wilson," *Look,* December 13, 1966, p. 50.

[25] William Bayard Hale, *The Story of a Style* (New York: B. W. Huebsch, 1920).

[26] Arthur S. Link, *Woodrow Wilson: A Brief Biography* (Cleveland: World, 1963); Seward W. Livermore, *Politics Is Adjourned* (Middletown, Conn.: Wesleyan University Press, 1966).

[27] See footnote 26, p. 139.

[28] See footnote 20, pp. 98–99.

[29] The veracity of this account is disputed by Bailey (Thomas A. Bailey, *Woodrow Wilson: The Great Betrayal* (Chicago: Quadrangle Books, 1963), p. 98), who calls Hoover unreliable. He claims that Hoover knew nothing of the President's pre-Conference ill health. Yet, Wilson would certainly not complain or act ill in front of the White House domestic staff. The theme of language was an important part of the President's symbolic system, and irrational attitudes toward motoring were to recur.

[30] See footnote 8, pp. 157–59.

[31] H. H. Kohlsaat, *From McKinley to Harding* (New York: Scribner's, 1923), p. 220.

[32] Sarajevo was the capital of Bosnia, an old province of the Turkish Empire annexed by Austria-Hungary in 1908 and claimed by Serbia.

[33] Speech in Des Moines, Sept. 6, 1919.

[34] Speech in Helena, Mont., Sept. 11, 1919.

[35] Speech in St. Louis, Sept. 5, 1919.

[36] Gilbert M. Hitchcock, Hitchcock Papers, on file, Library of Congress.

[37] See footnote 4, p. 145.

[38] See footnote 7, p. 38.

[39] See footnote 6, p. 94.

[40] See footnote 6, pp. 147–49.

[41] See footnote 21, p. 481.

[42] *Atlantic Monthly,* August, 1923, pp. 41–42.

APPENDIX

Chronology of Woodrow Wilson's Life

1856	December 28. Born in Staunton, Virginia.
1858	Family moved to Augusta, Georgia.
1870	Family moved to Columbia, South Carolina.
1874	Entered Davidson College.
1875	Returned home.
1875–79	College of New Jersey at Princeton.
1879	Entered University of Virginia Law School.
1880	Withdrew from Law School.
1883	Entered Johns Hopkins University.
1885	Married Ellen Axson. Ph.D. thesis.
1890	Professor of Jurisprudence at Princeton.
1902	President of Princeton University.
1906	Loss of vision in left eye.
1908	Beginning of Graduate School controversy.
1910	Resigned as President of Princeton. Elected Governor of New Jersey.
1912	Elected President of the United States.
1914	August. Death of first Mrs. Wilson.
1915	December. Married Edith Bolling Galt.
1916	Elected to Presidency for second term.
1917	Asked Congress for Declaration of War.
1918	January. Proclamation of Fourteen Points as a basis for World Peace.
1918	October. Appeal for election of a Democratic Congress.
1918	November. Loss of House and Senate to Republicans.
1918	November. Armistice.
1918	December. Sailed for Europe to attend Peace Conference.
1919	January. Opening of Peace Conference.
1919	April. Attack of influenza.
1919	June. Signing of Treaty at Versailles.
1919	August 19. Meeting with Senate Foreign Relations Committee.
1919	September 3. Beginning of Western trip.
1919	September 26. Stroke.
1920	February 13. Asked for resignation of Secretary of State Lansing.
1921	March. Retired to private life after inauguration of President Harding.
1924	February 3. Died.

7

A Symposium on Clinical Method in Historical Inquiry

In this essay on the nature of psychohistorical evidence, Erik Erikson also makes what Robert Coles calls a "pointed summary of his various interests, involvements, and ideas." Erikson begins by noting the need for careful methods in psychohistory, "an area in which nobody as yet is methodologically quite at home, but that some day will be settled and incorporated without a trace of border disputes and double names." The rest of the essay is (in part) an exploration of psychohistorical method, centering around the problems of evidence and evaluation that Erikson encountered in studying Gandhi.

The "Event" Erikson studied in *Gandhi's Truth: On the Origins of Militant Nonviolence* was the Ahmedabad textile mill strike of 1918, in which Gandhi applied his nonviolent technique of *satyagraha*—"a method of recognizing and mobilizing the forces of truth in the oppressor as well as in the oppressed." Gandhi's memoirs concerning the strike provide some of the most important evidence to be interpreted. Yet the "depth" interpretation cannot proceed in a vacuum. Erikson says:

One is almost embarrassed to point out what seems so obvious—namely, that in perusing a man's memoirs for the purpose of reconstructing past moments and reinterpreting pervasive motivational trends, one must first ask oneself at what age and under what general circumstances the memoirs were written, what their intended purpose was, and what form they assumed. Surely all this would have to be known before one could judge the less conscious motivations.

Erikson then provides a diagram pointing to different contexts in which a psychobiographer should consider the memoirs of his subject. One should ask at what stage in the subject's life they were written and how the moment at which they were written fits into the sequence of his life history. One must also ask about the state of his community as he wrote and about how this particular state of the community fits into the broader history of the community. Moreover, it is not only the subject (or as Erikson puts it, the "recorder" of the memoirs) whose acts should be scrutinized in these contexts. The evidence of those who followed, opposed, or witnessed the subject should be examined:

Our diagrammatic boxes, then, suggest the *relativity* governing any historical item— that is, the "concomitant variability" of passing moment and long-range trend, of individual life-cycle and communal development.

In the third and fourth sections of the essay, Erikson interprets Gandhi's account of the textile mill strike. But the interpretation, Erikson emphasizes, must be paired with systematic self-analysis by the psychobiographer. As an aid, he offers another chart showing the contexts in which the functions of "the review"— or the attempt to write psychobiography—should be considered. In the fifth section, Erikson asks whether Freud, in the study of Wilson he coauthored in some part with William Bullitt, lived up to these methodological standards and concludes that Freud did not. This warning of the need for self-analysis leads Erikson into an account of his own involvement with Gandhi and Freud, of the parallels between the two men, and of the significance to him of Gandhi's *satyagraha*.

The sixth section describes an interview with Gandhi's "counter-player" in the Event—the mill owner. Erikson gives a brilliant description of the difference between what one should expect of such an interviewee and what a therapist expects of a psychiatric client. In the seventh section, Erikson criticizes Victor Wolfenstein's interpretation of Gandhi's Salt-*Satyagraha* of 1930. Wolfenstein, a political scientist, had based a rather stereotyped interpretation of this campaign on Ernest Jones's assertion that "one of the two basic symbolic significances of salt is human semen." Wolfenstein concluded that Gandhi's attempt to free India from a British salt tax was a symbolic "reclaiming for the Indian people of manhood and potency." It is interesting to see the roles reversed, with Erikson, the psychoanalyst, arguing that no interpretation should overlook the compelling situational reasons why Gandhi chose the issue of salt.

Elusively and somewhat unclearly, in the eighth section, Erikson sets forth his theory of how uncommon men make history; how a man such as Gandhi seeks "the one way in which he (and he alone!) can reenact the past and create a new future in the right medium at the right moment on a sufficiently large scale." Erikson proposes that there must be a fit, an analogy, between the past a great man symbolically reenacts, the future he foresees, and the symbols that common people of his community can use to resituate themselves in a changing reality.

The "critical evaluations"—by three fellow psychiatrists—are not very critical but they are useful nonetheless. Robert Coles celebrates the importance of the essay, drawing attention to many of its significant features and the hints they provide of Erikson's continuing concerns.

Robert S. Liebert provides a representative example of how socially radical clinicians read Erikson and what implications they draw from his work. One should note here that while the radical critique of conservative interpretations of social phenomena serves a useful corrective function, the radical diagnoses (locating "superego lacunae" in the society rather than in the student activists) are as value-linked and, more important, undefined and unsupported as the conservative diagnoses. Thus, Liebert asserts that student activism is an "adaptive resolution" of the age-specific challenge to psychic integration that the threat of nuclear annihilation presented. This is clearly an interesting possibility, but it is an interpretation that makes no reference to data. If one asks (in Erikson's terms) about the functions of such a view, one cannot help noticing that it serves as an interpretive benediction of activism.

What Liebert's quite correct reading of Erikson brings out is that both Erikson and the conservative psychoanalysts are creating an ideology as they formulate methods for the analysis of history and society. Gandhi's *satyagraha* was a technique of social intervention that closely parallels psychoanalytic interpretation as a technique of clinical intervention, a point that Erikson makes more than once in his book on Gandhi.

Frederick Wyatt raises the more scholarly question of the liabilities of psychohistorical interpretation. He points to the clear perils of an interpretation such as the one Erikson makes of Gandhi's memoirs. On the other hand, Wyatt points to an advantage that the psychohistorian enjoys: he can test his hypotheses about motivational trends against the outcome while the therapist intervening in an ongoing life cannot.

ON THE NATURE OF PSYCHO–HISTORICAL EVIDENCE: IN SEARCH OF GANDHI

Erik H. Erikson

With Critical Evaluations by Robert Coles, Robert S. Liebert, and Frederick Wyatt

A field in-between the therapist and the historian that some have come to call the psychohistorical approach usually designates an area in which nobody as yet is methodologically quite at home, but that someday will be settled and incorporated without a trace of border disputes and double names. A psychohistorical analysis of the life of Gandhi—his relations with his father, his wife, his benefactor, his followers, his autobiography—is undertaken in an effort to understand the unity and the contradictions of the Mahatma.

About a decade ago, when I first participated in a *Daedalus* discussion, I represented one wing of the clinical arts and sciences in a symposium on Evidence and Inference.[1] I offered some observations of a "markedly personal nature," and this not only from predilection but because the only methodological certainty that I could claim for my specialty, the psychotherapeutic encounter, was "disciplined subjectivity." Of all the other fields represented in that symposium, I felt closest (so I cautiously suggested) to the historian: for he, like the clinician, must serve the curious process by which selected portions of the past impose themselves on our renewed awareness and claim continued actuality in our contemporary commitments. We clinicians, of course, work under a Hippocratic contract with our clients; and the way they submit their past to our interpretation is a special form of historicizing, dominated by their sense of fragmentation and isolation and by our method of restoring to them, through the encounter with us, a semblance of wholeness, immediacy, and mutuality. But as we, in our jargon, "take a history" with the promise of correcting it, we enter another's life, we "make history." Thus, both clinician and patient (and in psychoanalysis, at any rate, every clinician undergoes voluntary patienthood for didactic purposes) acquire more than an inkling of

Reprinted with permission of *Daedalus,* Journal of the American Academy of Arts & Sciences, Boston, Mass. Summer, 1968, "Philosophers and Kings: Studies in Leadership."

Much of the substantive analysis is incorporated in Erikson's book, *Gandhi's Truth: On the Origins of Militant Nonviolence* (New York: Norton, 1969).

what Collingwood claims history is—namely, "the life of mind" which "both lives in historical process and knows itself as so living."

Since that symposium, the former caution in the approach to each other of clinician and historian has given way to quite active efforts to find common ground. These have been confined for the most part to the joint study of the traditional affinity of case history and life history. But here the clinician is inexorably drawn into superpersonal history "itself," since he, too, must learn to conceive of, say, a "great" man's crises and achievements as communal events characteristic of a given historical period. On the other hand, some historians probably begin to suspect that they, too, are practitioners of a restorative art that transforms the fragmentation of the past and the peculiarities of those who make history into such wholeness of meaning as mankind seeks. This, in fact, may become only too clear in our time when the historian finds himself involved in ongoing history by an accelerated interplay of communication between the interpreters and the makers of history: Here, a new kind of Hippocratic Oath may become necessary. And as for him who would cure mankind from history itself—he certainly takes on the therapeutic job of jobs.

It is not my purpose, however, to blur the division between therapist and historian. Rather, I would like to try to delineate an in-between field that some of us have come to call the psychohistorical approach. Such a compound name usually designates an area in which nobody as yet is methodologically quite at home, but which someday will be settled and incorporated without a trace of border disputes and double names. The necessity to delineate it, however, becomes urgent when forward workers rush in with claims that endanger systematic exploration. Thus, today, psychoanalytic theory is sometimes applied to historical events with little clarification of the criteria for such a transfer. Such bravado can lead to brilliant insights, but also to renewed doubt in the specific fittedness and general applicability of psychological interpretation. I will, therefore, attempt to discuss here, in a manner both "markedly personal" and didactic, what parallels I have found between my clinical experience and the study of a circumscribed historical event.

Since the symposium on Evidence and Inference, my study *Young Man Luther* has also appeared;[2] and nothing could have better symbolized the methodological embarrassment on the part even of friendly critics than the stereotyped way in which editors, both in this country and in England, captioned the reviews of my book with the phrase "Luther on the Couch." Now clinicians are, in fact, rather sparing in the use of the couch except in a systematic psychoanalysis; yet, "on the couch" has assumed some such popular connotation as "on the carpet." And it so happens that Luther all his life was a flamboyant free associator and in his youth certainly often talked as if he *were* "on the couch." His urbane superior von Staupitz, could we inform him of the new uses of this adaptable furniture, would gladly testify to that. He recognized in the young monk's raving insistence that his repentance had not yet convinced God a "confession compulsion" altogether out of proposition to what the father confessor was ready to receive or to absolve; wherefore he told young Luther that *he* was resisting *God,* not God him. And with the recognition of an unfunctional resistance operative within the very act of "free" self-revelation, the confessor of old was on good clinical grounds.

The recognition of an inner resistance to some memories is, in fact, the technical basis for the whole theory of defense in psychoanalysis. As such, it is one of the five conceptions that Freud in one little-known dogmatic sentence calls "the principal constituents of . . . psychoanalysis."[3] To begin on didactic home ground, I will briefly discuss these fundamental assumptions, which have remained fundamental to all modifications of psychoanalysis and to its application in other fields. A "resisting" patient, then, may find something in himself obstrucing him in his very determination to communicate what "comes to his mind": Too much may come too fast, or too little too tortuously, if at all. For such *resistance,* Freud blamed the mechanism of *repression* and the fact of an *unconscious,* for what once has been repressed can reassert its right to awareness and resolution only in indirect ways: in the symbolic disguise of dreams and fantasies, or in symptoms of commission (meaning acts alien to the actor himself), or in symptoms of omission (inhibitions, avoidances).

On the basis of his Victorian data, Freud found "behind" repression and resistance primarily what he called the *aetiological significance of sexual life*—that is, the pathogenic power of repressed sexual impulses. But, of course, he included a wide assortment of impulses and affects in the definition of "sexual"; and he considered systematic attention to the *importance of infantile experiences* an intrinsic part of his method and his theory. The last two conceptions led to what has been called the Freudian revolution, although Freud has no more reason than have the fathers of other kinds of revolutions to acknowledge the "liberation" named after him.

But there is one more term, mentioned by Freud in the same study and called "neither more nor less than the mainspring of the joint work of psychoanalysis": *transference*—and for a good historical example of father transference, we again need look no further than Luther's relation to Herrn von Staupitz and the Pope. How he made this, too, historical in a grand manner is, for the moment, another matter. Transference is a universal tendency active wherever human beings enter a relationship to others in such a way that the other *also* "stands for" persons as perceived in the preadult past. He thus serves the reenactment of infantile and juvenile wishes and fears, hopes and apprehensions; and this always with a bewildering *ambivalence*—that is, a ratio of loving and hateful tendencies that, under certain conditions, change radically. This plays a singularly important role in the clinical encounter and not only in the dependent patient's behavior toward the clinician. It is also part of what the clinician must observe in himself: He, too, can transfer on different patients a variety of unconscious strivings which come from *his* infantile past. This we call *countertransference.*

All these seeming difficulties, however, are the very tools of the psychonanalyst. To a determined believer in free will, they may all sound like weaknesses, if not dishonesties, while together they are really an intrinsic "property" of the clinical situation. Relieved and resolved in each case, they are a necessary part of the evidence; and their elucidation is the only way to a cure. But are they also applicable to some aspects of historical research? Here the difficulties of a hyphenated approach become only too obvious, for in the absence of historical training I can only describe the way in which my clinical tools either hindered or proved handy in an attempt to reconstruct a historical event. Yet, it would seem that even the best trained historical mind could not "live in the historical process" without underscoring and erasing, professing and denying, even loving and hating and without trying to know himself as so living and so knowing. I may hope, then, that the predicaments to be described will remind the reader of his own experiences or of those recorded in the other contributions to this symposium. As for historical data proper, I can only try to introduce a psychological dimension into what would seem to be well-established rules of evidence.

II

Three times in the early sixties I visited the city of Ahmedabad in the Indian State of Gujarat. The first time I went on the invitation of some enlightened citizens in order to give a seminar on the human life cycle and to compare our modern conception of the stages of life with those of the Hindu tradition. My wife and I occupied a small house on the estate of an industrialist—the city being one of the oldest textile centers of the world. Nearby was the mill owner's marble mansion, always open for rest and work to men of the mind; in its very shadow was the simple house of his sister, a saintly woman called the Mother of Labor, in whose living room hung a portrait of Tolstoy inscribed for Gandhi. It came back to me only gradually (for I had known it when I was young) that this was the city in which Gandhi had lived for more than a decade and a half and that it was this mill owner and his sister (both now in their seventies) to whom Gandhi pays high and repeated tribute in his autobiography. They had been Gandhi's opponent and ally, respectively, in the dramatic event by which labor unionism was founded in India: the Ahmedabad textile strike of 1918.

At the age of forty-five Gandhi had returned to India "for good" in 1914, after having spent his student years in England and the years of his early manhood in South Africa. He had founded a settlement near Ahmedabad, the principal city of the province in which he had been born and had found a liberal benefactor in the man whom we shall simply refer to as "the mill owner" (as, in general, I will endeavor not to name in this paper individuals merely used for "demonstration"). Once settled, Gandhi had immediately begun to travel extensively to become familiar with the life of the masses and to find circumscribed grievances suited to his approach: the nonviolent technique which he had developed in South Africa and had called *Satyagraha*—that is, a method of recognizing and mobilizing the forces of truth and peace in the oppressor as well as in the oppressed. In 1917 he had found an opportunity to move in on the system of indigo growing in faraway Bihar in defense of the rights of the peasants there. And now, in 1918, he accepted at the mill owner's request the mediatorship in a wage dispute in the principal industry at home, in Ahmedabad. He had studied the situation carefully and had decided to accept the leadership of ten thousand workers, a decision which brought him into public, as well as personal, conflict with the mill owner and aligned him on the side of the mill owner's sister, who had been deeply involved in "social work" in the widest sense. In the weeks of this strike Gandhi developed, in deed and in words, his full technique, including even a brief fast. The whole matter ended in a compromise that nevertheless secured to the workers, in the long run, what they had asked for.

This story, then, seemed to harbor fascinating private, as well as public, issues. And it seemed significant that Gandhi would have chosen in the cataclysmic years 1917 and 1918 opportunities to demonstrate his kind of revolution in grievances involving first peasants and then workers and that he would do so on a local and even personal scale—visualize, in contrast, the global activities of other charismatic leaders in the concluding years of World War I. At the same time, in fact, the mill strike was hardly noted: "We cannot see what Mr. M. K. Gandhi can win, but we can well see that he might lose everything," wrote the leading newspaper in the area. And in his autobiography, written a decade later, the Mahatma makes relatively light of the whole event—a diffidence which he transmitted to his biographers. Yet, the very next year he would lead the first nationwide civil disobedience and become forever India's Mahatma.

Enter the psychohistorian: Having learned to esteem the mill owner and his family and having become convinced of the historical and biographic significance of the strike as well as of the "resistance" against it, I determined to study both.

First, then, a word on the record of the event as written by Gandhi himself about a decade after the strike. In a previous publication,[4] I have pointed to the general difficulties encountered in using Gandhi's autobiography for either historical or psychoanalytic purposes—not to speak of a combination of both. Maybe more so in translation than in Gandhi's native Gujarati in which it was written, the autobiography often impresses the reader as monotonous and moralistic to the point of priggishness, or, at any rate, as devoid of any indication of Gandhi's presence described by witnesses as energetic and energizing, challenging and teasing. And, indeed, the autobiography originally was not a book at all. It was written over a number of years in the form of "columns" for a biweekly primarily addressed to youth: Each column, like our traditional homilies, had to have a moral. Furthermore, these columns were written when the Mahatmaship of India, gained in the years after the strike, seemed already forfeited both by political fortune and by approaching old age: Gandhi had been jailed and set free only to face again a politically divided India. Temporarily as we now know, but at the time often with depressing finality, he had turned from rebel to reformer. A Hindu reformer approaching sixty must face fully what the autobiography's foreword clearly states: "What I want to achieve . . . is self-realization, to see God face to face, to attain *Moksha*." And *Moksha* in the Hindu life cycle means final renunciation and withdrawal. The autobiography is a testament, then, even though we now know that Gandhi's leadership had just begun.

One is almost embarrassed to point out what seems so obvious—namely, that in perusing a man's memoirs for the purpose of reconstructing past moments and reinterpreting pervasive motivational trends, one must first ask oneself at what age and under what general circumstances the memoirs were written, what their intended purpose was, and what form they assumed. Surely all this would have to be known before one can proceed to judge the less conscious motivations, which may have led the autobiographer to emphasize selectively some experiences and omit other equally decisive ones; to profess and reveal flamboyantly some deed or misdeed and to disguise or deny equally obvious commitments; to argue and to try to prove what seems to purify or confirm his historical role and to correct what might spoil the kind of immortality he has chosen for himself. Confessionlike remembrances often seem to be the most naively revealing and yet are also the most complex form of autobiography, for they attempt to prove the author's purity by the very advertisement of his impurities and, therefore, confound his honesty both as a sinner and a braggart.

As pointed out, past events make their often abrupt and surprising appearance in the psychoanalytic hour only as part of an observational situation that includes systematic attention to the reasons why they may come to mind just then: Factuality aside, what is their actuality in the developing relation of professional observer and self-observing client? It is, therefore, hard to understand how observers trained in clinical observation can accept an event reported in an autobiography—such as, say, Gandhi's account of his father's death—both as a factual event and as a naive confession without asking why the item came to mind in *its* au-

tonomous setting, the autobiography; and why, indeed, a particular form of autobiography was being practiced or newly created at that moment in history. Gandhi
himself states that he knew an autobiography to be a rather un-Indian phenomenon, which makes his own an all the more elemental creation comparable to
the confessions of St. Augustine and Abelard or to Rousseau's and Kierkegaard's
autobiographic works.

To put this diagrammatically and didactically, a psychohistorical reviewer
would have to fathom—in one intuitive configuration of thought if he can and
with the help of a diagram if he must—the *complementarity* of at least four conditions under which a record emerges.

Table 1
Functions of the Record

	I Moment	*II Sequence*
1. INDIVIDUAL	in the recorder's stage of life and general condition	in the recorder's life history
2. COMMUNITY	in the state of the recorder's community	in the history of the recorder's community

Under I-1, then, we would focus as if with a magnifying glass on one segment
of the recorder's life as a period with a circumscribed quality. Gandhi's autobiography served the acute function of demonstrating an aging reformer's capacity to
apply what he called truth to the balance sheet of his own failures and successes, in
order to gain the wisdom of renunciation for himself and to promote a new level of
political and spiritual awareness in his nation. But we would also have to consider
the special inner conflicts and overt mood swings that aggravated these, his often
withdrawn and "silent" years. Under I-2, we would consider all the acute circumstances in Indian history that would make Gandhi feel that he would find an echo
for his message in those segments of India's awakening youth who could read—or
be read to. Under II-1, we would remember that confession seems to have been a
passion for him throughout life and that his marked concern over *Moksha* began
in a precocious conscience development in childhood (which, in fact, he shared with
other *homines religiosi*). In II-2, however, we would have to account for the fact
that Gandhi's record, both in content and style, went far beyond the traditional
forms of self-revelation in India and bridged such confessionalism as St. Augustine's
or Tolstoy's awareness as Christians, as well as Rousseau's passionate and Freud's
systematized insight into the power of infantile and juvenile experience. From
the psychohistorical viewpoint, then, the question is not, or not only, whether a
man like Gandhi inadvertently proves some of Freud's points (such as the power
of the emotions subsumed under the term Oedipus complex), but why such items
that we now recognize as universal were reenacted in different media of representation (*including* Freud's dream analyses) by particular types of men in given periods of history—and why, indeed, their time was ready for them and their medium:
for only such complementarity makes a confession momentous and its historical
analysis meaningful.

Our diagrammatic boxes, then, suggest the *relativity* governing any historical
item—that is, the "concomitant variability" of passing moment and long-range
trend, of individual life cycle and communal development.

III

Let me now turn to the autobiography's rendition of the strike of 1918—the Event as I will call it from here on. There is besides Gandhi's retrospective reflections only one full account of it, a pamphlet of less than a hundred pages by the man who was then Gandhi's secretary.[5] Gandhi's own approach to the matter is even more casual and episodic and is, in fact, broken up by the insertion of a seemingly quite unrelated story.[6] This is the sequence: In a chapter (or installment) called "In Touch with Labor" Gandhi reports on the "delicate situation" in Ahmedabad where a sister "had to battle against her own brother." His friendly relations with both "made fighting with them the more difficult." But he considered the case of the mill hands strong, and he therefore "had to advise the laborers to go on strike." There follows a summary, less than one page long, of nearly twenty days of a strike during which he set in motion all the principles and techniques of his militant and nonviolent *Satyagraha*—on a local scale, to be sure, but with lasting consequences for Ahmedabad, India, and beyond. Then the story of the strike is interrupted by a chapter called "A Peep into the Ashram." Here the reader is entertained with a description of the multitude of snakes that infested the land by the river to which Gandhi, at the time of the strike, had just moved his settlement. Gandhi recounts how he and his Ashramites in South Africa, as well as in India, had always avoided killing snakes and that in twenty-five years of such practice "no loss of life [had been] occasioned by snake bite." [7] Only then, in a further chapter, does Gandhi conclude the strike story by reporting its climax—namely, his first fast in a public issue, in spite of which (or, as we shall see, because of which) the whole strike ended with what looked like a kind of hasty compromise. What was at stake then, and what was still at stake at the writing of the autobiography, was the purity of the nonviolent method: The mill owner could (and did) consider Gandhi's fast an unfairly coercive way of making the employers give in, whereas Gandhi did (and always would) consider a fast only justified as a means of persuading weakening supporters to hold out.

The technical question that arises here is whether the chapter that interrupts the account of the strike could be shown to signify an inner resistance against the whole story, comparable to what we observe and utilize in clinical work. Again and again, one finds, for example, that a child undergoing psychotherapy will suffer what I have called "play disruption"—that is, he will interrupt his play in some anxious manner, sometimes without being able to resume it. And often the very manner of disruption or the way in which play is resumed will suggest to the experienced observer what dangerous thought had occurred to the child and had ruined his playfulness. Or an adult in psychoanalysis will embark on a seemingly easy progression of free associations only to find suddenly that he has forgotten what he was about to say next or to interrupt his own trend of thought with what appears to be a senseless image or sentence "from nowhere." A little scrutiny can soon reveal that what had thus been lost or had intruded was, in fact, an important key to the underlying meaning of the whole sequence of thoughts—a key which more often than not reveals a repressed or suppressed sense of hate against a beloved person. I will later report on Gandhi's sudden awareness of such a disruption in another part of the autobiography.

What, then, could the nonkilling of snakes have to do with the Ahmedabad strike and with Gandhi's relation to the mill owner? Mere thematic play would suggest Gandhiites bent on nonviolence in the first column meet mill owners; in the second, poisonous snakes; and in the third, mill owners again. Do snakes, then, "stand for" mill owners? This could suggest to a clinician a breakthrough of Gandhi's anger against the mill owners—an anger that he had expressly forbidden himself, as well as the striking and starving workmen. If one can win over poisonous snakes by love and nonviolence, the hidden thought might be, then maybe one can reach the hearts of industrialists too. Or the suggestion might be more damaging—namely, that it would be more profitable to be kind to poisonous snakes than to industrialists—and here we remember that another Man of Peace, also using an analogy from the bestiary, once mused that big lazy camels might squeeze through where a rich man could not or would not. Was Gandhi's suppressed rage apt to be "displaced" in such a flagrant way? This would have to be seen.

There is, however, an explanation closer to historical fact and to the propagandistic purpose of the autobiography. He and the mill owner had been involved in a public scandal. Briefly, the mill owner had noted hordes of ferocious looking dogs around his factory on the outskirts of the city and had ascertained that the municipal police, knowing how Hindus feel about killing animals, were in the habit of releasing captured stray dogs outside the city limits. Since hydrophobia had reached major proportions in the area, the mill owner had requested the police to kill these dogs, and some obliging officer, for reasons of his own, had arranged for the carcasses to be carted away through the crowded city streets. Such is the stuff that riots are made of in India. But Gandhi did not hesitate to speak up for the mill owner, saying he himself would kill a deranged man if he found him massacring other people. He wrote in *Young India:*

The lower animals are our brethren. I include among them the lion and the tiger. We do not know how to live with these carnivorous beasts and poisonous reptiles because of our ignorance. When man learns better, he will learn to befriend even these. Today he does not even know how to befriend a man of a different religion or from a different country.[8]

In this prophetic statement we see the reptiles "associated" with carnivorous beasts; and from here it is only one step to the interpretation that Gandhi, before telling the story of how he had made concessions to the mill owner at the end of the strike, had to tell himself and his readers that his basic principles had not suffered on that other and better known occasion when he took the mill owner's side.

Was Gandhi "conscious" of such pleading with the reader? Probably, for the whole trend of thought fits well into the professed aim of his self-revelations: to sketch his "experiments with truth." But factual explanation (and here is the psychohistorical point) should not do away with the underlying and pervasive emotional actuality. For my story, the assumption of an ambivalence toward the mill owner is inescapable. In historical fact, it is an example of a mutual and manly acceptance of the Hindu *dharma*—that is, of the assignment to each man of a place within the world order that he must fulfill in order to have a higher chance in another life. If, as Gandhi would put it, "fasting is my business," then making money was that of the mill owner; and Gandhi could not have fulfilled his role of saintly politician (or, as he put it, "a politician who tried to be a saint") had he not had the financial support of wealthy men. This, the Marxists might say, corrupted him, while the Hindu point of view would merely call for a clean division of roles within a common search for a higher truth. The Freudian point of view, however, would suggest that such a situation might cause an unconscious "transference" of unresolved conflicts of childhood to the present.

Young Gandhi had, in varying ways, forsaken his caste and his father when he left to become an English barrister, and he had forsaken his older brother who had wanted him to join him in legal work when he had become a reformer. Such deviations from one's ancestral *dharma* are a grave problem in the lives of many creative Indians. At any rate, when he returned and settled down in Ahmedabad —the city in which both his native language and the mercantile spirit of his ancestors had reached a high level of cultivation—and when he again deviated grievously by taking a family of Untouchables into his *Ashram,* the mill owner alone had continued to support him. The mill owner, thus, had become a true brother; and anyone familiar with Gandhi's life will know how desperate at times was the "Great Soul's" never requited and never fully admitted search for somebody who would sanction, guide, and, yes, mother *him.* This is a complex matter, and it will be enough to indicate here that without the assumption of such a transference of the prime actor in my story to the principal witnesses, a brother and sister, I could not have made sense of the meaning of the Event in Gandhi's life— and of his wish to "play it down."

IV

Nobody likes to be found out, not even one who has made ruthless confession a part of his profession. Any autobiographer, therefore, at least between the lines, spars with his reader and potential judge. Does the autobiographic recorder then develop a kind of transference on the potential reviewer of his record? Gandhi did, as we shall see.

But before reporting this, let me ask another question: Does not the professional reader and reviewer, who makes it his business to reveal what others do or may *not* know about themselves, also feel some uncomfortable tension in relation to them? Yes, I think that he does and that he should know that he does. There are, of course, some who would claim that, after all, they are voyeurs merely in *majorem gloriam* of history or humanity and are not otherwise "involved" with their subjects. But such denial often results only in an interpretive brashness or a superior attitude toward the self-recorder who seems to reveal himself so inadvertently or to hide his "real" motivation so clumsily. A patient offers his motivation for full inspection only under the protection of a contract and a method; and the method is not complete unless the "doctor" knows how to gauge his own hidden feelings. If it can be assumed that the reviewer of self-revelations or of self-revealing acts and statements offered in nonclinical contexts also develops some form of irrational countertransference, that, too, must be turned to methodological advantage not only for the sake of his work, but also for that of his friends and his family.

I hope to have aroused just enough discomfort in the professional reader to make him share the sting I felt when in the course of my study I came once again across the following passage midway through Gandhi's autobiography: "If some busybody were to cross-examine me on the chapters I have now written, he could probably shed more light on them, and if it were a hostile critic's cross-examination, he might even flatter himself for having shown up the hollowness of many of my pretensions." [9] Here, then, we seem to have a real analogue to what I described above as "play disruption"; and, indeed, Gandhi continues with a momentary negative reaction to his whole undertaking: "I therefore wonder for a moment whether it might not be proper to stop writing these chapters altogether." After which he recovers, luckily, with a typically Gandhian form of self-sanction: "But so long as there is no prohibition from the voice within, I must continue the writing." There seems to be an awareness, however, of having given in to something akin to free association, though dictated by a higher power: "I write just as the spirit moves me at the time of writing. I do not claim to know definitely that all conscious thought and action on my part is directed by the spirit." Again, he recovers, however, and sanctions his own doings: "But on an examination of the greatest steps that I have taken in my life, as also of those that may be regarded as the least, I think it will not be improper to say that all of them were directed by the spirit." Now he can dismiss his "hostile" reader: "I am not writing the autobiography to please critics. Writing it itself is one of the experiments with truth." And he can distribute the blame for writing at all: "Indeed, I started writing [the autobiography] in compliance with their [his coworkers'] wishes. If, therefore, I am wrong in writing the autobiography, they must share the blame." This concluding remark is, I think, typical of the Gandhian half-humor so easily lost in translation; and humor means recovery.

To say more about this sudden disruption, I would have to know (according to my own specifications) exactly in what period of his life Gandhi wrote this particular installment of the autobiography. Was there a real snooper and critic in his life at the time? Or was the imaginary one an externalization of a second inner voice, one temporarily at odds with the one that inspired his every effort? Much speaks for the latter assumption, for the disruption follows a chapter called "A Sacred Recollection and Penance" in which Gandhi describes an especially cruel outbreak against his wife under circumstances (there were many in his life) both sublime and ridiculous. One, in South Africa, while cleaning her house, which has become a hostel, she has refused to empty a Christian Untouchable's chamber pot (*that* combination was too *much*), and Gandhi had literally shown her the gate. After such extreme and extremely petty moments something could cry out in him: What if all his professions of universal love, all his sacrifices of those closest to him by family ties for the sake of those furthest away (the masses, the poor, the Untouchables) were a "pretense?" So here, the reader and reviewer become an externalization of the writer's self-doubt; and I felt so directly appealed to that I began to think of how I might have explained these matters to him in the light of our clinical knowledge. Not without the sudden awareness of being older than he had been when he wrote that passage, I addressed him in an ensuing chapter explaining that, as a student of another lover of truth, a contemporary of his on the other side of the world, I had a more charitable term than "pretense" for the psychological aspects of his dilemma: namely, "ambivalence." I confronted him with another instance of petty and righteous cruelty and attempted to formulate a pervasive ambivalence: that his marriage at the age of thirteen to a girl of the same age and fatherhood in his teens had prevented him from making a conscious decision at an informed age for or against married life; that this "fate" had been foisted on him in the traditional manner by his father, whom he never forgave. Thus, a lifelong ambivalence toward his wife and children, not to speak of sexuality in general, had perpetuated a predicament in his life as well as in that of many of his followers: Are *Satyagraha* and chastity inseparable? That such conflicts in the lives of saintly men are more than a matter of mental hygiene, I need not emphasize here. Gandhi, I think, would have listened to me, but probably would have asked me teasingly why I had taken his outburst so personally. And, indeed, my impulsive need to answer him "in person" before I could go on with my book revealed again that all manner of countertransference can accompany our attempts to analyze others, great or ordinary.

And what, we must ask (and he might have asked), legitimizes such undertaking in clinical work? It is, of course, the mandate to help—*paired with self-analysis.* And even as we demand that he who makes a profession of "psycho-analyzing" others must have learned a certain capacity of self-analysis so must we presuppose that the psychohistorian will have developed or acquired a certain self-analytical capacity that would give to his dealings with others, great or small, both the charity of identification and a reasonably good conscience. Ours, too, are "experiments with truth."

I can offer, for such an ambitious aim, only another schema that lists the minimum requirements for what a reviewer of a record and of an event should be reasonably clear about (Table 2).

Table 2
Function of the Review

	I Moment	*II Sequence*
1. INDIVIDUAL	in the stage and the conditions of the reviewer's life	in the reviewer's life history
2. COMMUNITY	in the state of the reviewer's communities	in the history of the reviewer's communities

Under communities I here subsume a whole series of collective processes from which the reviewer derives identity and sanction and within which his act of reviewing has a function; there, above all, he must know himself as living in the historical process. Each community, of course, may call for a separate chart: the reviewer's nation or race, his caste or class, his religion or ideological party—and, of course, his professional field.

V

Did Freud live up to our methodological standards? His introduction to what we now know to have been the first psychohistorical essay—namely, the book on Wilson allegedly coauthored by him and William Bullitt[10]—does give an admirable approximation of what I have in mind. But not in the bulk of the book: for here he unwisely relied on Bullitt to review the record for him and to provide him with the data necessary for an application of the laws found in case histories to the life history of a public figure. In my review of this book,[11] I felt it necessary to explain the strange collaboration in this way: As a young man and before he became a doctor, so Freud himself tells us, he had wanted to be a statesman. His deep identification with Moses can be clearly read in his work. Did Bullitt awaken in the old and ailing man (who, in fact, was dying in exile when he signed the final manuscript) the fading hope that his life work, psychoanalysis, might yet be destined to become applicable to statesmanship? The task at hand, however, was obviously overshadowed by Freud's passionate feelings in regard to the joint subject, President Wilson. About this, Freud is explicit in his introduction, the only part of the book clearly written by him, all other handwritten contributions having been "lost" by Bullitt in one way or another. Freud declares that the figure of the American President, "as it rose above the horizons of Europeans, was from the beginning unsympathetic" to him and that this feeling increased "the more severely we suffered from the consequences of his intrusion into our destiny." Wilson's Fourteen Points had promised that a semblance of Christian charity, combined with political shrewdness, might yet survive the first mechanized slaughter in history. Could it be that the destruction or the dehumanization of mankind by the unrestricted use of superweaponry might be checked by the creation of a world democracy? What followed Versailles played into a pervasive trend in Freud's whole being: a Moses-like indignation at all false Christian (or other) prophecy. A proud man brought up in Judaism, I concluded, even if surrounded by the folklore and display of Catholicism, persists in the historical conviction that the Messiah has not yet appeared and persists with more grimness the more he has been inclined temporarily to give credence to the Christian hope for salvation. Such overall prejudice, however, even where clearly expressed, is methodologically meaningful only insofar as the slant thus given to the whole work is thereby clarified *and* insofar as it is vigorously counteracted by an adherence to the other criteria for evidence and interference—and for literary form. On the other hand, where a sovereign acknowledgment like Freud's introduction enters an alliance with a vindictive and tendentious case study clearly written by a chronically disappointed public servant such as Bullitt, then the whole work itself becomes a case study of a fascinating, but in its final form abortive, psychohistorical essay. The Wilson book can serve to illustrate, then, if somewhat by way of a caricature, the decisive influence on a bit of history that results from basic differences in *Weltanschauung* among actor, recorder, and reviewer—that is, a world view, a sense of existential space-time, which (as a venerable physicist acknowledged in my seminar in Ahmedabad) is "in a man's bones," no matter what else he has learned.

Freud's example leads me back to the days when I first heard of Gandhi and of Ahmedabad and maybe even of the mill owner—all of which remained latent until, at the time of my visit, it "came back to me" almost sensually in the occasional splendor and the pervasive squalor of India. In my youth I belonged to the class of wandering artists who—as some alienated and neurotic youths can and must in all ages—blithely keep some vision alive in the realities of political and economic chaos, even though, by a minute slip in the scales of fate, they may find themselves among the uniformed to whom killing and being killed becomes a sacred duty, or they may perish ingloriously in some mass furor.

As Wilson's image had set in the cruel night of post-Versailles, it was Gandhi's that then "rose above the horizon"—on the other side of the world. As described to us by Romain Rolland, he seemed to have that pervasive presence, always dear to youth, that comes from the total commitment (for that very reason) to the actuality of love and reason in every fleeting moment. The Event had been contemporaneous with Wilson's Fourteen Points; and if these Points were (and with variations still are) "Western democracy's answer to Bolshevism," so was Gandhi's *Satyagraha* (begun so locally) the East's answer to Wilson *and* to Lenin.

As for myself, I was to spend a lifetime finding an orientation in, and making a living from, the field created by Sigmund Freud. But when I decided in advanced years to study the Event—and all I can say is that at a certain time I became aware of having made that decision—I do not think that I set out merely to "apply" to Gandhi what I had learned from Freud. Great contemporaries, in all their grandiose one-sidedness, converge as much as they diverge; and it is not enough to characterize one with the methods of the other. As Freud once fancied he might become a political leader, so Gandhi thought of going into medicine. All his life Gandhi ran a kind of health institute, and Freud founded an international organization with the ideological and economic power of a movement. But both men came to revolutionize man's awareness of his wayward instinctuality and to meet it with a combination of militant intelligence—and nonviolence. Gandhi pointed a way to the "conquest of violence" in its external and manifest aspects and, in the meantime, chose to pluck out the sexuality that offended him. Freud, in studying man's repressed sexuality, also revealed the internalized violence of self-condemnation, but thought externalized violent strife to be inevitable. And both men, being good post-Darwinians, blamed man's instinctuality on his animal ancestry—Gandhi calling man a sexual "brute" and Freud comparing his viciousness (to his own kind!) to that of wolves. Since then ethology has fully described the intrinsic discipline of animal behavior and most impressively (in this context) the pacific rituals by which some social animals—yes, even wolves—"instinctively" prevent senseless murder.[12]

When I came to Ahmedabad, it had become clear to me (for I had just come from the disarmament conference of the American Academy) that man as a species cannot afford any more to cultivate illusions either about his own "nature" or about that of other species, or about those "pseudospecies" he calls enemies—not while inventing and manufacturing arsenals capable of global destruction and relying for inner and outer peace solely on the superbrakes built into the superweaponry. And Gandhi seems to have been the only man who was visualized *and* demonstrated an overall alternative.

Less nobly, I should admit that I must have been looking for a historical figure to write about. What could be more fitting than (as my student put it) letting "Young Man Luther" be followed by "Middle-Aged Mahatma"? And here I had witnesses: the survivors of a generation of then young men and women who had joined or met Gandhi in 1918, and whose life (as the saying goes) had not been the same since, as if one knew what it might have been. They included, besides the mill owner and his sister, individuals now retired or still in the forefront of national activity in industry, in the Cabinet, or in Parliament. These I set out to meet and to interview on my subsequent visits to India.

If all this sounds self-indulgently personal, it is spelled out here only far enough to remind the psychohistorian that his choice of subject often originates in early ideals or identifications and that it may be important for him to accept as well as he can some deeper bias than can be argued out on the level of verifiable fact or faultless methodology. I believe, in fact, that any man projects or comes to project on the men and the times he studies some unlived portions and often the unrealized selves of his own life, not to speak of what William James calls "the murdered self." The psychohistorian may owe it to history, as well as to himself, to be more conscious of what seems to be a *retransference* on former selves probably inescapable in any remembering, recording, or reviewing and to learn to live and to work in the light of such consciousness. This, incidentally, also calls for new forms of collaboration such as the father of psychoanalysis may have had in mind when he met the brilliant American diplomat.

To confound things a little further, there are also *cross-transferences* from one reviewer of the same subject to another. For example, in a book on Gandhi's main rivals for national leadership, *Tilak and Gokhale* (both of whom died before his ascendance), S. A. Wolpert[13] calls Gandhi a disciple of Gokhale, and, worse, calls Gokhale Gandhi's "guru." Now, Gandhi, while comparing Tilak with the forbidding ocean and Gokhale (his elder by three years only) with the maternal Ganges and while sometimes calling Gokhale his "political guru," certainly kept *the* guruship in his life free for his own inner voice: an important step in Indian self-conception. But why should Wolpert want to call *his* Gokhale *my* Gandhi's guru with such monotonous frequency—and why should this annoy me? The italics indicate the answer, which (as I would judge from my perusal of the literature on Luther) points to a pervasive aspect of a reviewer's "genealogical" identification with this subject as seen through his method, which may make history more entertaining, but rarely more enlightening unless seasoned with insight.

VI

In India, intellectual as well as political travelers could always count on being lodged with friends of means or with friends of friends, and the mill owner related the sayings of many interesting house guests—among them. Gandhi. He had offered me a terrace as a study, saying quietly, "Tagore has worked here." But to be a guest in a man's house is one thing; to be a reviewer of his place in history is another. When I returned to Ahmedabad to interview the mill owner regarding the mill strike, he became strangely distant and asked me to meet him at his office in the mill. This, he made clear, was business: What did I want?

I should say in general that the clinician turned historian must adapt himself to and utilize a new array of "resistances" before he can be sure to be encountering those he is accustomed to. There is, first of all, the often incredible or implausible loss or absence of data in the post-mortem of a charismatic figure, which can be variably attributed to simple carelessness or lack of awareness or of candor on the part of witnesses. Deeper difficulties, however, range from an almost cognitively ahistorical orientation—ascribed by some to Indians in general—to a highly idiosyncratic reluctance to "give up" the past. Here the myth-affirming and myth-destroying propensities of a postcharismatic period must be seen as the very stuff of which history is made. Where myth-making predominates, every item of the great man's life becomes or is reported like a parable; those who cannot commit themselves to this trend must disavow it with destructive fervor. I, for one, have almost never met anybody of whatever level of erudition or information, in India or elsewhere, who was not willing and eager to convey to me the whole measure of the Mahatma as based on one sublime or scandalous bit of hearsay. Then there are those whose lives have become part of a leader's and who have had to incorporate him in their self-image. Here it becomes especially clear that, unless a man wants to divest himself of his part in order to cure, purify, or sell himself —and there are always professions that receive and sanction such divestment—he must consider it an invested possession to be shared only according to custom and religion, personal style and stage of life. The interviewee, not being a client, does not break a contract with either himself or the interviewer in not telling the whole truth as he knows or feels it. He has, in fact, every right to be preoccupied with the intactness of his historical role rather than with fragmented details as patients and psychotherapists are—often to a fault. After all, this man had been

Gandhi's counterplayer in the Event, and he had (as Gandhi knew and took for granted) used all the means at his disposal to break the strike. About this he was, in fact, rather frank, while he seemed "shy" about those episodes that had proved him to be a gallant opponent and faithful supporter. What kind of "resistance" was *that?*

Let me be diagrammatic: The old man's insistence on anonymity turned out to be a lifelong one. In old newspapers I found more than one reference to his charitable deeds, which in feudal manner he had always considered his own choice and his own affair. "This is business, not charity," a union official quoted him as saying when he handed him a contribution; and it will be remembered that he did not identify himself when, as a young industrialist, he left money at the *Ashram* gate. Here was a lifelong trend, then, possibly aggravated by some sense of *Moksha* that supervenes both good deeds and misdeeds. It is not so easy to judge, then, what a man (and a foreigner) does not want to remember or does not want to say or cannot remember or cannot say.

By the same token, the old man's business-like attitude was later clarified in its most defensive aspects as resulting from an experience with an inquisitive visitor, while in general it seemed to reflect a sense of propriety as though he wanted to delineate what in this matter was "my business" and what his. I have already indicated that this same attitude pervaded even Gandhi's sainthood. When Gandhi said to his friends, who wanted to starve themselves with him, "Fasting is my business," he added, "You do yours." But, then, both he and the mill owner belonged to a cultural and national group referred to in India (admiringly as well as mockingly) as *banias*—that is, traders. And while the whole strike and its outcome are often considered a *bania* deal by Gandhi's many critics (Marxists, or Maharashtrians, or Bengalis), there is little doubt than Gandhi chose to unfold his whole *Satyagraha* technique first in a locality and with people who spoke his language and shared his brand of mercantile shrewdness. And behind such life styles there is always India and that larger framework of cosmic propriety, which is called *dharma*—that is, a man's preordained place in the cyclic order of things and their eventual transcendence. *Dharma* can excuse much wickedness and laziness, as can fate or God's will. But it will help determine, from childhood on, what a man considers proper and what out of line; above all, it provides the framework within which the individual can knowingly take hold of the law of *Karma,* the ethical accounting in his round of lives.

I felt, then, literally "put in my place" by the old man's "resistance." In fact, when he asked me after our first interview what, if anything, I had learned, I could only say truthfully that I had gotten an idea of what Gandhi had been up against with him and he with Gandhi. Only afterward did I realize how right I was and that the cause of my initial annoyance had been due to a certain parallel between Gandhi's and my relationship to the mill owner. Had I not gladly accepted the wealthy man's hospitality when I was a newcomer to India so that I could venture out into the dangers and horrors of that land from an initial position of friendship and sanitary safety? And had not Gandhi gladly accepted his financial support when he came back from South Africa, in many ways a newcomer to India after twenty-five years of absence? And had not both of us, Gandhi and I, developed a certain ambivalence to our benefactor? Here, a Marxist could find an opening for legitimate questions; and while he is at it, he might well consider the relationship of the social scientist to the foundations that support him. The common factor that interests us here, however, is the unconscious transference on any host—that is, the attribution of a father or older-brother role to anyone in whose home one seeks safety or in whose influence one seeks security. I should add that in my case this theme seems to be anchored in the infantile experience—and, strictly speaking, this alone make a real transference out of a mere thematic transfer—of having found a loving stepfather in an adoptive country. Every worker must decide for himself, of course, how much or how little he should make of such a connection, and how little or how much of it he should impose on his readers. But first, we must become aware of it.

Now an equally brief word on the other side of the coin—namely, the often sudden and unsolicited revelation of such highly personal material as dreams, memories, and fantasies in the course of interviews. In my case, these were offered by a number of informants in the more informal settings of social get-togethers. Accepting them with gratitude, I was always determined to make use of them only as an auxiliary source of insights, not to be attributed to individuals. I do not know, of course, whether revelations of this kind are common in such work or appeared in mine because my interviewees knew me to be a psychoanalyst. If this most personal data eventually proved to have some striking themes in common, I cannot say whether these themes are typically Indian or typical for men who had followed Gandhi. Here are the themes: a *deep hurt* that the informant had inflicted on one of his parents or guardians and could never forget, and an intense wish to *take care of abandoned creatures,* people or animals, who have strayed too far from home. I had secured from each interviewee the story of how he first met Gandhi only to learn with increasing clinical admiration how determinedly and yet cautiously Gandhi had induced his alienated young followers to cut an already frayed bond with their elders. Tentatively, then, I saw these revelations as an indirect admission of the obvious fact that followers can develop a more or less conscious sense of having vastly outdistanced their original life plan by serving a man who had the power to impose his superior *dharma* on his contemporaries, making a modernized use of the traditional need for a second, a spiritual, father. A resulting powerful ambivalence toward him is often overcompensated by the submissive antics of followership. And followership divides too: Gandhi's disciples had to accept what was his own family's plight—namely, that he belonged to all and to no one, like the mother in a joint family. Gandhi's was a unique maternalism, happily wedded in his case with a high degree of paternal voluntarism, but not always easily shared or tolerated by others.

Followers, too, deserve a diagram. Whatever motivation or conflict they may have in common as they join a leader and are joined together by him has to be studied in the full complementarity of Table 3. As to the last point, Gandhi was a

Table 3

	I Moment	*II Sequence*
1. INDIVIDUAL	the stage of life when they met the leader	lifelong themes transferred to the leader
2. COMMUNITY	their generation's search for leadership	traditional and evolving patterns of followership

master not only in the selection and acquisition of co-workers, but also in assigning them to or using them in different tasks and ways of life—from the position of elected sons and daughters in his ascetic settlement to that of revolutionary organizers all over India and of aspirants for highest political power, including the prime ministership, for which he "needed a boy from Harrow."

The monumental compilation of Gandhi's works[14] undertaken by the government of India (and now under the charge of Professor Swaminathan) permits us to follow Gandhi's acts, thoughts, and affects literally from day to day in speeches and letters, notes and even dreams (as reported in letters), and to recognize his own conflicts over being invested with that charismatic cloak, the Mahatmaship. That publication will permit us for once to see a leader in a life crisis fighting on two fronts at once: the individual past that marks every man as a defined link in the generational chain, and historical actuality. One thing is clear: On the verge of becoming the father of his nation, he did not (as he has been accused of having done) forget his sons, although the manner in which he did remember them was not without tragic overtones and consequences.

VII

The psychoanalyst, it seems, makes a family affair out of any historical event. Does anybody, we may ask, ever escape his internalized folk and learn to deal with the cast of his adult life on its own terms? The answer is yes and no. Certainly, where radical innovation depends on very special motivations and is paired with strong affect, there its impetus can be shown to draw on lifelong aspirations and involvements. It is true that the psychoanalytic method rarely contributes much to the explanation of the excellence of a man's performance—which may be just as well, for it permits the factor of grace to escape classification and prescription —but it may indicate what freed him for his own excellence or what may have inhibited or spoiled it. It so happens that the Ahmedabad Event *was* something of a family affair not only in that Gandhi's counter-players were a brother and a sister, but also because Gandhi here tried to do what is proverbially the most difficult thing for a leader—to be a prophet in his own country. The proverb, too, may gain a new meaning if we can locate the difficulty in the prophet's conflicts as well as in his "country's" diffidence. The very intimacy of my story may seem inapplicable to large events; yet the way Gandhi used his local successes to establish himself firmly as his whole nation's leader—a year later he would command nationwide civil disobedience against the British government—would seem to go to the core of his style as a leader. A man's leadership is prominently characterized by his choice of the proper place, the exact moment, and the specific issue that help him to make his point momentously. Here I would like to quote from a political scientist's work that has aroused interest and on which I have been asked to comment because it uses some "classical" psychoanalytic assumptions rather determinedly.

Victor Wolfenstein, in discussing Gandhi's famous Salt-*Satyagraha* of 1930, asks bluntly: "But why did Gandhi choose the salt tax from among his list of grievances as the first object of *Satyagraha?*" [15] This refers to the occasion when Gandhi, after his long period of political silence, chose (of all possible actions) to lead an at first small but gradually swelling line of marchers on a "sacred pilgrimage" from Ahmedabad to the Arabian Sea in order to break the law against the tax-free use of salt. Wolfenstein's answer is threefold: First, Gandhi "believed that of all British oppressions the salt tax was the most offensive because it struck the poorest people hardest. . . . By undertaking to serve or lead the lowliest self-esteem is raised." This refers to the assumption that Gandhi and other revolutionary leaders overcame a sense of guilt by acting not for themselves, but for the exploited. Wolfenstein's second point is that "the tax on salt constituted an oral deprivation, a restriction on eating." And it is true, Gandhi was preoccupied all his life with dietary prohibitions and dietary choices. But, then, Wolfenstein introduces psychoanalytic symbolism in a way that must be quoted more fully:

Another line of interpretation, which is consonant with the view I have been developing of Gandhi's personality, is suggested by Ernest Jones's contention that one of the two basic symbolic significances of salt is human semen. If it had this unconscious meaning for Gandhi, then we may understand his depriving himself of condiments, including salt, as a form of sexual abstinence, involving a regression to an issue of the oral phase. In the context of the Salt March, Gandhi's taking of salt from the British can thus be seen as reclaiming for the Indian people the manhood and potency which was properly theirs.

The choice of issues worthy of a *Satyagraha* campaign must interest us in past as well as in ongoing history, and Gandhi's choice of the salt tax has always impressed me as a model of practical and symbolic action. It pointed to a foreign power's interdiction of a vast population's right to lift from the long shorelines surrounding their tropical subcontinent a cheap and nature-given substance necessary for maintaining work capacity as well as for making bland food palatable and digestible. Here, Gandhi's shrewdness seemed to join his capacity to focus on the infinite meaning in finite things—a trait that is often associated with the attribution of sainthood. Wolfenstein's suggestion—that the power of this appeal is attributable to an unconscious sexual meaning of salt—while seeming somewhat ludicrous as an isolated statement, appears to have a certain probability if viewed in cultural context. Anybody acquainted with the ancient Indian preoccupation with semen as a substance that pervades the whole body and that, therefore, is released only at the expense of vitality, acuity, and spiritual power will have to admit that if there is an equation between salt and semen in the primitive mind, the Indian people more than any other could be assumed to make the most of it. I suggest, however, that we take a brief look at what E. Jones really said and what the place of his conclusions is in the history of psychoanalytic symbolism.

Jones's classical paper, "The Symbolic Significance of Salt in Folklore and Superstition," was written in 1928.[16] It really starts with the question of the meaning of superstitions that the spilling of salt at a table may bring ill luck and discord to those assembled for a meal. Jones brings together an overwhelming amount of data from folklore and folkcustom that indicates that salt is used in some magic connection with or as an equivalent of semen. A peasant bridegroom may put salt in his left pocket to insure potency; tribesmen and workmen may abstain from both salt and sex during important undertakings; Christian sects may be accused of "salting" the Eucharistic bread with semen—and so on. Jones's conclusion is that to spill salt "means" to lose or spill semen as Onan did: suggesting, then, the sexual model of an antisocial act.

But before we ask how salt may come to mean semen, it is only fair to state that through the ages it has had a powerful significance as itself. When other preservatives were not known, the capacity of salt not only to give pungent taste to the blandest diet, but also to keep perishable food fresh, to cleanse and cure wounds, and even to help embalm dead bodies gave it magic as well as practical value: The very word "salary" apparently comes from the fact that this clean, indestructible, and easily transportable substance could be used instead of money. That it comes from the great Sea, the mythical giver of life, makes salt also a "natural" symbol of procreation as well as of longevity and immortality, wit and wisdom, and thus of such incorruptibility as one fervently hopes will preserve the uncertain phenomena of friendship, loyalty, and hospitality. The use of salt on its own terms, then, for the ceremonial affirmation of mutual bonds would do nicely to explain the superstition concerning the unceremonious spilling.

Jones's conclusion is really rather cautious: "The significance naturally appertaining to such an important and remarkable article of diet as salt has thus been strengthened by an accession of psychical significance derived from deeper sources. The conclusion reached, therefore, is that salt is a typical symbol for semen. There is every reason to think that the primitive mind equates the idea of salt not only with that of semen, but also with the essential constituent of urine. The idea of salt in folklore and superstition characteristically represents the male, active, fertilizing principle."

In psychoanalysis, "deeper" always seems to mean both "sexual" and "repressed," an emphasis that made sense within Freud's libido theory—that is, his search for an "energy of dignity" in human life that would explain the fantastic vagaries of man's instinctuality and yet be comparable to the indestructible and commutable energy isolated and measured in natural science. In civilization, and especially in his day, he would find pervasive evidence of the systematic repression in children of any knowledge of the uses and purposes of the sexual organs and this most particularly in any parental context—a repression that no doubt used the pathways of universal symbolization in order to disguise sexual and, above all, incestual thoughts and yet find expression for them. Among these, early psychoanalysis emphasized paternal and phallic symbolism more than maternal; yet, if sexual symbolism did play a role in helping Gandhi, as he put it, "to arouse the religious imagination of an angry people," then the Indian masses, with all their stubborn worship of mother-goddesses, surely would have been swayed as much by the idea of free access to the fecundity of the maternal Sea as by the claim to male potency.

At any rate, the one-way symbolization suggested in psychoanalysis, by which the nonsexual always symbolizes the sexual, is grounded in the assumption that the erotic is more central to infantile and primitive experience than are the cognitive and the nutritional. But one wonders: Where survival is at stake, where sexuality is not so obsessive as it becomes in the midst of affluence, where sexual repression is not so marked as it became in the civilized and rational mind—could it not be that the symbolic equation of salt and semen is reciprocal? Could not the ceremonial linking of the two have the purpose of conferring on life-creating semen, a substance so easily squandered, the life-sustaining indestructibility of salt? This is, at the end, a question of determining the place of sexuality in man's whole ecology. But in the immediate context of the chronic semistarvation that has undermined the vitality of the Indian masses and considering the periodic threat of widespread death by famine, it would seem appropriate to assume, first of all, that salt means salt. In fact, the further development of psychoanalysis will have to help us understand the symbolic representation not only of repressed sexuality, but also of the ever-present and yet so blatantly denied fact of death in us and around us.[17] If reason will not suffice, then new forms of irrational violence will force us to consider the consequences of man's seeming ability to ignore not only the certainty of his own death, but also the superweaponry poised all around him to destroy the world he knows—literally at a moment's notice.

Sexual symbolism may help, I would agree, to understand superstition and symptoms such as, say, the often self-destructive food fads Gandhi indulged in: At one time, he excluded natural salt from his diet, while at another his friends had reason to tease him over his addiction to Epsom salts. In such matters, however, he was only the all-too-willing victim of a tremendous preoccupation with diet rampant during his student days in vegetarian circles in England as well as in the tradition of his native country, although he adorned this with his own concerns over the impact of diet on sexual desire. In deciding on the Salt March, however, he was obviously in command of his political and economic as well as his psychological wits. And in any context except that of irrationality clearly attributable to sexual repression, one should take any interpretation that explains a human act by recourse to sexual symbolism with a grain of salt.

VIII

A historical moment, we have been trying to suggest, is determined by the complementarity of what witnesses, for all manner of motivation, have considered momentous enough to remember and record and what later reviewers have considered momentous enough to review and rerecord in such a way that the factuality of the event is confirmed or corrected and actuality is perceived and transmitted to posterity. For recorders and reviewers alike, however, events assume a momentous character when they seem both unprecedented and yet also mysteriously familiar—that is, if *analogous events* come to mind that combine to suggest a direction to historical recurrences, be it divine intention someday to be revealed, or an inexorable fate to which man may at least learn to adapt, or regularities that it may be man's task to regulate more engineeringly, or a repetitive delusion from which thoughtful man must "wake up." Psychoanalysis is inclined to recognize in all events not only an analogy to, but also a regression to, the ontogenetic and phylogenetic past. This has proved fruitful in the clinical task of treating patients who suffered from "repressed reminiscenses"; but out of its habitual and dogmatic application has come what I have called the *originological fallacy,* which, in contrast to the teleological one, deals with the present as almost preempted by its own origins—a stance not conducive to the demonstration of developmental or historical probability.

Table 4

	I Moment	*II Sequence*
1. INDIVIDUAL	to a comparable individual at the corresponding stage of his development	to comparable individuals throughout their lives
2. COMMUNITY	in a corresponding stage of a comparable community	at comparable moments throughout history

The diagrammatic formula for a *historical analogy* would be that another event is considered equivalent to the one at hand because it happened.

Let me use as a first set of examples a thematic similarity between Gandhi's autobiography and that of the most influential Chinese writer of roughly the same period, Lu Hsün (1881–1937).

The memory from Gandhi's youth most often quoted to anchor his spiritual and political style in his oedipal relation to his father is that of his father's death. This passage is often referred to as a "childhood memory," although Mohandas at the time was sixteen years old and was about to become a father himself. One night his father, whom the youth had nursed with religious passion, was fast sinking; but since a trusted uncle had just arrived, the son left the nursing care to him and went to his marital bedroom in order to satisfy his "carnal desire," and this despite his wife's being pregnant. After a while, however, somebody came to fetch him: The father had died in the uncle's arms—"a blot," Gandhi writes, "which I have never been able to efface or to forget." A few weeks later his wife aborted. This experience represents in Gandhi's life what, following Kierkegaard, I have come to call "the curse" in the lives of comparable innovators with a similarly precocious and relentless conscience. As such, it is no doubt what in clinical work we call a "cover memory"—that is, a roughly factual event that has come to symbolize in condensed form a complex of ideas, affects, and memories transmitted to adulthood, and to the next generation, as an "account to be settled."

This curse, it has been automatically concluded, must be heir to the Oedipus conflict. In Gandhi's case, the "feminine" service to the father would have served to deny the boyish wish of replacing the (aging) father in the possession of the (young) mother and the youthful intention to outdo him as a leader in later life. Thus, the pattern would be set for a style of leadership that can defeat a superior adversary only nonviolently and with the express intent of saving him as well as those whom he oppressed. Some of this interpretation corresponds to what Gandhi would have unhesitatingly acknowledged as his conscious intention.

Here is my second example: The writer Lu Hsün, often quoted with veneration by Mao, is the founding father of modern China's revolutionary literature. His famous short story "Diary of a Madman" (1918), the first literary work written in vernacular Chinese, is a masterpiece not only (we are told) in the power of its style, but (as we can see) as a very modern combination of a precise psychiatric description of paranoia (Lu Hsün had studied medicine in Japan) and a nightmarish allegory of the fiercer aspects of traditional and revolutionary China. Later in an essay entitled "Father's Illness," Lu Hsün again mixes a historical theme—namely, the discrepancy of Western and Confucian concepts concerning a man's last moments—with the ambivalent emotions of a son. He had spent much of his adolescent years searching for herbs that might cure his father. But now death was near.

Sometimes an idea would flash like lightning into my mind: Better to end the gasping faster. . . . And immediately I knew that the idea was improper; it was like committing a crime. But as at the same time I thought this idea rather proper, for I loved my father. Even now, I still think so.[18]

This is the Western doctor speaking; but at the time a Mrs. Yen, a kind of midwife for the departing soul, had suggested a number of magic transactions and had urged the son to scream into his father's ear, so he would not stop breathing.

"Father! Father!"

His face, which had quieted down, suddenly became tense. He opened his eyes slightly as if he felt something bitter and painful.

"Yell! Yell! Quick!"

"Father!"

"What? . . . Don't shout . . . don't . . ." he said in a low tone. Then he gasped frantically for breath. After a while, he returned to normal and calmed down.

"Father!" I kept calling him until he stopped breathing. Now I can still hear my own voice at that time. Whenever I hear it, I feel that this is the gravest wrong I have done to my father.

Lu Hsün was fifteen at the time (to Gandhi's sixteen). He, like Gandhi, had come from a line of high officials, whose fortunes were on the decline during the son's adolescence. At any rate, his story clearly suggests that in the lives of both men a desperate clinging to the dying father and a mistake made at the very last moment represented a curse overshadowing both past and future.

It is not enough, however, to reduce such a curse to the "Oedipus complex" as reconstructed in thousands of case histories as the primal complex of them all. The oedipal crisis, too, must be evaluated as part of man's overall development. It appears to be a constellation of dark preoccupations in a species that must live through a period of infantile dependence and steplike learning unequaled in the animal world, which develops a sensitive self-awareness in the years of immaturity, and which becomes aware of sexuality and procreation at a stage of childhood beset with irrational guilt. For the boy, to better the father (even if it is his father's most fervent wish that he do so) unconsciously means to replace him, to survive him means to kill him, to usurp his domain means to appropriate the mother, the "house," the "throne." No wonder that mankind's Maker is often experienced in the infantile image of every man's maker. But the oedipal crisis as commonly formulated is only the infantile or neurotic version of a *generational conflict* that derives from the fact that man experiences life and death—and past and future—in terms of the turnover of generations.

It is, in fact, rather probable that a highly uncommon man experiences filial conflicts with such inescapable intensity because he senses in himself already early in childhood some kind of originality that seems to point beyond the competition with the personal father. His is also an early conscience development that makes him feel (and appear) old while still young and maybe older in single-mindedness than his conformist parents who, in turn, may treat him somehow as their potential redeemer. Thus he grows up almost with an obligation (beset with guilt) to surpass and to originate at all cost. In adolescence this may prolong his identity confusion because he must find the one way in which he (and he alone!) can reenact the past and create a new future in the right medium at the right moment on a sufficiently large scale. His prolonged identity crisis, in turn, may invoke a premature generativity crisis that makes him accept as his concern a whole communal body, or mankind itself, and embrace as his dependents those weak in power, poor in possessions, and seemingly simple in heart. Such a deflection in life plan, however, can crowd out his chances for the enjoyment of intimacy, sexual and otherwise, wherefore the "great" are often mateless, friendless, and childless in the midst of veneration and by their example further confound the human dilemma of counterpointing the responsibility of procreation and individual existence.

But not all highly uncommon men are chosen; and the psychohistorical question is not only how such men come to experience the inescapability of an existential curse, but how it comes about that they have the pertinacity and the giftedness to reenact it in a medium communicable to their fellow men and meaningful in their stage of history. The emphasis here is on the word *reenactment,* which in such cases goes far beyond the dictates of a mere "repetition-compulsion," such as characterizes the unfreedom of symptoms and irrational acts. For the mark of a creative reenactment of a curse is that the joint experience of it all becomes a liberating event for each member of an awe-stricken audience. Some dim awareness of this must be the reason that the wielders of power in different periods of history appreciate and support the efforts of creative men to reenact the universal conflicts of mankind in the garb of the historical day, as the great dramatists have done and as the great autobiographers do. A political leader like Mao, then, may recognize a writer like Hsün not for any ideological oratory, but for his precise and ruthless presentation of the inner conflicts that must accompany the emergence of a revolutionary mind in a society as bound to filial piety as China. In a man like Gandhi the autobiographer and the leader are united in one person, but remain distinct in the differentiation of reenactments in writing and in action. In all reenactment, however, it is the transformation of an infantile curse into an adult deed that makes the man.

Common men, of course, gladly accept as saviors *pro tem* uncommon men who seem so eager to take upon themselves an accounting thus spared to others, and who by finding words for the nameless make it possible for the majority of men to live in the concreteness and safety of realities tuned to procreation, production, and periodic destruction.

All the greater, therefore, can be the chaos that "great" men leave behind and often experience in themselves in the years following their ascendance. For the new momentum, which they gave to their time, may now roll over them, or their power to provide further momentum may wane from fatigue and age. Uncommon men, too, ultimately can become common (and worse) by the extent to which their solution of a universal curse remains tied to its ontogenetic version. The author of "Dairy of a Madman" at the end of a career as revolutionary writer himself died in paranoid isolation as, in hindsight, one would expect of a man who, all his life, could hear his own voice yelling into his dying father's ear. And Gandhi, who could not forgive himself for having sought the warmth of his marital bed while his father was dying, in old age indulged in behavior that cost him many friends. In Lear-like fashion, he would wander through the tempest of communal riots, making local peace where nobody else could and yet knowing that he was losing the power to keep India united. It was then that the widower wanted his "daughter" close (he had never had a daughter of his own) and asked some of his women followers to warm his shivering body at night. This "weakness" the septuagenarian explained as a test of his strength of abstinence, opening himself wide to cheap gossip. This story, too, will have to be retold in terms of life cycle and history.

What was once united by the power of charisma cannot fall apart without exploding into destructive furor in the leader or in the masses or in both. Here life history ends, and history begins in its sociological and political aspects. How a leader survives himself and how an idea survives a man, how the community absorbs him and his idea, and how the sense of wider identity created by his presence survives the limitations of his person and of the historical moment— these are matters that the psychohistorian cannot approach without the help of the sociologist in tradition-building and institution-forming. He, in turn, may want to consider the "metabolism" of generations and the influence of a leader's or an elite's image on the life stages of the led: Kennedy's rise and sudden death certainly would provide a modern model for such a study.

To return once more to my original interest in Gandhi: I have indicated what I have learned since about his personal idiosyncrasies as well as about his power of compromise. If some say that his ascendance was unfortunate for an India in desperate need of modernization, I cannot see who else in his time could have brought the vast backward mass of Indians closer to the tasks of this century. As for his lasting influence, I will endeavor to describe in a book his strategy (as enfolded in the Event) of challenging man's latent capacity for militant and disciplined nonviolence: In this, he will survive. In the meantime, I, for one, see no reason to decide whether he was a saint or a politician—a differentiation meaningless in the Hindu tradition of combining works and renunciation—for his life is characterized by an ability to derive existential strength, as well as political power, from the very evasion of all job specifications. In interviewing his old friends, however, I found ample affirmation of his agile and humorous presence, probably the most inclusive sign of his (or anybody's) simultaneous mastery of inner and outer events. And it is in his humor that Gandhi has been compared to Saint Francis. Luther understood such things even if he could not live them; and at least his sermons formulate unforgettably the centrality in space, the immediacy in time, and the wholeness in feeling that lead to such singular "events" as survive in parables—a form of enactment most memorable through the ages, although, or maybe just because, most effortless and least "goal-directed." Now a man has to be dead for quite a while before one can know what parables might survive him: In Gandhi's case, one can only say that the "stuff" for parables is there. Let me, in conclusion, compare two well-known scenes from the lives of Gandhi and Saint Francis.

Teasing was a gift and a habit with Gandhi throughout his life, and elsewhere I have pointed out the affinity of teasing to nonviolence.[19] It was after the great Salt March (he had been arrested again, and while he was in jail, his *Satyagrahas* had been brutally attacked by the police) that Gandhi was invited to talks with the Viceroy. Churchill scoffed at the "seditious fakir, striding half-naked up the steps of the Viceroy's palace, to negotiate with the representative of the King-Emperor." But the Viceroy, Lord Irwin, himself described the meeting as "the most dramatic personal encounter between a Viceroy and an Indian leader." When Gandhi was handed a cup of tea, he asked to be given a cup of hot water instead, into which he poured a bit of salt (tax-free) out of a small paper bag hidden in his shawl and remarked smilingly: "To remind us of the famous Boston Tea Party."

If we choose to insist on the symbolic meaning of salt and would see in his gesture a disguised act of masculine defiance—so be it. But such meaning would be totally absorbed in the overall artfulness with which personal quirk (Gandhi would not touch tea) is used for the abstention from and yet ceremonial participation in the important act of sharing tea at the palace, and yet also for the reenactment of a historical defiance, pointedly reminding his host of the time when the British taxed another invigorating substance and lost some colonies which, in independence, did rather well.

Whatever combination of overt and hidden meanings were enacted here in unison, the analogy that comes to mind is a scene from St. Francis' life, when he was asked for dinner to his bishop's palace. A place on the bishop's right was reserved for the ethereal rebel, and the guests were seated along well-decked tables. But Brother Francesco was late. Finally, he appeared with a small sack, out of which he took little pieces of dry dark bread and with his usual dancing gestures put one beside each guest's plate. To the bishop, who protested that there was plenty of food in the house, he explained that for *this* bread he had *begged* and that, therefore, it was consecrated food. Could there be a more delicate and yet finite lesson in Christianity?

The two scenes bespeak an obvious similarity in tone, and artfulness; but in order to make them true analogies, comparison is not enough. Other lifelong similarities in the two men could be enumerated and their respective tasks in their respective empires compared. Gandhi was no troubadour saint, but a tough activist as well as an enactor of poetic moments; and he was a strategist as well as a prayerful man. All this only points to the psychohistorian's job of specifying in all their complementarity the inner dynamics as well as the social conditions which make history seem to repeat, to renew, or to surpass itself.[20]

NOTES

[1] Erik H. Erikson, "The Nature of Clinical Evidence," in Daniel Lerner (ed.), *Evidence and Inference* (Glencoe, Ill.: Free Press, 1959); revised and enlarged in *Insight and Responsibility* (New York: Norton, 1964).

[2] Erik H. Erikson, *Young Man Luther* (New York: Norton 1958).

[3] Sigmund Freud, "An Autobiographical Study," *The Complete Works of Sigmund Freud* (London: Hogarth, 1959), p. 40.

[4] Erik H. Erikson, "Gandhi's Autobiography: The Leader as a Child," *The American Scholar* (Autumn 1966).

[5] Mahadav Desai, *A Righteous Struggle* (Ahmedabad).

[6] M. K. Gandhi, *An Autobiography* (Ahmedabad, 1927), Part 5, chaps. 20–22.

[7] An old Indian friend recounted to me an event taken almost for granted in those early days—namely, how young Vinoba Bhave (the man who in all these years has come and remained closest to Gandhi in spirit, style, and stature) sat by the *Ashram* grounds and a big and poisonous snake crawled under his shawl. He kept lovingly still, and another Ashramite quietly folded up the garment and took it to the riverbank.

[8] L. Fischer, *The Life of Mahatma Gandhi* (New York: Harper, 1950), p. 238.

[9] Gandhi, *An Autobiography,* Part 4, chap. 11.

[10] Sigmund Freud and William C. Bullitt, *Thomas Woodrow Wilson: Twenty-Eighth President of the United States—A Psychological Study* (Boston: Houghton Mifflin, 1967).

[11] Erik H. Erikson, *The New York Review of Books,* VII, 2 (1967); also *The International Journal of Psycho-Analysis* 3, XLVII (1967).

[12] "Psychoanalysis and Ongoing History: Problems of Identity, Hatred, and Non-Violence," *Journal of the American Psychiatric Association* (1965).

[13] S. A. Wolpert, *Tilak and Gokhale* (Berkeley: University of California Press, 1961).

[14] *Collected Works of Mahatma Gandhi* (Ahmedabad).

[15] Victor Wolfenstein, *The Revolutionary Personality* (Princeton, N.J.: Princeton University Press, 1967).

[16] Ernest Jones, *Essays in Applied Psychoanalysis* (London, 1951), Vol. 2.

[17] Robert Lifton, *Death in Life: Survivors of Hiroshima* (New York: Random House, 1967).

[18] Translated by Leo O. Lee for my seminar at Harvard from *Lu Hsün ch'üan-chi* (*Complete Works of Lu Hsün*) (Peking, 1956), Vol. II, pp. 261–62.

[19] Erik H. Erikson, "Gandhi's Autobiography: The Leader as a Child."

[20] This paper was presented in outline to the American Academy's Group for the Study of Psycho-Historical Processes at Wellfleet, Massachusetts, in 1966.

ERIKSON'S SEARCH FOR GANDHI

Robert Coles

In his study of Gandhi, Erik Erikson reveals his multifaceted past—clinician, psychoanalyst, case historian, life historian—and throws fresh light not only on his subject but also on the method of inquiry.

Sometimes in one paper a gifted scholar or writer who has written many papers or essays and a few books too comes up with a quiet and unselfconscious but pointed summary of his various interests, involvements, and ideas. Not that the author really means such a summary, and not that his essay or paper is all that comprehensive; but the hints and implications and allusions are there, and if they were all pursued the richness of a particular mind's life would be realized. I am thinking of Thomas Mann's essay, "Fantasy on Goethe," written late in life by a novelist who much earlier wrote *The Beloved Returns.* Mann's essay (like his novel) tells a lot about Goethe—but just as much about the author of *Buddenbrooks and Doctor Faustus* and *The Magic Mountain,* not to mention other essays on Goethe and on Germany, the nation whose language Goethe used, in company with Schiller and Wagner and Freud—Mann also wrote about them—and in company with Erik Erikson, who was working on *Young Man Luther,* a book about yet another German, when Thomas Mann died in 1955.

I believe Erikson's paper on Gandhi to be an achievement very much comparable to Mann's essay on Goethe. The paper was written presumably in late 1967 or early 1968 for the American Academy of Arts and Sciences; and the paper was part of a series of "studies in leadership," each one of which struggled with one of the central riddles of history: Who becomes the leader and in fact what is it that makes a leader after all? Many of the other studies (all published in the Summer 1968 issue of *Daedalus*) rely heavily on Erikson's work—and not only *Young Man Luther,* but the analysis of Hitler's imagery and Gorki's youth in *Childhood and Society,* and the brief but brilliant (come to think of it, very Shavian) analysis of George Bernard Shaw that first appeared in "Identity and the Life Cycle"—and at just the right moment in that monograph. But now Erikson, in a paper on Gandhi, seems called upon to look back on his own extraordinary career—yes, a career that has gradually supplied leadership to a generation of psychiatrists and psychoanalysts, and of late not a few historians or political scientists. Right off, for instance, we are reminded that "about a decade ago, when I first participated in a *Daedalus* discussion. I represented one wing of the clinical arts and sciences in a symposium on 'Evidence and Inference.' " Then, for several introductory pages the reader is given a quick but careful and constantly suggestive look at Erikson's professional past—as a clinician, a psychoanalyst, a man interested not only in case histories but life histories, and particularly the life histories of men like Martin Luther, who in turn make history.

Some powerful and touching things come forth in this first section of the paper, all the more powerful and touching because they are not forced upon the

Reprinted from *International Journal of Psychiatry,* 7 (July, 1969), 477–83.

reader, not made part of a lecture or a series of dogmatic assertions but really (and simply, and, of course, not so simply) *told*, told the way a good narrator, or perhaps a historian with a writer's sensibility, manages to tell, to get a whole lot of ideas and thoughts (yes, and difficult concepts) across without making the effort seem dull and exhausting—or, above all, banal. In a part of a sentence, for instance, the psychoanalyst and the historian are brought precisely and appropriately together in a way that long, heavy essays, even books, could not improve upon: ". . . for he [the historian] like the clinician, must serve the curious process by which selected portions of the past impose themselves on our renewed awareness and claim continued actuality in our contemporary commitments." Then, in an equally strong and evocative way we are asked to think of the struggle that patients make—and that with them their psychoanalysts also make—as something restorative and redemptive, as an achievement that cannot be measured in numbers and percentages, but has to do with "a semblance of wholeness, immediacy, and mutuality."

There he is, a scholar all right, writing in a journal issued by the American Academy of Arts and Sciences; and a psychoanalyst all right, able a few paragraphs later to give exact and well-rounded meaning to terms like "resistance" and "transference" and "countertransference"—yet, at the same time, someone rather more, someone willing to use psychology as Kierkegaard once did, as more recently Buber and Tillich did when they insisted that we all have a right to need and want more than a strict and supposedly "value-free"—is it really possible?—confrontation with our own "psychodynamics." We do indeed need to understand ourselves, become conscious of our mind's deviousness, of the hurt and sorrow and anger that we have known and forgotten and actually, ironically, never, never forgotten. But we also need to find ourselves become intact, feel life fully, and share what we feel and do with others. As Erikson keeps on emphasizing—here and in other papers and indeed books—we have to do something with our problems and tensions and anxieties; we have to put the past to use, as well as meet up with it and analyze it; we have to make history as well as "take" histories (as doctors) or learn about them as patients; and to get just the slightest bit dramatic, we have to find our destiny—which turns out to be more than the sum of a series of conflicts in the case of men like Luther and Gandhi, and in the case of more "ordinary" men too.

Gandhi certainly found his destiny in the course of a reasonably long lifetime, and Erikson follows his brief discussion of the assumptions psychoanalysts make about the human mind with an equally brief but significant reference to the repeated intersection of his own life with that of Gandhi's. In the early 1960s Professor and Mrs. Erikson went to Ahmedabad to lecture on the life cycle and indeed compare their ideas about life's way of unfolding with those of Hindu scholars and religious leaders. In Ahmedabad the Eriksons stayed in the guest house of a mill owner. But it so happened that this mill owner was a very special one: He had been Gandhi's opponent in the Ahmedabad textile strike of 1918, an event that marked the beginning of the trade union movement in India and an event that enabled Gandhi to test the meaing of and develop (in himself and in others) a capacity for *Satyagraha*, which is both a philosophy and a plan of action, and which aims itself at the powerful as well as the weak, the conqueror and the conquered, each of whom is considered somehow (given a demonstration of perseverence and faith and charity and unremitting, unbowed good will) responsive to ethical principles. "It came back to me only gradually," says Erikson of his first stay in Ahmedabad "(for I had known it when I was young) that this was the city in which Gandhi lived for more than a decade and a half and that it was this mill owner and his sister (both now in their seventies) to whom Gandhi pays high and repeated tribute in his autobiography."

The Eriksons were fortunate enough to meet the brother and sister, and apparently also felt very much touched by something else, perhaps Gandhi's spirit, still very much around, or perhaps their own memories of what Gandhi the leader did —not only for India but the entire world, many of whose two billion or so people still live in subjugation (even in so-called democracies) and still struggle for a greater degree of social and political freedom. Perhaps something else was at work too—and Erikson more or less suggests that was the case; I mean to say, perhaps the man who wrote *Young Man Luther* found in Ahmedabad not only reminders of yet another great moral and religious leader, but even access to people who saw and took part in an important historical moment, and seemed ready at least for a conversation or two with a psychoanalyst who tactfully finds a great deal of psychological significance in man's political deeds and ethical struggles.

"Enter then the psycho-historian," Erikson says as he announces this twofold (at least) intent to examine at once a series of deeds and the purposes of a man who gave those deeds a rather momentous quality—they were, in fact, forerunners to India's first nationwide episode of civil disobedience, after which the lawyer and sometimes agitator Mohandas K. Gandhi became India's great Mahatma, that is, in the eyes of millions, high-minded and of high soul beyond all other human beings. Ten years later Gandhi himself had written about that strike in Ahmedabad, so Erikson could fall back on the Mahatma's recollections as well as his own observations as a psychoanalyst really out in the "field"—in this case, half-way across the world, in a nation full of uncertainty and terrible misery and enormous pride and the grandest (as well as most awful) kinds of contradictions.

How does this psychohistorian (it can be argued the world's first and foremost one) go about his business? What does he "do" with Gandhi's memories of the Ahmedabad strike, or in fact with his hosts, who it turned out became his informants? For one thing, Gandhi's words are not seized upon, then single-mindedly analyzed and interpreted *on their own*. Instead it is asked (and we are told) what circumstances prompted the Mahatma to write down his thoughts and memories, for which readers, and in what literary form. "One is almost embarrassed to point out what seems so obvious," Erikson shyly begins—but then goes on to remind us how far behind we have all too often left the obvious: ". . . in perusing a man's memoirs for the purpose of reconstructing past moments and reinterpreting pervasive motivational trends, one must first ask oneself at what age and under what general circumstances the memoirs were written, what their intended purpose was, and what form they assumed. Surely all this would have to be known before one can proceed to judge the less conscious motivations. . . ." Sadly, not all psychoanalytic studies of writers or statesmen have demonstrated that kind of caution, breadth of vision, or plain good sense.

In Gandhi's autobiographical writings Erikson finds plenty of evidence that on the occasion of the Ahmedabad strike, and at other times too, the great Indian leader struggled valiantly with a number of contradictions: his larger desire to lead the poor and help them achieve the justice they needed; his particular relationship with the mill owner and his sister, who were generous and kind people (to Gandhi, but also to others), however rich and powerful they were; his sense of moral outrage as a true revolutionary hero, and his quiet need for the friendship and affection of those he knew well and liked; his tough, fighting spirit and his gentleness, his coyness, his playfulness, his desire to be approved and applauded and found lovable.

(Did not Gandhi spend the better part of his life trying to win over those he at some time defied and resisted and thwarted and drove to anger and despair?)

Gandhi rarely failed to take careful stock of his friends and enemies, who were often enough hard to tell apart, if his actions were to be the means of doing so. Erikson has no illusions that a Mahatma such as Gandhi would have failed to anticipate an effort to make something unpleasant out of all that autobiographical writing. So, in a paper subtitled "In Search of Gandhi" one comes across these rather ironic words: "Nobody likes to be found out, not even one who has made ruthless confession a part of his profession. Any autobiographer, therefore, at least between the lines, spars with his reader and potential judge." Of course, the whole point of Erikson's paper is to show exactly what that sparring is all about—why great men say and write the things they do (with posterity as well as a given moment very much in mind) and why those who make it their "business to reveal what others do, or may *not* know about themselves" come to some of their conclusions and make their record for future readers to see and think about. Erikson willingly challenges himself and no doubt brings up short any number of *his* readers by quoting what Gandhi had to say about those he knew would be waiting for his every word: "If some busy-body were to cross-examine me on the chapters which I have now written, he could probably shed more light on them, and if it were a hostile critic's cross-examination, he might even flatter himself for having shown up the hollowness of many of my pretensions."

Erikson admits to the "sting" he felt when he came across those words of Gandhi, but there is no evidence in this essay of his that a "search" for India's great man has ever given way to an assault upon him. Rather, Gandhi's generous, kind, and humorous side, yes, and his introspective side, come out again and again in this analysis by his Western biographer. As a matter of fact, at no time are we allowed to forget just that: Erik Erikson is a man of Europe and America, a psychoanalyst, a student of Freud's, a man born in the twentieth century and not the nineteenth; Gandhi was obviously different in many of those very respects that make up a significant part of (if the reader will excuse the expression) Erikson's *identity*. Nor will Erikson let the matter drop there. Indeed his purpose is to spell out such matters as carefully and thoughtfully as possible so that, for instance, we will not have to suffer yet again the absurd and insensitive and even malicious spectacle that goes under the name of "psychological study" of Woodrow Wilson, done by those supposed collaborators William Bullitt and Sigmund Freud.

In the middle of the paper Freud and Gandhi are actually brought together, and, at the same time, in a touching and revealing yet restrained way, the man who would do so in 1968 (and in 1969 at much greater length, by means of the book *Gandhi's Truth*) also tells us about himself—and, which is the whole point, tells us how important it is that a biographer have some sense of why and how he has come to seek out a particular historical figure. So, a discussion of Freud's ill-fated but instructive "relationship" with Mr. Bullit is followed by this: "Freud's example leads me back to the days when I first heard of Gandhi and of Ahmedabad and maybe even of the mill owner—all of which remained latent until, at the time of my visit, it 'came back to me' almost sensually in the occasional splendor and the pervasive squalor of India." Then follows an account of his youth, his memory of Romain Rolland's *Gandhi,* and eventually his decision to study the Mahatma's life—and in a way, of all ironies, learn more about *Freud* as well as Gandhi by so doing. After all, psychoanalysts say over and over again that we all can profit from being seen "objectively," which means being seen by someone who is distant and "uninvolved" enough to be able to take stock of things with reasonable accuracy. I believe that much of Erikson's work implicitly does this: by going out and getting to know American Indians, by getting a sense of men like Gorki or Shaw or Luther or Gandhi, and by always bringing them to Freud and Freud to them, psychoanalysis is given the wider and more "objective" historical and cultural context it deserves. The point then is not "merely to 'apply' to Gandhi what . . . is learned from Freud." Rather, there is something human (I suppose the word today is "existential") that transcends from time to time even the classes and castes and regions and cultures and continents and races that social scientists make so much of, as indeed they must, so long as they remember all that is meant by and hinted at throughout this astonishing, I would say—aware, I believe, of the word's significance—*revelatory* passage:

Great contemporaries, in all their grandiose one-sidedness, converge as much as they diverge; and it is not enough to characterize one with the methods of the other. As Freud once fancied he might become a political leader, so Gandhi thought of going into medicine. All his life Gandhi ran a kind of health institute, and Freud founded an international organization with the ideological and economic power of a movement. But both men came to revolutionize man's awareness of his wayward instinctuality and to meet it with a combination of militant intelligence—and nonviolence. Gandhi pointed a way to the "conquest of violence in its external and manifest aspect and, in the meantime, chose to pluck out the sexuality that offended him. Freud, in studying man's repressed sexuality, also revealed the internalized violence of self-condemnation, but thought externalized violent strife to be inevitable. And both men, being good post-Darwinians, blamed man's instinctuality on his animal ancestry—Gandhi calling man a sexual "brute" and Freud comparing his viciousness (to his own kind!) to that of wolves. Since then ethology has fully described the intrinsic discipline of animal behavior and most impressively (in this context) the pacific rituals by which some social animals— yes, even wolves—"instinctively" prevent senseless murder.

If those comparisons of Freud and Gandhi represent an almost exquisite distillation of a long, systematic inquiry, both psychoanalytic and historical in nature, there are other aspects of the paper that are no less memorable. Erikson is forthright, yet courteous and discreet, when he records his impressions of his informants, and like Gandhi, he can resort to a kind of humor that a phrase unmasks a million pretenses and stupidities, as for example: "And here I had witness: the survivors of a generation of then young men and women who had joined or met Gandhi in 1918 and whose life (as the saying goes) had not been the same since, *as if one knew what it might have been*" (italics mine). Or again: "The interviewee, not being a client, does not break a contract with either himself or the interviewer in not telling the whole truth as he knows it or feels it. He has, in fact, every right to be preoccupied with the intactness of his historical role rather than with fragmented details as patients and psychotherapists are—often to a fault." Speaking later on about that interviewee, the mill owner who was Gandhi's onetime (and only somewhat) antagonist, Erikson says this: 'When he asked me after our first interview what, if anything, I had learned, I could only say truthfully that I had gotten an idea of what Gandhi had been up against with him and he with Gandhi."

There is more, much more to this essay, in many respects one of the most important Erikson has ever written. A whole book is foreshadowed, and hopefully a whole profession taught how to go about its business with a little more intelligence and dignity. As always, Erikson shuns glib alternatives and easy categories. He makes gandhi neither a saint nor a politician—"a differentiation meaningless in the Hindu tradition of combining works and renunciation." Though Gandhi was no

St. Francis he was enough of one. Erikson compares both him and Freud to the Mahatma, and it is helpful in this century, when all people on this planet desperately need to come together and be healed and be part of something larger than this nation or that alliance, that a Western saint and a Western scientist and an Eastern Mahatma are shown not all that different.

And finally, for psychiatrists all over the world, not to mention their sometimes uncritical followers in various other disciplines, Gandhi's thought and deeds are looked at very instructively: "The psychoanalyst, it seems, makes a family affair out of any historical event. Does anybody, we may ask, ever escape his internalized folk and learn to deal with the case of his adult life on its own terms?" Erikson has been trying to answer that question for many years, by both doing the analysis that has to be (and ought to be done) done but stopping also to smile and make room for—well, for a lot of things: accident, mystery, grace, the turns and twists of all those individual destinies and collective "forces" that make up something called "history." No wonder, then, that Gandhi's march to the Arabian Sea, his effort to ridicule the British law that taxed salt, get such a careful but also delightfully humorous (and Gandhian) treatment from Erikson. Some analysts have declared that salt sybolizes semen, and that Gandhi's protest, including his refusal to use the condiment at all, had something to do with "sexuality" and "orality" and "regression." Neither Ernest Jones (who wrote about such psychoanalytic things) nor Victor Wolfenstein (who as a political scientist and biographer of Gandhi gives Jones's ideas a good deal of credence) are denied their right to be taken very seriously. Yet, Gandhi was a shrewd politician waging a very real struggle against very real injustices, including an outrageous and concrete and very unfair tax, a tax on salt, which millions of poor people both needed and couldn't afford. Therefore, ". . . before we ask how salt may come to mean semen, it is only fair to state that through the ages it has had a powerful significance as itself." And anyway: "The one way symbolization suggested in psychoanalysis, by which the nonsexual always symbolizes the sexual, is grounded in the assumption that the erotic is more central to infantile and primitive experience than are the cognitive and the nutritional. . . . But in the immediate context of the chronic semistarvation that has undermined the vitality of the Indian masses and considering the periodic threat of widespread death by famine, it would seem appropriate to assume, first of all, that salt means salt." Moreover, when Gandhi decided to lead the Salt March, ". . . he was obviously in command of his political and economic as well as his psychological wits." Indeed, ". . . in any context except that of irrationality clearly attributable to sexual repression, one should take any interpretation that explains a human act by recourse to sexual symbolism with a grain of salt."

Perhaps the point is a little overworked, but if so there is every cause. There comes a time when ideas become dogmas, and dogmas mercilessly and foolishly pronounced upon everyone and everything. Like others in our part of the world who have struggled to fashion new thoughts, new values, new ethical principles, Gandhi tried hard to take what was valuable in the Hindu scriptures and give it all a new life. In the opening passages of the *Gita* he saw a summons to *Satyagraha,* a summons he wanted others as well as himself to heed. It may well be that Erik Erikson has brought not only Gandhi's truth to life, but as well Freud's truth—for all too long the claimed property of any great man's worst (if most seductive) enemy, the tireless sycophants who also, alas, are part of history's story.

HISTORY AND PSYCHOANALYSIS

Robert S. Liebert

Erikson focuses on the ego synthesis of Gandhi as a leader—and of leadership in general. Applying the ego synthesis principle to current protests and dissatisfaction, the question arises as to where the ego deficiency lies—in institutions or in the activists.

History and psychoanalysis share the mutual goal of enabling us to understand human behavior in terms of the past. Twentieth-century historians have undertaken their reconstruction within the framework of sociological and economic theory in the main, largely ignoring that aspect of human behavior that is the manifestation of unconscious conflicts and the reworking of repressed impulses. Psychoanalytic theory is complex and part-time students, with no clinical experience, almost always employ it ineffectually. On the other hand, judging from the psychoanalytic literature, those who are proficient at the study of psychodynamics and the vicissitudes of the flow of psychic energy almost always focus on the microcosm of the single individual (and usually, following the medical model, an individual with psychopathology). The currents of economic, political, and social forces in which the single human being swirls are indeed complicated and with few exceptions, have been treated as confusing extra dimensions that are better off assigned to other disciplines, thereby preserving the elegance of the psychoanalytical model. In addition, the more private motivations of the individual members of these two groups of scholars, which separate them in preference in intellectual orientation, are institutionalized in the kinds of creative effort that are respected and rewarded within each of the disciplines.

In this remarkable essay, Professor Erikson moves back and forth over this seldom-traveled bridge between the lands staked out for themselves by the historians and by the psychoanalysts. Some future psychohistorian may well ask what enabled Erik Erikson to accomplish this, when most others floundered badly? One part of the answer, of course, resides in the realm of personal history and ego synthesis of Professor Erikson, as individual. However, in considering his creative contribution, Erikson as man cannot be separated from the needs that have become manifest at this phase of the evolution of the psychoanalytic movement—needs that grow out of the relationship of psychoanalytic insight to the sociopolitical nature of the times. Further, Erikson is concerned with the psychology of leadership at a time that many of us are increasingly concerned with the kind of leadership that emerges out of the political system in this country.

Erikson, who has been the leading theorist of the processes of adolescence and young adulthood as developmental stages, must also sense the increasing disenchantment of the youth of today with psychoanalysis. As they turn away from the arduous search for understanding their internal dynamics, to the search for their role in changing a society in deep trouble, psychoanalysis is to them diminishing in relevance. This is reflected in the progressively decreasing number of people

Reprinted from *International Journal of Psychiatry,* 7 (July, 1969), 484–87.

entering psychiatry who are interested, or at least, enthusiastic about psychoanalytic training. The question looms—can psychoanalysis clarify the issues that concern those who are actively dissatisfied with the state of the world and are interested in social change, or will it be useful primarily only as a therapeutic instrument and science of psychopathology?

Erikson casts light on the relationship between the crisis of the community and the crisis of the individual. Among the qualities in Erikson's orientation that might be noted as facilitating his success, perhaps most prominent is his emphasis on the ego actuality of the men who have succeeded in altering the course of their fellow-men's lives. Psychoanalysis developed out of the study of the maladaptive behavior of disturbed people, and, at times, we tend to view all unusual behavior through a psychopathological frame of reference. The laws of intrapsychic operation are applicable to all acts of leadership and political activism, but a concurrent determination must also be made as to nature and degree of pathology in the society, that the leader or activist is struggling to change, before certain judgments can be made regarding the health of the ego governing the political behavior. The emphasis in the essay is not focused on the regressive conflicts in Gandhi's behavior, although Erikson is aware of the forms and places in which they exert their influence. Rather, what is emphasized is the distinctive quality that enables leaders, in their public behavior, to change their world. It is the unique capacity of their ego to perceive external conditions and communal needs rationally and realistically and to integrate these perceptions with adaptive, original forms of action that happen also to fulfill the unconscious aims of the leader's life. A separation must be made by the psychohistorian in treating the great man as "homo politicus," and in his nonpolitical areas of life. With such men we may tease out all kinds of behavior that are symptomatic of neurotic and even psychotic processes at work, as, for example, in aspects of Gandhi's marriage. But in dealing with Gandhi in his role of leader, the presentation is not in terms of the more traditional formulation of compulsively patterned reenactments of the product of instinctual and intrafamilial vectors. Gandhi's harnessing and guiding the energies of the community by actions attuned to the communally felt needs is appreciated as healthy virtue. The discussion of the meaning of Gandhi's Salt-*Satyagraha,* when contrasted with Wolfenstein's more orthodox interpretation, illustrates this point. This approach is of importance in the current crisis of the social relevance of psychoanalysis, and it is at this point in the essay that Erikson states: "In fact, the further development of psychoanalysis will have to help us understand the symbolic representation not only of repressed sexuality, but also of the ever-present and yet so blatantly denied fact of death in us and around us. If reason will not suffice, then new forms of irrational violence will force us to consider the consequences of . . . the super-weaponry poised all around him to destroy the world he knows."

This issue of what level of psychic operation is causal is particularly timely because it is addressed regularly in the general sociopolitical literature that utilizes psychoanalytically derived motivational explanations for what is primarily political behavior. I am thinking here, for example, of conflicting views of the current student protest movement, an area of particular interest to me. It involves a significant segment of the youth challenging established authority, and often attempting to overthrow the current form and people in authority at the most immediate institution in their lives—their university. This raises an important question—is this radical protest the acting out of unsatisfactorily resolved psychodynamic conflicts in an essentially pathological way, or, is this rational action growing out of an accurate perception that the existing institutions and political processes provided for reform are incapable of correcting gross inequities and injustices of the society? Is this the primal horde rising to destroy the father, or behavior governed by a healthy flexible executive ego? Where are the superego lacunae—in the mainstream of society or the activists? I am setting up arbitrary and somewhat artificial poles, although there are authors who champion each of these explanations exclusively. Rather, radical action attracts to it students varying widely in both motivations and strength of psychological integration. This is reflected in a spectrum of political behavior from "idealistic" radicalism to "nihilistic" radicalism.

In understanding the "immediacy" and relatively "uncompromising" quality of today's radical and militant demands and tactics, Erikson serves well as a conceptual guide. The nonviolent technique, *Satyagraha,* of Gandhi not only creatively expressed and integrated themes of Gandhi's life, but ignited his followers because of the common circumstances and congruence of needs in their mutually related destinies at that period in history. The method and philosophy of mobilizing the "forces of truth and peace in the oppressor as well as the oppressed" has exerted seminal influence on the labor movement, civil rights movement, and antiwar movements until the past two or three years.

The change now, the abandoning of the techniques of Gandhi—and Gandhi influenced leaders such as Martin Luther King—by both large masses of black students and white radicals, is reflected in a different rhetoric, style, and timing that is a function of the very different nature of the formative psychosocial years for these "post-Hiroshima" youth. It becomes actualized in the face of contemporary events—the continuing war in Asia, the failure of the integrated civil rights movement, cities burning, and assassinations.

As Robert Jay Lifton, in the tradition of Erikson, has articulated, nuclear death means annihilation of life on earth, a barring of all paths to symbolic immortality. Thus, we are all faced with the possibility of sudden and absolute "termination." Depending on one's age, this historic event and ever-present threat has been integrated differently, at a particular developmental stage. To the youth of today, the age at which the threat of nuclear annihilation was assimilated, made it resolvable only by repression, denial, and isolation of effect. Yet, it emerges in multiple behavioral forms, among which student activism—black and white—is one adaptive resolution. We are witnessing new forms of individual character organization and ego integration—forms shaped by and consonant with the times. We are faced with the challenge of whether a science founded on the study of maladaptive behavior can be of service to us in understanding such contemporary social and political group behavior. This has been most successfully accomplished in the past in the study of historic mass pyschopathology as, for example, in Martin Wangh's penetrating study of the German genocide of Jews.

In pursuing this challenge, we are indebted to Professor Erikson, not only for his encouraging us to abandon the concept of a timeless fixity of character structure and to view "identity" as a changing, dynamic process related to changing historical forces. Erikson is not alone, or even the originator, in this. But, in picking the exceptional individual, the leader, and in then showing how that man uses his life history to resonate with his times, he advances our understanding of aspects of the most creative form of healthy ego functioning—social generativity. He brings the individual to history and history to the individual in a model that will stimulate all who endeavor to unravel the complexities of man's incredible sociopolitical behavior.

NOTES ON THE SCOPE OF THE PSYCHOHISTORICAL APPROACH

Frederick Wyatt

Psychoanalysis and history are relevant to each other, and a psychohistorical approach is valid. However, the limitations on one's mastery of universal knowledge impose a serious liability on the psychohistorical approach. An asset of the approach is that it deals with time completed and not with ongoing life, and can therefore test its conclusions against the chain of events.

Before setting out in search of Gandhi, Professor Erikson explains not only his purpose but also his own vantage point in discussing a significant event in the life of his notable subject. He defines his position by reflecting on the parallels in the intricate relationship between the historian and his subject on the one hand, and the psychotherapist and his patient on the other. This is as it should be, especially when interpretation—the endeavor of organizing the data of individual, or collective, history into a meaningful and plausible pattern—is concerned. It should be natural, therefore, to extend this principle to those who have been invited to comment on Erikson's undertaking. As a member of the Group for Psychohistorical Process I was there when he first presented his study of Gandhi. I found myself then, as on previous occasions, in accord with his ideas on the nature of psychohistorical evidence. The distance that time and the relegation to the printed word normally interpose have given me no reason to revise this opinion in any significant respect. It should not distract from the laudable aim of the *International Journal of Psychiatry* to make us clarify our common intellectual concerns by prompting us to critical debate, if I define my own purpose as *critical* only in the broadest sense of the term. Not being a historian, let alone a specialist on modern Indian history, I am not equipped to judge the specifically historical premises of Erikson's study. His discussion of the conditions governing the application of the principles of psychoanalytic psychology to historical studies I find exemplary. It points to all the elements of the psychohistorical approach, its inherent demands, its scope, and its equally inherent uncertainties. My purpose will, therefore, be to elaborate further on some questions in the psychological, and especially the psychoanalytic, approach to historical research.

Erikson's argument is anchored in the parallel between "historical" material emerging in an autobiography, such as Gandhi's, and similar events in a therapeutic session. The relevance of such an incident is obviously not limited to its own manifest claim to meaning—that which it seems to declare in ordinary language. Neither is it sufficiently understood if to the manifest any latent metaphorical significance is added merely by extrapolation. In either instance the relevance of the emerging idea needs to be examined in context and, usually, in more than one. One such context is that of the on-going present and its engagements, the other that of the factual as well as the metaphorical and analogical relationship of remember-

Reprinted from *International Journal of Psychiatry*, 7 (July, 1969), 488–92.

ing—its subject as well as the act itself—to the reporter's past. Another context is that of his social group, his society and culture, and their enduring and acute concerns. Finally, still another context comes from his relationship, conscious or not, to the person, or the people—Gandhi's Indian Youth, for instance—to whom he is reporting. It would be a poor therapeutic explanation if it limited itself to the manifest meaning of such an incident, and it would still have to be questioned if it did no more than invoke, by deduction, one of its universal analogical references, such as that to the Oedipus complex, or, as in a later example, to salt. The analogical spread of meaning issuing from resistance and its resolution in therapy usually contains the potential for pursuing the threads, that is, the drift of meaning in the ineffable coherence of the life history, along the several dimensions mentioned before. The observer-therapist needs but the will to do so, the requisite skills, and the necessary *Denkformen,* or concepts. The historical personality, no less than the history of any individual in this sense, can be properly understood only after the appropriate categories have become available. Common sense alone and the perennial popular psychology of household assumptions and time-honored clichés on which historians so often rely will not do the trick.

The argument of the traditional historian that the approaches of psychology are not germane to his purpose is as specious as the argument of the traditional psychoanalyst that social and historical contexts are not relevant for his understanding of motivation and conduct. History is nothing if not the conduct of individuals, molded and directed by the social system under whose push and pull they find themselves acting. History, inevitably, *is* psychology and sociology, and it is hard to imagine how this can be seriously doubted. Nor can psychoanalytic psychology hope to understand the conduct of individuals if it limits itself to a narrow, "monadic" concept of individual motivation, restricting itself to an ultraindividualistic, intraindividual schema of "instincts and their vicissitudes," disregarding the perfectly obvious disposition even of classical psychodynamic theory. Erikson's life work has shown this clearly enough.

The question is rather, how much the historian is willing to recognize this condition and if he does, how he will manage approaches for which he has not been trained. This applies, of course, just as much to the psychoanalyst who is not familiar with method and viewpoint of either history or the social sciences. To be sure, the psychoanalyst who intends to give this viewpoint its due need not be a historian; but he has to understand sufficiently how historians work and what they are after. The historian, on the other hand, will find it more difficult to use psychodynamic principles aptly and effectively for his purpose. Clinical competence is weighed in terms of experience. To this date we cannot clearly say what, exactly, this means in terms of cognitive facilities—better, in terms of the intellective use of the full range of one's own conscious and preconscious sensibilities. We can only say that it takes a lot of it, and that some individuals are better than others in gaining experience and, almost simultaneously, in using it.[1] At any rate, the basic condition of interdisciplinary work is to know enough so as to consult the right expert and ask him the right questions. We come here to one of the peculiar problems posed by the pitfalls of information in a subject matter not one's own. Perhaps it is rooted in the confident belief that a broad humanist education, by definition universal, will open up a variety of subjects if one only takes the trouble to read enough about them. The trouble is, however, not with the reading but with the limitations of universality. These in turn lead us to the observation that no subject matter is merely composed of data and the array of methods employed in obtaining them. Each field has peculiar ways of looking at human experience that rest on the use of specific concepts without being entirely defined and captured by them. The *approach* or *viewpoint* of a field of study consists of specific stresses and discriminations according to which the global, inchoate mass of primary experience is sifted. Acquiring the viewpoint of the field depends on extensive experience with the raw material of its subject, the documents of the historians, or the rambling reports of patients in therapy. It can, therefore, not well be substituted by reading up on the conclusions drawn from these premises by others. Competence in fields such as history or psychology also demands a working knowledge not only of its official engagements—its researches and results—but also its major dissensions and biases about the way questions should be asked and methods used. The history of creative argument in a field of study becomes part of its overall viewpoint. More pragmatically, it is indispensable for grasping the scope and the limitations of any single contribution to the study of the subject. In any event, the major prerequisite for the interdisciplinary work of the psychohistorian, or historian-psychologist, is in his grasp of the "viewpoint."

But to return to the question of interpretation: I suggested before that several corresponding themes of the individual and of his society can all issue quite naturally from the sudden remembrances of which Erikson spoke. Their predictable emergence is the hallmark of psychoanalytic therapy and, of course, its great opportunity for the joint reconstruction of the patient's past by him and the therapist, as well as the occasion for the main technique of therapeutic intervention, namely interpretation. Resistance and the emergence of seemingly disjunctive but, in fact, profoundly meaningful memories, and the revival of emotional sets both in remembering and reporting them (transference), also represent the common validation of the essence of psychoanalytic theory.

Here the therapeutic situation seems to have an enormous advantage over the reconstruction of lives in history. Gandhi's self-interruption may have had the purpose, as Erikson suggested, to give vent to his ambivalence for the mill owner, and show his secret disparagement, even though the comparison with the snakes has something of the characteristic, condescending benevolence of the obsessive moralist. It may also serve to rationalize the scandal about the dogs and behind it assert once more why Gandhi was right in supporting the mill owner when he agreed with his actions. But the incident could also point to a great many other subjects such as the characteristic inability of the obsessive personality to allow himself what he really wants to do. Worst of all, there's a whole plethora of possibilities in the dark void of the past at which we cannot even guess. Who knows what went on in Gandhi's mind between writing one installment of the autobiography and the drafting of the next? The past exists only insofar as it is remembered,[2] by whatever means and medium, but preferably in the memory of living people. And who could know the ruminations and phantasies of a highly differentiated person of restless energy if he has not divulged them in some way?

Here lies the greatest liability of the psychohistorical approach—it is devoid of the self-correction, and self-transcendence, implied in the diadic interplay of psychotherapy. Erikson shows convincingly that Luther behaved toward Staupitz as to God, or to a father, and, with his confessor's prudent help, also how he would have behaved had he gone through a therapy himself. But Luther was on nobody's couch, and Erikson spares no effort to make the difference clear.

We must simply accept it as one of the deficits of the psychohistorical method that it must apply to history what Freud gained from the interactional continuum with the patient; that is, to a situation largely populated by maladaptive and conflicted people but who were, as a rule, even less aware of their state than Luther was; above all, apply psychodynamic principles in the absence of an interactional continuum with a reasonably objective, reasonably sensitive trained observer. The psychohistorian must, therefore, rely on the universal applicability of psychoanalytic propositions and especially on the quasi-diagnostic relevance of typical acts and modes of expression. The interruption-and-emergence pattern is a good example. The connection between any manifest behavior and its motives is, however, always a bit precarious. It surely must vary with the styles of expression and action at different historical times and in different cultural contexts as it must vary among individuals. I have already referred to the essential uncertainty implied in the fact that there is no reliable access to the subjective awareness of an individual but the continued observant interaction of the therapist, which is, indeed, the unique methodological potential of the psychotherapeutic situation.

Having considered the liabilities of the psychohistorical approach we should now consider its assets. They are quite naturally implied in the method of studying history. At least under favorable circumstances the historian has the testimony of several observers for any single event and surely for the life of an historical personality whose biography he sets out to write. After examining the validity and probable distortion of each testimony he can balance them against each other and construct from them the most likely consistent and plausible image of the person or the event under scrutiny. What interferes with the "straight" psychological interpretations of the historical personality is precisely what offers the historian an extraordinary advantage. He usually deals with the past, that is, with time completed; and not, as the psychotherapist, with ongoing life. For the latter the past is a means to make sense of the present, and so equip his client thereby to build for himself a more orderly future. In this endeavor he can, of course, not foretell what opportunities and obstacles life will throw in his client's path. He can help him check the internal dangers of conflict, anxiety, and guilt and break with the heedless repetition of the same mistakes. But except for freeing his adaptive competence in general ways he cannot help him toward good fortune or protect him against adversity.

The historian, on the other hand, has the outcome of the story. He can test his ideas about the forces determining a life, or a chain of events, by reviewing them in the light of their effect. He has more opportunity thereby to study the individual and his growth, and his interdependence with his social and historical circumstances.[3] From his relatively distant vantage point he can watch the patterns of a life, or of a historical period assert themselves by their own force and inherent logic. Things seem to "fall into a pattern" also in history if we do not insist on imposing prematurely one of our own contriving; or if we do not interfere with it—as we have to in psychotherapy—by disproportionate attention to some aspect of experience against other equally relevant ones. There we are bound to maintain more attention to some qualities of the person, to the disadvantage of others which for the scope of his life may yet be equally important.

In this perspective the psychohistorical approach presents itself as a twin advance, by moving to a higher level of comprehension our understanding of the individual person, prompting us to recognize that he will always correspond with history—as if he were located in a set of concentric circles of which only the innermost represents his own subjective and, as it were, single-minded history. In return, this approach enables us to work for new synthesis between *Geschichts-*

schreibung, the study of history, and our knowledge of individual development and of the functioning of social systems. It is no accident either that we return to history in order to accomplish such a synthesis. It is, after all, the first and most elementary of the social sciences, intimating that man enters into his estate and becomes a person and a socius only when he becomes capable of acknowledging that he has a history himself and is part of a larger historical process.[4]

NOTES

[1] F. Wyatt, "The Meaning of Clinical Experience," *American Journal of Orthopsychiatry* 23:284–292, 1953.

[2] F. Wyatt, "The Reconstruction of the Individual and the Collective Past," in R. W. White (ed.), *The Study of Lives* (New York: Atherton Press, 1963), pp. 304–320.

[3] F. Wyatt, "A Psychologist Looks at History," *Journal of Social Issues* 17:65–77, 1961.

[4] Henry S. Murray, "Preparations for the Scaffold of a Comprehensive System," in Sigmund Koch (ed.), *Psychology: A Study of a Science* (New York: McGraw-Hill, 1959), vol. 3, pp. 7–54.

8

Intensive Case Studies of Members of the General Population

The essays on the analysis of individual political actors in selections five through seven take their examples from high- and middle-level political figures. This selection by Robert E. Lane demonstrates the fruitfulness of intensive study of members of the general population. Lane's depth interviews with fifteen working-class men are reported here in an analysis that could as readily have been located in the portion of this source book dealing with typology, since after diagnosing each of his subjects, Lane goes on to classify them in terms of the quality of their relationships with their fathers.

Here is Lane's own brief summary of his findings as presented in the abstract published with the article: "After a brief examination of 'typical' father-son relationships in several cultures, this study focuses on the youthful relationships with their fathers of fifteen normal working- and lower-middle-class men, information derived from depth interviews. Expressing rebellious feelings in political terms is completely alien to this sample—even for the four whose relationships with their fathers were damaged. Such damaged relationships, however, are associated with (1) limited political information (because of the need to concentrate on the self in the absence of an appropriate model), (2) authoritarianism, (3) inability to criticize legitimate public figures (because of a need to stifle anti-authority feelings), and (4) a pessimistic view of social improvement. The opposite characteristics, revealed in the majority of the sample, are said to be expressed in American political life and policy in specified ways."

FATHERS AND SONS:
FOUNDATIONS OF POLITICAL BELIEF

Robert E. Lane

Loosely speaking, there are three ways in which a father lays the foundations for his son's political beliefs. He may do this, first, through indoctrination, both overt and covert as a model for imitation, so that the son picks up the loyalties, beliefs, and values of the old man. Second, he places the child in a social context, giving him an ethnicity, class position, and community or regional environment. And, he helps to shape political beliefs by his personal relations with his son and by the way he molds the personality which must sustain and develop a social orientation. The combination of these three processes produces the "Mendelian law" of politics: the inheritance of political loyalties and beliefs. But while imitation and common social stakes tend to enforce this law, the socialization process may work to repeal it. It is the socialization process, the way in which fathers and sons get along with each other, that we examine in this paper.

Some perspective is gained by noting a number of possible models of the way fathers through their rearing practices may affect their sons' social outlook. The German model of the stern father who emphasizes masculine "hardness" and "fitness" in the son, and who monopolizes the opportunity for conversation at the dinner table, is one that has been explored at length.[1] The Japanese father, partially deified like his ancestors, strictly attentive to protocol and detail in the home, is another.[2] The Russian father image—the gruff, indulgent, somewhat undisciplined but spontaneous and warm individual—is a third.[3] And the American father is said to be more of a brother than a father, joined with his son under the same female yoke, uninspired but certainly not frightening.[4] Here is an image to compare with others and, as with the other models, its caricaturistic exaggeration nevertheless represents an identifiable likeness.

The father-son relationship may be explored with the help of data on the lives and politics of fifteen men interviewed recently at considerable length. These men represent a random sample drawn from the voting list of 220 citizens living in a moderate income housing development in an eastern industrial city. Out of fifteen asked, fifteen (prompted by a modest stipend) agreed to be interviewed, even though these interviews ranged from ten to fifteen hours, administered in from four to seven installments. The characteristics of the sample are as follows:

They were all white, married, fathers, urban, and eastern.
Their incomes ranged from 2,400 to 6,300 dollars (with one exception: his income was about 10,000 dollars in 1957).

Reprinted from *American Sociological Review,* 24, No. 4 (August, 1959), 502–11.
Professor Lane's note: "I wish to acknowledge financial assistance in the form of a Faculty Research Fellowship from the Social Science Research Council, a Fellowship at the Center for Advanced Study in the Behavioral Sciences, and a modest but indispensable grant from the former Behavioral Sciences Division of the Ford Foundation. This article is a revised version of a paper presented at the annual meeting of the American Political Science Association, September, 1958." Lane later wove this report into a full-length book based on the same sample of fifteen working-class men: *Political Ideology* (New York: Free Press, 1962).

Ten had working class occupations such as painter, plumber, policeman, railroad fireman, and machine operator. Five had white collar occupations such as salesman, bookkeeper, and supply clerk.

Their ages ranged from 25 to 54 years—most of them were in their thirties.

Twelve were Catholic, two Protestant, and one was Jewish.

All are native-born; their nationality backgrounds include: six Italian, five Irish, one Polish, one Swedish, one Russian (Jewish), and one Yankee.

All were employed at the time of the interviews.

Three concluded their schooling after grammar school and eight after some high school; two finished high school, one had some college training, and one went to graduate school.

The interviews were taped, with the permission of the interviewees, and transcribed for analysis. There was an agenda of topics and questions but the interviews were not closely structured, being conducted with probes and follow-up questions in a conversational style. The topics included: (1) current social questions, such as foreign policy, unions, taxes, and desegregation; (2) political parties; (3) political leaders and leadership; (4) social groups and group memberships; (5) ideological orientation toward "democracy," "freedom," "equality," and "government"; (6) personal values and philosophies of life; (7) personality dimensions—partially explored through standard tests; (8) life histories, including attitudes towards parents, brothers and sisters, school, and so forth.

In addition to the interviews, a group of tests were administered on anxiety, authoritarianism, anomie, information, and certain social attitudes.

The characteristics of the sample, as in any study, affect the relationships discovered. It should be stressed that this is a sample of men who, by and large, are well adjusted to society: they are married and have children, hold steady jobs, they are voters. This probably implies that any warping of personality which may have taken place in childhood was marginal. We are, then, dealing with the relationships of childhood experiences and political expression in a moderately "normal" group. We are not involved with the extremes of personality damage, or the bottom rung of the social ladder, or a highly socially alienated group. Unlike the studies of American Communists[5] or of nativist agitators,[6] this paper is concerned with middle and normal America, with more or less adjusted people. This is an important point because our findings differ in certain respects from those of other studies, but they do not necessarily conflict with them.

THE UNFOUGHT WAR OF INDEPENDENCE

The influence of the son's rebellious attitudes towards his father has often been said to be important in explaining radical movements, particularly "youth movements." The son's basic position is one of growing from complete dependence to independence. During the later stages of this growth he and his father each must make a rather drastic adjustment to the changing relationship called forth by the son's maturation. Under certain circumstances the son may rebel against the family and particularly against the father. Is this the typical American pattern—as Erikson denies? Unlike German youth, he argues, American youngsters do not rebel, although willing and able to do so, because the paternal discipline is not something to rebel against.[7]

We explored the question of rebellion, particularly in its political aspects, with our fifteen men and found that there was indeed very little evidence of the kind of relationship that Erikson describes in the German situation. Apparently, only rarely did a family-shattering clash of wills occur when the son thought himself old enough to behave as a man. The father-son opposition took relatively minor forms: the question of what hour to come in at night, the use of the family car, the son's conduct in school. Concerning the political expression of such rebellious feelings, there were strong indications that this subject remained on the periphery of the men's world of experience.

Although the major evidence comes from the biographical material, answers to a question on youthful rebellion or radicalism are revealing. Rapuano, an auto parts supply man with a rather undisciplined tendency to vent his aggression on social targets (Communists and doctors), responds in bewilderment and finally denies any such tendency. O'Hara, an oiler in a large factory and one of the more class-conscious interviewees, is confused and takes the question to mean rebellion against his brothers and sisters. Woodside, a policeman who rejected his father with venom, responds to an inquiry about his own youthful rebellion or radicalism:

I do remember through the depression that my folks mentioned that it seems as though more could have been done—that the parties should have made more means of work so that the poverty wouldn't be existing so much around you—and, not only around you —but with you yourself.

He turns the question of his own rebellion and radicalism into a family matter: the family was more or less disgruntled. Only one man, better educated than others, speaks of his own moderate radicalism in a way which could be interpreted as a search for independence from or opposition to his parents.

There are several reasons why political expression of youthful defiance failed to come off. One is the low salience of politics for the parents. Few of the men could remember many political discussions in the home and some were uncertain whether their parents were Democrats or Republicans. If the old man cared so little about politics, there was little reason to challenge him in this area. Another reason is that when there is a need to assert independence there are ways of doing it which come closer to the paternal (and generally American) value scheme. One of these is to quit school. Four or five men sought independence and the economic foundations for a life no longer dependent on paternal pleasure by leaving school shortly before they were ready to graduate—thus striking directly at the interests of parents determined to see their children "get ahead in the world." Of course this act had compensations for parents in need of money, but there seems to have been more of a genuine conflict of wills in this area than in any other. Quitting school, in some ways, is the American youth's equivalent of his European opposite of conservative parentage joining a socialist or fascist party.

Two reasons then for the apolitical quality of youthful revolt are the low salience of politics in the American home and the opportunity for rebellion in other ways. A third reason may be—to use a hyperbole—the relatively low salience of the father in the American scheme. We asked our men, "Who made the important decisions in your parents' household?" One replied that they were jointly made, two that their fathers made the important decisions, and twelve testified that mother was boss. The statement of Ruggiero, a maintenance engineer and supply man from a remarkably happy home, typifies the most frequent point of view:

"Which of your parents would you say was the boss in your family?"—I'd say my mother. My father was easy-going in the house. . . . We found that mother ran the house exactly the way she wanted to. She took care of the money, too. Paid all the bills. She still does.

Now it may be that from a child's perspective that Mother is usually boss. But the near unanimity on this point is convincing, all the more so because the accompanying comments generally show no overlord in the background. Even in this immigrant and second generation population Mom had taken over.[8] Why, then, rebel against Father?

There is a fourth reason for the generally low rate of political rebellion. In the American home a child is given considerable latitude. "Permissiveness" is the term used currently to express this idea and although the term and idea are in bad odor among some critics, it is clear that the prevailing standards of child care even twenty years ago allowed a degree of freedom in school, neighborhood, and home not generally prevalent in Europe or Asia.[9] To a large extent, the boy is on his own. This is Erikson's point, but we can illustrate it in detail. Thus Farrel, a man from a working class background whose schooling included graduate study, reports on his tendency to political radicalism in his youth: "I think there must also be the adolescent revolt aspect, which was never acute with me. . . . There was, as far as I was concerned, no necessity for it to be acute. I didn't feel hemmed in by my parents." Rapuano talks of his "reckless" youth in which he ran free with other boys, and some of the men speak of their parents' preoccupations that gave them opportunity to live a "free life." Many of the boys had earned money for their own as well as their families' use by selling papers, working in grocery stores, or cleaning up the school. Nor was this freedom attributable to parental indifference. When Rapuano was struck by a school teacher, his mother (*not* his father) visited the school to beat the teacher with a stick. A free child assured of supportive parental assistance when in need does not need to rebel.

A minority of four or five of these children, however, had suffered under controls which seem strict by most American standards.

FOUR MEN WHOSE FATHERS FAILED THEM

Although it is true that the symptoms of *rebellion* are rather slight and that its political expression is miniscule, it does not follow that the American son, particularly the son of immigrants, identifies with his father—introjects the paternal ideal, as the psychoanalysts might say—and accepts the male role as it has been played on the home stage. At least four of our fifteen men probably had experienced seriously damaged relations with their fathers and even in the roseate glow of remembered childhood do not like the old man. Interpretation of this situation must be circumspect, since people are supposed to love their parents and are even commanded to honor them. During the interviews, however, interstitial comments, reportorial selection of incidents, and graphic silences, as well as the explicit expressions of like and dislike, present a clear picture of father-son relations.

There are, of course, many varieties of both bad and good father-son relations. In these four cases of damaged relations we note two patterns. One is *identification without affection,* represented by only one case. The other, the *rejection pattern,* is illustrated by three cases. This section briefly pictures the father-son relationships of these four men. In the following sections their political expression is explored.

Identification Without Affection

The American youth, as we have noted, typically does not invest much emotional energy in a father rebellion on the European scale. But of course the latter does occur. And sometimes the process resembles the German pattern where the youth identifies with his father, struggles for his approval, gradually asserts himself against him as though assaulting a fortress, departs, and returns to be like him— another paternal fortress against his own son.

Sullivan, a railroad fireman and former semi-professional boxer follows this tradition. Now, at the age of 25, he stresses his respect for his father, but his report shows little affection. Of discipline he says:

He was pretty strict—very strict. He'd been brought up strict, and in an old Irish family there, and of course, all the way through school it was very strict [the father went to a Catholic seminary]. So he was pretty strict with me, more so than with the two girls.

When asked about his father's good points he responds in the same terms as though everything else were blotted out: "Well . . . (long pause) . . . his good points were that he knew when to be strict and when to be lenient." Except on the question of sports (where the father gave instruction, but nothing is said of a good time), there is little joy in this relationship.

Yet there is identification. The son has adopted his father's strict manner. Sullivan had left his family because his wife would not follow his orders about the management of the home; he now sees that the children should, properly, give instant obedience. His rebellion—and he did rebel—is over:

Oh, I knew everything when I was 19. Nobody could tell me nothing. Boy oh boy I found out, though. That's one thing my father would always try and . . . teach me things, and offer advice and so on. But no, I wouldn't listen. He told me especially about discipline and orders and so on. I never used to like to take orders. I don't think I was in the service a month when I wrote and told him, "Boy, you were right. You said some day I'm going to say that—and boy, you are." The service was a good thing for me.

Sullivan is a "hard" man to deal with, not mean, but there is a steely quality about him which reflects his experience in and exaltation of the Marine Corps, as well as his father's values.

Rejection of the Father

Unlike Sullivan, three others, Woodside, Dempsey, and DeAngelo, reject their fathers outright. There is no effort to cover over their feelings, to take back the criticism, undo the damage, unsay the words. Something within them is quite clear and solid on this matter and they are not shaken by fear or guilt at the thought of such rejection.

DeAngelo is a factory machine operative, whose father and mother separated when he was an infant; he subsequently acquired a step-father. Of his father, who lives in the same town, laconically he says: "I don't bother with him." Of his step-father:

He was a good guy when he was sober, but he was bad when he was drunk. I never had too much respect for him. . . . When he was drunk he wanted to argue, you know. But my mother was bigger than him—didn't have too much trouble taking care of him. After a while my mother left him, you know, and we were on our own.

DeAngelo narrowly missed reform school when in high school—from which the principal ordered him to leave, possibly through a misunderstanding. But some maternally inspired internal gyroscope kept him on an even keel through a series of such adversities. Today he is the father of six boys, a steady breadwinner, and union shop steward in the plant.

Woodside, a policeman with a conscience, remembers his childhood with horror because of the irresponsible drunken behavior of his father and particularly his father's "outside interests," women. He says, quite simply: "At one time I felt I'd hate my father—that if anything ever happened to him it would be a wonderful thing." But today he plays checkers with the pathetic old man and helps him when he's in trouble. He hated his father in the past for the beatings he gave his mother, the humiliation he brought on the household, and the physical suffering to the children: "It's a pretty gruesome thing to tell anybody that a father could neglect his kids so much. Believe me, a good many days I've seen where I had just water, and I was lucky to have water—for a meal for the whole day."

Dempsey is an older man who married a widow when he himself was 40, having previously lived with his mother and, until they were married, with his brothers. In comparison with DeAngelo and Woodside, his reactions to his father are more veiled and he identifies somewhat more with him. He thinks of him as "a hard working man, the same as I am now, and couldn't get much further than I probably will . . . although my hopes are probably a little bit higher." But through the veil we see more granite than flesh and blood:

"Did your father have a sense of humor?"—Well, that I couldn't say. As I say, we were never too chummy with him. He never was a fellow to be chummy with us children. . . . He was one of them guys—it had to be it, or there was no way out of it.

There apparently were few family outings, little fun, and strict curfews. What things did Dempsey admire about his father? "Only that he was a hard worker, and gave us a chance to do—to choose what we wanted to—at the time [reference to choice of religion in which they chose the mother's religion]. Outside of that he was a very hard man." And a few minutes later he repeats, "he was a hard—a very hard and stern man."

THE POLITICS OF FILIAL ALIENATION

Having examined a modal American pattern of father-son relationships and isolated four deviant cases, we turn to an inquiry into the politics of these latter four men.

Low Information and Social Interest

The question of political information is considered first, partly because it indicates the degree of interest in the social world outside oneself. Our measure of political information is made up of questions on local, national, and international institutions and events. The local events, in particular, are not usually learned in school, since they include such items as "Who is the local boss of New Haven?" and "How would you go about getting a traffic light put on your corner?"

It is therefore especially significant that these four men, concerning political information, rank as the four lowest of the fifteen cases.

There are several reasons for this. The loss or lack of a secure parental model encouraged each of these four to frame his own life style and to engage in the lifelong business of self-discovery. Each man is his own Pygmalion. More importantly, the development of a personal sense of security, of being a loved and wanted and respected person, which is a bulwark against psychic conflict, is lacking. This lack seems to be borne out by the evidence of severe anxiety in all four cases. Dempsey and DeAngelo rank among the four highest scorers on the "neurotic anxiety" scale. Sullivan ranks third on a social anxiety scale and shows evidence of severe sex-tension, as indicated by his top score in this area (and his marriage is breaking up). DeAngelo ranks fourth on this sex-tension scale. Woodside, while less troubled by sexual problems and not "neurotically" anxious, ties for first place on the scale of social anxiety; he is, by his own account and other evidence, a worrier, a searcher for all-around "security" and has somatic difficulties.

Anxiety can lead into politics as well as away from politics. People can defend themselves against anxiety by knowing more than others—or people may succumb to the demands of anxiety by knowing less. Generally in the American apolitical culture the anxious man does not employ politics as a defense against his conflicts. One of the little appreciated benefits of such a culture is the low premium on politics for the anxious and neurotic.

Authoritarianism

Three of the four men score strongly on authoritarianism: DeAngelo has the highest score in the group, and Sullivan and Woodside tie for fourth; only Dempsey's ranking is moderate. The genesis of authoritarianism and its close connection with father-son relations are well known. Here it is sufficient to note that in order to believe that people can live and work as cooperative equals or at least as trusting partners, a person must have experienced such a relationship. In their relations with their fathers, these men had no such experience.

Speak No Evil of the Political Leader

There is a third area of political outlook which seems to be shared by these four men with damaged father relations, a quality which in some measure sets them apart from the others. Although political lore would have it otherwise, people generally prefer to speak well of political leaders than to speak ill of them.[10] But the average citizen can criticize such leaders, designate those he dislikes, and weigh the good and bad points of each on occasion. Our four deviant cases found such criticism or even objectivity more difficult than the others.

Sullivan admires Monroe, Lincoln, Truman, and Eisenhower. He defends Truman against those who believe that his attack on the music critic was out of order. He defends Ike for the vacations he takes. When asked about political leaders he dislikes: "Well, from what I learned in history, Grant seemed to be pretty useless . . . [pause]. He didn't seem to do too much [mentions that he was a drunkard]. And [pause] I mean I don't dislike him, either, but—I don't dislike any of them." Question: "How about living leaders, or recent leaders, which of these would you say you had the least respect for?" Answer, after a pause: "Well [long pause], none that I could think of."

Dempsey likes Washington and Lincoln, and, when probed, Wilson and Truman, for whom he voted. Asked about "any particular feelings about Dewey" he says, "No, I wouldn't say that." Roosevelt was "a very good man." Eisenhower is also a "very good man, doing everything he possibly can." He can think of no mistakes he has made.

DeAngelo says he doesn't particularly admire any political leaders. But: "I like them. I mean I didn't think anything bad about them, y'know." Questioned about an earlier reference to Robert Taft, he replies:

Well, I mean, I thought for being President, I thought he'd be a little better in know-how and savvy than Eisenhower, y'know. I ain't got nothing against Eisenhower—he's good, he seems to be honest enough, but I don't . . . I don't . . . I don't think he should have run again because I think his health is—his health was good enough.

DeAngelo has trouble expressing his reservations about Eisenhower even on the question of health. When asked specifically about people he dislikes, distrusts, or thinks to be weak or wrong for the job: "Well, I don't know, not offhand."

Woodside's views are a little different. He likes Eisenhower but is more willing to discuss his weaknesses (particularly his signing of an order to execute a deserter). He likes MacArthur as a "big man" and mentions Lincoln favorably. Asked about his dislikes and those he thinks did a poor job, he mentions others' criticisms of Roosevelt but then rushes to his defense, except to say that he thinks Eisenhower is "a little bit more mannish" than Roosevelt. The only political leader he mentions unfavorably is Adlai Stevenson, who strikes him as a man who could say "yes" when he means "no."

With the possible exception of this last comment, these remarks convey three themes: (1) Conventional leaders like Washington, Lincoln, and Monroe are admired. (2) The independent leader who doesn't let outsiders tell him what to do is admired—Truman would stand for no nonsense (Sullivan), Stevenson is too much influenced by his advisors (Woodside). (3) Authority figures are not to be criticized—an especially important point.

These four men are not notably deficient in their general ability to criticize or to express hostility. Why, then, do these four, whose relations with their fathers are strained, find it so hard to criticize political leaders in a whole-hearted way?

In answering this question, Sullivan's case should be distinguished from the others. Sullivan feels guilty about his negative feelings toward the original political authority in the family. He cannot bring himself to express his hostility without quickly withdrawing his remarks and saying something of a positive nature. The expression of hostility to authority figures is painful and Sullivan simply avoids this pain.

The other three men express outright hostility toward or unrelieved criticism of their fathers. Why not also of political authority? In the first place, there is a carryover of fear from the childhood situation which has not been obliterated by the adult emancipation. Men do not easily forget those childhood moments of terror when the old man comes home drunk, abuses the mother, or gets out the strap to deal with the child in anger unalloyed with love. Secondly a combined worship and envy of strength exists, which father-hatred fosters in a child, for it is the father's strength in the family that penetrates the childish consciousness. Finally, there is the persistent belief in the futility and danger of countering and rebelling against authority. Although DeAngelo was a rebel in high school and was expelled and Woodside stood up to his father threatening him with a log behind the wood shed, both are successful now partly because they have curtailed these antiauthority impulses that threatened to bring disaster once before. Their consciences are composed of antirebellion controls; this is why, in part, they can be good citizens.[11]

Utopia and Conservatism

The basis for a hopeful view of the world lies in the self; the world is ambiguous on this point. In the self, the notion that we can move toward a more perfect society is supported by the belief that people are kindly by nature and considerate of one another. Moreover, when the idea of a better social order is developed even a little, the mind quickly turns to the nature of authority in such a society. Is there a kind of authority which is strong and directive, yet at the same time solicitous and supportive of the weak in their infirmities—in short, paternal?

We asked our subjects about the nature of their vision of a more perfect society (with results which must await detailed analysis). At the end of the discussion we inquired whether or not there is evidence that we are moving closer to such a society. Although the men were not asked if the world was possibly moving in the opposite direction, some volunteered this answer. Our fifteen men answered the questions on an ideal society as follows:

	Damaged Father-Son Relations	Others
We are moving closer to ideal society	0	8
We are not moving closer to ideal society	3	2
(volunteered) We are moving away from ideal society	1	1

The pattern is clear. Woodside first touches on the drift from a peacetime to a wartime society. Then speaking of only the peacetime society, "like we're in peace now, the society is about the same as it has been back along. . . . I would say that throughout history it has been about the same." Asked if people are happier now than they were a hundred years ago, he is reminded ironically of the phrase, "There's nothing like the good old days," and he digresses to say that people adjust so quickly to mechanical progress that their degree of satisfaction and dissatisfaction remains about constant.

Dempsey, as always, is more laconic. Asked the same question about possible progress toward a better society, he says: "No. I don't think so. I think we're going to stay on the same lines we are on right now."

And Sullivan: "Never. We'll never get any place close to it, I think." He first modifies his answer by noting that "prejudice" may decline but is skeptical because "you can't change human nature."

DeAngelo takes the dimmest view of all: "I don't think we'll ever get any closer [to a more perfect society]. We're getting farther and farther away from it, I guess. All indications are we're moving away from it. There's not enough people trying to make the world perfect." Asked why we are retrogressing, he cites what he regards as the drift away from religion and the rise of Communism. These are perhaps the two most convenient pegs today on which to hang a deeply rooted pessimism regarding the social order.

Contrast these views with those of five cases selected because of their close identification and warm relations with their fathers. One says flatly that "I don't think we're far from it." Another points out that the population increase will bring about troubles but he is hopeful because of the parallel increase of the proportion of good people. A third declares that every mistake we make teaches us something, hence the world is getting better. A fourth believes that a socialist society is developing, which he thinks is probably a "good thing" although socialism is not an "ideal" society. Only one of these five holds that such progress is unlikely, attributing this to the increase of governmental controls; but he adds, characteristically, "Maybe concurrently with such controls you're getting more of the things that most people seem to want made available to them."

FATHERS AND SONS—AND HISTORY

The state is "man writ large"; the family is a microcosm of society. The history of a nation may, in considerable measure, reflect the changes in the ways children and parents, sons and fathers, struggle to get along with one another. Some of the characteristics of a nation's politics may rest on the resolution of these struggles.[12] With this point in mind, we turn to certain aspects of American and foreign politics.

To recapitulate in American society: (1) "good" father-son relations are the norm; (2) of those youth with rebellious feelings against their fathers there are few for whom the rebellion takes political form; and (3) there is a tendency for moderately damaged father-son relations to be associated with relatively low levels of hope, interest, and capacity to criticize political leaders. There tendencies are revealed in what may be called the American political "style" in the following ways:

1. American politics is often said to embody a kind of consensualism in which both both sides tend to come together, rather than a bipolarization or radicalism. At the same time, campaigns become quite heated with highly critical comments passed between the partisans of one candidate and those of another. This situation parallels the qualities we find associated with sons of strong but nurturant fathers: lack of alienation but a capacity for outspoken criticism.

2. Compared with the citizens of other nations, the American citizen is reported to be relatively well informed about current events and civic matters. On the other hand, his intensity of concern is relatively low. He can exchange blows during campaigns and then accept the victory of the opposition without much trouble. This pattern (a considerable cultural achievement) is difficult, as we have seen, for the poorly socialized and again suggests an important family component in American democracy.

3. It is often noted that a strain of idealism exists in American international politics which distinguishes it from the hard-boiled realism of the Continent. Wilson's Fourteen Points, Roosevelt's Four Freedoms, and Truman's Point Four illustrate the character of this idealism, an idealism nourished by the hope that we can do away with war and establish a peaceful world order. Behind these beliefs and supporting them in their many expressions lies that quality of hope and trust which are forged in boyhood, when the son is apprenticed to a protective and loving father.

SUMMARY: SOME HYPOTHESES

With a humility based on an appreciation of the great variety of experience that goes into the making of political man, we suggest the following hypotheses.

1. Compared with other Western cultures, American culture discourages youthful rebellion against the father. It further discourages political expression of whatever rebellious impulses are generated. This is because: (a) There is less need to rebel in a permissive culture. (b) Rebellious impulses are less likely to be expressed against the father because of his relatively less dominant position in the family. (c) The low salience of politics for the father means that rebellion against him is less likely to be channeled into politics or political ideology. (d) The high salience of the father's ambition for the son (and the resulting independence) means that rebellion against the father is more likely to be expressed by quitting school and going to work, or by delinquent conduct.

2. Damaged father-son relations tend to produce low political information and political cathexis. This is because, *inter alia:* (a) Without an adult model the youth must give relatively greater attention to the process of self-discovery and expend greater energy in managing his own life problems. (b) Failure of father-son relationships creates anxiety which is often (not always) so preoccupying that more distant social problems become excluded from attention.

3. Damaged father-son relations tend to develop an authoritarian orientation.

4. Damaged father-son relations tend to inhibit critical attitudes toward political leaders because: (a) The damaged relations encourage an enduring fear of expressing hostility toward authority figures. (b) They stimulate a reverence for power over other values. (c) In children they provoke the belief that it may be useless to rebel or petition authority.

5. Damaged father-son relations discourage a hopeful view of the future of the social order because: (a) The damaged relations often give rise to a less favorable view of human nature. (b) They help to create skepticism about the possibility of kindly and supportive political authority. (c) They encourage a cynical view of the political process: it is seen in terms of corrupt men seeking their own ends.

6. The history, political style, and future development of a political community reflect the quality of the relationship between fathers and sons. The permissive yet supportive character of modal father-son relationships in the United States contributes to the following features of the American political style: (a) a relatively high consensualism combined with a capacity for direct and uninhibited criticism; (b) a relatively large amount of interest and political information combined with relatively low emotional commitment; and (c) a relatively strong idealism in foreign affairs (and in general social outlook).

NOTES

[1] See Bertram H. Shaffner, *Father Land, a Study of Authoritarianism in the German Family* (New York: Columbia University Press, 1948); David M. Levy, "Anti-Nazis: Criteria of Differentiation," in Alfred H. Stanton and Stewart E. Perry, eds., *Personality and Political Crisis* (Glencoe, Ill.: Free Press, 1951).

[2] See Ruth Benedict, *The Chrysanthemum and the Sword* (Boston: Houghton Mifflin, 1946).

[3] See Henry V. Dicks, "Observations on Contemporary Russian Behavior," *Human Relations* 5 (May 1952): 111–76.

[4] See Erik Erikson, *Childhood and Society* (New York: Norton, 1950).

[5] Gabriel Almond, *The Appeals of Communism* (Princeton: Princeton University Press, 1954); Morris L. Ernst and David Loth, *Report on the American Communist* (New York: Holt, 1952).

[6] Leo Lowenthal and N. Guterman, *Prophets of Deceit* (New York: Harper, 1949). For an interesting case analysis of father-son relationships and virulent fascism, see Robert Lindner, "Destiny's Tot" in his *The Fifty Minute Hour* (New York: Rinehart, 1955).

[7] Erikson, *op. cit.,* pp. 280–83.

[8] Compare Margaret Mead, *And Keep Your Powder Dry* (New York: Morrow, 1942).

[9] On this point, see Robert R. Sears, Eleanor E. Maccoby, and Harry Levin, *Patterns of Child Rearing* (Evanston, Ill.: Row, Peterson, 1957); and Robert J. Havighurst and Allison Davis, "A Comparison of the Chicago and Harvard Studies of Social Class Differences in Child Rearing," *American Sociological Review* 20 (August 1955): 438–42.

[10] In 1948 between a quarter and a third of a national sample could find nothing unfavorable to say about Truman or Dewey, but almost everyone could mention something favorable about both candidates. See Angus Campbell and Robert Kahn, *The People Elect a President* (Ann Arbor, Mich.: Survey Research Center, 1952); and Angus Campbell, Gerald Gurin, and Warren E. Miller, *The Voter Decides* (Evanston, Ill.: Row, Peterson, 1954).

[11] The view that men with damaged father-son relationships do not like to criticize authority figures may seem to fly in the face of a popular interpretation of radicalism. This contradiction is more apparent than real. The effect of failure of socialization on normal populations is more likely to be apathy than radicalism. (See, e.g., P. H. Mussen and A. B. Wyszinski, "Personality and Political Participation," *Human Relations* 5 (February 1952): 65–82.) There are exceptions, of course, since relationships are always expressed as probabilities. In radical groups, moreover, the tendency to criticize authority figures is focused on those who are seen as illegitimate, usurpers, or leaders who are considered to be weak. This was Woodside's approach to Stevenson, and it was precisely the latter's "weakness," his lack of decisiveness, which Woodside criticized. Our findings are complementary, not contradictory, to other similar studies in these respects.

[12] Melancholy experience suggests that it is prudent to note that I am not denying the importance of a nation's history or of its geography and economies, or of its current leadership, in shaping its destiny. I do not imply, for example, that German Nazism arose because of an authoritarian family pattern rather than the Versailles treaty, or Article 48 of the Weimar Constitution, or the weakness of von Hindenberg, or what not. Within Germany, however, those whose fathers forbade them from speaking at the dinner table were more likely to be Nazis than those whose fathers were more indulgent. (See Levy, *op. cit.*) German fathers were more likely to be repressive in this and other ways than fathers in certain other nations. The *combination* of defeat in World War I, the nature of German family life, and other factors, no doubt, helped to create a public responsive to Hitler's appeals.

9

A Scheme for Analyzing Intrapersonal
Conflict Resolution

Employing a variety of historical materials on the ways that various political actors have managed the intrapsychic requirements of making demanding, public commitments, Janis sets out a series of analytic categories for analyzing this important class of political action. Janis' paradigm differs from other schemes for analyzing choice in taking systematic cognizance of unconscious and preconscious as well as conscious levels of psychological functioning. For further elaboration of Janis' analytic categories and of the rather truncated list of hypotheses presented in this article, see "Motivational Factors in the Resolution of Decisional Conflicts," *Nebraska Symposium on Motivation,* 8 (1959), 198–231. Janis' analysis, like Lane's "Fathers and Sons" (Chapter 10), is germane to typological as well as to individual inquiries.

DECISIONAL CONFLICTS:
A THEORETICAL ANALYSIS

Irving L. Janis

This paper will present a set of theoretical constructs developed for the purpose of analyzing the psychological causes and consequences of decisional conflicts. Although the analysis is in terms of *intrapersonal* conflicts, it has many potential applications to politically relevant actions on the part of the leaders and representatives of organized groups and therefore may prove to be useful as a framework for studying certain aspects of *intergroup* conflicts.

At various points throughout this paper I shall attempt to indicate how the constructs might be taken into account by social scientists engaged in research on factors affecting the success or failure of peace treaties, nonviolence pacts, and other conciliatory agreements between hostile governments or rival organized groups. The historical examples to be cited come from biographical studies of men who were national leaders and key negotiators during the twentieth century, fo-

Reprinted from *Journal of Conflict Resolution,* 3, No. 1 (March, 1959), 6–27.

cusing especially on decision-makers during World War I, for whom rich documentary material has now accumulated from the publication of numerous secret records, letters, memoranda, and personal memoirs. At the end of the paper, the research implications of the theoretical analysis will be briefly discussed, with special reference to problems of operational research concerning ways and means of fostering the successful arbitration of international disputes.

I. PRELIMINARY ASSUMPTIONS AND DEFINITIONS

The term "decision" is used in this paper in a broad sense to refer to any act, symbolic or overt, which is socially defined as a commitment to carry out a specified task, to take on the responsibilities of a specified social role, or to execute a specified course of action in the future. The definition is intended to apply when the decision is made by a *representative* or *leader* acting on behalf of a group or organization, as well as when it is a purely private act affecting only the individual's private life.

The most clear-cut instances of commitment occur when the decision-maker anticipates that other people will become aware of his decision, will have the means for detecting deviations from it, and will have the power to censure, penalize, or apply other negative sanctions against him. Sometimes the social commitment is somewhat ambiguous, as when a person makes a private resolution about which other people either are not fully informed or are not interested. Such resolutions are referred to as "quasi-decisions" and will not be discussed in the present paper. The decisions which will occupy our attention are those for which commitment is unambiguous, in that the decision-maker knows that other people, whose disapproval he is motivated to avoid, are definitely counting on him to live up to his decision. A decision-maker's motivation to adhere to a legal contract, a formal agreement, or any informal decision that he regards as committing often stems not only from the fear of social censure but also from the desire to avoid two other types of deprivation as well: (*a*) formal or informal penalties resulting in loss of money, position, power, or other utilitarian values and (*b*) anticipated feelings of guilt or loss of self-esteem from violating internalized ethical standards with respect to keeping one's word. Thus, as Kurt Lewin has emphasized, decisions tend to be "frozen," in the sense that the person will be reluctant to reverse his decision or to violate the obligations that are implied by it.

Intrapersonal conflicts are partly attributable to the decision-maker's awareness of the *difficulties of reversing* an important decision such as getting married, accepting a new job, signing a business contract, or agreeing to a United Nations proposal on behalf of a government that he represents. It contributes to his reluctance *before* he commits himself, during the period when he is experiencing a *predecisional* conflict. After he has already committed himself, any desire to reverse the decision will give rise to a *postdecisional* conflict, which again arises partly from his awareness of the obligations entailed by his decision.

The term "decisional conflict," as used in this paper, refers to *opposing tendencies within an individual, which interfere with the formulation, acceptance, or execution of a decision.* The most prominent symptoms of such conflicts are hesitation, vacillation, subjective feelings of uncertainty, and overt manifestations of acute emotional tension whenever the given decision comes to the focus of attention. If a political leader develops acute tension symptoms of this type following a policy decision, he will tend to become so inefficient or inhibited that he is likely to fail to take the necessary steps to implement the decision in the way he originally intended. During a period when issues of war and peace are hanging in the balance, acute postdecisional conflict on the part of one or another of the main participants in international negotiations can drastically increase the chances of an outbreak of violence.

Intrapersonal conflicts, occurring both before and after a decision is reached, may be either the cause or the effect of *intergroup* conflicts. Ideological and policy disputes among political groups give rise to the well-known phenomena of "cross-pressures," which create intense postdecisional conflicts in a person who is affiliated with, or dependent upon, the contending groups, whenever he is required to commit himself on issues which implicate the clashing norms. Somewhat less frequently discussed are instances of the reverse causal sequence, where the intrapersonal conflicts of a decision-maker lead to an increase in intergroup hostility. Consider, for example, a powerful national leader who supports a pro-peace policy at a time when the government in which he holds executive office is under pressure from opposing groups to use force in an international dispute even at the risk of an all-out war. If the leader becomes acutely conflicted because of dramatic signs that some of his outstanding followers now object to his policy, he may prematurely abandon his persuasive efforts and make unnecessary concessions to the pro-war forces, with a corresponding increase in international tension. This is one of the main situations in the sphere of international relations on which psychological analysis of decision-making processes may shed some light. In particular, it may help to specify the conditions under which a leader's decisional conflicts will be most likely and least likely to lead to vacillation or to ineffectual execution of pro-peace policies.

A related type of problem is that of determining the psychological factors entering into the persistence and reversal of policy decisions among those political leaders who are opposed to peaceful settlements or who are openly pro-war in their policy orientation: What types of information and events will tend to augment their decisional conflicts in such a way that they will tend to become ineffective or neutralized?

A third type of problem—which is the main one discussed in the remainder of this paper—pertains to the decisional conflicts of any leader or representative who is in the role of negotiator and has the power to use his own judgment, without having to secure explicit instructions from other officials in the home government, in his attempts to arrive at a peaceful settlement with a rival nation through arbitration in a face-to-face conference. What are the main determinants of a negotiator's vulnerability to postdecisional conflicts when, after having arrived at a tentative agreement with his fellow negotiators, he encounters cross-pressures and setbacks because of opposition within his home government? Even when a seemingly definitive settlement has been reached at an international conference, subsequent postdecisional conflicts on the part of one or two of the key negotiators can have a markedly disruptive effect—resulting in procrastination or halfhearted efforts to put the agreement into operation and exploitation of "escape clauses." Perhaps even more damaging for the long-run reduction of intergroup hostility is the deterrent to subsequent arbitration of disputes—the development of a "burned-child" attitude which tends to arise in those conflicted negotiators who feel that they have overcommitted their governments and also in their opposite numbers from the rival governments, who are likely to resent intensely the "fizzling-out" of a promising agreement for which they had sacrificed time, energy, and prestige. The long-run outcome may be withdrawal reactions on the part of one or more of the negotiators who participated in the ill-fated agreement. This type of "withdrawal" includes any defensive effort on the part of the decision-maker to avoid repetitions of the frustrating episode by keeping away from subsequent negotiation situations. The withdrawal may take the form of refusing to continue in the role of negotiator, changing one's political position in such a way as to avoid being committed to enter into further negotiations, or even, in extreme instances, retiring from political life altogether.

The problem of preventing disruptive withdrawal reactions is especially relevant when the board of negotiators contains a number of men who feel that, despite the ideological and political differences between their countries, they share a common goal of bringing about a long-run reduction in violence on the international scene. If the continuing board of negotiators contains men who share fervent adherence to this goal and if they also share a strong preference for avoiding a mutually hostile approach to their disputes (e.g., openly admitting their intentions and refraining from humiliating their rivals), they are likely to develop a strong sense of *group identification* with respect to the board and its mission, which greatly increases the chances of their arriving at a creative solution to any new problems about which they confer. After having worked together over a long period of time, a board of negotiators will tend to evolve a type of "group culture" which greatly increases their cohesiveness and facilitates their capacity for working out mutually satisfactory agreements. But this favorable type of group culture, once formed, would be endangered and perhaps destroyed if several key members of the board of negotiators were to resolve their acute postdecisional conflicts, which are bound to arise from time to time, by disaffiliating from the board. Even those negotiators who genuinely adhere to an ethical code of nonviolence cannot be expected to be immune from the psychological needs that impel men to withdraw from the role at times when there is persistent and mounting tension created by postdecisional conflicts. Attaining the goal of a long-run reduction in international hostility, therefore, depends partly upon the degree to which the negotiators of international agreements can resolve their postdecisional conflicts without resorting to withdrawal reactions. This problem is one on which the analysis presented below has direct bearing.

II. CONTRASTING EXAMPLES: REACTIONS OF TWO NEGOTIATORS TO A MAJOR SETBACK

For illustrative purposes, it is worthwhile to examine the events immediately preceding America's entry into World War I from the standpoint of their impact on two key negotiators, Count Bernstorff and President Wilson.[1] For somewhat different reasons, the two men in 1916 were sincerely committed to a policy of ending the war between Germany and the Allies and of maintaining the neutrality of the United States. Early in 1917, a twofold crisis arose. First, the German government, ignoring all former agreements with the United States, opened up unrestricted U-boat warfare against neutral ships. Second, Zimmermann, the recently appointed foreign minister of Germany, sent the notorious telegram to Bernstorff, the German ambassador at Washington, giving instructions to induce Mexico to join with Germany in attacking the United States "to reconquer the lost territory in Texas, New

Mexico, and Arizona." This telegram, intercepted by the British intelligence service, created such a provocative effect when it was shown to Wilson that, according to his official biographer, "no single more devastating blow was delivered against Wilson's resistance to entering the War" (1, VI, 474). Following these events, Wilson was completely disillusioned, abandoned his role as peace negotiator, and became a vociferous proponent of war against the "natural foe of liberty." Bernstorff, on the other hand, did not abandon his pro-peace orientation but, rather, ardently pursued his efforts to convince the opposing German leaders at home that continuing the war would be tantamount to national suicide. He persisted despite the utter defeat of his unpopular policy at home, the loss of all effective support from his former colleagues, and the rebuffs he received from American officials when he became *persona non grata*.

Obviously, the significance of Germany's provocative actions would be quite different for any American leader than for a dissident, but loyal, German official. Nevertheless, by comparing certain characteristic differences in the way the two men approached the tasks of political decision-making, we may gain some insight into the psychological factors which contributed to Bernstorff's persistence as against Wilson's drastic reversal of policy following the blow to their joint efforts.

One of Bernstorff's main activities during the preceding year had been preparing detailed political analyses for his home government, which involved collecting information concerning the array of contending political forces in Germany and in the Allied countries as well as in the United States, for the purpose of appraising the chances of attaining one or another form of peace settlement. The memoranda he sent back to Germany in 1916, many of which were subsequently published in his memoirs, were filled with comments showing how keenly aware he was of the cleavages within each country, of the changes in relative strength of the contending groups within the United States, and of the shifts in the balance of power of the various pro- and anti-war factions within Germany. Moreover, Bernstorff prided himself on being unsentimentally objective in judging the political personalities with whom he was dealing. Summarizing his attitude toward Wilson, he states:

> I never once reckoned upon his personal friendliness towards ourselves; for I knew him too well to suppose him capable of pro-German tendencies. I expected nothing more from him than that he would play America's game—America's and no other country's—supported by the public opinion of the United States. American policy, however, pursued the object of a "Peace without Victory," from the standpoint of practical politics, in order that neither Germany nor England should attain to a superlatively powerful position [2, p. 333].

Bernstorff's continual efforts to maintain a high level of well-informed objectivity seems to have enabled him to approach each fresh crisis like a medical specialist who assimilates any new unfavorable development into his diagnostic appraisal as he confidently decides on appropriate emergency action. On a number of occasions, Bernstorff took the initiative without waiting for instructions from his home government, but, in so doing, he seems to have steeled himself in advance for possible rebuffs or failures. For example, when the "Lusitania" was torpedoed by U-boats and again a few months later when the "Arabic" was torpedoed, Bernstorff headed off a break in diplomatic relations by personally offering apologies and concessions which had not been cleared with the German government.

The German Ambassador's agreements were often resented by his colleagues in the home government, and on some occasions he was sharply reprimanded. But he claimed to have been quite unmoved by the negative feedback following agreements which exceeded his instructions. For example, Bernstorff asserts that, following the formal apology he made after the "Arabic" sinking, "I was once more taken to task—a matter that weighed little with me" (2, p. 159). Throughout his tenure in Washington, he was frequently frustrated when one after another of his achievements as a negotiator was being undermined because of the incompatible decisions by other German officials, about which he complained vociferously. He wrote: "My experiences in Washington as a result of [Chancellor] Bethmann's vacillations, made me feel disposed to give up the diplomatic service as soon as possible, for it can only be of any value when there exists a relation of confidence between the Ambassador and his Chief" (3, p. 106). The series of minor crises during 1915–16 seemed to have induced him to anticipate quite explicitly the undesirable outcomes that might follow from his unpopular decisions, as is implied by the above statement about having contemplated quitting the diplomatic service. It seems probable that his type of contemplation involves a psychological process of emotionally "working through" in advance the heavy blows that might be in store, as well as developing realistic cognitions concerning possible ways of minimizing the damage. This process of psychological preparation may have contributed to his capacity to avoid becoming excessively agitated or demoralized when the major crises of 1917 forced him to give up his post.

In contrast, Wilson was extremely shocked by the tremendous setback to his peace plans, becoming enraged and bitter. Frank L. Polk, the acting Secretary of State, who personally brought a copy of the Zimmermann telegram to the President on February 24, 1917, reported that Wilson showed much indignation and wanted to release the message immediately, without waiting to authenticate it and without any regard for the sensational effect it would have on the Congress and the American public. Bernstorff speaks of Wilson as having suddenly become incapable of an impartial attitude toward Germany: "He saw red whenever he thought of the Imperial Government and his repugnance against it knew no bounds. Even today the bitter feeling still rankles within him" (2, p. 316).

Wilson's surprise stemmed partly from his lack of information about the pro-war factions within the German government. Evidently he conceived of Germany as having a relatively homogeneous government and was unaware of the fact that very few of the leading officials shared the German Ambassador's views. Wilson's naïveté in this respect was a direct consequence of his deliberate refusal to make use of the channels of information that were available to him. According to Ambassador Joseph C. Grew's private papers (15), Wilson had little interest in hearing from American diplomats, habitually treating them like "office boys." In October, 1916, Wilson refused to see his ambassador to Germany for ten days when he came back to Washington at the request of Foreign Minister von Jagow (shortly before the latter was dismissed for his pro-peace position). When Wilson finally gave in, at the urging of the Secretary of State, he asked no questions but used the interview to lecture the ambassador on how to be friendly and "jolly the Germans." Nor did he read the letters sent to him from England by Ambassador Page, whom he regarded as hopelessly pro-Ally, since Wilson did not care to listen to opinions he did not welcome.

In addition to lacking interest in making informed and objective diagnoses, Wilson differed from Bernstorff in other respects as well. Evidently he avoided the type of contemplation that facilitates psychological preparation for future crises. Even though his series of peace proposals were repeatedly turned down by Germany and the Allies, he evidently gave little thought to what would happen if one of the belligerents attempted to use some of its other irons in the fire in an effort to win the war. This is indicated by the way Wilson handled his secret agreement with Bernstorff to help the German government maintain prompt communications with its ambassadors in North America. On December 28, 1916, Wilson authorized Germany to send messages in its own cipher, in both directions, over the United States State Department cable. This arrangement was intended to facilitate the exchange of notes bearing on peace negotiations, but it was a clear-cut violation of accepted international law concerning the behavior of neutral nations, and, of course, it involved the gamble that the Germans would not use it for their own purposes in pursuing the war against the Allies. At that time, Wilson was somewhat cool toward the Allies, despite America's heavy economic involvement on their side, because of their outright refusal to enter into negotiations for a peace without victory, and he felt willing to violate his obligations as a neutral on the grounds that his end justified the means. Tuckman writes:

> Secretary Lansing, who had to be informed because his department would be required to play the role of post office, was shocked to the core of his legal soul, even to rebellion, and each time the method was used he had to be personally ordered by the President, who was conscious only of the rectitude of his goal and careless of his methods, to comply. Wilson was perhaps less sensitive to a neutral's duties than to a neutral's rights. He considered himself justified in ignoring the obligations of neutrality because his mind was fixed on stopping the war. Aware that his object was noble, he did not imagine that anyone in Germany might make ignoble use of the channel he opened up for them. Lansing's objections to the procedure as unneutral he brushed aside as petty and legalistic. Besides, he had exacted Bernstorff's promise to confine the messages strictly to the issue of peace terms. Sharing the general impression of Bernstorff's new chief, Zimmermann, as a great liberal, honest backer, and friend of America, he apparently assumed that Bernstorff's pledge would cover Zimmermann's replies. In this impression he was strengthened by Colonel House, who assured him that the German government was at this moment "completely in the hands of the liberals" [15, pp. 129–30].

The intensity of Wilson's hostile reaction following disclosure of the Zimmermann telegram was probably augmented by his realization that the Germans had exploited the opportunity afforded by his earlier decision. According to Lansing, when the President learned that the message to induce Mexico to go to war was transmitted via the United States cable, he became outraged to the point of using intemperate language. Wilson's sense of injury was undoubtedly compounded of many different emotions, not the least of which may have been chagrin or guilt over his own lapse in unneutrally granting Germany the cable privilege, combined with intense embarrassment over the fact that the entire affair had become known to the British.

Wilson's biographers may find it quite easy to show how the particular features of Wilson's decision-making behavior that have been singled out in the above discussion are linked up with his chronic personality predispositions, which were manifested in a variety of ways long before and again after the fateful events of 1916–17. Nevertheless, it seems probable that if Wilson had been exposed to appropriate communications, the influence of these predispositions might have been checked to some extent, so that the severity of his disillusionment and the extreme degree to which he withdrew from his former role of international mediator might have been significantly reduced. Here I have in mind the possibility that during the year preceding the crisis this man's spontaneous insulating tendencies might not have been so completely dominant if the United States government had had a code of standard operating procedures such that any decision-maker in his role would be obliged to discuss with well-qualified colleagues the unintended consequences that could ensue from alternative decisions and to rehearse mentally a variety of potentially distressing setbacks that might require a shift in perspectives.

Present-day diplomats and statesmen in the United States as well as in Europe seem to resemble Bernstorff much more than Wilson in their approach to international negotiations, perhaps because of the object lessons derived from the latter's failures. There still remains, however, a wide range of individual differences in political diagnostic skills, in readiness to anticipate setbacks, and in the capacity to work through potential crises in advance. If dependable research data could be obtained concerning the personality strengths and weaknesses that are predictive of a decision-maker's capacity to tolerate reverses, the procedures for selecting personnel for key negotiation roles could probably be improved.

Moreover, if special procedures were developed for inducing the appropriate forms of psychological preparation, there would probably be considerable room for improving the long-run effectiveness of those decision-makers who already occupy important negotiation roles, by reducing the incidence of disruptive withdrawal reactions. Even men like Bernstorff might benefit from the application of special devices devised to facilitate psychological preparation. For example, a more complete working-through of the potential dangers inherent in making secret use of the American cable facilities might have alerted Bernstorff to the need for limiting the channel to discussions of peace proposals by agreeing to have all messages from Germany transmitted in the American code. In general, many men in public life who are hard-headed about taking account of the possible utilitarian losses and the initial reactions of other people are likely to neglect the long-run moral consequences, including foreseeable events that might ultimately generate self-reactions of guilt or remorse; the latter might have inclined them to modify their decisions before it was too late. Any new technique for aiding decision-makers to anticipate the major sources of subsequent regret might, therefore, have the added advantage of acting as a deterrent to violations of accepted ethical norms.

For the purpose of initiating productive research on the problems of selecting effective negotiators and of facilitating their predecisional thought processes, it seems worthwhile to take account of integrative theoretical conceptions from which testable hypotheses about cause-and-effect relationships can be derived. Although many different theoretical approaches in the behavioral sciences bear on the problems under discussion, no systematic theory has been developed as yet concerning the variables that enter into the resolution of decisional conflict. In the discussion which follows, I shall give a brief sketch of a theoretical framework which seems to be promising as a preliminary step in this direction.

III. ADDITIONAL ASSUMPTIONS

The sections which follow will introduce three sets of constructs corresponding to the following three aspects of decisional conflicts: (1) the dominant sources of decisional conflicts, (2) alternative psychological modes of resolving decisional conflicts, and (3) factors influencing the choice of the mode of resolution. The three sets of constructs are intended to serve as a preliminary set of categories for analyzing the psychological aspects of decision-making behavior. They are formulated in such a way as to be broadly applicable to all important life-decisions that have significant effects upon an individual's relationships to organizations and groups, as well as those pertaining to his personal life. Loosely speaking, the conflicts under consideration are always within a "single mind." The analysis may not be applicable, therefore, to many aspects of the policy-making decisions which are made collectively by *groups* of executives, administrators, legislators, or negotiators. Thus it will probably be of little value for predicting changes in group consensus, group cleavages, and other complex aspects of social collectivities which are not readily reducible to variables which describe the reaction tendencies of the individual participants. Despite this limitation, however, the constructs may help to illuminate many other important features of predecisional and postdecisional conflicts among the participants in collective decisions.

The main end in view which led me to develop these particular constructs was to try to integrate into a single conceptual scheme many of the diverse phenomena bearing on a person's attitude changes in relation to his overt social actions.[2] It seems to me that these constructs will prove to be particularly useful in conceptualizing the role of information and persuasive pressures in influencing a person's behavior in many diverse types of communication situations—such as psychotherapy, political propaganda, mass-media publicity, in-service training programs, formal organizational meetings, informal social gatherings, and daily conversations between casual acquaintances or between intimates. It is assumed that eventually it should be possible for social scientists to arrive at useful general laws concerning the conditions under which all such communications will and will not tend to influence a person's decisions (6). With this goal in mind, the constructs chosen to represent the various functional properties of decisional conflicts are those which seem useful for analyzing the way in which communications can affect predecisional and postdecisional attitudes and behavior. In the summary account given below, however, I shall refer to only a few potential implications of the constructs which bear most directly on the main problem described in the preceding sections of this paper—that of minimizing disruptive postdecisional conflicts among those governmental representatives who negotiate international agreements. In the present discussion, I shall call attention mainly to the implications which pertain specifically to the resolution of *postdecisional* conflicts. However, the basic assumptions, presented in the next three subsections, are intended to apply equally to pre- and postdecisional conflicts.

Sources of Decisional Conflict

ANTICIPATED CONSEQUENCES. All decisions are assumed to be oriented toward goals which involve the attainment of desired objectives or events and the avoidance of undesired objectives or events. The issues that are taken into account by the decision-maker involve, among other things, the anticipated *instrumental* effects of the decision in attaining a variety of ends, involving group goals as well as personal goals: e.g., "What will my group gain from this course of action? What will we lose? Will I personally gain or lose anything?" Thus the instrumental considerations may pertain to self-centered gratifications or to the goals of groups with which the decision-maker is identified or to both. All such instrumental considerations are referred to as *anticipations of utilitarian gains or losses*. During the predecisional period, these considerations are usually in the focus of awareness and play a major role in determining the course of action that is finally decided upon.

After the decision is made, the utilitarian gains or losses may turn out to be somewhat different from what had been expected beforehand, and new information may alter the person's overall revaluation of the utilitarian value of the decision. Such considerations affect the degree of satisfaction or dissatisfaction with the decision and can be a source of acute postdecisional conflict.

Utilitarian considerations do not exhaust the types of considerations that are taken into account by the decision-maker. A second major class of considerations, which sometimes conflict with utilitarian aims, involves the potential approval and disapproval of reference groups and reference persons who, in one way or another, are expected to evaluate the decision. (E.g., "What will my colleagues think of me if I commit our organization to this course of action? Will the executive board be satisfied with my decision? Will my supporters and followers stick with me? Will my friends and family feel that I did the right thing? And what will the 'old man' say?") All such considerations are designated as *anticipations of social approval or disapproval*. These anticipations sometimes have more importance than purely utilitarian considerations in determining the outcome of a decision.

Much of the new information that occurs after a political leader makes a decision pertains to the unfavorable reactions of reference persons and groups. Unanticipated postdecisional conflicts are frequently generated by a reappraisal of the magnitude or importance of disapproval from other power-holders with whom he is allied or from his own rank-and-file followers. However, if reality signs reinforce the decision-maker's expectations of general approval from the groups and persons that matter most to him, he will be inclined to stick with his decision at times when he encounters subsequent setbacks which convince him that the utilitarian loses will be higher than expected, even though he may have the opportunity to reverse his decision without suffering any special penalty. Kurt Lewin has emphasized the stabilizing effect of group support: "Only by anchoring his own conduct in something as substantial and superindividual as the culture of the group, can the individual stabilize his new beliefs sufficiently to keep them immune from the day-to-day fluctuations of moods and influences to which he, as an individual, is subject" (11, p. 59).

A third set of considerations has to do with *self*-reactions. Internalized moral standards, ego ideals, and basic components of the person's conscious self-image tend to be implicated by every important decision. Often these considerations are fleetingly thought about or perhaps occur only in daydream fantasies about consequences which do not manifestly refer to the decision itself. Nevertheless, it is assumed that for every vital decision some identifiable thought sequences occur that refer, at least in derivative form, to disturbing questions about changes in self-esteem (e.g., "Will I feel that my action is moral or immoral? Will I feel proud of myself or ashamed and guilty? Will I be living up to my ideals or letting myself down?"). All such considerations are referred to as *anticipations of self-approval or disapproval*. Although rarely appraised systematically by a decision-maker, such considerations are sometimes capable of arousing anticipatory guilt feelings which incline a person to reject a decision that is seemingly compatible with his utilitarian values and with the norms of the groups and persons with whom he is affiliated. This set of considerations can become a major source of postdecisional conflict, especially when the decision-maker has exerted such a strong effort to be objective and rational that he has deliberately ignored his own subjective feelings about the decision before committing himself to it.

The main reason for making the foregoing distinctions is the following:

Whereas all decisional conflicts share some of the same basic psychological features with respect to generating tension, there will, nevertheless, be important *differences in behavioral consequences,* depending upon whether the source of tension is an anticipated loss in the utilitarian, social, or self-sphere. More specifically, a somewhat different repertoire of conflict resolutions is expected in the average person for conflicts over utilitarian consequences as against conflicts over social or self-consequences. When I speak of a "conflict over utilitarian consequences," I mean that all social and self-considerations and perhaps also some of the utilitarian considerations are *dominant* in supporting the given decision but that there is at least one subdominant utilitarian consideration which inclines the person to reject the decision. For such conflicts, the modes of resolution may tend to be mainly in the sphere of cognitive changes, of the type which have been described by Festinger (4) in his recent studies of *cognitive dissonance-reduction.* For conflicts over social consequences, cognitive dissonance-reduction may also be involved but, as will shortly be described, other mechanisms of conflict resolution, such as compensatory behavior, may enter in. Finally, for conflicts over self-reactions, various guilt-reducing mechanisms, such as engaging in painful acts of expiation, may be dominant modes of conflict resolution.[3]

Sources of Motivation

The three types of anticipated consequences are assumed to affect the decision-maker's motivation to accept or reject (approach or avoid) a given decision. It is further assumed that the motivational impact of each of the three operates through three different psychological processes, which are distinguished because they can be stimulated in quite different ways and will have markedly different effects on decision-making behavior:

VERBALLY MEDIATED INCENTIVES. This refers to conscious thought sequences pertaining to means-consequences relationships. On the basis of prolonged social training and crossconditioning, certain symbol sequences have the functional properties of positive or negative *incentives* and are capable of modifying behavior in the same way as such physical incentives as food or painful stimulation. In contrast to the next two categories, these verbally mediated incentives can be readily modified by new information and impressive verbal arguments.

PRECONSCIOUS AFFECTIVE CHARGES. This refers to a certain class of *emotional impulses* which impel a person to approach or avoid a goal object. On the basis of emotional conditioning, social contagion, and direct experiences of frustration and gratification, every person has certain positive and negative emotional biases that are not wholly mediated by verbal thought sequences. For example, a sincere government official may be intellectually convinced of the validity of an equalitarian approach to social legislation but, nevertheless, make policy decisions which reflect a strong emotional bias in the direction of keeping various national or ethnic groups "in their place." In addition to chronic biases of this type, there are momentary emotional impulses that may also sway a decision-maker to make one choice rather than another. In President Truman's memoirs, for example, there are numerous indications that some of his decisions affecting international relations were partly influenced by transient affective reactions. During his controversy with General MacArthur over extending the war in Korea, Truman appears to have made his decision to dismiss the general for "insubordination" only after he became angered by a MacArthur press release which was felt to be "in open defiance" of his orders (17, p. 441). During negotiations with Churchill and Stalin at Potsdam, the bickering about a petty issue concerning the Yugoslav representatives annoyed Truman so much that he suddenly decided to inform them "that if they did not get to the main issues, I was going to pack up and go home. I meant just that" (16, p. 360).

There are also clear-cut indications in his memoirs (16, pp. 421–22) that following the news of the successful explosion of the A-bomb dropped at Hiroshima, Truman's reaction was marked elation combined with enthusiastic optimism about the war being over soon, an emotional state that may have contributed to his decision, as Commander-in-Chief, to issue an order to General Spaatz "to continue operations as planned" for a second demonstration of the destructiveness of the A-bomb on hundreds of thousands of people in another Japanese city.

The type of transient emotional impulses involved in the Truman examples, as well as the more chronic types of emotional biases, are frequently not "unconscious" in the Freudian sense of the term, because when the person is induced to scrutinize his own behavior, he is capable of becoming aware of the fact that he has affective reactions which do not fully correspond with his intellectual judgments. Hence the affective charge can be characterized as "preconscious," which is the term used by Freud to designate those "ideals" or "impulses" which the person is unaware of at the time that he takes actions but which he is capable of becoming aware of when he introspects about it or when he is given appropriate communications by others. Preconscious affective charges are thus assumed to be susceptible to change through current environmental influences. It is conceivable, for example, that certain of Truman's decisions would have been somewhat different if one or another of his advisers had induced him to reexamine the issues at times when he could be in a better position to take account of any disparities between his dispassionate appraisals of what was really at stake and his own spontaneous emotional feelings. In addition to social communications, a variety of situational factors may determine whether the affective charge exerts a strong or weak influence. For instance, the intensity of a person's fear of losing social status or of being censured by his group will depend partly upon whether the threat occurs suddenly, without any prior warning.

UNCONSCIOUS AFFECTIVE CHARGE. It is assumed that every source of gratification (positive goals) and every source of frustration or fear (negative goals) tends to evoke some degree of approach or avoidance motivation which remains *unconscious* because of repression and other defense mechanisms. As a consequence of disturbing socialization experiences and past psychological traumas, everyone is left with automatic anxiety reactions which prevent full awareness of certain motivational impulses and which also prevent the full use of verbal thought sequences for choosing the most appropriate action to be taken. Prime examples are the well-known instances of unconscious masochistic tendencies which incline a widow to make poor investments of her husband's life insurance money, entailing economic losses, social disapproval, and self-condemnation, even though she consciously wishes to avoid these damaging consequences.

Examples of the influence of unconscious avoidance needs can sometimes be inferred from personal documents written by national leaders about their political decisions. For example, the theme of avoiding cowardice and weakness comes up again and again in President Theodore Roosevelt's autobiographical writings, whenever he justifies his belligerent nationalistic actions. He states that his decision to seize Panama by force in 1903, without waiting for the ongoing international negotiations to arrive at a settlement of the purchase price for the canal rights, was unavoidable because otherwise he would have lost self-esteem over his "weak moral fiber" (13, pp. 566–67). He explained that a few years later, when he decided to risk war by sending the United States fleet on a demonstration cruise to the Far East, he avoided consulting with his cabinet, just as when he decided to take Panama, because "the duty of a leader is to lead and not to take refuge behind the generally timid wisdom of a multitude of councilors." And later on, as self-appointed leader of an "anti-Hun" interventionist crusade, he raged against Wilson's neutrality with epithets such as "yellow all through" (12, VIII, 1156). The content of his repeated protests strongly suggest that this man was often dominated by a powerful latent need to counteract passive-submissive tendencies. It seems quite probable that this type of reaction formation entered unconsciously into many of his pro-war decisions. Additional examples of the influence of unconscious motives on the policy decisions of political leaders can be found in studies by Harold D. Lasswell (9, 10).

Insofar as the main reasons for a given decision are unconscious, they will remain relatively uninfluenced by verbal persuasion or by the relatively simple methods of self-insight that can often enable a person to surmount his preconscious emotional biases.

IV. THE COMBINED SCHEMA

The three types of consequences and the three sources of motivation provide a 3×3 schema for representing the main factors that enter into decisional conflicts. This schema, represented in Table 1, can be regarded as a balance sheet for diagnosing predecisional and postdecisional conflicts. The chart can be visualized as having plus and minus entries in every cell, the pluses representing *approach* motivation (i.e., tendency to *accept* the given decision) and minuses representing *avoidance* motivation (i.e., tendency to *reject* the given decision). The pluses and minuses would have to vary in size to show the relative *magnitudes* of the various sources of approach and avoidance motivation.

If each of the nine cells were to contain relatively large pluses and only a small (or no) minus, there would be a *minimal* degree of decisional conflict. We would expect the decision-maker to make up his mind rapidly and to stick to his decision without having any qualms about it. However, if any one of the nine cells turns out to have a strong negative charge, then we are in the presence of a decisional conflict. The essential point of using this set of categories for analyzing decisional conflicts, as was mentioned earlier, is that different psychological causes and consequences are expected, depending upon which row and which column in the balance sheet contains the deviant motivational charge that is giving rise to the conflict. When one cell contains a minus charge, it is referred to as the "subdominant rejection tendency," whereas the other cells, containing positive charges, are referred to as "dominant acceptance tendencies." The modes of resolution will differ, depending upon which row contains a subdominant rejection tendency. The column it is in is also important because different behavioral consequences will ensue, depending upon whether the subdominant rejection tendency is mainly conscious, preconscious, or unconscious in character. If a policy-maker's fear of

Table 1
Schematic "Balance Sheet" For Conceptualizing Pre- or Postdecisional Conflicts*

Type of Anticipation (With Examples)	Source of Motivation		
	Verbally Mediated Incentive Value (Conscious Goals)	Preconscious Affective Charge	Unconscious Affective Charge
A. Utilitarian gains or losses: 　1. Preventing violence.......... 　2. Financial costs............. 　3. Aiding an ally............. 　. Etc. 　. 　. 　. 　n			
B. Social approval or disapproval: 　1. One's own political party..... 　2. An esteemed leader......... 　3. Colleagues................. 　4. A religious reference group... 　. Etc. 　. 　. 　n			
C. Self-approval or disapproval: 　1. Ethical norm: being honest... 　2. Ego ideal: being a "real man" 　3. Self-image: protector of the "weak"................... 　. Etc. 　. 　. 　n			

* The cells in this schematic balance sheet should be visualized as being filled with pluses (+) and minuses (−) of varying sizes to depict the strength of the motivation to accept or reject a given decision. The purpose of the balance sheet is not to predict *what* the decision will be but rather to predict other aspects of behavior by identifying the *main sources of conflict* with respect to a given decision (i.e., where are the *large minuses* located?).

social disapproval from a father figure is primarily based on verbally mediated incentives, it may be fairly easy to reduce the fear by corrective factual information from an authoritative source showing that the man in question really has no interest in the issue. If his fear is primarily based on preconscious mechanisms, however, it may be difficult to reduce it without employing some communications specially designed to provide self-insight (e.g., calling the policy-maker's attention to his attitude toward the father figure). Finally, if the fear stems from unconscious (repressed) sources, it may remain extraordinarily resistant to change unless the man obtains intensive psychotherapy or undergoes fundamental changes in his way of life which entail a series of corrective emotional experiences.

　　Thus a typology of decisional conflicts can be envisaged in terms of the type of subdominant consideration and the source of motivation, as represented by the nine cells in the table. This typology is proposed primarily as a research schema, with the expectation that studies designed to explore systematically each of the nine basic variations will provide a basis for making differential predictions.

This schema represents a considerable extension of psychological inquiry beyond the conventional discussions of decision-making. Classical economics, for instance, is concerned with only *one* cell (the upper left-hand one), and the other eight cells are typically ignored. In recent years, however, economists and other social scientists have become aware of the limitations of a purely rationalistic utilitarian approach to decision-making. Hill has stated:

Historically stemming from Utilitarianism, the traditional economic analysis of the business man's decision taking provides, like this famous theory itself, neither an adequate tool for the analysis of actual human behavior nor a practical guide to action. For it is based upon a concept of perfectly "rational" rather than actual behavior and tends to make assumptions about the kinds of decisions made, given that certain clearly defined goals are to be achieved and that complete knowledge exists about the means of achieving them. Thus the economist's interpretation of the business man's decision-taking behaviour has tended to postulate him as faced with a series of possible results. From this he is imagined to construct a probability distribution and to select that course of action which holds out the greatest hope of net gain. The difficulty with this is twofold. In the first place it ignores the multiplicity of social and psychological forces that, even given perfect knowledge, affect decision taking in the real world. In the second place it ignores the fact that in any given state of knowledge the calculation of even approximate probabilities may be impossible [5, p. 88].

One of the purposes of the theoretical assumptions presented in this paper is to conceptualize and to differentiate the "multiplicity of social and psychological forces" that are likely to affect anyone's economic and political, as well as personal, decisions. The nine-cell schema is intended to integrate the theoretical approaches and the empirical findings from several different disciplines, all of which have illuminated various aspects of decisional processes: (1) The appraisal of verbally mediated incentives pertaining to utilitarian gains and losses (the upper left-hand cell) has been the major preoccupation of recent specialists in *information theory* and *game theory,* as well as the central interest of *classical economists* and of a few psychologists who favor a narrow *cognitive theory* of human action. (2) The role of anticipated social approval and disapproval in influencing individual actions has been one of the major topics in the field of *social psychology* and *sociology*. Recent impetus has been gained from specialists in *group dynamics,* who have focused their theoretical and empirical studies on conformity factors and group norms in addition to utilitarian goals. Most of these studies are restricted to verbally mediated values, but some of the studies (such as those dealing with salient versus non-salient norms) also involve preconscious affective mechanisms. (3) One of the traditional problems of *psychoanalysis* and *dynamic psychiatry* has been the *unconscious* determinants of human actions (including all three cells in the last column). These disciplines have also made the pioneering studies of the role of internalized standards and self-concepts in regulating behavior (limited, however, mainly to the preconscious and unconscious mechanisms). More recently, psychologists who specialize in *personality research* have begun to explore some of the behavioral correlates of self-attitudes that are verbally mediated (lower left-hand cell).

These very general comments should suffice to call attention to the interdisciplinary potentialities of the ninefold schema.

V. MODES OF CONFLICT RESOLUTION

A decisional conflict will arise whenever there is at least one important (minus) consideration which goes counter to the dominant (plus) tendencies fostered by all (or most) of the others. A few functional properties of decisional conflicts are assumed to be relatively constant, irrespective of which type of consideration constitutes the subdominant minus tendency. One such property is the tension-inducing effect of high commitment to a decision. The degree of tension generated by any decisional conflict is assumed to depend not only on the strength of the motive that remains unsatisfied (whether in the sphere of utilitarian needs, social approval needs, or self-approval needs) but also on changes in the degree to which the person feels committed to adhere to the given course of action. The more committed the person is, the greater the degree of tension that will be generated by any new communication or event that arouses a subdominant rejection tendency.

Another common functional property of all decisional conflicts pertains to the consequences of the subjective discomfort and other symptoms of acute emotional tension. This state of tension, which occurs whenever there is a decisional conflict which implicates important personal or group goals, will motivate the person to work out some form of resolution whereby the subdominant (deviant) consideration can be ignored, minimized, or eliminated. For example, one of the main modes of resolution, which has recently been the subject of numerous research studies by Festinger and others, involves the *cognitive restructuring* of expectations concerning the ultimate positive values to be gained from a decision to which the individual feels committed. After making a decision, a person will seek information and use his argumentative powers in such a way as to convince himself of the unimportance of any subdominant minus consideration, whether it be fear of possible financial loss, of possible social censure, or of possible guilt feelings and remorse in the future. This mode of conflict resolution includes (a) *ignoring or avoiding information* which points to the potentially undesirable consequences; (b) *discounting communications and other reality signs* which show that there is a threat of losing something as a result of the decision; (c) *intellectually denying* those implications which would make one appreciate the threat; (d) *forgetting or unintentionally misinterpreting* the disturbing information that would make one acutely aware of the threat; (e) *inventing new reasons* as to why there will be *a marked gain* from having made the decision. Any one of these restructuring devices may help the decision-maker to reduce the conflict, at least temporarily, by enabling him to avoid thinking about or taking account of the disturbing threat. The long-run success of this mode depends upon whether or not one is exposed to unambiguous information pertaining to the threat.

Cognitive restructuring is assumed to be only one of many different modes of resolution that people use in an effort to alleviate the tensions generated by acute decisional conflicts. All modes of decisional conflict resolution represent the product of past learning experiences during which the person was motivated to eliminate a disturbing state of emotional tension stemming from similar decisional conflicts. For instance, early in life a child learns to perform certain conciliatory actions as a means of discharging tension which arises when an action he has taken elicits his father's stern disapproval. If a postdecisional conflict arises because of the threatened loss of a desired toy or some other object that satisfies a utilitarian goal, there is likely to be a considerable difference in the entire environmental situation, including the way in which the parents handle the child's distress and protests, so that he will tend to learn a different type of tension-reducing response. And, of course, for those postdecisional conflicts in which the main source of disturbance is the child's anticipatory sense of having failed to live up to his own internalized standards, still another set of readjustive responses will tend to be reinforced. These psychogenetic considerations are introduced here only to convey the reasons for expecting that a child's readiness to use one or another mode of conflict resolution and the effectiveness of any given mode in bringing about a sustained reduction in his emotional tension will be partly dependent upon the source of the decisional conflict. This is what was meant when it was asserted earlier that each person can be expected to display different modes of conflict resolution when the subdominant rejection tendency is in the sphere of anticipated social disapproval than when it is in the sphere of anticipated utilitarian loss or anticipated loss of self-esteem.

Once learned in the family, school, and peer-group setting, various modes of conflict resolution become habitual patterns of response, providing a repertoire of alternative adjustive tendencies that are available for coping with the more complex postdecisional conflicts which arise when the person occupies subsequent occupational and social roles in adult life. In the case of postdecisional conflicts over the anticipated social disapproval of a reference group or reference person, a number of common adjustive tendencies are assumed to characterize the majority of people, as a product of common socialization processes and the usual forms of social training that parents give their children in contemporary Western society.[4]

Cognitive restructuring of expectations concerning social consequences is only one of many alternative modes in the average person's repertoire. Among the other major modes of resolving conflicts over anticipated social disapproval are the following, all of which are assumed to be in everyone's repertoire. (These modes are described explicitly here because they constitute the dependent variables in the series of hypotheses in the next section on the conditions under which one as against another mode of resolution will be selected or preferred by the decision-maker.)

PERSUASIVE EFFORTS.   One way to cope with a threat of social disapproval which does not necessarily involve any cognitive restructuring, is to try to convince those who disapprove that one's own position is the correct one. If successful, this mode of resolution can be fairly permanent in eliminating a postdecisional conflict, because one need no longer fear the disapproval of those persons who have been persuaded to accept the same decision.

COMPENSATING ACTIONS.   Even when a man cannot convince the fellow members of an organization that his decision is correct, he can at least hope to convince them that he is a worthwhile person as a *member in good standing,* so that their disapproval should be temperate and not lead to any serious acts of formal censure or informal ostracism. Thus the person may take on difficult group tasks, make special sacrifices for the sake of the group, protest loudly his loyalty to the group, and so on—all of which may seem on the surface to be quite irrelevant to the decision in question. This compensatory mode of resolving tension about anticipated disapproval from a reference group can be effective in producing a long-term resolution of the postdecisional conflict if the decision-maker perceives himself as having succeeded in convincing the others that he is a valued member.

PRIVATE CONDEMNATION OF DISAPPROVED DECISION AND OF OTHER PERSONS WHO SUPPORT IT.   Even when a decision-maker regards his commitment as irreversibly binding, the shock of his group's intense disapproval may lead him to reconsider, condemn the decision, criticize himself for his bad judgment, and take steps to dissociate himself from those persons who currently support the decision. This mode of resolution may be tantamount to an extreme attempt at reconciliation, a remorseful appeal to the disapproving group for forgiveness. The effort to *undo* a binding agreement may lead the decision-maker to seek for escape clauses and to call attention to legal and administrative obstacles which would help to prevent the decision from being carried out in the way that was originally intended. Even if the decision-maker does not go so far as to join the opposition, he may condemn his own decision-making abilities and disqualify himself from making further decisions pertaining to the same issues. Thus he may resign from the decision-making body and generally withdraw from a decision-making role.

SUBSTITUTE-SEEKING ORIENTATION.   When a person perceives himself as being the object of social censure or if he is pessimistic about being able to ward off the disapproval of important people in the future, he will attempt to restore his damaged feelings by convincing himself that he is, nevertheless, still valued by other people, and especially by those people who are *closely linked* with the disapproving groups or persons. Just as the child turns to his mother for affection and reassurance if he cannot ward off his father's extreme disapproval, an adult will seek for approval from *substitute* social objects. If actually censured by his group, the decision-maker will find his defeat less bitter if he succeeds in gaining expressions of friendship and emotional support from at least a few persons who are members of the group or who are closely allied with it.

DISAFFILIATION FROM THE DISAPPROVING GROUP.   If the person fails in his efforts at warding off the sustained disapproval of a group and is unable to secure a satisfying balance of approval from substitute persons or subgroups, he will tend to become psychologically (if not officially) disaffiliated from the disapproving group. Another way to put it is that cathexis of the reference group will decrease and he will seek for other means to obtain the satisfactions that motivated his membership in the group. (It is assumed that essentially the same process of disaffiliation will occur with respect to a reference person, such as a respected leader, mentor, or spouse—the prototype for this process being the child's aggrieved reaction of turning away from his parent if he is subjected to a prolonged period of painful rejection.) Thus the decision-maker will no longer be oriented toward obtaining the approval of the reference group or of a substitute that is identified with it but, rather, will undergo an internal change whereby he loses interest in having the approval of the group. He will detach himself from the disapproving group so that it is no longer a reference group for him.

VI. FACTORS DETERMINING THE MODE OF RESOLUTION

The final *choice* of a mode of conflict resolution depends upon a number of predispositional and situational factors. (By "choice" here, I do not, of course, mean to imply that the readjustive processes under discussion are carried out in a deliberate, fully conscious way; rather, I conceptualize the choice of a mode of resolution as being sometimes a conscious appraisal but often the outcome of either preconscious or unconscious processes.) Some of the main determinants are singled out in the following series of sample hypotheses, which are intended to illustrate the ways in which the theoretical categories outlined above may prove to be useful for specifying relationships between dependent and independent variables.

Personality Factors

Personality characteristics may play an important role in determining the preferred mode of resolution. Power-oriented men with outgoing personalities have a strong preference for handling their postdecisional conflicts by winning over the opposition, whereas more depressive, guilt-ridden personalities are more inclined toward compensatory behavior and self-condemnation. The higher a man's chronic level of self-esteem, the lower the degree of tension evoked by any given sign of social disapproval from his reference groups and, corrspondingly, the greater the likelihood that (a) he will not introduce any marked degree of distortion into his cognitive restructuring of the social consequences of the decision and (b) his residual tension level will be sufficiently low that he will devote little or no energy to any other mode of conflict resolution.

Another example of relevant personality factors consists of those attributes which enter into the individual's general level of *stress tolerance,* including his capacity to withstand social disapproval without becoming inefficient or demoralized. The lower his level of social stress tolerance, the lower the probability that the decision-maker will be able to execute effectively any of his attempts at persuading others or of carrying out compensatory actions and hence the higher the probability that he will resort to the more extreme modes of resolution (condemnation of the decision or disaffiliation from the disapproving group).

Perceived Status and Vulnerability

The decision-maker's perception of his own status and power within the group will influence his expectations as to his vulnerability to negative sanctions from the group. If there are clear-cut signs that he is highly esteemed by the group and if he is in a high power position, he will feel relatively free from the more extreme forms of group punishment or censure. Such expectations, in turn, will make for a low intensity of tension generated by signs of potential disapproval, which, as previously stated, implies a low likelihood that any of the more extreme modes of conflict resolution will be adopted. The magnitude of perceived vulnerability to group punishment will tend to be low if a person (a) has high *formal status* within the organization, (b) receives *intragroup communications* which convey information to him about being highly esteemed by the group; and (c) is aware that the group has *institutionalized patterns or traditions* which foster cohesiveness despite heterogeneous opinions on policy issues. The latter factor is particularly interesting because little research has been done so far to discover the ways in which different institutional practices and traditions of an organization intentionally or unintentionally encourage its policy-makers to use certain modes of resolution and discourage them from using others. For example, the probability of using *persuasive efforts* to resolve postdecisional conflicts will undoubtedly increase if there are channels of communication open to the decision-maker so that he can hope to reach the key people or audience that he wants to try to convince. Similarly, there are some institutional practices or "operational codes" which foster the opportunity to engage in *compensatory* activities, whereas other codes may foster *condemnation of the decision* as the preferred mode of postdecisional conflict resolution. Institutionalized patterns involving toleration toward new factions and toward the loyal opposition would be expected to increase the chances that a decision-maker will find a satisfactory substitute within the group and thus reduce the chances of the most extreme forms of disaffiliation.

Energy-Consumption

The choice of a mode of resolution will depend partly on whether it requires less time and effort than alternative modes. Under conditions where little or no information is available about how a given reference group will react to a given decision, it is relatively easy to rely upon simple forms of cognitive restructuring. Persuasive efforts and compensatory actions are less likely to be used by a busy decision-maker if he is required to devote himself to these tasks as a part-time or full-time job. Disaffiliation from a major reference group (e.g., resigning from a long-held government post) is least likely to occur when it entails a complete readjustment in one's entire life-pattern, consuming 'a large amount of one's available energy. The *anticipation* of energy consumption (and related unfavorable consequences) will affect the person's *initial choice* of a mode of resolution. If the first, low-energy-consuming choice does not succeed, however, he can be expected to turn to a more energy-consuming mode which he expects will be more successful in resolving the conflict than the first mode turned out to be. For many situations of postdecisional conflict, the rank order of preference in terms of degree of energy consumption will probably correspond to the order in which the alternative modes were listed above, with cognitive restructuring being the most preferred and disaffiliation being least preferred.

Availability of Pertinent Information

When a person is in the throes of an acute postdecisional conflict, he will tend to seek for information that is relevant to his choice of a mode of resolution. Most pertinent of all is information as to which types of activity are most likely to be successful in warding off the threatened disapproval. For example, certain bits of information available to an organizational leader may make him feel that, although there is little chance of persuading fellow officers to support his policy, he can be quite optimistic about winning their esteem if he volunteers to take on certain additional administrative tasks, as a compensatory action.

Another important type of information consists of advance warnings. Awareness of the threat of potential disapproval in advance and especially before the decision has been made can be expected to influence the choice of the mode of resolution in several different ways. Elsewhere, I have described how advance warning facilitates psychological preparation and reduces the emotional impact of a stressful event when it subsequently occurs (7). Thus advance information can reduce the chances that signs of group disapproval during the postdecisional period will be overestimated or elicit transient aggressive reactions that give rise to thoughtless, impulsive actions and interfere with the effectiveness of any efforts at persuading other people. In general, the higher the degree of emotional tension generated by a postdecisional conflict, the lower the probability that the decision-maker will be capable of executing persuasive and compensatory activities effectively and hence the higher the probability that he will resort to the more extreme modes of condemning the decision or disaffiliating. Moreover, when detailed information is available about the prospects of group censure before it actually materializes, the decision-maker will be motivated to find out and to take account of the reasons for the opposition. He may then use this information to build into the decision the appropriate provisos which will enable him to disarm the opposition (or, at least, to anticipate that he is capable of convincing them of the soundness of his decision).

VII. RESEARCH IMPLICATIONS

The foregoing hypotheses call attention to a number of different variables and their interrelationships, the specification of which is facilitated by the theoretical categories discussed in the earlier sections. I have tried to formulate the sample hypotheses in such a way as to indicate the types of basic problems that I feel can be fruitfully investigated in research on psychological aspects of decision-making. In addition to the problems for basic research that have already been stated, there are numerous related ones that can be suggested on the basis of the same theoretical framework. From the assumptions that were used in constructing Table 1, we can postulate that there will be nine basic types of decisional conflicts. Each basic type consists of a unique array such that eight of the cells contain predominantly positive values, which collectively foster acceptance of the decision, whereas the ninth cell contains a sizable minus value, which constitutes a subdominant rejection tendency. For each of the nine primary types of decisional conflict, the following research questions can be posed:

1. What antecedent conditions (including personality attributes, status factors, communications, etc.) determine the probability that a high conflict of this type will arise?

2. What is the repertoire of resolutions for this type of conflict? That is, when this type of conflict occurs, what modes of conflict resolution are most frequently adopted by the population at large (and by various subpopulations)?

3. How and to what extent is each mode of resolution in the repertoire likely to have a disruptive effect, i.e., interfering with execution of the decision or with conscientious adherence to the main policies and values which the decision was intended to promote?

4. What types of information and what forms of psychological preparation have the effect of reducing the occurrence of the more disruptive modes of resolution for this type of conflict?

Operational research, as well as basic research, can be expected to furnish relevant data. Taking account of the various factors that are assumed to influence the choice of the mode of resolution, the following additional problems are suggested as examples of the questions that might be answered effectively if operational research studies in this area were conducted by research workers of the highest level of competence and ingenuity.

1. Assuming that the benign modes of resolution are generally fostered by having accurate information available to each international negotiator as to how each powerful sector of the home government and the public will react to the decisions he is working on: Can this function be fulfilled better than it is at present by delegating to each team of negotiators an information officer who is an expert on internal governmental politics or by extending the information services that are currently available to international negotiators?

2. Can some of the advance-warning functions be achieved by making available to international negotiators some new devices for pretesting their decisions? For example, would it be effective to have each government encourage its team of U.N. representatives to participate in preliminary role-playing sessions in which they "game" the international agreement and its consequences, in the same way that military experts carry out "war games" in which they take turns in playing the role of the high command of each of the opposing countries? Also is there some simple procedure for launching "trial balloons" in the form of predictions-of-agreements-to-come, which might circulate among a few key government officials, senators, and other influential persons whose reactions might reveal in advance the content of subsequent objections to an international agreement?

3. Can some new institutional patterns be devised that will encourage persuasive efforts and compensatory behavior as preferred modes of postdecisional conflict resolution? For example, would it be advantageous to give certain consulting prerogatives to key negotiators after they complete an important international agreement—such as giving them the time and occasion for conferring with whomever they wish within the home government?

4. Can the vulnerability of negotiators to social disapproval be minimized by adding some new elements to the definition of the role of representatives on international boards and selecting men for the role accordingly (analogous to Supreme Court Justices of the United States, who are recruited partly on the basis of their capacity to remain unaffected by social pressure or public clamor that is irrelevant to the decisions they are required to make).

This list is not intended as an exhaustive outline of operational research problems but rather to furnish a few illustrations of typical research questions for which the conceptual framework presented in this paper may prove to be of value. Such problems can probably be more sharply formulated, more adequately conceptualized, and more precisely evaluated if there is a concurrent development of *basic* research oriented toward evaluating the general set of research problems suggested by the theoretical analysis.

NOTES

[1] The factual statements and the characterizations of Bernstorff and Wilson were derived from the following sources: Baker (1), Bernstorff (2, 3), Lansing (8), Seymour (14), and Tuchman (15).

[2] This theoretical analysis was developed in connection with my research in the Yale Communication and Attitude Change Research Program.

[3] It must be recognized, of course, that the three types of anticipations are interrelated. For example, anticipation of social disapproval from a normative reference group may result in simultaneous anticipations of losing self-esteem. Nevertheless, it may often be possible to separate decisional conflicts according to the *predominating* consideration that goes counter to the decision.

[4] The remainder of this paper is devoted to hypotheses concerning the "social disapproval" category. Parallel hypotheses can also be formulated for the "utilitarian" and "self" categories, but such hypotheses require lengthy discussion and are much less relevant for research on the prevention of disruptive withdrawal reactions among international negotiators. They will therefore be presented elsewhere in separate papers.

REFERENCES

1. Baker, R. *Woodrow Wilson: Life and Letters*. 8 vols. New York: Doubleday Doran, 1927–39.
2. Bernstorff, J. *My Three Years in America*. London: Skeffington & Son, 1920.
3. ———. *Memoirs*. New York: Random House, 1936.
4. Festinger, L. *A Theory of Cognitive Dissonance*. Evanston, Ill.: Row, Peterson, 1957.
5. Hill, J. M. *Review of Uncertainty and Business Decisions,* by C. F. Carter, G. P. Meredith, and G. L. S. Shackle in *Human Relations,* VIII (1955), 88–89.
6. Hovland, C., Janis, I., and Kelley, H. *Communication and Persuasion*. New Haven, Conn.: Yale University Press, 1953.
7. Janis, I. *Psychological Stress*. New York: Wiley, 1958.
8. Lansing, R. *War Memoirs*. New York: Bobbs-Merrill, 1935.
9. Lasswell, H. *Psychopathology and Politics*. Chicago: University of Chicago Press, 1930.
10. ———. *Power and Personality*. New York: W. W. Norton, 1948.
11. Lewin, K. *Resolving Social Conflicts*. New York: Harper & Bros., 1948.
12. Morison, E. (ed.). *Theodore Roosevelt's Letters*. 8 vols. Cambridge, Mass.: Harvard University Press, 1954.
13. Roosevelt, T. *Autobiography*. New York: Macmillan, 1913.
14. Seymour, C. *The Intimate Papers of Colonel House*. 4 vols. Boston: Houghton Mifflin, 1926–28.
15. Tuchman, Barbara. *The Zimmermann Telegram*. New York: Viking Press, 1958.
16. Truman, H. *Memoirs, Vol. I: Year of Decisions*. New York: Doubleday, 1955.
17. ———. *Memoirs, Vol. II: Years of Trial and Hope*. New York: Doubleday, 1956.

PART THREE

Personality Analysis of Types of Political Actors

10

A Classification of Motivational Bases
of Attitudes and Their Consequences

Although the following paper concentrates on elucidating the motivational basis of attitude formation and change, Katz's formulations are more generally relevant to the analysis of political and other action, since all action that is not simply reflexive is likely to have an important attitudinal component. Katz, like M. Brewster Smith (Selection Two), advocates an approach to studying the relationships between attitudes and underlying patterns of psychological functioning in which the investigator seeks to establish the "functions" served by holding an opinion. For one individual, an opinion may serve largely cognitive functions, helping him to screen reality and respond to environmental demands; for another individual, the same opinion may serve largely ego-defensive functions, helping him to adapt to inner conflicts. The first of these individuals is likely to differ from the second in the conditions of opinion formation and change. This explicit focus on Katz's part on *variation* in motivational sources of action leads readily into classifications of types of actors and into multicase analyses of how one type of individual differs from another.

Katz suggests four major types of motivational—in his term, "functional"—sources of attitudes. As he put it in the original abstract summarizing his paper: "At the psychological level, the reasons for holding or for changing attitudes are found in the functions they perform for the individual, specifically the functions of adjustment, ego defense, value expression, and knowledge. The conditions necessary to arouse or modify an attitude vary according to the motivational basis of the attitude. Ego-defensive attitudes, for example, can be aroused by threats, appeals to hatred and repressed impulses, and authoritarian suggestion, and can be changed by removal of threat, catharsis, and self-insight. Expressive attitudes are aroused by cues associated with the individual's values and by his need to reassert his self-image; they can be changed by showing the appropriateness to the self-concept of new or modified beliefs. Brainwashing is primarily directed at the value-expressive function and operates by controlling all environmental supports of old values. Changing attitudes may involve generalization of change to related areas of belief and feeling. Minimal generalization seems to be the rule among adults; for example, in politics voting for an opposition candidate does not have much effect upon party identification."

THE FUNCTIONAL APPROACH
TO THE STUDY OF ATTITUDES

Daniel Katz

The study of opinion formation and attitude change is basic to an understanding of the public opinion process even though it should not be equated with this process. The public opinion process is one phase of the influencing of collective decisions, and its investigation involves knowledge of channels of communication, of the power structures of a society, of the character of mass media, of the relation between elites, factions and masses, of the role of formal and informal leaders, of the institutionalized access to officials. But the raw material out of which public opinion develops is to be found in the attitudes of individuals, whether they be followers or leaders and whether these attitudes be at the general level of tendencies to conform to legitimate authority or majority opinion or at the specific level of favoring or opposing the particular aspects of the issue under consideration. The nature of the organization of attitudes within the personality and the processes which account for attitude change are thus critical areas for the understanding of the collective product known as public opinion.

EARLY APPROACHES TO THE STUDY
OF ATTITUDE AND OPINION

There have been two main streams of thinking with respect to the determination of man's attitudes. The one tradition assumes an irrational model of man: specifically it holds that men have very limited powers of reason and reflection, weak capacity to discriminate, only the most primitive self-insight, and very short memories. Whatever mental capacities people do possess are easily overwhelmed by emotional forces and appeals to self-interest and vanity. The early books on the psychology of advertising, with their emphasis on the doctrine of suggestion, exemplify this approach. One expression of this philosophy is in the propagandist's concern with tricks and traps to manipulate the public. A modern form of it appears in *The Hidden Persuaders,* or the use of subliminal and marginal suggestion, or the devices supposedly employed by "the Madison Avenue boys." Experiments to support this line of thinking started with laboratory demonstrations of the power of hypnotic suggestion and were soon extended to show that people would change their attitudes in an uncritical manner under the influence of the prestige of authority and numbers. For example, individuals would accept or reject the same idea depending upon whether it came from a positive or a negative prestige source.[1]

The second approach is that of the ideologist who invokes a rational model of man. It assumes that the human being has a cerebral cortex, that he seeks understanding, that he consistently attempts to make sense of the world about him, that he possesses discriminating and reasoning powers which will assert themselves over time, and that he is capable of self-criticism and self-insight. It relies heavily upon

Reprinted from *Public Opinion Quarterly,* 24 (Summer, 1960), 163–204.

getting adequate information to people. Our educational system is based upon this rational model. The present emphasis upon the improvement of communication, upon developing more adequate channels of two-way communication, of conferences and institutes, upon bringing people together to interchange ideas, are all indications of the belief in the importance of intelligence and comprehension in the formation and change of men's opinions.

Now either school of thought can point to evidence which supports its assumptions, and can make fairly damaging criticisms of its opponent. Solomon Asch and his colleagues, in attacking the irrational model, have called attention to the biased character of the old experiments on prestige suggestion which gave the subject little opportunity to demonstrate critical thinking.[2] And further exploration of subjects in these stupid situations does indicate that they try to make sense of a nonsensical matter as far as possible. Though the same statement is presented by the experimenter to two groups, the first time as coming from a positive source and the second time as coming from a negative source, it is given a different meaning dependent upon the context in which it appears.[3] Thus the experimental subject does his best to give some rational meaning to the problem. On the other hand, a large body of experimental work indicates that there are many limitations in the rational approach in that people see their world in terms of their own needs, remember what they want to remember, and interpret information on the basis of wishful thinking. H. H. Hyman and P. Sheatsley have demonstrated that these experimental results have direct relevance to information campaigns directed at influencing public opinion.[4] These authors assembled facts about such campaigns and showed conclusively that increasing the flow of information to people does not necessarily increase the knowledge absorbed or produce the attitude changes desired.

The major difficulty with these conflicting approaches is their lack of specification of the conditions under which men do act as the theory would predict. For the facts are that people do act at times as if they had been decorticated and at times with intelligence and comprehension. And people themselves do recognize that on occasion they have behaved blindly, impulsively, and thoughtlessly. A second major difficulty is that the rationality-irrationality dimension is not clearly defined. At the extremes it is easy to point to examples, as in the case of the acceptance of stupid suggestions under emotional stress on the one hand, or brilliant problem solving on the other; but this does not provide adequate guidance for the many cases in the middle of the scale where one attempts to discriminate between rationalization and reason.

RECONCILIATION OF THE CONFLICT IN A FUNCTIONAL APPROACH

The conflict between the rationality and irrationality models was saved from becoming a worthless debate because of the experimentation and research suggested by these models. The findings of this research pointed toward the elements of truth in each approach and gave some indication of the conditions under which each model could make fairly accurate predictions. In general the irrational approach was at its best where the situation imposed heavy restrictions upon search behavior and response alternatives. Where individuals must give quick responses without adequate opportunities to explore the nature of the problem, where there are very few response alternatives available to them, where their own deep emotional needs are aroused, they will in general react much as does the unthinking subject under hypnosis. On the other hand, where the individual can have more adequate commerce with the relevant environmental setting, where he has time to obtain more feedback from his reality testing, and where he has a number of realistic choices, his behavior will reflect the use of his rational faculties.[5] The child will often respond to the directive of the parent not by implicit obedience but by testing out whether or not the parent really meant what he said.

Many of the papers in this issue, [Katz's article served as the introduction to a special number of *Public Opinion Quarterly* on "Attitude Change." Eds.] which describe research and theory concerning consistency and consonance, represent one outcome of the rationality model. The theory of psychological consonance, or cognitive balance, assumes that man attempts to reduce discrepancies in his beliefs, attitudes, and behavior by appropriate changes in these processes. While the emphasis here is upon consistency or logicality, the theory deals with all dissonances, no matter how produced. Thus they could result from irrational factors of distorted perception and wishful thinking as well as from rational factors of realistic appraisal of a problem and an accurate estimate of its consequences. Moreover, the theory would predict only that the individual will move to reduce dissonance, whether such movement is a good adjustment to the world or leads to the delusional systems of the paranoiac. In a sense, then, this theory would avoid the conflict between the old approaches of the rational and the irrational man by not dealing with the specific antecedent causes of behavior or with the particular ways in which the individual solves his problems.

In addition to the present preoccupation with the development of formal models concerned with cognitive balance and consonance, there is a growing interest in a more comprehensive framework for dealing with the complex variables and for bringing order within the field. The thoughtful system of Ulf Himmelstrand, presented in the following pages, is one such attempt. Another point of departure is represented by two groups of workers who have organized their theories around the functions which attitudes perform for the personality. Sarnoff, Katz, and McClintock, in taking this functional approach, have given primary attention to the motivational bases of attitudes and the processes of attitude change.[6] The basic assumption of this group is that both attitude formation and attitude change must be understood in terms of the needs they serve and that, as these motivational processes differ, so too will the conditions and techniques for attitude change. Smith, Bruner, and White have also analyzed the different functions which attitudes perform for the personality.[7] Both groups present essentially the same functions, but Smith, Bruner, and White give more attention to perceptual and cognitive processes and Sarnoff, Katz, and McClintock to the specific conditions of attitude change.

The importance of the functional approach is threefold. (1) Many previous studies of attitude change have dealt with factors which are not genuine psychological variables, for example, the effect on group prejudice of contact between two groups, or the exposure of a group of subjects to a communication in the mass media. Now contact serves different psychological functions for the individual and merely knowing that people have seen a movie or watched a television program tells us nothing about the personal values engaged or not engaged by such a presentation. If, however, we can gear our research to the functions attitudes perform, we can develop some generalizations about human behavior. Dealing with nonfunctional variables makes such generalization difficult, if not impossible.

(2) By concerning ourselves with the different functions attitudes can perform we can avoid the great error of oversimplification—the error of attributing a single cause to given types of attitude. It was once popular to ascribe radicalism in economic and political matters to the psychopathology of the insecure and to attribute conservatism to the rigidity of the mentally aged. At the present time it is common practice to see in attitudes of group prejudice the repressed hostilities stemming from childhood frustrations, though Hyman and Sheatsley have pointed out that prejudiced attitudes can serve a normative function of gaining acceptance in one's own group as readily as releasing unconscious hatred.[8] In short, not only are there a number of motivational forces to take into account in considering attitudes and behavior, but the same attitude can have a different motivational basis in different people.

(3) Finally, recognition of the complex motivational sources of behavior can help to remedy the neglect in general theories which lack specification of conditions under which given types of attitude will change. Gestalt theory tells us, for example, that attitudes will change to give better cognitive organization to the psychological field. This theoretical generalization is suggestive, but to carry out significant research we need some middle-level concepts to bridge the gap between a high level of abstraction and particularistic or phenotypical events. We need concepts that will point toward the types of motive and methods of motive satisfaction which are operative in bringing about cognitive reorganization.

Before we attempt a detailed analysis of the four major functions which attitudes can serve, it is appropriate to consider the nature of attitudes, their dimensions, and their relations to other psychological structures and processes.

NATURE OF ATTITUDES: THEIR DIMENSIONS

Attitude is the predisposition of the individual to evaluate some symbol or object or aspect of his world in a favorable or unfavorable manner. Opinion is the verbal expression of an attitude, but attitudes can also be expressed in nonverbal behavior. Attitudes include both the affective, or feeling core of liking or disliking, and the cognitive, or belief, elements which describe the object of the attitude, its characteristics, and its relations to other objects. All attitudes thus include beliefs, but not all beliefs are attitudes. When specific attitudes are organized into a hierarchical structure, they comprise *value systems*. Thus a person may not only hold specific attitudes against deficit spending and unbalanced budgets but may also have a systematic organization of such beliefs and attitudes in the form of a value system of economic conservatism.

The dimensions of attitudes can be stated more precisely if the above distinctions between beliefs and feelings and attitudes and value systems are kept in mind. The *intensity* of an attitude refers to the strength of the *affective* component. In fact, rating scales and even Thurstone scales deal primarily with the intensity of feeling of the individual for or against some social object. The cognitive, or belief, component suggests two additional dimensions, the *specificity* or *generality* of the attitude and the *degree of differentiation* of the beliefs. Differentiation refers to the number of beliefs or cognitive items contained in the attitude, and the general assumption is that the simpler the attitude in cognitive structure the easier it is to change.[9] For simple structures there is no defense in depth, and once a single item of belief has been changed the attitude will change. A rather different dimension of attitude is the *number and strength of its linkages to a related value system.* If an attitude favoring budget balancing by the Federal government is tied in strongly with a value system of economic conservatism, it will be more difficult to change than if it were a fairly isolated attitude of the person. Finally, the relation of the value system to the personality is a consideration of first importance. If an attitude is tied to a value system which is closely related to, or which consists of, the individual's conception of himself, then the appropriate change procedures become more complex. The *centrality* of an attitude refers to its role as part of a value system which is closely related to the individual's self-concept.

An additional aspect of attitudes is not clearly described in most theories, namely, their relation to action or overt behavior. Though behavior related to the attitude has other determinants than the attitude itself, it is also true that some attitudes in themselves have more of what Cartwright calls an action structure than do others.[10] Brewster Smith refers to this dimension as policy orientation[11] and Katz and Stotland speak of it as the action component.[12] For example, while many people have attitudes of approval toward one or the other of the two political parties, these attitudes will differ in their structure with respect to relevant action. One man may be prepared to vote on election day and will know where and when he should vote and will go to the polls no matter what the weather or how great the inconvenience. Another man will only vote if a party worker calls for him in a car. Himmelstrand's work is concerned with all aspects of the relationship between attitude and behavior, but he deals with the action structure of the attitude itself by distinguishing between attitudes where the affect is tied to verbal expression and attitudes where the affect is tied to behavior concerned with more objective referents of the attitude.[13] In the first case an individual derives satisfaction from talking about a problem; in the second case he derives satisfaction from taking some form of concrete action.

Attempts to change attitudes can be directed primarily at the belief component or at the feeling, or affective, component. Rosenberg theorizes that an effective change in one component will result in changes in the other component and presents experimental evidence to confirm this hypothesis.[14] For example, a political candidate will often attempt to win people by making them like him and dislike his opponent, and thus communicate affect rather than ideas. If he is successful, people will not only like him but entertain favorable beliefs about him. Another candidate may deal primarily with ideas and hope that, if he can change people's beliefs about an issue, their feelings will also change.

FOUR FUNCTIONS WHICH ATTITUDES PERFORM FOR THE INDIVIDUAL

The major functions which attitudes perform for the personality can be grouped according to their motivational basis as follows:

1. *The instrumental, adjustive, or utilitarian function* upon which Jeremy Bentham and the utilitarians constructed their model of man. A modern expression of this approach can be found in behavioristic learning theory.
2. *The ego-defensive function* in which the person protects himself from acknowledging the basic truths about himself or the harsh realities in his external world. Freudian psychology and neo-Freudian thinking have been preoccupied with this type of motivation and its outcomes.
3. *The value-expressive function* in which the individual derives satisfactions from expressing attitudes appropriate to his personal values and to his concept of

himself. This function is central to doctrines of ego psychology which stress the importance of self-expression, self-development, and self-realization.

4. *The knowledge function* based upon the individual's need to give adequate structure to his universe. The search for meaning, the need to understand, the trend toward better organization of perceptions and beliefs to provide clarity and consistency for the individual, are other descriptions of this function. The development of principles about perceptual and cognitive structure have been the contribution of Gestalt psychology.

Stated simply, the functional approach is the attempt to understand the reasons people hold the attitudes they do. The reasons, however, are at the level of psychological motivations and not of the accidents of external events and circumstances. Unless we know the psychological need which is met by the holding of an attitude we are in a poor position to predict when and how it will change. Moreover, the same attitude expressed toward a political candidate may not perform the same function for all the people who express it. And while many attitudes are predominantly in the service of a single type of motivational process, as described above, other attitudes may serve more than one purpose for the individual. A fuller discussion of how attitudes serve the above four functions is in order.

1. The Adjustment Function

Essentially this function is a recognition of the fact that people strive to maximize the rewards in their external environment and to minimize the penalties. The child develops favorable attitudes toward the objects in his world which are associated with the satisfactions of his needs and unfavorable attitudes toward objects which thwart him or punish him. Attitudes acquired in the service of the adjustment function are either the means for reaching the desired goal or avoiding the undesirable one, or are affective associations based upon experiences in attaining motive satisfactions.[15] The attitudes of the worker favoring a political party which will advance his economic lot are an example of the first type of utilitarian attitude. The pleasant image one has of one's favorite food is an example of the second type of utilitarian attitude.

In general, then, the dynamics of attitude formation with respect to the adjustment function are dependent upon present or past perceptions of the utility of the attitudinal object for the individual. The clarity, consistency, and nearness of rewards and punishments, as they relate to the individual's activities and goals, are important factors in the acquisition of such attitudes. Both attitudes and habits are formed toward specific objects, people, and symbols as they satisfy specific needs. The closer these objects are to actual need satisfaction and the more they are clearly perceived as relevant to need satisfaction, the greater are the probabilities of positive attitude formation. These principles of attitude formation are often observed in the breach rather than the compliance. In industry, management frequently expects to create favorable attitudes toward job performance through programs for making the company more attractive to the worker, such as providing recreational facilities and fringe benefits. Such programs, however, are much more likely to produce favorable attitudes toward the company as a desirable place to work than toward performance on the job. The company benefits and advantages are applied across the board to all employees and are not specifically relevant to increased effort in task performance by the individual worker.

Consistency of reward and punishment also contributes to the clarity of the instrumental object for goal attainment. If a political party bestows recognition and favors on party workers in an unpredictable and inconsistent fashion, it will destroy the favorable evaluation of the importance of working hard for the party among those whose motivation is of the utilitarian sort. But, curiously, while consistency of reward needs to be observed, 100 percent consistency is not as effective as a pattern which is usually consistent but in which there are some lapses. When animal or human subjects are invariably rewarded for a correct performance, they do not retain their learned responses as well as when the reward is sometimes skipped.[16]

2. The Ego-Defensive Function

People not only seek to make the most of their external world and what it offers, but they also expend a great deal of their energy on living with themselves. The mechanisms by which the individual protects his ego from his own unacceptable impulses and from the knowledge of threatening forces from without, and the methods by which he reduces his anxieties created by such problems, are known as mechanisms of ego defense. A more complete account of their origin and nature will be found in Sarnoff's article in this issue.[17] They include the devices by which the individual avoids facing either the inner reality of the kind of person he is, or the outer reality of the dangers the world holds for him. They stem basically from internal conflict with its resulting insecurities. In one sense the mechanisms of defense are adaptive in temporarily removing the sharp edges of conflict and in saving the individual from complete disaster. In another sense they are not adaptive in that they handicap the individual in his social adjustments and in obtaining the maximum satisfactions available to him from the world in which he lives. The worker who persistently quarrels with his boss and with his fellow workers, because he is acting out some of his own internal conflicts, may in this manner relieve himself of some of the emotional tensions which beset him. He is not, however, solving his problem of adjusting to his work situation and thus may deprive himself of advancement or even of steady employment.

Defense mechanisms, Miller and Swanson point out, may be classified into two families on the basis of the more or less primitive nature of the devices employed.[18] The first family, more primitive in nature, are more socially handicapping and consist of denial and complete avoidance. The individual in such case obliterates through withdrawal and denial the realities which confront him. The exaggerated case of such primitive mechanisms is the fantasy world of the paranoiac. The second type of defense is less handicapping and makes for distortion rather than denial. It includes rationalization, projection, and displacement.

Many of our attitudes have the function of defending our self-image. When we cannot admit to ourselves that we have deep feelings of inferiority we may project those feelings onto some convenient minority group and bolster our egos by attitudes of superiority toward this underprivileged group. The formation of such defensive attitudes differs in essential ways from the formation of attitudes which serve the adjustment function. They proceed from within the person, and the objects and situation to which they are attached are merely convenient outlets for their expression. Not all targets are equally satisfactory for a given defense mechanism, but the point is that the attitude is not created by the target but by the individual's emotional conflicts. And when no convenient target exists the individual will create one. Utilitarian attitudes, on the other hand, are formed with specific reference to the nature of the attitudinal object. They are thus appropriate to the nature of the social world to which they are geared. The high school student who values high grades because he wants to be admitted to a good college has a utilitarian attitude appropriate to the situation to which it is related.

All people employ defense mechanisms, but they differ with respect to the extent that they use them and some of their attitudes may be more defensive in function than others. It follows that the techniques and conditions for attitude change will not be the same for ego-defensive as for utilitarian attitudes.

Moreover, though people are ordinarily unaware of their defense mechanisms, especially at the time of employing them, they differ with respect to the amount of insight they may show at some later time about their use of defenses. In some cases they recognize that they have been protecting their egos without knowing the reason why. In other cases they may not even be aware of the devices they have been using to delude themselves.

3. The Value-Expressive Function

While many attitudes have the function of preventing the individual from revealing to himself and others his true nature, other attitudes have the function of giving positive expression to his central values and to the type of person he conceives himself to be. A man may consider himself to be an enlightened conservative or an internationalist or a liberal, and will hold attitudes which are the appropriate indication of his central values. Thus we need to take account of the fact that not all behavior has the negative function of reducing the tensions of biological drives or of internal conflicts. Satisfactions also accrue to the person from the expression of attitudes which reflect his cherished beliefs and his self-image. The reward to the person in these instances is not so much a matter of gaining social recognition or monetary rewards as of establishing his self-identity and confirming his notion of the sort of person he sees himself to be. The gratifications obtained from value expression may go beyond the confirmation of self-identity. Just as we find satisfaction in the exercise of our talents and abilities, so we find reward in the expression of any attributes associated with our egos.

Value-expressive attitudes not only give clarity to the self-image but also mold that self-image closer to the heart's desire. The teenager who by dress and speech establishes his identity as similar to his own peer group may appear to the outsider a weakling and a craven conformer. To himself he is asserting his independence of the adult world to which he has rendered childlike subservience and conformity all his life. Very early in the development of the personality the need for clarity of self-image is important—the need to know "who I am." Later it may be even more important to know that in some measure I am the type of person I want to be. Even as adults, however, the clarity and stability of the self-image is of primary significance. Just as the kind, considerate person will cover over his acts of selfishness, so too will the ruthless individualist become confused and embarrassed by his acts of sympathetic compassion. One reason it is difficult to change the character of the adult is that he is not comfortable with the new "me." Group support for such personality change is almost a necessity, as in Alcoholics Anonymous, so that the individual is aware of approval of his new self by people who are like him.

The socialization process during the formative years sets the basic outlines for the individual's self-concept. Parents constantly hold up before the child the model of the good character they want him to be. A good boy eats his spinach, does not hit girls, etc. The candy and the stick are less in evidence in training the child than the constant appeal to his notion of his own character. It is small wonder, then, that children reflect the acceptance of this model by inquiring about the characters of the actors in every drama, whether it be a television play, a political contest, or a war, wanting to know who are the "good guys" and who are the "bad guys." Even as adults we persist in labeling others in the terms of such character images. Joe McCarthy and his cause collapsed in fantastic fashion when the telecast of the Army hearings showed him in the role of the villain attacking the gentle, good man represented by Joseph Welch.

A related but somewhat different process from childhood socialization takes place when individuals enter a new group or organization. The individual will often take over and internalize the values of the group. What accounts, however, for the fact that sometimes this occurs and sometimes it does not? Four factors are probably operative, and some combination of them may be necessary for internalization. (1) The values of the new group may be highly consistent with existing values central to the personality. The girl who enters the nursing profession finds it congenial to consider herself a good nurse because of previous values of the importance of contributing to the welfare of others. (2) The new group may in its ideology have a clear model of what the good group member should be like and may persistently indoctrinate group members in these terms. One of the reasons for the code of conduct for members of the armed forces, devised after the revelations about the conduct of American prisoners in the Korean War, was to attempt to establish a model for what a good soldier does and does not do. (3) The activities of the group in moving toward its goal permit the individual genuine opportunity for participation. To become ego-involved so that he can internalize group values, the new member must find one of two conditions. The group activity open to him must tap his talents and abilities so that his chance to show what he is worth can be tied into the group effort. Or else the activities of the group must give him an active voice in group decisions. His particular talents and abilities may not be tapped but he does have the opportunity to enter into group decisions, and thus his need for self-determination is satisfied. He then identifies with the group in which such opportunities for ego-involvement are available. It is not necessary that opportunities for self-expression and self-determination be of great magnitude in an objective sense, so long as they are important for the psychological economy of the individuals themselves. (4) Finally, the individual may come to see himself as a group member if he can share in the rewards of group activity which includes his own efforts. The worker may not play much of a part in building a ship or make any decisions in the process of building it. Nevertheless, if he and his fellow workers are given a share in every boat they build and a return on the proceeds from the earnings of the ship, they may soon come to identify with the shipbuilding company and see themselves as builders of ships.

4. The Knowledge Function

Individuals not only acquire beliefs in the interest of satisfying various specific needs, but also seek knowledge to give meaning to what would otherwise be an unorganized chaotic universe. People need standards or frames of reference for understanding their world, and attitudes help to supply such standards. The problem of understanding, as John Dewey made clear years ago, is one "of introducing (1) *definiteness* and *distinction* and (2) *consistency* and *stability* of meaning into what is otherwise vague and wavering." [19] The definiteness and stability are pro-

vided in good measure by the norms of our culture, which give the otherwise per-
plexed individual ready-made attitudes for comprehending his universe. Walter
Lippmann's classical contribution to the study of opinions and attitudes was his
description of stereotypes and the way they provided order and clarity for a bewildering set of complexities.[20] The most interesting finding in Herzog's familiar
study of the gratifications obtained by housewives in listening to daytime serials
was the unsuspected role of information and advice.[21] The stories were liked "because they explained things to the inarticulate listener."

The need to know does not of course imply that people are driven by a thirst
for universal knowledge. The American public's appalling lack of political information has been documented many times. In 1956, for example, only 13 percent of
the people in Detroit could correctly name the two United States Senators from
the state of Michigan and only 18 percent knew the name of their own Congressman.[22] People are not avid seekers after knowledge as judged by what the educator
or social reformer would desire. But they do want to understand the events which
impinge directly on their own life. Moreover, many of the attitudes they have
already acquired give them sufficient basis for interpreting much of what they
perceive to be important for them. Our already existing stereotypes, in Lippmann's language, "are an ordered, more or less consistent picture of the world,
to which our habits, our tastes, our capacities, our comforts and our hopes have
adjusted themselves. They may not be a complete picture of the world, but they
are a picture of a possible world to which we are adapted." [23] It follows that new
information will not modify old attitudes unless there is some inadequacy or incompleteness or inconsistency in the existing attitudinal structure as it relates to the
perceptions of new situations.

The articles in this issue by Cohen, Rosenberg, Osgood, and Zajonc discuss
the process of attitude change with respect to inconsistencies and discrepancies in
cognitive structure.

DETERMINANTS OF THE ATTITUDE AROUSAL
AND ATTITUDE CHANGE

The problems of attitude arousal and of attitude change are separate problems.
The first has to do with the fact that the individual has many predispositions to
act and many influences playing upon him. Hence we need a more precise description of the appropriate conditions which will evoke a given attitude. The second
problem is that of specifying the factors which will help to predict the modification
of different types of attitude.

The most general statement that can be made concerning attitude arousal is
that it is dependent upon the excitation of some need in the individual, or some
relevant cue in the environment. When a man grows hungry, he talks of food. Even
when not hungry he may express favorable attitudes toward a preferred food if an
external stimulus cues him. The ego-defensive person who hates foreigners will
express such attitudes under conditions of increased anxiety or threat or when a
foreigner is perceived to be getting out of place.

The most general statement that can be made about the conditions conducive to attitude change is that the expression of the old attitude or its anticipated
expression no longer gives satisfaction to its related need state. In other words, it
no longer serves its function and the individual feels blocked or frustrated. Modify-

ing an old attitude or replacing it with a new one is a process of learning, and learning always starts with a problem, or being thwarted in coping with a situation. Being blocked is a necessary, but not a sufficient, condition for attitude change. Other factors must be operative and will vary in effectiveness depending upon the function involved.

AROUSING AND CHANGING UTILITARIAN ATTITUDES

Political parties have both the problem of converting people with antagonistic attitudes (attitude change) and the problem of mobilizing the support of their own followers (attitude arousal). To accomplish the latter they attempt to revive the needs basic to old attitudes. For example, the Democrats still utilize the appeals of the New Deal and the Republicans still talk of the balanced budget. The assumption is that many people still hold attitudes acquired in earlier circumstances and that appropriate communication can reinstate the old needs. For most people, however, utilitarian needs are reinforced by experience and not by verbal appeals. Hence invoking the symbols of the New Deal .will be relatively ineffective with respect to adjustive attitudes unless there are corresponding experiences with unemployment, decreased income, etc. Though the need state may not be under the control of the propagandist, he can exaggerate or minimize its importance. In addition to playing upon states of need, the propagandist can make perceptible the old cues associated with the attitude he is trying to elicit. These cues may have associated with them favorable affect, or feeling, though the related needs are inactive. For example, the fighters for old causes can be paraded across the political platform in an attempt to arouse the attitudes of the past.

The two basic conditions, then, for the arousal of existing attitudes are the activation of their relevant need states and the perception of the appropriate cues associated with the content of the attitude.

To change attitudes which serve a utilitarian function, one of two conditions must prevail: (1) the attitude and the activities related to it no longer provide the satisfactions they once did, or (2) the individual's level of aspiration has been raised. The Chevrolet owner who had positive attitudes toward his old car may now want a more expensive car commensurate with his new status.

Attitudes toward political parties and voting behavior are often difficult to change if there is no widespread dissatisfaction with economic conditions and international relations. Currently, however, the polls show that even Republicans in the age group over sixty are worried about increased costs of medical care and the general inadequacy of retirement incomes. Thus many old people may change their political allegiance, if it becomes clear that the Democratic party can furnish a program to take care of their needs.

Again the mass media play a role secondary to direct experience in changing attitudes directly related to economic matters. Once dissatisfaction exists, they can exert a potent influence in suggesting new ways of solving the problem. In the field of international affairs, mass media have a more primary role because in times of peace most people have no direct experience with other countries or their peoples. The threat of war comes from what they read, hear, or see in the mass media.

The area of freedom for changing utilitarian attitudes is of course much greater in dealing with methods of satisfying needs than with needs themselves. Needs change more slowly than the means for gratifying them, even though one role of the advertiser is to create new needs. Change in attitudes occurs more readily when people perceive that they can accomplish their objectives through revising existing attitudes. Integration of white and Negro personnel in the armed forces came to pass partly because political leaders and military leaders perceived that such a move would strengthen our fighting forces. And one of the powerful arguments for changing our attitudes toward Negroes is that in the struggle for world democracy we need to put our own house in order to present a more convincing picture of our own society to other countries. Carlson has experimentally demonstrated that discriminatory attitudes toward minority groups can be altered by showing the relevance of more positive beliefs to such individual goals and values as American international prestige and democratic equalitarianism.[24]

Just as attitudes formed in the interests of adjustment can be negative evaluations of objects associated with avoidance of the harmful effects of the environment, so too can attitudes change because of unpleasant experiences or anticipation of harmful consequences. The more remote the cause the one's suffering the more likely he is to seize upon a readily identifiable target for his negative evaluation. Public officials, as highly visible objects, can easily be associated with states of dissatisfaction. Thus there is truth in the old observation that people vote more against the candidates they dislike than for the candidates they like. In the 1958 elections, in a period of mild recession, unemployment, and general uneasiness about atomic weapons, the incumbent governors (the more visible targets), whether Republican or Democratic, fared less well than the incumbent legislators.

The use of negative sanctions and of punishment to change utilitarian attitudes is more complex than the use of rewards. To be successful in changing attitudes and behavior, punishment should be used only when there is clearly available a course of action that will save the individual from the undesirable consequences. To arouse fear among the enemy in time of war does not necessarily result in desertion, surrender, or a disruption of the enemy war effort. Such channels of action may not be available to the people whose fears are aroused. The experiment of Janis and Feshback in using fear appeals to coerce children into good habits of dental hygiene had the interesting outcome of a negative relationship between the amount of fear and the degree of change. Lurid pictures of the gangrene jaws of old people who had not observed good dental habits were not effective.[25] Moreover, the group exposed to the strongest fear appeal was the most susceptible to counter-propaganda. One factor which helps to account for the results of this investigation was the lack of a clear-cut relation in the minds of the children between failure to brush their teeth in the prescribed manner and the pictures of the gangrene jaws of the aged.

The necessity of coupling fear appeals with clear channels of action is illustrated by a study of Nunnally and Bobren.[26] These investigators manipulated three variables in communications about mental health, namely, the relative amount of message anxiety, the degree to which messages gave apparent solutions, and the relative personal or impersonal phrasing of the message. The high-anxiety message described electric shock treatment of the psychotic in distressing detail. People showed the least willingness to receive communications that were high in anxiety, personalized, and offered no solutions. When solutions were offered in the communication, there was more willingness to accept the high-anxiety message.

The use of punishment and arousal of fear depend for their effectiveness upon the presence of well-defined paths for avoiding the punishment, i.e. negative sanctions are successful in redirecting rather than suppressing behavior. When there is no clearly perceptible relation between the punishment and the desired behavior, people may continue to behave as they did before, only now they have negative attitudes toward the persons and objects associated with the negative sanctions. There is, however, another possibility, if the punishment is severe or if the individual is unusually sensitive. He may develop a defensive avoidance of the whole situation. His behavior, then, is not directed at solving the problem but at escaping from the situation, even if such escape has to be negotiated by absorbing extra punishment. The attitudes under discussion are those based upon the adjustive or utilitarian function, but if the individual is traumatized by a fearful experience he will shift from instrumental learning to defensive reactions.

AROUSAL AND CHANGE OF EGO-DEFENSIVE ATTITUDES

Attitudes which help to protect the individual from internally induced anxieties or from facing up to external dangers are readily elicited by any form of threat to the ego. The threat may be external, as in the case of a highly competitive situation, or a failure experience, or a derogatory remark. It is the stock in trade of demagogues to exaggerate the dangers confronting the people, for instance, Joe McCarthy's tactics with respect to Communists in the State Department. Many people have existing attitudes of withdrawal or of aggression toward deviants or outgroups based upon their ego-defensive needs. When threatened, these attitudes come into play, and defensive people either avoid the unpleasant situation entirely, as is common in the desegregation controversy, or exhibit hostility.

Another condition for eliciting the ego-defensive attitude is the encouragement given to its expression by some form of social support. The agitator may appeal to repressed hatred by providing moral justification for its expression. A mob leader before an audience with emotionally held attitudes toward Negroes may call out these attitudes in the most violent form by invoking the good of the community or the honor of white womanhood.

A third condition for the arousal of ego-defensive attitudes is the appeal to authority. The insecurity of the defensive person makes him particularly susceptible to authoritarian suggestion. When this type of authoritarian command is in the direction already indicated by his attitudes of antipathy toward other people, he responds quickly and joyously. It is no accident that movements of hate and aggression such as the Ku Klux Klan or the Nazi party are authoritarian in their organized structure. Wagman, in an experimental investigation of the uses of authoritarian suggestion, found that students high in ego-defensiveness as measured by the F-scale were much more responsive to directives from military leaders than were less defensive students.[27] In fact, the subjects low in defensiveness were not affected at all by authoritarian suggestion when this influence ran counter to their own attitudes. The subjects high in F-scores could be moved in either direction, although they moved more readily in the direction of their own beliefs.

A fourth condition for defensive arousal is the building up over time of inhibited drives in the individual, for example, repressed sex impulses. As the drive strength of forbidden impulses increases, anxiety mounts and release from tension is found in the expression of defensive attitudes. The deprivations of prison life, for example, build up tensions which can find expression in riots against the hated prison officials.

In other words, the drive strength for defensive reactions can be increased by situation frustration. Though the basic source is the long-standing internal conflict of the person, he can encounter additional frustration in immediate circumstances. Berkowitz has shown that anti-Semitic girls were more likely than less prejudiced girls to display aggression toward an innocent bystander when angered by a third person.[28] In a subsequent experiment, Berkowitz and Holmes created dislike by one group of subjects for their partners by giving them electric shocks which they though were administered by their partners.[29] In a second session, subjects worked alone and were threatened by the experimenter. In a third session they were brought together with their partners for a cooperative task of problem solving. Aggression and hostility were displayed by subjects toward one another in the third session as a result of the frustration produced by the experimenter, and were directed more against the disliked partner than toward an innocuous partner.

Studies outside the laboratory have confirmed the principle that, where negative attitudes exist, frustration in areas unrelated to the attitude will increase the strength of the prejudice. Bettelheim and Janowitz found that war veterans who had suffered downward mobility were more anti-Semitic than other war veterans.[30] In a secondary analysis of the data from the Elmira study, Greenblum and Pearlin report that the socially mobile people, whether upward or downward mobile, were more prejudiced against Jews and Negroes than were stationary people, provided that the socially mobile were insecure about their new status.[31] Though it is clear in these studies that the situation frustration strengthens a negative attitude, it is not clear as to the origin of the negative attitude.

Most research on ego-defensive attitudes has been directed at beliefs concerning the undesirable character of minority groups or of deviants, with accompanying feelings of distrust, contempt, and hatred. Many ego-defensive attitudes, however, are not the projection of repressed aggression but are expressions of apathy or withdrawal. The individual protects himself from a difficult or demanding world and salvages his self-respect by retreating within his own shell. His attitudes toward political matters are anomic: "It does not make any difference to people like me which party is in power" or "There is no point in voting because I can't influence the outcome." Threat to people of this type takes the form of a complexity with which they cannot cope. Thus, they daydream when the lecturer talks about economic theories of inflation or the public official talks about disarmament proposals.

The usual procedures for changing attitudes and behavior have little positive effect upon attitudes geared into our ego defenses. In fact they may have a boomerang effect of making the individual cling more tenaciously to his emotionally held beliefs. In the category of usual procedures should be included increasing the flow of information, promising and bestowing rewards, and invoking penalties. As has already been indicated, punishment is threatening to the ego-defensive person and the increase of threat is the very condition which will feed ego-defensive behavior. The eneuretic youngster with emotional problems is rarely cured by punishment. Teachers and coaches know that there are some children who respond to censure and punishment by persevering in the forbidden behavior. But what is not as well recognized is that reward is also not effective in modifying the actions of the ego-defensive person. His attitudes are an expression of his inner conflicts and are not susceptible to external rewards. The shopkeeper who will not serve Negroes because they are a well-fixated target for his aggressions will risk the loss of income incurred by his discriminatory reactions.

Three basic factors, however, can help change ego-defensive attitudes. In the first place, the removal of threat is a necessary though not a sufficient condition.

The permissive and even supportive atmosphere which the therapist attempts to create for his patients is a special instance of the removal of threat. Where the ego-defensive behavior of the delinquent is supported by his group, the social worker must gain a measure of group acceptance so as not to be perceived as a threat by the individual gang members. An objective, matter-of-fact approach can serve to remove threat, especially in situations where people are accustomed to emotional appeals. Humor can also be used to establish a nonthreatening atmosphere, but it should not be directed against the audience or even against the problem. Cooper and Jahoda attempted to change prejudiced attitudes by ridicule, in the form of cartoons which made Mr. Biggott seem silly, especially when he rejected a blood transfusion which did not come from 100 percent Americans.[32] Instead of changing their attitudes, the subjects in this experiment found ways of evading the meaning of the cartoons.

In the second place, catharsis or the ventilation of feelings can help to set the stage for attitude change. Mention has already been made of the building up of tension owing to the lack of discharge of inhibited impulses. When emotional tension is at a high level the individual will respond defensively and resist attempts to change him. Hence, providing him with opportunities to blow off steam may often be necessary before attempting a serious discussion of new possibilities of behavior. Again, humor can serve this purpose.

There are many practical problems in the use of catharsis, however, because of its complex relationship to other variables. In his review of the experimental work on the expression of hostility Berkowitz reports more findings supporting than contradicting the catharsis hypothesis, but there is no clear agreement about the mechanisms involved.[33] Under certain circumstances permitting emotional outbursts can act as a reward. In a gripe session to allow individuals to express their complaints, group members can reinforce one another's negative attitudes. Unless there are positive forces in the situation which lead to a serious consideration of the problem, the gripe session may have boomerang effects. The technique often employed is to keep the group in session long enough for the malcontents to get talked out so that more sober voices can be heard. Catharsis may function at two levels. It can operate to release or drain off energy of the moment, as in the above description. It can also serve to bring to the surface something of the nature of the conflict affecting the individual. So long as his impulses are repressed and carefully disguised, the individual has little chance of gaining even rudimentary insight into himself.

In the third place, ego-defensive behavior can be altered as the individual acquires insight into his own mechanisms of defense. Information about the nature of the problem in the external world will not affect him. Information about his own functioning may have an influence, if presented without threat, and if the defenses do not go too deep into the personality. In other words, only prolonged therapy can help the psychologically sick person. Many normal people, however, employ ego defenses about which they have some degree of awareness, though generally not at the time of the expression of such defenses. The frustrations of a tough day at work may result in an authoritarian father displacing his aggression that night on his family in yelling at his wife, or striking his youngsters. Afterward he may recognize the cause of his behavior. Not all defensive behavior, then, is so deep rooted in the personality as to be inaccessible to awareness and insight. Therefore, procedures for arousing self-insight can be utilized to change behavior, even in mass communications.

One technique is to show people the psychodynamics of attitudes, especially as they appear in the behavior of others. Allport's widely used pamphlet on the A B C's of Scapegoating is based upon the technique.[34] Katz, Sarnoff, and McClintock have conducted experimental investigations of the effects of insightful materials upon the reduction of prejudice.[35] In their procedure the psychodynamics of prejudice was presented in the case history of a subject sufficiently similar to the subjects as to appear as a sympathetic character. Two findings appeared in these investigations: (1) Subjects who were very high in defensiveness were not affected by the insight materials, but subjects of low or moderate defensiveness were significantly affected. (2) The changes in attitude produced by the arousal of self-insight persisted for a longer period of time than changes induced by information or conformity pressures. In a further experiment Stotland, Katz, and Patchen found that involving subjects in the task of understanding the dynamics of prejudice helped arouse self-insight and reduce prejudice.[36] McClintock compared an ethnocentric appeal, an information message, and self-insight materials, with similar results.[37] There was differential acceptance of these influences according to the personality pattern of the subject. McClintock also found a difference in F-scale items in predicting attitude change, with the projectivity items showing a different pattern from the conformity items.

Of practical concern are four general areas in which insufficient attention has been paid to the ego-defensive basis of attitudes with respect to the role of communication in inducing social change:

1. Prejudices toward foreigners, toward racial and religious outgroups, and toward international affairs often fall into this category. The thesis of the authors of *The Authoritarian Personality* that the defenses of repression and projectivity are correlated with racial prejudice has seen more confirmation than disproof in spite of the fact that not all racial prejudice is ego-defensive in nature. In a review of studies involving the California F-scale, Titus and Hollander report investigations where positive correlations were obtained between high scores on authoritarianism and prejudice and xenophobia.[38]

Of course not all the variance in social prejudice can be accounted for by ego-defensiveness. Pettigrew has shown that a sample of southern respondents was almost identical with a sample of northern respondents on the F-scale measure of authoritarianism, but the southern sample was much more negative toward Negroes with respect to employment, housing, and voting.[39]

Relations have also been found between authoritarianism and attitudes toward nationalism and internationalism. Levinson constructed a scale to give an index of internationalism which included such items as opinions about immigration policy, armaments, the get-tough with Russia policy, cooperation with Red China, our role in the UN, etc. This measure of internationalism correlated .60 with the F-scale.[40] A study by Lane in 1952 showed that a larger proportion of authoritarians than of equalitarians were against working toward a peaceful settlement of the Korean issue. The authoritarians either favored the bombing of China and Manchuria or else were for complete withdrawal.[41] And Smith and Rosen found such consistent negative relations between world-mindedness and the dimension of authoritarianism that they suggested in the interest of parsimony the two be considered as slightly different aspects of the same basic personality structure.[42]

2. A related area of attitudes consists of opinions toward deviant types of personalities, e.g. delinquents, the mentally ill, Beatniks, and other nonconformers.

The problem of the rehabilitation of the exconvict or the discharged mental patient is sometimes impeded by the emotional attitudes of the public toward individuals with a record of institutionalization.

3. Attitudes toward public health measures, whether the fluoridation of the water supply of a community, the utilization of X-ray examinations for the prevention of disease, or the availability of information about birth control, often have their roots in unacknowledged anxieties and fears. Davis, for example, believes that opposition to fluoridation is not so much a matter of ignorance of the specific problem as it is a function of a deeper attitudinal syndrome of naturalism.[43] Governmental interference with natural processes is regarded as the source of many evils, and this general ideology is tinged with suspicion and distrust suggestive of defensive motivation.

4. Apathy toward political issues and especially toward atomic weapons may reflect a defensive withdrawal on the part of some people. The information officer of a government agency or the public relations officer in charge of a health campaign faces the difficult problem of changing public attitudes which may satisfy different needs for different people. To present information designed to show the dangerous situation we are in may be effective for some people but may prove too threatening for others. What is needed in such cases is research which will get at the reasons why people hold the attitudes they do. There are times when dramatically confronting the public with the dangers of a situation may be more effective strategy than a more reassuring approach. But there are also occasions when the first strategy will merely add to defensive avoidance. Gladstone and Taylor presented communications to their students, two of which were news stories from the *New York Times*.[44] One reported speeches made by Malenkov and Khrushchev about the peaceful intentions of the Soviet Union but its readiness to crush aggressors. The second news story reported British reactions to the American opinion about the situation in Indo-China. A third communication concerned the H-bomb and its dangers. Students were previously tested on their susceptibility to being threatened. Those who were threat-prone tended to deny the truth of the points in the communications or to overlook them entirely. For these subjects the communications had no effect on existing attitudes.

The use of mass communication has been better adapted to supplying information and to emphasizing the advantages of a course of action than to changing defensive attitudes. A new field in communication to large publics is the creation of self-understanding, which so far has been pre-empted by personal advice columns. The specifics for this new development remain to be worked out, but they may well start with techniques based upon attitude research of the basic reasons for resistance to an objectively desirable program.

CONDITIONS FOR AROUSING AND CHANGING VALUE-EXPRESSIVE ATTITUDES

Two conditions for the arousal of value-expressive attitudes can be specified. The first is the occurrence of the cue in the stimulus situation which has been associated with the attitude. The liberal Democrat, as a liberal Democrat, has always believed in principle that an income tax is more just than a sales tax. Now the issue has arisen in his state, and the group in which he happens to be at the moment are discussing an increase in sales tax. This will be sufficient to cue off his opposition to the proposal without consideration of the specific local aspects of the tax problem. The second condition for the arousal of this type of attitude is some degree of thwarting of the individual's expressive behavior in the immediate past. The housewife occupied with the routine care of the home and the children during the day may seek opportunities to express her views to other women at the first social gathering she attends.

We have referred to voters backing their party for bread and butter reasons. Perhaps the bulk of voting behavior, however, is the elicitation of value-expressive attitudes. Voting is a symbolic expression of being a Republican or a Democrat. Party identification accounts for more variance in voting behavior than any other single factor.[45] Though there is a minority who consider themselves independent and though there are minor shifts in political allegiance, the great majority of the people identify themselves as the supporters of a political party. Their voting behavior is an expression of this self-concept, and it takes a major event such as a depression to affect their voting habits seriously.

Identification with party is in good measure a function of the political socialization of the child, as Hyman has shown.[46] An analysis of a national sample of the electorate in 1952 by Campbell, Gurin, and Miller revealed that of voters both of whose parents were Democrats, 76 percent identified themselves as Democrats, another 10 percent as independent Democrats, and 12 percent as Republicans.[47] Similarly, of those with Republican parents 63 percent considered themselves Republican and another 10 percent as independent Republicans. Attachment to party, Hyman suggests, furnishes an organizing principle for the individual and gives stability to his political orientation in the confusion of changing issues.

Even in European countries, where we assume greater knowledge of issues, political behavior is the symbolic expression of people's values. Members of the Labor party in Norway, for example, are little more conversant with the stand of their party on issues than are voters in the United States. In fact, the policy of their party in international affairs and armament in recent years has been closer to the views of Conservative voters than to their own. Nevertheless, they consider themselves supporters of the party which reflects their general values.

The problem of the political leader is to make salient the cues related to political allegiance in order to arouse the voters who consider themselves party supporters to the point of expressing their attitudes by voting on election day. One technique is to increase the volume and intensity of relevant stimulation as the election approaches. If the relevant cues could be presented to each voter on election day—for example, a ballot box in his home—then the appropriate behavior would follow. But the citizen must remember on the given Tuesday that this is election day and that he must find time to go to the polls. The task of party organization is to try to remind him of this fact the weekend before, to call him that very day by phone, or even to call for him in person.

Again, two conditions are relevant in changing value-expressive attitudes:

1. Some degree of dissatisfaction with one's self-concept or its associated values is the opening wedge for fundamental change. The complacent person, smugly satisfied with all aspects of himself, is immune to attempts to change his values. Dissatisfaction with the self can result from failures or from the inadequacy of one's values in preserving a favorable image of oneself in a changing world. The man with pacifist values may have become dissatisfied with himself during a period of fascist expansion and terror. Once there is a crack in the individual's central belief systems, it can be exploited by appropriately directed influences. The

techniques of brain washing employed by the Chinese Communists both on prisoners of war in Korea and in the thought reform of Chinese intellectuals were essentially procedures for changing value systems.

In the brain washing of Chinese intellectuals in the revolutionary college, the Communists took advantage of the confused identity of the student.[48] He had been both a faithful son and a rebellious reformer and perhaps even an uninvolved cynic. To make him an enthusiastic Communist the officials attempted to destroy his allegiance to his parents and to transfer his loyalty to Communist doctrines which could meet his values as a rebel. Group influences were mobilized to help bring about the change by intensifying guilt feelings and providing for atonement and redemption through the emotional catharsis of personal confession.

To convert American prisoners of war, the Communists made a careful study of the vulnerability of their victims. They found additional weaknesses through a system of informers and created new insecurities by giving the men no social support for their old values.[49] They manipulated group influences to support Communist values and exploited their ability to control behavior and all punishments and rewards in the situation. The direction of all their efforts, however, was to undermine old values and to supply new ones. The degree of their success has probably been exaggerated in the public prints, but from their point of view they did achieve some genuine gains. One estimate is that some 15 percent of the returning prisoners of war were active collaborators, another 5 percent resisters, and some 80 percent "neutrals." Segal, in a study of a sample of 579 of these men, found that 12 percent had to some degree accepted Communist ideology.[50]

2. Dissatisfaction with old attitudes as inappropriate to one's values can also lead to change. In fact, people are much less likely to find their values uncongenial than they are to find some of their attitudes inappropriate to their values. The discomfort with one's old attitudes may stem from new experiences or from the suggestions of other people. Senator Vandenberg, as an enlightened conservative, changed his attitudes on foreign relations from an isolationist to an internationalist position when critical events in our history suggested change. The influences exerted upon people are often in the direction of showing the inappropriateness of their present ways of expressing their values. Union leaders attempt to show that good union men should not vote on the old personal basis of rewarding friends and punishing enemies but should instead demand party responsibility for a program. In an experiment by Stotland, Katz, and Patchen there was suggestive evidence of the readiness of subjects to change attitudes which they found inappropriate to their values.[51] Though an attempt was made to change the prejudices of the ego-defensive subjects, individuals who were not basically ego-defensive also changed. These subjects, who already approved of tolerance, apparently became aware of the inappropriateness of some of their negative evaluations of minority groups. This second factor in attitude change thus refers to the comparatively greater appropriateness of one set of means than another for confirming the individual's self-concept and realizing his central values.

We have already called attention to the role of values in the formation of attitudes in the early years of life. It is also true that attitude formation is a constant process and that influences are continually being brought to bear throughout life which suggest new attitudes as important in implementing existing values. An often-used method is to make salient some central value such as the thinking man, the man of distinction, or the virile man, and then depict a relatively new form of behavior consistent with this image. The role of motivational research in advertising is to discover the rudimentary image associated with a given product, to use this as a basis for building up the image in more glorified terms, and then to cement the association of this image with the product.

AROUSING AND CHANGING ATTITUDES WHICH SERVE THE KNOWLEDGE FUNCTION

Attitudes acquired in the interests of the need to know are elicited by a stimulus associated with the attitude. The child who learns from his reading and from his parents that Orientals are treacherous will not have the attitude aroused unless some appropriate cue concerning the cognitive object is presented. He may even meet and interact with Orientals without identifying them as such and with no corresponding arousal of his attitude. Considerable prejudice in this sense is race-name prejudice and is only aroused when a premium is placed upon social identification. Since members of a minority group have many other memberships in common with a majority group, the latent prejudiced attitude may not necessarily be activated. Prejudice based upon ego-defensiveness, however, will result in ready identification of the disliked group.

The factors which are productive of change of attitudes of this character are inadequacies of the existing attitudes to deal with new and changing situations. The person who has been taught that Orientals are treacherous may read extended accounts of the honesty of the Chinese or may have favorable interactions with Japanese. He finds his old attitudes in conflict with new information and new experience, and proceeds to modify his beliefs. In this instance we are dealing with fictitious stereotypes which never corresponded to reality. In other cases the beliefs may have been adequate to the situation but the world has changed. Thus, some British military men formerly in favor of armaments have changed their attitude toward disarmament because of the character of nuclear weapons. The theory of cognitive consistency later elaborated in this issue can draw its best examples from attitudes related to the knowledge function.

Any situation, then, which is ambiguous for the individual is likely to produce attitude change. His need for cognitive structure is such that he will either modify his beliefs to impose structure or accept some new formula presented by others. He seeks a meaningful picture of his universe, and when there is ambiguity he will reach for a ready solution. Rumors abound when information is unavailable.

GLOBAL INFLUENCES AND ATTITUDE CHANGE

In the foregoing analysis we have attempted to clarify the functions which attitudes perform and to give some psychological specifications of the conditions under which they are formed, elicited, and changed. This material is summarized in the table on page 218. We must recognize, however, that the influences in the real world are not as a rule directed toward a single type of motivation. Contact with other peoples, experience in foreign cultures, group pressures, group discussion and decision, the impact of legislation, and the techniques of brain washing are all global variables. They represent combinations of forces. To predict their effectiveness in any given situation it is necessary to analyze their components in relation to the conditions of administration and the type of population toward which they are directed.

The Effect of Contact and Intercultural Exchange

Contact between peoples of different races, nations, and religions has been suggested as an excellent method of creating understanding and reducing prejudice. Research studies have demonstrated that such an outcome is possible but not that it is inevitable. People in integrated housing projects have developed more favor-

Determinants of Attitude Formation, Arousal, and Change in Relation to Type of Function

Function	Origin and Dynamics	Arousal Conditions	Change Conditions
Adjustment	Utility of attitudinal object in need satisfaction. Maximizing external rewards and minimizing punishments	1. Activation of needs 2. Salience of cues associated with need satisfaction	1. Need deprivation 2. Creation of new needs and new levels of aspiration 3. Shifting rewards and punishments 4. Emphasis on new and better paths for need satisfaction
Ego defense	Protecting against internal conflicts and external dangers	1. Posing of threats 2. Appeals to hatred and repressed impulses 3. Rise in frustrations 4. Use of authoritarian suggestion	1. Removal of threats 2. Catharsis 3. Development of self-insight
Value expression	Maintaining self identity; enhancing favorable self-image; self-expression and self-determination	1. Salience of cues associated with values 2. Appeals to individual to reassert self-image 3. Ambiguities which threaten self-concept	1. Some degree of dissatisfaction with self 2. Greater appropriateness of new attitude for the self 3. Control of all environmental supports to undermine old values
Knowledge	Need for understanding, for meaningful cognitive organization, for consistency and clarity	1. Reinstatement of cues associated with old problem or of old problem itself	1. Ambiguity created by new information or change in environment 2. More meaningful information about problems

able attitudes toward members of the other race;[52] the same findings are reported from children's camps,[53] industry,[54] and army units.[55] But some studies report increased prejudice with increased contact.[56] Obviously, contact as such is not a statement of the critical variables involved.

Contact carries with it no necessary conditions for alleviating the internal conflicts of the ego-defensive. If anything, the immediate presence of hated people may intensify prejudice. For less defensive people, contact with other groups depends upon the cooperative or competitive nature of the interaction. Prejudice against a minority can increase in a community as the minority grows in numbers and competes successfully with the majority group. Contact has increased but so too has prejudice. On the other hand, the successful effects of integrating white and Negro soldiers during World War II occurred under conditions of joint effort against a common enemy. Sherif has experimentally demonstrated the importance of cooperation toward common goals in a camp situation.[57] First he created two antagonistic groups of boys, established the identity of each group, and placed them in a series of competitive and conflicting situations. As a result the two groups felt mutual dislike and held negative stereotypes of each other. The groups then were brought together for a picnic, but the antagonistic attitudes persisted; food was hurled back and forth between the two gangs. Finally, superordinate goals were created by sending all the boys on an expedition during which the water supply broke down. Group differences were forgotten as the boys worked together to solve the common problem. Favorable interactions continued after the incident.

Contact, then, can change adjustive attitudes in the direction of either more positive or more negative evaluations depending upon whether the conditions of contact help or hinder the satisfaction of utilitarian needs. Contact can also change attitudes which serve the knowledge function, provided that little ego defensiveness and little competitiveness are present. The usual negative stereotypes toward other groups are gross simplifications and exaggerations of the characteristics of large numbers of human beings. Contact will provide richer and more accurate information about other people and will show them to be very much like members of one's own group.

A special case of contact is experience in a foreign culture. Our cultural exchange program is predicated upon the assumption that sending representatives of our nation abroad to teach, study, entertain, or work with the citizens of other countries and bringing their students, scientists, and representatives here will aid in international understanding and in mutually improved attitudes. The bulk of the research evidence supports this assumption. Reigrotski and Anderson have conducted one of the most extensive investigations in this area, involving interviews with sizable samples in Belgium, France, Holland, and Germany.[58] Foreign contact, as measured by visiting abroad and having friends and relatives abroad, was found to increase favorable images of other peoples and to make individuals more critical of their compatriots. But again we need to make more specific the conditions of such experiences as they relate to the motivations of the principals in the drama. The importance of such specification is documented by the findings of Selltiz, Hopson, and Cook, who interviewed some 348 foreign students in thirty-five colleges and universities in the United States shortly after their arrival and again five months later.[59] They found no relationship between amount of personal interaction with Americans and attitude change, and they suggest as one possible explanation that "other factors may be of overriding importance."

The importance of the utilitarian and value-expressive functions in attitude change through cross-cultural experience is indicated in the study of Watson and Lippitt of twenty-nine Germans brought here by the State Department for advanced study.[60] These visitors were interviewed while in the United States, shortly after their return to Germany, and six months after their return. They were eager to learn techniques which would help them with their own problems in areas where they regarded us as more expert. They were also willing to adopt new attitudes which were implementations of their own value systems. At first they had negative evaluations of American patterns of child rearing. However, they placed a high value on individualism and were ready to learn how to be successfully individualistic. When they saw the relation of the American child-rearing practices to individualism they developed favorable attitudes toward these practices.

Perhaps the reason most of the evidence suggests positive outcomes from cross-cultural experiences stems from the selective nature of the people engaged in visiting and traveling. Students and visitors who come from abroad come for specific purposes related to their needs and values. They do not come for the ego-defensive purposes of venting their aggression on a scapegoat or expressing their superiority, though some may come to escape problems at home. Once the visitor is in a foreign country, however, many circumstances can arouse ego-defensiveness. He is in a strange world where his usual coping mechanisms are no longer successful. He lacks the customary social support of his group. He may be forced to accept a lower status than he enjoys at home. The wife of the American Fulbrighter, who bears the brunt of the adjustment problem, may become defensive and negative toward the host country. The status problem is often in evidence when Indian scholars who enjoy privilege and position in their own country are reduced to the lowly status of a first-year graduate student. Another interesting issue arises with respect to the status of the country of the visitor as perceived by the people he meets in the host country. Morris studied 318 foreign students at U.C.L.A. and noted that finding one's country occupying a low status in America did not matter so much unless there was a discrepancy between the status expected and the status accorded.[61] Thus, if the visitor expected a moderately low evaluation he was not upset when he encountered it. But if with the same expectation he met an even lower evaluation, he was affected. Of the visiting students who found that their national status was higher than anticipated, some 66 percent held favorable attitudes toward the United States. Of those who experienced a relative loss in national status, only 38 percent were favorable.

Group Influences

In any practical attempt to change attitudes, social support and group influence assume first importance. The power of the group over the individual, however, needs to be assessed carefully with respect to the dynamics of the influence exerted. The concept of *group identification* points to an emotional tie between the individual and the group symbols. This can be a matter of individual incorporation of group values as expressing his own inner convictions, as in the case of the dedicated union member. Or it can result from the insecure person's attachment to the strength of the group to compensate for his own weakness. The concept of *reference group* implies less emotional attachment and suggests that many people turn to particular groups for their standards of judgment. In this narrow sense the reference group has the function of helping to supply cognitive structure for the individual's uncertainties. Sherif's early experiments demonstrated that in ambiguous situations people would turn to the group norms for support.[62]

Whatever definition is used for terms to describe the relation between the individual and the group, groups do serve all three of the functions described above. They also serve the fourth function of aiding the individual in his utilitarian attempt to maximize satisfactions. He gains recognition and other rewards through becoming a good group member. Since all four basic motivations can be present in group settings, we need to know the function involved if we are to predict the effectiveness of various types of appeal from the group. The defensive person can be used by the group more readily than the person motivated by utilitarian needs, who is more likely to want to use the group for his own purposes. The man who has internalized the group's values can be moved markedly by group leaders in the direction of their attainment but may prove to be very resistant to leaders who attempt to move him in the opposite direction.

Control over Behavior: Change Through Legislation

Attitudes can be expressed in overt action, but actions can also determine attitudes. Often behavior change precedes attitude change. People enter new groups, they take on new jobs, and in their new roles behave in a fashion appropriate to the expectations of those roles. In time they will develop attitudes supportive of the new behavior. Lieberman tested workers before and after their assumption of new roles as foremen and union stewards.[63] As workers they were very much alike in attitudes and beliefs. As foremen and stewards they quickly acquired the distinctive standards and values appropriate to the new roles.

Attitudes may change when people take on new roles for a number of reasons, but the two most likely causes are: (1) Both appropriate attitudes and appropriate behavior are necessary to receive the full rewards and anticipated benefits of the system the newcomers have entered. (2) It is confusing to have conflicting beliefs and behavior. Some people will maintain private attitudes at variance with their public behavior, but this becomes difficult if the public behavior has to be maintained fairly constantly.

The implications of the strategy of changing attitudes by requiring new behavior have long been recognized. Efforts are made, for example, to control juvenile delinquency by providing new recreational, educational, and social activities for teenagers; the critics in the group are given some responsibility for running these activities.

The use of legislation has been of special interest in the desegregation controversy. Its opponents contend that if change is to come about it should come about through education. Its advocates assert their belief in the efficacy of legislation. At least three conditions are important to the outcome of this debate: (1) Law in our culture is effective when directed against behavior and not against attitudes. We can legislate against specific discriminatory practices but not against prejudice as such. (2) Laws are accepted when the behavior is regarded as being in the public domain and not the private domain. People will not support measures directed at personal matters such as the length of women's skirts. (3) When the behavior is in the public domain, regulatory acts still may not work if they are not applied quickly and consistently. The basis of legal authority is in acceptance of what is properly legal. Hence if there is doubt, delay, and confusion in the administration of the law, with Federal authorities saying one thing and state authorities another, the legitimacy of the act is in question. Lack of powerful Federal legislation and a strong administrative enforcement program to implement the Supreme Court decision on desegregation gave local resistance a chance to form and to confuse the issue.

The problem of whether behavior is in the private or public domain is in good part a matter of public opinion and can be ascertained on borderline matters. Public schools, public housing, and government employment are, almost by definition, not in question. With respect to private housing there may be more of a question in the public mind, though it is recognized that the community has the right to pass zoning laws. Since people will resist legislation in what they regard as purely private matters, a survey of a representative sample of the public including both whites and Negroes can provide useful information.

Though legislation about desegregation can change behavior and the attitudes corresponding to it, the generalization to other attitudes and other forms of behavior is more difficult to predict.[64] The basic problem of the generalization of change will be considered in a later section.

Brainwashing

Though brainwashing methods are directed at changing the self-concept and its related values, they differ from other procedures by virtue of the complete control acquired over the individual. In a prisoner-of-war camp or in some institutions, the leaders have control over all information reaching their charges, all punishments and rewards, the composition of groups, and the formation of group life. Repressive methods and manipulation of people through reward and punishment are old devices. What is new in brainwashing is the more thorough use of old procedures, on the one hand, and the development of techniques for controlling group life with respect to both its formal and informal structure, on the other—a perverted group dynamics, in fact.

Eight procedures can be identified from the experience of the Korean camps.[65] (1) Leaders or potential leaders were segregated from the other prisoners, making group resistance to the Communists more difficult. (2) All ties and informational support from home were removed through systematic censorship of letters and materials from the outside world. (3) Distrust of their fellows was created among the prisoners through the use of informers and suspicion of informers. Generally, when formal group controls are in operation, informal communication and informal standards develop to protect the lowly against the decision makers. With potential ringleaders already screened out of the group and with the inculcation of fear of communication with comrades, no effective informal group structure developed. (4) Group life was made available to the prisoners if they participated in activities prescribed by the Communists. If a unit of men all participated in a study group they could then take part in a ball game or other group sport. Pressure to conform and participate in the discussion session was thus generated among the men themselves. At a later stage, self-criticism in group sessions was encouraged under threat of withholding the reward of group games. (5) The first instances of real or distorted collaboration by prisoners were used with telling effect upon their fellows. A testimonial from a prisoner or a lecture by a collaborator destroyed any illusion of group resistance and, moreover, made it seem pointless for others to resist further. (6) The Communists paced their demands so that they required little from the prisoner in the early stages. Once he made some concessions it was difficult for him to resist making further ones. (7) The Communists always required some behavioral compliance from the prisoners, no matter how trivial the level of participation. (8) Rewards and punishments were carefully manipulated. Extra food, medicine, and special privileges were awarded for acts of cooperation and collaboration. Punishments were threatened for acts of resistance, but only imprisonment was consistently used as a penalty.

These techniques were, of course, carried out with varying degrees of thoroughness and effectiveness in the different camps and at different stages of the war. Unfamiliarity with American culture on the part of many Chinese leaders made for difficulties in breaking down informal group processes of the prisoners, some of whom would indulge in ridiculous caricature during the self-criticism session. The overall effect of brainwashing was not so much the production of active collaboration and of ideological conversion to the Communist cause as it was the creation of apathy and withdrawal. The environment was so threatening that the prisoners resorted to primitive defense mechanisms of psychological escape and avoidance. There is some evidence to indicate that this apathetic reaction resulted in a higher death rate, since many men refused to marshal their strength to combat the rigors of the situation.

Perhaps the two most important lessons of the Korean experience are (1) the importance of central values in sustaining the ego under conditions of deprivation and threat and (2) the necessity of maintaining some form of group support in resisting the powerful manipulations of an opponent.

GENERALIZATION OF ATTITUDE CHANGE

Perhaps the most fascinating problem in attitude change has to do with consequences to a person's belief systems and general behavior of changing a single attitude. Is the change confined to the single target of the attitude? Does it affect related beliefs and feelings? If so, what types of related belief and feeling are affected, i.e. on what does the change rub off? Teachers and parents, for example, are concerned when a child acquires an immoral attitude or indulges in a single dishonest act, for fear of the pernicious spread of undesirable behavior tendencies. Responsible citizens are concerned about the lawless actions of extremists in the South in combatting integration, not only because of the immediate and specific implications of the behavior but because of the general threat to legal institutions.

Research evidence on the generalization of attitude change is meager. In experimental work, the manipulations to produce change are weak and last for brief periods, sometimes minutes and at the most several hours. It is not surprising, therefore, that these studies report few cases of change which has generalized to attitudes other than the one under attack. Even in the studies on self-insight by Katz et al., where the change in prejudice toward Negroes was still in evidence some two months after the experiment, there were no consistent changes in prejudice toward other minority groups.[66] In real-life situations outside the laboratory, more powerful forces are often brought to bear to modify behavior, but again the resulting changes seem more limited than one would expect on an a priori logical basis. Integration of whites and Negroes in the factory may produce acceptance of Negroes as fellow workers but not as residents in one's neighborhood, or as friends in one's social group. Significant numbers of Democrats were influenced by the candidacy of Dwight Eisenhower to help elect him President in 1952 and 1956, but, as Campbell et al. have established, this change in voting behavior did not rub off on the rest of the Republican ticket.[67] Most of the Democratic defectors at the presidential level voted for a Democratic Congress. Nor did they change their attitudes on political issues. And the chances are that this change will not generalize to other

Republican presidential candidates who lack Eisenhower's status as a national figure.

It is puzzling that attitude change seems to have slight generalization effects, when the evidence indicates considerable generalization in the organization of a person's beliefs and values. Studies of authoritarian and equalitarian trends in personality do find consistent constellations of attitudes. It is true that the correlations are not always high, and Prothro reports that, among his southern subjects, there was only a slight relationship between anti-Semitism and Negro prejudice.[68] But studies of the generalization hypothesis in attitude structure give positive findings. Grace confirmed his prediction that the attitudes people displayed in interpersonal relations toward their friends and colleagues carried over to their attitudes toward international matters.[69] He studied four types of reaction: verbal hostility, direct hostility, intropunitiveness, and apathy. People chraacteristically giving one type of response in everyday situations would tend to respond similarly in professional and international situations. Stagner concluded on the basis of his empirical investigation of attitudes toward colleagues and outgroups that the evidence supported a generalization theory rather than a displacement or sublimation theory.[70] Confirmation of the generalization hypothesis comes from a Norwegian study by Christiansen in which reactions were classified on two dimensions: (1) threat-oriented versus problem-oriented and (2) outward-directed versus inward-directed. Thus, blaming oneself would be a threat-oriented, inwardly directed reaction. Christiansen found that (a) people tend to react consistently toward everyday conflict situations, (b) they react consistently to international conflicts, (c) there is a correlation between reactions to everyday conflicts and to international conflicts, and (d) this correlation is lower than the correlations among reactions to everyday conflicts and among reactions to international conflicts, respectively.[71]

Three reasons can be suggested for the failure to find greater generalization effects in attitude change:

1. The overall organization of attitudes and values in the personality is highly differentiated. The many dimensions allow the individual to absorb change without major modification of his attitudes. A Democrat of long standing could vote for Eisenhower and still remain Democratic in his identification because to him politics was not involved in this decision. Eisenhower stood above the political arena in the minds of many people. He was not blamed for what his party did, as the Gallup polls indicate, nor did his popularity rub off on his party. In 1958, in spite of Eisenhower's urgings, the people returned a sizable Democratic majority to Congress. There are many standards of judgment, then, which pertain to content areas of belief and attitude. An individual uses one set of standards or dimensions for a political decision but will shift to another set when it is more appropriate.

2. The generalization of attitudes proceeds along lines of the individual's own psychological groupings more than along lines of conventional sociological categories. We may miss significant generalized change because we do not look at the individual's own pattern of beliefs and values. One man may dislike foreigners, but to him foreigners are those people whose English he cannot understand; to another person foreigners are people of certain physical characteristics; to a third they are people with different customs, etc.

People will utilize many principles in organizing their own groupings of attitudes: (a) the objective similarities of the referents of the attitudes, (b) their own limited experiences with these referents, (c) their own needs, and (d) their own ideas of causation and of the nature of proper relationships. Peak has used the concept of psychological distance and difference between events in psychological space to describe attitude structure and generalization.[72]

The liberal-conservative dimension, for example, may be useful for characterizing large groups of people, but individuals may differ considerably in their own scaling of attitudes comprising liberalism-conservatism. Some conservatives can stand to the left of center on issues of the legal rights of the individual or on internationalism. Social classes show differences in liberal and conservative ideology, the lower socioeconomic groups being more liberal on economic and political issues and the upper income groups more liberal on tolerance for deviants and on democratic values in interpersonal relationships. Stouffer found that during the McCarthy period the low-status groups were more intolerant, and other studies have shown more authoritarian values among these groups.[73]

3. Generalization of attitude change is limited by the lack of systematic forces in the social environment to implement that change. Even when people are prepared to modify their behavior to a considerable extent they find themselves in situations which exert pressures to maintain old attitudes and habits. The discharged convict who is ready to change his ways may find it difficult to find a decent job and his only friends may be his former criminal associates. It does not necessarily help an industrial firm to train its foremen in human relations if the foremen must perform in an authoritarian structure.

ASSESSMENT OF MOTIVATIONAL BASES OF ATTITUDES

If an understanding of the nature of attitudes and the conditions for their change depends upon a knowledge of their functional bases, then it becomes of first importance to identify the underlying motivational patterns. The traditional advertising approach is to give less attention to the research assessment of needs and motives and more attention to multiple appeals, to gaining public attention, and to plugging what seems to work. Multiple appeals will, it is hoped, reach some members of the public with an effective message. In political campaigns, there is more concern with gearing the approach to the appropriate audience. If the political party makes serious mistakes in its assessment of the needs of particular groups, it is not a matter of losing a few potential customers but of losing votes to the opposing party, and so losing the election. Political leaders are, therefore, making more and more use of public opinion polls and a number of the major candidates for high office enlist their own research specialists. So true is this that we may no longer have political conventions naming a dark-horse candidate for the presidency. If the leaders are not convinced by poll results that a candidate has a good chance to win, they are not likely to support him.

There are no reliable short-cuts to the assessment of the needs which various attitudes satisfy. Systematic sampling of the population in question by means of interviews or of behavioral observation is a necessity. A growing number of devices are becoming available to supplement the depth interview. Objective scales for determining personality trends, such as the F-scale or the Minnesota Multiphasic Inventory, have been widely used. Projective methods which call for the completion of sentences and stories or furnishing stories about ambiguous pictures are just beginning to be exploited. In a nationwide survey of attitudes toward public health, Veroff et al. successfully used a picture test to obtain scores for people with respect to their needs for achievement, for affiliation, and for power.[74] Methods for measuring motivation are difficult, but the basic logic in their application is essentially that of any research tool. If early abuses of these instruments do not prejudice the research field, they will in the future have almost as wide a use as the polls themselves. Moreover, polling methods can be adapted to measuring people's needs with indirect questions which have been validated against more projective tests.

In many situations inferences can be made about people's needs without elaborate measures. If farm income has fallen drastically in a given section of the country, or if unemployment has risen sharply in a certain city, obvious inferences can be drawn. The extent and depth of the dissatisfaction will be better known through adequate measurement.

Measures of the four types of motivational pattern discussed indicate wide individual differences in the extent to which the patterns characterize the person. Though all people employ defense mechanisms, there are wide differences in the depth and extent of defensiveness. And Cohen has shown that the need for knowledge varies even in a college population.[75] Subjects were assigned scores on their need to know by a questionnaire with forced-choice alternatives to a wide variety of hypothetical situations. One of three alternatives indicated a desire for more information. In the experimental situation which followed, one group was given fear-arousing communications about the grading of examinations and then given information about grading on the basis of the normal curve. Their need for information was thus aroused before the presentation of the information. A second group was given the information about grading on the basis of the curve and then given the fear-arousing communication. Measures were taken of the acceptance of the information at a subsequent period. The subjects who had scored low on need for knowledge were definitely affected by the order of presentation. When they received information before their anxieties had been aroused about grades, they were much less receptive than were the low-need scorers who had their anxieties aroused before they received the information. On the other hand, the subjects scoring high on the need to know were not affected by the order of the presentation. Their needs for knowledge were sufficiently strong that they were receptive to information without the specific need arousal of the experimental situation. In other words, the need to know, like other needs, varies in intensity among people as a characteristic of personality.

In spite of characteristic differences in the strength of needs and motives, we cannot predict attitude change with precision solely on the basis of measures of need. We must also have measures of the related attitudes. Knowledge of the need state indicates the type of goal toward which the individual is striving. But the means for reaching this goal may vary considerably, and for this reason we need to know the attitudes which reflect the evaluation of the various means. Farmers with depressed incomes may still vote for the Republican party if they have confidence in Nixon's farm program. Some need patterns furnish more direct predictions than others. The defensive person who is extrapunitive will be high in prejudice toward outgroups. Even in this case, however, his prejudices toward specific outgroups may vary considerably.

THE FACTOR OF GENERAL PERSUASIBILITY

We have emphasized the fact that appeals to change attitudes must be geared to the relevant motivational basis of the attitude. An opposed point of view would be that there is a general personality characteristic of persuasibility according to which some people are easier to convince than others no matter what the appeal. Hovland and Janis have tested this hypothesis in a series of experiments.[76] In one investigation ten different communications were presented to 185 high school students. The communications ranged from logical arguments to fear-arousing threats on five topics, on both the pro and con sides of the issue. In general there was some tendency for the acceptance of the influence of one communication to be associated with the acceptance of other influences. Of the 45 correlation coefficients for the ten communications, 39 were positive but only 11 were significant at the .01 confidence level and only 6 were over .40. Though there may be some general susceptibility to influence, it is apparently not a potent factor and accounts for a small amount of variance in attitude change. For certain purposes, however, it deserves consideration, especially in situations where attitudes are not supported by strong motivational patterns.

SUMMARY

The purpose of this paper was to provide a psychological framework for the systematic consideration of the dynamics of public and private attitudes. Four functions which attitudes perform for the personality were identified: the *adjustive function* of satisfying utilitarian needs, the *ego-defensive function* of handling internal conflicts, the *value-expressive function* of maintaining self-identity and of enhancing the self-image, and the *knowledge function* of giving understanding and meaning to the ambiguities of the world about us. The role of these functions in attitude formation was described. Their relevance for the conditions determining attitude arousal and attitude change were analyzed. Finally, constellations of variables such as group contact and legislative control of behavior were considered in terms of their motivational impact.

NOTES

[1] Muzafer Sherif, *The Psychology of Social Norms* (New York, Harper, 1936).

[2] Solomon E. Asch, *Social Psychology* (New York, Prentice-Hall, 1952).

[3] *Ibid.,* pp. 426–27. The following statement was attributed to its rightful author, John Adams, for some subjects and to Karl Marx for others: "those who hold and those who are without property have ever formed distinct interests in society." When the statement was attributed to Marx, this type of comment appeared: "Marx is stressing the need for a redistribution of wealth." When it was attributed to Adams, this comment appeared: "This social division is innate in mankind."

[4] Herbert H. Hyman and Paul B. Sheatsley, "Some Reasons Why Information Campaigns Fail," *Public Opinion Quarterly* 11 (1947): 413–23.

[5] William A. Scott points out that in the area of international relations the incompleteness and remoteness of the information and the lack of pressures on the individual to defend his views results in inconsistencies. Inconsistent elements with respect to a system of international beliefs may, however, be consistent with the larger system of the personality. "Rational-

ity and Non-rationality of International Attitudes," *Journal of Conflict Resolution* 2 (1958: 9–16.

[6] Irving Sarnoff and Daniel Katz, "The Motivational Bases of Attitude Change," *Journal of Abnormal and Social Psychology* 49 (1954): 115–24.

[7] M. Brewster Smith, Jerome S. Bruner, and Robert W. White, *Opinions and Personality* (New York, Wiley, 1956).

[8] Herbert H. Hyman and Paul B. Sheatsley, "The Authoritarian Personality: A Methodological Critique," in Richard Christie and Marie Jahoda, eds., *Studies in the Scope and Method of the Authoritarian Personality* (Glencoe, Ill., Free Press, 1954), pp. 50–122.

[9] David Krech and Richard S. Crutchfield, *Theory and Problems of Social Psychology* (New York, McGraw-Hill, 1948), pp. 160–63.

[10] Dorwin Cartwright, "Some Principles of Mass Persuasion," *Human Relations* 2 (1949): 253–67.

[11] M. Brewster Smith, "The Personal Setting of Public Opinions: A Study of Attitudes toward Russia," *Public Opinion Quarterly* 11 (1947): 507–23.

[12] Daniel Katz and Ezra Stotland, "A Preliminary Statement to a Theory of Attitude Structure and Change," in Sigmund Koch, ed., *Psychology: A Study of a Science,* vol. 3 (New York, McGraw-Hill, 1959), pp. 423–75.

[13] Ulf Himmelstrand, "Verbal Attitudes and Behavior," *Public Opinion Quarterly* 24 (Summer 1960): 224–50.

[14] Milton J. Rosenberg, "A Structural Theory of Attitude Dynamics," *ibid.,* pp. 319–40.

[15] Katz and Stotland, *op. cit.,* pp. 434–43.

[16] William O. Jenkins and Julian C. Stanley, "Partial Reinforcement: A Review and Critique," *Psychological Bulletin* 47 (1950): 193–234.

[17] See pp. 251–79.

[18] Daniel R. Miller and Guy E. Swanson, *Inner Conflict and Defense* (New York: Holt, 1960), pp. 194–288.

[19] John Dewey, *How We Think* (New York, Macmillan, 1910).

[20] Walter Lippmann, *Public Opinion* (New York, Macmillan, 1922).

[21] Herta Herzog, "What Do We Really Know about Daytime Serial Listeners?" in Paul F. Lazarsfeld and Frank N. Stanton, eds., *Radio Research 1942–1943* (New York, Duell, Sloan & Pearce, 1944), pp. 3–33.

[22] From a study of the impact of party organization on political behavior in the Detroit area, by Daniel Katz and Samuel Eldersveld, in maunscript.

[23] Lippmann, *op. cit.,* p. 95.

[24] Earl R. Carlson, "Attitude Change through Modification of Attitude Structure," *Journal of Abnormal and Social Psychology* 52 (1956): 256–61.

[25] Irving L. Janis and Seymour Feshback, "Effects of Fear-arousing Communications," *Journal of Abnormal and Social Psychology* 48 (1953): 78–92.

[26] Jum C. Nunnally and Howard M. Bobren, "Variables Governing the Willingness to Receive Communications in Mental Health," *Journal of Personality* 27 (1959): 38–46.

[27] Morton Wagman, "Attitude Change and the Authoritarian Personality," *Journal of Psychology* 40 (1955): 3–24. The F-scale is a measure of authoritarianism comprising items indicative of both defensiveness and ideology.

[28] Leonard Berkowitz, "Anti-Semitism and the Displacement of Aggression," *Journal of Abnormal and Social Psychology* 59 (1959): 182–88.

[29] Leonard Berkowitz and Douglas S. Holmes, "The Generalization of Hostility to Disliked Objects," *Journal of Personality* 27 (1959): 565–77.

[30] Bruno Bettelheim and Morris Janowitz, *Dynamics of Prejudice* (New York: Harper, 1950).

[31] Joseph Greenblum and Leonard I. Pearlin, "Vertical Mobility and Prejudice," in Reinhard Bendix and Seymour M. Lipset, eds., *Class, Status and Power* (Glencoe, Ill.: Free Press, 1953).

[32] Eunice Cooper and Marie Jahoda, "The Evasion of Propaganda: How Prejudiced People Respond to Anti-prejudice Propaganda," *Journal of Psychology* 23 (1947): 15–25.

[33] Leonard Berkowitz, "The Expression and Reduction of Hostility," *Psychological Bulletin* 55 (1958): 257–83.

[34] Gordon W. Allport, *The Nature of Prejudice* (Cambridge, Mass.: Addison-Wesley, 1954).

[35] Daniel Katz, Irving Sarnoff, and Charles McClintock, "Ego Defense and Attitude Change," *Human Relations* 9 (1956): 27–46. Also their "The Measurement of Ego Defense as Related to Attitude Change," *Journal of Personality* 25 (1957): 465–74.

[36] Ezra Stotland, Daniel Katz, and Martin Patchen, "The Reduction of Prejudice through the Arousal of Self-insight," *Journal of Personality* 27 (1959): 507–31.

[37] Charles McClintock, "Personality Syndromes and Attitude Change," *Journal of Personality* 26 (1958): 479–593.

[38] H. Edwin Titus and E. P. Hollander, "The California F-Scale in Psychological Research: 1950–1955," *Psychological Bulletin* 54 (1957): 47–64.

[39] Thomas F. Pettigrew, "Personality and Socio-cultural Factors in Intergroup Attitudes: A Cross-national Comparison," *Journal of Conflict Resolution* 2 (1958): 29–42.

[40] Daniel J. Levinson, "Authoritarian Personality and Foreign Personality," *Journal of Conflict Resolution* 1 (1957): 37–47.

[41] Robert E. Lane, "Political Personality and Electoral Choice," *American Political Science Review* 49 (1955): 173–90.

[42] Howard P. Smith and Ellen W. Rosen, "Some Psychological Correlates of World-mindedness and Authoritarianism," *Journal of Personality* 26 (1958): 170–83.

[43] Morris Davis, "Community Attitudes toward Fluoridation," *Public Opinion Quarterly* 23 (1959): 474–82.

[44] Arthur I. Gladstone and Martha A. Taylor, "Threat-related Attitudes and Reactions to Communication about International Events," *Journal of Conflict Resolution* 2 (1958): 17–28.

[45] Angus A. Campbell, Philip Converse, Warren Miller, and Donald Stokes, *The American Voter* (New York: Wiley, 1960).

[46] Herbert H. Hyman, *Political Socialization* (Glencoe, Ill.: Free Press, 1959).

[47] Angus A. Campbell, Gerald Gurin, and Warren Miller, *The Voter Decides* (Evanston, Ill.: Row, Peterson, 1954).

[48] Robert J. Lifton, "Thought Reform of Chinese Intellectuals: A Psychiatric Evaluation," *Journal of Social Issues* 13, No. 3 (1957): 5–20.

[49] Edgar H. Schein, "Reaction Patterns to Severe, Chronic Stress in American Army Prisoners of War of the Chinese," *Journal of Social Issues* 13, No. 3 (1957):21–30.

[50] Julius Segal, "Correlates of Collaboration and Resistance Behavior among U.S. Army POW's in Korea," *Journal of Social Issues* 13, No. 3 (1957): 31–40.

[51] Stotland, Katz, and Patchen, *op. cit.*

[52] Morton Deutsch and Mary E. Collins, *Interracial Housing: A Psychological Evaluation of a Social Experiment* (Minneapolis: University of Minnesota Press, 1951).

[53] Marian R. Yarrow, ed., "Interpersonal Dynamics in a Desegregation Process," *Journal of Social Issues* 14, No. 1 (1958): 1–63.

[54] Allport, *op. cit.*, pp. 274–76.

[55] Samuel A. Stouffer et al., *The American Soldier,* Vol. 1 (Princeton, N.J.: Princeton University Press, 1949), pp. 566–99.

[56] Muzafer Sherif and Carolyn W. Sherif, *An Outline of Social Psychology,* rev. ed. (New York: Harper, 1956), pp. 548–51.

[57] Sherif and Sherif, *op. cit.*, pp. 287–331.

[58] Erich Reigrotski and Nels Anderson, "National Stereotypes and Foreign Contacts," *Public Opinion Quarterly* 23 (1959): 515–28.

[59] Claire Selltiz, Anna L. Hopson, and Stuart W. Cook, "The Effects of Situational Factors on Personal Interaction between Foreign Students and Americans," *Journal of Social Issues* 12, No. 1 (1956): 33–44.

[60] Jeanne Watson and Ronald Lippitt, "Cross-cultural Experience as a Source of Attitude Change," *Journal of Conflict Resolution* 2 (1958): 61–66. Also, Jeanne Watson and Ronald Lippitt, *Learning across Cultures* (Ann Arbor, Mich.: Institute for Social Research, Research Center for Group Dynamics, 1955).

[61] Richard T. Morris, "National Status and Attitudes of Foreign Students," *Journal of Social Issues* 12, No. 1 (1956): 20–25.

[62] M. Sherif, *Psychology of Social Norms.*

[63] Seymour Lieberman, "The Relationship between Attitudes and Roles: A Natural Field Experiment." University of Michigan, 1954, unpublished doctoral dissertation.

[64] Stuart Cook, "Desegregation, A Psychological Analysis," *American Psychologist* 12 (1957): 11–13.

[65] Schein, *op. cit.*

[66] Stotland and Katz, *op. cit.*

[67] Campbell, Converse, Miller, and Stokes, *op. cit.*

[68] E. Terry Prothro, "Ethnocentrism and Anti-Negro Attitudes in the Deep South," *Journal of Abnormal and Social Psychology* 47 (1952): 105–08.

[69] H. A. Grace, *A Study of the Expression of Hostility in Everyday Professional and International Verbal Situations* (New York: Columbia University Press, 1949).

[70] Ross Stagner, "Studies of Aggressive Social Attitudes," *Journal of Social Psychology* 20 (1944): 109–20.

[71] Bjorn Christiansen, *Attitudes towards Foreign Affairs as a Function of Personality* (Oslo, Norway: Oslo University Press, 1959).

[72] Helen Peak, "Psychological Structure and Person Perception," in Renato Tagiuri and

Luigi Petrullo, eds., *Person Perception and Interpersonal Behavior* (Stanford, Calif.: Stanford University Press, 1958), pp. 337–52.

[73] Samuel A. Stouffer, *Communism, Conformity and Civil Liberties* (New York: Doubleday, 1955).

[74] Joseph Veroff, John W. Atkinson, Sheila C. Feld, and Gerald Gurin, "The Use of Thematic Apperception to Assess Motivation in a Nationwide Interview Study," *Psychological Monographs* 12, whole no. 499 (1960).

[75] Arthur R. Cohen, "Need for Cognition and Order of Communication as Determinants of Opinion Change," in Carl Hovland et al., eds., *The Order of Presentation in Persuasion* (New Haven, Conn.: Yale University Press, 1957), pp. 79–97.

[76] Carl I. Hovland and Irving L. Janis, eds., *Personality and Persuasibility* (New Haven, Conn.: Yale University Press, 1959).

11

The Logic of Political Personality Typologies

Psychological classifications or typologies, including those of political actors, range in complexity from rudimentary categorizations based on how individuals differ in terms of some single variable, such as aggressiveness or introversion, through complex "syndrome" typologies, in which people are classified in terms of intricately interwoven constellations of personal characteristics such as introversion-cum-shyness-cum-suppressed aggressiveness. Harold D. Lasswell is one of the few writers who has addressed himself systematically to the logic of constructing psychological typologies. In this highly condensed, demanding essay, Lasswell reviews a formulation he originally introduced in what continues to be a landmark in the personality and politics literature, his 1930 work, *Psychopathology and Politics*. He goes on to present an elliptical set of remarks summarizing various of his conceptual and theoretical proposals for the analysis of political personality. In reading this essay, it may be helpful to refer to the following benchmarks:

1. Lasswell's remarks under the initial subheading, "A Three-Fold Classification of Types," briefly set forth what could be described as three "levels" of psychological typology. He suggests that if political actors are initially classified in terms of some few "nuclear" characteristics and then further studied, it often will be possible to find more complex syndromes of further correlates associated with the nuclear defining characteristics. Once correlational analysis has generated such syndromes (or "co-relational" types), further classification will be possible in terms of the distinctive developmental histories that produced the syndromes (developmental types).

2. A second theme running throughout Lasswell's paper is the need for "functional" classifications: that is, classifications of actors in terms of the *actual* tasks they perform in the social order rather than in terms of the *conventional* labels society tacks onto them. Thus, Lasswell's "politician" or "power-centered personality" may be a bishop, a college president or a business magnate. In the special sense that Lasswell uses the term "politician," a local party official whose prime interest is to enhance his own sense of importance by symbolic gratification is *not* a "politician." This neologism seems to Lasswell to accomplish a crucial desideratum for personality-and-politics research. By isolating individuals with functionally similar nuclear characteristics, the analyst enhances his likelihood of discovering distinctive patterns of "co-relational" and developmental qualities.

3. A third aspect, the least readily accessible, is Lasswell's rather stark exposition of a set of analytic terms for describing (a) societies, (b) personality structures and dynamics, and (c) the societal processes that mold personality structure. Central in this formulation is Lasswell's long-standing convention of coding social and individual processes in terms of an analytically simplified list of

eight values that, to varying degrees, are present in the goals sought by social actors and in the actual outputs that emerge from their endeavors. (For purposes of political analysis it is, of course, the value of power that is of special importance.)

Complementing the analysis of individuals in terms of their values is psychological analysis in terms of the set of analytic criteria suggested in Lasswell's Table 2, Mechanisms of Conflict Resolution (page 235). Depending upon whether an individual employs repression, suppression, rejection, or resistance in dealing with an impulse, his inner personality patterns—for example, his needs for or aversions to power—may affect his behavior in different ways and with different degrees of effectiveness. The analyst of political personality, Lasswell suggests, can usefully study how such personality configurations arise by observing how the agents of socialization bestow rewards and deprivations on individuals of varying ages; Lasswell proposes using a standardized list of values, such as the eight-value list he has worked with, to identify the areas in which positive or negative sanctions are introduced in the course of socialization. In studying socialization, the personality-and-politics analyst, in effect, focuses on developmental typologies in the making.

4. Finally, Lasswell lists five questions for further study. Together, they constitute a proposal for massive trend analysis of the kinds of personality types emerging from the socialization processes that typify various societies as both the societies and their socialization processes change over time. Consistent with his long-standing advocacy of "policy science," Lasswell also proposes using this examination of the results of existing socialization processes in connection with critical analyses of the existing practices and the introduction of new practices calculated to produce more desirable results.

A NOTE ON "TYPES" OF POLITICAL PERSONALITY: NUCLEAR, CO-RELATIONAL, DEVELOPMENTAL

Harold D. Lasswell

Even a cursory inspection of the literature of the behavioral and social sciences indicates that the term "type" has a less luminous halo than it had when Carl Jung, for instance, was writing about "Psychological Types." We shall, however, presume on the syntactic and semantic sophistication of the age and use the term as a convenient label for a pattern that is at once contextual and empirical. The pattern is contextual because it is defined as referring to significant features of the social process; it is empirical because it is expected to sum up findings and to point the way to further research.

Reprinted from *Journal of Social Issues,* 24 (July, 1968), 81–91.

A THREEFOLD CLASSIFICATION OF TYPES

A *"nuclear"* type connects a political role with intense predispositions of the total personality (See Lasswell, 1930, especially chapter 4). The man who succeeds to an office in which he has no interest is at one end of the scale; the one whose whole life is focused on reaching the Presidency is at the other. We might provisionally introduce the term "politician" to characterize the individual whose life is focused on gaining office. (Later in the paper I shall develop a fuller delineation of an equivalent conception designed to deal with power-centered individuals—the "political personality.") Paralleling the notion of the "politician" as one whose life revolves around the pursuit of one particular value—that of power—we can functionally define other roles in terms of the pursuit of other values. Thus we might describe individuals whose lives are focused on the pursuit of enlightenment as "scientists," excluding from this classification those who happen merely conventionally to be called scientists, but who are primarily concerned with other values such as respect, well-being, power, etc.

A cross-sectional survey of those who play a particular role during a given period may show that "politicians" can be distinguished from "scientists," for example, in several ways. Thus "politicians" and "scientists" may come from different social strata and educational backgrounds, they may differ psychologically in a variety of ways—say, ability to tolerate ambiguity, cognitive style and willingness to engage in interpersonal relations. Such findings describe *"co-relational"* types; the data are not necessarily linked to an explanatory theory of how political personalities are formed. This is the province of *"developmental"* typologies. Thus we may find that the developmental experiences of "politicians" and "scientists" differ in distinctive ways. As political scientists our special responsibility is developmental, since political socialization, which is the transmitting and acquiring of political culture, includes the formation of political types.

In order further to exhibit the defining characteristics of nuclear, co-relational and developmental types and to show how they relate to each other, it is useful to quote an earlier discussion (Lasswell, 1930, 49–61).

> Political types may be set up on a threefold basis: by specifying a nuclear relations, a co-relation, and a developmental relation.
>
> What is meant by the choice of a nuclear relation may be illustrated by the concept of *Machtmensch* as elaborated by Eduard Spranger in his *Lebensformen*. . . . The gist of Spranger's generalization of the political man [politician or political type in the usage of this paper] is schematically expressible in terms of desire-method-success. The political man desires to control the motives of others; his method may vary from violence to wheedling; his success in securing recognition in some community must be tangible. These are the nuclear relations which are essential to the type definition. . . .
>
> [Such a type is] distinguished according to some nuclear relation among a few variables. The characteristics mode of elaborating such a type is to imagine a host of situations in which the type may be found and to describe the resulting picture. For these impressionistic methods it is possible to substitute a more formal procedure. Having chosen a central primary relation, it is possible to find, by reference to specific instances, the relative frequency with which other traits are associated with the nuclear ones. . . . The result . . . is to define "co-relational" (correlational) types. . . .
>
> Almost every nuclear and co-relational type carries developmental implications. The terms which are used to characterize motives have dynamic, genetic, formative coronas of meaning which, vaguely though they may be sketched, are emphatically present. When Michels says that a "Catonian strength of conviction" is one mark of the political leader, it is implied that if one pushed his inquiry into the adolescence,

childhood and even infancy of the individual that this ruling characteristic would be visible. Of course, Michels does not himself develop these implications; it is doubtful if he has tried to find the early analogues of the trait which he called "Catonian strength of conviction" on the adult level. But the dynamic penumbra of the term can lead empirical investigators to scrutinize the behavior of children from a new point of view. . . . Developmental types . . . describe a set of terminal, adult reactions and relate them to those critical experiences in the antecedent life of the individual which dispose him to set up such a mode of dealing with the world.

MODELS OF THE POLITICAL ORDER AND OF POLITICAL PERSONALITY

In order to guide the study of political types the scientific observer finds it essential to provide himself with a generalized scheme, a model, for use in searching out the "political" features in any social process, whether contemporary or historical, territorial or pluralistic. He also needs to use an exploratory scheme of "personality." I shall not elaborate the social process model in detail, since this has been done in other places.[1] The present focus is on "personality," particularly on the developmental study of political personality. It is, however, pertinent to recapitulate the principal contours of the social and political process.

A social process is characterized by mutual influencing: the *participants* are seeking to maximize[2] (optimalize) *values* (preferred outcomes) by using *institutions* affecting *resources*. The following eight terms are used to refer to values: power (P), the giving or receiving of support in the important decisions made in a social context; enlightenment (E), the giving or receiving of information; wealth (W), the giving or receiving of control over resources; well-being (B), similarly for access to safety, health and comfort; skill (S), similarly for opportunity to acquire and exercise talent; affection (A), similarly for love, friendship, loyalty; respect (R), similarly for recognition; rectitude (D), similarly for religion and ethics.

The conception of political personality that we suggest has the three major components shown in Table 1: a value focus, the patterning of behavior vis à vis

Table 1
Political Personality*

Political Personality = emphasizes the pursuit of power in preference to other values = utilizes specialized patterns to specify values = employs mechanisms to adapt internal perspectives and somatic operations.

* Compare with Lasswell, 1948, Chapters 2 and 3.

the value the individual is focused on and, finally, psychological and somatic components. The table indicates that when a person is relatively centered on the power value, he fits the definition of political personality. This defines according to nuclear type, since it presupposes knowledge of the behavior exhibited by the person in representative situations in the social process, plus understanding of his inner orientation. The simple fact that a role is performed that is conventionally perceived as political by the participants in the context does not warrant classifying a person among the political personalities. Nor, conversely, does failure to play a conventionally recognized political role necessarily imply that the person is not power oriented. Obviously the comprehensive appraisal of any social context must sample *all* value shaping and sharing processes, as they are *conventionally* understood, if the political personalities in the *functional* sense are to be identified. The point is implied when, as is sometimes the case, it is said that during the rapid growth phase of a private capitalistic economy the most power-centered persons engage in "business."

Thus, for analytic purposes, we may find ourselves categorizing as political types certain actors from a variety of conventionally designated institutions such as business, the church and the universities, and we may find ourselves excluding from the political type classification some bureaucrats, ward healers, elected officials and others who are usually thought of as political. For scientific purposes it is essential to use analytic tools that enable us to isolate functionally comparable types, since there is no reason to believe that the conventional classifications identify sufficiently comparable individuals for it to be possible *in principle* to find that the nuclear classification serves as an indicator of common co-relational, and developmental patterns.

In order to classify individuals functionally we need to employ a major distinction made in Table 1—the distinction between "values" and "specialized patterns." Individuals often use no such general categories of thought as power; they think in more concrete terms, such as wanting to be a senator, or to help their party win the election, or to win the war. The indispensable function of systematic categories is to provide the scientific observer with the tools necessary to make comparisons. They challenge the observer to discover the degree to which conventional perspectives and operations in one context have equivalents elsewhere. Hence it becomes possible to describe the value priorities from society to society, subgroup to subgroup, or from person to person. Thus, for example, Actor A, a medieval cleric, and Actor B, a nineteenth century American businessman, may exhibit similar "specialized patterns" focusing on the pursuit of power, even though A and B justify their behavior in quite different ways and neither employs a general category of thought referring explicitly to power. And in society A the institutions that are specialized to power may be commonly thought of as "churches," and in society B they may be thought of as "industries." In addition, contextual analysis may confirm the assertion that some societies give little encouragement to the pursuit of power in community decisions.

Principal "Mechanisms"

The reference in Table 1 to the "mechanisms" employed by the individual in internal adaptation covers all the modes by which "impulses" to complete an "act" are dealt with. One convenient scheme (presented in Table 2) underlines the principal mechanisms by which psychological conflicts are resolved. (All initiated

Table 2
Mechanisms of Conflict Resolution

a	
b	Rejection
c	
d	Suppression
e	
f	Repression
g	
h	Resistance

acts are not conflicting; some are facilitative or uninvolved.) A brief consideration of typical mechanisms for dealing with psychic conflict and of the personality structures to which they are related will take us to a discussion of how to analyze intrapersonal and environmental determinants of the development and persistence of political personality.

The break in each line in Table 2 indicates the passage from "unconscious" and "preconscious" events in the sequence to waking awareness (and somatic expression). Act b is shown as rejected, which means that a possible act completion (such as voting on a measure in which the individual has little interest) is overridden in favor of not voting. Act d is shown as suppressed. Suppression refers to the exclusion of an act from completion after an intense subjective conflict, such as a conflict between loyalty to two candidates who are one's close friends. Repression (act f) results from an exceedingly acute conflict that ends by establishing an internal inhibition against allowing the alternatives to reach full waking awareness (such as an intense urge to kill). Once established the inhibition operates as a resistance prior to awareness. However, the extensive clinical literature on "the return of the repressed" suggests that resisted (act h) impulses may obtain partial completion in the form of somatic symptom behavior (such as "accidentally" hitting someone) or in the form of symbol behavior. Among the many mechanisms that operate on symbolic events (subjectivities) rather than somatic expressions are "condensation," "detachment" (and so on). These may manifest themselves not only in dreams, jokes and slips of the tongue, but also, for example, in a political actor's choice of metaphors and other figures of speech.

At the several phases of inter-act adaptation various personality structures take form. The psychoanalytic distinctions, for instance, are pertinent here: the "super-ego" refers to the inhibiting and facilitating patterns that function prior to full waking awareness; the "ego" covers the "aware" patterns; the "id" refers to the impulses which are denied full subjectivity and expression, save at the cost of vivid anxiety. If, for example, the super-ego is excessively strict, repression may take its toll by generating apathy or otherwise inhibiting the channeling of impulse energies into action.

Political personalities can be profitably examined to discover the extent to which the completion of power-oriented acts is able to mobilize the *potential intensities* available to the personality system as a whole. Similarly, it is feasible to discover which specific institutional outcomes are the objects of power perspectives and operations as well as the inner mechanisms by which various act potentials are adapted within the total system.

Fundamental to dynamic analysis (developmental study) is the conception of political personality at any given cross-section of the career line as established by a process of relative value indulgence. Table 3 suggests how stability and instability of political personality dynamics may be analyzed in terms of the consistency of the political actor's expectations of and experiences with relevant positive and negative sanctions. Table 4 suggests how the actor's environment contributes to the stability of political personality.

For an example of what is implied by Tables 3 and 4, we may consider various of the slow-changing village societies of the globe. In such societies most preadults are successfully socialized to play adult roles by passing through sequences of interaction with the environment in which the preadult eventually integrates a stable system of perspective and operation (Table 3), and the social environ-

Table 3
Political Personality Dynamics

Political ⟶ when expected to
perspectives yield net value
and operations advantages
remain *stable* ⟶

when net value
advantages are
realized

Political ⟶ when expectations
perspectives are confused or
and operations contradictory
are *unstable* ⟶

when realized net
value advantages
are confused or
contradictory

ment provides the requisite flow of net value advantages, thanks to its appropriate expectations and realizations (Table 4).

A formulation of this kind, simple and obvious as it may seem, has yet to be corroborated in detail by suitable research. An instant's reflection reminds us of the vast complexity of the process in any society, and the difficulty that lies in the way of attempting to mobilize research talent, without creating a new "Navajo plus an anthropologist" pattern of culture; or of discovering how to make proper allowance for the impact of the new social context itself.

Table 4
Political Personality and Environment

A stable political personality depends on	*expectations* in the environment of net advantage from providing the indulgences required to sustain stability.
	the *realization* permitted by the environment of the net indulgences required.

In Illustration

As an illustration of the analytic strategy proposed here of contextual analysis of value indulgences and deprivations in order to explain personality development, consider, for a moment, the significance of an infant to those immediately involved with it. These comments are a free transcript of actual observations:

Think first of the infant as a source of *value indulgence* for the *mother*. If the mother has been doubtful of her adequacy as a woman, conception and birth may be experiences of enormous importance to her image of herself. Using abbreviations to employ the value categories introduced above, she may enjoy a continuing quiet euphoria, which is a positive state of well-being (B) that overwhelms any physical inconvenience or pain. She loves herself and also the image and the body of the child (A). She respects (R) herself; and she may have surges of religious feeling (D) for the mystery of life. Perhaps she perceives that a son is likely to safeguard her position in family decisions (P), and in obtaining the income from an estate (W). Motherhood may open up access to new sources of knowledge (E) and skill (S).

It is also relevant to explore the significance of an infant as a source of *deprivation* to the *mother*. If the child is sickly or deformed the humiliation (-R) and guilt (-D) may actually disturb the mental and physical health of the mother (-B). It may cost the love of the husband (-A), and put an end to the prospect of exercising power (-P), obtaining wealth (-W), or acquiring access to privileged sources of knowledge (-E), and skill (-S).

What value *indulgences* does an *infant* obtain from the mother? In the favorable case, nurture (B) and love (A); and a variety of opportunities that gradually encourage curiosity (E) and the discovery of latent aptitudes (S). Toys are early forms of wealth (W), as are the excretions. An environment willing to encourage initiative is providing a basic form of respect (R); approval for conformity ("good") introduces rudimentary components of appraisal in rectitude (D) terms. The strong willed child may exert a major impact on family decision (P) long before any conscious programs take shape.

An inventory of value *deprivations* is also essential to any comprehensive empirical investigation of a child. (I am omitting examples.) Moreover, the *timing* of value indulgences and deprivations must be clearly specified if their significance is to be brought out. And this makes it necessary to describe the *particular patterns* involved. To trace an interaction the observer must describe the initiator of an act and characterize the response of the environment in value terms. The scientific observer may say that *X* promises to support *Y,* noting that the promise of support is given according to the usual practice in the political culture of the relevant context. He goes on to recount that in response to this value indulgence, *Y* replies by granting *X* a value indulgence, perhaps in the form of a promise of support for his later candidacy. A more comprehensive examination may disclose many other value implications. *X* may be warmly greeted and applauded by party members who feared that he might be unwilling to go along with *Y's* nomination. These affection and respect responses might be supplemented by economic advantages (a contract for his construction company), disclosure of secret plans for development (enlightenment), opportunities to join a golf club (skill, etc.) and general commendation of his character (rectitude).

Confidential interviewing may indicate that, while the previous picture is correct as far as it goes, from *X's* point of view it omits many dimensions of the context. It leaves out the attacks made on him privately by disappointed supporters and friends and many other negative experiences.

The foregoing analysis calls attention to the complex interplay between values and practices, and indicates why the means at our disposal for investigation have a limited capability to disclose these relationships. Plainly, the evaluation of specific practices is subject to *external* and *internal* factors. The external changes are the indulgences and deprivations actually supplied by the environment. Obviously these depend on many factors beyond the deliberate control of the actors in the situation. The internal factors are the ego-indulging or depriving evaluations by the ego and superego; these "self by self" appraisals may continue for years with no external support (in fact, with deprivations by an environment in conflict with the standards applied by the conscience and the ego). Consider, for example, political prisoners who fail to change their convictions in spite of facing extreme deprivations in the environment of the concentration camp.

The theory of dynamic personality change implied in the foregoing can be summed up in these terms: *specific practices* (perceived as expressing a principal value) *result in external and internal value indulgences and deprivations that coincide with, or deviate from, net expectations prior to the outcome phase of action; expectations are modified according to results, save when the intensity with which expectations are sustained inhibits recognition of what has occurred; the rank ordering of major value categories is ratified or altered as the practices attributed to major categories rise or fall in value realization.*

The mechanisms conform to the same principles. For example, if a mechanism of rejection is applied to a specific practice and results in less than anticipated net advantage, the rejection will itself be altered on behalf of acceptance and expression.

When mechanisms, specific practices and values are not objects of relatively deliberate strategies, evaluations may occur at "unconscious" or "preconscious" levels, with the result that *image* components are little involved; instead, *moods* dominate the process.[3] The overwhelming probability is that the mood components are usually effective without becoming fully developed objects of imaged references.

QUESTIONS GENERATED BY THE FRAME OF REFERENCE

Imagine that we were omniscient, thanks to the observational methods at our disposal, and to the elegance of our theoretical system. What kinds of questions could we answer about personality and politics?

1. It would be possible to describe the intensity with which various political perspectives and operational patterns are supported or opposed within the personality system of representative (or atypical) groups throughout the body politic. These groups would be selected by culture (e.g., ethnic origin, urban-rural, regional); by class (upper, middle or lower position in terms of power, enlightenment, wealth, well-being, skill, affection, respect, rectitude); by interest (affiliation with groups that cut across culture and class lines, or fall short of including all members of these categories); by personality (e.g., by value priorities and institutional practices; and by mechanism).

2. Developmental patterns could be correctly predicted (retrospectively) for all nuclear and co-relational profiles. This means that we would have knowledge of the factors that condition the transfer of perspectives toward targets in the primary circle to secondary targets (from father to public political figures; from ideologies used in the family to ideologies employed in the public arenas). Among the conditioning factors would be deprivations in the primary circle that arouse pessimistic expectations regarding public persons, or, on the contrary, arouse compensatory evaluations of the beneficence of public life. At present very little can be said about this (Greenstein, 1965).

3. Examining available information (and estimates of the future), developmental constructs could be made of the actual course of the most probable future events.

4. On the basis of clarified goals for the body politic, policy objectives and strategies could be devised to develop the personality orientations most likely to realize and contribute to desired future results.

5. Among the policy recommendations would be the formation of appraisal and intelligence functions capable of feeding into the decision process a stream of information about the degree to which overriding objectives are being reached

(trends), the factor-combinations that explain favorable or unfavorable trends and projections of future developments.

The expansion of science and technology is such that the world has been taking giant strides toward developing comprehensive, selective and continuing self-observational institutions of the kind required. The tens of thousands of research specialists in the behavioral, social and biological sciences are, with minimum central administration or planning, studying the careers of each age group in politics and in all other sectors of social process. The computer revolution is introducing a data rich civilization equipped to provide more and more complete coverage.

Given the approximate character of the available methods for examining and explaining personality, it is especially relevant to consider the use of methods of appraisal that keep the developing context at the center of attention. By means of prototyping,[4] for instance, changes in practice can be explored systematically, while appraisal programs of "interlapping observation" keep developmental information up to date (McDougal, Lasswell, and Vlasic, 1963). Such are at least some of the far reaching implications of a configurative approach to the complexities of political personality.

NOTES

[1] For the present model see Lasswell and Kaplan, 1950 and McDougal, Lasswell and Vlasic, 1963.

[2] The maximizing principle may be strictly defined as in traditional economics, or more loosely defined, as in Simon, to require "satisfaction." See Simon, 1955.

[3] Dr. A. J. Brodbeck, with whom I am collaborating in a study of socialization, is especially concerned with the interplay of mood and image.

[4] See McDougal, Lasswell, and Vlasic, 1963, 268–273, and ch. 5.

REFERENCES

Greenstein, Fred I. *Children and politics.* New Haven: Yale University Press, 1965.

Lasswell, Harold D. *Psychopathology and politics.* (Paperback with afterthoughts by the author) New York: Viking Press, 1960; original, 1930.

Lasswell, Harold D. *Power and personality.* New York: Viking Press, 1962; original, 1948.

Lasswell, Harold D. and Abraham Kaplan. *Power and society.* New Haven: Yale University Press, 1963; original, 1950.

McDougal, M. S., Harold D. Lasswell and I. A. Vlasic. *Law and public order of space.* New Haven: Yale University Press, 1963.

Simon, Herbert A. A behavioral model of rational choice. *Quarterly Journal Economics,* 1955, 69, 99–118.

Spranger, Eduard. *Types of men: The psychology and ethics of personality.* Johnson Reprint, 1928.

12

The Use of Psychiatric Symptomatology
as a Basis for Classification

Three decades ago, Harold Lasswell indicated in *Psychopathology and Politics* how the "clinical caricature" of the relationship between personality and politics found in mental patients might provide instructive leads in the search for "typical subjective histories of typical public characters." "The clinical caricature," Lasswell said, "throws into imposing relief the constituent tendencies which make up the functioning person, and draws attention to their presence and processes."

Lasswell's lead remained almost entirely ignored until Rutherford undertook this study of the Elgin, Illinois State Mental Hospital. Rutherford not only took up Lasswell's suggestion that mental patients be studied, but also used the data to evaluate Lasswell's central hypothesis about political man.

Lasswell's well-known hypothesis was that the political man displaces his private motives onto public objects and rationalizes the resultant views and activities in terms of the public interest. Rutherford contrasts this hypothesis with a hypothesis derived from Robert Lane: "If an individual suffers from intrapsychic conflict, so much energy will be consumed by the struggle within the person that no surplus will remain to cope with conflict in the political arena. . . . Those experiencing intrapsychic conflict, then, would be expected to withdraw from political participation rather than project upon political objects. We would have this proposition: the higher the level of political participation, the greater the psychic energy need, the less the intrapsychic conflict, and, hence, the more rational the participant."

Rutherford then cites evidence that dictators (such as Hitler and Stalin) and other political participants who have been reliably identified as having paranoid tendencies clearly had energy available for political participation. Bureaucracies do not "filter out" irrational leadership since they are usually controlled by unscreened political appointees. Studies have shown that eighty-five percent of a variety of citizens manifest some psychopathological symptoms: "if some 85 percent of the population endure measurable psychopathology does the recruitment of political actives involve any 'selecting out?' " While others have been impressed by the overall positive correlations between socioeconomic status, political participation, and mental health, Rutherford points to the significance of a more selective correlation: in the high SES groups from which most political activists come, there is *no* significant correlation between activity in social organizations and mental health and, hence, probably no relationship between political participation (which correlates highly with activity in social organizations) and mental health. In other words, the evidence indicates that neurotics are not filtered out of political participation.

These questions divide "sick" from "well," but there is another way of approaching political participation: what kinds of personalities—wherever they stand on the mental health continuum—are attracted to political activity? Rutherford studied the patient-governed councils in milieu therapy wards of the Elgin State Mental Hospital and found that manic depressives and, especially, paranoid schizophrenics were impressively overrepresented on the leadership councils. Participation on the patient councils, moreover, correlated highly with outside political participation: "If paranoids emerge at both ends of a continuum running from totalitarian states to democratic proximate groups, this suggests a proposition that the paranoid is a general political type."

The paranoid is, above all, one who projects his internal conflicts; in this and other ways Rutherford shows that the paranoid fits Lasswell's description of the *homo politicus*. Nor does the paranoid contradict Lane's hypothesis, since his personality may remain relatively well integrated and his projective defenses serve to diminish his sense of *inner* conflict. Rutherford thus concludes that

The distinction of personality types for political participation should be, not between the mentally ill and the mentally well, but rather between internalizers and externalizers. The political world is a fertile area for the externalization of anxiety and intrapsychic conflict and, as such, tends to attract individuals with a need to find objects for projection and displacement.

Rutherford is sensitive to the difficulties of such "deviant case analysis." Rising above the difficulties, the article stands as something of a model of research in political psychology: the question is important, the conceptualization is clear, the method is resourceful, the technique good, and the findings unobvious and interesting.[1]

NOTE

[1] We reprint the article by Robert C. Tucker, "The Dictator and Totalitarianism," to which Rutherford refers, as selection 22.

PSYCHOPATHOLOGY, DECISION-MAKING, AND POLITICAL INVOLVEMENT

Brent M. Rutherford

In scholarly writings as well as in the popular press, a reader often finds himself presented with such phrases as "China's aggressive behavior," "Rhodesia's intransigence," and "narcissistic France." A familiar international relations text (Lerche and Said, 1963) offers "a discussion of the individual political actor (the state) and its foreign policy." Such anthropomorphic verbiage not only preserves the Hegelian concept of the monolithic *Volksgeist,* but also avoids many difficult yet crucial questions of the origins, motivations, and responsibility of national action.

This paper takes a reductionist approach to the study of national decision-making: it will focus on the individual decision-maker. Although he questions the utility of this approach, Sidney Verba (1961) has written: "It is a truism that all action within the international system can be reduced to the actions of individuals." It is not alleged that the study of individual behavior can provide a complete understanding of national behavior. However mediated by groups, economics, or other considerations, an understanding of individual behavior remains crucial to any adequate explanation of national or political behavior.

The decision-makers with whom I shall be concerned are all those who have any influence on the international system. From the Almond viewpoint, these would range from individuals with only the vaguest opinions to cabinet ministers and chief executives. By "psychopathology" I shall mean the study of and the existence of mental illness and aberration.[1] With regard to "political participation" I shall be concerned with differences in levels of identification and involvement in (Dahl) relationships that involve, to a significant extent, power rule or authority. By using levels of participation I avoid the somewhat artificial distinction between leaders and followers; furthermore, ordinal relationships yield a more elegant analysis than do dichotomies.

Finally, the notion of rationality, which is my fundamental concern, will serve to link psychopathology and decision-making with participation. I will seek to come to an understanding of some of the apparent contradictions between Lane's and Lasswell's conceptions of political man.

The Unity of Utility Problem

Perhaps the most often used proposition of decision-making theory posits that individuals are rational, and that rationality occurs when individuals make de-

From *The Journal of Conflict Resolution,* 10, No. 4 (December, 1966), 387–407.

The author notes: "For many helpful suggestions and criticisms of this paper I am indebted to David W. Minar, Thomas Milburn, and Richard C. Snyder, and especially grateful to Lee Anderson and Michael Shapiro." This acknowledgment constituted note one of the original; footnotes in this reprint are renumbered.

cisions which maximize their expected utility. This theory is represented by the formula:

$$EU_1 = (Ua \times Pa) + (Ub \times Pb) + \ldots + (Un \times Pn),$$

where:

> EU_1 is the expected utility of action 1;
> Ua, Ub, . . . , Un are the subjective utilities of the possible outcomes (a, b, . . . n) of action 1;
> Pa, Pb, . . . , Pn are the subjective probabilities of each of the possible outcomes (a, b, . . . n) occurring as a result of action 1.

Given this equation, a rational decision is made when the individual maximizes his utility: he will choose option 1 over option 2 when $EU_1 > EU_2$.

Patchen (1965), reviewing several theoretical works concerned with the limits of rationality in the maximization hypothesis, finds some writers (G. Snyder, 1960; Singer, 1963; M. Deutsch, 1961) who suggest limitations on the utility concept. Especially in conditions of threat, anxiety, crisis, and high tension, irrationality may arise from a failure to estimate relevant factors correctly, or from a failure to act appropriately on the basis of correct estimates. Such irrationality, it is suggested, may produce such behaviors as anxiety, stereotypes, self-esteem defense maneuvers, and social conformity pressures. Patchen goes on to review empirical investigations (Brim et al., 1962; Scodel, Ratoosh, and Minas, 1954; French and Raven, 1959) which describe various laboratory testing situations where subjects do not make their choices in the manner suggested by the maximization hypothesis. Especially remarkable is the fact that the subjects behaved "irrationally" under conditions which were much less stressful than situations of "threat, anxiety, crisis, and high tension." The proposition would appear to be that, regardless of situational conditions, some decision-makers do not always seek to maximize utility.

If the maximization-of-utility hypothesis is to be of even heuristic value in the study of political decision-making, it must cope with the problem of the unity of utility. The given model does provide a meaningful framework for understanding why Benjamin Franklin decided, on arriving in Philadelphia, to spend his last ten coppers on bread rather than eclairs. But suppose Franklin had been a public road commissioner charged with building a road from locus X to locus Y. The cheapest and most aesthetic route lies on a straight line from X to Y. Franklin owns a plot of land between X and Y, but off the shortest route, of which he would like to divest himself. Problem: given the maximization hypothesis, which option maximizes utility? In a situation where an individual is acting in a role for the political unit, his utility may not always coincide with the utility of the collectivity. Or, given a different context, a diplomat who has a need to displace aggression onto Asians may not be the person to negotiate a peace treaty with representatives of an Asian nation. The diplomat's personal utility is maximized by aggressive ideation, while the objective political utility is maximized by pacific behavior.

The problem of the unity of utility was anticipated by Harold D. Lasswell in his pioneering work, *Psychopathology and Politics* (1930; second edition, used here, 1960), although he used different terminology. Having studied a number of politicians who had become mentally ill, Lasswell concluded that the political actor—whether administrator, agitator, or theorist—connected his private motives and frustrations with public acts. He offered the general equation:

$$p \} d \} r = P$$

where: p = private motives
d = displacement onto public
objects
r = rationalization in terms of
public interest
P = the political man
} = "transformed into"

Following this formula, Lasswell concludes (1960, p. 262) that "the distinctive mark of the *homo politicus* is the rationalization of the displacement in terms of public interests." His early work in this field provided for a study of functional politics which would emphasize the elements of the political decision rather than the description of the legal and structural nature of the political office *per se*. Furthermore, the study of psychopathology and political participation focused attention on whole personality patterns and clusters of behavioral tendencies rather than on abstracted and isolated leadership traits. By bringing psychoanalytic considerations to political science, he opened the way for a systematic concern with the irrational in politics. (Here, it should be noted, I have shifted the definition of irrationality away from the maximization-of-utility scheme. In the new context it means the persistent inability to learn from experience, to the point where the individual shifts his conception of himself and his environment markedly away from some objective degree of normalcy.)

Criticism of Lasswell's formulation has clustered into two charges. First, the external validity of the study is questioned because factors which were found to operate in the case of mentally ill politicans may not be generalizable to those who are not mentally ill (McConaughy, 1950). Implicit in this criticism is the assumption that the mentally ill are clearly distinguishable from the mentally well. Second, the validity of Lasswell's claim that political man displaces personal frustrations onto public objects has been questioned. This reasoning (Lane, 1959, p. 123) runs thus: if an individual suffers from intrapsychic conflict, so much energy will be consumed by the struggle within the person that no surplus will remain to cope with conflict in the political arena. Interpersonal relations and ego strivings will thus suffer to a great extent. Those experiencing intrapsychic conflict, then, would be expected to withdraw from political participation rather than project upon political objects. We would have this proposition: the higher the level of political participation, the greater the psychic energy need, the less the intrapsychic conflict, and, hence, the more rational the participant.

PSYCHOPATHOLOGY AND THE DICTATOR

The task of separating political outputs into those stemming from system needs and those stemming from decision-makers' psychic personality needs is very difficult. In some cases, however, the distinction may be easier to make. We do find persons in whom substantial projection and irrationality are combined with a high level of political participation; and if such a description is valid for these persons, it tends to support Lasswell rather than his critics.

Robert C. Tucker, in an article following from his work on *The Soviet Mind* and *The Great Purge Trials,* concludes that the paranoid personality is the mark of the totalitarian dictator. He says (1965, p. 566) that the available evidence on Hitler and Stalin indicates that "in both instances we have to do with individuals whose personalities would be classified somewhere on the continuum of psychiatric conditions designated as paranoid, and in both instances the needs of the paranoidal personality were a powerful motivating factor in dictatorial decision-making." Defining a rational decision as one which is consonant with system needs, Tucker examines divergence from this kind of rationality in the Stalin era of Russian history. During 1936–1938 Stalin sought to cement his position in the Soviet state and Communist party by the plethora of terroristic activities known as the Great Purge. For example, the army alone lost three of its five marshals, 13 of its 15 commanders, 62 of its 80 corps commanders, and 110 of its 195 divisional commanders (Harcane, 1959, p. 618). This purge was in no sense a product of the system needs of the Soviet state, but rather a result of the private delusions of Stalin. His personal view of reality and history was conspiratorial in the internal, external, and ideological spheres. Tucker finds these conspiratorial delusions manifested not only in the purge trials but also in Stalin's *Short Course* on party history and in the extreme psychological warfare (especially the germ warfare motif) of the post-World War II period. In Lasswellian terms, Stalin's private motives and delusions of conspiracy were displaced upon public objects—the Communist party, internal relations, and foreign relations—and rationalized in terms of the public interest, the well-being and security of Russia.

It is also difficult to view Hitler's doctrine of an international Jewish conspiracy and the resulting genocide of millions as a system need. Historical anti-Semitism was, of course, persistent, and Hitler was able to recruit individuals whose delusions were consonant with his own and to persuade others of the rectitude of such delusions. Nevertheless, Hitler himself remained the central driving force behind the German *pogrom.* And the primary system need in the Nazi war effort—i.e., system survival —was certainly not aided by the diversion of resources to the extermination of the Jewish people. G. M. Gilbert, a clinical psychologist at the Nuremberg trials, was able to study materials relevant to Hitler's behavior as well as to examine his lieutenants. He concludes (1950, pp. 33–35 and 300–301) that Hitler's fear of a worldwide Jewish conspiracy was a nearly classic description of a paranoid delusional system. The case history is complete with the aggressive intransigence and the postures of self-righteousness and national righteousness taken by Hitler. Gilbert comes near to paraphrasing Lasswell when he concludes that Hitler ". . . learned to displace his psychological aggressions, to project his feelings of inferiority onto the most popular scapegoat of the time, and to structuralize his political attitudes on these defense mechanisms."

The extent to which the private needs of some political leaders can become transformed into the *raison d'être* of states can be roughly indicated by comparing national behaviors before and after the elimination of the leader. The death of Stalin would seem to account for most of the change within the Soviet system after 1953. Such a comparison is not possible in the German case, for Nazi Germany did not survive Hitler.

One cannot validly draw conclusions for a general theory of decision-making rationality from a study of Hitler or Stalin (or Mussolini).[2] Yet such studies show that some individuals with striking psychopathological manifestations do possess enough energy to participate at a high level in matters that are inherently conflictful. Their participation also seems to have been marked by persistent displacement and projection of private ideations upon public objects.

PSYCHOPATHOLOGY AND DEMOCRATIC PARTICIPATION

If there is plausible psychopathology in some noted totalitarian leaders, what can be said about the emergence of aberrant personalities in nontotalitarian situations? This question has not been treated in a systematic or provisionally complete manner. Some recent works (Tucker, 1965; Verba, 1961; Kaplan, 1965; Lasswell, 1954) do suggest elements of an answer. Tucker calls it "the theory of organizational rejection of aberrant personalities from leadership positions." The structure of the argument runs thus: (1) Modern society is increasingly dominated and controlled by bureaucratic organizations of which national government is the archetype. (2) The pressures of role conformity in the structural social situations inherent in such organizations tend to minimize the influence of individual personality factors. Actors within the bureaucracy are constrained by "colleagues, decision-making processes, and role expectations" (Kaplan, 1965, p. 359). It is emphasized that leaders with "well-integrated" personalities and those with "relatively few internal conflicts" will be selected by bureaucratic organizations, while "anxiety-ridden persons" will be selected out in the leadership recruitment process.

Tucker accepts this formulation as compatible with the emergence of totalitarian leaders. Hitler and Stalin are not seen as arising from established bureaucracies; rather, they seized control of "fighting organizations." Personality characteristics which may block an individual from bureaucratic leadership may serve as functional requisites for the leadership of fighting organizations.

It is interesting that a style of politics embodying characteristics basically congruent with those of Hitler and Stalin has been identified in political "fighting movements" in the United States. Hofstadter (1965) has seen a paranoid style of politics persisting in movements of suspicious discontent. Paranoid rhetoric has been an enduring factor in American politics—witness such early movements as the anti-Masonic, anti-Catholic, and nativist. Many abolitionists saw the antebellum United States enmeshed in a slaveholders' conspiracy, just as later Greenback and Populist writers saw menacing plots of international bankers. Such a trend may continue today in the extremes of the right and the left, as well as in both sides of the racial controversy: the Black Muslims and the White Citizens' Councils are probably more *politically* similar than dissimilar in view and style. If these movements are paranoid in rhetoric or manner, then certainly any explanation of leaders' origins cannot assert that paranoid politics is solely a phenomenon of totalitarian societies.

The possibility that aberrant personalities will be filtered out of positions of leadership in democratic bureaucracies, as suggested by the theory of organizational rejection, may be a specious issue. Governmental bureaucracies are rarely led by, and policy is rarely declared by, individuals incipient in the organization. Rather, such posts are filled by election or appointment, in either case circumventing the supposed filtering function of the organization itself. If the position is filled by election, the political party may be considered prone to adopt characteristics of the "fighting organization"—indeed, it *is* one at periodic intervals (election campaigns).

It is surprising that the topic of pathology among political participants, of such general interest to disciplines concerned with policy-making, has received so little investigation or even speculation. Some diagnoses of historical leaders have been attempted.[3] The difficulty is, of course that these diagnoses must rely on data which the clinician would regard as less than optimal. Even Rogow's (1963) recent study of an overt incident of aberration—the case of James Forrestal—was necessarily a reconstruction after the fact. McConaughy (1950) tested South Carolina legislators and found that they scored a mean of 32.8 on the neurotic tendency scale of the Bernreuter Personality Inventory. Because the population norm is given as 50.0, he concludes that his results throw doubt on the hypothesis that "politicians go into politics because of feelings of insufficiency or inferiority." There are, however, several problems with this study. Only eighteen of 170 legislators were tested, and we are not told how the eighteen were chosen. The scaling result may only indicate that the legislators had accomplished a successful tension-reducing displacement of "feelings of insufficiency or inferiority." Finally, the validity of the scale itself has been questioned.[4]

It seems evident that the existence of psychopathology in participants at different levels of activity in democratic situations remains an open question.

PSYCHOPATHOLOGY IN THE POPULATION

As all societies rest on tacit assumptions, perhaps the most widely held assumption in any society is, ultimately, that of its own sanity. Some individuals do suffer more or less from forms of mental illness, but there is little doubt as to the general level of societal mental health. When a person becomes mentally ill society views it as a strictly individual incident and a rather surprising exception, i.e., deviation. Such persons, whatever the frequency of their maladies, are thought to pose no threat to the assumption of societal sanity.

If it is important to inquire about the degree of psychopathology at different levels of political participation, it is also important to inquire about the degree of psychopathology in the population from which the participants come. If filtering does occur—whether by organizational selection, self-selection (the anxiety hypothesis), or selection by a perceptive electorate—at what rate must it occur? The rate of rejection of aberrant personalities need not be high if psychopathology is rare in the population. But if psychopathology is widespread, the efficacy of selection procedures (if they exist at all) must come increasingly into question.

Almost every text concerned with abnormal psychology (cf. Wolff, 1950, pp. 3–14 and 432–44; Coleman, 1956, p. 421) emphasizes that the mentally ill cannot be clearly distinguished from the mentally well. The difference is not a cleft but a gradual slope. Behaviors of different individuals range in imperceptible gradations from normal to abnormal. Sigmund Freud was greatly interested in the existence of neurotic tendencies in individuals who function well in society. In *The Psychopathology of Everyday Life* he demonstrated how the same forces he found operative in neurosis were also found in faulty acts of daily life—forgetting names, slips of the tongue, the *déjà vu,* etc. The gap between the neurotic and the normal is more semantical than real.

Fortunately there is more on this subject than Freud's impressions of the several hundred patients with whom he was familiar. The Midtown Manhattan study (Srole et al., 1962) by the Cornell Medical School was designed to determine the actual prevalence of mental disturbance in society, that is, nontreated psychopathology. Using the techniques of what could best be termed social psychiatry, the investigators drew a probability sample of 1,666 Manhattan residents and interviewed them extensively. Only 18.5 percent of the respondents were found to be free of measurable psychopathologic tendencies. (When diagnoses differed, the healthier rank was used.) Of the remainder, none was institutionalized and only 5.4 percent were receiving professional care. This study is probably representative of urban populations, but the rate of psychological impairment found in Manhattan is not, apparently, peculiar to urban centers. The Sterling County Study (Leighton, 1956) of psychiatric disorder and sociocultural environment has sought to discover and treat mental illness in a rural county in Nova Scotia. This study found measurable pathology in 84.5 percent of its nonurban population. Two studies of school children (cited in Christiansen, 1956) in Scandinavia have reached similar conclusions: H. Wall estimates that neurotic conflict is measurable in 86 percent of a normal sample in Copenhagen; G. Jonssen concluded that of 220 boys in Stockholm only 21 percent could be classified as being without any nervous symptoms or behavior problems.

Despite the diversity of populations, methodologies, definitions, and criteria, and despite the independence of the studies themselves, these findings are in remarkable agreement: about 85 percent of the population can be considered to have manifest degrees of psychopathology. Two contrasting hypotheses can then be considered: (1) If political participants are selected randomly from their populations, about 85 percent may be expected to exhibit psychopathology. (2) If political participants are selected with mental health as a criterion, organizational rejection must filter out the majority of aspirants.

It is unfortunate that the Midtown study did not include an assessment of political activity. If it had, the viability of the two hypotheses could be determined. However, organizational activity of the respondents did receive attention, and there are good grounds for relating this to political participation. In his recent review of the literature, Milbrath (1965, p. 17) found more than twenty surveys which supported the proposition that "persons who are active in community affairs are much more likely than those not active to participate in politics." Almond and Verba (1963, pp. 300–22), in their study of social and political culture in the United States, Great Britain, Germany, Italy, and Mexico, found that where levels of political participation are higher, the level of social and organizational activity is much higher also.

Table 1
Mental Health Risk and Organizational
Membership by Socioeconomic Status

Number of Organizations	Low SES Percent	R	Mid SES Percent	R	High SES Percent	R
0	63.6	.62	57.9	.53	43.5	.43
1	23.3	.55	24.8	.44	18.9	.40
2	6.8	.49	5.4	.50	11.3	.44
3	2.4	.46	4.7	.48	10.2	.36
4	0.4	ns	2.5	.34	5.9	.40
5+	0.6	ns	1.6	ns	10.2	.39
Total cases	544		556		560	

Source: Langner and Michael (1963), p. 287.

While correspondence between political participation and activity in social organizations is not exact, comparison is useful. In an elaboration of the Midtown study, an indication of mental health risk (R) was derived from diagnostic evaluations of the respondents.[5] If people with tendencies toward psychopathology (higher

R level) withdraw rather than participate, the expectation is that the mental health risk (R) would decrease as organizational membership increases. Table 1 shows that this is confirmed only for the low and middle socioeconomic groups; in the high group the differences in R are trivial and the relationship is not linear. It is from the high socioeconomic group, of course, that most political participants are recruited.

THE RESEARCH

From the studies cited thus far, some pertinent questions emerge regarding the possibility of rational decisions on political problems. To what degree may political decision-makers separate their political roles from their personal motivations and personalities? If some 85 percent of the population endure measurable psychopathology, does the recruitment of political actives involve any "selecting out"? If the totalitarian leader can be typified as a paranoid personality, may democratic leaders too be assigned to a diagnostic classification? And if these questions are important, how would the social scientist proceed to investigate them?

In the best of all possible research worlds, the researcher interested in psychology and politics would be invited to administer all types of projective techniques, questionnaires, inventories, and analytic interviews to all levels of political participants. This was an early plea of Lasswell's (1929), but few political scientists have considered psychopathology even relevant to the study of politics. Only McConaughy has approached the problem among democratic political participants and his study, as noted above, was limited to eighteen South Carolina legislators. Political participants are not amenable to the assessment of their mental health. Indeed, Dean Rusk (1960) would deny that such an approach is a legitimate method or could produce significantly relevant results. Despite the work of Lasswell and Nathan Leites (1948), Richard Snyder (1962, p. 122) has lamented that "the state of research and theory on personality and decision role in the field of foreign policy is primitive indeed. . . ."

The next best strategy would be to study individuals whose psychopathologies are already known and who are free to participate in political situations. The first condition could always have been met in psychiatric hospitals. Only very recently, however, has meaningful participation been available to psychiatric patients. This has taken place with the introduction of milieu therapy (Artiss, 1962; Cumming and Cumming, 1962; Jones, 1954), which attempts to minimize the differences between the hospital environment and the social environment to which the patient will return. It is hoped that lessening the gulf will smooth the transition in both directions. Milieu therapy contrasts markedly with the authoritarian approach that formerly dominated hospital administrations.[6] In the latter type of hospital, custodial procedures prevailed; socialization of patients was minimal, except in staff-organized activities; spontaneity was considered a threat to established authority. Underlying milieu therapy is the principle that each person should be given the opportunity to express himself in his own manner and style, limited only by the rules that guide society in general.

Central to the milieu program is the ward government, which follows from another milieu principle—that the patients should maintain initiative and self-determination even in possible conflict with staff and administrators. Each milieu council, which consists of the patients of the ward meeting in their political capacities, has a freely elected chairman and secretary. Meetings are held at least once a week, and patients may or may not be required to attend. Although staff members may be present, the meeting and officers are free from staff control or sanction and, in fact, frequently challenge the authority, wisdom, and professional training of the staff. The functions of the councils are usually broad and cover such areas as dispensing funds allotted to the ward, requesting special monies for special projects, organizing and planning social events, making ward regulations, invoking and dispensing sanctions for patients breaking ward regulations, and—in some instances —advising for the discharge of patients. In effect, then, the ward council is a direct democracy exercising an authoritative allocation of values: a system which may justifiably be termed political.

The research reported below is a study of political participation in ward council government within a psychiatric hospital, and this necessarily limits the generalizability of the findings. That deficiency is balanced, however, by the accuracy of the available diagnoses and data, far exceeding what could be elicited through interviews alone, and by the economy with which these data are obtained. The institutional setting assures the stability of variables which otherwise could only be assumed to be stable or randomly distributed.

METHOD

After several visits to the hospital to observe council meetings in progress, and after a pretest in the women's wards, the research proceeded in four stages.

(1)   Male milieu wards were identified from all those at the hospital. A 16 percent random sample was drawn from each of the twelve milieu wards to determine the diagnostic typologies characteristic of the milieu population. These were easily obtained from patient files. Where there was any ambiguity, a staff psychologist[7] reviewed the entire file and rendered his conclusions.

(2) The participants in each ward were interviewed. Both a quota and a random sample were drawn. The council chairman and secretary were included in each ward. Four other residents—about an 8.5 percent sample—in each ward were randomly selected for interviewing.

The content of the interview schedule was dictated by the scope of the research. Level of political participation, interest in political participation, and interest in political questions prior to hospitalization were ascertained. Respondents' positions on the Campaign Activity Index (Campbell et al., 1960) and the index of political efficacy (Campbell et. al., 1954) were obtained. Since political activity is a function of social position as well as of personal factors, information was elicited which would enable the researcher to estimate respondents' socioeconomic status by Hollingshead's two-factor index of social position. Finally, in an effort to control for the distortion which might be expected to prevail in a psychiatric settting, information was elicited which could be checked by other means (e.g., patients' files).

At the end of each interview each respondent completed a questionnaire consisting of three scales. Because of the expectation of paranoia, the paranoid (Pa) scale of the Minnesota Multiphasic Personality Inventory was administered. Concern about distortion led to the inclusion of a validity scale from the MMPI. The lie (L) scale consists of a group of items that will make the respondent appear in a favorable light but are unlikely to be truthfully answered in the socially acceptable direction (e.g., "I do not always tell the truth," and "Once in a while I laugh at dirty jokes"). Better to understand the results of the Bernreuter Personality Inventory with the South Carolina legislators, the third part of the questionnaire consisted of 25 items from that inventory which are most discriminating in a total of 125 items measuring neurotic tendency.[8]

(3) The files of the respondents were then examined. Checks were made for distortion, and a staff psychologist sharpened some vague diagnoses.

(4) The final stage in the field research was devoted to assessing the level of ward council participation and the level of mental health of each respondent. Judges were selected from those staff personnel who regularly attended council meetings and were acquainted with the respondents. Three independent rankings of participation were obtained for each ward. One ranking was obtained from one of the three attendants who are with the respondents eight hours a day, six days a week. Another ranking was obtained from the professional staff, either the social worker or the occupational or recreational therapist. The third ranking came from another staff member in either of these two categories. The agreement among judges was high, with a median rank order correlation of .914. The mental health ranking was done by the staff psychologist or psychiatrist assigned to each ward. Each respondent was thus ranked in comparison with the other five respondents from his ward on both participation level and mental health level.

RESULTS

The twelve male milieu wards had about 50 residents each. Ninety-three men were sampled to assess diagnostic typologies characteristic of the ward population. In the interviewing stage, two persons refused to be interviewed; two terminated before completion; and three were not responsive to the questions. These seven persons were replaced in the sample. A total of six respondents from each of the 12 wards yielded 72 completed interviews: 12 with council chairmen, 12 with secretaries, and 48 with other ward members.

The members of the councils were more heterogeneous than homogeneous. One respondent had never registered to vote; another had been a school board member. One was an attorney and another an electrical engineer, while still another was a laborer who had never held one job for as long as two months. The mean age was 37.44 years, but the standard deviation of 15.20 years suggests diversity. The median number of years spent at the hospital was 2.4, but the range was from two days to 37 years.

Regarding distortion, a thorough comparison of information obtained from respondents and that obtained from hospital files, which is compiled from sources other than the patient, revealed only trivial differences. A comparison of the results of the MMPI lie scale with norms established for that scale indicates that the Elgin respondents were as veracious as the general population ($x = 4.57$, $s = 2.97$) at the 52nd percentile. The expectation is that distortion is not significantly different in the Elgin study from that encountered in other survey research situations.

Another problem in the present study is the degree to which participation in council meetings may be compared to participation in other settings. If there is any agreement among the scholars interested in political participation, it is on the importance of socioeconomic status. Milbrath (1965, pp. 113–20) cites more than 35 research works which support the proposition that higher status persons are more likely to participate in politics than lower status persons. The relationship between socioeconomic status and political campaign activity persists with a tau beta correlation of .25 between the two variables. It has also been found that a sense of political efficacy is perhaps the best single predictor of all personal factors which explain participation. Milbrath (1965, pp. 56–57) cites research work in five different nations which suggests a tau beta correlation of .27 between participation and sense of political efficacy. If participation patterns among Elgin respondents are similar to those prevailing elsewhere, efficacy and participation should be significantly correlated with campaign activity.

Table 2 indicates the percentages of Elgin respondents who mentioned ever participating in a political campaign, and these are cross tabulated with socio-

Table 2
Percentage at Two Levels of Campaign Participation by Socioeconomic Status,
Efficacy, and Levels of Council Participation

		Campaign Participant	Campaign Nonparticipant	
SES:	High	35.9	3.0	
	Med.	33.3	15.2	$X^2 = 16.60$
	Low	30.8	81.8	$p < .001$
	Total	100.1	100.0	Tau C = .492
Efficacy:	High	46.2	18.8	
	Med.	38.5	53.1	$X^2 = 6.09$
	Low	15.5	28.1	$p < .05$
	Total	100.1	100.0	Tau C = .298
Council participation:	High	56.4	6.1	
	Med.	28.3	39.4	$X^2 = 22.49$
	Low	15.4	54.5	$p < .001$
	Total	100.1	100.0	Tau C = .593
Number of cases		39	33	

economic status, level of personal efficacy, and the ranked level of participation in council meetings. We see that campaign participation is significantly associated with the variables which predict political participation in other situations in national samples. Although correlational levels are somewhat higher, there is no apparent deviance among Elgin respondents in the salient factors of participation. Furthermore, the table shows that respondents who had been political participants before coming to Elgin continued to be high participants in the ward council meetings. Factors relevant to political participation would therefore seem to be salient in council participation too. We may therefore consider council participation to be fundamentally comparable to participation in other settings.

What light can the Elgin study shed on the theory of organizational rejection of aberrant personalities and on Robert Lane's hypothesis that individuals with personality disturbances would tend to withdraw from social situations, including political confrontations? Of the 72 persons in the Elgin sample, only 26 had not been members of a club, organization, or other institutionalized group. Thirteen respondents were members of a single organization; 20 belonged to two organizations; five reported membership in three; four belonged to four; and four acknowledged membership in five or more organizations. When we recall that state hospital populations involve an overrepresentation of lower levels of socioeconomic status, the fact that 64 percent of our sample reported having belonged to at least one organization is remarkable.

Besides activity in organizations, the level of political interest is a key factor in the motivation to participate politically. Respondents were asked: "Would you say that you are highly, moderately, slightly, or not at all interested in political questions?" This same query has been asked in national samples (e.g., Campbell et al., 1960, p. 104), and Table 3 compares these results with those from the Elgin

Table 3
Percentage of Population and Elgin Respondents
at Different Levels of Expressed Political Interest

	Population Sample*		Elgin Milieu Sample	
	N	Percent	N	Percent
High interest	459	27.2	20	27.8
Moderate interest	627	37.2	21	29.2
Slight interest	367	21.8	15	20.8
No interest	230	13.6	16	22.2
Total cases	1683	100.0	72	100.0
	$X^2 = 3.10$		$.30 < p < .50$	

*Source: Campbell et al. (1960), p. 104.

sample. The national sample was asked this question during a presidential campaign, so it is especially notable that the level of interest is not higher. Furthermore, the Lane hypothesis suggests that the level of interest among the mentally ill should be markedly lower than that in the general population. A chi-square goodness of fit test shows, however, that the distribution of Elgin patients is not significantly different from that of the national sample. We are thus led to the tentative conclusion that there is little difference in political interest between individuals in society and individuals with severe mental illness.

Interest in political questions, as an attitudinal component, is carried over into overt behavior. The Elgin respondents were asked if they had been registered to vote and, if so, how often they had voted. Of the 52 registered respondents, 26 reported voting in "nearly all elections"; 11 said they had voted in "only major elections"; 12 voted only in presidential elections; and only three, although registered, had never voted. Thus the transfer from expressed interest to activity appears consonant with expectations.

As important as political interest and voting are in a democratic society, they are activities rather low on any decision-making spectrum. The differing levels of the spectrum have been summarized by Milbrath in *Political Participation* (1965, pp. 16–22) and are shown in Table 4 along with the percentage of the population which has been found to be active at each level, and the figures for the Elgin sample. Although the population percentages are based on male and female respondents and the Elgin sample is male only, Milbrath (1965, p. 130) reviews works which indicate that sex differences are minimal or mixed in the more modern nations and among the higher status groups. The rankings are a hierarchy because they express the intermediate steps between voting and holding public office, and because they express a hierarchy of costs to the participant. Requirements including time, personal commitment, and energy increase as one moves from each level to the next higher level. It is because of the energy component that, by Lane's hypothesis, persons suffering from intrapsychic disturbance would tend to withdraw rather than participate. Yet Table 4 indicates little difference in distribution between the population and the Elgin sample. Trying to proselytize another voter, exhibiting buttons or automobile stickers, and especially attendance at political rallies seem somewhat more popular among Elgin respondents than among the general population. The comparison suggests that, particularly at lower and medium levels of political participation, individuals with severe mental illness take part as frequently as the general population.

Table 4
Elgin Study Respondents Compared to Population Percentages
on Hierarchy of Political Involvement

	Population Percent*	Patients Percent	Patients Cases
Holding political office		1.4	1
Being a candidate	1	—	—
Soliciting funds		—	—
Attending caucus or strategy meeting		—	—
Being an active member of a party		—	—
Contributing time in campaign	4–5	8.3	6
Attending political rally		27.8	21
Contributing money	10	8.3	6
Contacting public officials	13	7.2	10
Using button or auto sticker	15	38.9	28
Attempting to sway another to vote a certain way	25–30	52.8	38
Voting	40–70	72.2	52
Apathetics	30–60	27.8	20

* Source: Milbrath (1965), p. 18.

The Elgin respondents show no tendency to engage in extremist or fighting-group politics. In response to the question, "Do you generally think of yourself as a Republican, Democrat, or what?" fifty-two patients identified with one of the two major parties; nineteen leaned toward one or the other party but preferred independence; only one person insisted that he was a member of the International Workers of the World and would always remain such. The Elgin respondents appear to be thoroughly involved in all levels of participation in the mainstream of American democratic politics.

If the Elgin people seem to be no different from others in their levels of participation, how does ward council participation relate to mental health? Taking all the councils together, we find a signficant relationship (tau beta correlation .294) between judged participation rank and clinical judgment of mental health rank. The magnitude of the correlation is interesting in that mental health is probably the greatest single status component which the Elgin respondents possess. The therapeutic environment stresses that the primary goal is mental health; the celebrity is the former patient who returns on visiting day. While a high degree of mental health is certainly no barrier to participation, neither is mental health any substantial prerequisite for participation. It should be noted here that the Bernreuter scale used in other research to conclude that legislators had superior mental health failed, in the Elgin study, to show any significant relationship between respondent scores and the clinician's ranking of mental health.[9] Furthermore, high L scorers tend to "lie good"; high Bernreuter scorers supposedly show worse mental health. A correlation of $-.497$ (p $<$ .01, t $=$ 22.02) was found between the lie score and the Bernreuter scale. This would seem to indicate that those who wish to put themselves in a good light, to "lie good," are able to manipulate their scores on the Bernreuter to appear more "good" or healthy. Scores on the Bernreuter are a better indication of how the respondent wishes to appear than of his objective degree of mental health. In partial summary, then, the Elgin study seems to indicate that mental health is not a requisite for participation.

If the totalitarian leader can be typified as a paranoid personality, do leaders in democratic contexts tend to be of the same diagnostic type? Table 5 compares

Table 5
Comparison of Elgin Milieu Population and Leader Diagnostic Typologies

Diagnostic Type	Milieu Population Sample		Milieu Council Leaders	
	N	Percent	N	Percent
1. Sociopathic	1	1.1	1	4.2
2. Personality trait disturbance	4	4.3	0	—
3. Manic-depressive	3	3.2	5	20.8
4. Involutional psychotic reaction	7	7.5	0	—
5. Schizophrenic schizo-affective	6	6.4	1	4.2
6. Catatonic schizophrenic	5	5.4	0	—
7. Paranoid schizophrenic	11	11.8	11	45.8
8. Undifferentiated schizophrenic	31	33.3	5	20.8
9. Simple schizophrenic	6	6.4	0	—
10. Hebephrenic schizophrenic	2	2.2	0	—
11. Mental deficiency	4	4.3	0	—
12. Chronic brain syndrome	13	14.0	1	4.2
Total cases	93	99.9	24	100.0

$$X^2 = 30.28 \text{ with } 4 \text{ df}, p < .001$$

the milieu council leaders with the milieu population sample in terms of diagnostic type. A discussion of the characteristics of these types is beyond the scope of this paper.[10] However, the typologies are ordered according to Melanie Klein's (1955) theory about the positions of various types of psychopathology. We see that the distribution for the council leaders (chairmen and secretaries) is markedly different from that of the mileu population from which they were selected.[11] Manic-depressive and schizophrenic-paranoid types are overrepresented among the leaders. Blumel (1950) noted that the American politicians he treated in the 1930s were frequently manic-depressives. Still more interesting, however, is the prevalence of individuals on the paranoid continuum in the council leadership. Although only 12 percent of the milieu patient population are paranoiac, fully 46 percent of the leaders are; this is an overrepresentation of nearly 400 percent.[12] If paranoids emerge at both ends of a continuum running from totalitarian nation-states to democratic proximate groups, this suggests a proposition that the paranoid is a general political type.

THE PARANOID AS A POLITICAL TYPE

In this section the characteristics of paranoia and their nexus with decision-making and participation will be discussed.[13] In the official classification of the American Psychiatric Association (1956), paranoid reactions are defined as disorders which exhibit persistent delusions, usually persecutory or grandiose, without the presence of hallucinations. Intelligence is well preserved; behavior and emotional response are consistent with the patient's ideas. Under paranoid reactions, two subgroups are distinguished: paranoia and paranoid states. Paranoia is characterized by an intricate and internally logical system of persecutory and/or grandiose delusion. The system is more or less isolated and does not interfere with the remainder of the personality. Paranoid states are not as elaborate as in paranoia and not as fragmented and bizarre as in schizophrenia. There is no personality deterioration, as there is among paranoid schizophrenes.

The paranoid does not conform to the popular conception of mental illness— loss of contact with reality, loss of control of elementary impulses, and regressive behavior and attitudes. Hallucinations, false sensory perceptions without actual external stimulus, are not an element of paranoia, but delusions are. A delusion is a belief which is without consensual validation in the individual's social group. The paranoid maintains his intelligence, personality, and logical powers.

The dynamics of paranoia are fairly well agreed upon: projection and aggression, yet with great sensitivity to social norms. Projection is the basic mechanism in all types of paranoid reaction; there is a minimum of accepted guilt, anxiety, and awareness of conflict. The organization of the personality is continually strengthened, but at the cost of rigidity. The paranoid personality often gives the impression of self-sufficiency, superiority, and certainty. No powers of argument or reasoning can convince the paranoid of the error of his beliefs.

If these impressions of paranoia are correct, they are consonant with conditions which have been considered present or requisite in political participation. Lasswell's notion that displacement and projection are characteristic of *homo politicus* could serve as a description of the primary defense mechanism of paranoia. Senses of ego strength, self-confidence, competence, and effectiveness which have been found as correlates of political participation (Milbrath, 1965, pp. 76–77) are also descriptive of the paranoid personality.

The Lane hypothesis that "well-integrated" personalities with "relatively few internal conflicts" will participate more frequently, while "anxiety-ridden persons" will not seek leadership roles, is not contradicted by the prevalence of paranoid participants. The paranoid personality projects and displaces guilt and anxiety; it is integrated to such an extent that societal consensus and perceptual validation are not required in order to sustain a belief. Then both the Lane hypothesis and the Lasswell hypothesis are probably correct, except that Lane seems to assume that anxiety is the only manifestation of psychopathology. The distinction of personality types for political participation should be, not between the mentally ill and the mentally well, but rather between internalizers and externalizers. The political world is a fertile area for the externalization of anxiety and intrapsychic conflict and, as such, tends to attract individuals with a need to find objects for projection and displacement.

The remarkable stability and integration of the paranoid delusional belief system were the objects of an ingenious study by Rokeach (1964), in which three schizophrenic paranoids, each believing himself to be the one true Christ, were confronted with the existence of the other two. Their paranoid systems were repeatedly challenged by continued contact with one another, by contrived communications from individuals important to the subjects, and by other strategies. Despite these efforts, and despite transitory strategic retreats by the subjects from their delusions, the self-indentification and the beliefs of the three Christs remained substantially unchanged.

In addition to this characteristic of an unshakable belief system, another characteristic—paranoid suspicion—has been viewed by Hoffer (1951; second edition, used here, 1962, p. 114) as functional to mass movements. The ill will and spying which he finds rife in these movements seem actually to integrate the followers.

"The surprising thing is that this pathological mistrust within the ranks leads not to dissension but to strict conformity. . . . Strict orthodoxy is as much the result of mutual suspicion as of ardent faith."

I do not intend to suggest here that high political participants are psychotic paranoids; rather, I suggest that substantial elements of paranoid behavior and belief may be prevalent among higher level participants. A political environment may be especially propitious for *particular* paranoid behaviors in individuals not otherwise to be characterized as paranoid in type. Higher participants may tend toward paranoid methods of dealing with their political world.

Different degrees of psychopathology are often visualized as a continuum extending from the normal through character disorder and psychoneurosis to psychosis. These different categories involve fundamental differences, and yet a basically similar defense mechanism may be seen operating throughout the continuum. For example, the limited use of projection by normal persons stands next to the predominant use of it by persons with a maladaptive character disorder; this use of projection may turn into xenophobia as a psychoneurotic phobic reaction, and into paranoia as a psychotic reaction.

Langner and Michael (1963, pp. 412–13) estimated from the Midtown study the probable neurotic and psychotic reactions at different levels of stress. The two resulting graphs present an interesting picture (see Figure 1). The high socioeconomic status group seems to avoid psychotic adaptation no matter how high their stress scores, yet they are much more prone to neurotic adaptation, for the same stress scores, than the lower socioeconomic status group. Given equal stress scores and the assumption that these "psychic hammer blows" occur with equal magnitude and frequency in each socioeconomic level, the group from which most political participants are recruited has a very high probability of neurotic adaptation. Individuals at these higher socioeconomic levels choose, or probably learn, to bend under stress rather than run the risk of breaking.

When an individual has not been successful in goal achievement and tension reduction, i.e., when he has received a psychic hammer blow, he may adopt several adaptive or maladaptive behaviors. The selection of these behaviors (Krech and Crutchfield, 1948) is based on the learning and internalization of these methods early in life, and is largely unconscious. When adaptive behaviors cannot be implemented—as is frequently true in the political world—maladaptive behaviors may be the resort. Thus an integrated picture emerges of the upper socioeconomic person: he participates politically to a high degree, but he also has a high degree of psychic malleability, using mechanisms which frequently include rationalization, aggression, and projection to contend with his environment.

It would appear that any explanation of national decision-making must—if it is to describe the real world—distinguish between the decision-maker's subjective utility and the objective utility of the collectivity. Lasswell's description of political man as an externalizer who rationalizes and displaces his personal motivation onto public objects is supported.

CONCLUSION AND IMPLICATIONS

Certain cautions must be expressed about the Elgin findings. The sample sizes were exploratory rather than definitive. The research was conducted at a single state hospital and the characteristics of milieu therapy, the patient population, and

Figure 1

Proportions of probable psychotics and probable neurotics, by socioeconomic status
(SES), at different stress scores.

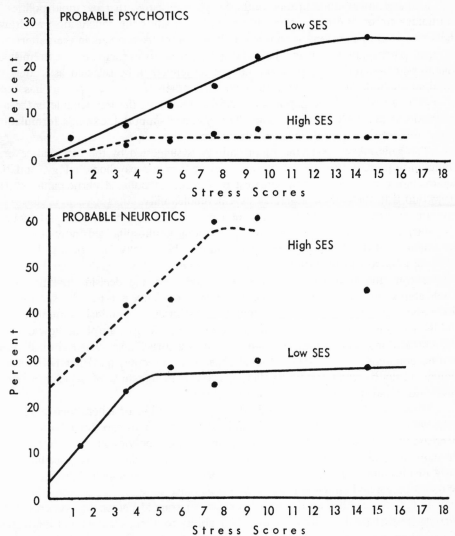

Source: Langner and Michael (1963), pp. 412–13.

preferences for a possible diagnostic style can only be controlled by research at
other institutions. In no event can the findings of a study of a psychotic population
be considered preferable to accurate and thorough research on nonhospitalized
individuals. Finally, we simply do not know the extent of impairment of judgment
in subjects whom the community psychiatry studies describe as manifesting some
degree of psychopathology.

This paper began by contrasting two decision models, the maximization-of-
utility model and the Lasswell displacement model. It was suggested that the first
of these assumed a unity of utility between the decision-maker and the organization.
The Lasswell notion that personality needs—even abnormal ones—were merged
with political outputs was compared with the theory that organizations reject
aberrant personalities.

Some evidence was noted that the totalitarian dictator is frequently of a paranoid personality type and, as such, is seen to rationalize private motives in terms of public interest. In addition, a paranoid style of politics seems to be a continuing part of the political scene in the United States, suggesting that paranoid politics is not unique to totalitarian contexts. From the Elgin study the conclusion was drawn that even psychotic persons are not markedly different from others in the patterns of political participation, nor are they especially prone to participate in extremist or "fighting-group" politics. Paranoiac individuals tended to be selected as leaders of proximate democratic groups more often than other diagnostic types. It has been argued here that the more paranoid a decision-maker is, the less tenable is the assumption of the unity of utility. The Elgin findings support Lasswell's formulation of political man as a displacer and externalizer.

The generalizability of the Elgin findings is suggested by the fact that several community psychiatry studies have revealed widespread psychopathology, and the social class which furnishes the greatest proportion of political participants is also the group with the highest degree of psychic malleability.

Future research along the lines indicated by the Elgin study would include identification of paranoid personality types among nonhospitalized individuals, and investigation of the degree to which paranoia may be socially functional rather than incapacitating to the individual.

Beyond the immediate concerns of participation and decision-making, other implications may be noted. Since the paranoid personality is especially sensitive to detrimental communications about himself, structures of political communication are relevant for further study. The paranoid person seeks to control the flow of such communications, and he may be restive about any surveillance centered on himself and his communications. Organizational concern with secrecy may thus be relevant. Paranoia may be an important mediating variable in the study of decision-makers' perceptions and misperceptions of public opinion.

If modern society is characterized by great division of labor, then a general distribution of trust is needed as each individual's ability to care for his own needs decreases. The absence of widespread paranoia might be viewed as a requisite for developing societies. In advanced societies, on the other hand, as responsibility for decisions becomes more difficult to assess, societal paranoia may be both a correlate of development and an obstacle to continued advance.

Finally, if decision-makers tend to possess paranoid personality systems, with attendant belief rigidity and suspicion, their ability to adopt creative and innovative perspectives may be curtailed. The ability of their organizations to enter into trustful relations with other organizations may likewise be curtailed. The peculiar rhetoric of disarmament is a possible case in point.

NOTES

[1] "Psychopathology" should not be confused with "psychopathy" or, as more recent usage prefers, "sociopathy." The latter two terms refer to behavior which is predominantly amoral or antisocial.

[2] Mussolini's decision to commit Italy to the invasion of Ethiopia is examined from the viewpoint of psychological motivation by Kirkpatrick (1964).

[3] Some examples: Nebuchadnezzar is found to have suffered from lycanthropy, a disorder in which he thought himself to be a wolf or a wild beast; Saul, king of Israel, suffered from

manic-depressive episodes (Coleman, 1956, p. 20). Cromwell is diagnosed as exhibiting paranoid delusions; Gandhi, as an obsessive-compulsive; and Napoleon, as a hypomaniac (Blumel, 1950, pp. 65–97).

[4] Wesman (1952) has found the Bernreuter especially vulnerable to "lying good."

[5] Langner and Michael, 1963. For their discussion of the computation of this index, see pp. 85–116.

[6] The milieu program described in this paper is that operative at Elgin State Hospital, Elgin, Illinois. I am indebted to Dr. Warner Teteur and Dr. Phillip Bower and staff for their open-door policy and their many kindnesses to me. Elgin was selected as a research site because of its propinquity to the writer's university and because its milieu program is well developed. Field work there was completed in March and April 1965.

[7] I am indebted to psychologist Kenneth Karrels for help here and in other phases of the project.

[8] This shortened scale adds a constant to eliminate items scored as minus quantities. The short scale correlated .864 with the whole scale, and has a Kuder-Richardson 20 reliability coefficient of .917.

[9] Following is the analysis of variance relating the shortened Bernreuter N-1 scale and the clinically judged mental health rank for the Elgin sample:

Source of variance	DF	SS	MS	F
Health rank	5	18,941	3,788.2	1,0699
Error	66	233,693.5	3,540.8	
Total	71	252,634.5		

An F ratio of 1.07 for 5 and 66 degrees of freedom is not significant.

[10] The nomenclature used here follows the American Psychiatric Association's (1952) suggestions.

[11] A chi-square goodness of fit test, with categories one to six and nine through twelve combined, shows that the leaders are significantly different with respect to diagnosis.

[12] The stability of this relationship is shown by a partial replication completed a year and a half later. It was assumed that the ratio of diagnostic types in the patient population had not changed; only the leaders were studied. Although only three of the original leaders remained in office, the circulation of leaders did not affect the marked overrepresentation of paranoid schizophrenics. Thirty-six percent of the new leadership group were of this diagnostic type—fewer than originally, but more than three times the expected frequency.

[13] This is drawn largely from Norman Cameron's (1959) discussion of "Paranoid Conditions and Paranoia," in *The American Handbook of Psychiatry*.

REFERENCES

Almond, G. A., and S. Verba. *The Civic Culture*. Princeton, N.J.: Princeton University Press, 1963.

Artiss, K. L. *Milieu Therapy in Schizophrenia*. New York: Grune and Stratton, 1962.

Blumel, C. S. *War, Politics and Insanity*. (2d ed.) Denver, Colo.: World Press, 1950.

Brim, O. G., et al. *Personality and Decision Processes*. Stanford, Calif.: Stanford University Press, 1962.

Cameron, N. "Paranoid Conditions and Paranoia." In S. Arietie ed., *American Handbook of Psychiatry*. Vol. II. New York: Basic Books, 1959.

Campbell, A., P. Converse, W. Miller, and D. Stokes. *The American Voter*. New York: Wiley, 1960.

Campbell, A., G. Gurin, and W. Miller. *The Voter Decides*. Evanston, Ill.: Row, Peterson, 1954.

Christiansen, B. *Attitudes Toward Foreign Affairs as a Function of Personality*. Oslo: Oslo University Press, 1959.

Coleman, J. C. *Abnormal Psychology and Modern Life*. (2d ed.) Chicago: Scott Foresman, 1956.

Cumming, J., and E. Cumming. *Ego and Milieu: Theory and Practice of Environmental Therapy*. New York: Atherton Press, 1962.

Deutsch, M. "Some Considerations Relevant to National Policy," *Journal of Social Issues* 17 (1961), 57–68.

French, J. R. P., Jr., and B. Raven. "The Bases of Social Power." In D. Cartwright ed., *Studies in Social Power*. Ann Arbor: University of Michigan Press, 1959.

Freud, S. *Psychopathology of Everyday Life.* Translated by A. A. Brill. New York: Macmillan, n.d.

Gilbert, G. M. *Psychology of Dictatorship.* New York: Ronald Press, 1950.

Harcane, S. *Russia: A History.* (4th ed.) Chicago: Lippincott, 1959.

Hoffer, E. *The True Believer* (1951). New York: Mentor, 1962.

Hofstadter, R. *The Paranoid Style in American Politics.* New York: Knopf, 1965.

Jones, M. *The Therapeutic Community.* New York: Basic Books, 1954.

Kaplan, M. A. "Old Realities and New Myths," *World Politics* 17 (January 1965), 334–67.

Kirkpatrick, Ivone. *Mussolini: A Study in Power.* New York: Hawthorn Press, 1964.

Klein, M. *New Directions in Psychoanalysis.* New York: Basic Books, 1955.

Krech, D., and R. S. Crutchfield. *Theory and Problems of Social Psychology.* New York: McGraw-Hill, 1948.

Lane, R. E. *Political Life.* Glencoe, Ill.: Free Press, 1959.

Langner, T. S., and S. T. Michael. *Life Stress and Mental Health.* New York: Free Press of Glencoe, 1963.

Lasswell, H. D. *Psychopathology and Politics* (1930). (2d ed.) With afterthoughts by the author. New York: Viking Press, 1960.

———. "Selective Effect of Personality of Political Participation." In R. Christie and M. Jahoda (eds.), *Studies in the Scope and Method of "The Authoritarian Personality."* Glencoe, Ill.: Free Press, 1954.

———. "The Study of the Ill as a Method of Research into Political Personalities," *American Political Science Review* 23 (November 1929), 996–1001.

Leighton, D. C. "The Distribution of Psychiatric Symptoms in a Small Town," *American Journal of Psychiatry* 112 (1956), 716–23.

Leites, N. "Psycho-Cultural Hypothesis about Political Acts," *World Politics* 1 (October 1948), 102–19.

Lemert, E. M. "Paranoia and the Dynamics of Exclusion," *Sociometry* 25 (March 1962), 2–20.

Lerche, C. O., Jr., and A. A. Said. *Concepts of International Politics.* Englewood Cliffs, N.J.: Prentice-Hall, 1963.

McConaughy, J. B. "Certain Personality Factors of State Legislators in South Carolina," *American Political Science Review* 44 (December 1950), 897–903.

Milbrath, L. W. *Political Participation: How and Why Do People Get Involved in Politics?* Chicago: Rand McNally, 1965.

Patchen, M. "Decision Theory in the Study of National Action: Problems and a Proposal," *Journal of Conflict Resolution* 9, 2 (June 1965), 164–76.

Rogow, A. *James Forrestal: A Study of Personality, Politics and Policy.* New York: Macmillan, 1963.

Rokeach, M. *Three Christs of Ypsilanti.* New York: Knopf, 1964.

Rusk, D. "The President," *Foreign Affairs* 38 (1960), 353–69.

Scodel, A., P. Ratoosh, and J. S. Minas. "Some Personality Correlates of Decision-Making under Conditions of Risk," *Behavioral Science* 4 (1959), 19–28.

Singer, J. D. "Inter-Nation Influence: A Formal Model," *American Political Science Review* 57 (1963), 420–30.

Snyder, G. H. "Deterrence and Power," *Journal of Conflict Resolution* 4, 2 (June 1960), 163–78.

Snyder, R. C. "Some Recent Trends in International Relations Theory and Research." In Austin Ranney (ed.), *Essays on the Behavioral Study of Politics.* Urbana: University of Illinois Press, 1962.

Srole, L., et al. *Mental Health in the Metropolis: The Midtown Manhattan Study.* New York: McGraw-Hill, 1962.

Tucker, R. C. "The Dictator and Totalitarianism," *World Politics* 17 (July 1965), 555–83.

Verba, S. "Assumptions of Rationality and Non-Rationality in Models of the International System," *World Politics* 14 (October 1961), 93–117.

Wesman, A. G. "Faking Personality Test Scores in a Simulated Employment Situation," *Journal of Applied Psychology* 36 (1952), 112–13.

Wolff, W. *The Threshold of the Abnormal.* New York: Hermitage House, 1950.

13

Systematic Analysis of Clinical Data

P sychoanalytic therapy continues to be by far the most intensive means of gaining insight into individual psychic functioning, including aspects of psychological functioning that may well be important but not easily observable by less intensive procedures. Yet numerous methodological problems hedge efforts to determine the validity of psychoanalytic observations and interpretations. Furthermore, it is difficult to employ data of such idiosyncratic richness as the usual products of psychoanalytic therapeutic interviews for the tasks of typological classification that are required in research that seeks to advance general propositions. The essay that follows is a proposal for the systematic, critical analysis of psychoanalytic data on a multi-case basis, thus making empirical study of political types through psychoanalysis in principle possible.

PRIVATE DISORDER AND THE PUBLIC ORDER: A PROPOSAL FOR COLLABORATION BETWEEN PSYCHOANALYSTS AND POLITICAL SCIENTISTS

Fred I. Greenstein

In 1938 Lasswell wrote an article entitled "What Psychiatrists and Political Scientists Can Learn from Each Other." [1] It is noteworthy that he was able to state his theme in the form of a declarative sentence rather than a question. The intellectual atmosphere of the 1930s and 1940s seems to have been more congenial than that of the present age of specialization to suggestions that psychiatrists might find it fruitful to exchange views and collaborate with investigators in the various social sciences. To take one example, the volumes of *Psychiatry* for those years are liberally sprinkled with contributions not only by Lasswell but also by such scholars as Edward Sapir, Talcott Parsons, and Ruth Benedict. And many of the articles from within the psychiatric guild were also directed to social issues, including politics. But not long ago Rogow examined the thirty-five most recent issues

From *The Psychoanalytic Quarterly,* 37 (1968), 261–81. Reprinted with slight revisions.

of four leading psychiatric journals and found very little indeed in the way of inter-disciplinary bridging with the social sciences—of a total of two hundred sixty-two articles in the four journals "only seven were concerned with the social sciences however broadly defined." [2]

This paper suggests a research strategy through which one variety of social scientist—the political scientist—might profitably collaborate with one variety of psychiatrist—the psychoanalyst. My proposal is for a continuing, systematic effort to use the distinctive vantage point of psychoanalytic therapy to clarify the familiar hypothesis that people's reactions to the public order and its symbols are influenced by the private order and disorder of their psyches and, particularly, by the ways they have earlier learned to respond to the private authorities of their childhoods. In other words, that, in Lasswell's famous formula, "private motives" become displaced on public objects and "rationalized in the public interest." [3]

I will confine much of my discussion to proposing a research design addressed to one of the many problems that might be investigated in a collaborative effort by political scientists and psychoanalysts to study the private symbolism of public objects: the problem of how various members of the public orient themselves to-ward the American Chief Executive. The way the public is disposed to respond to the President—its propensity to follow him, reject him, or ignore him—is of obvious interest to political scientists. This matter also has been of occasional in-terest to psychoanalysts. As a preface to my proposal, it will be useful to indicate a way in which the existing social science literature on citizens' orientations to the President presents a puzzle, then to summarize the scattered psychoanalytic evi-dence on the citizens' orientations to the President, indicating both why that evi-dence appears to be highly relevant to solving the puzzle in the social science litera-ture and why, as a result of existing conventions for reporting case materials, the psychoanalytic evidence is, in fact, frustratingly incomplete for that purpose.

THE PRESIDENT AS A SYMBOL: SOCIAL SCIENCE RESEARCH

There is an interesting closeness of fit between what seems to be missing in the partially completed mosaic of political science data on public orientations toward the President and the observations in the scattered psychoanalytic case reports on the topic. It is a commonplace of political science literature on the presidency that one aspect of the Chief Executive's role is his status as a symbolic personification of the nation.[4] In this capacity, the literature points out, he is a nonpartisan figure, above the political fray. The specific manifestations of this symbolic aspect of his role range from decorous ceremonies like the lighting of the White House Christmas tree through such grim occasions as President Roosevelt's "day of infamy" speech on December 8, 1941. A skilful President must excel at the intricate task of bal-ancing the demands for dignified neutrality connected with his symbolic Head of State status and the more partisan, combative demands imposed by the exigencies of winning support for his program. Mishandling of either side of the role can impede the President in the other; by the same token, success in either may be additive.

But to what degree *is* the President a meaningful symbol for most Americans? From the standpoint of one set of research findings that have been accumulating over the years, we might well conclude that the President's importance as a symbol has been grossly overrated. It has frequently been shown that the great bulk of the American electorate (like the electorates of other nations) is extraordinarily inattentive to the sphere in which the President exercises leadership. Public opinion polls have shown again and again that most citizens on most occasions are far more interested in day-to-day happenings in their immediate environment than in the remote political happenings to which they are exposed through mass communications media. For example, most voters are unable to name their Congressman or Senator or the leading Cabinet officials, such as the Secretary of State, much less indicate what these individuals have been doing. Many of the rudimentary facts that must be known if a citizen is to follow national events with anything of the acuteness with which baseball fans follow the great American sport are unknown to most citizens; for example, the length of Congressmen's terms, the composition of the Supreme Court, the provisions of the Bill of Rights.[5]

Occasionally, however, the President is the object of widespread and profoundly emotional responses that suggest he has an extremely important symbolic value for citizens. The most striking of these occasions is when an incumbent President dies. Beginning with the assassinations of Presidents Lincoln, Garfield and McKinley, and continuing through the deaths by natural causes of Harding and Roosevelt and the assassination of Kennedy—the historical record suggests that in each of these instances, from Lincoln's death on, the demise of the man filling the presidential role has occasioned widespread public grief and mourning. No comparable responses are produced by the deaths of other public officials, or of ex-Presidents or nonpolitical celebrities (except on the part of very limited segments of the population, as in the case of teenagers' reaction to the death of entertainment celebrities). While some of the responses to President Kennedy's death certainly were related to the horror of assassination and to his youth, the public response seems to have been much the same in the two preceding instances of natural deaths of Presidents in office—Roosevelt and Harding. This makes it clear that the reactions are not merely to the man or to the mode of his death but rather are to the fact that *the President* has died.[6]

How do we reconcile the seeming inconsistency between widespread indifference to the sphere of activity in which the President is a leader and profound emotional response to his death? What explains this manifestation on a mass scale of a phenomenon that psychoanalysts encounter among individual patients—*an emotional reaction that seems to be far out of proportion to our prior impression of the individual's emotional investment in the object?*

Let us consider a variety of empirical observations in the political science literature that seem relevant to resolving this paradox. 1. Although public information on politics and political figures may be low, "the President is by far the best known figure on the American political scene." 2. "The status of President is accorded great respect in American society." 3. "The President ordinarily is the first public official to come to the attention of young children." 4. "Even before they are substantively informed about the President's functions, children believe that he is exceptionally important—and that he is benign." 5. Adults also "normally have a favorable view of the President's performance (although not so automatically positive a view as that held by children)." 6. "There is a significant tendency for citizens to rally to the support of the President, particularly when he acts in times of international crisis." 7. "Citizens seem to perceive and evaluate the President as a person, rather than in terms of his policy commitments or his skills in the specialized tasks of leadership." [7]

These fragments take us part of the way toward resolution of the paradox.

In effect, they soften the impression that the President is not a widespread object of public awareness, interest, and sympathy; compared with other actors in the political system, he is. But something of the puzzle remains. Why should citizens be so disturbed at the death of a distant figure—someone they have never even met? The National Opinion Research Center survey of reactions to President Kennedy's death found, for example, that forty-three percent of a national sample of adults experienced loss of appetite during the four days following the assassination; forty-eight percent reported insomnia; twenty-five percent headaches. Anxiety symptoms such as rapid heart beat and perspiring were reported by many respondents. Interestingly, at the time of what would seem to have been a particularly tense and potentially far more threatening event in the distant environment (the Cuban missile crisis), comparable research showed no increase in these somatic symptoms.[8] During this crisis, the nation seemed to be at the edge of the abyss, whereas on November 22, 1963, a single public official had died and his successor was installed within the day. Why then should the latter event be by far the more disturbing?

It is here that the fragments of psychoanalytic and other psychiatric data assume an interest. If it can be shown that, at an unconscious level, people are in fact deeply emotionally attached to the President, this will contribute to an explanation of their "disproportionate" grief at his death. In effect, we can conclude that the grief was not disproportionate to the "true" feelings of citizens toward the President. And we may also have obtained a "handle" for understanding certain less remarkable, but still puzzling, aspects of public behavior toward the Chief Executive. For example, why is it that the level of public support for the President usually goes up when he takes some decisive action in the international arena, even if the action is like the Bay of Pigs invasion, one which would seem to have been a fiasco?

PSYCHOANALYTIC EVIDENCE ON THE PRESIDENT'S SYMBOLIC MEANING

There was no question in Freud's mind that a variety of public authority figures— kings, generals, religious leaders—can serve important unconscious functions. He returned to this topic at various stages of his career—in *Totem and Taboo* (1912), *Group Psychology and the Analysis of the Ego* (1921), and shortly before his death in *Moses and Monotheism* (1939). In the latter, he succinctly advanced a psychoanalytic explanation of why the great man should rise to significance. "We know that in the mass of mankind there is a powerful need for an authority who can be admired, before whom one bows down, by whom one is ruled and perhaps even ill-treated. We have learnt from the psychology of individual men what the origin is of this need of the masses. It is a longing for the father felt by everyone from his childhood onwards, for the same father whom the hero of legend boasts he has overcome. And now it may begin to dawn on us that all the characteristics with which we equipped the great man are paternal characteristics, and that the essence of great men for which we vainly searched lies in this conformity." [9]

Freud relied largely upon historical, ethnographic, and literary materials for his observations about the private, unconscious influences on individuals' orientations toward public authority, and he did not comment on public orientations toward the particular authority figure we are concerned with here, the American President. A political scientist, interested in what psychoanalysis can contribute to resolving the seeming inconsistency between rather scant day-to-day reactions to the President and massive reactions to his death, is likely to insist on direct observational data. Can such evidence be adduced, drawing on the observational vantage that is distinctive to psychoanalysis—the psychoanalytic interview?

Let us look narrowly at evidence of adult psychoanalytic patients' reactions to presidential death, rather than canvassing the literature generally for fugitive references to patients' responses to Presidents and other authority figures. There have been only three published reports of patients' reactions under these circumstances, although I have been assured that many other analysts found similar evidence. In each case the report indicates that the analyst found material emerging in the sessions after the President's death that clearly pointed to an unconscious symbolic linkage of the President to the patient's childhood authority figures.

The earliest of these published papers was by a political scientist, Sebastian de Grazia.[10] It summarizes the reactions of thirty patients of two psychoanalysts (Blitzsten and Emch) to the death of President Roosevelt. For the moment I shall simply quote those statements in de Grazia's sparse report which refer to ways in which the patients' responses to the President's death bore on their orientations toward childhood authority figures.

> All persons made explicit linkages of the President with the father figure. Some said, "I felt like I did when my father died." More persons, however, said, "I felt worse than I did when my father [or mother] died." All persons in pursuing associations further made linkages with an original sexless mother imago. In this latter context, many persons mentioned the President's paralytic incapacity. . . .
>
> All analysands became aware that over the past years the President had unconsciously substituted for the parental imagos and in this manner had affected their attitudes and manner toward him. . . .
>
> Living parents were discussed by those few patients who had a mother or father alive. At least temporarily there seemed to be less hostility expressed toward . . . living . . . parents.

The second of the three reports is by Sterba[11] and also deals with reactions to President Roosevelt's death, in this case by five patients, all of them male and liberal Democrats. While no indication is given of the patients' ages, they probably were younger than those de Grazia reported on, since four out of five had living parents.

Sterba gives only a single datum on each patient—the reports they gave of dreams on the night of the President's death or the following night. Each patient reported a dream in which there was no manifest reference to the late President. Common symbolic elements ran through the dreams. In every case the dream involved augmentation of the patient's masculinity and independence of authority. Male authority figures were overcome (one patient breaks the sword of an attacking older male adversary; a delinquent boy is accused of dismembering a policeman), or the patient was suddenly free to express sexuality. Sterba's patients, unlike those reported in de Grazia's paper, evidently did not perceive the unconscious symbolic connection of President-parent. Or if they made such a connection it was not in relation to their dream reports and therefore not discussed in the paper. "The patients did not spontaneously link up their dreams with the President because the resistance against recognition of the negative feeling towards the father figure of the late President was too strong, and thus the connection had to be demonstrated to them."

The single report I have seen of adult psychoanalytic patients' reactions to President Kennedy's death is by Kirschner, who reports on the behavior in therapy of eight women.[12] "These eight women, while in therapy for a variety of reasons . . . could be described as a rather homogeneous group in many respects. They might all be considered 'good' neurotic patients: they were all between thirty to fifty-five years of age, middle- to upper-middle-class, above average in intelligence, motivated, well-intact, introspective individuals. Politically, they were all liberal Democrats, and had all voted for JFK. . . . Each had lost one or both parents (in six cases, the father); and unresolved hostility and ambivalence toward the deceased parent(s) figured importantly in their respective therapies."

Kirschner observed that: "Almost without exception, the eight female patients in the present study described their initial reaction to the news of the assassination as 'exactly the same' as their response when first told of a parent's death. . . ."

In addition, at least two of his parents contrasted their highly idealized favorable views of Kennedy with unsympathetic accounts of their fathers. In the first example it is not clear whether the contrast was made explicitly by the patient, or whether it is the analyst who has made the juxtaposition. "One woman who in therapy could only describe her father in the blackest terms . . . related the death of JFK to the 'loss of a heroic figure—a shiny knight on a white charger.' Another woman, who had perceived her father as a passive, dull, nonentity, discussed her feelings about JFK as follows: 'He represented to me the things I always wanted my own father to be—a great intellect, forceful; a person of dignity who commanded the respect and esteem of others.'

"Almost without exception, these patients noted that they were able to express more grief and tears for President Kennedy than for their own parents. Typical comments were as follows: 'I had the luxury of grief I couldn't express for my own father'; 'I told my husband I released more tears for President Kennedy than when Poppa died. The tears were for my father. I buried Poppa again. . . .'"

EVIDENCE AND INFERENCE IN THE THREE REPORTS

The brief summary of these three case reports shows why the possible contribution of psychoanalysis to resolving the enigma of public orientations to the President has been less than completely realized. Let us suppose that the psychoanalytic reports on reactions to the presidential deaths, rather than being serendipitous observations reported by unconnected investigators, had been part of a planned, coordinated effort by psychoanalysts, and their colleagues in other relevant fields, to compile week-to-week observations of their patients, for a continuing survey of the private meanings of individuals' reactions to the wider environment. Such a suggestion was made by Lasswell: "Psychiatrists do not, as a rule, record the role of secondary symbols [such as political attitudes] in relation to the personality structure which they observe. Once they understand the nature of the problem to which these data are precious, they may take care to preserve, rather than to ignore or to discard, material . . . so fully exposed by their special procedure." [13]

Such a collective investigation, particularly if it had the partial aim of communicating with sympathetic investigators outside of the specialized area of psychoanalysis, might help to remedy a number of deficiencies which make the three sets of case histories on reactions to presidential deaths less than fully satisfactory as sources of evidence on the unconscious significance of the President as a parent surrogate. Six deficiencies that might be remedied are:

1. Sample Size

Although the case studies are exceptionally suggestive, they are based on a small number of individuals; a total of forty-three, eight of them the patients of a single therapist at the time of Kennedy's assassination, thirty-five the patients of three therapists at the time of Roosevelt's death.

2. Sample Representativeness

As any specialist in sampling will confirm, the absolute size of a sample is less important than its representativeness. The latter is best assured by the use of impersonal statistical techniques through which the cases are selected at random, but, if necessary, certain compromises are possible; for example, purposive, stratified sampling. The cases summarized here are conspicuously unrepresentative—so much so that even comparisons among the three reports are perilous in the extreme. Apart from the obvious observation that patients in any psychiatric situation (much less psychoanalytic patients) are "unrepresentative," these patients probably were not even an accurate microcosm of the psychoanalytic analysand population. No information is given about the background of the thirty patients reported on by de Grazia. Sterba's five patients were probably young men and liberal Democrats. Kirschner's eight patients were middle-aged women and liberal Democrats.

3. Uniformity of Reporting

Sterba reports exclusively on the dreams of five patients, giving his interpretations of the dreams and alluding briefly to the fact that he met with resistances from the patients in presenting interpretations to them. There is no reference to dreaming in the thirty patients de Grazia reports on; rather, he refers to their spontaneous references in the therapy hours to the President's death and alludes to their further associations without presenting details. Kirschner presents some of both kinds of material. We do not know whether Sterba or Kirschner had other patients who showed different behavior; we do not know if any of the thirty patients of Blitzsten and Emch reported dreams. An observer interested in systematizing this material would need to know more in a more fully comparable fashion about the reactions at various levels of all of the four therapists' patients, as well as the patients of other therapists and, ideally, of nonpatient populations.

4. Full Accounts of Variability of Reaction

Small sample case reports of the sort discussed here tend to emphasize the uniformities in the subjects' responses, at the expense of an account of types of variation. The number of respondents is so small that those variations that are reported appear as individual idiosyncracies rather than as subpatterns of response which might be of interest to explain. This greatly reduces the usefulness of the reports as sources of hypotheses that might be tested by appropriately designed and controlled experimental research. The experimental psychologist is typically interested in variables rather than uniformities. He wants to test hypotheses which take the form: if the variable X is present, then the outcome Y will (is more likely to) occur.

The lack of emphasis on variation is particularly noticeable in de Grazia's report, which frequently refers to responses of "all" the analysands, sometimes with respect to behavior that we would expect to be at least somewhat variable in a group of thirty patients. "All analysands spontaneously began their hour talking about the events . . . ; all persons made explicit linkages of the President with the father figure . . . ; analysts were immediately asked by all analysands, 'Have you heard the news?' and then, 'How do you feel about it?' Upon being told that the analyst felt grieved, the analysands invariably demonstrated a sense of relief . . . ; the President's wife was referred to by all persons . . . ; all persons expressed great incredulity that the event had actually occurred. . . ." [14]

Attention to variability should enable us to go beyond such simple formulations as "the President serves as a father (or more generally parent) figure" to hypotheses raising more specific questions. Under what circumstances? To what degree? For what individuals? In what manner? Not only are there probably differences in the degree to which Presidents serve as unconscious parent surrogates from individual to individual and from President to President but, as Lasswell once pointed out, there are probably quite different ways in which the generalization of early orientations toward authority can occur. Depending upon other contingencies, individuals may differ in the degree to which conscious and unconscious hostility and affection is experienced toward their own parents, and the patterns of orientations toward the parents may either be directly generalized to remote authorities such as the President, or the generalization may take a compensatory form involving either idealization of the President or unconsciously motivated hostility toward him.[15]

5. Distinguishing Obervations Based on the Patient's Spontaneous Responses from Therapeutic Communication and from Interpretations of the Observational Material of the Psychoanalytic Interview

No doubt there is much truth to the assertion often made by psychoanalysts that the understanding of psychoanalytic theory and case reports by laymen, including academic social scientists, is inevitably limited by processes of resistance. Resistance certainly is a partial cause of much of the lay scepticism toward psychoanalytic explanation. In addition, there are tendencies on the part of at least some laymen toward excessive credulity—willingness to accept virtually any psychoanalytic explanation on faith. Above and beyond such irrational barriers to the intelligent assessment of psychoanalytic assertions by political scientists, the conventions according to which psychoanalytic material is reported also contribute to restricting the amount of effective interchange between psychoanalysis and the various social science disciplines, all of which have been in a continuing process of perfecting their procedures for gathering and assessing data.

Much of what is reported in psychoanalytic journals seems to the outside observer, even to the observer with far more than usual sympathetic interest in psychoanalysis, to be arbitrary and unconvincing. There are two problems faced by the outsider who wishes to draw upon psychoanalytic reports, but does not want to have to take the interpretations made in these reports on faith (if only so that he can more effectively transmit the psychoanalytic findings and hypotheses to other of his professional colleagues who are more typical in their scepticism toward psychoanalysis).

First, the case reports too rarely distinguish between the spontaneous emanations of the patient and material that emerges from the interaction between patient and therapist. One would assume that special caution is necessary in accepting the latter as evidence: for example, it must occasionally be true that an analyst offers an incorrect interpretation, which the patient compliantly accepts. I suspect that some of the most convincing evidence in support of certain of the more controversial psychoanalytic hypotheses—such as the hypotheses connecting Presidents and fathers—arises in therapy contexts which, if carefully reported, would reveal that suggestion by the therapist could not possibly be responsible for the finding (unsolicited free associations, patients' own interpretations of their dreams, slips of the tongue, etc.).

Second, and more generally, the elliptical mode of presentation of the typical case report too often fails to lay before the reader the precise phenomenology of the psychoanalytic interview and to indicate precisely what evidence from the interview is leading to what interpretations. Thus, I am unable to determine from de Grazia's report the full pattern of behavior on the part of patients leading to de Grazia's assertion that "linkage" was made with an "original sexless mother imago." Another example: the interpretations in psychoanalytic case reports of statements of negation by parents as "denial"—i.e., as assertions concealing an unconscious motivation directly opposite that of their manifest content—are one of the more common sources of derisive criticism from outside the psychoanalytic fraternity. Yet I am sure that partially implicit and partially explicit criteria underlie such interpretations, and that when analysts interpret a negation as denial they do so on the basis of observational evidence that distinguishes one negative statement by a patient from another (e.g., the intensity and nature of the affect expressed in making the denial). By failing to make both the observational data and the inferential steps more explicit, psychoanalysts not only reduce the credibility of their reports; they also probably fail to engage in sufficiently stringent examination of their own methodology. One consequence may often be an unwarranted scepticism by many social scientists about all psychoanalytic interpretations and findings; this is likely to contribute to the failure on the part of psychoanalysts to incorporate psychodynamic notions into research to which such notions might well prove to be relevant.

THE PROPOSAL

I propose a continuing, systematic inventory of ways in which psychoanalytic patients of varying characteristics and in varying treatment situations respond to the events of the secondary environment. From the standpoint of the tack taken in this paper such a continuing investigation would emphasize responses to political authority figures and particularly the President. But it clearly would be possible to produce a similar inventory of patients' reactions to any type of wider-society events that impinge upon citizens through mass media and also to the inner significance of whatever political experience they may be exposed to in their immediate environments.

It would be enormously interesting to have a progressively expanding catalogue of psychodynamic insights into public response to phenomena such as war, civil defense, international politics, electoral contests, racial conflict in the cities, etc. Let me indicate in a very general way some of the possible desiderata of a study aimed at assembling such an inventory. My purpose, in effect, is to suggest how we might collect material of the sort presented in the three case studies on reaction to presidential deaths in a fashion that avoids the shortcomings of uncoordinated case study reports.

1. The sample of subjects would be fairly sizable. Sample size would be determined, apart from restrictions imposed by the number of analysts participating in the investigation and their patient loads, by the number of cases needed for a minimally satisfactory statistical treatment of the data. The study of male homosexuals sponsored by the Society of Medical Psychoanalysis and reported by Bieber and associates, which serves as my model in many of the suggestions that follow, reported on two hundred six patients, the data being contributed by seventy-seven psychoanalysts.[16]

2. Sample representativeness is as important as sample size. It certainly would not be feasible, and probably not desirable, to attempt to stratify the sample population along the lines of a cross-section of the American population. A preferable strategy would be to select cases with a view to building up sufficiently large comparison groups to test hypotheses about the effects of varying social and psychological characteristics on the various connections between personality and political behavior to be studied. However, it is desirable to estimate the degree to which the sample is representative of various nonpatient populations, by careful comparison of the sample with census and other demographic statistics. This, incidentally, would probably have the side effect of generating a more satisfactory account than presently is available of who is receiving psychoanalytic treatment.

3. A main point of departure from the technique of the Bieber study is that this investigation would, in effect, be a continuing panel study. In other words, rather than depending upon a single interview schedule at one point in time, data would be reported periodically on the same group of subjects. The occasions for collecting new data would be when events occurred in the wider environment that are likely to impinge upon the patients' emotional lives. One can only guess at the valuable insights into reactions to President Kennedy's assassination—and therefore more generally into the psychology of leader-follower relations—that might have been gained if such a data-gathering enterprise had been underway in 1963. It also would be important, of course, to establish the kinds of events that do *not* have emotional effects. As in all panel surveys, attrition of respondents would pose difficulties, but various ways of compensating partially for this difficulty are possible: initial selection of a large sample; emphasis on detailed analysis of the early data-gathering waves; adding similar cases to match the lost respondents and reporting both the reconstructed sample and the residual original respondents.

4. A second point of difference from the Bieber study would be a greater emphasis on reporting the phenomenology of the psychoanalytic interview in detail, so that a careful distinction is made between the three classes of statements referred to above: spontaneous patient reactions, reactions elicited as a part of the interaction with the therapist, and interpretations. This will make it possible to exhibit the findings along a sliding scale ranging from data that should be of interest to any student of the phenomenon being reported on, to data that will be more credible to psychoanalysts and others committed to psychoanalytic modes of

analysis. Even social scientists who are not particularly committed to psycho-analysis should find it necessary to take account of behavior in the psychoanalytic interview itself as observational material of some interest and in need of ex-planation.

5. Such a project would of course call for central facilities for planning and coordinating the research. I would assume that the core investigators would be a team of psychoanalysts and social scientists; that after the initial planning stages it would be important to delegate decisions about what information to request from the contributing therapists to a small steering committee that was in a position to deliberate rapidly and communicate requests for data swiftly. It also would be important to report back to the contributing therapists regularly, since the added information about one's patients' comparative "standing" in the larger patient population would be one of the important incentives for taking part in such an endeavor. A useful base from which such a study could be directed might be some university facility, such as the Inter-University Consortium for Political Research in Ann Arbor, the National Opinion Research Center in Chicago, or the Yale Office for Advanced Political Studies in New Haven.

6. A final suggestion involves developing techniques to estimate the degree to which the responses reported are a consequence of the selective factors that lead patients into therapy. An obvious possibility is use of physicians in training analyses as control groups. It would also be possible to use control groups of respondents drawn by survey techniques from the general nonpatient population, matching on a variety of social and psychological characteristics, and then administering standard survey questionnaires to both the patient and nonpatient samples. As a side effect, this could lead to a particularly worthwhile contribution to research technology: by comparing patients' questionnaire responses with their responses in therapy it might be possible to determine where and under what circumstances the survey technique fails to elicit responses reflecting the deeper meanings of the secondary environment.

AN OBJECTION AND ITS IMPLICATIONS

There are many practical obstacles standing in the way of such a proposal for interdisciplinary cooperation. However, even a modest effort, fulfilling only a part of the proposal, would take us far ahead of the present state of knowledge. One reason for being dubious about the likely results of any such enterprise is the objection I most often encounter in suggesting such a proposal to psychoanalysts.

The reasons for scepticism are summed up in the comment of one analyst: "I would not know that the political world existed if I did not read the news-papers." In other words, one may well be sceptical less about the practicality of my proposal than about the possibility that it will turn up findings of any interest. There evidently are wide variations in the degree to which political events impinge upon regular proceedings of psychoanalytic treatment. At the other extreme from the analyst who never "sees" politics in the treatment situation is the published report of Renneker that among a total of forty-two patients in treatment with him during the 1948, 1952, and 1956 elections, not only was politics invariably evident in the course of treatment, but also "there was *always* some sort of meaningful relationship between the voting history of the patient and the *dominant* parent." [17] A middle ground is struck by analysts who comment that they rarely deal explicitly with political material, but that public happenings sometimes are evident at some symbolic level. One analyst commented that he regularly was able to observe current news events appearing in disguised form in dream reports, although this level of the patients' output did not normally enter into the treatment.

It appears that this variability in the degree to which the different analysts' patients are likely to respond to public events in private terms results from factors related to the analysts themselves—their own assumptions about whether such hidden meanings are to be expected and are of interest and of relevance to treatment. The same reference to the President might be considered interesting and therapeutically constructive by one analyst and time-wasting resistance by another. This would affect both the analysts' memory of what had occurred in the session and whatever cues he inevitably provided to the patient about the appropriate lines of association to dwell upon in therapy. If this is the case, the differences in the degree to which secondary environment symbols appear in the associations of different analysts' patients might in itself be of interest to study: in effect, the analyst would be one of the variables of the investigation, just as the experimenter is increasingly being thought of as the "hidden variable" in experimental research on small groups.

In addition, if the effects of wider environment events on patients and on the content of the psychoanalytic interview are as indirect as the comments of the third analyst quoted above indicates, we will need to do more than simply observe explicit political material that emerges during therapy. It may be that the effects of the wider environment will manifest themselves in complexly disguised forms. Consider, for example, the possibility of providing some central collection agency of the sort I have been proposing with the dream reports and fantasies produced by a large patient population on the days prior to and just after some event such as Khrushchev's deposal, a presidential inauguration, or one of the recent episodes of racial violence. Is it not likely that some systematic, if disguised, effects of these happenings would be evident?

SUMMARY AND CONCLUSIONS

There has been a decline in recent years of interdisciplinary efforts to apply psychiatric insights and findings to the explanation of social—and especially political—phenomena. After reviewing the puzzling pattern of social science data on the symbolic meaning of the American President to citizens, I have suggested why scattered psychoanalytic evidence on this topic, if systematically expanded and validated, might provide a missing link in our explanatory account of how the public orients itself toward the President. However, the several existing psychoanalytic case reports on public orientations toward the President (as shown by reactions to the death of a President in office) fall short of adequacy in terms of evidence and inference. A systematic, continuing program for accumulating understanding about the symbolic values to citizens of events in the wider environment (including the persons and activities of the President)—a program of the sort proposed here—would do much to eliminate the methodological inadequacies.

The great discoveries of Freud, while in one sense pervasively influential in both modern society and modern social science, in another sense have had far too little impact. In particular, the social sciences have had little benefit from the central procedures of psychoanalysis: the prolonged one-to-one relationship of therapist to patient, which continues to be the deepest and longest of the interviewing techniques; free association; and the meticulous examination of overt and covert mental life. For a student of politics, some of the earliest, most old-fashioned pre-ego psychology innovations of psychoanalysis may still be among the most interesting (which is not to deprecate more recent advances). Conscious attitudes and beliefs are studied very well, and with rewarding findings, with existing techniques at the disposal of the political scientist, anthropologist, sociologist, and academic psychologist.

However, students of politics frequently encounter knots that do not unravel at the bidding of interviewers at the doorstep with questionnaires in hand. Especially knotty and difficult to explain are the circumstances in which the behavior of citizens or their leaders is "disproportionately" emotional: for example, deep grief and profound mourning at the death of a public figure one has never met and may have voted against; or murderously violent impulses toward an individual of another skin pigmentation. The hope that we will find the sources of these seemingly inexplicable reactions—and that from this knowledge, will eventually come the possibility of accomplishing on a much larger scale what psychoanalysis attempts to accomplish with Sisyphean effort, patient by patient—seems to justify proposals to foster closer and more fruitful cooperation between psychoanalysts and other students of mankind.

NOTES

[1] Harold D. Lasswell, "What Psychiatrists and Political Scientists Can Learn from Each Other," *Psychiatry* 1 (1938), 33–39.

[2] Arnold Rogow, "Psychiatry as a Political Science," *Psychiatric Quarterly* XL (1966), 319–32.

[3] Harold D. Lasswell, *Power and Personality*. New York, Norton, 1948, pp. 229–30. Press, 1930) reprinted in *Political Writings of Harold D. Lasswell* (Glencoe, Illinois: Free Press, 1951), pp. 75–76.

[4] Clinton Rossiter, *The American Presidency* (2nd ed.; New York: New American Library, 1960), pp. 14–17.

[5] Fred I. Greenstein, *The American Party System and the American People* (Englewood Cliffs, New Jersey: Prentice-Hall, 1963); 2nd ed., 1970).

[6] Fred I. Greenstein, "Popular Images of the President," *American Journal of Psychiatry* CXXII (1965), 523–29.

[7] For the source of these assertions and expansions on them, see *ibid.*

[8] Norman M. Bradburn and David Caplovitz, *Reports on Happiness* (Chicago: Aldine, 1965), p. 78.

[9] Freud, *Moses and Monotheism* (1939 [1934–1938]), Standard Edition, XXIII, p. 109.

[10] Sebastian de Grazia, "A Note on the Psychological Position of the Chief Executive," *Psychiatry* VIII (1945), 267–72.

[11] Richard Sterba, "Report on Some Emotional Reactions to President Roosevelt's Death," *Psychoanalytic Review* XXXIII (1946), 393–98.

[12] David Kirschner, "Some Reactions of Patients in Psychotherapy to the Death of the President," *Psychoanalytic Review* XLI (1964–1965), 125–29. (See also *Behavioral Science* X (1965), 1–6). For reports on the reactions of children in therapy, see Martha Wolfenstein and Gilbert Kliman, eds., *Children and the Death of a President: Multi-Disciplinary Studies* (New York: Doubleday, 1965).

[13] Lasswell, "What Psychiatrists and Political Scientists Can Learn from Each Other," *op. cit.*, pp. 33–39.

[14] de Grazia, "A Note on the Psychological Position of the Chief Executive," *op. cit.*, pp. 267–68.

[15] Harold D. Lasswell, *Power and Personality* (New York: W. W. Norton, 1948), pp. 156–59.

[16] Irving Bieber, et al., *Homosexuality: A Psychoanalytic Study* (New York: Basic Books, 1962).

[17] Richard E. Renneker, "Some Psychodynamic Aspects of Voting Behavior" in Eugene Burdick and Arthur J. Brodbeck, eds., *American Voting Behavior* (Glencoe, Illinois: Free Press, 1959), pp. 399–413.

14

A Psychometric Analysis of Connections Between Personality and Political Orientation

Over the years, numerous studies have been reported in which some quantitative index of political orientation or political behavior was correlated with one or more of the psychometric procedures for measuring personality disposition. The 1930s were a heyday for such research. As Smith, Bruner, and White point out in their careful review of such "trait-attitude correlational" studies,[1] the mountain of published work produced scarcely a molehill of reliable insight into such matters as the personality characteristics of radicals, conservatives, pacifists, internationalists, politicians and so on.

In part, such studies suffered from the inevitable difficulty of satisfactory measurement. Statistical relationships are bound to be weak and unstable when phenomena of considerable complexity and subtlety are studied by means of necessarily crude indexes of both the independent and dependent variables. But much of the psychometric literature also has suffered from inadequate conceptualization and from the failure to anticipate what relationships ought *in principle* to be expected to exist. By and large, one should not expect to find gross, broad-gauged connections differentiating all individuals who happen to have a particular broad political characteristic from all other individuals. Rather, distinctive personality profiles are likely to be evident when investigators further distinguish the precise form of the political characteristic (for example, not radicalism in general, but intense radical activism) and the situational context in which it manifests itself (such as whether the radical is a revolutionary operating in a hostile environment or a conforming member of a college peer group in which radicalism is fashionable). William J. McGuire's remarks on the study of personality and susceptibility to social influence (which happens also to be the topic of this selection) apply generally to connections between personality and sociopolitical patterns:

It is highly likely that personality factors will interact with various other classes [of factors] . . . in affecting influenceability. Hence, although we should seek the most general relationships in mapping the domain of personality-influenceability interrelations, it is likely that these will tend to be interaction effects, rather than condition-free main effects of single personality variables.[2]

This selection by Di Palma and McClosky uses an outstanding body of data on American political leaders and members of the general electorate collected by McClosky in the 1950s. Several important, methodologically fastidious papers resulting from the study, which is soon to be described in a book-length presentation, have been reported. This selection is instructive as a guide to future investigators in that it is built on a base of carefully tested psychometric procedures and is analyzed with precisely the kind of theoretical sophistication necessary to anticipate relationships between personality and political orientations and behavior.

The reader is urged to take careful note of how the authors employ the term "conformity." As they make clear, they are not focusing on conformity in the pejorative sense of "yielding compulsively to group pressures," but rather in the sense of being in the mainstream of one's social context.

NOTES

[1] M. Brewster Smith, Jerome S. Bruner and Robert W. White, *Opinions and Personality* (New York: Wiley, 1965), pp. 8–11.

[2] William J. McGuire, "Personality and Susceptibility to Social Influence," in Edgar F. Borgatta and William W. Lambert, eds., *Handbook of Personality Theory and Research* (Chicago: Rand McNally, 1968), p. 139. An "interaction effect" is a contingent relationship —that is, a statistical relationship between two variables that is evident only when one or more additional variables are present.

PERSONALITY AND CONFORMITY: THE LEARNING OF POLITICAL ATTITUDES

Giuseppe Di Palma and Herbert McClosky

Why do some men embrace society's values while others reject them? Is conformity a general trait, more uniformly manifested by some people than by others? What social or psychological forces lie behind the tendency to conform or deviate?

Although these questions obviously have significance for the conduct of political life, they have received far less attention from political scientists than from scholars in other disciplines such as psychology and sociology. In view of current challenges to the legitimacy of existing political institutions, the mounting debate over the acceptable limits of protest, and the growing disdain for democratic decision-processes shown by some segments of the population, the need for political scientists to understand the nature and sources of conformity and deviation has become, if anything, more urgent. We hope, in the present paper, to explore the psychological—and to some extent the social and political—meaning of conformity

Reprinted from *American Political Science Review*, 64 (December, 1970) pp. 1054–73. In the original publication of this article, the authors acknowledge the following: This is publication A108 of the Survey Research Center, University of California, Berkeley. The research was conducted under grants to Herbert McClosky from the Social Science Research Council and supported in part by Public Health Service Research Grant MH-05837, from the National Institutes of Health. David Koff assisted in the planning and tabulation stages of the project, and Ellen Siegelman offered her valuable advice at the later stages. We owe a special debt to Paul Sniderman for his many penetrating suggestions concerning both the intellectual content and editorial style of the manuscript.

and deviation as reflected in citizen responses to political beliefs. To that end we will review briefly the present state of psychological theory and research on conformity behavior; suggest, in light of our own research findings, some ways in which current psychological explanations might be modified and extended to account for conformity and deviation within the mass public; and furnish data that might help to explain why individuals who have different personality characteristics and who occupy different roles in the society are likely to accept or reject political norms.

Until recently, most writers who dealt with conformity and deviation were concerned to evaluate them morally rather than to investigate them scientifically. Discursive treatments of the subject tend even today either to reify these concepts or to treat them as moral universals, appraising them as good or bad according to the particular bias of the author. Rarely is it recognized in such discussions that conformity and deviation are terms of relationship that take their meaning from the contexts in which they occur and from the combination of forces that happens in the particular instance to give rise to them. In practice, of course, everyone is to some degree both conformer and deviant, adhering to certain community and group standards but not to others.

Not all acts of conformity spring from the same motivations. Some arise from a tendency to yield to intimidation and some from hunger for approval and group solidarity; others, however, result from the ubiquitous human need to reduce moral and perceptual ambiguity, and still others from a rational assessment of the social realities and a recognition that accommodation to society's standards can help to bring about mutually desired goals. Thus, conformity to social norms may only occasionally signify deference, servility, obsequious surrender, or weakness of character—just as deviation or resistance to norms may only occasionally represent a superior conscience, personal independence, or courage to defy Establishment pressures. In short, conformity and deviation are descriptive terms that merely denote one's response to norms; they can be morally appraised only with reference to their particular motivation and consequences. We shall also see that conformity—defined as the acceptance of majority beliefs—is not necessarily the same as gullibility, yea-saying, suggestibility, or even, for that matter, persuasibility.

Whether desirable or undesirable, conformity to community and group standards is, in any event, "natural." Few social science findings have been more firmly and repeatedly confirmed than those revealing man's vulnerability to group pressure and his responsiveness to group norms.[1] Through association with family, peers, and other reference groups, and through the routine mechanisms of socialization (e.g. imitation, modelling, indoctrination, reinforcement), one learns which standards society prizes and one conforms to them, for the most part, without reflection.

How effectively these values are transmitted will partly depend on one's proximity to the cultural mainstream and partly on one's individual personality characteristics. A mounting body of experimental and other evidence has shown that not everyone is equally susceptible to group pressure or persuasion.[2] It is with these differences—particularly the relation of personality differences to the adoption of social norms—that we are mainly concerned in this paper. By examining the data collected in two field surveys, we hope to show how personality variables affect the acceptance or rejection of community beliefs. In addressing this question, we also hope to gain further insight into the nature of conformity and deviation in natural settings.

THEORY AND PREVIOUS RESEARCH

The most prolific and systematic research on susceptibility to influence has been carried on by the psychologists, chiefly through small group experiments. Three major experimental traditions have evolved—those of conformity, persuasibility, and suggestibility.[3] In the typical *conformity* (or convergence) experiment, psychological pressure is exerted upon a subject to induce him to yield to a group standard. No effort is made, however, to win him over by persuasive arguments; instead, he is confronted by group opinions or perceptions discrepant with his own. The measure of his conformity is the distance he moves toward the position held by the group.[4] Although variations occur in the type of stimulus or group structure employed, almost all conformity experiments aim to assess the subject's susceptibility to group influence. In the typical *persuasibility* (or attitude change) experiment, the subject is exposed to arguments and communications deliberately designed to persuade him to shift his beliefs in the direction of the message.[5] Here too the experiments vary in detail: in some the source of the communication is revealed, in others concealed; in some the source is congenial, in others inimical. The message employed may be threatening or reassuring; it may be delivered in written form, or via recording, film, or face-to-face communication. Some persuasibility studies are conducted in the laboratory, and some in actual field situations. Studies of *suggestibility* (which are least relevant for our purposes) have mainly been concerned with motor and sensory responses to influence inductions, focusing upon such phenomena as body sway, odor suggestibility, sensory hallucinations, and hypnotizability.[6]

Research involving these concepts has yielded an abundant, complex, but not altogether consistent set of findings. In general, however, the studies show that personality and cognitive characteristics affect conformity and deviation in important ways. For example, in conformity experiments of the type pioneered by Asch and Crutchfield,[7] the subjects most likely to yield to group influence are those who are least well integrated psychologically and hence most poorly equipped to interact effectively with others. Subjects possessing superior intellect and creativity submit to misleading majority judgments less often than others do. The ability to withstand pressure is also related to ego-strength and self-awareness: Those who resist erroneous majority judgments usually have greater self-esteem than those who yield to them.[8] Presumably they are, among other things, less apprehensive about social disapproval.

Other personality characteristics often correlated with yielding in the conformity experiments include rigidity, dogmatism, conventionality, and authoritarianism.[9] Individuals characterized by these traits prove especially vulnerable in stressful or unpredictable situations. Their need for certitude may incline them to be negativistic and unmovable when *they* are in command, but submissive and receptive to influence when *others* wield the power and when compliance rather than resistance is the more likely to produce order and predictability. Compared with the Independents, the Yielders are also found to be less trusting and outgoing toward others. Although they crave social approval, they are less tolerant of those who disagree with them.[10] They are less poised than the Independents and have more poorly developed social skills. They generally score lower on dominance, responsibility, and achievement orientation. In short, while the Yielders may seem on the surface to be cooperative and even submissive, clinical measures reveal them to be comparatively hostile and socially maladapted.

Some of these traits also turn up as correlates of *persuasibility* in the research on attitude change and communication conducted by Hovland and his associates. Here the picture is even more complicated, the correlations lower, and the results more inconclusive. As in the conformity experiments, subjects with low self-esteem are more susceptible to persuasion and more likely to alter their opinions in the direction of the influence.[11] But even this relationship is confounded, for when the message is highly complicated or threatening, these subjects are more likely to resist persuasion and to retain the views they initially held.[12] Conclusions about the relationship between persuasibility and such personality attributes as aggressiveness, authoritarianism, and social isolation are still more equivocal. Correlations are found in some experiments but not in others, depending upon the types of participants, procedures, and measures used in the study.[13] Although Hovland and others believe that persuasibility is a general trait (i.e. a predisposition "reflecting an individual's susceptibility to influence from many different sources, on a wide variety of topics, and irrespective of the media employed"),[14] its relation to other motivational predispositions appears, from present evidence, to be tenuous and complex.

One need not look far to find the reasons for these uncertainties: the act of yielding to, or resisting, influence is never simple and can rarely be understood by reference to any single explanatory variable. In order to conform, an individual must be located where he can receive the message, and he must have enough interest and cognitive skill to comprehend it. His judgment will be swayed by his estimate of the source's trustworthiness, prestige, and authority, and (where content is relevant) by his feelings about the substance of the communication. He will also be affected by the context, e.g. whether the task is easy or difficult; whether clues are furnished that indicate how he is expected to respond; whether he is called upon to undergo a genuine, enduring shift in viewpoint or merely to comply publicly; whether the group to which he must respond is unanimous or divided in its judgments; and whether he has reason to feel psychologically "threatened" if he fails to comply.

Nor is the relation between conformity and a given personality trait invariably monotonic.[15] Interaction effects are common: a strong personality need may affect one's susceptibility to influence far differently than would a milder version of the same need. For example, anxiety in moderate degree often serves to motivate learning (and hence may increase persuasibility), whereas severe anxiety can be so crippling as to impede learning. A person low in self-esteem may readily open his mind to reassuring messages but close it to threatening ones, whereas a person high in self-esteem may be accessible to both. Sometimes an individual's personality traits work at cross purposes in shaping his response to influence: one trait (say low self-esteem) may lead him to yield, but another (say personality disorganization) may make it difficult for him to detect accurately what is being communicated and which influence to yield to.

Another complication is that susceptibility to influence often depends upon learning history and reinforcement as well as upon personality characteristics.[16] The rewards and punishments available in any given situation can strongly determine whether the behavior elicited will be deviant or conformist. Many who belong to and are reinforced by "deviant" sub-cultures will diverge from society's norms regardless of their personality needs; others will, for similar reasons, conform.

A further complication is that a given influence attempt may have different consequences in different settings—for example, in a laboratory as compared with a natural setting. These settings affect both the credibility of the rewards and punishments one encounters and the earnestness with which one confronts the research task. They also determine the number and types of communications one receives. In most laboratory experiments, the participants are treated not as individuals but as experimental *subjects*—which means either that they are all treated interchangeably or that their treatment is determined solely by their preassigned role in the experiment; the differences in their individual *personality* configurations are usually ignored. Outside the laboratory, however, people are treated differentially according to their status and their particular cognitive and personality characteristics. Some people will thus be exposed to more frequent, more varied, and more intense communications than others. Obviously, these differences in treatment and exposure will determine how often one encounters the beliefs circulating in the society, and how effectively one learns whether to embrace or reject a given standard.

The intimacy and relatively uncomplicated structure of most conformity experiments also set them apart from natural settings in ways that may be critical for the learning of norms. In the laboratory, the task is usually simple, the stimulus is difficult to ignore, the direction of the group pressure is unmistakable and the extent to which one's views are shared by the other participants is readily ascertained. In the larger society, by contrast, such matters are more difficult to decipher. Many who deviate from conventional standards are not aware that they are doing so. Confronted by a bewildering array of opinions, values, attitudes, assertions, etc., they are often unable to recognize which standards the society approves and which ones it disapproves. Their interactions with others about public questions are often so random and casual that they have little sense of being "pressured" from *any* direction. While laboratory experiments on influence characteristically compel them to face alternatives and to make choices, a large, complex society permits them to ignore or remain neutral on many questions. The society also furnishes an extraordinary variety of groups in which individuals with deviant or unpopular outlooks can find a home, enabling them to believe that theirs is the "true" or accepted standard. Thus, the inducements to conform to or deviate from group norms can be dramatically different in the two contexts.[17]

A final complication grows out of the differences in the several types of susceptibility to influence. Experimental findings indicate that the intercorrelations among suggestibility, conformity (in the Asch sense), and persuasibility are weak. While the three concepts superficially resemble one another and are sometimes used interchangeably by investigators, they may spring from very different personality dynamics and they often describe very different forms of behavior. For example, a subject with sufficient intellectual discernment to yield to a reasoned argument in a persuasibility experiment is likely to be sufficiently perspicacious to resist the erroneous majority judgments in a standard conformity experiment.[18] Many people adhere strongly to group norms without being unusually susceptible to persuasion. The two, in fact, commonly work in opposite directions, e.g., the stronger one's initial loyalty to a group's norms, the more one resists efforts to persuade one to deviate from those norms.[19]

The above qualifications are not meant to deny that some people are more susceptible to persuasive influence than others. They do, however, lead us to question whether all manifestations of yielding to influence should be placed under a single rubric and considered simply as different expressions of the same general predilection. Indeed, conformity may be a behavior category so broad as to be almost equivalent with the concept of learning itself, rather than an identifiable, specific propensity or personality trait that some people possess in significantly greater measure than others.

HYPOTHESES AND PROCEDURES

In the present study we are concerned not with conformity in small groups or laboratory settings but with the influences governing the acceptance or rejection of the dominant political and social values of the society. For this purpose we have defined conformity and deviation operationally as the degree to which individual Americans subscribe to the beliefs held by more than 70 percent of the American people (as measured by survey data). Although this definition differs in certain respects from the definition employed in laboratory studies of conformity (for example, it lacks an explicit reference to possible conflict between a subject's initial beliefs and the forces pressing on him to shift his views), it does contain the two key ingredients in the definition of conformity: 1) subjective concurrence with norms, and 2) objective social pressure—however covert and unsystematic—to adopt the dominant, or majority, view. We consider it plausible to assume that even highly complex, pluralistic societies make a considerable effort to persuade their members to accept prevailing norms. Pressure to conform is implicit in the mere circulation and repetition of majority beliefs, and it is often made explicit in the innumerable group interactions in which those beliefs are directly expressed and reinforced. For convenience we shall refer to persons who embrace (or reject) a disproportionate number of society's beliefs as "conformers" (or "deviants").[20]

In a free and highly diversified society, even moderately informed individuals will encounter and grapple with a bewildering array of beliefs on numerous public questions—all pretending to some measure of legitimacy. Not everyone, however, has equal opportunity or equal capacity to learn which of these beliefs the society approves. The *opportunity* to acquire a society's norms depends on how closely one is stationed to the communications mainstream, and whether one associates with people who reinforce those norms. The *capacity* to absorb and understand what is being communicated depends on education, sensitivity to public affairs, cognitive skills, personality structure, and so on.

Personality structure can affect the learning process—and hence conformity and deviation—in various ways. It can promote or impede social learning *directly,* by enhancing or impairing one's cognitive performance; or *indirectly,* by regulating the nature and extent of one's interactions with others. Given the extraordinary profusion and complexity of beliefs available in modern society, numerous opportunities arise for individuals to select (or avoid) opinions that serve psychological needs. Personality disorders, for example, can determine what an individual hears and what he blocks out; they can distort judgment and cause him to misread signals and messages. Personality traits that affect social adaptation can shape one's interactions with others so as to impede or promote the learning of norms. Highly defensive, hostile, or paranoid individuals will have more difficulty discerning what others expect them to believe, and will often be unaware that their beliefs diverge from the standard; they will therefore lack incentive for bringing their views into line. Certain personality needs may also lead to a behavior pattern that Crutchfield has called "counterformity"—a tendency to dissent compulsively from the group out of negativistic, hostile, and recalcitrant motives. The counterformist not only resists but is "repelled by the group norms; he seeks to *widen* disagreement between himself and the group . . . to repudiate the group's beliefs or actions even when he perceives that the group is right." [21]

In summary, the tendency to conform to, or deviate from, a society's prevailing attitudes is a function of a complex set of influences, the most significant of which are the following:

1. Social and geographic location, which affect one's opportunity to encounter the beliefs that circulate in the society, and to have them reinforced.

2. Cognitive abilities, which govern one's *capacity* to comprehend those beliefs.

3. Personality characteristics, which influence the clarity, accuracy, and posture with which one perceives and assimilates communications on public questions.

4. Social-psychological factors, which affect social adaptability, including the ability to interact effectively with others, to be aware of the demands of the social environment, etc.

Specifically then, deviation from majority attitudes should increase with (a) impaired ability or opportunity to encounter and comprehend communications on public questions; (b) personal isolation or estrangement from social institutions and opinion networks; (c) cognitive deficiencies; (d) personality malintegration; and (e) social maladaptation.

Obviously, these hypotheses are fairly broad and could be qualified in several ways. Some people, for example, echo conventional beliefs not because they are informed but because they are intellectually impoverished and respond mindlessly to the opinions they encounter. Others may be receptive to communications on public affairs but, owing to a skeptical turn of mind, question much of what they hear. The college educated, having greater opportunity and capacity to learn the norms than do the less educated, are more likely to respond to the actual content of the beliefs they encounter and, when they deviate at all, are less likely to do so because of personality impediments to effective cognitive performance. Although the hypotheses stress cognitive, personality, and social adaptability factors, other influences (source, content, reference groups, etc.) also affect conformity and deviation. Then, too, conformity does not always stem from the same psychological motives: some individuals may yield out of dependency, others out of personal strength that enables them to accommodate to majority views without threat to their sense of autonomy. These and other cautions suggested earlier are sobering, but their importance for the arguments in this paper can be assessed by the reader after reviewing the findings.

Procedures

The items used to measure conformity were selected from the attitude scales employed in two lengthy questionnaires developed by McClosky for surveys of the general populations of Minnesota and the United States.[22] Both questionnaires contained extensive item pools—539 items in the one case and 390 in the other. Some were personality items and others were attitude statements. All were of the agree-disagree type. One questionnaire was administered during the middle 1950's to a cross-section sample of 1082 Minnesota adults, and the other several years later to a national cross-section sample of 1484 adults.

In constructing the conformity measure, we initially selected from each pool every item that had been either endorsed or rejected by at least 70 percent of respondents from all educational backgrounds—college, high school, and grade school. Our reason for introducing an education hurdle was to insure that the measure would not be education-bound, but would consist of items widely favored (or opposed) by adults in *all* social strata. Approximately 100 items from each item pool met this initial test. These items were then examined and sorted by a panel of 30 judges (drawn from Berkeley staff members and graduate students from the Political Science Department and the Survey Research Center) to select those that clearly reflected political, economic, or social attitudes. The items that survived this sifting were then further screened to reduce subject-matter duplications, to achieve maximum diversity of content, and to eradicate, if possible, any traces of systematic ideological bias.[23] We also tried to correct for possible acquiescent response set by selecting as nearly as practicable an equal number of items on which the majority had agreed and disagreed.

Two indices for measuring attitude conformity were yielded by these procedures, one from the national survey and the other from the Minnesota survey. The national index consisted of 27 items—16 Agree and 11 Disagree items; the Minnesota index contained 33 items—17 Agree and 16 Disagree items. Twenty-one of the 27 items used in the national index also turned up in the Minnesota index. Scalability, of course, was not a criterion in selecting the items for either index.

Sample items from the conformity indices, and the direction of majority preference, follow:

Our freedom depends on the private enterprise system. (Agree)
By belonging to the UN we are running the danger of losing our constitutional right to control our own affairs. (Disagree)
It's the common people who have really made this country great. (Agree)
The idea that everyone has a right to his own opinion is being carried too far these days. (Disagree)
I think it is more important to vote for the man than for the party. (Agree)
There is nothing wrong with a man trying to make as much money as he honestly can. (Agree)
Politicians can't afford to be frank with the voters. (Disagree)
When a community pays a teacher's salary it has the right to tell him exactly what and how to teach. (Disagree)
There is less opportunity in this country than there used to be. (Disagree)
We need a strong central government to handle modern economic problems efficiently. (Agree)
We almost have to restrict the amount of goods we let into this country because labor is so cheap in most other nations. (Agree)
To bring about great changes for the benefit of mankind often requires cruelty and even ruthlessness. (Disagree)
The farmland of this country should be redivided so that no one can own land except the people who actually do the farming. (Disagree)
Poor people should look out for themselves. (Disagree)
No matter what crime a person is accused of, he should never be convicted unless he has been given the right to face and question his accusers. (Agree)

Each respondent was given a conformity score reflecting the sum of his answers to these and the other items in the index. Whenever he answered an item as the majority did (i.e. whenever he was among the 70 per cent or more who agreed, or disagreed, with the item) he was assigned a score of one; whenever he rejected the majority's view, he was assigned a score of zero. The scores on the

Minnesota conformity index ranged from 15 to 33, with a mean of 27.7; the scores on the national index ranged from 11 to 27, with a mean of 21.8. To facilitate the analysis, each index was broken into five levels—extreme conformers, moderate conformers, middle, moderate deviants, and extreme deviants—with the cutting points chosen to keep the number of extreme conformers and deviants fairly small and "pure" but large enough to make statistical comparison possible. In the present paper we have simplified the analysis by excluding the respondents who fell into the middle of the distribution; since they neither conformed nor deviated, little was to be gained by including them. (We have, however, run correlations among the variables in which we included the middle group. These correlations merely express, in different form, the same results reported in this paper.) The frequency distributions for the two indices are shown in Table 1.

Table 1
Distribution of Respondents on Indices of Conformity-Deviation

	Minnesota Survey General Population Sample (N = 1082)			National Survey General Population Sample (N = 1484)		
Level of Conformity	Range of Scores	Number of Respondents	Percentage of Respondents	Range of Scores	Number of Respondents	Percentage of Respondents
Extreme Deviants	15–21	50	4.7	11–17	98	6.6
Moderate Deviants	22–25	179	16.6	18–19	147	9.9
Middle	26–29	511	47.6	20–24	920	62.0
Moderate Conformers	30–31	269	24.1	25–26	279	18.8
Extreme Conformers	32–33	73	7.0	27	40	2.7
		1082	100 %		1484	100 %

In the tables that follow, we have compared people who largely conform to majority opinion with those who largely deviate from it. The independent variables are the social adjustment, personality, and cognitive characteristics of the respondents, as measured by a number of scales. Most of these scales (Tables 2–6) may be considered "psychological" scales, although not all reflect personality in the same degree. Some of the scales, especially those in Tables 2 and 3, are heavily "social" in content; others, including most (though not all) of the scales in Tables 4 and 5, reflect "personality" characteristics in greater measure. Some of the scales, in short, might be designated as "social-psychological," others as "clinical-psychological." Containing on the average nine items each, the scales were independently developed for inclusion in a battery of psychological tests employed in previous research on political behavior.[24]

In Tables 2–5, mean scores are presented on selected psychological variables for each of the four levels of conformity and deviation. Given our hypotheses and the implicit explanatory model, it might have been more appropriate to turn the tables around and to show conformity in its actual role as the dependent variable. However, since we wanted to compare conformers and deviants as such, we chose to retain these categories intact and to present the comparisons as shown in the tables.

In assessing the findings, the reader should keep in mind that the Minnesota and national surveys, although utilizing many of the same measures, were conducted five years apart on samples drawn from two different universes. They were also separately analyzed. Thus the results derive from two entirely independent studies —one, in effect, replicating the other.

FINDINGS

Social Adaptation

The most consistent finding in both surveys is that those who conform to the majority outlook are distinctly better adjusted than those who reject that outlook. With only minor exceptions, the data in Table 2 show that social adjustment variables bear a strong and largely monotonic relationship to conformity-deviation. People who are generally satisfied with their lives, who identify with the society and believe they understand it, who do not feel personally isolated, who do not especially fear the future, and who have a strong sense of social responsibility—tend to accept majority beliefs more often than do those who have adapted less successfully. These findings hold for both the Minnesota and national samples.

While the data in Table 2 are fairly straightforward, their interpretation is more open to conjectiure. Social maladaptation is in some measure a function of personality traits that independently influence one's ability to recognize and understand the norms. Hence the connections just observed might in part be a product of common underlying personality factors. There is reason to believe, however, that they are also the direct result of one's capacity for social adaptation as such; as the internal evidence of the present research bears out repeatedly, almost any impediment to social interaction or communication reduces the probability that one will encounter and acquire the values held by most other members of the community.

Although this connection may seem obvious after the fact, it is neither logically nor psychologically inevitable. In the absence of data, one might easily predict that the poorly adjusted would be *more,* rather than less, likely to embrace majority outlooks because they fear further separation from the society and therefore seek out opinions that are conventionally anchored. If such influences are at work, they are outweighed by the relative inability of the socially maladjusted to connect with the majority culture and to comprehend its attitudes.

The results on social adaptation hold for both the well-educated and less-educated respondents, but the differences between the conformers and deviants are generally larger and more consistent among those who have not attended college. Among the college educated, such attributes as cognitive capacity, political awareness, and opportunity for communication are more uniformly adequate to the tasks of social learning; hence, deviations from conventional beliefs, while still reflecting maladjustment to some extent, also reflect greater attention to the content of the beliefs to be embraced or rejected.

Cognitive Capacities

We have suggested that agreement with a society's prevailing beliefs may in part be a function of cognitive skills. The assumption here is that intellectual styles and abilities affect both the motivation and capacity to receive and comprehend persuasive communications. If, to borrow McGuire's phrase, cultural norms are, in effect, "obscure, subtle, persuasive messages" which seep in over time,[25] they will in some measure be learned by everyone—but not by everyone

Table 2
Mean Scores on Measures of Social Adaptation for Four Levels of Conformity-Deviation for Minnesota and National General Population Samples

Level of Conformity	Minnesota Survey (N = 1082)			National Survey (N = 1484)		
	Gen. Pop.	Non-Coll.	College	Gen. Pop.	Non-Coll.*	College**
Alienation						
Ext. Deviants	4.68 (50)	4.74 (47)	— (2)	4.27 (98)	4.31 (89)	3.35 (8)
Mod. Deviants	3.10(179)	3.30(148)	2.16(31)	3.78(147)	3.91(117)	3.35 (29)
Mod. Conformers	1.95(269)	1.94(175)	1.97(91)	2.35(279)	2.42(187)	2.12 (90)
Ext. Conformers	1.75 (73)	1.82 (39)	1.58(33)	1.73 (40)	1.85 (27)	2.12 (13)
Anomy						
Ext. Deviants	6.72	6.83	—	5.83	6.04	3.43
Mod. Deviants	4.97	5.37	3.06	5.57	6.08	3.43
Mod. Conformers	2.73	3.06	2.00	3.61	3.88	3.14
Ext. Conformers	2.19	2.87	1.39	3.60	3.56	3.14
Bewilderment						
Ext. Deviants	5.06	5.13	—	Scale Not Included		
Mod. Deviants	3.96	4.11	3.23			
Mod. Conformers	3.07	3.18	2.81			
Ext. Conformers	2.93	3.13	2.70			
Community Identification						
Ext. Deviants	3.52	3.51	—	Scale Not Included		
Mod. Deviants	4.10	4.11	4.06			
Mod. Conformers	4.48	4.58	4.27			
Ext. Conformers	4.63	4.72	4.52			
Folksiness						
Ext. Deviants	3.30	3.26	—	Scale Not Included		
Mod. Deviants	3.54	3.61	3.19			
Mod. Conformers	3.77	3.77	3.75			
Ext. Conformers	4.19	4.38	3.94			
Life Satisfaction						
Ext. Deviants	3.54	3.36	—	3.51	3.51	4.30
Mod. Deviants	4.18	3.96	5.23	3.79	3.62	4.30
Mod. Conformers	4.94	4.77	5.25	4.73	4.59	4.97
Ext. Conformers	5.14	5.15	5.18	4.28	4.00	4.97
Pessimism						
Ext. Deviants	3.32	3.36	—	3.36	3.40	2.78
Mod. Deviants	2.79	2.75	3.00	3.28	3.42	2.78
Mod. Conformers	1.92	1.92	1.93	2.27	2.27	2.33
Ext. Conformers	1.68	1.79	1.52	2.48	2.33	2.33
Social Responsibility						
Ext. Deviants	4.02	3.94	—	4.45	4.29	6.32
Mod. Deviants	5.23	4.97	6.48	5.11	4.80	6.32
Mod. Conformers	6.86	6.83	6.96	6.82	6.59	7.26
Ext. Conformers	7.01	6.85	7.30	6.65	6.52	7.26
Status Frustration						
Ext. Deviants	4.32	4.34	—	4.38	4.47	3.00
Mod. Deviants	3.09	3.28	2.19	3.76	3.95	3.00
Mod. Conformers	2.59	2.69	2.40	2.83	2.82	2.74
Ext. Conformers	2.37	2.67	2.00	2.63	2.85	2.74

* Totals for the general population are in a few instances slightly larger than the combined college and non-college totals, because education was not adequately ascertained for a few respondents.

** Owing to the small size of the N's for the Extreme Deviants and Extreme Conformers in the national college sample, we have, in this and subsequent tables, combined the Extreme and Moderate Deviants, and the Extreme and Moderate Conformers, and entered the mean scores only for the combined samples.

equally. The intellectually adept will pay closer attention to public affairs and will usually have a better sense of what is valued and likely to be rewarded. They will read the signals more accurately and have a more acute grasp of the intention or meaning of a given public communication.[26] They will detect and respond to persuasive influences that are scarcely perceptible to less alert minds.

Whether these expectations mainly result from raw intelligence, or from cognitive style and disposition, is not clearly known. The experimental findings on the relation of intelligence to conformity and persuasion are inconclusive. Crutchfield and other investigators find meaningful correlations in the conformity experiments, but Hovland and his associates, in their persuasion experiments, do not.[27] McGuire, in analyzing the available research, observes that a positive relation between intelligence and persuasibility is more likely to emerge when reception is complex and comprehension difficult.[28] The weakness of the connection in some situations may be due to the play of conflicting motivations that cancel each other out: superior intelligence may alert an individual to the message, but may also make him more wary of being manipulated and more resistant to arguments that do not satisfy his intellectual standards.

Data relating to the effects of cognitive disposition on our measure of conformity are presented in Table 3. Although no direct tests of intelligence were

Table 3
Mean Scores on Measures of Cognitive Disposition for Four Levels of Conformity-Deviation for Minnesota and National General Population Samples

Level of Conformity	Minnesota Survey (N = 1082)			National Survey (N = 1484)		
	Gen. Pop.	Non-Coll.	College	Gen. Pop.	Non-Coll.	College
Acquiescence						
Ext. Deviants	7.52 (50)	7.68 (47)	— (2)	6.39 (98)	6.57 (89)	4.10 (8)
Mod. Deviants	5.31(179)	5.74(148)	3.23(31)	6.00(147)	6.46(117)	(29)
Mod. Conformers	4.11(269)	4.46(175)	3.32(91)	3.89(279)	4.14(187)	3.49 (90)
Ext. Conformers	3.53 (73)	3.97 (39)	2.85(33)	3.98 (40)	3.81 (27)	(13)
Political Awareness						
Ext. Deviants	2.78	2.55	—	Scale Not Included		
Mod. Deviants	3.53	2.99	6.10			
Mod. Conformers	5.14	4.49	6.45			
Ext. Conformers	5.44	4.69	6.36			
Intellectuality						
Ext. Deviants	3.06	2.89	—	3.97	3.81	5.97
Mod. Deviants	3.88	3.51	5.61	4.20	3.76	
Mod. Conformers	5.20	4.83	5.98	5.36	5.00	6.00
Ext. Conformers	5.59	4.85	6.52	5.05	4.86	
Mysticism						
Ext. Deviants	5.46	5.60	—	Scale Not Included		
Mod. Deviants	4.89	5.20	3.42			
Mod. Conformers	3.37	3.68	2.73			
Ext. Conformers	3.26	3.72	2.70			

included in the surveys, several scales were available which measure some aspect of intellectual performance. Their relationship to conformity is generally positive, although stronger in the non-college than in the college samples.

As Table 3 indicates, the conformers are generally more oriented toward intellectual activities than are the deviants, and they attain higher scores on an achievement test of political and social awareness. They also score lower on Aquiescence (this index was mainly designed to test response set, but because it was constructed as a battery of 19 pairs of incompatible items, it also measures the ability to think consistently and discriminatingly).[29] The conformers also have significantly lower scores on the Mysticism scale, which taps the propensity to embrace nonrational, nonscientific, and nonlogical explanations of ordinary phenomena—a propensity that appears from the internal evidence of the study to be most characteristic of people who are intellectually uncritical.

The general thrust of these findings is consistent with other data in our surveys which indicate that the deviants, both college and non-college, have failed to absorb the values of the "American Creed"—tolerance, faith in freedom and democracy, political and social equality, procedural rights, etc.—as effectively and thoroughly as have the conformers of comparable education.[30] They are also more prejudiced, more politically cynical, and more responsive to extreme Right-Wing and Left-Wing values—values which the majority, and especially the majority among the educated, strongly reject. That learning capacity should affect these judgments is entirely plausible. Many deviants seem unable to conform even when they want to. In the non-college group, for example, the deviants value conventionality (as measured by our conventionality scale) more than the conformers do. They also profess stronger love of country and greater respect for traditional values. (These findings, however, are less consistent among the college-educated group.) Apparently, the intellectual and psychological failings that initially led some individuals to misread or reject prevailing norms also keep them from discovering how divergent their beliefs actually are. Their inability to utilize the social validation process effectively apparently prevents them from seeing—and hence remedying—their failures to conform.

Note, finally, that the negative correlation between Acquiescence and Conformity adds credence to the claim that conformity (as herein defined) is by no means the same as yea-saying, suggestibility, or gullibility. It suggests, in fact, that the relation is inverse. An individual who affirms belief after belief regardless of content—indeed, regardless of whether one belief contradicts another—is less likely than someone of greater discrimination to recognize which of the innumerable beliefs he encounters have been approved, or rejected, by the society. Being suggestible does not necessarily make him conformist; on the contrary, it makes him vulnerable to many aberrant opinions that a more perspicacious mind would shun.

Self-Esteem

Few personality clusters have received as much attention from students of conformity behavior as self-esteem—the evaluation an individual places upon himself. People *low* in self-esteem are guilt-ridden, cautious, morbidly afraid of failure, chronically anxious, and psychologically vulnerable. People *high* in self-esteem, by contrast, feel a sense of command over themselves and their immediate environment; they are well-integrated, candid, and willing to take risks.

The major assumption about self-esteem and susceptibility to influence is that those who lack self-esteem are highly vulnerable to group pressures. Presumably they will capitulate to pressure either because they fear ridicule if they should prove to be "wrong," or because they yearn for group approval and a sense of interpersonal solidarity. Lacking self-confidence, they are in any event inclined to doubt the worth of their own judgments. For these and other reasons, individuals low in self-esteem have tended under experimental conditions to be uncommonly responsive to group influence. However, the relationship between self-esteem and yielding is not always monotonic, for the anxiety that often attends low self-esteem can function either to inhibit or potentiate persuasibility, depending upon the magnitude of the anxiety aroused by the stimulus.[31]

We predicted that anxiety, and low ego-strength in general, would serve to impede the learning of community norms. The very traits that might lead people with low self-esteem to yield in a laboratory would, in the maelstrom of the complex larger society, insulate them against influence. Lacking self-assurance, such people tend to withdraw from social interactions and avoid "involvement" in group activities.[32] McGuire suggests that they are frequently preoccupied with themselves and too distracted to attend closely to outside communications.[33]

In Table 4 we present data on scales that tap various facets of self-esteem. Need Inviolacy, for example, measures vulnerability to psychological exposure and the fear of being unmasked; the other scales reflect one's sense of personal

Table 4
Mean Scores on Personality Measures of Self-Esteem for Four Levels of Conformity-Deviation for Minnesota and National General Population Samples

Level of Conformity	Minnesota Survey (N = 1082)			National Survey (N = 1484)		
	Gen. Pop.	Non-Coll.	College	Gen. Pop.	Non-Coll.	College
Dominance						
Ext. Deviants	2.26 (50)	2.15 (47)	— (2)	3.27 (98)	3.21 (89)	5.12 (8)
Mod. Deviants	3.35(179)	3.08(148)	4.65(31)	3.58(147)	3.11(117)	5.12 (29)
Mod. Conformers	4.43(269)	3.77(175)	5.76(91)	4.06(279)	3.71(187)	4.69 (90)
Ext. Conformers	4.85 (73)	4.13 (39)	5.70(33)	4.23 (40)	4.26 (27)	4.69 (13)
Guilt						
Ext. Deviants	5.12	5.23	—	4.92	5.00	3.62
Mod. Deviants	4.70	4.82	4.10	4.76	5.06	
Mod. Conformers	3.87	4.10	3.40	3.97	3.97	4.05
Ext. Conformers	3.75	4.03	3.33	4.05	3.89	
Manifest Anxiety						
Ext. Deviants	4.50	4.47	—			
Mod. Deviants	3.96	4.05	3.48	Scale Not Included		
Mod. Conformers	3.20	3.28	3.01			
Ext. Conformers	3.10	3.18	2.94			
Need Inviolacy (Ego Vulnerability and Defense)						
Ext. Deviants	4.04	4.13	—	3.45	3.55	2.38
Mod. Deviants	3.20	3.36	2.39	3.54	3.81	
Mod. Conformers	2.54	2.67	2.23	2.57	2.63	2.35
Ext. Conformers	2.11	2.10	2.12	2.10	2.33	
Personality Disorganization						
Ext. Deviants	4.04	4.11	—			
Mod. Deviants	3.02	3.18	2.26	Scale Not Included		
Mod. Conformers	2.30	2.45	2.00			
Ext. Conformers	2.29	2.31	2.24			
Self-Confidence						
Ext. Deviants	2.94	2.89	—			
Mod. Deviants	3.26	3.04	4.32	Scale Not Included		
Mod. Conformers	3.99	3.63	4.69			
Ext. Conformers	3.62	3.13	4.21			

security and command (Dominance and Self-Confidence), propensity to heightened feelings of shame and regret (Guilt), and a proclivity toward excessive worry, restlessness, inability to concentrate, and pervasive feelings of uncertainty (Manifest Anxiety and Personality Disorganization).

Among the non-college populations in both the national and Minnesota studies, the deviants consistently show up as having less self-esteem than do the conformers. Among the college educated, however, the prediction is supported in only four of the nine instances in which the connection is tested (Dominance, Guilt, Anxiety, and Need Inviolacy—all in the Minnesota sample). No differences turn up in three instances and reversals appear in the other two. We can only guess at the exact meaning of these instances of disconfirmation, but the evidence from our own and other research suggests that the better educated have sufficient ability and opportunity to learn the community norms despite personality needs that are in other ways disabling. Then, too, they are likely, as we have observed, to weigh the content of beliefs more carefully—which in the case of a content-diversified index would tend to flatten differences further.

Rigidity and Aggression

The relation of personality rigidity and aggression to conformity and persuasibility has also been explored experimentally, but with equivocal results. In general, experiments on conformity have usually hypothesized positive correlations with rigidity, hostility, and authoritarianism; while experiments on communication and persuasion have sometimes predicted positive and sometimes negative correlations. One can reason either way: that hostile and rigid subjects should be more authoritarian and hence ready to submit to conformity pressures; or, alternatively, that they should prove especially recalcitrant in resisting efforts to persuade them to shift their point of view.

Unfortunately the research findings from the experimental literature are not sufficiently consistent to resolve these issues. Crutchfield [34] and others have found positive correlations between conformity and such personality dispositions as hostility and authoritarianism. Linton and Graham [35] have found persuasibility to be related to the aggressive and submissive aspects of authoritarianism but not to authoritarianism as a whole. Other investigators [36] contend that authoritarians yield in conformity experiments principally when the message is so simple and easily understood that individual differences in capacity for attention and comprehension are negligible. Still others [37] find that persuasibility among aggressive individuals may depend on whether the communication is benign or punitive. Janis and Hovland believe that "personal rigidity" may chronically lead subjects to refuse to accept persuasive messages. [38] In short, the existing research bears out the complexities that surround the interplay of these variables and underscores our earlier observation that the connection between conformity and personality structure is rarely a simple linear relation that can be predicted apart from the context in which they coexist.

In light of our own earlier research, we expected to find rigidity and hostility correlating negatively with the adoption of majority values—largely because these personality traits tend to retard social learning and hinder the social interactions through which beliefs are disseminated. [39] If the members of a society acquire its norms through gradual assimilation—through the repeated exchange of ideas, the clarification of subtle distinctions, and the modification of opinions resulting from the interplay of divergent views—one can plausibly assume that people gripped by hostile and inflexible needs will engage less often in these activities and will be less likely to learn what the society really believes. Unusually hostile or inflexible people, moreover, tend to be insensitive to the qualifications, contingencies, and nuances that are inherent in many social norms—an incapacity that can easily lead to misunderstandings or misapplications of those norms.

Table 5
Mean Scores on Personality Measures of Aggression and Rigidity for Four Levels of Conformity-Deviation for Minnesota and National General Population Samples

Level of Conformity	Minnesota Survey (N = 1082)			National Survey (N = 1484)		
	Gen. Pop.	Non-Coll.	College	Gen. Pop.	Non-Coll.	College
F Authoritarianism						
Ext. Deviants	5.12 (50)	5.23 (47)	— (2)	6.41 (98)	6.67 (89)	3.62 (8)
Mod. Deviants	4.70(179)	4.82(148)	4.10(31)	6.33(167)	6.72(117)	(29)
Mod. Conformers	3.87(269)	4.10(175)	3.40(91)	5.23(279)	5.52(187)	4.05 (90)
Ext. Conformers	3.75 (73)	4.03 (39)	3.33(33)	5.23 (40)	5.19 (27)	(13)
Faith in People						
Ext. Deviants	2.04	1.98	—	Scale Not Included		
Mod. Deviants	2.71	2.83	2.13			
Mod. Conformers	3.86	4.01	3.56			
Ext. Conformers	4.37	4.15	4.64			
Hostility						
Ext. Deviants	6.40	6.55	—	4.14	4.33	3.05
Mod. Deviants	4.74	4.99	3.58	3.93	4.09	
Mod. Conformers	2.89	3.05	2.53	3.08	3.14	2.66
Ext. Conformers	2.53	2.90	2.00	3.10	3.19	
Intolerance of Ambiguity						
Ext. Deviants	6.00	6.26	—	5.76	5.96	4.11
Mod. Deviants	5.64	5.85	4.61	5.64	5.96	
Mod. Conformers	4.40	4.73	3.69	4.31	4.55	3.85
Ext. Conformers	3.82	3.90	3.73	4.23	4.26	
Paranoid Tendencies						
Ext. Deviants	6.40	6.55	—	5.37	5.54	3.89
Mod. Deviants	4.74	4.99	3.58	5.31	5.60	
Mod. Conformers	2.89	3.05	2.53	3.04	3.25	2.66
Ext. Conformers	2.53	2.90	2.00	2.88	2.81	
Rigidity						
Ext. Deviants	3.74	3.83	—	3.62	3.75	2.35
Mod. Deviants	3.21	3.36	2.48	3.28	3.47	
Mod. Conformers	3.05	3.12	2.89	2.99	3.01	2.94
Ext. Conformers	2.56	2.95	2.06	2.72	2.67	
Tolerance						
Ext. Deviants	4.60	4.51	—	4.77	4.60	6.24
Mod. Deviants	5.30	5.22	5.68	5.39	5.21	
Mod. Conformers	6.41	6.33	6.57	6.61	6.50	6.85
Ext. Conformers	6.66	6.46	6.91	7.10	7.15	

The data in Table 5 generally confirm these expectations. In all but two instances (the scores on Authoritarianism and Rigidity for the national college-educated sample) the deviants are more hostile and inflexible than the conformers. They are more paranoid (a projected expression of hostility), more intolerant of people whose traits or opinions they disapprove of, more distressed by ambiguity, more punitive, and more jaundiced in their estimates of other people. Contrary to the claims in the popular literature, those who conform in matters of political belief (as distinguished from those who merely glorify conformity) are less motivated than the deviants by a desire to force everyone to obey prescribed standards.

SUMMARY AND DISCUSSION

The findings from the two surveys reported in this paper confirm the hypothesis that conformity-deviation—defined operationally as agreement or disagreement with prevailing American beliefs on diverse social and political subjects—is significantly related to personality factors. Those who preponderantly conform to majority attitudes are by substantial margins better adapted socially and psychologically than those who preponderantly reject them. They are more intellectually oriented, more politically aware, and more proficient in their cognitive skills. They exhibit greater self-esteem and less anxiety than the deviants, and are less motivated by aggression and inflexibility.

The evidence is consistent with the hypothesis that the conformers are both more able and more likely to encounter and comprehend the norms—contingencies which the experimental research shows to be of central importance in effecting communication and persuasion. They are more accessible to interaction, less withdrawn or socially isolated, and more strongly motivated to receive and respond to information on public questions. Although we have not tested the communication process directly, we think it plausible to infer from the evidence that the deviants, more often than the conformers, have missed or misread communications on public norms—an inference consistent with the findings from our previous research on the correlates of anomy, isolationism, extreme Right-Wing and Left-Wing radicalism, and other outlooks which diverge from prevailing American attitudes.[40]

Despite the pronounced tendency of the findings, some puzzling questions remain. One question, for example, concerns the meaning of the deviant responses: Are they genuine expressions of deviant belief or should they be regarded instead as "non-attitudes"—i.e., labile or casual responses by people so little interested in the substance of the items that they score as deviant largely by answering erratically or randomly?[41] Might there even be reason to believe that many of the deviants would show up as conformers if tested on another occasion?

There is little doubt that some people respond to questionnaire items—as they do to the public opinions they encounter in their daily activities—without much thought. Indeed, it is an argument of this paper that many people hold nonconforming attitudes not because they are led by superior sensitivity to weigh alternatives and to reject conventional views, but mainly because they have been so imperfectly socialized that they are either indifferent to many social issues or unable to recognize what the society believes. This is not to say, however, that their responses to attitude items are entirely random or casual, for one could not then explain the distinct pattern of correlations yielded by the research reported here—a pattern predictable from theory, consistent with our earlier research on other deviant attitudes, and reproduced here in two independent studies conducted several years apart on samples from two different universes.[42]

Even if we assumed that some respondents *had* attained deviant scores on the Conformity index by answering randomly or thoughtlessly, they could not, by replying in this fashion, have achieved the highly patterned, and often extreme, scores on the numerous personality and attitude scales with which the Conformity index is correlated. Since the items from the various measures were scrambled and presented to the respondents in a single, unstructured item pool, it would be highly implausible to suppose that they responded randomly or heedlessly to the items that were later selected for the Conformity index while replying carefully and "accurately" to the numerous other items with which the Conformity items were intermingled. The assumption that indifferent respondents might be accounting for the results becomes still less tenable when one considers that such respondents would turn up not only among the deviants but also among the conformers, if only because they can be expected, *ceteris paribus,* to encounter majority views more often than they encounter minority views—when they encounter them at all. Note, finally, that no measure employed here has consisted merely of a single item or question; all have been multiple item batteries or scales, averaging close to nine items each for the independent variables and between 27 and 33 items for the dependent Conformity indices. This feature, of course, greatly reduces the possibility that scores at either extreme could be achieved randomly or without reference to actual attitude content.[43]

Let us assume for the sake of the argument, however, that some of the deviants are in fact expressing non-attitudes or responding randomly. Are the results markedly different for those respondents who are more thoughtful, more discriminating, more informed, and more concerned with public questions?

We have already seen (Tables 2–5) that while the differences between well-educated conformers and deviants are usually smaller than they are for the less-educated, the pattern of differences is generally similar for both samples. In Table 6 we have put the issue to two other, more severe, tests. There we present data on two narrowly restricted subsets of respondents—those who, on an achievement test, display high levels of political awareness and understanding; and those who score close to the median on the Acquiescence index,[44] and who therefore appear to have answered the items with greater care and discrimination. Neither group is likely to have responded randomly or thoughtlessly.

Both Awareness and Acquiescence are measures of cognitive capacity and, as we have seen, are correlated with conformity—one positively, the other negatively. Neither, however, is an exhaustive measure of this capacity, for not only are they imperfect as measures, but other factors, such as personality structure, can and often do have an independent, direct affect on the clarity and understanding with which norms are learned. Thus, respondents with similar scores on Awareness (or Acquiescence) may still differ somewhat in their ability to read communications correctly and discern their implications. Controlling for these measures, we therefore assumed, should reduce the magnitude of the differences between conformers and deviants but not eradicate them entirely. This assumption proved, on the whole, correct.

The results confirm that the psychological differences between conformers and deviants reported for the total sample (and shown in Table 6 in percentage form) hold in most instances even for the more thoughtful and politically informed respondents—although they are, as predicted, smaller for the more narrowly defined subsamples. The differences that emerge are in the predicted direction, and are consistent with the general findings in all but a few instances. Moreover, in 20 of the 25 comparisons with middle Acquiescence controlled, and in 16 of the 25 comparisons with high Awareness controlled, the differences remain large enough to

Table 6
Conformers and Deviants Compared, Controlled for Middle Acquiescence
and High Awareness—Minnesota Survey Only
(Percentages Down)

Scales	Total Minnesota Sample		Middle Acquiescence Sample		High Awareness Sample	
	Deviants N = 229	Conformers N = 342	Deviants N = 58	Conformers N = 128	Deviants N = 54	Conformers N = 160
ALIENATION						
% High	40.2	16.4*	34.5	18.0*	25.9	14.4*
% Low	21.4	47.7	19.0	48.4	25.9	52.5
ANOMY						
% High	56.8	10.8*	53.4	8.6*	25.9	3.7*
% Low	19.7	53.2	13.8	54.7	46.3	63.1
BEWILDERMENT						
% High	48.0	21.6*	36.2	18.7**	14.8	16.4
% Low	19.2	41.5	15.5	39.1	42.6	46.2
COMMUNITY IDENTIFICATION						
% High	14.8	24.0***	15.5	28.9	14.8	20.6
% Low	35.8	20.8	36.2	22.7	37.0	21.9
FOLKSINESS						
% High	21.4	32.2**	24.1	36.7	14.8	34.4**
% Low	49.3	35.4	39.7	32.0	59.3	35.0
LIFE SATISFACTION						
% High	24.0	42.1*	22.4	46.9**	40.7	47.5
% Low	40.2	24.9	39.7	24.2	24.1	20.0
PESSIMISM						
% High	60.7	26.9*	58.6	30.5**	53.7	26.2*
% Low	17.0	42.1	22.4	36.7	22.2	41.2
SOCIAL RESPONSIBILITY						
% High	10.5	36.3*	17.2	33.6*	20.4	40.6**
% Low	59.3	18.4	56.9	20.3	31.5	15.6
STATUS FRUSTRATION						
% High	44.1	27.8*	32.8	29.7	35.2	19.4
% Low	18.3	29.2	24.1	28.9	29.6	36.9
ACQUIESCENCE						
% High	51.1	21.9*	—	—	22.2	10.6**
% Low	23.6	40.6	—	—	59.3	47.5
POLITICAL AWARENESS						
% High	15.3	34.2*	8.6	35.9	—	—
% Low	61.1	26.6	60.3	21.1	—	—
INTELLEC-TUALITY						
% High	15.7	48.5*	15.5	46.9*	35.2	58.7*
% Low	52.8	17.8	50.0	14.8	27.8	10.0
MYSTICISM						
% High	59.8	24.6*	46.6	21.9**	31.5	16.9**
% Low	11.4	32.5	15.5	34.4	25.9	46.9

Table 6 (Cont.)

Scales	Total Minnesota Sample		Middle Acquiescence Sample		High Awareness Sample	
	Deviants N = 229	Conformers N = 342	Deviants N = 58	Conformers N = 128	Deviants N = 54	Conformers N = 160
DOMINANCE						
% High	21.0	51.2*	19.0	53.9*	42.6	63.7*
% Low	42.8	20.8	41.4	14.1	11.1	13.1
GUILT						
% High	39.7	20.8*	32.8	16.4**	25.9	14.4
% Low	24.9	47.7	25.9	51.6	40.7	53.1
ANXIETY						
% High	33.2	14.9*	25.9	14.8	24.1	11.2
% Low	20.5	31.3	24.1	35.2	27.8	32.5
NEED INVIOLACY						
% High	49.3	24.3*	36.2	20.3**	31.5	19.4
% Low	27.5	54.4	39.7	63.3	48.1	61.2
PERSONALITY DISORGANI-ZATION						
% High	43.2	24.3*	36.2	23.4	29.6	18.7
% Low	21.8	36.5	34.5	39.1	31.5	35.6
SELF-CONFIDENCE						
% High	22.7	37.1*	20.7	38.3***	29.6	50.0***
% Low	35.4	22.5	41.4	22.7	25.9	14.4
F. AUTHORI-TARIANISM						
% High	44.5	14.3*	39.7	10.9*	9.3	5.6
% Low	17.9	38.0	8.6	36.7	46.3	46.9
FAITH IN PEOPLE						
% High	10.5	40.1*	10.3	35.9*	18.5	40.6*
% Low	52.0	20.5	48.3	22.7	53.7	23.1
HOSTILITY						
% High	60.7	33.0*	56.9	37.5***	33.3	27.5
% Low	19.7	42.7	22.4	42.2	42.6	50.0
INTOLERANCE FOR AMBIGUITY						
% High	60.7	27.8*	58.6	23.4*	37.0	18.1**
% Low	16.2	36.5	10.3	35.9	46.3	45.6
PARANOIA						
% High	59.8	19.6*	53.4	17.2*	31.5	13.7**
% Low	13.1	46.8	12.1	40.6	29.6	51.9
RIGIDITY						
% High	49.8	35.7**	36.2	39.1	25.9	26.2
% Low	26.6	33.9	29.3	32.8	46.3	41.9
TOLERANCE						
% High	22.7	51.5*	27.6	57.8*	31.5	56.9*
% Low	60.3	20.2	55.2	19.5	51.9	17.5

Note: % Middle has been omitted to conserve space.
* Chi Square for table significant at or below .001 level.
** Chi Square for table significant at or below .01 level.
*** Chi Square for table significant at or below .05 level.

be significant, by chi square test, at or well below the .05 level of significance—despite the severity of the controls and the reduction in sample size. Similar tables, controlling for Acquiescence, were also computed for the *national* sample, with results at least as strong as those reported here, and in some cases (e.g., rigidity and status frustration) markedly stronger.

Divergence from majority norms among the more sophisticated respondents, of course, can scarcely be explained by reference to distance from communication networks, lack of information, or insufficient opportunity to encounter the norms. For some, it doubtless represents a considered, philosophically anchored rejection of the established society and its values. For others, however, it appears to be strongly associated with cognitive and personality impairments that hinder effective communication and the accurate learning of norms, or that lead, in some cases, to a "counterformist" rejection of prevailing standards.

Since the data from the two surveys reported in this paper were gathered in the middle and late '50's, one may ask whether they would hold with equal force today. Defiance of traditional norms and accepted standards appears to be more common in the '60's than in the decades that preceded it. In certain quarters today, nay-saying is "in," and may itself have become the norm. Today's deviants then, may conceivably differ in crucial ways from those described in this paper.[45] The question, of course, cannot be settled without a new study of comparable design on comparable samples. There are, nevertheless, reasons to expect that the results of such a study would be similar to those reported here. For one thing, historical studies of values indicate that a society's basic beliefs are extraordinarily tenacious and change extremely slowly. For another, even if the norms *had* changed dramatically in the space of a decade, the social-psychological processes by which people become aware of and acquire norms can scarcely have changed much. No matter what beliefs prevail in a society, some people will be better placed, better adapted, better trained, and better disposed than others to discern and appreciate them.

A final question concerns the apparent conflict between the findings reported in this paper and those turned up by Crutchfield in his personality assessment of subjects who conform in an Asch-type laboratory experiment. A comparison of the personality profiles of conformers and deviants in the two studies reveals that the *deviants* in our study closely resemble the *conformers* in the Crutchfield experiment. Despite the seeming inconsistency, we believe that the findings of the present study are not only congruent with Crutchfield's but in a curious way confirm them. Both Crutchfield's conformers and our deviants suffer cognitive and personality deficiencies that lead to distorted perceptions, heightened anxiety, narrowness and inflexibility of focus, defective capacity for observing situations accurately, insensitivity to signals that indicate how one is expected to respond, and defective antennae that prevent them from sensing what is happening and how they are supposed to react. That such people conform in the one study and deviate in the other largely reflects the differences in the two situations and research tasks.[46] In the conformity experiment, the stimulus and the research task are simple, the source is identifiable, the pressure is tangible, the direction of the influence is unmistakable, and the means of satisfying the demands and relieving one's internal conflicts are or appear to be immediately available—namely, by conforming to the majority judgment. In the society at large, however, one encounters innumerable, varied, and often conflicting messages, many of them issuing from unknown sources and most of them difficult to comprehend; the pressure to conform is frequently diffuse, intangible, and indirect; the way to resolve conflicting pressures is often unclear or unavailable; the reinforcements for choosing the "correct" alternative are uncertain and sporadic—in short, one is beleaguered by the sheer number and variety of influences that compete for recognition. Under these conditions, those least able to master the environment are most likely to become the "deviants." In the Asch-Crutchfield experiments they are most likely to become the "conformers."

All this points up the risks in assuming that all forms of conformity (or deviation) are phenotypically or genotypically equivalent. Much depends on the source, the context, the reference group, the content, and the like. Even the several forms of susceptibility to influence are only weakly, and somtimes negatively, correlated. In speaking of conformity and deviation, one needs to take into account much more than the simple question of whether an individual yields to or resists influence. When one observes this behavior, he has merely begun the inquiry.

NOTES

[1] For reviews of the research see especially William J. McGuire, "Personality and Susceptibility to Social Influence," in E. F. Borgatta and W. W. Lambert, eds., *Handbook of Personality Theory and Research* (Chicago: Rand McNally), 1968, Chap. 24, pp. 1130–1187; William J. McGuire, "The Nature of Attitudes and Attitude Change," in Gardner Lindzey and Elliot Aronson, eds., *Handbook of Social Psychology*, 2nd ed. (Reading, Mass.: Addison-Wesley), 1968, Vol. 3, Chap. 21; Vernon L. Allen, "Situational Factors in Conformity," in Leonard Berkowitz, ed., *Advances in Experimental Social Psychology*, Vol. 2 (New York: Academic Press), 1965, pp. 133–176; I. A. Berg and B. M. Bass, eds., *Conformity and Deviation* (New York: Harper), 1962; Arthur R. Cohen, *Attitude Change and Social Influence* (New York: Basic Books) 1964; Carl I. Hovland and Irving L. Janis, eds., *Personality and Persuasibility* (New Haven: Yale University Press), 1959. See also E. P. Hollander and R. H. Willis, "Some Current Issues in the Psychology of Conformity and Non-Conformity," *Psychological Bulletin*, Vol. 68, 1967, pp. 62–76.

[2] See, for example, Solomon E. Asch, "Effects of Group Pressure Upon the Modification and Distortion of Judgments," in Harold Guetzkow, ed., *Groups, Leadership and Men* (Pittsburgh: Carnegie Press), 1951, pp. 177–190; McGuire, "Personality and Susceptibility," *loc. cit.;* Hovland and Janis, *Personality and Persuasibility*; Richard S. Crutchfield, "Conformity and Character," *American Psychologist*, Vol. 10, 1955, pp. 191–198; Frank Barron, "Some Personality Correlates of Independence of Judgment," *Journal of Personality*, Vol. 21, March, 1953, pp. 287–297.

[3] Cf. McGuire, "Personality and Susceptibility," *op. cit.*, pp. 1131–1136.

[4] Leading examples of this experimental tradition are Solomon E. Asch, "Studies in Independence and Conformity: I. A Minority of One against a Unanimous Majority," *Psychological Monographs*, Vol. 70, No. 9, 1956; Muzafer Sherif, "Group Influence upon the Formation of Norms and Attitudes," in Eleanor E. Maccoby *et. al.*, eds., *Readings in Social Psychology*, 3rd ed. (New York: Holt, Rinehart, and Winston), 1958, pp. 219–232; Crutchfield, *op. cit.*

[5] The major research in this field has been conducted by the "Yale School" under the direction of Carl I. Hovland. Three illustrative publications are Carl I. Hovland *et. al.*, *Communication and Persuasion* (New Haven: Yale University Press), 1953; Carl I. Hovland *et al.*, *The Order of Presentation in Persuasion* (New Haven: Yale University Press), 1950; Hovland and Janis, *Personality and Persuasibility*.

[6] E. R. Hilgard, *Hypnotic Susceptibility* (New York: Harcourt, Brace), 1965; McGuire, *loc. cit.*

[7] See also R. D. Tuddenham, "Correlates of Yielding to a Distorted Group Norm," *Journal of Personality*, Vol. 27, 1959, pp. 272–284; Francis Di Vesta and D. Cox, "Some Dispositional Correlates of Conformity Behavior," *Journal of Social Psychology*, Vol. 52, 1960, pp. 259–268; Crutchfield, "Conformity and Character," *op. cit.;* Crutchfield, "Detrimental Effects of Conformity Pressures on Creative Thinking," *Psychologische Beitrage,* Vol. 6, 1962, pp. 463–471; Crutchfield, "Independent Thought in a Conformist's World," 1962, mimeographed; Crutchfield, "Personal and Situational Factors in Conformity to Group Pressure,"

1957, mimeographed; Frank Barron, "The Psychology of Imagination," *Scientific American,* September, 1958.

[8] Crutchfield, "Conformity and Character," *loc. cit.;* Barron, "The Psychology of Imagination," *loc. cit.;* Tuddenham, "Correlates of Yielding," *loc. cit.;* M. L. Hoffman, "Some Psychodynamic Factors in Compulsive Conformity," *Journal of Abnormal and Social Psychology,* Vol. 48, 1953, pp. 383–393; H. C. Kelman, "Effects of Success and Failure on Suggestibility in the Autokinetic Situation," Vol. 45, 1950, pp. 267–285; Di Vesta and Cox, *op. cit.;* Leo Levy, "A Study of Some Personality Attributes of Independents and Conformers," *Diss. Abst.,* Vol. 19, 1959, p. 1823.

[9] Crutchfield, "Conformity and Character"; Tuddenham, "Correlates of Yielding"; Hoffman, "Some Psychodynamic Factors"; Halla Beloff, "Two Forms of Social Conformity: Acquiescence and Conventionality," *Journal of Abnormal and Social Psychology,* Vol. 56, 1958, pp. 99–104; W. Wells *et al.,* "Conformity Pressure and Authoritarian Personality," *Journal of Psychology,* Vol. 42, 1956, pp. 133–136; David Marlow, "Some Personality and Behavioral Correlates of Conformity," *Diss. Abst.,* Vol. 20, 1959, pp. 2388–2399.

[10] Di Vesta and Cox, *op. cit.;* Marlow, *op. cit.;* Kelman, *op. cit.;* Crutchfield, "Conformity and Character," *loc. cit.;* Leo Levy, *op. cit.;* K. R. Hardy, "Determinants of Conformity and Attitude Change," *Journal of Abnormal and Social Psychology,* Vol. 54, 1957, pp. 289–294; H. B. Linton, "Dependence on External Influence: Correlates in Perception, Attitudes and Judgment," *Journal of Abnormal and Social Psychology,* Vol. 51, 1955, pp. 502–507; D. W. Bray, "The Prediction of Behavior from Two Attitude Scales," *Journal of Abnormal and Social Psychology,* Vol. 45, 1950, pp. 64–84; J. S. Mouton *et al.,* "The Relationship Between Frequency of Yielding and the Disclosure of Personal Identity," *Journal of Personality,* Vol. 24, 1956, pp. 339–347; Tuddenham, *op. cit.*

[11] Irving L. Janis, "Personality Correlates of Susceptibility to Persuasion," *Journal of Personality,* Vol. 22, 1954, pp. 504–518; Irving L. Janis, "Anxiety Indices Related to Susceptibility to Persuasion," *Journal of Abnormal and Social Psychology,* Vol. 51, 1955, pp. 663–667; Irving L. Janis and Donald Rife, "Persuasibility and Emotional Disorder," in Carl I. Hovland and Irving L. Janis, eds., *Personality and Persuasibility,* Chap. 6; Arthur R. Cohen, "Some Implications of Self-Esteem for Social Influence," *ibid.* Chapter 5.

[12] A. F. Gollob and James E. Dittes, "Effects of Manipulated Self-Esteem on Persuasibility Depending on Threat and Complexity of Communication," *Journal of Personality and Social Psychology,* Vol. 2, 1965, pp. 195–201; Richard Nisbett and Andrew Gordon, "Self-Esteem and Susceptibility to Social Influence," *Journal of Personality and Social Psychology,* Vol. 5, 1967, pp. 268–276; Owen Silverman, Leroy H. Ford, Jr., and John B. Morganti, "Interrelated Effects of Social Desirability, Sex, Self-Esteem, and Complexity of Argument on Relationship between Self-Esteem and Persuasibility, *Journal of Abnormal and Social Psychology,* Vol. 64, 1962, pp. 385–388; James M. Dabbs, Jr., "Self-Esteem, Communicator Characteristics and Attitude Change," *Journal of Abnormal and Social Psychology,* Vol. 69, 1964, pp. 173–181; Homer H. Johnson, James M. Torcivia, and Mary Ann Poprick, "Effects of Source Credibility on a Relationship between Authoritarianism and Attitude Change," *Journal of Personality and Social Psychology,* Vol. 9, 1968, pp. 179–183.

[13] For a discussion of some of the inconclusive and contradictory results see McGuire, "Personality and Susceptibility," *loc. cit.;* Hovland and Janis, *Personality and Persuasibility,* Chap. 11. See also Mortimer H. Appley and George Moeller, "Conformity Behavior and Personality Variables in College Women," *Journal of Abnormal and Social Psychology,* Vol. 66, 1963, pp. 284–290; Richard D. Tuddenham, "Studies in Conformity and Yielding: II. The Influences Upon a Judgment of a Grossly Distorted Norm," Technical Report No. 2, 1957, University of California, Berkeley, N.R. 170–259; Halla Beloff, *op. cit.;* N. S. Endler, "Conformity Analyzed and Related to Personality," *Journal of Social Psychology,* Vol. 53, 1961, pp. 271–283; Ivan D. Steiner, "Personality and the Resolution of Interpersonal Disagreements," in B. Maher, ed., *Progress in Experimental Personality Research,* Vol. 3, (New York: Academic Press), 1966, pp. 195–239; Homer H. Johnson *et al., op. cit.;* Homer H. Johnson and Ivan D. Steiner, "Some Effects of Discrepancy Levels on Relationships between Authoritarianism and Conformity," *Journal of Social Psychology,* Vol. 73, 1967, pp. 199–205; Ivan D. Steiner and Joseph S. Vannoy, "Personality Correlates of Two Types of Conformity Behavior," *Journal of Personality and Social Psychology,* Vol. 4, 1964, pp. 307–315; Ralph Barocas and Leon Gorlow, "Self-Report, Personality Measurement, and Conformity Behavior," *Journal of Social Psychology,* Vol. 71, 1967, 227–234.

[14] Hovland and Janis, *Personality and Persuasibility,* p. 225.

[15] William J. McGuire, "Personality and Susceptibility," see especially pp. 1143–48.

[16] See for example, Norman S. Endler and Elizabeth Hoy, "Conformity as Related to Reinforcement and Social Pressure," *Journal of Personality and Social Psychology,* Vol. 7, 1967, pp. 197–202.

[17] We are not, of course, claiming that the laboratory context is unreal, synthetic, or in any other way inappropriate to the study of conformity and persuasibility. We are saying,

rather, that the findings turned up in a laboratory context, however valid for *that* context, may not take the same form or hold with the same force in some situations encountered in the larger society. As we shall see, the same principles can apply in both contexts, but manifest themselves quite differently.

[18] H. C. Kelman, "Compliance, Identification, and Internalization: Three Processes of Attitude Change," *Journal of Conflict Resolution,* Vol. 2, 1958, pp. 51–60; Robert P. Abelson and Gerald L. Lesser, "The Measurement of Persuasibility in Children," in Hovland and Janis, *Personality and Persuasibility,* Chap. 7; Bert T. King, "Relationships between Susceptibility to Opinion Change and Child-rearing Practices," *op. cit.,* Chap. 10; B. W. Harper and Richard D. Tuddenham, "The Sociometric Composition of the Group as a Determinant of Yielding to a Distorted Norm," *Journal of Psychology,* Vol. 58, 1964, 307–311; R. R. Sears, "Dependency Motivation," in M. R. Jones, ed., *Nebraska Symposium on Motivation* (Lincoln, Nebraska: University of Nebraska Press), 1963, pp. 25–64. McGuire, *op. cit.,* especially pp. 1141–1142.

[19] Lucille Nahemow and Ruth Bennett, "Conformity, Persuasibility and Counternormative Persuasion," *Sociometry,* Vol. 30, 1967, pp. 14–25; H. H. Kelley and E. H. Volkart, "The Resistance to Change of Group Anchored Attitudes," *American Sociological Review,* Vol. 17, 1952, pp. 453–465.

[20] We are, of course, aware that many who deviate from society's values will conform to the values of their respective subcultures. Correspondence to national norms, thus, is only one of several ways by which one might assess conformity to political beliefs in the society. For some purposes it may not even be the most interesting way. Except for a crude categoric grouping by level of education (see below), we could not, in the present context, analyze the responses of each individual with respect to the several substrata that might be relevant to his political beliefs. We have, nevertheless, investigated conformity and deviation within certain political subcultures, e.g., conformity to party beliefs among the active members of the Democratic and Republican parties, and will report the findings in a later publication. There is a depressing paucity of research on conformity and deviation within various political subcultures, a gap which we hope future investigators will fill before long.

[21] David Krech, Richard S. Crutchfield, and E. L. Ballachey, *Individual in Society* (New York), 1962, p. 507.

[22] Many of the items came from a battery of personality and attitude scales jointly developed by Paul E. Meehl, Kenneth E. Clark, and Herbert McClosky for earlier surveys of political belief, affiliation, and participation.

[23] To this end we decreed that no more than two items could be drawn from the same attitude scale; as it worked out, the items in each of the indices came from at least 20 different scales. It also turned out that the norms selected for use in the final measure were widely accepted by adults not only at different educational levels but also in different age groups and in different size communities. In the non-college sample, conformity to the national norms was higher among younger people than among older ones, and higher among residents of larger communities than smaller ones—results that are consonant with the findings reported below. Among those who have attended college, however, the correlations between age, size of community, and conformity with national norms are mixed and inconclusive—which is to say that the response to these values is more homogeneous among the college-educated.

[24] The nature and validation of these scales has been set forth in earlier papers. See, for example, Herbert McClosky, "Consensus and Ideology in American Politics," *American Political Science Review,* Vol. 58, June, 1964; Herbert McClosky, Paul J. Hoffman, and Rosemary O'Hara, "Issue Conflict and Consensus among Party Leaders and Followers," *American Political Science Review,* No. 2, June, 1960; Herbert McClosky and John H. Schaar, "Psychological Dimensions of Anomy," *American Sociological Review,* February, 1965; Harrison Gough, Herbert McClosky, and Paul E. Meehl, "A Personality Scale for Social Responsibility," *Journal of Abnormal and Social Psychology,* Vol. 47, January, 1952.

[25] McGuire, "Personality and Susceptibility," *op. cit.*

[26] Irving L. Janis and Carl I. Hovland, "Postscript: Theoretical Categories for Analyzing Individual Differences," in Hovland and Janis, *op. cit.,* pp. 258–259.

[27] Carl I. Hovland and Irving L. Janis, "Summary and Implications for Future Research," in Hovland and Janis, *op. cit.,* p. 237; Gardner Murphy *et al., Experimental Social Psychology* (New York and London: Harper), 1937, p. 930; Carl I. Hovland *et al., Communication and Persuasion* (New Haven: Yale University Press), 1953, pp. 181–184.

[28] William J. McGuire, "Personality and Susceptibility," *op. cit.,* pp. 1141–1142.

[29] In the Minnesota study, the Agree and Disagree items in the Conformity index are closely balanced out. These results, therefore, cannot be interpreted as an artifact of response set. Furthermore, in the national study, this result is achieved despite the bias in the Conformity index in the opposite direction, i.e. it contains 16 Agree and 11 Disagree items.

Hence, other things being equal, the Conformers might be expected to score *higher* than the Deviants on Acquiescence, but, in keeping with our prediction, they score lower.

[30] Since some of the items used in the Conformity index were taken from the scales measuring attitudes toward these values, the relation between conformity-deviation and these attitude scales partly reflects overlapping item content. However, the differences between conformers and deviants on these and other attitude measures cited in the paragraph are larger than could be accounted for by item overlap alone.

[31] See, for example, William J. McGuire, "Personality and Susceptibility to Social Influence," *op. cit.,* pp. 1142–1143. For a recent review of the relation between anxiety and learning generally, see Janet Taylor Spence and Kenneth W. Spence, "The Motivational Components of Manifest Anxiety: Drive and Drive Stimuli," in Charles D. Spielberger, ed., *Anexiety and Behavior* (New York: Academic Press), 1966, Chap. 12, pp. 21–26; and Charles D. Spielberger, "The Effects of Anxiety on Complex Learning and Academic Achievement," in Spielberger, *op. cit.;* S. Sarason, K. Davidson, F. Lighthall, R. Waite, and B. Ruebush, *Anxiety in Elementary School Children* (New York: Wiley), 1960.

[32] See, for example, Morris Rosenberg, *Society and the Adolescent Self-Image* (Princeton: Princeton University Press), 1965; Stanley Coopersmith, "Studies in Self-Esteem," *Scientific American,* February, 1968, Vol. 218, pp. 96–106, and *The Antecedents of Self-Esteem* (London: W. H. Freeman & Co.), 1967.

[33] McGuire, "Personality and Susceptibility to Influence," *loc. cit.*

[34] Crutchfield, "Conformity and Character," *loc. cit.*

[35] Harriet Linton and Elaine Graham, "Personality Correlates of Persuasibility," in Hovland and Janis, *Personality and Persuasibility,* pp. 69–101.

[36] See, for example, Homer H. Johnson *et al.,* "Effects of Source Credibility," *op. cit.*

[37] Walter Wise and B. J. Fine, "The Effect of Induced Aggressiveness on Opinion Change," *Journal of Abnormal and Social Psychology,* Vol. 52, 1956, pp. 109–114.

[38] Janis and Hovland, "Postscript," *op. cit.,* p. 257.

[39] Herbert McClosky, *Political Inquiry* (New York: Macmillan), 1969, pp. 74 and 87.

[40] McClosky, *ibid.,* Chaps. 2 and 3.

[41] Cf. Philip E. Converse, "Attitudes vs. Non-Attitudes: Continuation of a Dailogue," paper read at Seventh International Congress of Psychology, Washington, D.C., 1963 (mimeo).

[42] Similar correlation patterns have also emerged from our study of deviation and conformity among Democratic and Republican party leaders toward the dominant beliefs of their respective parties. For a preliminary report of these findings, see "The Influence of Personality on Political and Social Attitudes," *Mental Health Program Reports*–3, National Institute of Mental Health, Chevy Chase, Maryland, January, 1968, pp. 105–106.

[43] Converse, *loc. cit.*

[44] We have chosen the Minnesota, rather than the national survey for this test, partly because it contains all the scales considered in the earlier tables; partly because it includes the Awareness scale, which was omitted from the national survey; and partly because the numbers of Agree and Disagree items in its Conformity index were more closely balanced.

[45] For a recent study of one such deviant subculture, see David Whittaker and William A. Watts, "Personality Characteristics of a Nonconformist Youth Subculture: A Study of the Berkeley Non-Student," *Journal of Social Issues,* Vol. 25, 1969, pp. 65–89. The members of this special, rather exotic, but by no means homogeneous community resemble our deviants in certain respects (e.g. they are, compared with enrolled students, more "socio-emotionally maladjusted," alienated, anomic, personally less integrated, express lower self-esteem and greater anxiety, etc.); but they differ in important other respects (e.g. they are more autonomous, freer in their impulse expression, and have a more experimental, intellectual, and complex orientation toward social experience.)

[46] Support for this interpretation may be inferred from a newly published study by Laurence J. Gould, "Conformity and Marginality: Two Faces of Alienation," *Journal of Social Issues,* Vol. 25, 1969, pp. 39–63. Gould finds that the highly alienated (who closely resemble our deviants, e.g. more acquiescent, more suspicious, more expressed pathology, less self-esteem, and, of course, more alienated) also conform more in an Asch-type experiment. They also exhibit less curiosity about the reasons for their own judgements and those of the majority, "are less sensitive to the feelings of others [and] are less likely to be 'tuned in' to the more subtle and informal norms in any given social situation." See also Melvin Seeman, "An Experimental Study of Alienation and Social Learning," *American Journal of Sociology,* Vol. 49, 1963, pp. 270–284.

15

An Overview of the Authoritarianism Typology

As noted in the introduction to Selection 10, there are simple and complex personality typologies. The classical example of a complex typology in personality-and-politics research is the widely discussed, controversial notion of authoritarianism. The 1950 publication of a lengthy research report on the psychology of anti-Semitism led first to massive psychological research employing the psychometric procedures devised in that study. In the long run, the 1950 report produced one of the more conceptually and empirically gnarled controversies in the history of the behavioral sciences. At the center of the controversy was the hypothesis advanced in the original research: that a personality syndrome, reflecting a diverse array of seemingly disparate surface manifestations, could be identified and traced to certain distinctive underlying psychodynamic needs—needs to repress hostile impulses toward authority which find their outlet (by reaction formation) in excessive deference to authority and compensatory hostility to nonauthoritative, socially disadvantaged members of society. Thus anti-Semitism was held to be simply a single manifestation of a more ubiquitous personality tendency and one of great interest to the student of politics.

At least part of the exceptionally confused and confusing debate on the nature and measurement of "authoritarianism" (and indeed on the usefulness of such a construct at all) was caused by the unthinking use of a mechanically imperfect measuring device—the famous (or infamous) F-scale. But this unreflective reliance on a particular measuring procedure was, in turn, partly the result of the puzzling diffuseness of the original 1950 research report, the 990-page volume entitled *The Authoritarian Personality*, by Theodore Adorno, Else Frenkel-Brunswik, Daniel Levinson and Nevitt Sanford. At no single place in that work could a succinct, internally consistent account of the authors' theory be found, but their measuring scales were readily available.

The following essay, which has been out of print for some time, is by far the most extensive and internally consistent exposition by one of the original authors of their formulation. This paper has the further merit of having appeared after some subsequent confirming research, which the author summarizes, and after much of the more important controversy engendered by *The Authoritarian Personality* (including the paper by Shils, which is reprinted as Selection 16) was available for Sanford to comment on.

As originally published, Sanford's essay was preceded by the following remarks:

Dr. Sanford and his co-workers in *The Authoritarian Personality* studies have regarded their work as a contribution to the knowledge of personality in general and not, as many have seen the work, as mere studies in prejudice. These studies were an effort to focus on the problems of social discrimination an approach that combined psychoanalytic theory of personality, clinical methods for the diagnosis of personality, and modern social-psychological devices for opinion and attitude measurement. The authors of the study, however, believe the title for their book was an unhappy choice inasmuch as the work deals more specifically with potential fascism than with actual authoritarianism.

In the present work, Dr. Sanford is concerned with criticism which has been directed toward *The Authoritarian Personality*. Readily admitting the "psychoanalytic bias" which many reviewers found in the original work, he still believes that the current trend toward unification in theory does find needed expression in this work. Much of the criticism directed toward the work was based on the critics' expecting far more from the study than the authors intended or expected. The chief hope of the authors is that the method of approach exemplified in *The Authoritarian Personality* studies may be employed in the discovery and elucidation of other patterns of personality.

THE APPROACH OF "THE AUTHORITARIAN PERSONALITY"

Nevitt Sanford

INTRODUCTION

That "The Authoritarian Personality" should have a place in a book on theories of personality is a little surprising and very pleasing. It is surprising because the volume published under this title has been regarded by its authors primarily as an empirical study, one which yielded results that were susceptible to interpretation according to diverse points of view. It is pleasing to see this work included in this book because the authors of *The Authoritarian Personality* have always chosen to regard it as a contribution to the knowledge of personality in general, and not merely as a study in prejudice. It is true that the volume was published as one of a series called *Studies in Prejudice*, and it has most often been mentioned in connection with the problem of social discrimination. Actually, we came to conceive of a central structure in personality which had a determining role not only in overt prejudice but in various areas of behavior: social attitudes, political behavior, role taking in groups, and so on. It is this conception or, better, this aspect of the work, which has turned out to be most significant.

It is important to note at the outset that *The Authoritarian Personality*, the book, and the authoritarian personality, the concept, are two different things. Authoritarian personality is the name for a "type" of personality or a personality syndrome that is, supposedly, fairly common in the world today. Different writers conceive of the "type" or syndrome somewhat differently, and the work of describing the organization that exists in fact is far from having been completed. Experience has shown that *The Authoritarian Personality* was not a very happy title for the book. It will be obvious to anyone who reads the volume that it has to

From James L. McCary, ed., *Psychology of Personality* (New York: Grove Press, 1959; originally published by Logas Press, 1956), pp. 255–319.

do mainly with potential fascism, and that the title was not thought of until after the writing was virtually finished. This title was supposed to convey the idea that the main concern was with a pattern of personality organization, and to indicate the similarity of the work to that of Fromm (25) and of Maslow (38) who had written about the "authoritarian character." But the title has led to misunderstandings. For example, since authoritarian personality has become almost a household term, it is not infrequently asked why, in such a large study of this personality type, a more systematic method of study was not used or why more of the common manifestations of this type in action were not covered. The answer, of course, is that we were not studying the authoritarian personality; we set out to study anti-Semitism, arrived eventually at the conception of potential fascism in the personality, and finally chose *The Authoritarian Personality* as a connotative title.

The Authoritarian Personality has no systematic position such as that presented by factor theory, psychoanalysis, field theory or even culture-personality theory; but it is not eclectic either. The "psychoanalytic bias" which so many reviewers have found in our work is readily admitted; yet it does seem fair to say that the current trend toward unification in theory finds expression in this work.

Unification is expressed in the backgrounds of the authors and in the very fact of their collaboration. European sociology and American social psychology, nonpsychoanalytic dynamic theory of personality, field theory, neo-Freudian theory, training in experimental, statistical and clinical methods were, in addition to classical psychoanalysis, well represented in the backgrounds of the research workers; and the study was a more or less deliberate attempt to bring to bear upon a single phenomenon, anti-Semitism, a diversity of skills and points of view. Yet there was never any serious problem concerning "agreement on fundamentals," if, indeed, any necessity for such agreement was ever felt. The common orientation to psychoanalysis and the common interest in social phenomena seem to have been enough to hold the work together.

Classical psychoanalysis has, however, shown no eagerness to clasp the work to its bosom. And there is good reason for this because more support was received from psychoanalysis than was given it. Even though psychoanalysis was fundamental to the whole endeavor and the research is replete with confirmations of psychoanalytic hypotheses (in the sense that things came out as if those hypotheses were true), the work as a whole could not be assimilated into the classical psychoanalytic system. This is because the bulk of the research had to do with matters about which psychoanalysis has had little or nothing to say, that is, the everyday behavior of large samples of normal people.

There is no purely psychoanalytic theory of anti-Semitism; attempts to produce one have yielded something that was not essentially different from the psychoanalytic theory of a great many other things. This is due to the fact that one cannot go directly from depth psychology to complex social behavior. Between the unconscious impulse or complex and the overt act or openly expressed attitude, a great many other factors of personality and of the contemporary social environment intervene. It is precisely at this point that most attempts at theory-making, in the work under consideration, have been directed.

In order to explain complex social behavior it is necessary to weigh the contributions of unconscious impulse, unconscious defense, preconscious response readiness, rational deliberation, social stimuli of the moment and the perceptions of these, and to formulate the interactions among these different kinds of variables.

Thus it is that most of the theoretical work on the authoritarian personality belongs to what, from the point of view of psychoanalysis, may be called ego psychology. Our major concern has been with the ways in which the ego manages or fails to manage the impulse life, the way it strives to make sense for itself of the complex social world. There has been concern too with what might be called "other-directed psychoanalysis," if one might use this term to describe modern attempts to formulate the roles of peer groups, social institutions, the contemporary social environment generally, in determining central personality structures.

But this concern with what, from the classical psychoanalytic point of view, would have to be called the superficial does not mean that there has been an inclination to leave "the basic" strictly alone. The study of relatively large numbers of normal people by clinical procedures, procedures designed to produce the kind of material upon which psychoanalytic theories were originally based, constitutes a severe test of certain psychoanalytic propositions. The questions of what is "normal" and what is human nature begin to loom very large.

One is led to wonder whether certain patterns of character development which classical psychoanalysis has treated as universal in the species are not, instead, products of certain patterns of social organization or even social pathology. This question may be asked about certain aspects of superego development in authoritarian personalities. Similarly, this is not the first time that workers using modern clinical methods with normal people have been struck by how much "pathology" there is in the normal. One finds in normal people the kinds of disturbed childhood environments, infantile fixations, unconscious complexes, mechanisms of defense, that have commonly been regarded as indices of psychopathology. This means that there has had to be a new accent on those positive adjustive devices by which the normal person, with a normal amount of morbidity, keeps functioning. It turns out that the differentiation between the adequately functioning person and the neurotically handicapped one is more subtle than has often been thought. This is another reason for a special accent upon ego psychology.

However, there has been no watering down of psychoanalysis in *The Authoritarian Personality*. Its excursions into ego psychology and its accent upon determinants of behavior other than depth-psychological ones are in no sense substitutions for the older psychoanalytic propositions. As indicated above, the concern was largely with areas of the person and of behavior to which classical psychoanalysis does not apply. When it comes to areas where psychoanalysis does apply, such as in the understanding of neurosis itself or in the treatment of psychosis, classical psychoanalysis is given its due. The real watering down of psychoanalysis in recent years must be attributed to those psychoanalysts and psychoanalytically oriented psychologists who have sought to apply to everyday behavior concepts and theories originally designed to explain the operation of deep unconscious processes in neurosis and psychosis. This has meant that some of these concepts and theories have been stretched to a point where they have become almost meaningless.

In the work under consideration, there has been no hesitation to modify classical psychoanalytic theory when this seemed called for by research findings. This was very rarely done because, first, at the level of personality with which the authors were working, there was rarely any opportunity to apply a crucial test to any psychoanalytic proposition; and, second, as background, as general orientation, as a source of ideas for hypotheses to explain the phenomena observed, little fault was found with psychoanalysis.

It should be pointed out here that, in so far as a new theory has been concocted in *The Authoritarian Personality*, it has been of the low order or even *ad hoc* variety. Although in the beginning there was a general background of theory, with a certain sense of theoretical direction, it was found repeatedly that it was necessary to invent a particular theory to explain observed facts, and then to proceed to collect more facts to test that theory. It will be a long time before the very general, loosely cohering, theoretical approach embodied in *The Authoritarian Personality* can be made into a true theoretical system. I would suggest, however, that, when this is accomplished, there will then exist the long-sought "general theory of action."

One more point about theory. In the research there were encountered the most persistent problems of personology, e.g., the problems of personality organization, of "types," of levels of functioning, of genetic vs. contemporary determination of personality. The authors of *The Authoritarian Personality* hope that in these areas there has been a contribution not only to theory but also to knowledge of personality functioning.

Let us turn now to an outline of what these pages are intended to cover. I should like to begin with an account of how the research culminating in *The Authoritarian Personality* was started and how it was conducted. This story has not been fully told before. I offer it now as a means for correcting certain common misapprehensions and as a basis for some comment about current research practice in this country.

Then we may proceed immediately to a description of the major pattern of personality that emerged from the research. More particularly, we shall consider how the F (for potential fascist)-syndrome was arrived at, the details of its content, and the basic ideas underlying it. After considering some clinical studies of the F pattern, we shall discuss the attempts to reduce the pattern to its essential elements (factor analysis and cluster analysis), and this will lead to a consideration of the general theory of the syndrome and of personality "types." Here will be presented the types of authoritarian and nonauthoritarian personality structures suggested by our study, and this will be followed by empirical studies of differentiation within the extremes, and of similarities between the extremes, on the F scale.

Differentiating sharply between personality and behavior, there will be next an attempt to evaluate the roles of personality and of situational factors in determining overt prejudice, and more than this, an attempt to formulate the interaction of personality and situation in producing various phenomena of behavior. The general formulation will be exemplified by considering how authoritarianism in the personality is expressed in such social roles as parent, husband or wife, political leader, teacher, group member.

In discussing the origins of the F-syndrome it is necessary to accent, as was done in the research, the development of the individual in the setting of family life with particular reference to early events. The data to be presented consist mainly of what adults subjects had to say about their childhoods. But it is possible to make sense of these unreliable reports by considering them in relation to the general knowledge of development and, particularly, in relation to more recent studies, including studies on children—and so to evolve a more or less coherent theory. Recognizing, however, that the childhood experiences of the subjects must have depended in considerable part upon the total social situation in which their parents lived, and noting variations in the incidence of authoritarianism from one culture or subculture to another, it becomes clear that an account of the origins of authoritarian personality must include attention to broad historical and cultural forces. Although one cannot go so far beyond the limits of his own discipline without trepidation, these larger determinants must be considered.

In the summing up, there will be an attempt to evaluate the researches on the authoritarian personality and to consider therapy, both individual and social.

The study of the authoritarian personality actually began in 1943 as a result of an anonymous donation made for a study of anti-Semitism.

This writer, together with Herbert Conrad and others, had been engaged in some studies of personality factors in relation to certain aspects of "war morale," using John Harding's morale scale (29) and, later, local scales of our own design having to do with optimism-pessimism with respect to the war (11, 12). Scale scores were related to life history data, personality scale items, projective questions and a TAT story, particular attention being paid to extreme scorers. Interpretation from a psychoanalytic viewpoint was frequently employed. A study of anti-Semitism fitted in well with this pattern of research.

It seemed that the place to begin the study was with the construction of a suitable instrument for measuring anti-Semitism. Then scores on the scale could be related to questionnaire data bearing on personality and sociological factors, as had been done in the studies of morale mentioned above. By the early spring of 1944, the scale was ready for publication, together with a certain amount of validating data gathered by administering the scale, together with the general questionnaire, to several samples of college students (36). The basic material of this paper and much of the thinking that went into it—mostly Daniel Levinson's work—appear in Chapter III of *The Authoritarian Personality*.

Meanwhile, also in the fall of 1943, this author had met Dr. Max Horkheimer, director of the Institute of Social Research, which had moved after Hitler's revolution from Frankfort to Columbia University. This institute had published in 1936 the well-known *Studien über Autorität und Familie*, which linked psychological dispositions with political leanings and contained some of Erich Fromm's early work on the sado-masochistic character. It was still pursuing theoretical and empirical studies of anti-Semitism and allied phenomena. Dr. Horkheimer, keenly interested in bringing to bear upon the theories being developed by his institute some of the quantitative methods of American social psychology, made some funds available to the anti-Semitism project. These funds made it possible for us to invite Dr. Else Frenkel-Brunswik and Dr. Suzanne Reichard to join the project part-time and to begin the task of making clinical studies of subjects scoring at the extremes on the anti-Semitism scale.

There now followed a most exciting and creative period. All four staff members conducted interviews; and, in the conferences which followed these experiences with key subjects, it was difficult to get the floor, so great was the need to express ideas concerning the personality dynamics of the anti-Semite. Dr. Frenkel-Brunswik concentrated on the analysis of the interview material. Here her grasp of psychoanalytic theory, her broad experience with the analysis of qualitative material and her insistence upon conceptual clarity were richly rewarding. Dr. Reichard made a special study of the Rorschach responses, and Dr. Levinson continued to give a large part of his time to the development of questionnaire methods for getting at personality and ideology. Before the end of summer, 1944, the paper, "Some Personality Correlates of Anti-Semitism" (22), was ready for publication and Reichard had written up her study of Rorschach responses (43).

Meanwhile Horkheimer had become director of the newly established Department of Scientific Research of the American Jewish Committee (A.J.C.). This department had been set up with the object of initiating and stimulating fundamental studies of prejudice, and it was natural that Horkheimer should wish to further the research in Berkeley which had already profited from his help and in which he firmly believed. The idea now was that T. W. Adorno, long-time member of the Institute of Social Research and close associate of Horkheimer, should participate actively in the research, sharing its direction, and that there should be continued exploration for personality correlates of anti-Semitism, using both more intensive clinical studies and quantitative studies with large samples.

The financial support of the A.J.C. would insure that the several senior researchers could devote more time to this work, that some assistants could be employed, and that continuity would be assured for at least three years. The A.J.C. were offering their support to *exploratory* researches which were to be carried forward by empirical methods. They never asked for, nor did they receive, any statement of a research design, nor were they offered more than a general idea of the kinds of findings that might be made. They knew only that approved quantitative methods were being used and that the thinking of the group was guided by psychoanalysis and by the broad social theories of Drs. Horkheimer and Adorno. They never indicated what they wanted us to do or what they hoped the research would find out.

Thus, the group members were always free to pursue hunches or to follow up whatever was suggested by a particular finding. Full advantage was taken of this. The proposition that anti-Semitism has a functional aspect, that is to say, is put in the service of the needs of the individual, was hardly a research hypothesis; it was, in this instance, an assumption, like the assumptions that "behavior is goal-directed," or "the organism functions as a whole." To arrive at testable hypotheses in keeping with his general assumption required some doing as well as some thinking; as indicated above, the best hypotheses were for the most part conceived *after* data were collected rather than before; and then some, but not all, of these hypotheses were tested by further data collection.

From the beginning to the end, the research was loosely organized. Of the senior researchers only Dr. Levinson ever devoted full time to the project, and he for only three years. Dr. Adorno lived in Los Angeles and carried on his collaboration by correspondence and visits to Berkeley. When the grant from the A.J.C. was made, Dr. Frenkel-Brunswik began working half time on the project while continuing to carry out her duties at the Institute of Child Welfare. Late in 1944 she began her own study of prejudice in children, also with the support of the A.J.C., a study that was carried on concurrently with, and after the conclusion of, this project. In July 1945, I started working half time on the project. Previously I had been busy full time with the Psychology Department of the university, the Institute of Child Welfare and the Office of Strategic Services.

Just as the group enjoyed maximum freedom as far as relations with the A.J.C. were concerned, so each member enjoyed a great deal of autonomy within the group. The result was that in pursuit of particular ideas or interests there was a tendency to go off in various directions and to set up outposts in some fairly remote areas. Nevertheless, everyone shared the same theoretical outlook and there was always a central line of attack: the development of scales that would express in quantitative terms expanding conceptions of what prejudice involves, clinical study of individuals scoring at the extremes on these scales, and the subsequent revision of the scales. Further financial assistance was received from the Social

Science Research Council, the Rosenberg Foundation, the Research Board of the University of California and the Graduate Division of Western University. That it was possible to produce a book, instead of writing a series of papers, was due not so much to any original "master plan" as to our shared underlying theory and the fact that our diverse investigations turned up similar results, or results that permitted the same general line of interpretation.

In this light it is a little odd, if not flattering, that this work should be evaluated according to the standards which ordinarily hold for researches, in well-tilled fields, which set out to provide a crucial test of some familiar hypothesis. Some critics write about *The Authoritarian Personality* as if it were the research project which we might well have begun along about the time we decided to write a book about the data already collected. This, of course, is not an excuse for mistakes made in handling data and in their interpretation. There is, however, a good answer to the rather surprising charges of Shils (*58*). He assumes, first, that the group set out to do a large study of authoritarianism as it is conceived of today (he refers to the work as a "monumental research *into* [italics mine] *The Authoritarian Personality*"), and, second, that any truly knowledgeable person setting out to investigate this phenomenon in 1943–44 would have seen that "authoritarianism of the left" was just as important as "authoritarianism of the right"; that the insufficient attention given to the former must have been due, therefore, either to political naivete or to political bias or, more likely, to both. It should be recalled here that the F scale, which the group and others in recent years have called a "measure of authoritarianism," was not designed until the late spring of 1945, and that what we had primarily in mind at the time was an aggregation of scale items that would predict anti-Semitism and ethnocentrism without mentioning the names of any minority groups. The difference between the way Shils and the group itself view this work is well illustrated by the fact that, whereas both refer to "pseudo-conservative" as an *ad hoc* conception, the group does so proudly while he does so contemptuously. The group has regarded this conception as a valuable fruit of the exploratory-empirical approach. Shils seems to think that it should have been arrived at intuitively or, better still, from consultation with political scientists and included in the original "design."

There is a place for the exploratory study. Consider, for example, *Explorations in Personality* (*41*). Methodologically primitive according to present-day standards but a mine of suggestiveness for, up to now, about eighteen years. "Exploratory study" does not mean a self-conscious "preliminary study" or a casual, free-floating observational study; but a study that goes after facts, becomes involved with data, while permitting thinking about those data, or insights derived from them, to determine the next stage of data collection. It is a study in which curiosity about what lies over the next hill becomes the determining motive, and which is therefore willing to "travel light," not waiting for the proper development of base camps. Very probably, neither *Explorations in Personality* nor *The Authoritarian Personality* could have been produced without the kind of financial support—or a lack of such support—that gave real freedom to the investigator, nor could they have been produced had the investigators been wedded to the kind of methodology which such writers as Hyman and Sheatsley (*32*) regard as the ideal. The impression is strong today that research becomes more and more design-centered—rather than content-centered—more and more conventionalized. Somebody is always taking the joy out of it. As a friend said after looking over the Hyman and Sheatsley exercise, "These 'scientists' make me nervous." Yet, I do not wish to encourage any widespread revolt against the scientific superego of today, however externalized it may have become. Obviously, there are times when it is necessary to submit to this discipline, and the critique of Hyman and Sheatsley is so penetrating, so permeated with good will, that the temptation to submit is strong. However, what really must be watched in the methodological experts is their tendency to inject their own philosophy or theoretical biases under the guise of methodological orthodoxy. For example, Hyman and Sheatsley, in reproaching us for neglecting national norms in some of our interpretations of responses to scale items, presumably base their remarks purely on methodological principles; actually they are promoting social relativism, a point of view specifically rejected in the study. Methodological cobblers ought to stick to their lasts.

No one would argue that there is some kind of necessary affinity between originality—or whatever it takes to break new ground—and methodological laxity. Mistakes which our group made in the management of data were not due to any ideological objection to statistical or experimental rigor. They were due rather to ignorance, lack of skill, and, apparently, failure to secure the right advisors. Still, it is doubtful that greater methodological purity or rigor, or adherence to the advice of the most advanced experts—even Hyman or Sheatsley—would have made any crucial difference in the general results and conclusions of our work.

The Authoritarian Personality has been called by highly responsible critics "monumental," "a classic," "a milestone" in social research. This can be interpreted as a rather severe criticism of social psychology and personology. What have our people been doing then? It ought not to be so difficult to produce a work like *The Authoritarian Personality*. All that is really essential is a reasonably comprehensive theoretical framework, curiosity, and freedom—freedom from hampering research conventions, from the conventional expectations of sponsors and from the aspiration to produce a monumental work. Then one simply follows one nose, so to speak. Instead of saying, "This experiment raises more questions than it answers," and then turning attention to something else, one proceeds to try to answer a few of those questions—and later questions raised by this new effort. If the pattern which emerges in the end has such coherence that it appears to have been put in at the beginning, so much the better. There is no good reason why work which proceeds in this way should not maintain high standards in sampling, in generalization, in the collection and analysis of data, but even so it is inevitable that much of it will have to be followed up and checked by more exacting methods. There is a difference between exploratory research as used here and the conventional hypothesis-testing research which is so common today. It is no criticism of the latter to say that there is need for more "explorations in personality."

THE F SCALE

Although the idea of constructing a scale for measuring potential fascism in the personality appeared at a relatively late stage in these explorations, it still came at a time when the focus of attention was upon anti-Semitism and prejudice. A Likert-type scale for measuring ethnocentrism (E) had been constructed and studied in relation to anti-Semitism (A-S). This scale, which embraced hostility to various intra- and extra-national outgroups as well as the tendency to overestimate and to glorify the ingroup, correlated so highly with anti-Semitism, .80, that it seemed reasonable to view this latter as, mainly, a manifestation of general ethnocentrism.

Ethnocentrism, in the group's thinking, had become something very general indeed. Not only did it include generalized outgroup rejection and exaggerated ingroup loyalty but also such defects in thinking as stereotypy, rigidity, and rationailzation; it was a way of looking at groups and group relations that was, in the long run at least, maladaptive; it had begun to take on the aspect of a fundamental psychological problem.

The high correlation between A-S and E meant that it would be possible to go on studying anti-Semitism without having to rely on the original A-S scale itself. This scale had evoked protests both from a local chapter of the Anti-Defamation League, who considered that the instrument spread anti-Semitism, and from the dean of a graduate school, who objected to "the pro-Semitic bias" in this research. From whatever point of view it was seen, this scale did tend to bring the matter of prejudice painfully into the open and it was used with reluctance, particularly in groups that included Jews. But the same considerations held for members of other minority groups. The real need was for an instrument that would measure prejudice without appearing to have this aim and without mentioning the name of any minority group.

The idea of the F scale was a product of thinking about the A-S and E scales. An effort was being made to abstract from the A-S and E scale items the kinds of psychological dispositions—fears, anxieties, values, impulses—being expressed, the thought being that a systematic covering of this ground might suggest additional E items. There were certain general themes in the item content: e.g., Jews were "extravagant," or "sensual" or "lazy" or "soft"; or Jews were mysterious, strange, foreign, basically different; or minority groups generally failed to come up to ordinary standards of middle-class morality. It was as if the subject, in agreeing with these scale items, was not so much considering Jews or other minority group members as expressing concern lest other people "get away" with tendencies which he himself had to inhibit, or anxiety lest he be the victim of strange forces beyond his control, or lest his moral values, already somewhat unstable, be undermined. And since, apparently, items expressing these kinds of preoccupation were agreed with consistently by some subjects regardless of the minority groups involved, would not these subjects agree with such items even though no minority group were mentioned at all? In short, why not have a scale that covered the psychological content of the A-S and E scales but did not appear to be concerned with the familiar phenomena of prejudice? Certainly this fitted in with Leo Loewenthal's memorable if somewhat exaggerated dictum: "Anti-Semitism has nothing to do with Jews."

It cannot really be claimed that this notion came as the result of a deliberate quest for an instrument that would be less awkward to administer to groups of varied ethnic backgrounds, although it came at a time when the need for such an instrument was keenly felt and this implication of the new notion was more or less immediately seen. Furthermore, this notion was conceived at a time when the group was prepared to exploit it to the full. Interviews with subjects scoring high on A-S and E had suggested many psychological characteristics of the highly prejudiced subjects, and whereas many of these characteristics had not yet found a place in the A-S or E scales there was no reason why they should not. And now, since attention was going to be directed to items expressing the general outlook of the highly prejudiced individual, it was possible to make use of the vast literature on Nazism and Fascism and, particularly, the ideas represented by Dr. Adorno and the Institute for Social Research. Finally, it was possible to make explicit a theoretical assumption which, actually, had been a guide to the group's thinking for some time.

The essence of this assumption was that some of the deeper needs of the personality were being expressed by agreement with prejudiced statements. If this were true, then these needs should express themselves in other ways as well. If, for example, a subject's tendency to attribute weakness to Jews sprang from his own underlying fear of weakness, that fear might also express itself in an over-accent upon his own strength and toughness. Thus, scale items having to do with the supposed weakness of Jews or of other people and items expressing exaggerated strength and toughness would correlate positively in a population of men because agreement with both kinds of items commonly sprang from the same underlying source, fear of weakness. All of us were accustomed to this kind of thinking in terms of levels of functioning in the personality; it had loomed large in earlier work of Frenkel-Brunswik (20) and of Sanford (52). It is, of course, essentially psychoanalytic.

Given this way of looking at things, the task became one of imagining what personality needs were commonly expressed in overt prejudice, and then thinking of other surface manifestations of these same needs. The intention was, of course, to gain access to those other manifestations by means of scale items. Here it was possible to make good use of the existing literature on anti-Semitism and Fascism. Fromm (25), Erikson (16), Maslow (38), Chisholm (7), Reich (42), and Stagner (59) were among the writers who influenced us the most, although heaviest reliance was on the group's own earlier explorations. The central personality trends which were expected to be most significant were those which emerged from the analysis of clinical material and those which, as hypothetical constructs, seemed best to explain the consistency of response to the A-S and E scales.

CONTENT OF THE F SCALE

For every item of the F scale there was a hypothesis or, more usually, several hypotheses stating the nature of its supposed connection with prejudice. And there were hypotheses concerning the relations of these items one to another, theorizing having led the group more and more toward the conceptualization of a *pattern* of personality that predisposed the individual to prejudice and fascism.

Here it seems worth while to go into some detail, for progress in an understanding of authoritarianism will come from the closest involvement with the subtle workings of this and similar trends in the personality.

Conventionalism

First consider the idea of *conventionalism*. It was observed in our conversations with anti-Semitic subjects that most of their accusations against Jews were couched in conventionally moralistic terms. This theme was also pronounced in the original A-S scale items. It may be recalled that Hitler made this same type of accusation when addressing midde-class audiences. Our thought here was that we were dealing not so much with bad experiences with Jews or with adaptation to a general climate of opinion as with a need to adhere strictly to conventional, middle-class values, a disposition to feel anxious at the sight of or the thought of any violation of these values—something that could be attributed to instability in the individual's own value system. It is important to note that conventionalism refers not merely to conformity with middle-class values but to *rigid* adherence to such values, to an *over*accent upon them and to responsiveness to contemporary *external* social pressure. Items expressive of this trend invited the subject to go *all out* in his support of conventional values, e.g., "A person who has bad manners, habits, and breeding can hardly expect to get along with decent people."

Authoritarian Submission

Submission to authority, desire for a strong leader, subservience of the individual to the state, had for some time been put forward as important aspects of the Nazi creed. It was thus natural that these themes should be taken into account in a search for the correlates of prejudice. *Authoritarian submission,* as we termed the hypothetical generalized disposition of personality, was conceived of not as a balanced, realistic respect for valid authority but as an exaggerated, emotional need to submit. This seems well represented in the item: "Every person should have a deep faith in some supernatural force higher than himself to which he gives total allegiance and whose decisions he obeys without question." Here, as with conventionalism, the individual is assumed to be oriented toward external powers or agencies of control rather than under the direction of a conscience of his own.

Authoritarian Aggression

Authoritarian submission is closely related, conceptually, to *authoritarian aggression.* Both attitudes, according to theory, spring from underlying hostility toward ingroup authorities, originally the parents. The individual strives to keep this hostility in check by overdoing in the direction of respect, obedience, gratitude toward the ingroup authorities and by displacing the underlying hostility toward these authorities onto outgroups. This is the most essential connection between authoritarian submission and ethnocentrism. But it appears that the tendency to displace hostility is more general than that seen in the common forms of prejudice; the greatest variety of people and actions are likely to become the objects of condemnation. The connection of this hostility and its original source is seen in the fact that the kinds of things for which the individual would punish other peoples are the same as those for which he was punished or for which he feels in his heart he deserves to be punished. But he has identified himself with the ingroup authorities of his childhood, and found in the tendency to punish wrongdoing in others a safe, and fairly well-sanctioned, outlet for his aggression. The items chosen to represent authoritarian aggression offer the subject a chance to favor condemnation, total rejection, stern discipline or severe punishment as ways for dealing with a variety of people and forms of behavior; e.g., "Sex crimes, such as rape and attacks on children, deserve more than mere imprisonment; such criminals ought to be publicly whipped, or worse."

Anti-intraception

It was common to note in the interviews of more prejudiced subjects, and in some of the A-S and E scale items with which they heartily agreed, disapproval of a free emotional life, of the intellectual or theoretical, of the impractical. These were things they tended to attribute to their outgroups. And there was theory at hand to explain the relations of these attitudes to prejudice and to the personality trends just discussed. The individual who had been forced to repress hostility against his parents and others who appeared to be strong, and who was thus forced into submissiveness which impaired his self-respect, would naturally be required to maintain a narrow range of consciousness. Self-awareness might threaten his whole scheme of adjustment. He would be afraid of genuine feeling because his emotions might get out of control, afraid of thinking about human phenomena because he might, as it were, think the wrong thoughts. The term *anti-intraception* was borrowed from Murray et al. *(41)*. It stands for a general attitude of impatience with and opposition to feelings, fantasies, speculations and other subjective or "tender-minded" phenomena. A sample item: "When a person has a problem or worry, it is best for him not to think about it, but to keep busy with more cheerful things."

Superstition and Stereotypy

The narrowness of consciousness just referred to appeared also to be a major source of both *superstition* and *stereotypy,* two tendencies which loomed large in our early clinical studies of highly prejudiced individuals. Superstitiousness indicates a tendency to shift responsibility from within the individual onto outside forces beyond one's control. It suggests a narrow area within which there is a conscious sense of self-determination, a broad area of unconscious forces which are projected onto the external world, to appear to the individual as mystical or fantastic determinants of his fate. Stereotypy is the tendency to think in rigid, oversimplified categories, in unambiguous terms of black and white, particularly in the realm of psychological or social matters. It was hypothesized that one reason why people, even those who are otherwise "intelligent," resort to primitive explanations of human events is that so many of the ideas and observations needed for an adequate account are not allowed to enter into the calculations: because they are affect-laden and potentially anxiety producing they could not be included in the conscious scheme of things. The assumption here is, of course, that many of the common phenomena of prejudice were superstitions or stereotypes. The present task was to devise scale items that would express these tendencies without reference to minority groups, e.g., "It is entirely possible that this series of wars and conflicts will be ended once and for all by a world-destroying earthquake, flood, or other catastrophe."

Power and Toughness

As suggested above, the state of affairs in which the individual has to submit to powers or agencies with which he is not fully in sympathy leaves him with a nagging sense of weakness. Since to admit such weakness is to damage self-respect, every effort is made to deny it. These include the projection of weakness onto outgroups according to the formula "I am not weak, they are," and the use of the mechanism of overcompensation, according to which the individual seeks to present to the world an aspect of *power and toughness*. Accent on the strong-weak, dominant-submissive, leader-follower dimension in human relations is, of course, a familiar feature of the Nazi outlook. In our experience it appeared that the "power complex" contained elements that were essentially contradictory. Whereas the power-centered individual wants to have power, he is at the same time afraid to seize it and wield it. He also admires power in others and is inclined to submit to it, but is at the same time afraid of the weakness thus implied. A common solution for such a person is to align himself with power figures, thus gratifying both his need to have power and his need to submit. By submitting to power he can still somehow participate in it. The following is a sample of the items designed to represent this theme: "Too many people today are living in an unnatural, soft way; we should return to the fundamentals, to a more red-blooded, active way of life."

Destructiveness and Cynicism

Although authoritarian aggression provides a very broad channel for the expression of underlying hostile impulses, it seemed that this might not be enough for many of the prejudiced subjects. We supposed that they harbored, as a result of numerous externally imposed restrictions upon the satisfaction of their needs, a great deal of resentment and generalized hostility, and that this would come into the open when it could be justified or rationalized. *Destructiveness* and *cynicism* was the term for rationalized, ego-accepted aggression, not including authoritarian aggression. Cynicism was regarded as a form of rationalized aggression: one can the more freely be aggressive when he believes that everybody is doing it and, hence, if he wants to be aggressive he is disposed to believe that everybody is similarly motivated, e.g., that it is "human nature" to exploit and to make war on one's neighbors. It seemed a fairly safe assumption that such undifferentiated aggressiveness could be directed against minority groups with a minimum of external stimulation.

Projectivity

The mechanism just described is, of course, a form of projection. And it will have been noted that this unconscious defensive device has had an important place in our earlier related theory making, particularly in the discussion of authoritarian aggression and of superstition. Indeed, projection has a crucial role in the whole theory of prejudice as a means for keeping the individual's psychological household in some sort of order. The most essential notion is that impulses which cannot be admitted to the conscious ego tend to be projected into minority groups—convenient objects. In constructing the F scale, the concern was with a readiness to project, with *projectivity* as a general feature of the personality, considered independently of the object onto which the projection was made. Hence, the items expressive of this tendency were designed to tap any preoccupation with "evil forces" in the world, with plots and conspiracies, germs, sexual excesses.

Sex

Concern with *sex* seemed to deserve a certain amount of special consideration. Inhibitions in this sphere, and moral indignation with respect to the sexual behavior of other people, had been noted in the interviews with our prejudiced subjects; sexual immorality was one of the many violations of conventional values which they attributed to minority groups. Ego-alien sexuality was conceived then as a part of the picture of the typical prejudiced person, and included in the F scale were several items having to do with belief in the existence of "sex orgies" and with the punishment of violators of sex mores.

In summary, there were nine major personality variables which, by hypothesis, were dynamically related to overt prejudice.

1. *Conventionalism.*   Rigid adherence to conventional middle-class values.

2. *Authoritarian Submission.*   Submissive, uncritical attitude toward idealized moral authorities of the ingroup.

3. *Authoritarian Aggression.*   Tendency to be on the lookout for, and to condemn, reject and punish people who violate conventional values.

4. *Anti-intraception.*   Opposition to the subjective, the imaginative, the tender-minded.

5. *Superstition and Stereotypy.*   The belief in mystical determinants of the individual's fate; the disposition to think in rigid categories.

6. *Power and Toughness.*   Preoccupation with the dominance-submission, strong-weak, leader-follower dimension; identification with power figures; exaggerated assertion of strength and toughness.

7. *Destructiveness and Cynicism.*   Generalized hostility, vilification of the human.

8. *Projectivity.*   The disposition to believe that wild and dangerous things go on in the world; the projection outward of unconscious emotional impulses.

9. *Sex.*   Ego-alien sexuality; exaggerated concern with sexual "goings on," and punitiveness toward violators of sex mores.

THEORY UNDERLYING THE F SCALE

In their theoretical work on the F scale the research group leaned heavily upon the concepts of superego, ego, and id. It was considered that these features of the personality have characteristic modes of functioning in the ethnocentric subject. As a first approximation, one might say that in the highly ethnocentric person the superego is strict, rigid and relatively externalized, the id is strong, primitive and ego-alien, while the ego is weak and can manage the superego-id conflicts only by resorting to rather desperate defenses. But this general formulation would hold for a very large segment of the population and, thus, it is necessary to look more closely at the functioning of these parts of the person in the authoritarian syndrome.

In considering the variables which entered into the theory underlying the F scale, it may be seen that the first three—Conventionalism, Authoritarian Submission, and Authoritarian Aggression—all have to do with superego functioning. The accent is upon external reinforcements of strict superego demands, and upon punishment in the name of those authorities to whom the subject has submitted.

Anti-intraception, Superstition and Stereotypy, and Projectivity may be regarded as manifestations of a relatively weak ego. Anti-intraception involves the primitive defensive mechanisms of repression, denial, keeping things ego-alien. Superstition shows an inclination to shift responsibility onto the external world, as if the ego were giving up its attempts to predict and control, while Stereotypy is an attempt to deal with complex events by means of oversimplified categories. Projectivity is the consistent use of another relatively primitive mechanism of defense.

Power and Toughness is another manifestation of ego weakness, involving as it does an over-accent upon the conventionalized aspects of the ego, e.g., the emphasis on "will power"; but this variable, like Destructiveness and Cynicism, and Sex, also expresses with a minimum of indirectness the activity of id tendencies.

However, superego, ego and id can be separated in this fashion only arbitrarily.

In actuality, the functioning of any one of these agencies depends at any moment upon the activities of the other two; and everyday behavior, expressed attitudes and values, are not readily classifiable as manifestations of superego, ego or id but are to be understood as expressions of the relationships among these agencies. This, at any rate, was the thinking that went into the F scale. Consider the item: "He is indeed contemptible who does not feel an undying love, gratitude, and respect for his parents." On the surface, this item expresses authoritarian aggression and authoritarian submission and, hence, might be classified as primarily a superego item. But the theory was that agreement with this extreme statement might well mask an underlying hostility toward the parents. To put this differently, it was hypothesized that unconscious hostility toward the parents was a distinguishing feature of the highly ethnocentric person, and the problem was to determine how this tendency might give itself away in an attitude scale. One answer was through signs of a reaction formation, this mechanism being a common one in the highly ethnocentric person. Thus the present item has to do with an interplay of superego, ego and id: an underlying unconscious, ego-alien tendency, coming mainly from the id, has led to anxiety of punishment (superego) which the ego seeks to ward off or reduce by transforming the forbidden tendency into its opposite. But this is not all. This is merely the authoritarian submission expressed in the item. "He is indeed contemptible" is authoritarian aggression. The ego must, so to speak, be doubly sure that punishment is avoided and it must see to it that the original id tendency finds some sort of gratification; hence, it joins forces with the punitive agency, imputes the "badness" to other people who may then be freely aggressed against in good conscience.

Or consider the item: "The wild sex life of the old Greeks and Romans was tame compared to some of the goings on in this country, even in places where people might least expect it." Here it is assumed that underlying sexual tendencies, inhibited because of a strict superego, have found through the ego's work some expression in fantasies, which, however, can be enjoyed or tolerated only when other people, and not the self, are the actors and when the fantasies are accompanied by moral indignation.

Now it is not suggested that the whole authoritarian personality structure is somehow embedded in each F scale item. But it is fair to say that theory of the kind just indicated lay behind the writing of each item, and that, according to this theory, the F pattern is a structure whose features are so closely interrelated that a clear expression of one permits quite reasonable inferences concerning the activity of the others. Perhaps the items just used are among the best for making this point, but all the F scale items should be viewed from this standpoint.

The F scale works as if the superego, ego, id theory were correct, and there is no doubt but that without this theory the scale would not have been constructed. On the other hand, it cannot be claimed that such results as have been obtained could not be explained as well in other terms.

CLINICAL STUDIES OF THE F PATTERN

In trying to understand the inner workings of the F-syndrome one is not, of course, limited to consideration of the F scale. The interviews and projective techniques which yielded the hypotheses underlying the F scale also yielded some of the most convincing evidence concerning the truth of those hypotheses. To consider an example, the interviews, like some questionnaire material, showed unmistakably that the tendency to glorify his parents was a distinguishing feature of the highly ethnocentric subject. And the interviews also gave evidence of ambivalence in this subject's relationship with his parents. It was usually not long after the statements of glorification that a note of complaint or self-pity began to creep into the interview. How might one demonstrate that overt glorification of the parents is functionally related to underlying hostility toward them? One way would be to use a projective technique to obtain an independent measure of the latter and see if the two vary together. Unfortunately, this is not simple. What are the TAT signs of repressed aggression? Certainly not the frequency and intensity of aggressive actions by heroes of the stories. These seem to be, for the most part, indications of aggression that is accepted by the ego; it is more pronounced in the low scorers than in the high scorers on the F scale. But Betty Aron (2) did conclude that there was more *ego-alien* aggression against the parents in the stories of high scorers, the indications being such things as the frequency with which parent figures were the victims of affliction or death and the frequency and intensity of aggression against parental figures on the part of characters with whom the storyteller was not identified. Thus, to arrive at diagnoses of deep-lying tendencies on the basis of the TAT requires *interpretation*. Although Aron's work goes a long way toward the objectification of such interpretation, and although it argues persuasively for a functional relationship between overt glorification and underlying hostility, it remains in need of independent validation.

The same considerations hold for the Projective Questions. The material elicited by this procedure is for the most part on the same level of personality as the F scale. Responses to the open-ended questions could easily be—and they sometimes were—translated into F scale items. Thus the Projective Questions yielded a large amount of material that confirmed independently the F scale findings on the difference between ethnocentric and nonethnocentric subjects. But, more than this, the material from the Projective Questions called for interpretation, for the conceptualization of underlying trends that would explain the pattern of overt expression.

Two of the Projective Questions were as follows:

1. We all have times when we feel below par. What moods or feelings are the most unpleasant or disturbing to you?
2. There is hardly a person who hasn't said to himself: "If this keeps up I'll go nuts." What might drive a person nuts?

These two questions, like the six others used, brought out numerous differences between highs and lows on the E scale. The "lows" are disturbed by conscious conflict and guilt feelings, frustrations of love and dependence, consciousness of hostility toward loved objects, and they suppose that people are "driven nuts" by inner psychological states or by a dominating environment. The "highs," on the other hand, are more disturbed by violations of conventional values, by self or others or by a threatening or nonsupporting environment; they are also more disturbed by, and state that people are "driven nuts" by, what Levinson called "rumblings from below."

According to Levinson, "These responses refer to situations or bodily conditions which, by inference though not explicitly, tend to bring out ego-alien trends such as passivity, anxiety, and hostility." Examples, from the subjects' responses, are: "Quietness, boredom, inactivity"; "When at a party everything is quiet and dead as a morgue"; "Lack of work or anything to do, causing restlessness and lack of self-confidence." How does one know that such responses as these are signs that the subject is struggling with id tendencies, such as passivity and hostility, which might break into the open unless the anti-intraceptive defenses of keeping busy, having excitement, not thinking too much, are employed to the full? One does not *know*, of course, but this formulation seems to go a long way toward explaining why it is that the very same subjects who feel that they must keep busy are also most concerned about the dangers to mental health of "overwork," "too long hours," "mental fatigue," "undertaking too much." The very activities which ward off the bad impulses may, if persisted in too long, intensify those impulses and increase the danger of a breakthrough. The point to be emphasized is that, when one is working with a theory that postulates levels of personality, he need not suppose that his hypothetical "deeper tendencies" are, so to speak, things which he will one day get his hands on. Even in psychoanalytic practice these deeper tendencies are rarely revealed directly; they are the stuff of interpretations, not just those which the analyst offers the patient but those which he makes for himself. In other words, psychoanalysis, like the research reported in *The Authoritarian Personality*, makes maximum use of hypothetical constructs. The "correctness," or one might better say the usefulness, of the psychoanalytic formulation is gauged by its service in making sense of a great diversity of material and in predicting what a patient will do next. And it is the same in such research as this: does the formulation explain the relationships observed and does it permit the prediction of responses in particular types of situations? The truth of such formulations may rarely be demonstrated to the satisfaction of all, but one may hope to creep up on it.

The largest amount of clinical material in *The Authoritarian Personality* was derived from interviews, the analysis of which is reported in great detail in chapters by Else Frenkel-Brunswik, William Morrow and Maria Levinson. As critics have pointed out, the statistical relationships based on the analysis of interview material from the regular sample of subjects are seriously in need of cross-validation. Criticisms of the methodology in Frenkel-Brunswik's chapters have often been severe, but these are precisely the chapters that most people turn to for an elucidation of the inner working of the potentially fascist pattern, for here they find richness, complexity and comprehensiveness. There is a paradox here. The interviews were not conducted with any thought to their later quantitative analysis. They were going to be used for exploratory purposes and, later, as the basis for case studies that would exemplify some of the patterns that emerged from the other procedures. When it became apparent, however, that certain differences between "high" and "low" ethnocentric subjects appeared regularly in the interview material it seemed that comparisons in quantitative terms would be an aid to description. This, as it turned out, was asking for trouble, for what was essentially clinical work now became subject to the standards for criticism which hold for small sample statistical studies.

Morrow, in his study of prison inmates, used his interview material only for case studies and thus escaped such criticism as was directed toward Frenkel-Brunswik, while Levinson in her study of psychiatric clinic patients analyzed the regular intake interviewers in a way that was methodologically impeccable. The fact that all these approaches led to about the same conclusions concerning the structure and functioning of the F-syndrome probably has made more of an impression upon the authors than upon many readers, who have tended to take chapters or procedures or special studies one at a time and to ask whether they really showed what was claimed. Or perhaps the same general bias on the authors' part pervaded all of these investigations. At any rate, it was not suggested that the numerous findings concerning the dynamics of the F-syndrome did not need to be followed up by other workers.

The picture of potential fascism in the personality was considerably expanded by these clinical studies. All of the major variables of the F scale appeared in these studies. But there were many others besides. Although the procedure was to convert clinical findings into scale items whenever possible, many such findings were still to come in long after a place had been reached when it seemed wise to stop changing the F scale.

It may be well to mention briefly, on the basis of findings from the clinical procedures, some additional features of the potentially fascist pattern: relative inability to accept blame; a tendency to view interpersonal relations in terms of power and status rather than in terms of love and friendship; a manipulative attitude toward other people; the inability or the unwillingness to deal with the indefinite, the ambiguous or the merely probable; tendency to treat property as an extension of the self; tendency to see the real self and the ideal self as essentially the same, and signs of self-contempt underlying this self-overestimation; self-pity; rigidity in adjustment; constriction of fantasy; concreteness of thinking; less differentiated emotional experience; undifferentiated conception of the opposite sex; relative absence of a value for achievement for its own sake; ego-alien dependency; tendency in emotional crises to emphasize somatic rather than psychological complaints.

Perhaps some of these characteristics overlap, or might be reduced to, some of the variables of which the F scale took account. Perhaps not. What, indeed, *are* the essential or "basic" elements of the pattern under consideration? This is a question to be dealt with shortly. The chief point here is that the F scale does not pretend to cover all the facets of the potentially fascist pattern, and that with attention to the findings just described one could construct a second F scale that overlapped but little with the present one but performed in much the same way in relation to other measures. And this is to say nothing of the expansion of the F pattern in the hands of other workers.

STATISTICAL ANALYSIS OF THE F PATTERN

The question of what are the basic elements in authoritarianism calls, of course, for statistical analysis. The F scale in its final form comprised 30 items and had a split-half reliability of .90 in a sample of 517 college women. The average inter-item correlation was .13; the average item-total scale correlation .33. A factor analysis hardly seemed justified. No empirical support was found for the hypothetical clusters—authoritarian submission, anti-intraception, and so forth. Christie and Garcia (*10*), however, have discovered empirical clusters which do resemble rather closely the hypothetical ones. These workers performed a statistical analysis of the tetrachoric intercorrelations of F scale items for two samples matched for socioeconomic factors: the one comprising 57 male and female students at the University of California; the other, 57 male and female students at "Southwest City." The first sample yielded 7 clusters, the second, 8, all of which were very similar to those hypothesized. But there were difficulties. Some of the items fell into no clusters, and individual items generally fell into different clusters in the two samples. The authors suggest—probably correctly—that the latter phenomenon is largely due to the fact that the items are so vague that they quite frequently mean different things to different people, and, hence were organized differently in groups representing somewhat different cultures. This research seems to indicate that the discovery of "pure" attributes of general authoritarianism with the use of the present F scale items is probably impossible.

A suggestion for further work in this area would be that, in place of further analysis of the present F scale, one perform the analysis with an instrument three or four times as long. Perhaps the authors of *The Authoritarian Personality* did not place enough stress on the extreme condensation of the F scale. Concerned with predicting anti-Semitism by means of a conveniently brief instrument, and convinced that the best way to do this was through taking account of a large number of theoretically significant ideas, we frequently made a simple item serve several important hypotheses and consistently eliminated items that came too close to duplicating others. This is hardly the way to explore a broad area with a view to sorting out any pure elements that might lie there. A greatly lengthened F scale could easily be composed of discarded items, items suggested by later clinical findings, and items written by other workers in the course of constructing scales that correlate with F.

An indication of what is possible may be found in some work now being carried on by the Mellon Foundation project at Vassar College. A group of 441 college freshmen were administered both the F and the E scales. In addition, they responded to 677 true-false items from various personality tests. Of these true-false items, 178 had sufficient correlation with F and enough variance to comprise an experimental scale. Further item selection resulted in a 124-item scale which correlated .78 with F and .53 with E. (The correlation between E and F in this sample was .59. Cross-validation of the scale a year later with a new sample of 402 college freshmen gave a correlation with F of .74.)

(Incidentally, this work offers a comment on the familiar suggestion that since high scores on the F scale are obtained by agreeing with statements, the instrument measures not potential fascism but the tendency to agree with foolish statements. It may be, of course, that this latter tendency is indeed an important aspect of the potential for fascism. However, in the Vassar sample of 441 subjects, of 353 items unrelated to F, 56 percent were marked "true" more often by high scorers on F than by low scorers, whereas 91 percent of the 124 items in the new scale were scored in the "true" direction. Apparently, in this sample, a general tendency to agree does not distinguish subjects who score high on F.)

Here is, at least, the possibility of developing an equivalent form of the F scale, something that may be of considerable practical value, particularly in work that requires a great deal of "before and after" testing. A new F scale is needed for other reasons. The present one is becoming too familiar to the present generation of college students, and, more than this, it contains too much "ideology." For example, it was possible for a group of New York City educators to condemn the instrument as a piece of subtle propaganda for Freudianism, Deweyism, and other "bad" things. The new items certainly have the merit of being ideologically neutral; they all come from such personality scales as the MMPI, the California Psychological Inventory, and the Maslow Scale for Dominance Feeling in Women.

In content, the 124 items range over a wide area. In one exposition of the new scale, where our concern was to show something of the breadth and complexity of authoritarianism, we had occasion to mention 28 variables each of which was exemplified by a few items. And since all of these items are relatively simple and unequivocal, in contrast to those of the original F scale, it was fairly easy to classify them under 11 headings. Most of the major psychological dispositions having a place in the original theory of the F scale are represented, with the exception of "Power and Toughness." Although a good many items of this latter type appear among the 677 used in this study, none was correlated with F in this sample of college women. Thus it is possible to conclude that "power and toughness" is not a feature of the F pattern in middle- and upper-middle-class young women, however important it might be in men or in a large sample of the general population.

A factor analysis or cluster analysis of these 124 items would be very interesting. The task, though formidable, is not impossible, and its performance might proceed a long way toward the discovery of the more essential elements in the rapidly expanding F picture. It must be borne in mind that this 124-item scale is not the same thing as F, the correlation between the two being only .74. But this correlation could be raised, partly by further item selection and partly by finding new items that covered the content of F.

AUTHORITARIANISM AS A SYNDROME

There is a need to know, of course, not only the essential elements of F but how these elements are organized. Is F one very general factor that dominates a large number of minor ones, or a structure embracing a limited number of loosely cohering major variables, or an aggregation of truly independent factors? In *The Authoritarian Personality* there was an inclination to stress the conception of one very general factor and a variety of relatively minor ones. Individuals were thought to differ both with respect to the amount of this general factor and with respect to minor factors which entered significantly into the picture. The same view would seem to hold for the 124-item scale discussed above. That one general factor could account for much of the variation of items was indicated by the homogeneity coefficient [Kuder Richardson formula, 20] of .88 and by the fact that the distribution, which appeared to be normal, filled the possible range, 0–124, rather compactly.

Speaking of a general factor and of minor factors does not, however, imply thinking in terms of classical factor theory. The F pattern has repeatedly been referred to as a "syndrome." This conception came from Murray (41), who gives major credit to L. J. Henderson; it had a central place in the analysis of data in *Physique, Personality and Scholarship* (52), and the thinking here about the matter may not have matured very much since the publication of that work. *Syndrome* is a concept from clinical medicine; it refers to a complex of functionally related variables. In the ideal case, the variables are so related that a change in one will usually be accompanied by a change in the others. A syndrome might consist of factors that correlate zero in general population; in fact, it could exist in one and only one individual. Its existence, in such an instance, would be demonstrated when the experimental variation in one constituent leads to variation in the others. In other words, dynamic relationship and correlation in a population of individuals are two different things. Some syndromes are apparently fairly common among individuals in our society, and in these cases the dynamically related variables will be found to show some intercorrelation. The statistical conception of a general factor is not inappropriate here because a syndrome by definition has a unitary character, and one may explain correlations of the constituent variables with each other and with the total score on the basis of their common embeddedness in the total structure.

It is highly important to note, however, that the coherence of the variables in a syndrome may be quite loose. A variable which in one individual has a functional role in a given syndrome may in another individual be absent from that syndrome. The same variable may appear in different syndromes, its nature being modified by the character of the complex in which it is found. And, particularly important syndromes themselves, though conceived as unitary structures, enjoy no true independence; their nature too will depend upon the still broader context of personality within which they have their being.

Thus it is that individuals may exhibit the same syndrome in about the same degree and yet differ among themselves in numerous significant ways. It is not proper to speak of an individual as "an authoritarian personality," thus implying that this is all one needs to know about him. No syndrome can ever totally embrace a person. Even when authoritarianism is pronounced, what emerges in behavior will depend upon what other syndromes are present. The closest one can come to speaking of a type of person is to note that in that person some broad and complex syndrome stands out above all the other known patterns. And one may speak of types of authoritarianism. Authoritarianism may vary from one individual to another according to which of the constituent variables are relatively pronounced, a matter which may depend upon what other factors are at work in the personality. Some of these variations in authoritarianism may be common in large populations.

It is perhaps in keeping with current trends in psychology that almost all the work on the F scale and on authoritarian personality trends has taken the direction of further inquiry *into* the syndrome rather than that of asking about broader contexts of personality within which the authoritarian pattern might have a place. The accent in the follow-up studies has been more upon the similarities of authoritarian personalities to one another than upon the differences among them, upon correlation within the F scale and with the F scale—rather than upon variables which might be related to authoritarianism in some subjects but not in others.

It had been thought that one of the most promising leads for further research contained in this work would concern the suggested "types" or subvarieties of high and low authoritarianism. Evidently only two studies bear directly on this problem. Dombrose and Levinson (*14*) differentiated empirically between low authoritarians who tended to favor "militant" programs of democratic action and low authoritarians who tended to favor "pacifistic" programs. The former obtained lower scores on the ethnocentrism scale than did the latter.

Rokeach (*45*) found that he could distinguish low scorers on ethnocentrism who were markedly dogmatic from those who were less so. He had in his earlier study on the relations of rigidity and ethnocentrism noted that some of his low extremes exhibited a rigid approach to problem-solving which resembled that found more characteristically in his high extremes. These results seem quite consistent with what *The Authoritarian Personality* has to say about "The Rigid Low Scorer." Frenkel-Brunswik and her associates (*21*), in their continuing study of prejudice in children, have added some empirical support for the distinction between a more constricted, conventional pattern of authoritarianism and a more psychopathic one.

It may be well to review briefly here the typology of authoritarianism and nonauthoritarianism which appears in *The Authoritarian Personality*. There is still hope that further research in this area may yet be stimulated. This typology is largely the work of Adorno, and is based upon clinical observation and analysis. It is a modification and extension of a typology of anti-Semites worked out and published by the Institute of Social Research (*33*).

There are six distinguishable patterns among the high authoritarians and five among the lows. It is to be emphasized that high authoritarianism is, in the view of this study, essentially *one* syndrome; what differentiates the "subsyndromes" is the emphasis on one or another of the variables that appear in the overall structure. The patterns found among the lows seem to be relatively more "independent." This is in keeping with the fact that the highs were more alike as a group than were the lows. Although potential fascism appears to be essentially one structure, there are a variety of ways in which it may, so to speak, be avoided.

HIGH AUTHORITARIANISM

The varieties of high authoritarianism were labeled, by Adorno, *Surface Resentment, Conventional, "Authoritarian," Tough Guy, Crank,* and *Manipulative*.

Surface Resentment

Surface Resentment is not on the same logical level as the other high patterns. It refers not so much to any deep-lying tendency in the personality as to a state of affairs in which the individual is provoked to prejudiced and authoritarian modes of behavior by externally imposed frustrations.

The Conventional

The Conventional pattern emphasizes conventional values and determination by external representatives of the superego. Individuals exhibiting this pattern would be very slow to engage in any of the more violent expressions of prejudice; they would be equally slow to oppose or to condemn such expressions if this meant "to be different."

The "Authoritarian"

The "Authoritarian" pattern is probably the purest instance of potential fascism as that picture emerged from the research. It is also very similar to Eric Fromm's conception of the "sado-masochistic character." The subject achieves his social adjustment by taking pleasure in obedience and subordination, while remaining ambivalent toward his authorities. Part of the repressed hatred of authority is turned into masochism and part is displaced onto outgroups.

The Tough Guy

The Tough Guy pattern, as might be expected, has the accent on "power and toughness" and "destructiveness and cynicism." One may find at a deeper level either the type of structure described by Erikson (*16*), in which a successful insurrection against the hated father is made possible through adherence to the gang leader or "older brother," or, the true psychopathic organization in which there is a basic disturbance in object relations and failure in superego formation, the individual being prepared to do anything to protect himself against what he perceives to be a hostile world.

The Crank

The outstanding feature of the Crank is "projectivity," with "superstition and stereotypy" also looming large. According to theory, individuals exhibiting this pattern have reacted to early frustrations by withdrawing into an inner world, one that has been built in considerable part upon denials of reality. They concentrate upon self-aggrandizement and the protection of their self-conception by projective formulas.

The Manipulative

In the Manipulative pattern "anti-intraception" is extreme. There is a marked deficiency of object-cathexis and of emotional ties. In the extreme case people become objects to be handled, administered, manipulated in accordance with the subject's theoretical or practical schemes.

LOW AUTHORITARIANISM

The patterns found among subjects low in potential fascism were labeled *Rigid, Protesting, Impulsive, Easygoing* and *Genuine Liberal.*

The Rigid

The Rigid Low appeared to have most in common with the overall High pattern. The main idea here is that the absence of prejudice, instead of being based on concrete experience and integrated within the personality is derived from some general external, ideological pattern. To quote Adorno, "The latter kind of low scorers are definitely disposed toward totalitarianism in their thinking; what is accidental up to a certain degree is the particular brand of ideological world formula that they chance to come into contact with. We encountered a few subjects who had been identified ideologically with some progressive movement, such as the struggle for minority rights, for a long time, but with whom such ideas contained features of compulsiveness, even of paranoid obsession, and who, with respect to many of our variables, especially rigidity and total thinking, could hardly be distinguished from some of our high extremes."

The Protesting

In the *Protesting* low authoritarian the decisive feature is opposition to whatever appears to be tyranny. The subject is out to protect the weak from the strong.

One might say that he is still fixated at the level of the normal Oedipus complex. Here, perhaps, belong those individuals who can lead or at least be effective in revolts but who can find nothing to do once the revolt has met with success.

The Impulsive

In the *Impulsive* low authoritarian unconventionality is the outstanding theme. Here the subject is able not only to be different but to sympathize with what is different, to look upon it as if it promised some new kind of gratification. For whatever reason, it appears that id impulses, with the exception of destructive ones, are allowed rather free expression. In some cases it seems that the rational ego is lined up with the id, in others that the individual is driven to gratify id impulses in order to gain proof that this may be done without catastrophic consequences.

The Easygoing

The *Easygoing* pattern is the opposite of the Manipulative high authoritarian one. It is marked by imagination, capacity for enjoyment and a sense of humor that often assumes the form of self-irony. The subject in whom this pattern stands out is reluctant to make decisions or to commit himself and extremely unwilling to do violence to any person or thing. He seems to be governed by the idea of "live and let live." Theory concerning the etiology of this pattern puts the accent on the absence of traumatic experiences and upon pleasant relations with the mother and other females.

The Genuine Liberal

The *Genuine Liberal* is close to the psychoanalytic ideal, representing a balance of superego, ego and id. This pattern has features in common with those just described. As in the Impulsive pattern, there is relatively little repression, the subject sometimes having difficulty in controlling himself, but his emotionality is directed toward other people as individuals. As in the Protesting nonauthoritarian, there is identification with the underdog, but this is not compulsive or overcompensatory. And like the Easygoing type the Genuine Liberal is close to reality and relatively free of stereotypy, but he lacks the element of hesitation and indecision. Since his opinions and values are most essentially his own, in the sense of being integral to the personality, he stands rather in contrast to the Rigid low scorer, although there may well be an element of rigidity in the firmness of his convictions. Perhaps the outstanding features of this pattern are ethical sensitivity and value for independence. The subject in whom it is highly developed cannot "keep silent" in the face of something wrong; he resists any interference with his personal convictions and beliefs, and he does not want to interfere with those of others.

There is a question as to the existence of a pattern of nonauthoritarianism in which liberal values and opposition to prejudice are aspects of a well internalized religious conscience. A major conclusion from our study of ethnocentrism in relation to religious attitudes and group memberships was that the "genuinely" religious, as opposed to conventionally religious, person tended to be low on ethnocentrism. According to the present typology a genuinely religious person might exhibit the Protesting or even the Genuine Liberal pattern. It might well be, however, that neither of these patterns does justice to the person in whom nonauthoritarianism is mainly the expression of a superego that insists upon values and standards of Christianity.

This typology deserves a great deal of study and empirical testing. As far as the present work goes, there is the most empirical support for the differentiation between the Conventional and the Tough Guy types of authoritarianism. The differences found by this study between the sample of authoritarian prison inmates and those of authoritarian college and professional people were quite obvious, though they were by no means great enough to obscure the common features.

Closely related to this matter of differentiation within the extremes is the question of possible similarities between one extreme and the other. This question has aroused very considerable interest in recent years. Other workers have been quick to grasp the significance of our conclusion that in authoritarianism one deals with a way of thinking, a way of looking at the world, that can vary independently of the content of ingroups or outgroups. This means that authoritarianism might cut across any existing dimension of political ideology, a matter that certainly invites investigation. Again, our data were collected in 1944–45; and by the time the book was published attention in the United States, scientific as well as popular, had shifted decidedly from fascism to communism. In the absence of empirical psychological studies that throw much light on the emotional appeal of communism, our book has been examined with this purpose in mind. Unfortunately, *The Authoritarian Personality* does not contain very much that is useful here. Obligated to study anti-Semitism in American subjects in 1944–45, the authors did not feel called upon to give communism any special attention. They did, to be sure, point up the problems arising out of the complexity of the right-left dimension in political ideology. Early in the research it was discovered that politico-economic conservatism (PEC) is a relatively poor predictor of anti-Semitism. The correlation was .43 in the first 295 subjects. And, the correlation of conservatism with ethnocentrism and with potential fascism was, in all the various groups of subjects, around .50, on the average. We concluded that "It is clear that political ideologies do not fall neatly along a simple liberalism-conservatism dimension; that the relation between ethnocentrism and 'conservatism' is extremely complex." (*1, p. 183*) Attention was drawn to various subvarieties of rightist and leftist ideologies that could be found in the sample, and to the need for research in this area, while the search for other—more promising—predictors of anti-Semitism was continued.

In order to accent the complexity of the conservatism-ethnocentrism relationship and to dramatize the differences among conservatives—and to counteract, perhaps, the then widespread tendency to regard all conservatives as "bad"—a highly conservative young man was chosen as the subject of a case study that would exemplify the low extremes on ethnocentrism and potential fascism, and contrast with the case of another conservative young man who was at the opposite extreme on these dimensions. Nowadays it is possible that some researchers in this position would seek to find two political leftists to represent the "high" and the "low" authoritarian patterns. It would not be so easy to identify them if one selected on the basis of the E, F, and PEC scales by themselves, for extreme leftists almost always obtain extremely low scores on the F as well as on the E scale. (The low E-PEC correlation is due chiefly to the variability of the conservatives; apart from the genuine equalitarianism of the extreme leftists, these subjects are likely to have the particular kind of political sophistication that enables them to "see through" the test and to bring their responses into line with their overall ideology of the moment.) As indicated above, it was clinical study that permitted the delineation of the *Rigid* low scorer and the noting of authoritarian trends in his makeup. Next in order of similarity to the high-authoritarian pattern was the *Protesting* low scorer, whose rather compulsive need to go against external authority, the father image, suggested that he was caught in the same dilemma as many of the high scorers, but was seeking a different kind of solution of the Oedipus complex.

Meanwhile there has appeared a certain amount of quantitative work in this area. Rokeach (*46*) has reported similarity between the high and the low extremes on prejudice with respect to the tendency to favor "reification of thinking." Rokeach (*45*) also constructed a scale for measuring dogmatism and showed that this factor cut across the left-right continuum. This brings to mind Eysenck's (*17*) isolation of a "tough-mindedness" factor that also cuts across the conservative-radical dimension.

It is noteworthy that these similarities of extreme rightists and extreme leftists, and other similarities that have been mentioned, i.e., Rigidity and Stereotypy—and still others that might well be hypothesized, e.g., Anti-intraception and Manipulativeness—lie mainly in formal traits rather than in the contents of imagery or in broad motivational directions. This seems to be in keeping with the fact that, in the tendency to equate fascism and communism, the accent has been on similarities in method, and on the fact that means tend to be substituted for ends. Such considerations as these could easily lead to an overestimation of the similarities in the emotional appeals of fascism and communism in countries where the leftist parties are weak and despised. It used to be, before communism became established as a world power, that psychoanalysts quite regularly found in their bolshevist patients and acquaintances an intense Oedipus fixation, something that would stand rather in contrast to the *inverted* Oedipus situation which seemed to characterize potential fascists. It seems reasonable enough to suppose that an individual in whose personality the inverted Oedipus theme was central would find life in a state dominated by a communist bureaucracy to his liking or that he might be attracted by the power attributes of communism abroad or by the prospect of losing himself in a strong communist movement at home. As one surveys the scene in the United States today, he is struck by the similarities between the communists and cultist anti-communists, the more so since both insist on attacking liberals. But to neglect the differences between these two groups would be to miss something very interesting and significant. At the level of social and political action there are certainly marked differences, and it seems advisable to retain the hypothesis that these reflect differences at a deep level, in the type of resolution of the Oedipus complex for example, instead of standing as superficial variations upon a common authoritarian theme. The need, of course, is for investigation of leftist zealots by methods as comprehensive as those that have been employed with potential fascists.

AUTHORITARIANISM AS A DETERMINANT OF BEHAVIOR

It is important to note that the authoritarian structure is a structure of *personality,* and that personality is by no means the same thing as behavior. Authoritarianism in personality is a matter of dispositions, readinesses, potentialities; whether or not it is expressed in behavior will depend upon numerous other factors including those of the social situation. It was for this reason that this research was regarded primarily as a study of *susceptibility,* in the individual, to fascist propaganda. Underscored was the view that it is on the level of behavior, mainly, that measures for combating or controlling prejudice will have to be undertaken, the understanding of personality offering nothing more than suggestions as to which measures might be effective with which subjects in which circumstances. Nevertheless, the concentration on personality was intense, the enthusiasm for it obvious; so it is not surprising or particularly unjust that reviewers should say that this study "neglected the social." It is, of course, wrong to characterize the work as a "personality approach" in contradistinction to other kinds of approach, as if there had been an attempt to explain in terms of personality factors the whole phenomenon of prejudice, or as if these various "approaches"—personological, sociological, economic, historical—were competing for the honor of sole determinant and that one or another would sooner or later win the day. The question is, what is the role of personality in prejudice? How does personality interact with various other kinds of factors in producing the manifest phenomenon?

That personality is of very great importance in prejudice is rather forcefully argued by the high correlations—around .70 on the average—between the F scale, on the one hand, and the A-S and E scales, on the other. Since much has been known about the social correlates of prejudice, and since economic interpretations have been predominant for a long time, these high correlations have been objects of the closest scrutiny. Every possible source of spuriousness has been explored. Today the important fact is that the correlation has stood up in numerous replications of this work. The E and F scales have by now been administered to numerous groups of the greatest variety in various parts of the United States, and in no case has the investigator failed to obtain a substantial correlation between the E and F scales. Thus one is spared the necessity of defending in detail a methodology employed ten years ago.

There is one point having to do mainly with the interpretation of the E-F correlation that seems interesting. Naturally, a correlation of .83 between a measure of "prejudice" (E) and a measure of "deep personality trends" (F) in a group of 154 middle-class women—to mention one sample—comes as something of a shock to the social scientist long accustomed to considering "prejudice" as mainly a function of contemporary social and economic factors. What seems a little odd is that reactions have taken the direction of questioning the methods by which such correlations were obtained rather than the more promising direction of questioning the validity of the E scale. The usual approach has been to regard E as a criterion measure and to inquire whether all the rules were followed in discovering personality correlates of it. But the important fact is that the E scale is itself a personality measure. True enough, when it is viewed as an ordinary measure of prejudice, the scale has much face validity, filled as it is with plainly negative beliefs and hostile attitudes respecting a variety of minority groups; but, seen in the light of the concepts and theory employed, it also has face validity as a measure of personality, filled as it is with unmistakable expressions of such tendencies as extrapunitiveness, conventionalism, and compartmentalization in thinking.

This explains why it is that this scale predicts external criteria such as rigidity in problem-solving or lack of progress in psychotherapy as well as, if not better than, the F scale. Since, in the thinking of this research ethnocentricism and potential fascism are expressive of the same trends in a person, the E-F correlation is as easily regarded as a reliability coefficient as it is a validity coefficient. A reliability coefficient of .83—or .87, to mention the highest E-F correlation obtained

—does not seem extraordinarily high. As for the validity of the E scale, its value as a predictor of such overt behavior as direct verbal or physical attacks upon members of minority groups remains something of a question. All that can be claimed for it is that it probably predicts as well as any other verbal instrument.

When F is correlated with other measures of prejudice, coefficients somewhat lower than those reported above are obtained. Thus, for example, Campbell and McCandless (6) report a correlation of .60 between the F scale and their own Xenophobia scale, and a correlation in the same sample, of 179 college students, of .73 between F and E. It has been suggested that this correlation between the personality measure and a completely independent measure of xenophobia might well represent the true degree of relationship between personality and prejudice. This conclusion would not be found disturbing. It must be pointed out, however, that xenophobia is not the same thing as ethnocentrism. The Campbell and McCandless instrument was limited to items referring to English, Japanese, Jews, Mexicans, Negroes; the E scale gave as much attention to "patriotism," or ingroup overestimation, and to a variety of minorities other than ethnic ones as it gave to Jews or Negroes. Before admitting that the difference in size between E-F correlations and correlations between F and other measures of prejudice is due to an element of spuriousness in results, one should require that this other measure cover the same ground as the E scale.

It does appear that E-F correlations in recent investigations have been running somewhat lower than those perviously reported. It seems not unlikely that, when truly adequate sampling has been completed, the degree of relationship will have settled down in the neighborhood of .60, rather than .70. At the same time, however, one must reckon with a sort of "self-destroying prophesy." Prejudice has been the subject of an enormous amount of public discussion since 1944–45 when the data of this research were collected. The present study work has had a place in this discussion. Open expressions of prejudice have been increasingly frowned upon, so that one might well expect an increased discrepancy between verbal manifestation and underlying disposition. In any event, with respect to the overt phenomena of prejudice, one may well be content with the 25 to 35 percent of the total variance which may safely be ascribed to personality.

But it is not merely as a predictor of prejudice that authoritarianism should be considered. As a central structure of personality, authoritarianism may be expected to influence behavior in a wide variety of situations; or, more correctly, as a system of response readiness more or less ingrained in the person, authoritarianism may be expected to express itself somehow in most of the individual's behavior.

Numerous investigations have been concerned with empirical correlates of the F scale; they have asked whether subjects scoring high on the F scale respond to some other test, or in some other situation in the way that authoritarian subjects might, by hypothesis, be expected to respond. Thus, for example, F. H. Sanford (49) studied 963 individuals, a representative sample of the population of greater Philadelphia, by means of a standard interview that included a short authoritarianism scale, and reported that subjects exhibiting more authoritarianism were less inclined to participate in political affairs, less likely to join community groups, less likely to become officers in the groups they did join, more reluctant to accept responsibility; and that they had characteristic ways of perceiving leaders, characteristic preferences among leaders and characteristic attitudes toward their fellow followers. Gump (28) showed that high scores on the F scale were closely associated with disapproval of President Truman's dismissal of General MacArthur, and Milton (*40*) has reported a correlation of .73 between F scale score and tendency to prefer "authoritarian" candidates for the United States presidency (e.g., MacArthur vs. Stevenson). But since the findings of these studies all rest upon self-reports, they were better regarded merely as indices of the same factors that the F scale measures rather than as measures of that instrument's validity.

In another group of studies the F scale has been used in connection with the currently widespread interest in the relations of personality and mental processes. Examples would be Rokeach's (*44*) finding that his more authoritarian subjects were more rigid in their approach to the solutions of arithmetical reasoning problems, Block and Block's (*5*) finding that their more authoritarian subjects showed a stronger tendency to establish norms in an experiment involving the autokinetic phenomenon and Fisher's (*18*) report that the visual memory image changed more, in the direction of simplicity and symmetry, in his more authoritarian subjects. These studies not only have the merit of having established correlations with measures that were entirely independent of the F scale but they seem to offer rather forcible arguments that authoritarianism is highly central to the personality.

Although the authoritarian syndrome as put forward here embodies a number of variables that seem to belong mainly in the area of cognitive functioning, e.g., stereotypy, projectivity, its major emphasis is upon factors in the realm of social relations: authoritarian submission, accent on power relations, and so forth. Accordingly, there has been some demand for evidence that F scale score is predictive of overt behavior in social situations. There is a certain irony in the fact that what was always of the least concern in this study has been the ground for some of the most persistent criticism of it. From a great deal of first-hand observation it was known that subjects high and subjects low on anti-Semitism differed in numerous very obvious ways in their overt social behavior. For example, the project's secretary, a good observer to be sure, could tell with considerable accuracy from a subject's telephone conversation about an appointment whether she was dealing with a "high" or "low," and if any doubt remained it was almost always dispelled by noting that subject's dress and manner when he or she appeared at the office.

The F scale was designed to be a convenient device for setting forth in crudely quantitative fashion some of the more important of the observed differences. So, the question, "Will the F scale differentiate groups of people who show authoritarian traits in their behavior from groups who do not show such traits?" is not one that has troubled the group very much. Still, one does not wish his attitude in this matter to be classed with that of Freud when he wrote that certain experimental confirmations of the repression hypothesis "could do no harm."

Science must from time to time prove the obvious, and it may be an error to treat lightly, for just a moment, the dangers of subjective bias and, particularly in the present case, of contamination of the observer. All this is leading up to a report of the fact that Eager and Smith (*15*) have now shown, in a manner that will be to everyone's satisfaction, that a short authoritarianism scale is a predictor of the actual behavior of camp counselors. Boys and girls at a summer camp were asked to guess which of a number of statements applied to which of the counselors. On the basis of the guesses the counselors were divided into two groups, a relatively authoritarian one and a relatively equalitarian one. It was found that the former had significantly higher F scale scores than did the latter.

An even more impressive validation study is that of McGee (*39*), who secured very careful estimates of the authoritarianism of teachers, as shown in their performances throughout the school year, and found a correlation of .60 between these estimates and scores on the F scale obtained at the beginning of the year. However, the most gratifying evidence of the validity of this work has been the publication of Henry Dicks' study of the German prisoners of war (*13*). Here is an entirely independent research that reports numerous findings, respecting not only the general structure of the F-syndrome but the details of its workings, that are remarkably similar to those of the present study.

Also in the realm of social behavior, but apparently having most to do with factors of ego strength, particularly intraception, are demonstrations of relationships between the authoritarian pattern and unreceptiveness to psychotherapy (*Barron, 3*) and unwillingness to volunteer for psychological experiments (*Rosen, 48*).

There is no doubt about it; the F scale really correlates with other measures. Is any other instrument as safe a bet for the M.A. candidate who wants a personality measure that differentiates subjects performing differently in an experimental situation? Apparently not. It is suggested that the reason for this is that personality is organized, and the F scale respects that organization. It is based upon some insight into, or at least preoccupation with, one area of organized functioning in the personality. It might be called a *psychological* scale. It taps central dispositions of personality by deliberately taking into account some of the ways in which such dispositions are related dynamically to diverse surface manifestations. Since it is of the very essence of personality organization that infinitely diverse performances are motivated in part by fewer more basic dispositions, and since the evidence is that the F scale has succeeded in getting hold of some of the later, reports of many more empirical correlates of F should be expected.

Besides offering evidence for the validity of the F scale, the work described above contributes to the definition, and to an understanding, of the F pattern. The F scale was not intended to be, and it most certainly did not prove to be, a unidimensional scale. (The whole effort was directed to producing an instrument that would correlate with other indices of potential fascism and a concentration on purity of dimension might well have defeated this purpose.) We conceived of, and the evidence is that there exists in fact, a pattern of loosely cohering variables of personality.

It could be said of all the above studies that they improve the picture either by bringing in elements not observed by us (e.g., tendency to avoid social activities and membership in face-to-face groups), or by offering usable measures of factors noted clinically but not measured previously (e.g., the tendency to premature closure). Other work has taken the direction of studying in great detail certain particular attributes of the over-all pattern. Thus, misanthropy (*Adelson and Sullivan, 1*), rigidity (*Gough and Sanford, 27*), dogmatism and opinionation, (*Rokeach, 45*), and traditional family ideology (*Levinson and Huffman, 35*) have been more or less isolated and scaled. The unidimensionality of these scales is open to question, but they have been shown to have some validity. To give various other features of the authoritarian pattern this same kind of treatment would appear to be a worthy undertaking.

Further work on the relations of the personality syndrome to behavior might well be directed to the ways in which authoritarianism is expressed in some of the most common social roles—politician, parent, teacher, student, spouse, and the like—and inquire how authoritarianism of personality might be expressed in them. A few indications will have to suffice here.

The authoritarian political leader is a fairly familiar subject. Many of the ideas for the F scale were derived from consideration of the copious literature on the Nazi leadership. It seems that American demagogues exhibit pretty much the same pattern as the Nazis, as far as individual personality is concerned. Perhaps the point to emphasize now is that it takes a great deal more than authoritarian personality trends, however pronounced, to make a totalitarian leader: special abilities, the times, the receptivity of the people, should be mentioned, to say nothing of innumerable chance factors.

The authoritarian political follower was, of course, the primary concern of *The Authoritarian Personality*. In this regard the need for dissemination of knowledge is about as great as the need for knowledge itself. It is asked on every hand: "How do you explain the appeal of McCarthyism?" With all due respect to history, the international situation and the nature of the American political institutions, it might be suggested that what this country needs is a sort of *Reader's Digest* version of *The Authoritarian Personality*.

A number of good studies have related authoritarianism in personality to leadership and followship in general. F. H. Sanford (*49*), for example, in the study referred to earlier, educed evidence that subjects high on authoritarianism tended to prefer strongly directive leaders of status and power and to exhibit toward them an attitude of "bargaining dependency." There were also indications that the more authoritarian subjects tended not to accept responsibility; they do, however, "accept the leadership role but appear to regard a leadership position more as an opportunity to control people than as a mandate to serve them." Hollander (*31*), in a recent paper, reports that in a group of 268 naval cadets, subjects high on authoritarianism tended not to be nominated by their peers for the hypothetical position of "student commander," the correlation being −.23.

It is necessary, of course, to distinguish between authoritarian behavior in leadership roles and authoritarianism in the personality; and it must be noted that the two do not necessarily go together. Conceivably, a person with strong authoritarian personality trends may, in an academic leadership position, bend over backward to keep things nice and democratic. Conversely, Lewin et al. (*37*) showed some time ago that a very democratic teacher may, without difficulty, deliberately create an autocratic social climate. Still, one would expect that, in general, those leadership roles in which authoritarian behavior is more or less required by the needs and expectations of the followers would tend to attract individuals in whose personalities authoritarianism loomed large, just as strongly authoritarian personalities might be expected sooner or later to put their own stamp upon the roles they chanced to assume.

The role of teacher is certainly one that serves well to elicit any authoritarianism in the personality. The strict adherence to senseless rules, the disposition to treat minor infractions as if they were major ones, the device of punishing the whole class for the misbehavior of one member—the picture is familiar. It is important to distinguish carefully between the responsible assumption of authority, which, though it may sometimes require stern measures, is always in the service of cultural goals that are shared by teacher and students, and authoritarianism, which springs from the needs—often the near panic—of the teacher alone. This has been done elsewhere (*51*).

It is important to note, too, the very large role of the situation in determining the authoritarian behavior of teachers. Consider the familiar situation in which the teacher is afraid of the principal, the principal of the superintendent, the superintendent of the school board, while the children are afraid of nobody. Some school setups are enough to bring out authoritarianism in almost anyone who has to stay within them. But there is no reason to doubt that those who are predisposed by virtue of personality will be the first to exhibit such behavior or will do so most vividly in the end.

Perhaps the authoritarian student is but a special case of the authoritarian follower. But the problem would seem to be one of particular interest and importance because of the role of authoritarianism in resistance to learning and in determining the conditions under which learning occurs. It appears that when the subject matter has to do with the concrete, the objective, the physical, and the teaching is straightforward and authoritative, the authoritarian student may do very well. But when the concern is with human events and experiences, and the teaching is of the sort that is designed to change attitudes, then there is likely to be considerable difficulty. Here it is not so much that the student is inclined to learn only by rote or to take things upon authority, but that he does not want to learn anything that would disturb the somewhat precarious adjustment that he has already made.

The difficulty for the educator lies in the fact that, when authoritarian students are presented with a nondirective, flexible approach in teaching and a free, unstructured environment, they are likely to leave the field. Goldberg and Stern (26), for example, found that ethnocentrism in freshmen at a liberal university was predictive of dropping out of school in the first quarter. On the other hand, directive teaching and a highly structured situation, which such students find congenial, are likely to intensify the very attitudes that one might like to change. Much work will have to be done in this area before one may know how to apply in the case of each student the right mixture of direction and permissiveness, of freedom and authority, of extraceptiveness and intraceptiveness in subject matter for the fullest possible realization of educational goals.

Concerning the role of the parent, apparently individuals with marked authoritarian personality trends adopt toward their children the same attitudes and practices that they characteristically adopt toward other people. Levinson and Huffman's Traditional Family Ideology Scale (35) contains items which express in a context of child training and family relations many of the same underlying attitudes and values that characterize the F-syndrome. The scale correlates .73 with the F scale. Kates and Diab (34), using the E and F scales in conjunction with the USC Parent Attitude Survey, found that in mothers ethnocentrism and authoritarianism were significantly related to dominant and possessive attitudes toward children, while in fathers authoritarianism was related to ignoring attitudes. One may, however, sound a note of optimism at this point. There is convincing evidence that an enormous change in child-training methods, a change in the direction of less authoritarianism, is taking place in this country. Even the highly authoritarian parent is open to suggestions where his children are concerned; there is enough involvement and enough uncertainty about what to do so that the authority of the mass media makes a very considerable impact.

The Levinson and Huffman scale also contains items expressive of that traditional pattern of husband-wife relationship in which the husband is supposed to be dominant, determined, adventurous, while the wife is submissive, timid, moralistically, long-suffering. The high correlation of this scale with F confirms many observations contained in *The Authoritarian Personality*. Clinical experience shows that authoritarianism is an important factor in marital maladjustment. It is common for the authoritarian male with his overcompensatory insistence upon the manly virtues to seek a girl with the attributes of a clinging vine, and for the authoritarian woman to be attracted by a determined go-getter. Naturally the two have an affinity one for the other, but in marriage both are likely to be disappointed. Underneath the sweet façade of the clinging vine there is, too often, aggression and exploitiveness, while the go-getting features of her spouse are too often a mask for dependence and passivity. The case one most often sees in practice is that of the less authoritarian wife who is wondering what she can do about her more authoritarian husband. This is not to say there are not cases in which the authoritarianism of one partner is meshed with the masochism of the other in a relationship that is durable if not very happy. This whole area is much deserving of intensive study.

And the same might be said for various other social roles—physician, patient, counselor, counselee, employer, employee, military officers and enlisted men. The need is for research that combines sociological analysis—for example, of the requirements of the role and of the social system within which it has a place—with intensive studies of the individuals who take the roles. Where the focus of attention is upon behavior in the role, personality trends such as authoritarianism may be considered to be among the determining factors. Where the concern is with selection for the role, personality determinants will loom considerably larger. It may very well turn out that individuals with pronounced authoritarian personality trends are better suited than other people for certain roles that are necessary in a society such as this one. If personality itself is under study, then, of course, one must study behavior in various roles; here, sociological knowledge of the roles will help reveal those consistencies of behavior from which underlying personality structures are inferred.

But perhaps this is enough to support the argument with which the discussion of roles started, namely, that authoritarianism as a central structure in personality is sufficiently generalized so that it finds expression in virtually any of the individual's activities. To quote from a recent paper by Milton Rokeach (*47*), ". . . authoritarianism may well be observed within the context of any ideological orientation, and in areas of human endeavor relatively removed from the political or religious arena . . authoritarianism can be recognized as a problem in such areas as science, art, literature and philosophy. . . ."

Perhaps this discussion should not be closed without the comment that just as authoritarianism in personality helps to determine behavior in many varied situations, so there are situations which seem well-calculated to elicit authoritarian behavior. Thus Christie (*9*) has educed evidence that F scale scores of certain army trainees increased as they became adjusted to military life. Eager and Smith (*15*), in the study referred to earlier, observed that some camp counselors scored higher on F at the end of the season than they did at the beginning, as if insecurity or impatience, stimulated by some unexpectedly unruly children, had provoked authoritarian aggression.

This line of thought has been employed in an attempt to explain the behavior of the Regents of the University of California during the period of the oath controversy (*56*, p. 30):

As the struggle proceeded the Regents, of course, became more and more totalitarian in their actions. This, I think, is best understood in field-theoretical terms. They were in a position corresponding somewhat to that of a teacher before a rebellious and misunderstood class. The more things threatened to get out of hand the more rigid they became, and the more rigid they became the greater was the actual danger of a break-out somewhere, and so on. [But, be it noted, it was added that] the stronger the disposition [in the personality] the earlier did a Regent adopt a rigid attitude toward the rebellious faculty.

THE GENESIS OF AUTHORITARIANISM IN PERSONALITY

The major hypothesis guiding our investigations into the origins of authoritarianism was that such central structures of personality had their beginnings in experiences of early childhood. It must be granted, however, that the evidence on this was of a rather indirect sort: it was limited to what our subjects *said* about their childhoods. Naturally such retrospective accounts were distorted by the subjects' contemporary outlook. Nevertheless, it was possible to make reasonable inferences about what actually happened. Sometimes the reference was to more or less objective events or circumstances which the subject apparently had no reason to invent or magnify; sometimes, with knowledge of common modes of distortion, one could, so to speak, read between the lines and arrive at a reasonably convincing picture of the childhood in question. By taking the many differences between the reports of subjects scoring high and those scoring low on the F and E scales and considering these in the light of contemporary knowledge and theory of personality development, it was possible to put together a plausible account.

It may be helpful at this point to sketch very briefly the contrasting accounts of childhood by high- and low-authoritarian subjects. High-authoritarian men more often described their father as distant and stern, while the "lows" tended to describe him as relaxed and mild. High-authoritarian women characteristically saw the father of their childhoods as hard-working and serious, while low-scoring women more often perceived him as intellectual and easygoing. The mother of high-scoring subjects, both male and female, was more often said to be kind, self-sacrificing and submissive, while the mother of low-scoring subjects were more often described as warm, sociable and understanding. High-scoring men tended to accent the mother's moral restrictiveness, low-scoring men her intellectual and aesthetic interests. High-scoring women more often described their mothers as models of morality, restricting and fearsome, while low-scoring women were more often able to offer realistic criticism of their mothers.

In general, high scorers gave a less differentiated picture of their parents than did the lows. The tendency of the former was to offer a somewhat stereotyped and idealized picture at the beginning of the interview but to allow negative features to make their appearances when there was questioning about details; while the latter more often undertook an objective appraisal with good and bad features mentioned in their place.

When it came to the matter of the relations between the parents, the tendency of the high scorers was to deny any conflict, the lows usually describing some conflict in more or less realistic terms. High-scoring men usually described their homes as being dominated by the father; low-scoring men more often described homes in which there was general orientation toward the mother.

Discipline in the families of the more authoritarian men and women was characterized in their accounts by relatively harsh application of rules, in accordance with conventional values; and this discipline was commonly experienced as threatening or traumatic or even overwhelming. In the families of subjects low on authoritarianism, on the other hand, discipline was more often for the violation of principles, and the parents more often made an effort to explain the issues to the child, thus enabling him to assimilate the discipline.

In view of the more authoritarian subject's obvious inclination to put as good a face as possible upon his family and his childhood situation, we were inclined to assume that such negative features as appeared in his account were probably to be taken more or less at their face value; that is, to believe that the high authoritarians came, for the most part, from homes in which a rather stern and distant father dominated a submissive and long-suffering but morally restrictive mother, and in which discipline was an attempt to apply conventionally approved rules rather than an effort to further general values in accordance with the perceived needs of the child.

This view of the matter seems to be in accordance with the findings of a recent quantitative study by Harris et al. *(30)*. These workers showed that the parents of prejudiced children tended in their answers to a questionnaire to emphasize obedience, strict control, the inculcation of fear and the like significantly more than did the parents of relatively unprejudiced children.

The real need here, of course, is for longitudinal studies in which developmental trends in children are observed against a background of actual events and practices in the home. The closest to this ideal so far would appear to be the work of Frenkel-Brunswik and her associates. These workers have measured prejudice in children as young as 10 years and have obtained information on family background, handling of discipline, and childhood events by means of visits to the home and extensive interviews with the parents: Frenkel-Brunswik writes *(21,* p. 236):

> A preliminary inspection of the data supports the assumption made in *The Authoritarian Personality* that warmer, closer and more affectionate interpersonal relationships prevail in the homes of the unprejudiced children; the conclusions concerning the importance of strictness, rigidity, punitiveness, rejection vs. acceptance of the child seem to be borne out by data from the children themselves. . . .
>
> In the home with the orientation toward rigid conformity, on the other hand, actual maintenance of discipline is often based upon the expectation of a quick learning of external, rigid and superficial rules which are bound to be beyond the comprehension of the child. Family relationships are characterized by fearful subservience to the demands of the parents and by an early suppression of impulses not acceptable to the adults.

In this picture of parents and their discipline are very probably the major sources of the most essential features of the authoritarian personality syndrome, the superego's failure to become integrated with the ego, and certain crucial shortcomings in the ego's development. Discipline that is strict and rigid and, from the child's point of view, unjust or unreasonable may be submitted to, but it will not be genuinely accepted, in the sense that the child will eventually apply it to himself in the absence of external figures of authority. There also is good reason to believe that authoritarian discipline, of the sort described above, acts directly to prevent the best ego development. Where the child is not allowed to question anything, to participate in decisions affecting him, nor to feel that his own will counts for something, the stunting of the ego is a pretty direct consequence. It is for this reason that, when it comes to talking with parents about the prevention of authoritarianism and ethnocentrism in children, the recommendation is: "Treat the child with respect—especially after he is about two years old and begins to show signs of having a will of his own." This has nothing to do with permissiveness, nor does it work against the maintenance of high standards. Naturally the parent has to put certain things across; but, if he is to get acceptance and not mere submission, he must at least recognize that he is dealing with another human being.

GENERAL FORMULATION OF THE AUTHORITARIAN PERSONALITY SYNDROME

It seems worth while, now, to attempt a formulation in hypothetical terms of the overall F pattern, a formulation that seems to order most of the statistical facts and clinical observations made, which may, it is hoped, serve as a guide to further research.

A very strict and punitive superego is behind the inability to admit blame or to bear guilt found in the F-syndrome. It is this inability that makes it necessary for the subject to put blame onto others who may then be hated in the way that he would hate himself were he to become conscious of his own impulses. This superego is not integrated with the ego but stands much of the time in opposition to it. Indeed, the ego would get rid of it altogether if it could. And sometimes it almost succeeds. It is this state of affairs that permits one to speak of the superego in the F-syndrome as rigid. It either works in a total, all-out fashion, when one may observe strict adherence to conventional standards, strict obedience to the authorities of the moment accompanied by feelings of self-pity, or it works apparently not at all, as in a high school sorority initiation, or in the riots of sailors in San Francisco on V-J Day, or in children in an authoritarian classroom when the teacher is away. These examples show the great importance of external agencies, be they authority figures or the social groups of the moment. Wishing to be free of the punitive superego, the individual is always ready to exchange it for a suitable external agency of control; and if this external agency offers gratification of id needs at the same time, as in the crowd where anything goes because "everybody is doing it," or, as in the case of the authoritarian leader who says, "there is your enemy," then the way is open to generally regressive behavior.

The key notion here is the failure of the superego to become integrated with the ego. It is quite likely that the chief opponent of authoritarianism in the personality is an internalized superego that *is* genuinely integrated with the ego. Yet it must be admitted that something very similar to what has just been said about superego functioning in the F-syndrome has been put forward in psychoanalytic writings as a theory of superego functioning in general. Indeed, there is some justification for Fromm's (*24*) allegation that the Freudian superego is an "authoritarian superego." Insofar as the Freudian superego is limited to that which is built up through "identification with the aggressor," as described by Anna Freud (*23*) in particular, Fromm is quite right. But Freud had many other things to say about the superego, and probably never did arrive at a theory which satisfied him.

The interesting theoretical question here concerns the role of identification with the aggressor in the genesis of the superego in the authoritarian structure. On first view, this formulation seems made to order for what is known of the F-syndrome. The individual manages his ambivalent feelings toward his punitive parent by identifying himself with that parent, by actually internalizing the punitiveness, now receiving masochistic satisfaction through submission to parent figures and sadistic gratification through the punishment of others. The question here is whether, or to what extent, this "authoritarian superego" is truly *inside* the personality. There is much to be said for the view elsewhere (*50*) that the superego in the authoritarian pattern derives from infantile projections and introjections, that through failures in ego development it remains as an unconscious source of extreme anxiety, and that it is in order to escape this anxiety or in the hope of getting rid of its source that the individual must seek and have an authority.

The underlying drives that have loomed largest in these discussions, as they did in the research, are aggression, dependence, submission, passivity and homosexuality. Not only were these drives hypothesized in order to explain the interconnectedness of surface manifestations, but clinical studies also provided a mass of evidence that these were the crucial motivating forces in the more authoritarian subjects. Whether one speaks of id tendencies here depends upon his definition of that concept. One is inclined to say that these are id tendencies, for, though they have undoubtedly been in considerable part built up through experience, they are certainly primitive, impulsive, childish and alien to the ego. The important thing is that these drives were repressed in childhood and hence were no longer accessible to the maturing effects of experience. It is for this reason that the subject acts as if any expression of depedence were the equivalent of a total descent into infantilism, as if any show of hostility against the parents were a giveaway of the wish to destroy them altogether. Given drives which are felt to have such potency, it is natural that anxiety should frequently be acute and that extreme measures for warding it off should have to be taken.

But subjects who are relatively free of authoritarianism also have to deal with aggression against parents, with dependence, passivity and homosexual trends. Indeed, there is nothing to indicate that these tendencies are less strong in them than in the more authoritarian subjects; the difference lies in the way these tendencies are managed. This is a matter of ego functioning. Because of the various failures in this department, such as the extreme narrowness of consciousness, rigidity of functioning, and use of primitive mechanisms of defense, that distinguish the more authoritarian subjects, there is justification for speaking of their greater ego weakness. But the weakness of the ego cannot be considered apart from the size of the task that it has to perform. There is in the authoritarian pattern the picture of an ego that is in constant danger of being overwhelmed either by emotional impulses from within or authoritative demands from without. In these circumstances it must devote itself to its last-ditch defenses, so to speak, being in no position to undertake any forward movements. When one asks what is crucially determining in this pattern, he finds himself accenting now the underlying impulses, now the demands and threats, now the ego weakness itself. However he looks at it, he perceives a single structure, the several features of which are mutually dependent.

THE HISTORICAL MATRIX OF AUTHORITARIANISM

The above accounts of the genesis of authoritarianism in the individual personality put the emphasis upon early experiences in the family. Now it is necessary to ask what makes parents behave in the ways that apparently promote authoritarianism in their children? It will not do merely to say they are authoritarian themselves, thus pushing things back indefinitely into the past. One must consider that family life, within which personality develops, is constantly under the impact of various complex social and historical factors. In what times and places, under what general sociological conditions, or what conditions of cultural change, or stability, is the development of authoritarian personalities favored or discouraged? This is a critically important matter about which there is very little exact knowledge.

Very much has, of course, been written about the importance of German institutions, or perhaps better, the breaking up of certain institutions—in the genesis of authoritarian and fascist personalities before and during the time of Hitler; but there is much here that remains mysterious. And it is not so easy to carry over knowledge of the German case so that it helps to explain the incidence of authoritarian personality in the United States. The kind of research that is called for is well exemplified in the work of Bjorklund and Israel (4), who relate modal personality and family structure to other aspects of the social process, such as growing industrialization and urbanization; and that being undertaken by the Institute for Social Research at Oslo in which authoritarianism, among other things, is being studied in seven different nations.

When it is said that authoritarian personality structure has its genesis in family life that, in its turn, goes forward under the influence of social conditions and processes, one means that the attitudes and practices of parents with respect to their children may be responses to stimuli of the moment. Such stimuli might arouse or set in motion such beliefs and policies as those found by Harris et al. (30) in the parents of prejudiced children. It is easy to imagine, for example, middle-class parents, who have climbed rapidly, and who have been made to feel insecure with respect to their new-found status, directing toward their children precisely that type of desperate, unreasonable control that has seemed to be most important in the genesis of the authoritarian syndrome. For that matter, one can understand such parental behavior resulting from a loss of status and of self-respect, as was so common in Germany in the aftermath of World War I.

Therapeutic Considerations

Authoritarianism, it appears, may be heavily influenced by the external field forces. This is of crucial importance to any consideration of what to do about the problem. It would be a sad state of affairs indeed if one were forced to conclude that the only thing that could be done was to give intensive psychotherapy to all people in whom authoritarianism in personality was highly developed. Actually, the stress upon personality *structure* has not been intended to suggest something fixed and solid and impregnable to influence from outside. Not only is authoritarianism in personality conceived of as more or less normally distributed; it is further believed that almost anyone is capable of having his authoritarianism evoked by sufficiently strong stimuli. The structure itself exists within a larger dynamic organization of personality, the whole of which is in some kind of interaction with the contemporary environment. Little enough, to be sure, is known about the conditions of change or of fixity in such a structure; but it is safe to assume that it is accessible to study by experimental methods. Christie (8), for example, has shown that rigidity in problem solution—something which has appeared to be a factor in authoritarian personality structure—increases as a function of experimental frustration.

One may conceive of two opposite approaches to the problem of how to reduce authoritarianism and prejudice; and it may well be that progress will be made in the degree that these two approaches become integrated. The extreme of the one approach is individual psychotherapy; the extreme of the other would be attempts at manipulating the social situation without understanding of the people who live in it.

It should be remarked concerning individual psychotherapy, on authoritarianism of personality, not only that it is impractical but that it is very difficult. The person high on F rarely seeks, but rather resists the idea of psychotherapy; and once a start has been made, the technical problems are trying. One case (57) has been reported that is fairly representative of the psychopathic type of high scorer on F. Four years of therapy with this individual produced no satisfactory progress. To establish any kind of relationship that would involve him in the therapy was difficult enough; and, when a relationship was finally established, it was, as one might expect, an authoritarian one. With the therapist in the role of authority and this patient in the role of authoritarian follower, any progress in the analysis was exceedingly difficult; he would either act out his new role or else leave the situation altogether.

The study with a view to the ultimate control of situations that evoke or inhibit authoritarian behavior is perhaps somewhat more hopeful. Attention will have to be given to every type of social structure ranging from the small group to the society at large. This is a task in which all of the social sciences might well take part. Unless, however, these studies of the social complex take account of the potentialities and readinesses within the individuals involved, the major implication of *The Authoritarian Personality* will have been lost.

It may be hoped that knowledge gained from the intensive study of individuals can be combined with knowledge of group structure and functioning to form an integration of the opposing approaches mentioned above. What group structures, what institutional patterns, what cultural trends appeal to or serve to counteract authoritarian tendencies in personality?

At the present time, group psychotherapy and certain experiments in education seem to offer the best samples of the integration being urged. Freedman and Sweet (19) have recently offered evidence that patients with many features of the F pattern actually respond better in certain forms of group psychotherapy than they do in individual therapy. And many workers are exploring the possibilities of bringing into the classroom some of the techniques for involving the subject and for removing resistance that have been developed in connection with individual psychotherapy. This is a field of great promise as well as great difficulty.

It is not argued, of course, that such an approach is likely to be effective with extreme cases of authoritarianism. Obviously, however, most people are not extreme but "middle" on F, and one may suppose that they are prepared to move in either direction. For them, education in general seems to have some effect, as is indicated by the fact that scores on F and E tend to decrease as amount of education increases. There is evidence that experience with the psychological and social sciences is particularly effective. This is what knowledge of authoritarian personality trends would lead one to expect. Awareness of self and of one's relations to social processes works directly against authoritarianism; one might hope that educational offerings, having such awareness as their objective, will be enormously expanded, as they might easily be.

The preceding remarks have concerned authoritarianism in the adult personality. The prevention of authoritarianism in children is a different, and more hopeful, matter. As has been indicated, knowledge of the kind of child training that favors ego development and the internalization of standards is becoming very widespread in this country, particularly in the middle classes, and a movement toward nonauthoritarian principles and practices is being pushed along by the mass media of communication. The coming of age of another generation might mark an appreciable falling off in the amount of authoritarianism in this country.

CONCLUSION

The Authoritarian Personality was an effort to bring to bear upon the problem of social discrimination an approach that combined psychoanalytic theory of personality, clinical methods for the diagnosis of personality, and modern social-psychological devices for opinion and attitude measurement. The major contribution of the work was the empirical elucidation of the F or Authoritarian personality syndrome. It was shown that prejudice and other social attitudes and ideological trends were functionally related one to another and to this central structure. The conclusion was that these manifestations cannot be fully understood apart from the total personality of the individual who exhibits them. The elucidation of the F-syndrome involved not only the discovery of the major elements or factors that comprise it but the application of a variety of concepts for formulating the way in which personality is organized. Of particular importance was the conceptualization of levels of personality and of the conditions of communication among the levels. These, and other concepts from psychoanalytic, dynamic psychology, were not tested in any crucial way; but so consistent were the findings with them, that one could be left with little doubt as to their power and productivity.

Research that has used *The Authoritarian Personality* as its point of departure has tended, on the whole, to confirm the findings reported there. This research has both sharpened and expanded the picture of the content of the syndrome, and it has demonstrated the relations of this structure to behavior in a wide variety of situations. It has not, unfortunately, *deepened* knowledge of authoritarianism in personality. The accent has been upon quantitative studies of large groups of subjects and a few variables at a time. Such studies are important and economical; but sooner or later one must get back to the individual. A pressing need at this moment is for systematic, comprehensive and carefully conducted interviews with subjects representing the total range of scores on F, and for a method of analysis sufficiently rigorous to provide crucial checks on some of the very numerous propositions concerning the genesis and inner workings of the authoritarian personality syndrome. Such interviews, combined with a variety of projective techniques, would undoubtedly turn up additional variables and provide new insight into the dynamics of authoritarianism. Finally, one might hope that the method of approach exemplified in *The Authoritarian Personality* might be employed in the discovery and elucidation of other patterns of personality.

REFERENCES

1. Adelson, J., & Sullivan, P. Ethnocentrism and Misanthropy. *American Psychologist,* 7, 1952, 330 (abstract).
2. Adorno, T., Frenkel-Brunswik, E., Levinson, D., & Sanford, R. N. *The Authoritarian Personality.* New York: Harper, 1950.

3. Barron, F. X. *Psychotherapy as a Special Case of Personal Interaction: Prediction of its Course.* (Ph.D. dissertation, University of California, Berkeley, 1950.)

4. Bjorklund, E., & Israel, J. The Authoritarian Ideology of Upbringing. Mimeographed. Sociologiska Institutionen, Uppsala, Sweden, 1951.

5. Block, J., & Block, J. An Investigation of the Relationship between Intolerance of Ambiguity and Ethnocentrism. *Journal of Personality* 19, 1951, 303–11.

6. Campbell, D., & McCandless, B. Ethnocentrism, Xenophobia, and Personality. *Human Relations* 4, 1951, 185–92.

7. Chisholm, G. B. The Reestablishment of Peacetime Society. *Psychiatry* 9, 1946, 3–21.

8. Christie, R. *The Effect of Frustration upon Rigidity in Problem Solution.* (Ph.D. dissertation, University of California, Berkeley, 1949.)

9. ————. Changes in Authoritarianism as Related to Situational Factors. *American Psychologist* 7, 1952, 307–8 (abstract).

10. ————, & Garcia, J. Subcultural Variation in Authoritarian Personality. *Journal of Abnormal Social Psychology* 46, 1951, 457–69.

11. Conrad, H., & Sanford, N. Scales for the Measure of War-Optimism: I. Military Optimism II. Optimism on the Consequences of the War. *Journal of Psychology* 16, 1943, 285–311.

12. ————, & Sanford, N. Some Specific War Attitudes of College Students. *Journal of Psychology* 17, 1944, 153–86.

13. Dicks, H. Personality Traits and National Socialist Ideology. *Human Relations* 3, 1950, 111–54.

14. Dombrose, L. A., & Levinson, D. J. Ideological "Militancy" and "Pacifism" in Democratic Individuals. *Journal of Social Psychology* 32, 1950, 101–30.

15. Eager, J., & Smith, B. A Note on the Validity of Sanford's Authoritarian-Equalitarian Scale. *Journal of Abnormal Social Psychology* 47, 1952, 265–67.

16. Erikson, E. H. Hitler's Imagery and German Youth. *Psychiatry,* 5, 1942, 475–93.

17. Eysenck, H. Primary Social Attitudes As Related to Social Class and Political Party. *British Journal of Sociology* 2, 1951, 198–209.

18. Fisher, J. The Memory Process and Certain Psychosocial Attitudes with Special Reference to the Law of Prägnanz: I. Study of Non-Verbal Content. *Journal of Personality* 19, 1951, 406–20.

19. Freedman, M., & Sweet, B. A Theoretical Formulation of Some Features of Group Psychotherapy and Its Implications for Selection of Patients. *International Journal of Group Psychotherapy* 4, 1954, 355–68.

20. Frenkel-Brunswik, E. Motivation and Behavior. *Genetic Psychological Monographs* 26, 1942, 121–265.

21. ————. Further Explorations by a Contributor, in *Studies in the Scope and Method of the Authoritarian Personality,* ed. R. Christie & M. Jahoda. Glencoe, Ill.: Free Press, 1954.

22. ————. & Sanford, N. Some Personality Correlates of Anti-Semitism. *Journal of Psychology* 20, 1945, 271–91.

23. Freud, A. *The Ego and the Mechanisms of Defense.* New York: International Universities Press, 1946.

24. Fromm, E. *Man for Himself.* New York: Rinehart, 1947.

25. ————. *Escape from Freedom.* New York: Farrar & Rinehart, 1941.

26. Goldberg, S., & Stern, G. The Authoritarian Personality and Education. *American Psychologist* 7, 1952, 372–75 (abstract).

27. Gough, H., & Sanford, N. Rigidity as a Psychological Variable. Mimeographed. University of California, Institute of Personality Assessment and Research, Berkeley, 1952.

28. Gump, P. Anti-Democratic Trends and Student Reaction to President Truman's Dismissal of General MacArthur. (Unpublished paper.)

29. Harding, J. A Scale for Measuring Civilian Morale. *Journal of Psychology* 12, 1941, 101–10.

30. Harris, D. B., Gough, H. G., & Martin, W. E. Children's Ethnic Attitudes: II. Relationship to Parental Beliefs Concerning Child Training. *Child Development* 21, 1950, 169–81.

31. Hollander, E. P. Authoritarianism and Leadership Choice in a Military Setting. *American Psychologist* 8, 1953, 368–69.

32. Hyman, H., & Sheatsley, P. The Authoritarian Personality—a Methodological Critique, in *Studies in the Scope and Method of the Authoritarian Personality,* ed. R. Christie & M. Jahoda. Glencoe, Ill.: Free Press, 1954.

33. Institute of Social Research, ed. M. Horkheimer. *Studies in Philosophy and Social Science,* Vol. 9, 1941.

34. Kates, S., & Diab, L. Authoritarian Ideology and Child-Rearing Attitudes. *American Psychologist* 8, 1953, 378 (abstract).

35. Levinson, D., & Huffman, P. Studies in Personality and Ideology: Theory and Measure-

ment of Traditional Family Ideology. Mimeographed. Harvard University, Cambridge, 1952.

36. ———, & Sanford, N. A Scale for the Measurement of Anti-Semitism. *Journal of Psychology* 17, 1944, 339–70.

37. Lewin, K., Lippitt, R., & White, R. Patterns of Aggressive Behavior in Experimentally Created Social Climates. *Journal of Social Psychology* 10, 1939, 271–99.

38. Maslow, A. H. The Authoritarian Character Structure. *Journal of Social Psychology* 18, 1932, 401–11.

39. McGee, H. Measurement of Authoritarianism and Its Relation to Teachers' Classroom Behavior. (Ph.D. dissertation, University of California, Berkeley, 1954.)

40. Milton, O. Presidential Choice and Performance on a Scale of Authoritarianism. *American Psychologist* 7, 1952, 597–98 (abstract).

41. Murray, H. A., et al. *Explorations in Personality.* New York: Oxford University Press, 1938.

42. Reich, W. *The Mass Psychology of Fascism.* New York: Orgone-Institute Press, 1946.

43. Reichard, S. Rorschach Study of the Prejudiced Personality. *American Journal of Orthopsychiatry* 18, 1948, 280–86.

44. Rokeach, M. Generalized Mental Rigidity as a Factor in Ethnocentrism. *Journal of Abnormal Social Psychology* 43, 1948, 259–78.

45. ———. Dogmatism and Opinionation on the Left and on the Right. *American Psychologist* 7, 1952, 310 (abstract).

46. ———. Prejudice, Concreteness of Thinking, and Reification of Thinking. *Journal of Abnormal Social Psychology* 46, 1951, 83–91.

47. ———. The Nature and Meaning of Dogmatism. *Psychological Review* 61, 1954, 194–204.

48. Rosen, E. Differences between Volunteers and Non-Volunteers for Psychological Studies. *Journal of Applied Psychology* 35, 1951, 185–93.

49. Sanford, F. H. *Authoritarianism and Leadership.* Philadelphia: Stephenson Bros., 1950.

50. Sanford, N. The Dynamics of Identification. *Psychological Review* 62, 1955, 106–18.

51. ———. Dominance *versus* Autocracy, and the Democratic Character. *Childhood Education,* November, 1946.

52. ———, Adkins, M., Cobb, E., & Miller, B. Physique, Personality and Scholarship. *Monograph on Sociological Research in Child Development* 8, 1943, 1–705.

53. ———, Conrad, H., & Frank, K. Psychological Determinants of Optimism Regarding the Consequences of the War. *Journal of Psychology* 22, 1946, 207–35.

54. ———, & Conrad, H. Some Personality Correlates of Morale. *Journal of Abnormal Social Psychology* 38, 1943, 3–20.

55. ———, & Conrad, H. High and Low Morale as Exemplified in Two Cases. *Character and Personality* 13, 1944, 207–27.

56. ———. Individual and Social Change in a Community under Pressure: The Oath Controversy. *Journal of Social Issues* 9, 1953, 25–42.

57. ———. Identification with the Enemy: A Case Study of an American Quisling. *Journal of Personality* 15, 1946, 53–58.

58. Shils, E. Authoritarianism: "Right" and "Left," in *Studies in the Scope and Method of The Authoritarian Personality,* ed. R. Christie & M. Jahoda. Glencoe, Ill.: Free Press, 1954.

59. Stagner, R. Fascist Attitudes: Their Determining Conditions. *Journal of Social Psychology* 7, 1936, 438–54.

16

A Classical Critique of the
Authoritarianism Typology

This well-known essay by Shils is an example of the occasional instance when a critique of a major work, in its own right, has come to be recognized as a seminal clarification of the issues raised in that work. There is no need to summarize Shils' fluent statement, but among his many assertions, the reader should note two aspects of his remarks that are of especially broad implication for the study of personality and politics.

First, in the assertion that provides his title: Shils argues that the personality type equated with *right-wing* extremism by the authors of *The Authoritarian Personality* is also consistent with attachment to such *left-wing* authoritarian doctrines as the dogmatic Stalinism, which was one of the readily available belief options during the period immediately following World War II, when the original research on authoritarian personality patterns was conducted. But this is an argument that extends far beyond the specific issues of the authoritarian personality type. Shils is advancing a methodological assertion similar to Lasswell's emphasis on the desirability of studying the personalities of individuals who perform "functionally similar" roles (see introduction to Selection 11). His argument suggests that, even *in principle,* there is no reason to expect strong connections between underlying psychological dispositions and particular substantive political beliefs that happen to be held by some socially defined conglomeration of human beings. However, it *is* reasonable to expect to find strong connections once the analyst identifies patterns of belief and behavior that seem similar in terms of the contributions they might be expected to make to the psychic economy of the individual who holds them (also see the "functionalist" discussions by Smith and Katz in Selections 2 and 10 and the Browning and Jacob empirical analysis in Selection 21).

The second (and related) aspect emerges in Shils' incisive observations on the connection between personality needs and role performance. This aspect of his discussion complements the theoretical essays by Bendix and Levinson reprinted in the first portion of this anthology. Not only does Shils point out that individual behavior in actual institutional roles entails a good bit more than simply extensions of personality dynamics; he also specifies, in considerable detail, the precise ways that role and personality are likely to interconnect under varying, specifiable circumstances.

AUTHORITARIANISM: "RIGHT" AND "LEFT"

Edward A. Shils

By the end of the nineteenth century, it was widely believed in continental Europe and in the United States that political institutions and activities could be described as either "radical" or "conservative." Each term had its synonyms and each admitted of variations in both directions. Radicalism moved off in one direction towards socialism, evolutionary and revolutionary, and ultimately towards anarchism, and in the other direction towards liberalism and the moderate position. On the other side, conservatism by accentuating its peculiar characteristics became reactionary, or it could modify itself in the opposite direction and move towards the "center." Radicalism was "left" and conservatism was "right." Continental and later British and American political intellectuals came to accept the validity of the dichotomy of right and left in political life even where it did not use the terminology which flourished particularly in radical and socialist circles. Every political programme could, it was thought, be placed on this scale and be fairly judged.

The view rested, especially among socialists, on the belief that fundamentally each of the main political positions formed a coherent and indissoluble unity. Thus, for example, conservatism, according to this notion, was characterized by attachment to private property, hostility towards universal male or adult suffrage, rejection of freedom of association and assembly for working men, an acknowledgment of the rightfulness of self-enrichment by individual exertion, a repugnance for humanitarian and social welfare legislation, devotion to economic and social inequality derived from a belief in the inequality of human qualities and achievements, disapproval of state regulation of private economic activity, etc. This was called the point of view of the Right. And each element in it was thought to be peculiar and necessary to the right-wing outlook.

In contrast to it stood the point of view of the Left. This entailed a general derogation of private property, a preference for political democracy including the universal enjoyment of all civil liberties, a rejection of pecuniary goals and standards, the espousal of humanitarian goals to be achieved through social legislation, the aspiration towards economic and social equality based on a sense of the fundamentally equal dignity of all men and preference for the collective organization or regulation of economic life. The Left also believed in progress and therefore welcomed change. It was antagonistic towards religious institutions and beliefs and it had great faith in science as the liberator and benefactor of humanity. It believed that man's individual merit and not family connections should determine his position in life. The Right was opposed to the Left in all these respects and in all others. The opposition on every point was accentuated by the fact that the mere contention of the value of some institution or practice by the Right made it into a target of leftist criticism. For example, patriotism or loyalty to the national state found its counterpart in the Marxist claim that the workingman has no fatherland. The seating arrangements in legislative chambers, ranging from extreme left to extreme

Reprinted with permission of The Macmillan Company from *Studies in the Scope and Method of The Authoritarian Personality,* by Richard Christie and Marie Jahoda, eds., pp. 24–49. Copyright by The Free Press, a Corporation 1954.

right, seemed to confirm the inevitable nature of this continuum of political outlooks.

Nor can there be any doubt that in the decades surrounding the turn of the century in continental political life this simplification did have a certain descriptive truth. There are good reasons for it. Continental domestic politics through much of the nineteenth century, centered to a large extent around the ideals of the Liberal Enlightenment and the "ideas of 1789." Particularly to the Radical or Liberal parties or movements, which were usually in opposition and therefore remote from the complex of fine and overlapping differences which separate those political parties which are in the actual arena of political power, did it appear as if all parties were located along the continuum of right and left. "Leftist" parties in opposition tended often to define their own position on an issue simply by taking what they thought was the diametrically opposite position to that of their ruling opponents. This strengthened the conviction that right and left were the two basic directions of political life which pervaded the entire outlook of every party and group and it gave to each the appearance of necessary and unavoidable unity.

The Bolshevik Revolution did not seem at first to constitute an infringement on this classification. It was obviously the achievement of a group which stood at the extreme left and which refused to admit that any other group could be more left than it. Demands for more revolutionary action from within its own ranks were labelled as "infantile leftism." More revolutionary demands emanating from outside its ranks were derogated as petit-bourgeois romanticism or adventurism and therewith transferred "rightward" on the continuum. To observers among the western intellectuals, the Bolshevik claims recommended themselves as wholly just. The Bolsheviks were seeming to realize the most extreme leftist program by equally leftist methods. Many liberal and socialist intellectuals in the decade after the first world war did not see anything fundamental to censure in the Bolshevik regime. Even though to some of them a few actions seemed regrettable, such as the terror and the suppression of all opposition parties, that seemed to them to be only a tactical necessity which an obnoxious *ancien regime* and a ruthless counter-revolution justified and made expedient. Bolshevism seemed to be on the road to the realization of the classical programme of the socialist Left and the Stalin Constitution of 1935 seemed to give veracity to this interpretation.

The appearance of fascism in Italy and Germany caused little embarrassment to those whose political *Weltanschauung* was built within the framework of the Right-Left continuum. The Marxist interpretation of fascism as the penultimate stage in the polarization of all political life into the extreme Right and the extreme Left prevailed almost universally in the 1930s in many intellectual circles. Fascism was seen as an accentuation of bourgeois conservatism, a conservatism driven to desperation by the inevitable crisis of capitalism. It was devoted to private property, opposed to political democracy and humanitarianism, it was inegalitarian and antiscientific and it sought to stabilize the existing social order. The fact that it sought to introduce fundamental changes in the status quo which it was alleged to be stabilizing was less of an embarrassment than the fact that its elite did not consist for the most part of big business men or that it instituted a far reaching scheme of regulations of private business enterprise.

This was not the first time that Marxists were embarrassed by the insufficiency of the Right-Left scheme. Tory Radicalism in nineteenth century Great Britain and the social legislation of Bismarckian Germany had both created difficulties for the Marxist viewpoint. The former had been dismissed as an amalgam of romanticism and hypocrisy, the latter as *State* Socialism and hence fraudulent. Georges Sorel's ideas which contained elements conventionally associated with both right and left were written off by Marxists as Fascist.

Ingenious and erudite Marxist writers in the late '30s and early '40s sought to overcome the embarrassment for their system of thought by the argument that nazism was the servant of German capitalism. Through resourceful arguments they sought to demonstrate the capitalistic nature of nazism while at the very same time rendering the interpretation insecure by the impressive body of data which they presented.

During this time, however, events in the Soviet Union, particularly the "purges," the abortion laws, the introduction of school fees, the restriction of progressive education, the persistence and growth of pronounced inequalities in income and status, the reemergence of patriotism as an official policy—these and many other backslidings from the purest ideals of leftist extremism placed a further burden upon the now rickety structure of right and left as a scheme for political analysis.

What had been looked upon as a seamless unity was turning out to be a constellation of diverse elements which could be recombined in constellations which had not for many years been imagined. Hostility towards private property was now seen to be capable of combination with anti-Semitism, inequality, the repression of civil liberties, etc. Welfare legislation was seen to enter into combination with political oligarchy, the elimination of civil liberties was combined with an increase in equalitarianism. In short, what had once appeared to be a simple unidimensional scheme now turned out to be a complicated multidimensional pattern in which there were many different political positions. The attachment to private property was now perceived as compatible both with sympathy with humanitarianism and with a disapproval of welfare legislation, the respect for civil liberties could fit with either socialism or capitalism, equalitarianism could go with either democracy or oligarchy. But above all, the two poles of the continuum Right and Left which were once deemed incompatible and mutually antagonistic were discovered to overlap in many very striking respects.

Fascism and Bolshevism, only a few decades ago thought of as worlds apart, have now been recognized increasingly as sharing many very important features. Their common hostility towards civil liberties, political democracy, their common antipathy for parliamentary institutions, individualism, private enterprise, their image of the political world as a struggle between morally irreconcilable forces, their belief that all their opponents are secretly leagued against them and their own predilection for secrecy, their conviction that all forms of power are in a hostile world concentrated in a few hands and their own aspirations for concentrated and total power—all of these showed that the two extremes had much in common.

The prejudice however dies very hard. Even those of us who have seen the spurious nature of the polarity of "right" and "left" still find it hard to dispense with it. There has been no recoalescence or regrouping of the constituent ideas of our political outlook which is at once sufficiently simple and convenient for our use. In general conversation we still use these terms although we know that they are at most a shorthand which will have to be replaced by particulars as soon as the discussion is joined.

The obsolete belief that all political, social and economic philosophies can be classified on the Right-Left continuum however dies very hard. A recent and very instructive instance of this steadfast adherence to the Right-Left polarity is the monumental investigation into *The Authoritarian Personality*. An examination of the manner in which political preconceptions enter into one of the most elaborate social-psychological investigations hitherto undertaken illuminates important problems of procedure in social research and offers opportunities for the further interpretation of a body of rich data. The Left-Right dichotomy is present not only in the general interpretive chapters written by Professor Adorno but even in the severely empirical chapters written by Professor Levinson and Dr. Sanford. The entire team of investigators proceeds as if there were an unilinear scale of political and social attitudes at the extreme right of which stands the Fascist—the product and proponent of monopoly-capitalism and at the other end what the authors call the complete democrat who—as I shall presently demonstrate—actually holds the views of the non-Stalinist Leninist.[1]

The antidemocrat or proto-Fascist—the authoritarian personality—is distinguished by anti-Semitism, ethnocentrism and politicoeconomic conservatism. He is rigid in his beliefs—although no evidence for this is presented—he makes frequent use of stereotypes in his political perceptions and judgments, he is sympathetic with the use of violence against his enemies, he distinguishes sharply between his "ingroup" and the "outgroups" which he interprets as menacing his security. More concretely he shares the most commonplace of the vulgar cliches about Jews, foreigners, reformers, homosexuals, intellectuals, and he admires strong men, business men, successful men, manly men who have no tender side or who allow it no play in their lives.

At the other extreme is the democrat who is sympathetic with the outcasts, the underprivileged, the discriminated against ethnic minorities, who sees through the hollowness of patriotism, who is alert to the defects of politicians and the selfishness of business men; governmental control of economic life appears to him necessary and just. He thinks wealth is not a great good, science the source of truth and progress. Indeed according to the expectations of Professor Levinson, he rejects every tenet of the antidemocrat's faith and *by implication* believes the opposite. I stress the denotative nature of the democratic beliefs as this study views them because the positive beliefs of the "democrat" are seldom presented in the questionnaire (only the "politicoeconomic conservatism" scale contains positive items). For the most part "democrats" are distinguished from "antidemocrats" through their rejection of a considerable series of illiberal opinions which are the stock in trade of the xenophobic fundamentalist, the lunatic fringe of the detractors of the late President Roosevelt. The more extreme opinions, in great measure, are those expressed before the war by the fanatical publishers of periodicals of tiny circulation and short lives, by the would-be leaders of the small conventicles of nativist saviors of the United States from Jewish and foreign influences and by American Legionnaires when on a campaign of righteousness. Those who reject these opinions are residually defined as "democrats"; the positive opinions they are expected to approve in the politicoeconomic conservatism questionnaire are most often the commonplaces of the "left" intelligentsia—of those who approved the New Deal and more particularly those who in the late '40s sympathized with Mr. Henry Wallace and the Progressive party. The positive items on the P.E.C. questionnaire are Wallaceite cliches to which at the time Communists and fellow travellers gave their assent as well as persons of humane sentiments who did not share the more elaborate ideology of the Stalinoid and fellow-travelling followers of the Progressive "line." [2] The questionnaire, concerned as it legitimately was to distinguish nativists and fundamentalists from others, put all those rejecting the nativistic-fundamentalist view expressed in each questionnaire item into the same category—distinguishing them only with respect to the strength of their disagreement. This failure to discriminate the substantially different types of outlook which could be called liberal, liberal collectivist, radical, Marxist, etc., is not just the outcome of the deficiency of the questionnaire technique in general nor does it arise from carelessness. It flows from the authors' failure to perceive the distinctions between totalitarian Leninism (particularly in a period of Peoples Front maneuvers), humanitarianism and New Deal interventionism.[3]

II

Opinion surveys are in themselves of no great importance in increasing our understanding of human behavior and the failure to measure the distribution of authoritarian attitudes would not of itself be especially interesting apart from the striking text which it provides for observations concerning the influence of political ideas and preferences on the categories of empirical analysis in the social sciences. In *The Authoritarian Personality,* however, this narrowness of political imagination, this holding fast to a deforming intellectual tradition, has greater significance. *The Authoritarian Personality* in its two major sections—in the sections by Levinson, Sanford and Dr. Else Frenkel-Brunswik—follows a quite highly integrated plan of analysis. The extreme cases of democratic and antidemocratic outlook (the High and Low Scorers on the various scales) which Dr. Frenkel-Brunswik analyzed more intensively were selected by virtue of their performance on the questionnaires. As a result it is highly probable that a number of authoritarians of the "Left" have been included among those who scored "low" in Anti-Semitism, Ethnocentrism, Political-Economic-Conservatism or Fascism. In her analysis Dr. Frenkel-Brunswik concentrated on the interpretation of the major differences between the deeper dispositions of the High Scorers and the Low Scorers and paid practically no attention to the Low Scorers in the questionnaire who in clinical interviews showed the traits of the High Scorers.[4]

Among the 35 low scorers, there were at least five "leftist." In most of the categories of deeper cognitive and emotional disposition in which Low Scorers differ from High Scorers, there is almost always a significant number of Low Scorers whose deeper dispositions are closer to the High Scorer than to the Low Scorer. In conformity with the preconceived idea that authoritarianism is a characteristic of the Right and the corresponding notion that there is no authoritarianism on the "Left," there is no analysis of these deviant Low Scorers. It would be presumptuous to assert that it was always the same low scoring individuals who repeatedly received the high ratings in the clinical interviews and that these deviant low scorers were in the main the five "leftists" [5] among the Low Scorers. It is however a reasonable interpretation, which would justify a reexamination of the original data.

Even if, however, these five "leftists" were not the deviant "highs" among the Low Scorers, the investigators' belief that authoritarianism and its concomitants belongs to the Right and that the Right and Left, being at the two poles of the continuum, can never meet, has prevented them from seeing what appears to be very evident to a more detached eye.

The material gathered and the hypothesis employed by the Berkeley investigators provides a most valuable approach to the study of Bolshevism and to the reevaluation of the idea of the political spectrum.

But the investigators accept the view that political opinions are located on a right-left continuum and because their political conceptions are exceedingly unsophisticated, they have described political, social and economic attitudes by sets of concrete cliches expressed in the phraseology of current usage.

Obviously a Fascist who says that the Jews have monopolized almost all the important posts in the government is concretely different from the Bolshevik who asserts that the small circle of big business men control not only the economic life but the intellectual, political and religious life of the country. Concretely these two views are very different—one we know to be the usual paranoid anti-Semitism—the other sounds like a somewhat crude social science proposition in which many intellectuals in the West believe. Yet looked at from another point of view, they are strikingly similar. Both aver that a small group has with doubtful legitimacy concentrated the power of the country in their hands.

The Berkeley group have emphasized, among others, the following deeper tendencies of the authoritarian of the Right:

a) Extreme hostility towards "outgroups";
b) Extreme submissiveness towards the "ingroups";
c) The establishment of sharp boundaries between the group of which one is a member and all other groups;
d) The tendency to categorize persons with respect to certain particular qualities and make "all or none" judgments;
e) A vision of the world as a realm of conflict;
f) Disdain for purely theoretical or contemplative activities;
g) A repugnance for the expression of sentiments, particularly sentiments of affection;
h) Belief that oneself and one's group are the objects of manipulative designs and that oneself and one's group can survive only by the manipulation of others;
i) The ideal of a conflictless wholly harmonious society in contrast with an environing or antecedent conflictful chaos. There are other properties as well but these will serve for illustrative purposes.

Anyone well acquainted with the works of Lenin and Stalin,[6] or with European and American Communists of recent decades, will immediately recognize that the cognitive and emotional orientations enumerated above correspond very closely to the central features of the Bolshevik *Weltanschauung*. Let us examine briefly their Bolshevik form in the order in which we have listed them:

a) The demand for complete and unqualified loyalty to the Party.
b) The insistence on the necessary conflict of interests between the working class of which the Party is the leader and all other classes and the need for unrelenting conflict against these other classes, even in times of apparent truce and cooperation.
c) The continuous application of the criteria of Party interests in judging every person and situation and the need to avoid eclecticism in doctrine and opportunism and compromise in practice.
d) The stress on the class characteristics of individuals and the interpretation of their actions in the light of their class position exclusively.
e) The belief that all history is the history of class conflict.
f) The denial of the existence of pure truth and attack on those who espouse pure science or "art for art's sake."
g) The belief that the expression of sentiment is an expression of weakness and that it interferes with the correct interpretation of reality and the choice of the right course of action.
h) The belief in the ubiquitousness of the influence of "Wall Street," the "City," the "Big Banks," "Heavy Industry," "200 families," etc. and their masked

control over even the most remote spheres of life and the counter-belief in the necessity to penetrate organizations and achieve complete control over them.

i) The ideal of the classless society, without private property in the instruments of production and hence without conflict, the "realm of freedom" where man will cease his alienation and become truly human.

There are important differences between the two authoritarianisms and we shall deal with some of these below. But what is so impressive is their very far-reaching overlap. Let us take for example the specific items in the F (fascism) scale employed for the discrimination of persons with Fascist potentialities from those who are free of such potentialities.

Let us begin with the statements indicative of "Authoritarian Submission" [7] which is defined as a "submissive, uncritical attitude towards idealized moral authorities of the ingroup."

"1. Obedience and respect for authority are the most important virtues children should learn.

"4. Science has a place but there are many important things that can never possibly be understood by the human mind.

"8. Every person should have complete faith in some supernatural power whose decisions he obeys without question.

"21. Young people sometimes get rebellious ideas but as they grow up they ought to get over them and settle down.

"23. What this country needs most, more than laws and political programmes is a few courageous, devoted, tireless leaders in whom the people can put their faith.

"42. No sane, normal, decent person could ever think of hurting a close friend or relative."

Agreement with these sentences is indicative of belief in the rightness of submission to familial, political and religious authorities. At first glance, they appear to have nothing to do with the Communist attitude. They counsel respect for the family, and a refusal of respect for the powers of science. Modern revolutionaries including the Communists, especially outside the Soviet Union, have long been inclined toward the denial of familial authority and a conviction of the potency of science. There is a very obvious similarity concerning faith in political leaders who serve their followers with an unresting devotion. The Communist adulation of Stalin and of the national Party leaders could certainly not be exceeded by the awe in which Hitler was held by fervent Nazis—and the attitudes towards these two leaders, which party functionaries in Nazi Germany and the Soviet Union have tried to arouse in their respective peoples, through propaganda, certainly have very much in common.

But even where there are genuine surface differences, as with regard to family and science, there are also some similarities in the deeper dispositions associated with these particular concrete beliefs. It is one of the Berkeley group's most valuable hypotheses, for which there is plausible evidence, that the loyalty and submissiveness of the authoritarian personality (the High Scorer) is a reaction-formation against his hostility towards his parents' and particularly towards his father's authority, which he experienced, whether correctly or not, as harshly repressive. The Low Scorers on the other hand either reject their parental authority openly and without fear or, as deviant Low Scorers, they respect parental authority in the same manner as the Rightist Authoritarian High Scorer. Thus at the level of the deeper depositions, the two types of authoritarians share the same attitude towards their familial authorities. Indeed, in the matter of alleged victimization by parents, an unusually large number of eight of the low scorers felt they had been victimized by their parents while none of the Low Scorers expressed contrary opinions. Likewise five of the Low Scorers were capricious rebels against their parents—an attitude selected by the investigators as indicative of an authoritarian disposition. We see then that as far as hostility towards parents is concerned, there are Low Scorers who have the same overt attitude as the High Scorers. More fundamentally, moreover, the refusal to acknowledge the sacredness of parental authority exists in both groups. The difference arises on the level of the conscious expression of sentiment in which there is a genuine difference—a difference which should not however obscure the equally genuine similarity.

Furthermore, is the difference as it bears on our main thesis, as wide as the interpretation presented in the preceding paragraph would allow? The concentration of loyalty and obedience in the relationship with the political leader, such as is demanded of and actually given by many Communists, is all encompassing. The "left" authoritarians would deny familial authority, not as the liberal tradition sought, on behalf of the freedom of the individual, but rather on behalf of the authority of the Party and of the Party leader. Communists in western countries preach the relaxation of family loyalties where these interfere with loyalty to the Party and they exploit and manipulate them where they can for the benefit of the Party. This is not to say that in those circles, wittingly or unwittingly, permeated by the outlook of the Liberal Enlightenment and which have furthermore experienced the relaxation of kinship ties produced by many developments in modern society, there is not a genuine belief that for the benefit of the individual's freedom and the development of his individuality, there should be a minimum of parental authority. All I wish to do here is to point out that the anti-familistic sentiments which find freer expression in the leftists' authoritarian personality than they do in the rightists' personality are different in their nature from the preference for looser family ties sought by moderate liberalism. The latter is what mainly engages Dr. Frenkel-Brunswik's attention and it is an error to confuse it with the rebellious type of antifamilism which is found among the Low Scorers.

We must also examine the difference between the High and Low Scorers concerning their attitudes towards science. There is a clear difference between these two groups in this explicit approval of science. The High Scorers are more superstitious and are more sympathetic to the claims of religious authority while practically none of the Low Scorers are antagonistic towards science. Is this not also a real difference between the two authoritarianisms? It might be. We should however recall that for the Communist who vigorously proclaims the "scientific" basis of his convictions, science is not the discovery of truths hitherto unknown by an individual scientist working freely within the framework of a scientific tradition; it is rather the corroboration of the truth of the writings of Marx, Engels, Lenin, and more recently, Stalin. The tradition of liberalism and revolutionism are both "scientistic" but the science to which western Communists give their allegiance today is as authoritarian as their other beliefs. Once more, therefore, the affinity between "right" and "left" emerges and here too it could probably have been perceived by the Berkeley group were they themselves not so enmeshed in their doctrine.

The preoccupation with power is another feature of the "antidemocratic" outlook according to the findings of *The Authoritarian Personality*. They define this as a "preoccupation with the dominance-subordination, strong-weak, leader-follower dimension; identification with power figures; overemphasis upon the conventionalized attributes of the ego; exaggerated assertion of strength and toughness." [8] The presence or absence of this syndrome is tested by agreement with the following assertions:

"2. No weakness or difficulty can hold us back if we have enough will power.

"13. What the youth needs most is strict discipline, rugged determination, and the will to work and fight for family and country.

"19. An insult to our honour should always be punished.

"22. It is best to use some pre-war authorities in Germany to keep order and prevent chaos.

"23. What this country needs most, more than laws and political programmes, is a few courageous, tireless, devoted leaders in whom the people can put their faith.

"26. People can be divided into two distinct classes: the weak and the strong.

"28. Most people don't realize how much our laws are controlled by plots hatched in secret places." [9]

For the most part, these items are quite discriminating between High and Low Scorers. Here too, however, the concrete content of the assertions—mainly cliches abominated by "progressive intellectuals"—blurs the distinction between leftist authoritarians and reasonable persons of humanitarian, equalitarian dispositions. In any case, careful examination of the deeper elements in the test sentences reveal numerous points of affinity with leftist authoritarianism. The stress on the value of persistence and determination is always present in the Communist image of the true Bolshevik, of the effective Party member who works on, even against great odds, sustained by confidence in the final victory. The importance accorded to discipline likewise figures centrally in the Communist doctrine of the good Party member. The difference here is that the right totalitarian whose reaction-formations are very strong, represses his rebellious sentiments towards family and country and instead gives them his loyalty; the Communist whose hostility against these collectivities is unrepressed, subjects himself to the discipline of the Party.

The dichotomy between the weak and the strong is also of course very prominent in Communist thought. The weak, the declining lower middle classes, are worthy only of contempt—only the powerful class enemy is worthy of being taken seriously. In Communist thought the weakness/strength dichotomy is almost as fundamental as the Party/non-Party dichotomy. The Communist fascination by power is manifest in a common tendency to exaggerate the strength of the powerful and the weakness of the weak.

Finally, with respect to the belief in conspiracies in modern society—the Leninist-Stalinist theory of politics is scarcely less conspiratorial than the Protocols of the Elders of Zion. In the latter instance it is the Jews who are the conspirators, in the former, the leaders of the bourgeoisie, once British and now American. It is the Communists who believe that wars are brought about by small cliques of munitions makers and bankers, that a small number of business men control the press in order to guarantee the power of their class and that economic life itself in western society is controlled by a small number of monopolists whose actions and decisions are hidden from the public eye. It is through these conspiratorial actions that the bourgeoisie conducts the class struggle and it is through a sharply defined band of professional revolutionaries inspired by Leninist doctrine that the working class defends itself and contends for its own class interests.

III

In the preceding section we have argued that the questionnaires were designed to disclose not the authoritarian personality as such but rather the "Right"—the nativist-fundamentalist authoritarian. This restriction of range of interest we believe rested on the proposition that political opinions are distributed on a unilinear scale and that the Left being at the other end of the scale from the Right was of necessity its opposite in every respect. Finally we have contended that as a result of this restriction of attention, the investigators have failed to observe that at the left pole of their continuum, there is to be found an authoritarianism impressively like the Authoritarianism of the Right.

It is our view that the resemblance becomes vividly apparent once we move from the level of the questionnaire to that of the data provided by the interview. This is so because the contents of the questionnaire are composed of the concrete cliches of nativist thought and the negative cliches (with a few positive cliches) of "progressive" thought during the period when the Communist followed a Peoples Front policy. As a product of the wartime collaboration, Communist tactics and a well intentioned lack of political and economic sophistication, the intellectual currency of American humanitarian liberalism for some years was much influenced by a Marxist outlook.

If we go below the surface of the concrete cliche to the deeper cognitive and emotional dispositions, such as Dr. Frenkel-Brunswik observed through her clinical interviews, the analogies and incongruities in rightist and leftist authoritarianism would become much more obvious. We shall now select some of the major categories which she employs to pursue our search for similarities a little further, and while doing so to formulate some of the major differences.

We have already asserted that both authoritarianisms were characterized by hostility towards parents. That of the Right is usually covered over by respect as a reaction-formation but like that of the Left it often breaks out into capricious rebellion.

Among Low Scorers we find a sizable minority (seven) who think that they were "victimized" by their siblings, a belief even more common among the High Scorers. Six Low Sorers reject their siblings[10] allegedly on grounds of principle, a symptom of left authoritarianism which tends to justify all its actions in terms of general principles in contrast with the more emotional justifications of the rightist authoritarian when his defensive reaction-formation against his own rebelliousness breaks down. Both authoritarianisms reveal reaction-formations against their hostility towards siblings—the rightists by idealizing their actual siblings, and the leftists by rejecting their actual siblings but constructing the spurious sibling relationship of comradeliness with their fellow members of the Party, in which exploitation and manipulation of comrades, especially new recruits, is covered with protestations of solidarity. Leninist ideology which asserts the solidarity of the working classes across national boundaries, without a trace of benevolent sentiment such as could be found among more humanitarian socialists, certainly conforms with this interpretation.

A very substantial difference between the two authoritarianisms seems to exist regarding the sex. Those on the "Right" combine great preoccupation with sexual activity with a very tense demand for sexual purity and propriety. The leftists, aided by the liberal tradition of weakening repressive sexual conventions in favor of a freer expression of affection between the sexes, do not insist on sexual purity and propriety in the same way. Much less emotion is aroused by sexual behavior which deviates from conventions, e.g. homosexuality. Both are below the surface antipathetic to "bourgeois" sexual morality but as in the case of hostility, alienation from or rebellion against the parents, the leftists feel much less need to defend themselves from the painful emotions aroused by this antipathy. Nonetheless, even among the Low Scorers, there were as many as ten who followed the High Scorers' pattern of "rejection of the id" and seven who shared the rightist authoritarian pattern of sharply distinguishing between sexuality and love.[11]

In their attitudes towards other persons, left and right authoritarianisms again reveal basic similarities. Both are distrustful and suspicious. As many as six of the Low Scorers show this authoritarian trait and the behavior of Communists gives repeated evidence of a deep lying suspicion even towards comrades, to say nothing of their contempt and distrust for persons outside the Party. The need in which every comrade stands to scrutinize his actions and those of his closest associates in the Party to discover and eradicate traces of "deviations" is a part of this generalized distrust, for which the assertions of comradeliness and fraternal solidarity are only reaction formations.

Rightist authoritarians prefer a hierarchical scale of human beings and in this they show their aggressiveness and contempt towards their inferiors and their submissiveness towards their superiors—both of whom they sharply distinguish from themselves. Liberalism has historically been more equalitarian but it is only at the revolutionary extreme that we find an intense claim for complete equality. Doctrines are often adopted only because they are part of a cultural tradition or because they conform with more general standards which are embedded in that tradition, but they can also be espoused because they function as a reaction-formation in the face of practices which diverge widely from the imperatives of the doctrine. So it seems to be with the equalitarianism which Dr. Frenkel-Brunswik finds in such predominance among her Low Scorers. The rigid hierarchy of the Communist party, the very strong feelings about the moral inferiority of various classes, the contempt for non-Communists—these are hardly the benign equalitarianism which the Berkeley group think is characteristic of the "left" sector of the political continuum.

Dr. Frenkel-Brunswik also finds the disposition to blame others (extra-punitiveness) to be characteristic of rightist authoritarianism in contrast with the relative freedom from guilt feelings or excessive guilt feelings which she finds among the Low Scorers. Excessive guilt feelings and the denial of one's own guilt are however very intimately related to one another. The latter is often only the mechanism of defense brought into play by the strength of the former. Does not Communist doctrine and daily practice attribute the ills of the world to the actions of the non-Communists, and does not this usual self-exculpation from the responsibility for every error and defeat alternate in the history of Communism with extraordinary outbursts of confessions of guilt in persons who had previously exceeded all others in attributing guilt to the rest of the world? Are not the Communist "trials"—not just the famous purges, but those which take place regularly within even the smaller units of Communist parties—organized demands for self-accusation—and do they not often succeed in eliciting the now well-known catalogues of vices of which errant Communists accuse themselves? Hence although some of the manifestations may be different and although the jargon is certainly different, it does not seem reasonable to deny that there are fairly close affinities between the two authoritarianisms in this respect too.

One final instance of the affinity will be selected. The rightist authoritarians are correctly asserted to be "intolerant of ambiguity." They demand definitiveness and freedom from vagueness in distinctions which they regard as crucial. Their beliefs must be unqualified; there must be no doubt and there must be no restrictions to the validity of their beliefs. Their actions too must be unequivocal and always on the right side of the clearly defined boundary which separates good and evil. Six of the Low Scorers possess this "intolerance of ambiguity" and although it is unjustified on the basis of the data available at present[12] to impute it to the five leftists included among the Low Scorers, it is certainly justifiable to regard this characteristic as a very important one in leftist authoritarianism. It is of course a common property of alienated sects of many kinds, religious, political and literary, but it is especially noticeable in leftist sectarianism and particularly in the Communist party. There, no judgment can be left in suspension, there must always be a clear prescription which lays down the correct "line." Indeed the very conception of a *correct line* springs from the need never to confront an ambiguous situation. This is of course closely related to the need for clear boundaries to which we have already referred. The Bolshevik rule that when temporary tactical collaboration with other groups is necessary, the greatest pains must be taken to retain the complete identity of the Party and to avoid any trend of collaboration which at any point might approximate a genuine fusion provides evidence that the "intolerance of ambiguity" in the definition of situations is certainly not a monopoly of the authoritarianism of the Right.

The same process of assimilation of the extremes of right and left which we have performed on the preceding pages could be continued for many others of the deeper cognitive and emotional dispositions which are treated by Dr. Frenkel-Brunswik. We have dealt with most of the more important ones. Further examination would only repeat and refine what we have already set forth: great affinities in most of the underlying dispositions (except for sexual preoccupations) and superficial differences connected with the different concrete objects of love and hatred which the authoritarians select or which arise from differences in the strength and frequency of certain defensive mechanisms such as repression and reaction-formation.

The authors of *The Authoritarian Personality* have demonstrated in a more plausible manner than any previous investigators that there is a determinate relationship between particular attitudes towards public objects and symbols and "deeper" cognitive and emotional attitudes or dispositions.[13] There are many technical scientific questions concerning the adequacy of the canons of precise interpretation of the interview data, and earlier sections of this paper have criticized the conceptual scheme used in the analysis of political orientations. Nonetheless the consistency of the results as well as the statistical significance of many of the more important differences provide grounds for accepting their claim that general disposition and particular concrete political attitudes are intimately related.

The authors are not however content with this conclusion. Their interest is to estimate the probability of fascism in the United States. By their analysis of personality structures, they seek to predict which types of persons will accept Fascist propaganda and become Fascists. They assume except for a few passages where the Marxist heritage reasserts itself that political behavior is a function of deeper personality characteristics. Social structure only plays the role of setting off the chain of personality-impelled actions. Once these are started, political activity and the political system take their form directly from the content of the impulses and beliefs of those participating in them.[14] The entire discussion is very remote from the actual working of institutions—the interviewers did not seek to obtain information about how the subjects actually behaved in their workshops or offices, in their churches and voluntary associations, in their trade union meetings, etc. The authors tell us nothing of the *actual* roles of their subjects and for this reason, they encounter no obstacles to their view that political conduct follows from personality traits.

Yet it is obvious that this is so only within very broad limits and under rather special circumstances. The expectations of our fellow men are certainly of very great weight in the determination of our conduct—to varying degrees, of course, depending on our responsive capacities or our social sensitivity. Persons of quite different dispositions, as long as they have some reasonable measure of responsiveness to the expectations of others will behave in a more or less uniform manner, when expectations are relatively uniform. Naturally not all of them will be equally zealous or enthusiastic about the action which they perform in accordance with the expectations of particular colleagues, superiors and inferiors who are present and in accordance with the expectations symbolized in abstract rules, traditions and material objects. To a large extent, large enough indeed to enable great organizations to operate in a quite predictable manner, they will conform despite the possibly conflicting urges of their personalities. The foreign policy of a country is not ordinarily a direct and primary resultant of the personality of the foreign minister even though aspects of his personality will enter into his policy. The traditions of his country, the realistic perception of the international situation and of the situation with which he is presented by his civil servants, the expectations of his colleagues in the government, the demands of the leaders of his party who wish to be reelected as well as his own conceptions of justice, of the national interest, of superior and inferior nations, etc.—all weigh in the balance in which policy is decided. The position of a civil servant or a business executive in the middle ranks of the hierarchy of this organization is even more restrictive of the range of freedom enjoyed by the personality qualities of the individual than is that of a leader or high official.

Now it is certainly true that these actions are not completely divorced from the personality of the actor. He must have sufficient sensitivity to the expectations of others, he must be capable of understanding the symbols in his situation. He must be oriented towards the approval of his colleagues and of his constituency and he must have some degree of reality-orientation which enables him to persist in a course once undertaken. Other qualities are necessary too for this capacity to act in a diversity of situations but they are all compatible with a fairly wide range of variation in such categories as tolerance of ambiguity, distrust and suspicion, preoccupation with sexual concerns, aggressiveness towards outgroups, and others of the sort dealt with by the Berkeley group. The Berkeley group has no realization of the extent and importance for the proper functioning of any kind of society of this kind of adaptiveness to institutional roles. For them conformity is only compulsive conformity, adherence to conventions is rigid conventionalism, both of which are obviously more closely related to the substantive content of the dispositional system than the ordinary run of conformity and respect for conventions which enables any society to run peacefully and with some satisfaction to its members.

Their belief that personality traits dominate public behavior has more truth when we turn to situations which have no prior organization, where there is, in other words, no framework of action set for the newcomer by the expectations of those already on the scene. A new political party, a newly formed religious sect will thus be more amenable to the expressive behavior of the personalities of those who make them up than an ongoing government or private business office or university department with its traditions of scientific work. Personality will play a greater part in positions of leadership than in positions in the lower levels of an organization, because by the nature of the organization the higher positions have a greater freedom from elaborate expectations of fixed content. Personality structure will also be more determinant of political activities when the impulses and the defenses of the actors are extremely intense, e.g., when the compulsive elements are powerful and rigid or when the aggressiveness is very strong.

However, even when we have made these qualifications, the fact remains that it takes more than one set of personality characteristics to make a political movement,—even one which has the more favorable conditions we have just stated. The middle west and southern California are well strewn with small-scale nativist-fundamentalist agitators of the type which might be called Fascist. Yet they have never had any success in the United States despite their numbers and despite the existence in the middle and far western population of a vein of xenophobia, populist, antiurban and antiplutocratic sentiment, distrust of politicians and intellectuals—in fact very much of what the Berkeley group would regard as the ingredients of fascism. Since an *Ethos* or general value system are not the same as differentiated behavior in a system of roles, these people have never been able to constitute a significant movement.

The failure of American nativism to organize its potential followers in the United States has been a consequence of a lack of organization skill in its aspirants to leadership, by the unstable and fluctuating relationships of the anti-authoritarian and the authoritarian components in the personalities of their followers and their consequent inability to sustain loyalty. They have had the necessary orientation or *Ethos* but they have lacked the minimum capacities to act in the roles necessary for a movement or an institution.

The internal organization of the various nativist groups in the United States has always been extremely loose, while the interconnections among the groups have despite repeated efforts to establish some degree of unity, been perhaps even more tenuous. The nativist leaders have almost without exception been characterized by their inability to organize an administrative apparatus for their movements, or to hire or attract others to do the work for them. The organization of an administrative apparatus involves a minimum of the capacity to trust other individuals and to evoke their trust and affection to an extent sufficient for them to pursue the goals set by the organization or its leaders. American nativistic-fundamentalistic agitators have lacked this minimum of trust even in those who share their views.

In the main, nativist leaders have been personalities who were driven into their "vocation" by strong paranoid tendencies or what is now called an authoritarian personality. Their paranoid tendencies have, however, been so diffuse in their objects, that even their own fellow nativists have been looked upon as potential agents of deprivation. Where the leader has been either so distrustful of others or, in order to overcome his fear of his own impotence, maintains in himself certain illusions of omnipotence, he seeks to do everything in the organization. It is usually too much for him. Especially since his aggressiveness keeps intruding into his efforts to do the routine work of his group. Demanding affection and loyalty, and fearing it when it is given, the aspirants to nativist leadership in the United States have had a hard row to hoe.

Their intense and self-inhibiting demands for affection and their interpretation of any failure as a deliberately inflicted deprivation are exacerbated because the normal modes of social ascent are closed to them. In the United States, the person with diffuse aggressiveness is likely to fail in his efforts to enter any of the occupations demanding persistent routine effort or offering high rewards of creativity in the exercise of authority. Hence, the paranoid tendencies of the nativist agitators which must have been generated quite early in their careers are accentuated by failures suffered during their adult years. Practically none of the nativist leaders could be called a reasonably successful individual in the conventional sense except perhaps for one who despite his external vocational success is alleged to have suffered for a long time from his social rejection at Harvard on account of his negroid appearance.

The impulsiveness which has driven these men into extremely aggressive behavior and speech has likewise prevented them from developing the flexible self-control required to build the administrative machinery in their organizations. They have been people who are driven by their immediately pressing impulses to take instantaneous action: their defenses, although strong on one side are completely open on the flank. They hate authority, for example, sufficiently for them to build up by reaction-formation a belief that the best society is one in which there is a great concentration of authority—but they cannot control their anti-authoritarianism in actual situations. Hence the movements remain small because they cannot tolerate leaders and any effort to unify the fragments is attacked as the gesture of a menacing authority. Their poor reality-orientation led them to think that they were constantly on the verge of success and therefore to underemphasize those techniques necessary to consolidate their position for a long slow movement.

An examination of the physical state of their offices and files, even among the more successful ones, has revealed extreme disorder, and they themselves in their offices show impatience and irrationality in the use of their equipment. The manner in which they transacted business, as revealed both by observation and from their correspondence has indicated inability to conduct coherent, continuous discourse. The frequent quarrels among the leaders within a group have testified to their undisciplined, unchanneled aggressiveness. Their local followership and indeed even their more remote followership have been based largely on a direct unilateral personal relationship between the leader and the group. There is no hierarchical structure of the sort which is absolutely necessary if the actions of large numbers of people are to be coordinated. The leaders and their lieutenants who come and go seem to be incapable of the sustained continuous work of the "wardheeler" who also uses direct personal contact as a means of control.

Public meetings were often conducted in an informal unplanned manner—more like a religious revival in a storefront church—without any of the highly organized arrangements employed so successfully by the Nazis in calling forth the awe and devotion among their followers. At a meeting in Chicago organized by G. L. K. Smith, for example, the speakers strolled in individually, stopping to chat with the audience; during the speeches there was a constant movement to and from the platform. The speakers were too informal to inspire discipline among their followers, and the movement gave the appearance of being limited in size by the number of people with whom the leaders could personally be acquainted while the difficulties in personal relationships of these persons imbued with the authoritarian ethos meant there had to be a constant turnover in membership.

The hostilities of the nativists flow out against all groups who appear distinguishable from themselves. The symbol "national" and "Christian" [15] seem hardly adequate to bind such random aggressiveness which by its very diffuseness prevents unification and solidarity.

Despite the intensity of their animosities against those who diverge from the standards of nativist Americanism, the nativists have not on the whole appeared to be persons who have been capable of separating their love and hate components, and to attach them to objects in a persisting manner. The amount of attachment to objects, to say nothing of affection or congeniality of which they have been capable, has not offered the possibilities of sustaining a continuously ongoing organization. Furthermore, inasmuch as there has been no formal authority to articulate their actions, and to tie them to the organization, their spontaneous affection for their fellow members has had to carry a burden far too heavy for its meager supply. It is entirely possible that these same people with their prickly antiauthoritarianism and their universally diffused distrust, could not have sustained the structure of a more formal hierarchical body even as well as they do the present internal organizational disorder of the nativist sects.

This brief summary of certain features of American nativist organization and personality structure hardly supports the Berkeley group's views that a large number of authoritarian personalities as such could produce an effective authoritarian movement. Movements and institutions, even if they are authoritarian, require both more and less than authoritarian personality structures. On the other hand, a liberal democratic society itself could probably not function satisfactorily with only "democratic liberal personalities" [16] to fill all its roles.

The tasks of a liberal democratic society are many and many different kinds of personality structures are compatible with and necessary for its well being. Even authoritarian personalities are especially useful in some roles in democratic societies and in many other roles where they are not indispensable, they are at least harmless.

The fact that there is no point to point correspondence of personality and social role does not however mean that they have no approximate relationship to one another. The task of social research in this field is to clarify and make more determinate the scope of this relationship. *The Authoritarian Personality* both by its very solid achievement and its very significant deficiencies has contributed towards our progress in the solution of this task.

NOTES

[1] The authors themselves occasionally sense the difficulties of their position and seek to remedy them by the introduction of ad hoc concepts such as "pseudo-conservative" and "pseudo-democrat." These categories are not however introduced in a systematic way into either their quantitative or their clinical analyses.

[2] Some of the positive items in the P.E.C. questionnaire are cited herewith:

First form 36: "It is the responsibility of the entire society, through its government, to guarantee everyone adequate housing, income and leisure." (p. 158)

44: "The only way to provide adequate medical care is through some programme of socialized medicine." (p. 158)

52: "It is essential after the war to maintain or increase the income taxes on corporations and private individuals." (p. 158)

53: "Labor unions should become stronger by being politically active and by publishing labor newspapers to be read by the general public." (p. 158)

Second form 9: "Most government controls over business should continue after the war." (p. 163)

15: "If America had more men like Henry Wallace in office we would get along much better." (p. 163)

43: "The government should own and operate all public utilities (transportation, gas, and electric, railroads, etc.)." (p. 163)

84: "Poverty could be almost entirely done away with if we made certain basic changes in our social and economic system." (p. 163)

[3] It might be pointed out that the investigators' failure to analyze in a differentiated manner the fundamentally heterogeneous outlooks which they group in the leftward sector of their continuum leads them into the same error as their antagonists, the Authoritarians of the Right, Senator McCarthy, the leading spirit of the House Un-American Affairs Committee, the Senatorial Committee on Internal Security, and their likeminded colleagues and supporters.

[4] We shall not discuss Frenkel-Brunswik's interpretation of the major differences between High and Low scorers except to say that we regard them on the whole as in the right direction and as a valuable extension of the work done on German Nazi prisoners of war.

As in Dr. Sanford's interpretation of the cases of Mack and Larry, two typical high and low scorers, there is a tendency in Dr. Frenkel-Brunswik's analysis to overinterpret the material. The exceptionally sensitive and subtle mind at work in these interpretations tends to widen differences more than seems necessary for any except rhetorical purposes. The two young men chosen to illustrate the extreme antidemocrats and extreme democrats are both quite moderate in their views as compared with nativist fire-eaters one encountered before the war or even the ordinary supporters of the New and Fair Deals who were common in university classrooms over the past two decades. Likewise, in the case of Dr. Frenkel-Brunswik's interpretations, they make certain traits far more pronounced than they are likely to be in reality.

In a work of this sort it is however difficult to avoid this overstress. For one thing, our language for the description of small differences among human beings and social situations is far too crude—sociological and political concepts are too gross and the concepts of psychoanalytic derivation were developed in a field in which the symptoms to which the terms applied were much more fully developed than they were in these relatively run-of-the-mill subjects. Moreover, working with the doubtful hypothesis that the tests were selecting and analyzing potential Fascists and anti-Fascists, there is a readiness to interpret the rudimentary events of the present in categories more appropriate to the hypothetically more massive events which have not yet emerged but which the hypothesis predicts.

[5] p. 300.

[6] For a very useful collection of excerpts from the writings of Lenin and Stalin arranged in categories similar to those used in the present analysis, cf. Leites, Nathan, *A Study of Bolshevism* (Glencoe, Ill.: The Free Press, 1953).

[7] Table 7 (VII) (p. 255)

[8] p. 256.

[9] p. 256.

[10] We do not know whether these six are included in the seven who feel victimized by their siblings.

[11] p. 392.

[12] p. 462.

[13] The evidence concerning the operation of the mechanisms of repression and reaction-formation is much less convincing than the evidences about the deeper dispositions but it is plausible. The operation of these mechanisms must be adduced in order to bring systematic coherence into the data gathered in the clinical interviews.

[14] The ambiguity of the discussion of the role of personality in political institutions and movements, and of the Authoritarian political and social system is so great that an exegesis of their views would serve little purpose.

[15] The fantasies of nativist fundamentalist Protestantism in the period between the wars were among the elements which prevented the unification of two of the main strands of nativism. The fundamentalists were about as anti-Catholic as they were antagonistic to any other institution or symbol. This antagonism prevented, for example, the unification of Father Coughlin and Huey Long's organizations, the two largest, even though they made overtures to one another. The war, and especially the pre-war isolationist agitation seemed temporarily to overcome this antagonism. The anti-British Catholic Irish were found to have numerous points of affinity with the anti-British Protestant nativists. Since the British were allied with international bankers, and the Protestant nativists saw this as well as anyone, they were for a time at least, able to sink their antipathies towards the Catholics out of their greater hatred for the British, the Jews, the war mongers, etc.

[16] From which the "leftist Authoritarians" have been separated.

17

The Relationship Between Personality Type and Behavior in Situational Contexts

The sophisticated, technically advanced research report that follows appeared a decade and a half after publication of *The Authoritarian Personality*. From this report, one gets a sense both of how much and how little progress had been made on the original issues that concerned the authors of *The Authoritarian Personality*. The "much" includes a highly elaborated measurements technology, which is further advanced by the research here reported, and numerous empirical findings on various types of "authoritarianism," using diverse instruments and populations. The "little" is evident from the fact that, in 1965, it was still necessary to produce a fully convincing demonstration that the basic psychological configuration described in the 1950 book "really exists." Such a demonstration is one of the contributions of the present paper. Furthermore, the issue connected with the study of authoritarianism that is most important for the study of personality and politics—namely, that of how the authoritarian syndrome influences actual behavior (or *if* it does)—was still imperfectly documented. Many of the methodological "nuts and bolts" of this report will be beyond the understanding of those not trained in relevant aspects of psychology. However, even the untrained reader should be able to follow the general lines of the author's argument and data presentation. The following summary points are designed to help the lay reader:

1. The article is concerned with two matters: (a) Does "authoritarianism," in fact, constitute a recognizable, measurable, phenomenon? This is the problem of establishing "construct validity." (b) Do authoritarian personality traits influence actional behavior in real-world settings? This is the problem of determining whether the authoritarian construct has "predictive validity."

2. The measurement problem arises, among other things, from the debacle that resulted from the unidirectional wording of the original measuring instrument used to identify authoritarians—the F-scale questionnaire. "High-F" authoritarian scores were attainable by answering "agree" (rather than "disagree") to a series of assertions about man and his works, such as "children should be seen and not heard." Rather late in the day (after a good bit of research had already been published), it was discovered that some high-scorers on the F-scale were simply people who tend to respond favorably to any pontifical statement—the people would also have acquiesced to assertions such as "children should be allowed to express themselves freely in the presence of adults."

3. One of Smith's accomplishments was the development of a new version of the authoritarianism scale which (via reversals of wording and the conventions for scoring) appears to eliminate sheer acquiescence tendencies from the final score. A further and more striking accomplishment was attained by employing a procedure for scoring themes in open-ended qualitative interviews conducted by psychiatrists.

Neither the psychiatrists nor the psychologists who converted the psychiatrists' reports to quantitative personality assessment scores were aware of Smith's theoretical interests; nevertheless, these psychiatrist-psychologist teams produced descriptive clinical profiles of the interviews that appeared to fit the characterological portrait originally presented in *The Authoritarian Personality* and (especially important) to correlate closely with high scores on Smith's "improved" authoritarian scale. The clinical scores also correlated (but much less well) with the older measure of authoritarianism in spite of the tendency of that measure to tap acquiescence as well as authoritarianism. As an added bonus, a portion of Smith's findings complemented the findings of a group of investigators who had been studying the phenomenon of acquiescence in its own right.

4. Even assuming that there *are* individuals who exhibit the authoritarian personality characteristics described in the previous two selections in this anthology, it remains to be shown that psychological authoritarianism—tendencies to defer to higher authority, to be punitive toward people "lower" in the social order, and to be intolerant of ambiguity, etc.—has an actual impact on behavior. As many of the selections in this anthology suggest (including Shils' classic critique of *The Authoritarian Personality*), situational pressures may lead psychologically diverse individuals to behave uniformly. In fact, Smith finds virtually *no* correlation between authoritarianism scores on the part of Peace Corps teachers and the job ratings they received as a result of the way they performed their tasks in the field in Ghana.

Does this mean that authoritarianism is *never* likely to influence role behavior? Not at all. Smith goes on in an exceptionally detailed and careful discussion to show why it is likely that other psychological characteristics of the Peace Corps teachers who scored higher than their colleagues on Smith's authoritarianism measures would have muted the effect of their authoritarian proclivities. None of Smith's subjects were more than moderate authoritarians. They were people who had volunteered for the Peace Corps experience and therefore were probably much more favorably disposed to their work than a more typical person who might happen to have authoritarian personality characteristics would be. Probably even more important, the highly structured and indeed "authoritarian" nature of the teaching situation in Ghana was likely, in many respects, to be congenial to an individual with authoritarian proclivities. More generally, the Ghanese teaching situation appears to have been a good example of a role with requirements that, if not likely to impose "uniform" behavior on the part of individuals with diverse personalities, were at least capable of accommodating a wide spectrum of psychological types.

AN ANALYSIS OF TWO MEASURES
OF "AUTHORITARIANISM" AMONG
PEACE CORPS TEACHERS

M. Brewster Smith

As the flood of research that followed the appearance of *The Authoritarian Personality* (Adorno, Levinson, Sanford, & Frenkel-Brunswik, 1950) abates, one can take little satisfaction in the accretion that remains to substantive social psychology. Beginning with the classical critique by Hyman and Sheatsley (1954), research on "authoritarianism" as measured by the F scale has been heavily preoccupied with technical issues; with some notable exceptions (e.g., Rokeach, 1960) the substantive issues that gave interest and importance to the monograph have been lost to sight in the beguiling pursuit of methodologically oriented research. Now that the necessary technical clean-up job is largely done, however, the original substantive questions are hardly settled: what is the status of "authoritarianism" as a personological syndrome, and what is its significance for important social orientations and behavior?

Keenly aware of such unfinished business, I seized the opportunity to include measures of authoritarianism in a battery of procedures administered to a group of 58 Peace Corps volunteers in training on the Berkeley campus in the summer of 1961, 50 of whom were to teach in secondary schools in Ghana as the first Peace Corps contingent to go overseas. The rationale seemed clear-cut: the qualities of flexibility, interpersonal sensitivity, humanistic orientation, and the like, commonly ascribed to persons who are low in authoritarianism, would seem to be ingredients of an effective performance in the Peace Corps, while alleged authoritarian traits such as rigidity, ethnocentrism, and conventionality should interfere with effective performance. In these predictions, the consideration weighed heavily that the unfamiliar intercultural setting of Peace Corps duty would require novel adjustments on the part of all the volunteers, as would the teaching job itself for the majority of them who had had no substantial experience in teaching.

By hindsight, the expectation of a simple, direct relationship between authoritarianism and performance in the Peace Corps shows a certain naivete, which it is one of the purposes of this paper to dispel. Obviously, many factors besides authoritarianism might be expected to contribute to the effectiveness of Peace Corps teachers—factors of intelligence, technical competence, commitment, and personal stability, among others. More generally, the broad theoretical and methodological question of how to conceive the relationship between core personality and overt social behavior is involved. As Couch (1962) has pointed out in an incisive discus-

Reprinted from *Journal of Personality,* 33 (1965), 513–35. Smith's acknowledgements constitute the first footnote in the article: "Written during tenure as Special Research Fellow of the National Institute of Mental Health and Fellow of the Center for Advanced Study in the Behavioral Sciences. The research was supported by Contract No. PC–(W)–55 with the Peace Corps, which, of course, is not to be held responsible for my conclusions. I am indebted to Dr. Raphael S. Ezekiel, Dr. Susan Roth Sherman, Dr. James T. Fawcett, and Cigdem Cizakca Kagitcibasi for assistance in the study, which in the case of the first two mentioned approached full collaboration. This is part of a larger study of experience and performance in the Peace Corps on which a volume is in preparation."
Footnotes have been renumbered.

sion of this issue, not only a person's deeper motives but also his characteristic defenses and the press of his perceived environment need to be taken into account.

It might be argued that an "ego" variable like authoritarianism, concerned with a person's ways of relating both to his impulse life and to the social world, should be less subject to Couch's (1962) strictures than, say, a motivational variable such as need for aggression. As compared with inferred states of inner need, its theoretical status lies closer to overt behavior. Even so, the likelihood remains that the person's manifest behavior may deviate from that which would best fit his authoritarian dispositions, as a result either of his inner reasons to censor and guide his behavior or of environmental pressures to which he is exposed.

Empirically, the limited available evidence confirms the complexity of relationships between authoritarianism and social behavior. Thus, Haythorn, Couch, Haefner, Langham, and Carter (1956), in their study of discussion groups composed of persons high or low in authoritarianism, found the variable to be related to differences in leader and member behavior that accorded well with the theory of authoritarianism (though a number of differences that might have been expected failed to emerge). On the other hand, the paradoxical results found by Katz and Benjamin (1960) for biracial work groups—e.g., among white subjects, high authoritarians were more favorable than lows to their Negro partners—seem to call for explanation in terms of defensive processes of "leaning over backwards" or of differential responsiveness to the norms perceived to apply in the experimental setting. Additional empirical study is badly needed before the considerations that govern the relationship between authoritarian dispositions and overt social behavior can be disentangled. The follow-up study of the Peace Corps teachers provides relevant data.

For the volunteers tested in training, ratings of their subsequent performance overseas were obtained, and their experience as teachers in Ghana was explored in detail in long tape-recorded interviews conducted with them at their schools near the end of their first and second years of service.[1] Transcriptions of the interviews were subsequently rated in a complex Q-sort procedure by graduate students in psychology who were otherwise unacquainted with the volunteers or with the hypotheses under investigation.

These voluminous materials can thus be brought to bear on two major questions: At the time of training, how were the volunteers who scored high in authoritarianism distinguished personologically from those who scored low? And in what respects was authoritarianism, as measured during training, related to performance overseas? The first issue pertains to the construct validity of the measures. The second bears on their predictive validity, though not decisively in view of the many other factors on which success in the Peace Corps must also depend. After describing briefly the measures of authoritarianism, the remainder of this paper is organized around these two themes.

MEASURES OF AUTHORITARIANISM

Derived F

The principal measure of authoritarianism was derived from the SSRC S-A schedule.[2] This inventory, developed for the study of "stereopathy" (Stern, Stein, & Bloom, 1956)—a concept essentially synonymous with "authoritarianism"—is comprised of two forms of 100 items each in which the direction and style of item wording are systematically varied. Form P860 is composed of "personality" items similar to those in the MMPI and CPI; form 1860 of "ideology" items is similar to those in the original F scale. Each form in turn is made up of 10 scales of 10 items apiece. Items for four of the scales in each form are worded in the stereopathic direction. In two of these, items are worded as categorical generalizations; in two, they are given qualified, probabilistic phrasing. In each of these pairs, one scale is comprised of items that are expressed in relatively "violent" terms, one of items expressed in more "moderate" terms. Four corresponding scales in each form are composed of items worded in the nonstereopathic direction. Each form contains two additional nonstereopathic scales comprised of "antiviolent" items, as distinct from both violence and moderation: one scale of "categorical" items, one of "qualified" ones. In each form, items from the ten scales are interspersed with one another according to a standard pattern. Ss responded to each item on a six-point continuum, ranging from strongly disagree to strongly agree. A neutral response was not allowed, and the rare cases in which Ss failed to respond to an item were arbitrarily given a score of 3.5.

Preliminary correlational and cluster analysis of scores on the twenty scales called the validity of the "personality" scales into question: three of the stereopathy scales in this form turned out to have high loadings on the cluster defined by the first four nonstereopathy personality scales.[3] We therefore confined all further analysis to the "ideology" scales of form 1860, which manifestly belonged to the domain sampled by the F scale and were indeed based on an item pool drawn from the research literature on the measurement of authoritarianism.

Cluster analysis of these scale scores could not effectively disentangle stereopathy from acquiescence. Since we sought a measure of authoritarianism that was independent of acquiescence and had no special interest in the other stylistic variables of item phrasing, we took advantage of the balanced construction of the schedule. Discarding the pair of nonstereopathic antiviolence scales (for which there was no corresponding stereopathic version), we followed the example of Christie, Havel, and Seidenberg (1958) to obtain rational derived measures of authoritarianism and acquiescence from appropriate sums and differences of the eight scale scores for which there were formally matched stereopathic and nonstereopathic versions. Specifically, a Derived Acquiescence score was computed as the sum of S's raw scores on all eight of the ten-item scales. For 57 Peace Corps volunteers in training, the mean was 244.4 (SD, 24.7), compared with a theoretical neutral point of 280. The average response tendency thus fell somewhat on the nonacquiescent side for this sample of item content. A score for authoritarianism, here labeled Derived F, was similarly obtained by subtracting the sum of S's raw scores on the four nonstereopathy scales from the sum of his scores on the four corresponding scales that were worded in the stereopathic direction, arbitrarily adding 400 to avoid negative numbers. The group mean was 336.8 (SD, 29.0), on the nonauthoritarian side of the theoretical neutral point of 400.

Levinson F

A related instrument then being administered to several Peace Corps training groups provides a second but generally inferior measure of authoritarianism. This was a 24-item version of the F scale, composed of 12 items from the original F scale and 12 items relating to "traditional family ideology" (Levinson & Huffman,

1955).[4] Conventional scoring of items from one to seven was employed, four representing the theoretical neutral point. For the 58 volunteers in training, the mean score on this "Levinson F scale" was 66.7 (*SD*, 18.9), substantially on the non-authoritarian side of the theoretical neutral point, 96.

The Levinson F scale shares with the scales employed in *The Authoritarian Personality* the technical defect that all items are worded in the authoritarian direction. It is thus of interest that while our measures of Derived F and Derived Acquiescence are constructed to be independent of one another ($r = -.02$), Levinson F correlates .66 with Derived F and .41 with Derived Acquiescence. (In each case, $N = 57$.) These results correspond generally with estimates in the literature concerning the contribution of acquiescent response set to F-scale scores based on unidirectional items.

CONSTRUCT VALIDITY

The Personological Criterion

Experimental procedures in the psychiatric assessment of Peace Corps volunteers that were employed with the Ghana group are the basis for our personological criterion. Early in the training period, each volunteer was seen in two 50-minute appraisal interviews by psychiatrists from the Langley-Porter Neuropsychiatric Institute. Seven psychiatrists participated in the interviewing, each seeing 16 or 17 volunteers on a schedule that as far as possible varied the pairing of psychiatrists who interviewed the same volunteer and also the psychiatrists' participation in first and second interviews. Upon completion of each interview, the psychiatrist made various ratings with which we are not presently concerned. He also wrote a narrative summary of the interview. When typed, the summaries ranged from one to three pages of single-spaced narrative description.[5] Inspection of these summaries indicated that the psychiatrists' skills had been used more fully and appropriately here than in the case of the ratings, and that the summaries would thus provide rich material on the volunteers as they appeared to psychiatric interviewers before overseas service. Where the two summaries on a given volunteer diverged from one another, the reader often experienced a stereoscopic-like effect in which the person interviewed seemed to emerge three-dimensionally from the discrepant perspectives. Our problem was to convert the qualitatives narratives into a form amenable to quantitative treatment.

The *Q*-sort method, employing the California *Q* set (Form III) (abbreviated CQ) as developed by Block (1961), seemed ideally suited to the purpose. The CQ deck consists of 100 items printed on separate cards, to be sorted by judges in a fixed distribution according to the extent to which each item is saliently descriptive of a given person or saliently uncharacteristic of him. The items, developed by Block in the course of extensive research with diverse groups, in effect provide a theoretically neutral common language for the dynamic characterization of personality.

Three graduate students in psychology,[6] working independently of one another, read the pair of summaries for each trainee and then sorted the CQ set to characterize him. The correlations between the *Q* sorts of the three judges for a given volunteer provide an estimate of the reliability of these judgments. Across the three pairs of judges, the mean interjudge correlation (via Fisher's *z* transformation) was .61. The composite Q descriptions across the three judges provide our criterion data; by the Spearman-Brown formula, an average reliability coefficient of .82 corresponds to this level of interjudge correlation.

Derived F

From the group of 57 trainees, subgroups respectively high and low in authoritarianism were selected, in terms of the 19 highest (350–419) and 20 lowest (279–324) in the Derived F score. Mean composite ratings for the two subgroups on each of the 100 CQ items were then compared by t test. The results are summarized in Table 1. Correspondence with the formulations of *The Authoritarian Personality* is remarkable. In view of the fact that the psychiatrists' appraisal interviews were in no way focused on authoritarianism nor was the CQ set specially

Table 1
Comparison of Peace Corps Volunteers Who Are High and Low in Derived F,
in Terms of Q Sort of Summaries of Psychiatric Appraisal Interviews

Items for which the more authoritarian group had significantly higher means
Significant at .01 level:
    9. Is uncomfortable with uncertainty and complexities.
   25. Tends toward overcontrol of needs and impulses; binds tensions excessively; delays gratification unnecessarily.
   41. Is moralistic. (N.B. Regardless of the particular nature of the moral code.)
   76. Tends to project his own feelings and motivations onto others.
Significant at .05 level:
    7. Favors conservative values in a variety of areas.
   13. Is thin-skinned; sensitive to anything that can be construed as criticism or any interpersonal slight.
   49. Is basically distrustful of people in general; questions their motivations.
   86. Handles anxiety and conflicts by, in effect, refusing to recognize their presence; repressive or dissociative tendencies.
Significant at .10 level:
   12. Tends to be self-defensive.
   87. Interprets basically simple and clear-cut situations in complicated and particularizing ways.
Items for which the less authoritarian group had significantly higher means
Significant at .01 level:
   62. Tends to be rebellious and nonconforming.
   98. Is verbally fluent; can express ideas well.
Significant at .05 level:
    3. Has a wide range of interests. (N.B. Superficiality or depth of interest is irrelevant here.)
   53. Various needs tend toward relatively direct and uncontrolled expression; unable to delay gratification.
   60. Has insight into own motives and behavior.
   66. Enjoys esthetic impressions; is esthetically reactive.
   83. Able to see to the heart of important problems.
   96. Values own independence and autonomy.
Significant at .10 level:
    8. Appears to have high degree of intellectual capacity. (N.B. Whether actualized or not. Originality is not necessarily assumed.)
   16. Is introspective and concerned with self as an object. (N.B. Introspectiveness per se does not imply insight.)
   28. Tends to arouse liking and acceptance in people.
   51. Genuinely values intellectual and cognitive matters. (N.B. Ability or achievement are not implied here.)

devised for its portrayal, such close correspondence speaks forcefully for the construct validity of Derived F as a measure of authoritarianism.

Levinson F

The same analytic approach was applied to high and low subgroups of 19 trainees each in terms of scores on the Levinson F test. Scores for the "highs" ranged from 75 to 114, for the "lows" from 30 to 55. Based on 24 rather than 80 items, its scores should be less reliable. We have also seen reason to believe that they are confounded by acquiescent response set. Table 2 shows the results of the analysis.

Table 2
**Comparison of Peace Corps Volunteers Who Are High and Low in Levinson F,
in Terms of *Q* Sort of Summaries of Psychiatric Appraisal Interviews**

Items for which the more authoritarian group had significantly higher means
Signifiant at .05 level:
  13. Is thin-skinned; sensitive to anything that can be construed as criticism or any interpersonal slight.
  41. Is moralistic. (N.B. Regardless of the particular nature of the moral code.)
  63. Judges self and others in conventional terms like "popularity," "the correct thing to do," social pressure, etc.
Significant at .10 level:
  7. Favors conservative values in a variety of areas.
  89. Compares self to others. Is alert to real or fancied differences between self and other people.
Items for which the less authoritarian group had significantly higher means
Significant at .01 level:
  3. Has a wide range of interests. (N.B. Superficiality or depth of interest is irrelevant here.)
  39. Thinks and associates to ideas in unusual ways; has unconventional thought processes.
  66. Enjoys esthetic impressions; is esthetically reactive.
Significant at .05 level:
  8. Appears to have a high degree of intellectual capacity. (N.B. Whether actualized or not. Originality is not necessarily assumed.)
  51. Genuinely values intellectual and cognitive matters. (N.B. Ability or achievement are not implied here.)
  57. Is an interesting, arresting person.
Significant at .10 level:
  20. Has a rapid personal tempo; behaves and acts quickly.
  62. Tends to be rebellious and nonconforming.

In view of the positive correlation between Levinson F and Derived F, one would expect a somewhat similar set of items to emerge as differentiating the subgroups. Inspection of Table 2 indicates that such is indeed the case: moralism, hypersensitiveness to criticism, and conservatism remain characteristic of the highs, and conventionality is added; the lows continue to be described as intelligent, unconventional, nonconforming, esthetically oriented, and as having a wide range of interests. But substantially fewer items differentiate significantly, and the portrait of the "authoritarian personality" is somewhat blurred in comparison with the one that arises from the comparisons based on Derived F. Derived F is clearly the better measure in terms of construct validity.

Derived Acquiescence

It will be remembered that the Derived Acquiescence score was a byproduct of the method by which a purified measure of authoritarianism was extracted from the SSRC S-A schedule. Delineation of the characteristic features of extreme subgroups in terms of this variable has interest in its own right; it also helps to clarify the consequences of confounding authoritarianism and acquiescence, as in Levinson F. Table 3 presents the items that discriminate between high and low

Table 3
Comparison of Peace Corps Volunteers Who Are High and Low in Derived Acquiescence, in Terms of *Q* Sort of Summaries of Psychiatric Appraisal Interviews

Items for which the more acquiescent group had significantly higher means
Significant at .01 level:
    58. Enjoys sensuous experiences (including touch, taste, smell, physical contact).
    67. Is self-indulgent.
Significant at .05 level:
    18. Initiates humor.
    53. Various needs tend toward relatively direct and uncontrolled expression; unable to delay gratification.
    73. Tends to perceive many different contexts in sexual terms; eroticizes situations.
    80. Interested in members of the opposite sex. (N.B. At opposite end, item implies *absence* of such interest.)
Significant at .10 level:
    15. Is skilled in social techniques of imaginative play, pretending, and humor.
    56. Responds to humor.
Items for which the less acquiescent group had significantly higher means
Significant at .05 level:
    25. Tends toward overcontrol of needs and impulses; binds tensions excessively; delays gratification unnecessarily.
    36. Is subtly negativistic; tends to undermine and obstruct or sabotage.
    48. Keeps people at a distance; avoids close interpersonal relationships.
Significant at .10 level:
    37. Is guileful and deceitful, manipulative, opportunistic.
    49. Is basically distrustful of people in general; questions their motivations.
    65. Characteristically pushes and tries to stretch limits; sees what he can get away with.

subgroups of 19 trainees each. (Ranges of scores for high and low subgroups were 256–293 and 161–233, respectively.)

The items that distinguish the more acquiescent volunteers seem in general to be congruent with Couch and Keniston's picture of the "yeasayer" (1960) as tending toward impulsiveness and undercontrol; the three items that differentiate the less acquiescent subgroups at the .05 level correspond to characteristics of Couch and Keniston's "naysayers," although the suggestion of manipulativeness and distrust in this group seems new. Since overcontrol is at once part of the picture of high authoritarianism and of low acquiescence, the partial confounding of authoritarianism and acquiescence in measures based on unidirectionally worded instruments like the Levinson F scale can only obscure the view that such instruments afford of the personality correlates of authoritarianism.

RELATIONSHIP TO OVERSEAS CRITERIA

We now turn to the question of predictive validity: was authoritarianism as measured in training related to the volunteers' performance as Peace Corps teachers in

Ghana? The follow-up study provides a variety of criterion measures available for 49 volunteers (28 men and 21 women) for the first year of service, and for 44 volunteers (27 men and 21 women) for the second year. These somewhat smaller groups included the full range of scores on both measures of authoritarianism found in the larger group who were tested during training.

Overseas Criteria

The criterion measures fall into three categories: overall evaluative ratings, peer nominations, and scores factorially derived from the analysis of the transcribed interviews.

Overall evaluations. At the end of the volunteers' first year of duty, the Peace Corps representative in Ghana and his deputy representative completed a routine administrative rating form on each volunteer, which included a five-point scale of "overall evaluation." The first-year evaluation scores to be employed here combine the ratings by these two administrators with ratings made on the same scale by the two field interviewers, working jointly after the completion of their field work, but before examining the transcribed interview records. (See Smith, Fawcett, Ezekiel, & Roth, 1963, pp. 22–23.) These composite ratings are thus not fully independent of the interview data. With a possible "best" score of 15, the mean was 10.2 (*SD,* 2.6). At the end of the second and final year, only ratings by the Peace Corps representative on a similar five-point scale are available. On this version, one represented the most favorable rating, five the least favorable. For the entire group, the mean rating was 2.6 (*SD,* 0.9). These scores, appropriately reflected, correlated .79 with the combined first-year evaluations just described, and .71 with the first-year ratings made by the same judge.

PEER NOMINATIONS.   In the field interviews conducted near the end of the first year of service, each volunteer was asked to name several volunteers "who are doing a particularly good job." A simple tally of the number of mentions received by each volunteer provided an additional crude criterion (mean, 4.5; *SD,* 5.1). This index correlated .61 with first-year evaluation and .58 with second-year evaluation (when the sign of the latter is appropriately reversed). No peer nominations are available for the second year.

INTERVIEW Q-SORT FACTOR LOADINGS.   The primary source of data in the larger follow-up study was derived from *Q* sorts of the transcripts of the field interviews—amounting to some 200 double-spaced pages of typescript for each volunteer —made by 12 advanced graduate students in psychology who were otherwise unfamiliar with the volunteers and with the preconceptions of the investigator.[7] We are here concerned with *Q* sorts made on the basis of reading both years' interviews (giving precedence to status as of the final year in cases of evident change). These sorts were done with two specially prepared sets of items that had passed through several revisions: a deck of 65 items pertaining to the volunteer's role perceptions, personal agenda, and role performance; and a deck of 64 items characterizing the volunteer's personality structure and processes while overseas, as displayed through the job-focussed interview.[8] Depending on the degree of interjudge agreement achieved by the first pair of raters to *Q* sort a case, from two to six judges contributed to each of the composite Q-sort ratings that underlie the criterion measures with which we are presently concerned. On the basis of the average interjudge correlations for each case (computed via Fisher's *z* transformation and corrected by the Spearman-Brown formula according to the number of judges contributing to a given composite), the role performance Q set was judged with a mean reliability of .76, the personality set with a mean reliability of .68.

We were interested in employing the composite ratings on the two Q sets to identify distinguishable major patterns of personal orientation and performance in Peace Corps service. To this end, we computed the matrix of interperson correlations for each of the two sets and carried out a Q-oriented principal components factor analysis on each matrix. Inspection of the items receiving high and low factor scores on the first principal components in the two analyses indicated the highly evaluative character of each. On the basis of the distinctive item content, we labelled the first component in the analysis based on the personality Q set "Self-confident maturity," and the first component in the role performance analysis "Competent teaching in Africa." The loadings received by individual volunteers on these factors provide additional evaluative criteria, which are essentially uncorrelated with peer nominations and only modestly related to the overall evaluations. Loadings on the first personality factor correlate .31 with first-year evaluation, .35 with second-year evaluation (both significant at $p < .05$); whereas loadings on the first role performance factor correlate .17 and .26, respectively, with first-and second-year evaluations. Individual loadings on the two P-1 factors are closely correlated with one another ($r = .89$).

The role performance factors V-1 to V-3 and personality factors V-1 to V-6 in Table 5 were obtained through varimax rotation. As defined by the content of the Q-sort items with high and low factor scores on each, these represent coherent patterns in terms of which volunteers resembled or differed from one another in their approach to the Peace Corps role and in their personal functioning as inferred from the field interviews. By way of illustration, Table 4 presents for inspection the items that have distinctively high and low factor scores on role performance factor V-1, "Constructive involvement with Africa." Similar illustrations of factors derived from the personality Q set may be found in Tables 6 and 7.

Again, each volunteer's loading on a given factor was used as a score to index his resemblance to that particular factor pattern. These factor loading scores could then be employed in R-oriented analyses correlating the patterns with other variables, among them our scores on authoritarianism.

The Relationship Between Authoritarianism and Overseas Criteria

The data bearing on the predictive validity of the two measures of authoritarianism are given in Table 5. Correlations with first- and second-year evaluations, with peer nominations, and with the evaluative P-1 factors derived from the field interviews all approximate zero. The initial expectation that low authoritarianism, however measured, should be predictive of good performance in the Peace Corps is clearly refuted for this group of teachers in Ghana.

The argument might be advanced, however—and the data of the larger study give it strong support—that global indices of effective performance merge psychologically divergent ways of doing a better or poorer job in the Peace Corps into a single resultant score. Perhaps if these disparate routes to favorably or unfavorably evaluated performance can be disentangled, relationships to predictor variables might emerge that are obscured in the case of overall evaluations. The varimax factor patterns derived from the interview Q sorts allow us to examine this possibility.

Consider first, in Table 5, the correlations of authoritarianism with the vari-max factor loadings based on the Q set for role performance. Factor V-1 identifies a pattern that mainly concerns the quality of the volunteer's intercultural and interpersonal relations with his students and with other Ghanaians. The distinguish-

Table 4
Interview Q-Sort Items Defining Role Performance Factor V-1,
"Constructive Involvement with Africa"

Item No.	Items with High Factor Scores	Score
56.	His African experiences have increased his concern with race relations in the U.S.	67.6
10.	Generally likes his students, treats them with warmth and understanding.	64.7
38.	Has established intimate, continuing relationships with adult Africans.	63.7
34.	Enjoys or admires Ghanaian style of living.	63.5
24.	In his appraisal of Ghanaian life and institutions, is sympathetically critical; forms his own judgments with due regard to historical and cultural differences.	63.2
45.	Is on friendly terms with many Ghanaians (apart from students). (N.B. Disregard depth of the relationship.)	63.0
19.	Has developed close, personal relationships with some of his students.	61.4
22.	Committed to carrying out his job as Peace Corps teacher to the best of his ability.	61.3
32.	In anticipating his return he is concerned with interpreting Ghana and/or West Africa to Americans.	61.1
9.	Judges Ghanaian governmental policies and actions in terms of the needs of Ghana. (Regardless of approval or disapproval.)	60.9
63.	Views his teaching in terms of its contribution to the personal welfare or develop-ment of his students.	60.5
16.	Views his teaching in terms of its contribution to the development of Ghana.	60.4
25.	As a result of his experience in Ghana his thoughts and feelings about America show increased depth and perspective.	60.1
	Items with Low Factor Scores	
15.	Has little real interest in Ghana.	25.0
54.	Feels mostly negative about Ghanaians he has met, really doesn't like them very much.	28.0
51.	Reacts to his students as a category or as types, rather than as individuals. (N.B. Regardless of degree of warmth or liking.)	31.0
6.	Shows lack of tact in relations with students.	32.4
13.	Tends to be condescending toward his students.	34.0
21.	His whole life has centered on the school compound.	34.2
18.	His personal problems of finding himself take priority for him over the tasks of the Peace Corps assignment.	35.0
43.	Tends to identify with the authoritarian and punitive aspects of the Ghanaian educational system.	35.3
37.	Gets exasperated by [some Ghanaian characteristics].	37.4
11.	Incompetent in his understanding of the major subject matter that he has to teach.	39.1

ing items are given in Table 4. It is particularly in this aspect of the Peace Corps role that theory might lead one to expect differences between volunteers who differ in their scores on authoritarianism. Though the correlation with Derived F is in the right direction whereas that with Levinson F is not, the relationship remains negligible. The content of the two remaining role performance factors has no obvious relationship to authoritarianism, so the insignificant correlations into which they enter are less surprising.

Correlations with the factor patterns that emerged from the Q set descriptive of personality functioning overseas present a somewhat different picture. Again we find that the measures of authoritarianism are quite unrelated to the pattern (V-1) that highlights interpersonal openness, tolerance, and sensitivity (loadings on this factor correlate .74 with loadings on factor V-1 from the role-performance set). There is a suggestion of a relationship, though at a level short of statistical signifi-

Table 5
Correlations of Measures of Authoritarianism with Indices of Performance and Personality Functioning Overseas, among Peace Corps Teachers in Ghana
($N = 44$ except for first-year evaluation and peer nominations, for which $N = 49$)

Index	Derived F	Levinson F
First-year evaluation	.01	−.08
Second-year evaluation[a]	−.08	−.18
Peer nominations (first year only)	−.03	−.23
Factor-loading scores derived from Q sorts of field interviews:		
Role performance:		
P-1 "Competent teaching in Africa"	−.10	.13
V-1 "Constructive involvement with Africa"	−.16	.14
V-2 "Exclusive teaching commitment"	.20	.03
V-3 "Limited commitment"	.06	.08
Personality:		
P-1 "Self-confident maturity"	−.07	.08
V-1 "Interpersonally sensitive maturity"	.06	.14
V-2 "Intellectualizing future orientation"	−.38**	−.15
V-3 "Self-reliant conventionality"	.23	.22
V-4 "Dependent anxiety"	.14	.05
V-5 "Controlling responsibility"	.03	.05
V-6 "Self-actualizing search for identity"	−.26*	−.33**

[a] The sign of the correlation has been reversed so that a positive correlation would mean that high scores on authoritarianism are accompanied by favorable ratings.
* $p < .10$
** $p < .05$

cance, with factor V-3, "Self-reliant conventionality." The prominence of conventionality among the items characterizing this pattern might lead one to expect such a relationship, but equally prominent ingredients of matter-of-fact, self-confident, solid dependability are not parts of the theoretical portrait of the authoritarian. Negative correlations that reach statistically acceptable levels for at least one of the measures appear, however, for factors V-2, "Intellectualizing future-orientation," and V-6, "Self-actualizing search for identity." The items that define these factors are given in Tables 6 and 7.

In terms of their distinctive item content, both of these patterns involve a somewhat self-preoccupied, future-oriented outlook; they appear to characterize a person who is in good communication with himself and finds the topic interesting, one for whom the search for identity is still a prominent part of the agenda of young adulthood. All of this agrees nicely with theoretical expectations about persons low in F. Otherwise the patterns are divergent. Volunteers with high loadings on V-2 seem in general to have the upper hand in the identity struggle: they are forceful and self-confident and know very well where they are going. The articulately intellectualized stance that is particularly characteristic of this pattern is accompanied by a lack of intensity or enthusiasm. In contrast, the volunteers who correspond most closely to the V-6 pattern seem to be in the midst of a post-adolescent turmoil that is centered on problems of identity. They are intense, unconventional and impulsive, a bit confused and chaotic, not at all sure of themselves or of what the

Table 6
Interview *Q*-Sort Items Defining Personality Factor V-2,
"Intellectualizing Future Orientation"

Item No.	Items with High Factor Scores	Score
39.	Characteristically maintains a highly articulate intellectual formulation of his situation and problems.	73.9
58.	Can communicate freely about self.	70.8
22.	Has long-term goals.	69.0
12.	The two-year limit on his commitment has been salient for him in helping him accept and adapt to his situation.	67.1
6.	Has a complex, well-differentiated picture of his own future.	66.5
24.	Envisions a challenging and demanding personal future.	66.3
10.	Is actively striving toward a clearer, more complex or mature sense of identity.	65.7
50.	Feels his own life is important, that it matters what he does with his life.	64.6
4.	Can assert himself in a forceful manner when he feels he should.	64.6
57.	Generally self-confident.	62.8
45.	Is emotionally labile, given to highs and lows.	61.4

Items with Low Factor Scores

42.	Intense, tends to involve self deeply.	25.5
54.	Tends to expect little of life, pessimistic.	27.9
32.	Feels a lack of worth; has low self-esteem.	33.0
38.	Nurturant; enjoys helping the younger or less adequate.	33.1
43.	Unsure just who he is or who he ought to be or how he fits into the world.	35.8
30.	Characterized by zeal and enthusiasm.	37.1
16.	Would be unable to accept help from others when in need.	39.1

Table 7
Interview *Q*-Sort Items Defining Personality Factor V-6,
"Self-Actualizing Search for Identity"

Item No.	Items with High Factor Scores	Score
50.	Feels his own life is important, that it matters what he does with his life.	72.8
3.	Devotes much of his energy to a deliberate program of self-improvement (creative activity, study, etc.).	72.5
42.	Intense, tends to involve self deeply.	72.3
9.	Is aware of his own feelings and motives.	67.5
23.	The values and principles which he holds directly affect what he does.	65.5
11.	Copes with the novelty of the Ghanaian experience by seeking relationships, activities, and settings that let him continue important personal interests.	63.8
43.	Unsure just who he is or what he ought to be or how he fits into the world.	63.1
25.	Impulsive; undercontrolled. (N.B. Opposite implies overcontrolled.)	60.5
10.	Is actively striving toward a clearer, more complex or mature sense of identity.	60.1

Items with Low Factor Scores

8.	Basically a dependent person; characteristically leans upon others for support.	28.7
40.	In times of stress, would characteristically tell himself that the troubles will soon blow over.	28.7
59.	Accepts difficulties as inherent in the situation, is not bothered by them.	28.8
61.	Conventional in thought and actions.	29.7
51.	When the going is rough, would tend to take a long-run view.	33.5
53.	When things go badly, would tend to stand back and look at the situation objectively.	35.1
6.	Has a complex, well-differentiated picture of his own future.	35.3
18.	A major component of his stance has been his assumption that one meets one's daily obligations as a matter of course.	37.6
31.	When discouraged, would tend to talk over his problems with somebody else.	39.4
64.	Tends to be preoccupied with matters of physical health.	39.6

future may offer. But they are working on the problem hard and constructively, if somewhat erratically: self-cultivation and improvement stand high on their personal agenda.

As the data in Table 5 indicate, our measures of authoritarianism correlate only modestly even with these patterns. In spite of reasons to prefer Derived F to Levinson F, the former measure does not enter into strikingly higher correlations. To round out the picture, we may ask what is the bearing of the patterns described by factors V-2 and V-6 on evaluated performance in the Peace Corps. The answer is clear: very little. As compared with V-1, which accounts for 26.5 percent of the common factor variance, V-2 accounts for only 12.7 percent, V-6 for 6.5 percent. And loadings on the factors have little to do with evaluations of performance.

	First-year Evaluation	Second-year Evaluation	Peer – Nominations	P-1 (Role Perf.)	P-1 (Personality)
Correlations with V-2	.01	.09	−.04	.48	.57
Correlations with V-6	−.10	.08	.04	−.15	−.11

V-2 does correlate significantly $(p < .01)$ with the evaluative first principal component factors from both Q sets, but this relationship, rather suspect because it is rooted in the same interview data as rated by the same judges, is not supported by results for the other criteria. Otherwise, the results are null.

Results of analyses of the interview Q sorts at the item level may be noted briefly for the sake of completeness. When the Q-sort ratings received by subgroups of volunteers who scored high or low in Derived F $(N = 16$ and 15, respectively) are compared by t test, only a chance proportion of items emerges as differentiating significantly at the .05 level or better. In general, such differences as do appear fall in the expected direction:

> *Items for which the more authoritarian group had significantly higher means:*
> *Role Performance Deck*
> (none)
> *Personality Deck*
> > 31. When discouraged, would tend to talk over his problems with some-
> > one else. $(p < .05)$
> > 61. Conventional in thought and actions. $(p < .01)$
> *Items for which the less authoritarian group had significantly higher means:*
> *Role Performance Deck*
> > 64. Has an intelligent grasp of the problems of political and economic
> > development in Ghana. $(p < .05)$
> *Personality Deck*
> > 3. Devotes much of his energy to a deliberate program of self-improve-
> > ment (creative activity, study, etc.) $(p < .05)$
> > 39. Characteristically maintains a highly articulate intellectual formula-
> > tion of his situation and problems. $(p < .01)$

What, then, are we to say about the predictive validity of our measures of F in this Peace Corps setting? Do the modest correlations with the V-2 and V-6 personality patterns require us to qualify the negative answer given by all other criteria? Hardly. In the first place, the relationship was not *predicted*, even though it seems reasonable enough after the fact. More important, although scores on these patterns were obtained at a later time, in a different setting, by a very different method from those characterizing our measures of authoritarianism, the correlations seem to be interpretable more legitimately as extensions of our data on the *construct* validity of the measures than as evidence for their predictive validity. Like the pencil-and-paper instruments for measuring F and the congruent evidence from the psychiatrists' appraisal interviews, the content of the V-2 and V-6 patterns pertains especially to how the volunteers conceive and feel about their selves and worlds. It tells us much less about what they characteristically *do,* about the kinds of relationships that they establish. In this connection, the failure of the F measures to predict standing on the V-1 personality and performance patterns involving open, nurturant, tolerant, and empathic relationships and low ethnocentrism must be taken seriously. The evidence before us would seem to support the view of Derived F, and to a lesser degree Levinson F, as good measures of a coherent mode of presentation of self *to* self and others, the bearing of which on consequential interpersonal relations and behavior remains to be shown.

DISCUSSION

With the data in hand that refute our initial expectation about the bearing of authoritarianism on the performance of Peace Corps teachers, we must ask if our predictions put the claims for authoritarianism to a fair test. By hindsight, there are several considerations that require us to qualify our conclusions. On the one hand, these pertain to possible effects of self-selection, and on the other, to unanticipated features of the situation of secondary school teachers in Ghana.

One possibility that comes immediately to mind is that the Peace Corps sample, after all, is a very special group, self-selected in ways that might well reduce the correlations obtained between measures of authoritarianism and other variables. There are two issues here. The narrower one concerns the effects of a restricted range in authoritarianism scores, as such. Although the central tendency of the group was toward low F scores, substantial variability remained, enough to permit the clear relationship that we have seen to emerge with the Q-sort judgments of the psychiatrists' summaries. Sheer restriction of range seems inadequate to account for the consistently negative predictive results.[9] But other consequences of self-selection for Peace Corps duty in Africa cannot be discounted so readily.

If one assumes, for the moment, that the conception of F developed in *The Authoritarian Personality* is entirely valid, the high-scoring young people who volunteered to spend two years in a foreign land teaching young Africans under the auspices of an as yet unknown Peace Corps must have been quite atypical of young people in the population at large who would earn similar scores. The prominent special features of the prospective Peace Corps assignment may well have led to self-selection that reduced the normally to be expected correlation between authoritarianism scores and ethnocentrism or prejudice, while leaving intact some of the other personological ingredients of the syndrome. That something of the sort may indeed have happened can be given at least anecdotal support. One of the higher-scoring women in the group, whose outlook on self and world impressed the field interviewer as a close replica of the authoritarian personality, was notable for her genuine friendship with an American Negro and an East Indian. The residue of authoritarians who volunteered for Ghana may largely exclude those who would have manifested the expected interpersonal and intercultural handicap.

Acquaintance with the actual situation of secondary school teachers in Ghana, acquired in the course of the field work of the study, also throws light on a degree of naiveté in the initial expectation of a direct relationship between authoritarianism and Peace Corps performance. In the lives of volunteers overseas, the teaching job loomed much larger and intercultural relations rather less prominently than the investigator had anticipated. Most of the volunteers lived on the compounds of modern residential schools. Often the school compound became a small, engrossing world, one heavily committed to modern western ways, from which the teacher might make forays into the surrounding environment of traditional and modern Africa, but at his own pace and only when he could get free from demanding job commitments that were likely to tie him closely to the compound. Under these circumstances, and contrary to expectation, the phenomena of "culture shock" as described by anthropologists were not prominent among the volunteers. In this respect, the qualities supposedly measured by tests of authoritarianism were clearly less relevant to successful adjustment than they had seemed initially.

As for the teaching job itself, here too the criterion situation presented some surprises. The Ghanaian secondary school is patterned on British models, with differences arising from the cultural novelty and high status of formal education. The authority of the headmaster approaches the absolute; the status distance between master and pupil is great and is marked by many symbols of formal respect. The expectations of students are heavily geared toward didactic presentations, toward "notes" that are dictated and memorized. Classroom discipline is rarely a problem; other infractions are customarily dealt with through an elaborate system of penalties that may include corporal punishment. All told, the Ghanaian school atmosphere is probably much more authoritarian than any experienced by the volunteers in the course of an American education. How such a setting affects the relevance of the teacher's own authoritarian dispositions is not clear, but the problem of prediction is obviously more complex than the investigator had assumed.

A final word is in order lest these findings for Peace Corps teachers be generalized unduly. More than half the volunteers in the Peace Corps are assigned to teaching jobs, like Ss in the present study. Even for these, there is a question of generalization. For 41 volunteers teaching in Nigeria, Mischel (1965) reports a correlation of $-.45$ ($p < .01$) between scores on the identical 24-item Levinson F scale and criterion ratings. There is reason to believe that the situation of volunteers in Nigeria closely resembled that of volunteers in Ghana. Other kinds of projects, particularly those concerned with community development, surely make substantially different psychological demands. Traits such as flexibility and tolerance of ambiguity, part of the portrait of persons who score low in authoritarianism, would seem to be essential for a volunteer who is left to define and discover a job for himself and must put up with long periods of apparent uselessness. The definiteness and predictability of a teacher's core obligations in the classroom may have served to blur the relevance of our measures to performance in Ghana.

The study of Peace Corps teachers in Ghana leaves us, then, with encouraging evidence for the construct validity of Derived F as a measure of authoritarianism. As for predictive validity in this particular setting, our evidence is negative. But the closer look at the criterion situation to which these results have led us questions the fairness of our predictive test. Pending the availability of appropriate comparative evidence from other performance settings, we must ourselves tolerate ambiguity for a while longer.

SUMMARY

Two measures of "authoritarianism" were given to 58 Peace Corps volunteers in training. High scorers differed from low scorers essentially as theory would predict on ratings based on psychiatric appraisal interviews. For 44 volunteers completing two years' teaching in Ghana, scores on authoritarianism were correlated with overall evaluative ratings, peer nominations, and scores on factor patterns derived from Q sorts of long transcribed interviews conducted near the end of the first and second years of duty. Authoritarianism was unrelated to evaluations, to peer nominations, and to factorial patterns describing role performance. It was modestly correlated in a negative direction with scores on two personality factor patterns: "Intellectualizing future orientation" and "Self-actualizing search for identity." The lack of relation to performance criteria is discussed.

NOTES

[1] The interviews were done by Dr. Raphael S. Ezekiel and the author. First-year interviews averaged about four hours; second-year interviews, two and one-half to three hours.

[2] This unpublished inventory was developed by Richard Christie, Hugh Lane, Nevitt Sanford, George Stern, and Harold Webster. I am indebted to Drs. Webster and Stern for making copies available for use in this study. A copy of the items of form 1860, together with a scoring key, has been deposited as document number 8332 with the ADI Auxiliary Publications Projects, Photoduplication Service, Library of Congress, Washington 25, D.C. A copy may be secured by citing the document number and by remitting $1.25 in advance for photoprints or for 35 mm. microfilm. Make checks or money orders payable to: Chief, Photoduplication Service, Library of Congress.

[3] The details of this analysis are given in Appendix A to Progress Report, April, 1963, "Summary of analysis of data collected during training, Summer, 1961," by Susan Roth, on file with the Peace Corps.

[4] A copy of the 24-item scale, as used, has been filed with the American Documentation Institute. See n. 3 above.

[5] I am indebted to Dr. M. Robert Harris for making these summaries available.

[6] I am indebted to Dan and Jeanne Peterman and to Naomi Litt Quenk for conscientious service as judges. They were otherwise unacquainted with the volunteers or with the hypotheses of the study.

[7] The details of this procedure are described in Ezekiel (1964). A summary of the analytic procedures employed and of the Q-oriented factors obtained from the factor analysis of the interperson correlations is also given by Ezekiel. A full exposition will be provided in the volume being prepared on the larger study.

[8] A third Q set was also employed to characterize the volunteer's view of his situation, its challenges and limitations, frustrations and satisfactions. Ratings obtained on it were not technically suitable for the kind of factor analysis that was done with the other Q sets and are not relevant to the present problem.

[9] However, the central tendency toward low authoritarianism has the result that our t-tests compared very low scorers with medium scorers. The tendencies of the extreme "lows" toward impulsiveness or under-control may have counterbalanced the advantages that accrued from their low-authoritarian virtues.

382   **Personality Analysis of Types of Political Actors**

REFERENCES

Adorno, T. W., Frenkel-Brunswik, Else, Levinson, D. J., & Sanford, N. *The authoritarian personality*. New York: Harper, 1950.

Block, J. *The Q-sort method in personality assessment and psychiatric research*. Springfield, Ill.: Charles C. Thomas, 1961.

Christie, R., Havel, Joan, & Seidenberg, B. Is the F scale reversible? *Journal of Abnormal and Social Psychology*, 56 (1958): 143–59.

Couch, A. S. The psychological determinants of interpersonal behavior. In S. Coopersmith (Ed.), *Personality research*. Proceedings of the XIV International Congress of Applied Psychology. Copenhagen: Munksgaard, 1962. Vol. 2, 111–27.

Couch, A. S., & Keniston, K. Yeasayers and naysayers: Agreeing response set as a personality variable. *Journal of Abnormal and Social Psychology*, 60 (1960): 151–74.

Ezekiel, R. S. *Differentiation, demand, and agency in projections of the personal future: A predictive study of the performance of Peace Corps teachers*. Unpublished doctoral dissertation, University of California, Berkeley, 1964. Ann Arbor, Mich.: University Microfilms.

Haythorn, W., Couch, A., Haefner, D., Langham, P., & Carter, L. F. The behavior of authoritarian and equalitarian personalities in groups. *Human Relations* 9 (1956): 57–74.

Hyman H. H., & Sheatsley, P. B. "The authoritarian personality"— A methodological critique. In R. Christie and Marie Jahoda (Eds.), *Studies in the scope and method of "The authoritarian personality."* Glencoe, Ill.: Free Press, 1954. Pp. 50–122.

Katz, I., & Benjamin, L. Effects of white authoritarianism in biracial work groups. *Journal of Abnormal and Social Psychology*, 61, (1960): 488–560.

Levinson, D. J., & Hoffman, P. E. Traditional family ideology and its relation to personality. *Journal of Personality*, 23 (1955): 251–73.

Mischel, W. Predicting the success of Peace Corps volunteers in Nigeria. *Journal of Personality and Social Psychology*, 1, (1965): 510–17.

Rokeach, M. *The open and closed mind*. New York: Basic Books, 1960.

Smith, M. B., Fawcett, J. T., Ezekiel, R., & Roth, Susan. A factorial study of morale among Peace Corps teachers in Ghana. *Journal of Social Issues*, 19, No. 3 (1963): 10–32.

Stern, G. G., Stein, M. I., & Bloom, B. S. *Methods in personality assessment*. Glencoe, Ill.: Free Press 1956.

18

Typological Analysis of Political Leaders

One of the most politically sophisticated and psychologically suggestive typological analyses of political actors is the fourfold classification reported a number of years ago by James David Barber in a study based on interviews with state legislators.[1] In the course of poring over questionnaire data and depth interviews, Barber found himself generating a classification on the two dichotomous variables of (a) the member's attitude toward his membership in the legislative group, as indicated by willingness to return to the legislature for additional terms, and (b) his level of activity in the legislature, as shown by various objective indicators of legislative behavior.

		Activity in Legislature	
		High	Low
Attitude toward legislative membership	positive	Lawmakers	Spectators
	negative	Advertisers	Reluctants

Barber found a remarkable degree of variation in the motives and behavior of the legislators, but was able to isolate a good bit of patterning by means of his typology. For example, the legislators Barber calls the Lawmakers—those members who are both active in the legislature and positively oriented to it—proved to have strong needs to engage in intelligent problem-solving based on rational canvassing of alternatives. Each of the remaining three types also tended to exhibit distinctive patterns of needs and distinctive political styles—needs and styles that were generally not pointed toward achieving policy goals in the legislature. The antithesis of the lawmakers, those members who were both inactive and uncommitted to the legislature, tended to be in office to fulfill a dutiful obligation. These are Barber's Reluctants. His inactive but committed Spectators exhibited an other-directed tendency to be dependent upon their political participation for signs of emotional reassurance. Finally, the active but uncommitted Advertisers tended to be "young men on the make"—exploitative types whose political activity was a way of obtaining personal attention and career advancement.

The present work is one of several preliminary reports of Barber's effort to modify, extend and expand on his typology in applying it to American Presidents. Unlike state legislators, individuals who reach the eminence of the presidency are not likely to be uncommitted to their institutional role. But Barber has found that an individual's broad outlook on other people and on life can be classified in terms of whether his dispositions express themselves in a generally positive or in a generally negative fashion. This provides a surrogate for the variable "commitment to office" and enables Barber to go on and extend his classification to Presidents. In what follows, Barber seeks to classify and to analyze several twentieth century presidents in terms of his hypotheses about how political styles develop drawing on the available biographical record. He discusses Truman (active-positive), Taft (passive-positive), Eisenhower (passive-negative), and Johnson and, provisionally, Nixon (active-negative).

Professor Barber's original abstract of his own paper reads as follows:

President Nixon has already displayed a distinctive political style in relating to his White House advisors. This paper sets forth a "paradigm of accentuations" for analyzing Presidential performance. It then illustrates with four cases the interplay of character and style in shaping Presidents' personal relations, each case exemplifying one character type. The paper concludes with a tentative exploration of Nixon's personal relations style and the danger that poses for one of his character. The broad purpose is to move toward an empirically-supported theory of Presidential behavior that will contribute to more rational candidate selection and institutional design.

NOTE

[1] James David Barber, *The Lawmakers: Recruitment and Adaptation to Legislative Life* (New Haven, Conn.: Yale University Press, 1965).

THE INTERPLAY OF PRESIDENTIAL CHARACTER AND STYLE: A PARADIGM AND FIVE ILLUSTRATIONS

James David Barber

The President is a lonely figure in the midst of a crowd of helpers. He must share the work; he cannot share the core responsibility. He may try, as Harding did, to escape this tension by surrounding himself with advisors he can give in to, but he finds in that strategy no way out when their counsel is divided. He may, as Wilson did, seek escape by turning inward, with a private declaration of independence, but only at the risk of mistake and failure in ventures where cooperation is essential. The endless speculation about who has the President's confidence—and who is losing it and who gaining it as issues shift—reflects a general recognition that the way a President defines and relates to his close circle of confidants has significance for policy. Detailed studies tend to confirm this general opinion, in such relationships as Wilson with House, Franklin Roosevelt with Howe and Hopkins, and Eisenhower with Sherman Adams. Obviously important policy choices involve several major factors; this is one of them.

Revised version of a paper prepared for delivery at the 65th Annual Meeting of the American Political Science Association, September, 1969 under the title "The President and his Friends." A portion of the paper was later published in *The Washington Monthly*, 1, No. 9 (October, 1969), 33–54, under the title "Analyzing Presidents: From Passive-Positive (Taft) to Active-Negative (Nixon)." Professor Barber, who provided the new title, wishes to express his thanks to Fred I. Greenstein and Nelson W. Polsby for comments. The version in *The Washington Monthly* also appears in *Inside the System* (New York: Praeger, 1970).

The variations suggest that designing advice-making machinery for "the President"—that is, the right system for all future Presidents—may be beside the point. For example, a system which mobilizes intellectuals through ad hoc commissions will not work for a President who is disdainful of intellectuals and suspicious of commissions. The structure must fit the man if it is to be effective. The hard question is how to produce that fit. That requires a way of anticipating the ways a President's needs, values, and habits are likely to connect with alternative advisory relationships. In turn, that calls for concepts which will highlight, amidst the flux of individual idiosyncracies, those characteristics most relevant for discerning regularities in the man's links with his friends at the office.

In this paper, I will first suggest a general mapping scheme for successive approximations to understanding Presidential behavior. This is advanced very tentatively as a framework to be corrected and supplemented as individual cases are analyzed. Second, I will concentrate on one area of the map: the relations between character and style in the President's adaptation to the interpersonal aspects of his role. Four cases will be reviewed briefly. Third, I will present an estimate of President Nixon's performance in this area, with attention to the possibilities for attenuating the dangers inherent in his character-style combination.

The ultimate purposes of these explorations are to develop an explanatory theory of Presidential behavior and to use that theory for assessing candidates in the future.

A GENERAL MAPPING SCHEME FOR UNDERSTANDING PRESIDENTIAL BEHAVIOR

The scheme outlined below is best considered as a paradigm of accentuations, in this sense of Harold Lasswell's:

We note first the importance of recognizing what is meant by the *accentuation* of power. Accentuation is a conception of cultural relativity, and it implies that the political type developed in one setting may attach very different importance to power from that given to it by the political type elsewhere. . . . [R]elative stress on power is what we mean by its accentuation.[1]

Figure 1
A Paradigm of Accentuations

Stages of Definition	Factors in Experience and Performance			Key Developmental/ Indicative Phase
	(A) Words	(B) Work	(C) Persons	(D)
1. Character	Criteria of self-judgment	Orientation toward action	Affective response to self and others	Childhood
2. World View	Ideological investments	View of social causality	View of human nature, loyalties	Adolescence
3. Style	Rhetoric	Decision management	Personal relations	Early adulthood
4. Climate of Expectations	Legitimizing	Politicizing	Normalizing	Nomination and campaign
5. Power Situation	Public Support	Washington Support	White House Support	Election and inauguration

In this setting—within a given political culture and a given political role—we are interested in identifying the kinds of accentuations most likely to be important for the man's performance as President. So it is not a matter of some qualities being present and others absent, but of the relative strength of and the balance among the relevant qualities. Furthermore this scheme is, at this stage, closer to Lasswell's ideas of a "developmental construct" than to his characterization of "scientific propositions." That is, it projects probable trends and continuities as they develop in the life history and points to possible indicators of those trends. From these initial posings we may be able to move on to explanatory hypotheses, suggesting why certain continuities occur.

"Factors in Experience and Performance" refers to three broad dimensions of life as an enterprise in which the individual receives from and acts upon his world. In analyzing the opportunities the Presidential role affords, I found it useful to focus on the President's rhetoric—his relating to public audiences, on decision management—his relating to the flow of details and demands for choice he encounters, and on personal relations—his relating to the close circle of advisors and opponents who surround him. Identification of these simple parts of the President's role led into explorations of the larger dimensions of words, work and persons in pre-Presidential life histories. By that route I began to see how the President's rhetoric, for example, traced back to the meanings public expressiveness had had in the development of his style as he emerged from relative obscurity to relative prominence, usually in early adulthood; how that in turn drew content from the ideological investments he had developed as he learned a way of connecting his beliefs with those of his culture, particularly in adolescence; and how these beliefs had grown out of an even earlier set of learnings about who one is and ought to be.

Similarly the dimension I call "work" sensitizes the observer to connections among all the ways an individual relates himself to action and effort: most basically whether his fundamental character tends toward making his environment, or complying with its demands, or withdrawing from adaptive effort, or some relatively more flexible combination and alternation of these stances. In terms of the world view, the question translates into how he comes to view the pace and development of change in the larger world and how he relates his sense of his own development to that. Is it that life rolls on from age to age the same, as it seemed to Coolidge? Or is all flux and confusion and fad as Harding appears to have felt? Or is there some mysterious key to grace, some magic moment when the right move will shake the world? These assumptions about social causality tend to reinforce or conflict with the practical habits a man pursues as he learns what kind of work succeeds for him.

Similarly the "persons" factor embraces one's core appreciation of oneself and significant others as fundamentally loveable or not; one's connection of these feelings with a view of human nature as various or unitary, attractive or repulsive, trustworthy or devious, and with one's special loyalties, memberships, and identifications; and one's style of behavior in dealing with the human environment.

Freud said that to be happy is to love and to work, to which must be added: to believe. Somehow every man answers these questions in his life: What is worth believing? What is worth trying? Who is worth loving? More concretely: Presidents must adapt to intense role demands that they communicate guidance, operate productively, and cooperate closely with others. These adaptive opportunities represent parts of larger contexts in which the search for meaning and purpose, the discovery of a style of acting, and the extension of personal trust and affection are critical.

The "Stages of Definition" refer to an additive sequence by which progressive clarifications of behavior can be obtained. Thus character is seen as a general stance toward the self and the environment; world view adds the content of differentiated beliefs about reality; and style focuses on the processes by which character and world view are translated into patterns of activity. Empirical variations show the indeterminacies in this sequence—there are compulsive liberals and compulsive conservatives, hopeful and skeptical rhetoricians, specialists in personal relations who are deeply aggressive and those who are deeply loving, etc. Isolating these stages analytically is meant to simplify actual complexity without falling into the trap of a characterological reductionism. Furthermore they enable one to grasp the importance of learning and habit development without losing sight of the more fundamental character forces which energize these life-historical accretions.

The right-hand column, "Key Developmental/Indicative Phase," suggests (somewhat ambiguously) a dynamic and an evidential proposition. Dynamically, the *primary* life-stage in which character is formed is childhood, the *primary* time of focusing on an identity which links one with larger social meanings is adolescence, and the *primary* stage for adopting lasting habit patterns for success in a particular arena of life is early adulthood. The emphases expresses my awareness that these developmental stages are times of special accentuation, not final, isolated freezings. Cases will differ in the sharpness with which development occurs. For example, it now seems to me that the President with compulsive tendencies is far more likely to have developed a political style in some relatively short, dramatic period of compensation than is the President with tendencies toward a pattern of compliance. Nevertheless, it remains to be seen how widely the hypothesized linkage between life-stages and personal development holds.

The "Indicative" element suggests a different, evidential proposition. Leaving aside when a stage of personal definition may in fact develop, we are also interested in economical ways to draw together the evidence for comparisons among cases. The question is one of the clarity of our vision as observers rather than the reality of the process being observed. For example, a person's propensity for perceiving the world as a jungle may have been growing in him for a long time, but may emerge with special vividness in adolescence, making the theme much more visible (in biographies, for instance) than it was or will be later in his story.

I have said nothing yet of the fourth and fifth rows in this paradigm of accentuations, "Climate of Expectations" and "Power Situation." These represent far leaps in time beyond the first three and even farther leaps in terms of my own understanding; they are preliminary guesses about distinctions that may turn out to be important. They refer to the President's perceptions of the basic state of the political environment as he moves into office. I think every Presidential election year defines a climate of expectations, a widely-shared sense of the time's most critical needs. This climate tends to stress some combination of three themes. In a "legitimizing" period, the attentive public shows a central concern for morality in politics, for cleansing the government, for reversing trends toward deteriorations of trust. Often this concern takes a nonpartisan or antipartisan thrust: the need is for good character in the Presidency, for a man who will rise above politics, a man of all the people, a Solomon, an Eisenhower. But much of the energy behind this theme is reactive; there is a sense that politicians have poisoned the well of national loyalty (1952?), that immorality threatens the national conscience (1928?), that some bizarre distortion of values may lead the nation away from its established traditions (1964?). The answer is a man of high principle who will restore respect and confidence in the fundamental moral rightness of democratic leadership. (Such a man is not always available.)

Alternatively the climate of expectations may stress changes or confirmations of policy trends, demands to politicize the nation in the sense of emphasizing a programmatic direction. The question at the forefront of public attention is "Which way for America?" The President is made to think he has a mandate to implement a partisan program. He is expected to perform as a representative of his party or faction, whether that means expanding the role of the government in meeting human needs or removing deadening government restrictions on the nation's energies. The emphasis is less on virtue, more on power. Such elections (1912, 1924, 1936, 1948, 1960 ?) tend to polarize the electorate along partisan, programmatic lines. In such elections, about half the people lose. The President is apt to enter (or reenter) office ready to implement a "mandate."

A third type of climatic emphasis is the appeal for rest, the desire for a breathing space, a peaceable time, an end to troubles and conflicts. The stress is on well-being as a value. In memory of 1920, I call this theme "normalizing." The appeal is for relief from the worries, the social anxieties, the unwanted uncertainties the nation has been experiencing, not on moral uplift or partisan programs. There was much of this dona-nobis-pacem feeling about 1968—and in 1932.

For legitimizing, the people want father; the election should be a coronation. For politicizing, big brother, empowered in a victory celebration. For normalizing, mother and Thanksgiving dinner.[2] The columnar placement of these climate of expectation themes should be obvious by this point.

A President's character, world view, and style may or may not fit well with the climate of expectations he confronts. Similarly the power situation he faces has different implications for different Presidents. For example, an activist President bent on redirecting the nation's course cares much more about the shape of power than does a President who intends to change little or nothing. The alignment of political forces a President encounters as he moves into office—the structure of power opportunities—breaks down conveniently into the public arena in which his rhetoric plays the main part, the Washington community of Congress, the Court, the bureaucracy, the lobbies, etc. in which he may struggle for favorable decisions, and the close crew of assistants in and around the White House with whom he interacts intimately. A survey of the power situation would acquire explanatory meaning only in the light of the President's style and purpose. The usual mistake is to think that every President is hungry for all the power he can get.

We reach for a map when we want to get somewhere. Until some question of relationships among or configurations within some locale is defined, the above map is useful only to highlight important factors which might otherwise be forgotten. So far, I have explored the functioning and formation of a highly distinctive rhetorical style,[3] developed a similar but comparative analysis of the styles of two "weak" Presidents,[4] and prepared a short study of direct resonances between character and political events—direct in the sense that the usual mediating function of style is bypassed.[5] Throughout these studies I am trying to maintain a focus on possibilities for prediction (so that, eventually, candidates can be assessed) and on the significant political consequences of various Presidential performances. In this paper, I want to look at interactions of character and style—ways in which a set of politically relevant adaptive habit patterns (style) may conflict or concord with a President's basic character orientation. As mentioned previously, style adoptions in early adulthood occur in a context where character comes together with a particular set of historical circumstances which may or may not facilitate a style consonant with all aspects of that character. For instance, Hoover clearly belongs among the compulsive characters in the Presidency; there is much evidence of his driving energy, depressed mood, orientation toward manipulating his environment, his ambition and his problems with controlling aggression. These forces fed his conscious desire to use the Presidency for positive achievement, for reshaping his environment. The Hoover character was in these ways similar to the Andrew and Lyndon Johnson characters, for example. But Hoover's style, developed when he emerged as a campus political leader at Stanford, was centered in the management of decisions (through careful work on details) and personal relations (gaining acceptance for pre-packaged proposals in small groups). Rhetoric played virtually no part in his first independent political success at Stanford, where he failed English four years running and was famous for his shyness. In the Presidency, Hoover had to speak, though he hated the office's demands for dramatization. His driving ambitions ran head on into his rhetorical blankness and he had to invent some way to reach beyond this stylistic gap to get at the public. Lacking the guidance of successful experience in rhetoric, he drew upon his character-rooted sense that words are essentially devices for persuasion—propaganda weapons rather than symbols for realities or terms of commitment. The result was a rhetoric of reassurance, a pollyanna optimism so obviously out of line with national conditions that it's main effect was to increase, not allay, national anxieties. In this case, then, a marked imbalance in style opened the way for the emergence of character forces. Forced to perform, but lacking habits, the President fell back on character.

"Character" comes from the Greek word for engraving; it is what life has marked into a man's being. "Style" is the stylus or instrumentation by which a man marks his environment. A complete character and style analysis for any individual political leader requires a close examination of his life history, with special attention to periods in which self-esteem is linked with experiments in adaptation. For comparative purposes, however, it is useful to begin with cruder first approximations, sorting the Presidents into rough types as tending to accentuate certain broad character and style features.

The general character tendencies are indicated by a combination of two simple dimensions, activity-passivity and positive-negative affect toward one's activity. These are independent dimensions; they interact to produce four types:[6]

Active-positive. The combination represents a congruence between action and affect typically based on relatively high self-esteem and relative success in relating to the environment. There is an orientation toward productiveness as a value and an ability to move flexibly among various orientations toward action as rational adaptation to opportunities and demands. The self is seen as developing over time toward relatively well-defined personal goals. The emphasis on rational mastery in this pattern can lead to mistakes in appreciating important political irrationalities.

Active-negative. The basic contradiction is between relatively intense effort and relatively low personal reward for that effort. The activity has a compulsive quality; politics appears as a means for compensating for power deprivations through ambitious striving. The stance toward the environment is aggressive and the problem of managing aggressive feelings is persistent. The self-image is typically vague and temporally discontinuous. Life is a hard struggle to achieve and hold power, hampered by the condemnations of a perfectionistic conscience.

Passive-positive. This is the receptive, compliant, other-directed character whose life is a search for affection as a reward for being agreeable and cooperative rather than personally assertive. The contradiction is between low self-esteem (on grounds of feeling unloveable, unattractive) and a superficial optimism. A hopeful attitude helps the person deny inferiority and elicit encouragement from others. The dependence and fragility of this character orientation make disappointment in politics likely.

Passive-negative. The factors are consistent but do not account for the presence of the person in a political role. That is explained by a character-rooted orientation toward doing dutiful service; the compensation is for low self-esteem based on a sense of uselessness. Typically the person is relatively well-adapted to certain nonpolitical roles, but lacks the experience and flexibility to perform effectively as a political leader. The tendency is to withdraw from the conflict and uncertainty of politics to an emphasis on vague principles (particularly prohibitions) and procedural arrangements.

A first approximation to a President's style is simply the configuration of energy investments among rhetoric, decision management, and personal relations. The emphasis is captured crudely in the way he allocates his time, and somewhat more precisely in the way he allocates his attention and emotion. Beyond such allocations are the accentuations within each style area. A rhetorical specialist like Woodrow Wilson, for example, may shape his sermons quite differently from other rhetoricians like Andrew Johnson or John F. Kennedy. These variants are likely to be linked to the experience in early adulthood of the man's first independent political success, that period of style adoption in which he found marked infusions of confidence from relative success, a relatively new and special relationship to group life, and a relatively sudden emergence from obscurity to wider attention. A scanning of the life-historical context in which these early changes occurred, and of the ways they got worked out in subsequent political situations adds closer approximations.

Enough conceptualizing. I want to turn now to the four cases, noted in Figure 2, of Taft, Truman, Eisenhower, and Johnson, with a provisional set of

Figure 2
Typology of Presidential Character

		Level of Activity	
		Active	Passive
Affect toward his activity	positive	Truman	Taft
	negative	L. Johnson (Nixon)	Eisenhower

observations on Nixon in order to illustrate how character and style interactions help to explain peculiarities in the President's personal relations.

SOME PRESIDENTIAL CASES

William Howard Taft: Passive-Positive

What lends drama to Presidential performances is the interplay of character and style. Consider William Howard Taft. In character, Taft was from the beginning a genial, agreeable, friendly, compliant person, much in need of affection from wife, family, and friends. He fits the passive-positive category most closely, with his slow-moving pace and his optimistic grin. Taft endured several illnesses and a severe accident during childhood. His family was remarkable for its close, affectionate relationships. I think he was spoiled. His father expected his children to do well in school, and Will did. By his Yale days he was a big, handsome campus favorite, with many friends but no really intimate ones. By his twenties he was a fat man. Always sensitive to criticism and anxious for approval, he repeatedly entered new offices with a feeling of personal inadequacy to the tasks before him. He was a humane friend of the men and women around him. His mother often said that "the love of approval was Will's besetting fault." As Secretary of War under Theodore Roosevelt, he won the President's approval by complying willingly with every assignment and by repeatedly expressing his devotion to him.

Taft's political style developed in his career as a lawyer and judge. By a series of family connections and historical accidents (Taft said he always had his plate turned right side up when offices were being handed out), he found his way into the judiciary and adopted the style of the legalist, the law-worshipper. He found the bench comfortable and secure, stable and safe, honorable and respected. He developed a decision-management style based firmly in a narrow, literal, conservative concept of a judge's relationship to the law. Principles were applied to cases to give verdicts, period.

The conflict between Taft's character and style was largely latent until after he became President in 1909. In the White House he had to choose between loyalty and law. His biographer, Henry F. Pringle, wrote that:

Indeed, one of the astonishing things about Taft's four years in the White House was the almost total lack of men, related or otherwise, upon whom he could lean. He had no Cabot Lodge. He had no Colonel House. For the most part he faced his troubles alone.

Again there is the pattern of his earlier years: many friends, no intimates. And from his character came also his worshipful, submissive orientation toward Theodore Roosevelt, which he continued to express in letters and conversation as President. "I can never forget," he wrote to Roosevelt from the White House, "that the power that I now exercise was a voluntary transfer from you to me, and that I am under obligation to you to see to it that your judgment in selecting me as your successor and in bringing about the succession shall be vindicated according to the standards which you and I in conversation have always formulated."

Taft saw himself as a follower of TR—but not as an imitator of the TR style. "There is no use trying to be William Howard Taft with Roosevelt's ways," he wrote. Taft had learned, as a lawyer and judge, to manage decisions by the application of legal principles: "Our President has no initiative in respect to legislation given to him by law except that of mere recommendation, and no legal or formal method of entering into argument and discussion of the proposed legislation while pending in Congress," Taft said in a post-Presidential lecture in which he disagreed explicitly with Roosevelt's view that the "executive power was limited only by specific restrictions and prohibitions appearing in the Constitution." This was more than a matter of intellectual principle. Taft's judicial stance worked—as long as he was in judicial roles—to protect him from the fires of controversy. But in the White House, he abhorred the heat of the kitchen. As his Presidential aide wrote, "I have never known a man to dislike discord as much as the President. He wants every man's approval, and a row of any kind is repugnant to him."

President Taft had once told an aide that "if I only knew what the President [i.e., Roosevelt—for a long time Taft referred to TR this way] wanted . . . I would do it, but you know he has held himself so aloof that I am absolutely in the dark. I am deeply wounded." But Taft's character-rooted affectionate loyalty to Roosevelt inevitably came into conflict with Taft's legalistic style. The initial issue was the Ballinger-Pinchot controversy over conservation policy. The details are not important here. What is significant to this discussion is that Taft attempted to solve a broad but intensely political conflict within his Administration through a strict application of the law. As he wrote of the controversy at the time: "I get very impatient at criticism by men who do not know what the law is, who have not looked it up, and yet ascribe all sorts of motives to those who live within it."

Slowly he began to see the Roosevelt Presidency as less than perfection, flawed by irregular procedures. He tried to find a way out which would not offend TR. But as criticisms from TR's followers mounted, negative references to Roosevelt crept into Taft's correspondence. The two managed to maintain a surface amiability in their meeting when Roosevelt returned from Africa, but as Roosevelt began making speeches, Taft found more and more cause for Constitutional alarm. When Roosevelt attacked property rights and then the Supreme Court, Taft became edgy and nervous. He lost his temper on the golf links. He began criticizing Roosevelt in less and less private circles. The man who had written in 1909 that "my coming into office was exactly as if Roosevelt had succeeded himself," wrote in 1912 of "facing as I do a crisis with Mr. Roosevelt."

The crisis came a piece at a time. In 1911, Taft still hoped to avoid a fight, though he saw Roosevelt as "so lacking in legal knowledge that his reasoning is just as deficient as Lodge's." Roosevelt continued to criticize. Taft stuck by his legal guns. However, he confided to his chief aide, Archie Butt: "It is hard, very hard, Archie, to see a devoted friendship going to pieces like a rope of sand."

By the end of 1911, it was clear that TR would not support Taft for reelection. As Pringle says of Taft's mood:

He was heartsick and unhappy. "If I am defeated," he wrote, "I hope that somebody, sometime, will recognize the agony of spirit that I have undergone." Yet Taft remained in the contest. He fought to the limit of his too-tranquil nature because he envisioned the issue as more than a personal one. The "whole fate of constitutional government," he said, was at stake.

Roosevelt attacked "legalistic justice" as "a dead thing" and called on the people to "never forget that the judge is as much a servant of the people as any other official." At first Taft refrained from answering what he privately called TR's "lies and unblushing misrepresentations," but in April of 1913, confessing that "this wrenches my soul" and "I do not want to fight Theodore Roosevelt," he defended himself in public:

Neither in thought nor word nor action have I been disloyal to the friendship I owe Theodore Roosevelt. . . . I propose to examine the charges he makes against me, and to ask you whether in making them he is giving me a square deal.

Taft's nerves were shattered by the ordeal of attacking TR, that man "who so lightly regards constitutional principles, and especially the independence of the judiciary, one who is so naturally impatient of legal restraints, and of due legal procedure, and who has so misunderstood what liberty regulated by law is. . . ." Exhausted, depressed and shaken, Taft was found by a reporter with his head in his hands. He looked up to say, "Roosevelt was my closest friend," and began to weep.

In 1912 the Republican party split apart and the Democrats captured the government.

The break between Taft and Roosevelt had numerous levels and dimensions; one of those was clearly the conflict within Taft between his legalistic style and his submissive character. Taft's decision-management approach—the application of principles to cases—served him well, both before and after he was President. It failed him as President. If he had had a different character, he might have pushed Roosevelt aside as soon as he won the Presidency, as Woodrow Wilson did the New Jersey bosses when he won his governorship. As it was, Taft nearly tore himself apart—and did help tear his party apart—by hanging onto his leader long after Roosevelt had, in Taft's eyes, broken the law.

Harry S. Truman: Active-Positive

Harry S. Truman belongs among the active-positive Presidents. His activity is evident; beginning with a brisk walk early in the morning, he went at the job with all his might. And despite occasional discouragement, he relished his experience. His first memory was of his laughter while chasing a frog across the backyard; his grandmother said, "It's very strange that a two-year-old has such a sense of humor." When Democratic spirits hit the bottom in the 1948 campaign, Truman said, "Everybody around here seems to be nervous but me." And he played the piano.

Although he was in his sixties throughout his long stay in the White House, he put in 16 to 18 hours a day at Presidenting, but "was fresher at the end than I was at the beginning," according to Charles Ross. Truman often got angry but rarely depressed. Once he compared the criticism he got with the "vicious slanders" against Washington, Lincoln, and Andrew Johnson. Truman expressed his buoyancy under attack in these words (quoted in William Hillman's *Mr. President*):

So I don't let these things bother me for the simple reason that I know that I am trying to do the right thing and eventually the facts will come out. I'll probably be holding a conference with Saint Peter when that happens. I never give much weight or attention to the brickbats that are thrown my way. The people that cause me trouble are the good men who have to take these brickbats for me.

And then there is that ultimate, almost implausible indication of persistent optimism: he is said to have enjoyed being Vice President (for 82 days). The White House staff called him "Billie Spunk."

Truman had a strong father (nicknamed "Peanuts" for his short stature) and an affectionate mother. The family had more than its share of difficulties, especially financial ones. They moved several times in Harry's early years. His severe vision problem kept him out of school until he was eight, and at nine he nearly died of diphtheria. But he appears to have come through it with an unusually strong store of self-confidence, ready to endure what had to be, ready to reach out when opportunities presented themselves. He drew on a home in which the rules said: Do the right thing, Love one another, and By their fruits shall ye know them. When he telephoned his mother to ask if she had listened to his inauguration as Vice President on the radio, she answered: "Yes. I heard it all. Now you behave yourself up there, Harry. You behave yourself!"

Truman's drive for decisions, his emphasis on results, his faith in rational persuasion, his confidence in his own values, his humor about himself, and his ability to grow into responsibility all fit the active-positive character. The character shows itself as an orientation, a broad direction of energy and affect, a tendency to experience self and others in a certain way. Truman attacked life; he was not withdrawn. He emphasized his independence; he was not compliant. He laughed at himself; he was not compulsive (though he showed some tendencies in that direction). His character thus provided a foundation for the transcendence of his defenses, for devoting his attention to the realities beyond himself.

Style is what he built on those foundations. Truman's style developed in two main spurts. "So far as its effect on Harry Truman was concerned," his biographer writes, "World War I released the genie from the bottle." He had worked in a bank, farmed, taken a flier on an oil-drilling enterprise, joined the Masons, and fallen in love with Bess Wallace. The family was having financial difficulties again. His father died in 1914, when Harry was 30. At the outbreak of the war, he joined the National Guard and was elected lieutenant by his friends. Sent away from home to Oklahoma, he became regimental canteen officer, with Eddie Jacobson as his assistant. The other Ft. Sill canteens had heavy losses, but the Truman-Jacobson enterprise returned 666 percent on the initial investment in six months. In charge for the first time, Truman had shown that he could succeed through careful management. Later in France, he was put in charge of a rowdy flock of Irish pranksters loosely organized as a field-artillery battery. One former officer who could not control the men had been thrown out of the Army; another had broken down under the strain. Upon assuming command, Truman recalled later, "I was the most thoroughly scared individual in that camp. Never on the front or anywhere else have I been so nervous." Alfred Steinberg, in *The Man from Missouri,* gives this account of how Truman handled himself:

"Men," he told the sergeants and corporals, "I know you've been making trouble for your previous commanders. From now on, you're going to be responsible for maintaining discipline in your squads and sections. And if there are any of you who can't, speak up right now and I'll bust you back right now."

Truman did his own reconnaissance at the front, to get his information first-hand. When his troops broke and ran under fire in "The Battle of Who Run":

"I got up and called them everything I knew," said Truman. The curses that poured out contained some of the vilest four-letter words heard on the Western Front. Said Father Curtis Tiernan, the regiment's Catholic chaplain, who was on the scene, "It took the skin off the ears of those boys." The effect was amazing, Padre Tiernan recalled with pleasure. "It turned those boys right around."

"Captain Harry" came out of the war with the respect and admiration of his men. He had learned that his angry voice could turn the tide and that he could decide what to do if he got the facts himself and paid attention to the details. Most important, his style developed around intense loyalty in personal relations: everything depended on the stick-togetherness of imperfect allies.

After the war, Truman and Jacobson opened their famous haberdashery, serving mostly old Army buddies. An Army friend who happened to be a Missouri Pendergast got him into politics—not against his will. He ran for county judge and won; his performance in that office reconfirmed his faith in hard personal campaigning and in careful, honest business practice. During the campaign he was charged with voting for a member of the other party and he answered with his speech:

You have heard it said that I voted for John Miles for county marshal. I'll have to plead guilty to that charge, along with 5,000 ex-soldiers. I was closer to John Miles than a brother. I have seen him in places that made hell look like a playground. I have seen him stick to his guns when Frenchmen were falling back. I have seen him hold the American line when only John Miles and his three batteries were between the Germans and a successful counterattack. He was of the right stuff, and a man who wouldn't vote for his comrade under circumstances such as these would be untrue to his country. I know that every soldier understands it. I have no apology to make for it.

These experiences reinforced and confirmed an emphasis Truman had grown up with. "If Mamma Truman was for you," he said, "she was for you, and as long as she lived I always knew there was one person who was in my corner." Throughout his political life Truman reiterated this for-me-or-against-me theme:

"We don't play halfway politics in Missouri. When we start out with a man, if he is any good at all, we always stay with him to the end. Sometimes people quit me but I never quit people when I start to back them up."

[To Admiral Leahy:] "Of course, I will make the decisions, and after a decision is made, I will expect you to be loyal."

[Margaret Truman, on her father's philosophy:] ". . . 'the friends thou hast and their adoption tried, grapple them to thy soul with hoops of steel'. . . ."

[From Truman's own memoirs:] "Vinson was gifted with a sense of personal and political loyalty seldom found among the top men in Washington. Too often loyalties are breached in Washington in the rivalries for political advantage."

[Truman on Tom Pendergast:] "I never deserted him when he needed friends. Many for whom he'd done much more than he ever did for me ran out on him when the going was rough. I didn't do that—and I am President of the United States in my own right!"

[Truman to Harry Vaughn:] "Harry, they're just trying to use you to embarrass me. You go up there, and tell 'em to go to hell. We came in here together and, God damn it, we're going out together!"

[Of Eisenhower's refusal to stand up for Marshall:] "You don't kick the man who made you."

What did this emphasis on loyalty mean for the Truman Presidency? The story of Truman's wrangles with aides high and low is well known. Conflicts, misunderstandings, scandals, and dismissals piled up: Byrnes, Wallace, Ickes, Louis Johnson, J. Howard McGrath, Morgenthau, MacArthur, Baruch, Clifford vs. Steelman, and the ragtag crew of cronies and influenceables typified by Harry Vaughan. The landscape of the Truman administration was littered with political corpses. Both Presidential candidates in 1952 promised to clean up what Eisenhower called "the mess in Washington."

I think Patrick Anderson, in *The President's Men,*[7] is right when he sees the key to Truman's loyalty troubles "in the man himself, not in those who so poorly served him." Anderson continues:

> Truman once said that his entire political career was based upon his World War I experience, upon the friends he made and the lessons he learned. It was as an army captain under fire in France that Harry Truman first learned that he was as brave and as capable as the next man. He learned, too, the rule that says an officer must always stand by his men. Perhaps he learned that rule too well; in later years he seemed to confuse standing by Harry Vaughan when he was under fire from Drew Pearson with standing by the men of the 35th Division when they were under fire from the Germans at Meuse-Argonne and Verdun.
>
> After the war, he was a failure as a businessman; his success came in politics. It must have galled Truman that he owed his political success to the corruption-ridden Pendergast machine. But he kept quiet, he kept his hands clean, he learned to mind his own business. That may be another lesson he learned too well. The most simple, most harsh explanation of Truman's tolerance is just this: You can take the politician out of the county courthouse, but you can't take the county courthouse out of the politician.
>
> But it is not that simple. Another reason Truman stood by Vaughan and the others was no doubt simple political tactics: If you fire a man, you in effect admit wrongdoing; if you keep him, you can continue to deny it. More than by politics, however, Truman seems to have been motivated by stubborn loyalty to his friends. It was a sadly misguided loyalty, for Presidents owe a loyalty to the nation that transcends any allegiance to erring friends. Roosevelt understood this instinctively; Truman would not recognize it. Truman's dilemma was complicated by the fact that his nature was more sentimental than that of any of the other recent Presidents. It is often helpful for a President to be a ruthless son-of-a-bitch, particularly in his personal relationships; this, for better or worse, Truman was not.

There appears to have been a lapse in communication in each of Truman's "breaks" with such high-level personages as Wallace, Byrnes, Baruch, and Mac-Arthur. Truman believed that he had made clear to the other fellow just how he must change his behavior; each of the others believed that Truman had endorsed him in the course he was pursuing. Truman seems to have been slowly, and then radically, disillusioned with men in whom he had placed his trust. He was not able to realize that the loyalties around a President are not black and white—as they are in battle or in a Missouri political campaign—but rather shade off from Vaughan-like sycophancy at one end of the spectrum to MacArthur-like independence at the other. For Truman, loyalties were hard and brittle; when they broke they broke. Before he became President, he had, after all, been the chief of loyal subordinates only twice: in the Army and as a "judge" in Missouri. It was natural for him to revert back to those times when he was again in charge.

In terms of our character and style analysis, Truman shows one form of danger inherent in the political adaptation of the active-positive type. To oversimplify what is really much more complicated: the character who has overcome his own hang-ups, who has leaped over the barriers between himself and the real world, whose bent is toward rational mastery of the environment, is likely to forget, from time to time, that other persons, publics, and institutions maintain themselves in rather messier ways. In another context I have said this type may want a political institution "to deliberate like Plato's Academy and then take action like Caesar's army," neglecting the necessities of emotional inspiration and peaceful procedure. The type is also vulnerable to betrayal when he assumes that others who seem to share his purposes will see those purposes precisely as he does and govern their actions accordingly. He is especially prone to this mistake with respect to the active-negative type who is, on the surface, like him in many ways.

Truman's style exaggerated these characteristic vulnerabilities. What he had learned of himself when he was under 20 was shaped and channeled by what he learned of life when he was over 30. Character fed style, style digested character. Amid many Presidential successes, most of his failures can be traced to a particular way in which style reinforced character trends.

Dwight D. Eisenhower: Passive-Negative

Eisenhower as President is best approximated in the passive-negative category, in which tendencies to withdraw predominate. On a great many occasions in the biographies, Eisenhower is found asserting himself by denying himself; that is, by taking a strong stand against the suggestion that he take a strong stand.

No, he would not get down in the gutter with Joseph McCarthy; no, he would not stop the Cohn and Schine highjinks. Franklin Roosevelt had usurped Congressional powers, he thought, and he would not do that: "I want to say with all the emphasis at my command that this Administration has absolutely *no* personal choice for a new Majority Leader. *We* are not going to get into *their* business." When "those damn monkeys on the Hill" acted up, he would stay out of it. Press conferences were another Rooseveltian mistake: "I keep telling you fellows I don't like to do this sort of thing." Was he under attack in the press? "Listen," Eisenhower said, "anyone who has time to listen to commentators or read columnists obviously doesn't have enough work to do." Should he engage in personal summitry on the international front? "This idea of the President of the United States going personally abroad to negotiate—it's just damn stupid."

With a new Cabinet, wouldn't it make sense to oversee them rather carefully? "I guess you know about as much about the job as I do," he told George Humphrey. His friend Arthur Larson wrote that Eisenhower found patronage "nauseating" and "partisan political effect was not only at the bottom of the list—indeed, it did not exist as a motive at all." In 1958 the President said, "Frankly, I don't care too much about the Congressional elections." Eisenhower disliked speechmaking (he had once been struck by lightning while delivering a lecture). Urged to address some meeting, he would typically say, "Well, all right, but not over 20 minutes." Sherman Adams writes that Eisenhower "focused his mind completely on the big and important aspects of the questions we discussed, shutting out with a strongly self-disciplined firmness the smaller and petty side issues when they crept into the conversation." In other words, he did not so much select problems upon which to concentrate as he selected an *aspect* of all problems—the aspect of principle.

When someone aggravated Eisenhower, he would "write his name on a piece of paper, put it in my lower desk drawer, and shut the drawer." When it came time to end his four-pack-a-day cigarette habit, "I found that the easiest way was just to put it out of your mind."

Eisenhower's tendency to move away from involvements, to avoid personal commitments, was supported by belief: "My personal convictions, no matter how strong, cannot be the final answer," he said. The definition of democracy he liked best was "simply the opportunity for self-discipline." As a military man he had detested and avoided politics at least since his first command, when a Congressman had pressed him for a favor. His beliefs were carved into epigrams:

He that conquereth his own soul is greater than he who taketh a city.

Forget yourself and personal fortunes.

Belligerence is the hallmark of insecurity.

Never lose your temper except intentionally.

It is the tone, the flavor, the aura of self-denial and refusal that counts in these comments. Eisenhower is not attacking or rejecting others; he is simply turning away from them, leaving them alone, refusing to interfere.

His character is further illuminated by his complaints, which cluster around the theme of being bothered. His temper flared whenever he felt that he was either being imposed upon or interfered with on matters he wanted others to handle. He "heatedly gave the Cabinet to understand that he was sick and tired of being bothered about patronage." "When does anybody get any time to think around here?" he complained to Adams. Robert Donovan said of Eisenhower: "Nothing gets him out of sorts faster than for a subordinate to come in and start to hem and haw about a decision. He wants the decision and not the thinking out loud." Eisenhower felt that his 1955 heart attack was triggered when he was repeatedly interrupted on the golf links by unnecessary phone calls from the State Department. In 1948, when he finally managed to stop the boomlet for his nomination, he said he felt "as if I've had an abscessed tooth pulled." He told a persistent reporter as the 1948 speculations continued: "Look, son, I cannot conceive of any circumstance that could drag out of me permission to consider me for any political post from dogcatcher to Grand High Supreme King of the Universe."

Why, then, did Eisenhower bother to become President? Why did he answer those phone calls on the golf links? Because he thought he ought to. He was a sucker for duty and always had been. Sentiments which would sound false for most political leaders ring true for Eisenhower:

My only satisfaction in life is to hope that my effort means something to the other fellow. What can I do to repay society for the wonderful opportunities it has given me?

. . . a decision that I have never recanted or regretted [was the decision] to perform every duty given me in the Army to the best of my ability and to do the best I could to make a creditable record, no matter what the nature of the duty.

. . . in trying to explain to you a situation that has been tossed in my teeth more than once (my lack of extended troop duty in recent years), all I accomplished was to pass up something I *wanted* to do, in favor of something I thought I *ought* to do.

He did not feel a duty to save the world or to become a great hero, but simply to contribute what he could, in the best way he was able. From the family Bible readings, from the sportsmanship of a boy who wanted nothing more than to be a first-rate athlete, from the West Point creed, Eisenhower felt, amid questions about many other things, that duty was a certainty.

In all these respects, and also in his personal comradeliness, Eisenhower fits the passive-negative (or "reluctant") type. The orientation is toward performing duty with modesty; the political adaptation is characterized by protective retreats to principle, ritual, and personal virtue. The political strength of this character is its legitimacy. It inspires trust in the incorruptibility and the good intentions of the man. Its political weakness is its inability to produce, though it may contribute by preventing. Typically, the passive-negative character presides over drift and confusion, partially concealed by the apparent orderliness of the formalities. Samuel Lubell caught the crux of this character when he saw in Eisenhower "one man's struggle between a passion for active duty and a dream of quiet retirement."

Eisenhower's political style, particularly his style in personal relations, channeled these character forces in an interesting way. At West Point he was a minor hell raiser (eventually ranking 125th in a class of 164 in "conduct") and a dedicated athlete until an injury, incurred because he would not tell a sadistic riding instructor that he had a weak knee, removed him from competition. He missed combat in World War I and kicked around for a good many years in staff jobs and football coaching; he served seven years on the staff of that flamboyant self-dramatist, Douglas MacArthur, for whom Eisenhower learned to make a newly-developing kind of military administration work.

The old structure of military command—the hierarchy—was giving way to a system less like a pyramid, more like a floating crap game, a system of interdependent functional specialties—teams—that had to be brought together around new technological and strategic concepts. Eisenhower mastered the skills this system increasingly demanded, particularly the ability to coordinate, to gather together the right threads into the right knot. It was *this* style, the style of the modern administrative team-cordinator, that stuck with Eisenhower on into his White House years. The danger of his "military mind" was not that he would be a martinet, a MacArthur; here Harry Truman misestimated him. It was Eisenhower's command habit of central coordination that shaped his behavior. The President, he said,

must know the general purpose of everything that is going on, the general problem that is there, whether or not it is being solved or the solution is going ahead according to principles in which he believes and which he has promulgated; and, finally, he must say "yes" or "no."

The well-known staff system Eisenhower put into the Presidency was designed to leave him free to coordinate at the highest level. The trouble was that the level got higher and higher, more and more removed from the political battlefield, until, in his second term, Eisenhower had to break through a good many layers and circles to get at the controls of policy.

In the Army, Eisenhower's brand of coordination went forward in a context of command; the colonels were dependent on the generals. An order announced (after however much coordination) was an order to be executed. Not so in politics, where promulgation is just the beginning. In an Army at war, coordination takes place behind the advancing flag: the overriding purposes are not in question. Not so in the political "order" where the national purpose is continually questioned and redefined.

When Eisenhower had to deal with military matters as President, such as Lebanon and the Suez crisis, he could act with celerity and precision. He took his greatest pride in the fact that there had been eight years of peace during his administration. But at the same time his character and style fit together to contribute —along with many external factors—to a long list of less happy incidents and trends (Dixon-Yates, Dullesian brinksmanship, the Faubus and U-2 bumbles, the McCarthy contagion). He didn't mean it this way, but when Eisenhower said that "our system demands the Supreme Being," he was probably right.

Lyndon B. Johnson: Active-Negative

For this generation of President-watchers, it would be tedious to document President Lyndon B. Johnson's difficulties in personal relations. The bully-ragging, the humiliations visited upon the men around him, are nearly as familiar as his rages against the Kennedy clan. By mid-1966 it was hard to find an independent voice among his intimate advisors. What had happened to a political style whose cornerstone was the expert manipulation of personal relations?

Johnson experienced his first independent political success as a student at Southwest Texas State Teachers College. Lyndon's mother pushed the boy to get an education; when he was four years old she persuaded the local schoolteacher to let him attend classes. In 1924, he graduated from high school at 15, the youngest of the six-member senior class as well as its president. That year he had lost an important debating contest ("I was so disappointed I went right into the bathroom and was sick"). The year before the family had moved back to a farm in Johnson City and stayed "just long enough for Daddy to go broke," Lyndon's sister recalled.

After high school, Lyndon told all his friends he was through with school forever, despite his mother's urgings to go on. That summer he tried a clerical job for a few weeks but got discouraged and came home. Then Lyndon and two friends left home for California in an old car. A year and a half later, thin, broke, and hungry, he came back and found a job on a road gang for a dollar a day. There was some beer and girls and fights; once his mother looked at his bloodied face and said, "To think that my eldest-born should turn out like this." By February, 1927, Lyndon had had enough: "I'm sick of working with just my hands, and I'm ready to try working with my brain. If you and Daddy can get me into a college, I'll go as soon as I can." On borrowed money, he set off for San Marcos.

Johnson's intense ambition—and his style in personal relations, rhetoric, and decision management—took shape in his college years. The academic side of life did not trouble him much at unaccredited Southwest Texas Teachers; he attacked his courses "with an intensity he had never before revealed." But his main energies went into operating, getting on top of the institution. President Evans got him a job collecting trash, but Lyndon soon cajoled his way into a position as assistant to the President's secretary, with a desk in the outer office. In *Sam Johnson's Boy,* Alfred Steinberg continues the story:

> According to Nichols [the secretary], what next unfolded was flabbergasting. Lyndon jumped up to talk to everyone who came to the office to see Evans, and before days passed, he was asking the purpose of the visit and offering solutions to problems. The notion soon spread that it was necessary to get Lyndon's approval first in order to see Dr. Evans. At the same time, faculty members came to the conclusion that it was essential for them to be friendly to Lyndon, for they believed he could influence the president on their behalf. This erroneous idea developed because the school lacked a telephone system tying President Evans' office with those of department heads, and when the president wanted to send a message to a department head or a professor, he asked his part-time aide, rather than Nichols, to run with a note. Lyndon's tone and attitude somehow gave the impression he was far more than a messenger.

Soon this student assistant was slapping the president on the back, accompanying him to the state capitol, answering mail, and writing reports to state agencies. "Lyndon," President Evans said, "I declare you hadn't been in my office a month before I could hardly tell who was president of the school—you or me."

Johnson was off and running. Blackballed by the dominant fraternity, he helped start a rival one, the White Stars, who won campus elections in part by Johnson's energetic behind-the-scenes campaigning and in part by fancy parliamentary tactics. Johnson sold more Real Silk socks than his customers had use for. He became a star debater, significantly in a system where he and his partner had to prepare both sides of each question because the assignment of negative or affirmative turned on the flip of a coin just before the debate. Johnson's strength was in finding the opponents' key weakness, and then exploiting it to the hilt. Later he began to win office: president of the press club, senior legislator of his class, student council member, secretary of the Schoolmakers Club, editor of the newspaper. His editorials were full of positive thinking. They came out for courtesy, "honesty of soul," and the Fourth of July, along with some more personal sentiments:

Personality is power; the man with a striking personality can accomplish greater deeds in life than a man of equal abilities but less personality.

The great men of the world are those who have never faltered. They had the glowing vision of a noble work to inspire them to press forward, but they also had the inflexible will, the resolute determination, the perfectly attuned spiritual forces for the execution of the work planned.

The successful man has a well-trained will. He has under absolute control his passions and desires, his habits and his deeds.

There are no tyrannies like those that human passions and weaknesses exercise. No master is so cruelly exacting as an indulged appetite. To govern self is a greater feat than to control armies and forces.

Ambition is an uncomfortable companion many times. He creates discontent with present surroundings and achievements; he is never satisfied but always pressing forward to better things in the future. Restless, energetic, purposeful, it is ambition that makes of a creature a real man.

In 1928, Johnson left college with a two-year teaching certificate. He returned a year later after having served, at the age of 20, as principal of an elementary school in Cotulla, Texas. As principal (over five teachers and a janitor), Lyndon was in his first chief executive position. His friendly biographers report he was "a firm administrator, a strict disciplinarian, and a good teacher." He insisted that Mexican children speak only English, and he required his teachers to keep constant supervision of the students. Laziness or misbehavior "was likely to bring some form of punishment. A hard worker himself, Johnson expected others to work with equal energy and determination. He was persistent, sometimes high-tempered, energetic, aggressive and creative." His march into the classroom each morning was the signal for the students to sing out:

> How do you do, Mr. Johnson,
> How do you do?
> How do you do, Mr. Johnson,
> How are you?
> We'll do it if we can,
> We'll stand by you to a man.
> How do you do, Mr. Johnson,
> How are you?

Mr. Johnson spanked at least one boy who ridiculed his walk. His energy was incredible. He introduced school assemblies, interschool public-speaking contests, spelldowns, baseball games, track meets, parental car pools for transporting children, coached debating and basketball at the high school, organized a literary society, courted a girl who taught 35 miles away, and took courses at the Cotulla extension center.

Enough. Johnson's style—the whirlwind energy, the operator-dominator personal relations, the idealistic rhetoric, the use of information as an instrument—all of it was there when he emerged from road-gang bum to big wheel in the world of San Marcos and Cotulla. Obviously personal relations was at the core of his style. It displayed itself in two interesting variations: Johnson on the make, and Johnson in charge. In the first he was the operator who repeated, as secretary to a conservative Congressman and as Senate party leader, the story of his San Marcos takeover, showing a remarkable ability to expand his roles—and his influence—through energetic social manipulation. Johnson in charge used domination successfully, forcing subordinates into conformity.

I think Johnson's character infused this stylistic pattern with a compulsive quality, so that he was virtually unable to alter it when it proved unproductive. Clearly Johnson belongs among the active-negative characters. His fantastic pace of action in the Presidency was obvious. He was also characteristically discouraged much of the time. On the wall of his Senate office he hung this quotation from Edmund Burke:

Those who would carry on great public schemes must be proof against the worst fatiguing delays, the most mortifying disappointments, the most shocking insults, and worst of all, the presumptuous judgment of the ignorant upon their designs.

He was, he said, "the loneliest man in the world," "the most denounced man in the world," for whom "nothing really seems to go right from early in the morning until late at night," who was "not sure whether I can lead this country and keep it together, with my background." Even at the height of his success—at the close of the remarkable first session of the 89th Congress—Johnson, convalescing from a gallstone operation, complained:

What do they want—what *really* do they want? I am giving them boom times and more good legislation than anybody else did, and what do they do—attack and sneer! Could FDR do better? Could anybody do better? What *do* they want?

Johnson's remarkable effectiveness *in situations where the social environment provided direction* is not to be doubted. As Senate Democratic Leader he reached the high point of success in consensus-building by catching issues at the right stage of development, mapping the terrain of Senatorial opinion, and manipulating members' perceptions and expectations to get bills passed. The raw materials were given: Johnson did not take a stand, he worked with the range of stands he found among other members, pushing here, pulling there, until he had a workable configuration of votes. "I have always thought of myself as one who has been moderate in approaching problems," he said. But "moderation"—like Eisenhower's middle-of-the-road—is a relational concept definable only in terms of the positions others take. In the legislative setting, Johnson *had* to work that way. In the Presidency, Johnson had around him, not a circle of Senatorial barons, each with his own independence and authority, but a circle of subordinates. There his beseeching for knowledge of "what they *really* want," his feeling that "no President ever had a problem of doing what is right; the big problem is knowing what is right," and especially his plea to his advisors that "all you fellows must be prudent about what you encourage me to go for," indicated the disorientation of an expert middleman elevated above the ordinary political marketplace.

Put crudely: Johnson's style failed him, so he fell back on character. There he found no clear-cut ideology, no particular direction other than the compulsion to secure and enhance his personal power. As his real troubles mounted, he compounded them by so dominating his advisors that he was eventually left even more alone, even more vulnerable to the exaggerations of his inner dramas, until he took to wondering aloud: "Why don't people like me?" "Why do you want to destroy me?" "I can't trust anybody!" "What are you trying to do to me? Everybody is trying to cut me down, destroy me!"

Richard Nixon: Active-Negative*

The description accompanying Richard Nixon's figure at the Fisherman's Wharf Wax Museum in San Francisco calls the President "industrious and persistent," "ambitious and dedicated from childhood." Like Woodrow Wilson, Herbert Hoover, and Lyndon B. Johnson, Nixon in the early months of his Presidency seemed happy in his work.

He began cautiously. Recognizing the national mood as calling for peace and quiet, empowered by a narrow, minority victory in the election, and confronting a Congress and a bureaucracy dominated by Democrats, he opted for an undramatic beginning. He devoted much of his attention in these early days to gathering around him the men who would help him shape a program, and in arranging them in relation to his own style of operation.

The recruitment process had its difficulties—Nixon received refusals from his first choices for Secretaries of State, Defense, and Treasury and Attorney General: his friend Finch had decided not to accept the Vice Presidential nomination: Warren Burger was at least fifth on his list of candidates for Chief Justice. But it was probably Nixon's own preference which brought together in the Cabinet a collection of competent, quiet, relatively obscure men whose "extra dimensions" he had to describe to the unknowing national audience, and in the White House a crew of younger lieutenant-colonel types leavened with two brilliant Harvardians. He intended to disperse power in his administration. In 1968 he had said: "Publicity would not center at the White House alone. Every key official would have the opportunity to be a big man in his field." If so, their reputations would be made, largely, within and through the Nixon Administration.

Nixon's Presidential style was not entirely clear as of September, 1969; he had not yet been through the fires of large-scale political crisis. But a few features emerged that seemed likely to persist. In several ways, Nixon appeared to have adopted a judge-like stance:

• He takes up one case at a time and tries to dispose of it before moving on to the next case.

• He relies on formal, official channels for information and advice. In his ABM decision, for example, "Although he instructed his aides to seek out all sides of the argument, the President appears to have had little direct contact with opponents or advocates of the missile system outside his own circle." Senators and scientists opposed to the ABM sought out Kissinger, who prepared a "devil's advocate" paper.

• At official meetings, Nixon is the presider, the listener who keeps his own counsel while other members of the group present their cases and options and briefs, like lawyers in a court. He asks questions; he himself rarely tosses out suggestions for critical comment.

• Evidence in hand, he retires to his chambers (usually a small room off the Lincoln bedroom), where he may spend hours in complete solitude reaching his decision.

* I have not changed the following speculations to reflect events after September 1969. The subsequent Carswell and Haynesworth cases, Nixon's reactions to the Vietnam Moratoria, his much noticed isolation in 1970, the invasion of Cambodia and his continuing conflict with the Senate, do not, in July 1970, seem inconsistent with this interpretation.

• He emerges and pronounces the verdict.

By September 1969, this system had already produced some Presidential stumbles. Decisions or near-decisions taken in this fashion had to be reversed or abruptly modified as they set off political alarms. There was the $30,000 job for Nixon's brother Edward; Franklin Long and the National Science Foundation directorship; Willie Mae Rogers's appointment as consumer consultant; the Knowles appointment; the nomination and then withdrawal of Peter Bove to be Governor of the Virgin Islands; the shelving and then unshelving of the "hunger" question; the backing and filling regarding desegregation guidelines; and the various changes in the Job Corps. In these cases "decisions" came unglued in the face of indignant and surprised reactions from the press, interest groups, and Congress. The resignation of Clifford Alexander and the appointment of Senator Strom Thurmond's protégé as chief White House political troubleshooter seemed to indicate inadequate consultation, as did certain exaggerations by Secretary Laird on defense and Attorney General Mitchell on "preventive detention." On the ABM, Nixon emerged, despite his victory, with about half the Senate confirmed in opposition. These bobbles may be seen, some years hence, as nothing more than the inevitable trials of shaking down a new crew. Through them all, Nixon's popularity with the public rose.

It is the isolation, the lonely seclusion adopted consciously as a way of deciding, that stands out in Nixon's personal-relations style. That style was defined, in its main configurations, at the time of his first indepedent political success in 1946.

Following a childhood marred by accident, severe illness, the deaths of two brothers, and much family financial insecurity, Richard Nixon made his way to the Law School of Duke University, where he succeeded as a student but failed in his fervent desire to land a position in New York or Washington upon his graduation in 1937. Instead, his mother arranged a place for him in a small Whittier firm, where he spent the late 1930's in a practice featuring a good deal of divorce and criminal law, holding town attorney office, and serving as a trustee of Whittier College. He and "a group of local plungers" gambled $10,000 to start a frozen-orange-juice company which went broke after a year and a half. In 1938, he proposed to Pat Ryan; they were married in 1940 and took an apartment over a garage.

After Pearl Harbor he worked briefly in the OPA tire-rationing office in Washington before entering the Navy as a lieutenant junior grade—at which, Nixon remembered in 1968, his "gentle, Quaker mother . . . quietly wept." He met William P. Rogers in the Navy. He served as a supply officer in the South Pacific, where he ran a kind of commissary, called "Nixon's Hamburger Stand." When he returned from the war, he struck acquaintances as unusually contemplative, "dreaming about some new world order," possibly feeling guilty about his " 'sin' of serving in the armed forces." Then there was an unexpected outburst: at a homecoming luncheon for some 30 family and friends, an elderly cousin gave an arm-chair analysis of the war. Suddenly Richard leaned across the table and cursed the old man out. Talk stopped. His folks were amazed. Nixon thought no one there would ever forget this uncharacteristic outburst.

He was returning to be, in his own words, "Nothing . . . a small-time lawyer just out of the Navy." Then, as he was winding up his service in Baltimore, he received a call from a Whittier banker asking if he would run for Congress against Jerry Voorhis. He accepted almost immediately. The year was 1945; Nixon was

32. He flew back to California and appeared in his uniform before the Republican group; he brought along a collection of pictures he had had taken, in his lieutenant commander's uniform, for use in the campaign. He impressed the group with his calm, crisp answers. They took him as their candidate in what seemed like a hopeless campaign against the popular Voorhis. In his letter of acceptance he said he planned to stress "a group of speeches." Voorhis's "conservative reputation must be blasted," he said. His campaign became an aggressive rhetorical performance in which he won with little help from anyone else.

Nixon's success at this period was independent of his parents; it was his first clearly political commitment in a personal sense; it was then, he wrote later, that "the meaning of crisis [took] on sharply expanded dimensions"—a fine paraphrase of Alexander George's concept of the expansion of one's "field of power." Perhaps most important is the independence dimension: he had tried several times to make it into the big time in a big city away from home and now he had achieved that.

The shape of Nixon's style, confirmed in his subsequent success with the Hiss case, was clear in its general outline at this point. Close inter-personal relations were simply not very important to his success. He was, and remained, a loner. His style was centered in speaking and in hard work getting ready to speak. Later he attributed his victory over Voorhis to three factors: "intensive campaigning; doing my homework; and participating in debates with my better-known opponent." From then on, Nixon was primarily a man on his own—a hard-working, careful student of one issue or case at a time, continually preparing for a public presentation, highly sensitive to his rhetorical style and the reactions of audiences to him. Throughout his career, including his stint with Eisenhower, Nixon was never a full-fledged member of a cooperative team or an administrator used to overseeing the work of such a team. He stood apart, made his own judgments, relied on his own decisions.

All this should have made it evident that Nixon in the Presidency would (a) develop a rhetorical stance carefully attuned to his reading of the temper of the times (and of the public's reaction to him), (b) work very hard at building a detailed case to back up each of his positions, and (c) maintain a stance of interpersonal independence and individual final authority with respect to his Cabinet and his White House staff.

It is the way this style interacts with Nixon's character which is of interest here. Despite his current air of happy calm, similar in many ways to the early Presidential experience of others of his type, Nixon belongs, I think, among the active-negative Presidents. On the activity side there is little doubt. Nixon has always been a striver, an energetic doer who attacks his tasks vigorously and aggressively. He has often driven himself to gray-faced exhaustion. But even the less demanding 1968–69 Nixon schedules leave him on the side of activists, in contrast, to, say, Taft, Harding, Coolidge, and Eisenhower.

As for his affect toward his experience, I would put more stock in the way he has typically felt about what he was doing over a lifetime than I would put in his current euphoria. Over more than 20 political years, Nixon has seen himself repeatedly as being just on the verge of quitting. Furthermore, on many occasions he has experienced profound depression and disappointment, even when he was succeeding. As a new Congressman, he said he had "the same lost feeling I had when I went into military service." With the Hiss case victory, "I should have felt elated. . . . However, I experienced a sense of letdown which is difficult to describe or even to understand." Running for the Senate in 1950 he was a "sad but earnest underdog." The Nixon Fund episode in 1952 left him "gloomy and angry;" after the Checkers speech, he said, "I loused it up, and I am sorry. . . . It was a flop," and then he cried. He was "dissatisfied" and "disappointed" in his Vice Presidency; in "semi-shock" at Eisenhower's heart attack; he found the President's 1956 hesitations about him "an emotional ordeal"; he was "grim and nervous" in 1960, and he exploded bitterly and publicly after his 1962 defeat.

There have been a few piano-thumping exceptions, but the general tone of Nixon in politics—even when he has not been in a crisis—has been the doing of the unpleasant but necessary. It is this lifelong sense that the burdens outweigh the pleasures which must be set up against the prospect of a new Nixon continuing to find the White House a fun place. In the introduction to *Six Crises,* Nixon writes, "I find it especially difficult to answer the question, does a man 'enjoy' crises?" He goes on to say that he had not found his "fun," but that "surely there is more to life than the search for enjoyment in the popular sense." Crisis engages all a man's talents; he loses himself in a larger cause. Nixon contrasts enjoyment with "life's mountaintop experiences"—what he calls the "exquisite agony" of crisis. When Nixon begins to feel pleasantly relaxed, or playfully enjoying, I think, some danger sign goes up, some inner commandment says no, and he feels called back into the quest for worlds to conquer.

There are many more aspects of Nixon's character that fit the active-negative type: the unclear and discontinuous self-image; the continual self-examination and effort to construct a "Richard Nixon;" the fatalism and pessimism; the substitution of technique for value; the energies devoted to controlling aggressive feelings; the distrust of political allies; and, most of all, the perpetual sensitivity to the power dimensions of situations. I think that if Nixon is ever threatened simultaneously with public disdain and loss of power, he may move into a crisis syndrome. In that case, the important resonances will be direct ones between character and the political environment; style would play a secondary part. But in the ordinary conduct of the Presidency (and there are long stretches of that), Nixon's personal-relations style may interact with his character to produce a different kind of danger, a kind the President and his friends could, I think, steer away from.

The danger is that Nixon will commit himself irrevocably to some disastrous course of action, as, indeed, his predecessor did. This is precisely the possibility against which Nixon could defend himself by a stylistic adjustment in his relations with his White House friends. Yet it is made more likely than it need be by the way he appears to be designing his decision-making process in the critical early period of definition.

It may seem that the danger of the Nixon Presidency lies not in exaggeration but in timidity, that his administration will turn out to be more Coolidgean than Johnsonian. Yet unless there has been a fundamental change in his personality (as Theodore White and others think there has been), Nixon has within him a very strong drive for personal power—especially *independent* power—which pushes him away from reliance on anyone else and pulls him toward stubborn insistence on showing everyone that he can win out on his own. Throughout his life he has experienced sharp alternations between periods of quiet and periods of crisis. These discontinuities in his experience have contributed to the uncertainties nearly all observers have felt in interpreting the "real" Nixon. On the one hand, he is a shrewd, calm, careful, proper, almost fussily conventional man of moderation, a mildly self-deprecating common-sense burgher. On the other hand, he has been a fighter, a rip-snorting indignant, a dramatic contender for his own moral vision. To say that the first theme traces to his mother and the second to his father is but the beginning of an explanation of a pattern in which alternation has substituted for resolution. The temptation for one of his character type is to follow a period of self-sacrificing service with a declaration of independence, a move which is necessary exactly because it breaks through the web of dependencies he feels gathering around him.

Add to this character a style in which intimacy and consultation have never been easy and in which isolated soul-searching is habitual. Add to that an explicit theory and system of decision-making in which the President listens inquiringly to his committees of officials (who have been encouraged in their own independence), then retires to make his personal choice, then emerges to announce that choice. The temptation to surprise them all and, when the issue is defined as critically important, to adhere to it adamantly is exacerbated by the mechanisms of decision. Add also hostile reporters given unusual access, an increasingly independent Senate, a generationally-polarized nation, and a set of substantive problems nearly impossible to "solve" and the stage is set for tragic drama.

Another President once dismissed Nixon as a "chronic campaigner." In a campaign, day by day, the product is a speech or other public appearance. The big decisions are what to say. In the Presidency, rhetoric is immensely important, but preliminary: the product is a movement by the government. To bring that about Nixon needs to succeed not only with the national audience (where the danger of impromptu, "sincere" commitment is already great) and with the audience of himself alone (where the danger of self-deception is evident), but also with that middle range of professional President-watchers in Washington. Managing their anticipated reactions requires not only the development of "options," but widening circles of consultation around a tentative Presidential decision—in other words, consultation *after* the President has reached a course of action satisfactory to him. It is at that point that the President's friends can help him most. For it is not true in the Presidency that, as Nixon wrote of 1960: "In the final analysis I knew that what was most important was that I must be myself."

CONCLUDING REMARKS

Lives are complicated. In the hope of improving our predictions about Presidents, it is worth trying to discern the key regularities. This may bring us to the point where we can look over a field of candidates and say, with a confidence beyond common sense, where the main problems and possibilities are likely to lie. I think the way to get to that point is by broad, comparative categorization and the slow work of filling in the connections among factors.

In this essay, I have concentrated on relations between two factors, character and style, focusing on the personal relations aspect of style. In discussing character, I have said little of its deeper dimensions, of the innermost meanings of words, work, and persons. I believe it would (and may) be possible to show how early experience shapes political character. For example, it seems likely that the power-oriented, compulsive character grows out of early power deprivations, particularly a helpless vulnerability to erratic external forces, while the compliant, affection-oriented character may develop from early experience in which unrealistically high expectations of affectionate nurturance are established. But the origins are both less certain and less important than the result, and the result—the political character—can be discerned in its main features by the relatively simple scheme described above. In this sense, the research is behavioral, not psychoanalytic.

Style, as in the cases summarized, confronts character on the one side and the Presidency on the other, with a set of habits anchored in early adult success. The early congruences in adapting to other political (in the widest sense) roles push the new President to try again what worked for him before. But the new role is unique; the old combination may add up in a different way. The main disparities are definable, probably predictable, and possibly preventable.

Character plus style is only a slice of the problem. In the larger map sketched earlier, there are many other combinations that need exploring, both in the realm of theory and down below in the messier search for similarities in real experience.

NOTES

[1] Harold D. Lasswell, *Power and Personality* (New York: Viking, 1962), 32–33.

[2] There is a curious periodicity in these themes historically, possibly reflecting the reactive quality of political change. The mystic could see the series politicizing-legitimizing-normalizing marching in fateful repetition beginning in 1900. Although this sequence does call for a politicizing "Big Brother" election in 1984, the pattern is too astrological to be entirely convincing.

[3] "Adult Identity and Presidential Style: The Rhetorical Emphasis," *Daedalus* (Summer 1968).

[4] "Classifying and Predicting Presidential Styles: Two 'Weak' Presidents," *Journal of Social Issues* 24, No. 3 (1968).

[5] "Will There be a 'Tragedy of Richard Nixon'?" forthcoming.

[6] For a fuller development of this typology in another context, see *The Lawmakers* (New Haven, Conn.: Yale University Press, 1965).

[7] Patrick Anderson, *The President's Men* (Garden City, N.Y:. Doubleday, 1968), 105.

19

Social Change and Personality Type Change

At the time this article appeared, early in the sequence of student protest politics during the 1960s, its findings on who student activists were and what they were responding to in their socialization experience were by no means the conclusions that many commentators on "a generation in revolt" had expected. Through repeated subsequent confirmation, Flacks' portrait of the student activist has come to seem less surprising—at least for the period of student activism Flacks studied. During subsequent years, as many protests turned violent, there was a question as to whether student (and nonstudent) activists were being drawn from the personality types Flacks found.[1] Yet Flacks' careful inquiry into the roots of protest at several clearly defined levels of analysis is still a model for thinking and research.

The article is organized so that one can easily distinguish macro-level assumptions about what structural factors may lie behind protest and micro-level research findings on what can specifically be shown to be true of the protesters. The broader macro-level discussion informs the more detailed micro-level research: the findings gain significance from the wider context. Flacks cites, for example, the expectation of observers in the 1950s that an "intensification of the pattern of middle class conformism" would result from "changing patterns of childrearing prevalent in the middle class. The democratic and 'permissive' family would produce young men who knew how to cooperate in bureaucratic settings." Flacks draws (as one can in retrospect) the more contemporary conclusions about the possible anti-conformity significance of the "permissive" family. In setting forth his conception of the student rebel, Flacks has constructed a suggestive and useful ideal type by a most unmechanical and imaginative use of empirical research.

NOTE

[1] See Jeanne H. Block, Norman Hahn, and M. Brewster Smith, "Socialization Correlates of Student Activism," *Journal of Social Issues,* 25 (No. 4, 1969), 143–77 and the sources there cited.

THE LIBERATED GENERATION:
AN EXPLORATION OF THE ROOTS
OF STUDENT PROTEST

Richard Flacks

As all of us are by now aware, there has emerged, during the past five years, an increasingly self-conscious student movement in the United States. This movement began primarily as a response to the efforts by southern Negro students to break the barriers of legal segregation in public accommodations—scores of northern white students engaged in sympathy demonstrations and related activities as early as 1960. But as we all know, the scope of the student concern expanded rapidly to include such issues as nuclear testing and the arms race, attacks on civil liberties, the problems of the poor in urban slum ghettoes, democracy and educational quality in universities, the war in Vietnam, conscription.

This movement represents a social phenomenon of considerable significance. In the first place, it is having an important direct and indirect impact on the larger society. But secondly it is significant because it is a phenomenon which was unexpected—unexpected, in particular, by those social scientists who are professionally responsible for locating and understanding such phenomena. Because it is an unanticipated event, the attempt to understand and explain the sources of the student movement may lead to fresh interpretations of some important trends in our society.

RADICALISM AND THE YOUNG INTELLIGENTSIA

In one sense, the existence of a radical student movement should not be unexpected. After all, the young intelligentsia seem almost always to be in revolt. Yet if we examine the case a bit more closely I think we will find that movements of active disaffection among intellectuals and students tend to be concentrated at particular moments in history. Not every generation produces an organized oppositional movement.

In particular, students and young intellectuals seem to have become active agents of opposition and change under two sets of interrelated conditions:

When they have been marginal in the labor market because their numbers exceed the opportunities for employment commensurate with their abilities and training. This has most typically been the case in colonial or underdeveloped societies; it also seems to account, in part, for the radicalization of European Jewish intellectuals and American college-educated women at the turn of the century (Coser, 1965; Shils, 1960; Veblen, 1963).

When they found that the values with which they were closely connected by virtue of their upbringing no longer were appropriate to the developing social reality. This has been the case most typically at the point where traditional authority has broken down due to the impact of Westernization, industrialization, modernization. Under these

Reprinted from *Journal of Social Issues*, XXIII, No. 3 (1967), 52–75. Footnotes have been renumbered.

conditions, the intellectuals, and particularly the youth, felt called upon to assert new values, new modes of legitimation, new styles of life. Although the case of breakdown of traditional authority is most typically the point at which youth movements have emerged, there seems, historically, to have been a second point in time—in Western Europe and the United States—when intellectuals were radicalized. This was, roughly, at the turn of the century, when values such as gentility, laissez faire, naive optimism, naive rationalism and naive nationalism seemed increasingly inappropriate due to the impact of large scale industrial organization, intensifying class conflict, economic crisis and the emergence of total war. Variants of radicalism waxed and waned in their influence among American intellectuals and students during the first four decades of the twentieth century (Aaron, 1965; Eisenstadt, 1956; Lasch, 1965).

If these conditions have historically been those which produced revolts among the young intelligentsia, then I think it is easy to understand why a relatively superficial observer would find the new wave of radicalism on the campus fairly mysterious.

In the first place, the current student generation can look forward, not to occupational insecurity or marginality, but to an unexampled opening up of opportunity for occupational advance in situations in which their skills will be maximally demanded and the prestige of their roles unprecedentedly high.

In the second place, there is no evident erosion of the legitimacy of established authority; we do not seem, at least on the surface, to be in a period of rapid disintegration of traditional values—at least no more so than a decade ago when sociologists were observing the *exhaustion* of opportunity for radical social movements in America (Bell, 1962; Lipset, 1960).

In fact, during the Fifties sociologists and social psychologists emphasized the decline in political commitment, particularly among the young, and the rise of a bland, security-oriented conformism throughout the population, but most particularly among college students. The variety of studies conducted then reported students as overwhelmingly unconcerned with value questions, highly complacent, status-oriented, privatized, uncommitted (Jacob, 1957; Goldsen, et al, 1960). Most of us interpreted this situation as one to be expected given the opportunities newly opened to educated youth, and given the emergence of liberal pluralism and affluence as the characteristic features of postwar America. Several observers predicted an intensification of the pattern of middle class conformism, declining individualism, and growing "other-directedness" based on the changing styles of childrearing prevalent in the middle class. The democratic and "permissive" family would produce young men who know how to cooperate in bureaucratic settings, but who lacked a strongly rooted ego-ideal and inner control (Miller and Swanson, 1958; Bronfenbrenner, 1961; Erikson, 1963). Although some observers reported that some students were searching for "meaning" and "self-expression," and others reported the existence of "subcultures" of alienation and bohemianism on some campuses (Keniston, 1965a; Trow, 1962; Newcomb and Flacks, 1963), not a single observer of the campus scene as late as 1959 anticipated the emergence of the organized disaffection, protest and activism which was to take shape early in the Sixties.

In short, the very occurrence of a student movement in the present American context is surprising because it seems to contradict our prior understanding of the determinants of disaffection among the young intelligentsia.

A REVOLT OF THE ADVANTAGED

The student movement is, I think, surprising for another set of reasons. These have to do with its social composition and the kinds of ideological themes which characterize it.

The current group of student activists is predominantly upper middle class, and frequently these students are of elite origins. This fact is evident as soon as one begins to learn the personal histories of activist leaders. Consider the following scene at a convention of Students for a Democratic Society a few years ago. Toward the end of several days of deliberation, someone decided that a quick way of raising funds for the organization would be to appeal to the several hundred students assembled at the convention to dig down deep into their pockets on the spot. To this end, one of the leadership, skilled at mimicry, stood on a chair, and in the style of a Southern Baptist preacher, appealed to the students to come forward, confess their sins and be saved by contributing to SDS. The students did come forward, and in each case the sin confessed was the social class or occupation of their fathers. "My father is the editor of a Hearst newspaper, I give $25"! My father is Assistant Director of the ———— Bureau, I give $40." "My father is dean of a law school, here's $50"!

These impressions of the social composition of the student movement are supported and refined by more systematic sources of data. For example, when a random sample of students who participated in the anti-Selective Service sit-in at the University of Chicago Administration Building was compared with a sample composed of nonprotesters and students hostile to the protest, the protesters disproportionately reported their social class to be "upper middle," their family incomes to be disproportionately high, their parents' education to be disproportionately advanced. In addition, the protesters' fathers' occupations were primarily upper professional (doctors, college faculty, lawyers) rather than business, white collar, or working class. These findings parallel those of other investigators (Braungart, 1966). Thus, the student movement represents the disaffection not of an underprivileged stratum of the student population but of *the most advantaged sector* of the students.

One hypothesis to explain disaffection among socially advantaged youth would suggest that, although such students come from advantaged backgrounds, their academic performance leads them to anticipate downward mobility or failure. Stinchcombe, for example, found high rates of quasi-delinquent rebelliousness among middle class high school youth with poor academic records (Stinchcombe, 1964). This hypothesis is not tenable with respect to college student protest, however. Our own data with respect to the antidraft protest at Chicago indicate that the grade point average of the protesters averaged around B-B+ (with 75% of them reporting an average of B or better). This was slightly higher than the grade point average of our sample of nonprotesters. Other data from our own research indicate that student activists tend to be at the top of their high school class; in general, data from our own and other studies support the view that many activists are academically superior, and that very few activists are recruited from among low academic achievers. Thus, in terms of *both* the status of their families of origins *and* their own scholastic performance, student protest movements are predominantly composed of students who have been born to high social advantage and who are in a position to experience the career and status opportunities of the society without significant limitations.

THEMES OF THE PROTEST

The positive correlation between disaffection and status among college students suggested by these observations is, I think, made even more paradoxical when one examines closely the main value themes which characterize the student movement. I want to describe these in an impressionistic way here; a more systematic depiction awaits further analysis of our data.

Romanticism: There is a strong stress among many Movement participants on a quest for self-expression, often articulated in terms of leading a "free" life—i.e., one not bound by conventional restraints on feeling, experience, communication, expression. This is often coupled with aesthetic interests and a strong rejection of scientific and other highly rational pursuits. Students often express the classic romantic aspiration of "knowing" or "experiencing" "everything."

Anti-authoritarianism: A strong antipathy toward arbitrary rule, centralized decision-making, "manipulation." The antiauthoritarian sentiment is fundamental to the widespread campus protests during the past few years; in most cases, the protests were precipitated by an administrative act which was interpreted as arbitrary, and received impetus when college administrators continued to act unilaterally, coercively or secretively. Antiauthoritarianism is manifested further by the styles and internal processes within activist organizations; for example, both SDS and SNCC have attempted to decentralize their operations quite radically and members are strongly critical of leadership within the organization when it is too assertive.

Egalitarianism, populism: A belief that all men are capable of political participation, that political power should be widely dispersed, that the locus of value in society lies with the people and not elites. This is a stress on something more than equality of opportunity or equal legal treatment; the students stress instead the notion of "participatory democracy"—direct participation in the making of decisions by those affected by them. Two common slogans—"One man, one vote"; "Let the people decide."

Anti-dogmatism: A strong reaction against doctrinaire ideological interpretations of events. Many of the students are quite restless when presented with formulated models of the social order, and specific programs for social change. This underlies much of their antagonism to the varieties of "old left" politics, and is one meaning of the oft-quoted (if not seriously used) phrase: "You can't trust anyone over thirty."

Moral purity: A strong antipathy to self-interested behavior, particularly when overlaid by claims of disinterestedness. A major criticism of the society is that it is "hypocritical." Another meaning of the criticism of the older generation has to do with the perception that (a) the older generation "sold out" the values it espouses; (b) to assume conventional adult roles usually leads to increasing self-interestedness, hence selling-out, or "phoniness." A particularly important criticism students make of the university is that it fails to live up to its professed ideals; there is an expectation that the institution ought to be *moral*—that is, not compromise its official values for the sake of institutional survival or aggrandizement.

Community: A strong emphasis on a desire for "human" relationships, for a full expression of emotions, for the breaking down of interpersonal barriers and the refusal to accept conventional norms concerning interpersonal contact (e.g., norms respecting sex, status, race, age, etc.). A central positive theme in the campus revolts has been the expression of the desire for a campus "community," for the breaking down of aspects of impersonality on the campus, for more direct contact between students and faculty. There is a frequent counterposing of bureaucratic norms to communal norms; a testing of the former against the latter. Many of the students involved in slum projects have experimented with attempts to achieve a "kibbutz"-like community amongst themselves, entailing communal living and a strong stress on achieving intimacy and resolving tensions within the group.

Anti-institutionalism: A strong distrust of involvement with conventional institutional roles. This is most importantly expressed in the almost universal desire among the highly involved to avoid institutionalized careers. Our data suggest that few student activists look toward careers in the professions, the sciences, industry or politics. Many of the most committed expect to continue to work full-time in the "movement" or, alternatively, to become free-lance writers, artists, intellectuals. A high proportion are oriented toward academic careers—at least so far the academic career seems still to have a reputation among many student activists for permitting "freedom."

Several of these themes, it should be noted, are not unique to student activists. In particular, the value we have described as "romanticism"—a quest for self-expression—has been found by observers, for example Kenneth Keniston (1965b; 1967), to be a central feature of the ideology of "alienated" or "bohemian" students. Perhaps more important, the disaffection of student activists with conventional careers, their low valuation of careers as important in their personal aspirations, their quest for careers outside the institutionalized sphere—these attitudes toward careers seem to be characteristic of other groups of students as well. It is certainly typical of youth involved in "bohemian" and aesthetic subcultures; it also characterizes students who volunteer for participation in such programs as the Peace Corps, Vista and other full-time commitments oriented toward service. In fact, it is our view that the dissatisfaction of socially advantaged youth with conventional career opportunities is a significant social trend, the most important single indicator of restlessness among sectors of the youth population. One expression of this restlessness is the student movement, but it is not the only one. One reason why it seems important to investigate the student movement in detail, despite the fact that it represents a small minority of the student population, is that it is a symptom of social and psychological strains experienced by a larger segment of the youth—strains not well understood or anticipated heretofore by social science.

If some of the themes listed above are not unique to student activists, several of them may characterize only a portion of the activist group itself. In particular, some of the more explicitly political values are likely to be articulated mainly by activists who are involved in radical organizations, particularly Students for a Democratic Society, and the Student Non-violent Coordinating Committee. This would be true particularly for such notions as "participatory democracy" and deep commitments to populist-like orientations. These orientations have been formulated within SDS and SNCC as these organizations have sought to develop a coherent strategy and a framework for establishing priorities. It is an empirical question whether students not directly involved in such organizations articulate similar attitudes. The impressions we have from a preliminary examination of our data suggest that they frequently do not. It is more likely that the student movement is very heterogeneous politically at this point. Most participants share a set of broad orientations, but differ greatly in the degree to which they are oriented toward ideology in general or to particular political positions. The degree of politicization of student activists is probably very much a function of the kinds of peer group and organizational relationships they have had; the underlying disaffection and tendency toward activism, however, is perhaps best understood as being based on more enduring, preestablished values, attitudes and needs.

SOCIAL-PSYCHOLOGICAL ROOTS OF STUDENT PROTEST: SOME HYPOTHESES

How, then, can we account for the emergence of an obviously dynamic and attractive radical movement among American students in this period? Why should this movement be particularly appealing to youth from upper-status, highly educated families? Why should such youth be particularly concerned with problems of authority, of vocation, of equality, of moral consistency? Why should students in the most advantaged sector of the youth population be disaffected with their own privilege?

It should be stressed that the privileged status of the student protesters and the themes they express in their protest are not *in themselves* unique or surprising. Student movements in developing nations—e.g., Russia, Japan and Latin America— typically recruit people of elite background; moreover, many of the themes of the "new left" are reminiscent of similar expressions in other student movements (Lipset, 1966). What is unexpected is that these should emerge in the American context at this time.

Earlier theoretical formulations about the social and psychological sources of strain for youth, for example the work of Parsons (1965), Eisenstadt (1956), and Erikson (1959), are important for understanding the emergence of self-conscious oppositional youth cultures and movements. At first glance, these theorists, who tend to see American youth as relatively well-integrated into the larger society, would seem to be unhelpful in providing a framework for explaining the emergence of a radical student movement at the present moment. Nevertheless, in developing our own hypotheses we have drawn freely on their work. What I want to do here is to sketch the notions which have guided our research; a more systematic and detailed exposition will be developed in future publications.

What we have done is to accept the main lines of the argument made by Parsons and Eisenstadt about the social functions of youth cultures and movements. The kernel of their argument is that self-conscious subcultures and movements among adolescents tend to develop when there is a sharp disjunction between the values and expectations embodied in the traditional families in a society and the values and expectations prevailing in the occupational sphere. The greater the disjunction, the more self-conscious and oppositional will be the youth culture (as for example in the situation of rapid transition from a traditional-ascriptive to a bureaucratic-achievement social system).

In modern industrial society, such a disjunction exists as a matter of course, since families are, by definition, particularistic, ascriptive, diffuse, and the occupational sphere is universalistic, impersonal, achievement-oriented, functionally specific. But Parsons, and many others, have suggested that over time the American middle class family has developed a structure and style which tends to articulate with the occupational sphere; thus, whatever youth culture does emerge in American society is likely to be fairly well-integrated with conventional values, not particularly self-conscious, not rebellious (Parsons, 1965).

The emergence of the student movement, and other expressions of estrangement among youth, leads us to ask whether, in fact, there may be families in the middle class which embody values and expectations which do *not* articulate with those prevailing in the occupational sphere, to look for previously unremarked incompatibilities between trends in the larger social system and trends in family life and early socialization.

The argument we have developed may be sketched as follows:

First, on the macro-structural level we assume that two related trends are of importance: one, the increasing rationalization of student life in high schools and universities, symbolized by the "multiversity," which entails a high degree of impersonality, competitiveness and an increasingly explicit and direct relationship between the university and corporate and governmental bureaucracies; two, the increasing unavailability of coherent careers independent of bureaucratic organizations.

Second, these trends converge, in time, with a particular trend in the development of the family; namely, the emergence of a pattern of familial relations, located most typically in upper middle class, professional homes, having the following elements:

(a) a strong emphasis on democratic, egalitarian interpersonal relations
(b) a high degree of permissiveness with respect to self-regulation
(c) an emphasis on values *other than achievement;* in particular, a stress on the intrinsic worth of living up to intellectual, aesthetic, political, or religious ideals.

Third, young people raised in this kind of family setting, contrary to the expectations of some observers, find it difficult to accommodate to institutional expectations requiring submissiveness to adult authority, respect for established status distinctions, a high degree of competition, and firm regulation of sexual and expressive impulses. They are likely to be particularly sensitized to acts of arbitrary authority, to unexamined expressions of allegiance to conventional values, to instances of institutional practices which conflict with professed ideals. Further, the values embodied in their families are likely to be reinforced by other socializing experiences—for example, summer vacations at progressive children's camps, attendance at experimental private schools, growing up in a community with a high proportion of friends from similar backgrounds. Paralleling these experiences of positive reinforcement, there are likely to be experiences which reinforce a sense of estrangement from peers or conventional society. For instance, many of these young people experience a strong sense of being "different" or "isolated" in school; this sense of distance is often based on the relative uniqueness of their interests and values, their inability to accept conventional norms about appropriate sex-role behavior, and the like. An additional source of strain is generated when these young people perceive a fundamental discrepancy between the values espoused by their parents and the style of life actually practiced by them. This discrepancy is experienced as a feeling of "guilt" over "being middle class" and a perception of "hypocrisy" on the part of parents who express liberal or intellectual values while appearing to their children as acquisitive or self-interested.

Fourth, the incentives operative in the occupational sphere are of limited efficacy for these young people—achievement of status or material advantage is relatively ineffective for an individual who already has high status and affluence by virtue of his family origins. This means, on the one hand, that these students are less oriented toward occupational achievement; on the other hand, the operative sanctions within the school and the larger society are less effective in enforcing conformity.

It seems plausible that this is the first generation in which a substantial number of youth have both the impulse to free themselves from conventional status concerns *and can afford to do so*. In this sense they are a "liberated" generation; affluence has freed them, at least for a period of time, from some of the anxieties and preoccupations which have been the defining features of American middle class social character.

Fifth, the emergence of the student movement is to be understood in large part as a consequence of opportunities for prolonged interaction available in the university environment. The kinds of personality structures produced by the socializing experiences outlined above need not necessarily have generated a collective response. In fact, Kenneth Keniston's recently published work on alienated students at Harvard suggests that students with similar characteristics to those described here were identifiable on college campuses in the Fifties. But Keniston makes clear that his highly alienated subjects were rarely involved in extensive peer-relationships, and that few opportunities for collective expressions of alienation were then available. The result was that each of his subjects attempted to work out a value-system and a mode of operation on his own (Keniston, 1965b; and this issue).

What seems to have happened was that during the Fifties, there began to emerge an "alienated" student culture, as students with alienated predispositions became visible to each other and began to interact. There was some tendency for these students to identify with the "Beat" style and related forms of bohemianism. Since this involved a high degree of disaffiliation, "cool" noncommitment and social withdrawal, observers tended to interpret this subculture as but a variant of the prevailing privatism of the Fifties. However, a series of precipitating events, most particularly the southern student sit-ins, the revolutionary successes of students in Cuba, Korea and Turkey, and the suppression of student demonstrations against the House Un-American Activities Committee in San Francisco, suggested to groups of students that direct action was a plausible means for expressing their grievances. These first stirrings out of apathy were soon enmeshed in a variety of organizations and publicized in several student-organized underground journals—thus enabling the movement to grow and become increasingly institutionalized. The story of the emergence and growth of the movement cannot be developed here; my main point now is that many of its characteristics cannot be understood solely as consequences of the structural and personality variables outlined earlier—in addition, a full understanding of the dynamics of the movement requires a "collective behavior" perspective.

Sixth, organized expressions of youth disaffection are likely to be an increasingly visible and established feature of our society. In important ways, the "new radicalism" is *not* new, but rather a more widespread version of certain subcultural phenomena with a considerable history. During the late nineteenth and early twentieth century a considerable number of young people began to move out of their provincial environments as a consequence of university education; many of these people gathered in such locales as Greenwich Village and created the first visible bohemian subculture in the United States. The Village bohemians and associated young intellectuals shared a common concern with radical politics and, influenced by Freud, Dewey, etc., with the reform of the process of socialization in America—i.e., a restructuring of family and educational institutions (Lash, 1965; Coser, 1965). Although many of the reforms advocated by this group were only partially realized in a formal sense, it seems to be the case that the values and style of life which they advocated have become strongly rooted in American life. This has occurred in at least two ways: first, the subcultures created by the early intellectuals took root, have grown and been emulated in various parts of the country. Second, many of the *ideas* of the early twentieth-century intellectuals, particularly their critique of the bourgeois family and Victorian sensibility, spread rapidly; it now seems that an important defining characteristic of the college-educated mother is her willingness to adopt child-centered techniques of rearing, and of the college educated couple that they create a family which is democratic and egalitarian in style. In this way, the values that an earlier generation espoused in an abstract way have become embodied as *personality traits* in the new generation. The rootedness of the bohemian and quasi-bohemian subcultures, and the spread of their ideas with the rapid increase in the number of college graduates, suggests that there will be a steadily increasing number of families raising their children with considerable ambivalence about dominant values, incentives and expectations in the society. In this sense, the students who engage in protest or who participate in "alienated" styles of life are often not "converts" to a "deviant" adaptation, but people who have been socialized into a developing cultural tradition. Rising levels of affluence and education are drying up the traditional sources of alienation and radical politics; what we are now becoming aware of, however, is that this same situation is creating new sources of alienation and idealism, and new constituencies for radicalism.

THE YOUTH AND SOCIAL CHANGE PROJECT

These hypotheses have been the basis for two studies we have undertaken. Study One, begun in the Summer of 1965, involved extensive interviews with samples of student activists and nonactivists and their parents. Study Two, conducted in the Spring of 1966, involved interviews with samples of participants, nonparticipants and opponents of the tumultuous "anti-ranking" sit-in at the University of Chicago.

Study One—The Socialization of Student Activists

For Study One, fifty students were selected from mailing lists of various peace, civil rights, and student movement organizations in the Chicago area. An additional fifty students, matched for sex, neighborhood of parents' residence, and type of college attended, were drawn from student directories of Chicago-area colleges. In each case, an attempt was made to interview both parents of the student respondent, as well as the student himself. We were able to interview both parents of 82 of the students; there were two cases in which no parents were available for the interview, in the remaining 16 cases, one parent was interviewed. The interviews with both students and parents averaged about three hours in length, were closely parallel in content, and covered such matters as: political attitudes and participation; attitudes toward the student movement and "youth"; "values," broadly defined; family life, child-rearing, family conflict and other aspects of socialization. Rating scales and "projective" questions were used to assess family members' perceptions of parent-child relationships.

It was clear to us that our sampling procedures were prone to a certain degree of error in the classification of students as "activists" and "nonactivists." Some students who appeared on mailing lists of activist organizations had no substantial involvement in the student movement, while some of our "control" students had a considerable history of such involvement. Thus the data to be reported here are based on an index of Activism constructed from interview responses to questions about participation in seven kinds of activity: attendance at rallies, picketing, canvassing, working on a project to help the disadvantaged, being jailed for civil disobedience, working full-time for a social action organization, serving as an officer in such organizations.

Study Two—The "Anti-Ranking" Sit-in

In May, 1966, about five hundred students sat-in at the Administration Build-ing on the campus of the University of Chicago, barring the building to offical use for two and a half days. The focal issue of the protest, emulated on a number of other campuses in the succeeding days, was the demand by the students that the Uni-versity not cooperate with the Selective Service System in supplying class standings for the purpose of assigning student deferments. The students who sat-in formed an organization called "Students Against the Rank" (SAR). During the sit-in, an-other group of students, calling themselves "Students for a Free Choice" (SFC) circulated a petition opposing the sit-in and supporting the University Administra-tion's view that each student had a right to submit (or withhold) his class stand-ings—the University could not withhold the "frank" of students who requested it. This petition was signed by several hundred students.

Beginning about 10 days after the end of the sit-in, we undertook to interview three samples of students: a random sample of 65 supporters of SAR (the pro-testers); a random sample of 35 signers of the SFC petition (the anti-protesters); approximately 60 students who constituted the total population of two randomly selected floors in the student dormitories. Of about 160 students thus selected, 117 were finally either interviewed or returned mailed questionnaires. The interview schedule was based largely on items used in the original study; it also included some additional items relevant to the sit-in and the "ranking" controversy.

Some Preliminary Findings

At this writing, our data analysis is at an early stage. In general, however, it is clear that the framework of hypotheses with which we began is substantially sup-ported, and in interesting ways, refined, by the data. Our principal findings thus far include the following: [1]

Activists tend to come from upper status families.   As indicated earlier, our study of the Chicago sit-in suggests that such actions attract students predominantly from upper-status backgrounds. When compared with students who did not sit-in, and with students who signed the anti-sit-in petition, the sit-in participants reported higher family incomes, higher levels of education for both fathers and mothers, and overwhelmingly perceived themselves to be "upper-middle class". One illustrative finding: in our dormitory sample, of 24 students reporting family incomes of above $15,000, half participated in the sit-in. Of 23 students reporting family incomes below $15,000, only two sat-in.

Certain kinds of occupations are particularly characteristic of the parents of sit-in participants. In particular, their fathers tend to be professionals (college faculty, lawyers, doctors) rather than businessmen, white collar employees or blue-collar workers. Moreover, somewhat unexpectedly, activists' mothers are likely to be employed, and are more likely to have "career" types of employment, than are the mothers of nonactivists.

Also of significance, although not particularly surprising, is the fact that activists are more likely to be Jewish than are nonactivists. (For example 45% of our SAR sample reported that they were Jewish; only about one-fourth of the non-participants were Jewish). Furthermore, a very high proportion of both Jewish and non-Jewish activists report no religious preference for themselves and their parents. Associated with the Jewish ethnicity of a large proportion of our activist samples is the fact the great majority of activists' grandparents were foreign born. Yet, despite this, data from Study One show that the grandparents of activists tended to be relatively highly educated as compared to the grandparents of nonactivists. Most of the grandparents of nonactivists had not completed high school; nearly half of the grandparents of activists had at least a high school education and fully one-fourth of their maternal grandmothers had attended college. These data suggest that relatively high status characterized the families of activists over several generations; this conclusion is supported by data showing that, unlike nonactivist grandfathers, the grandfathers of activists tended to have white collar, professional and entre-preneurial occupations rather than blue collar jobs.

In sum, our data suggest that, at least at major Northern colleges, students involved in protest activity are characteristically from families which are urban, highly educated, Jewish or irreligious, professional and affluent. It is perhaps particularly interesting that many of their mothers are uniquely well-educated and involved in careers, and that high status and education has characterized these families over at least two generations.

Activists are more "radical" than their parents; but activists' parents are decidedly more liberal than others of their status. The demographic data reported above suggests that activists come from high status families, but the occupational, religious and educational characteristics of these families are unique in several important ways. The distinctiveness of these families is especially clear when we examine data from Study One on the political attitudes of students and their parents. In this study, it should be remembered, activist and nonactivist families were roughly equivalent in status, income and education because of our sampling procedures. Our data quite clearly demonstrate that the fathers of activists are disproportionately liberal. For example, whereas forty percent of the nonactivists' fathers said that they were Republican, only thirteen percent of the activists' fathers were Republicans. Only six percent of nonactivists' fathers were willing to describe themselves as "highly liberal" or "socialist", whereas sixty percent of the activists' fathers accepted such designations. Forty percent of the nonactivists' fathers described themselves as conservative; none of the activists' fathers endorsed that position.[2]

In general, differences in the political preferences of the students paralleled these parental differences. The nonactivist sample is only slightly less conservative and Republican than their fathers; all of the activist students with Republican fathers report their own party preferences as either Democrat or independent. Thirty-two percent of the activists regard themselves as "socialist" as compared with sixteen percent of their fathers. In general, both nonactivists and their fathers are typically "moderate" in their politics; activists and their fathers tend to be at least "liberal", but a substantial proportion of the activists prefer a more "radical" designation.

A somewhat more detailed picture of comparative political positions emerges when we examine responses of students and their fathers to a series of 6-point scales on which respondents rated their attitudes on such issues as: US bombing of North Vietnam, US troops in the Dominican Republic, student participation in protest demonstrations, civil rights protests involving civil disobedience, Lyndon Johnson, Barry Goldwater, congressional investigations of "un-American activities", full socialization of all industries, socialization of the medical profession.

Table 1 presents data on activists and nonactivists and their fathers with

Table 1
Students' and Fathers' Attitudes on Current Issues

	Activists		Nonactivists	
Issue	Students	Fathers	Students	Fathers
Percent who approve:				
Bombing of North Vietnam	9	27	73	80
American troops in Dominican Republic	6	33	65	50
Student participation in protest demonstrations	100	80	61	37
Civil disobedience in civil rights protests	97	57	28	23
Congressional investigations of "un-American activities"	3	7	73	57
Lyndon Johnson	35	77	81	83
Barry Goldwater	0	7	35	20
Full socialization of industry	62	23	5	10
Socialization of the medical profession	94	43	30	27
N	34	30	37	30

respect to these items. This table suggests, first, wide divergence between the two groups of fathers on most issues, with activist fathers typically critical of current policies. Although activists' fathers are overwhelmingly "liberal" in their responses, for the most part, activist students tend to endorse "left-wing" positions more strongly and consistently than do their fathers. The items showing strongest divergence between activists and their fathers are interesting. Whereas activists overwhelmingly endorse civil disobedience, nearly half of their fathers do not. Whereas fathers of both activists and nonactivists tend to approve of Lyndon Johnson, activist students tend to disapprove of him. Whereas activists' fathers tend to disapprove of "full socialization of industry", this item is endorsed by the majority of activists (although fewer gave an extremely radical response on this item than any other); whereas the vast majority of activists approve of socialized medicine, the majority of their fathers do not. This table provides further support for the view that activists, though more "radical" than their fathers, come predominantly from very liberal homes. The attitudes of nonactivists and their fathers are conventional and supportive of current policies; there is a slight tendency on some items for nonactivist students to endorse more conservative positions than their fathers.

It seems fair to conclude, then, that most students who are involved in the movement (at least those one finds in a city like Chicago) are involved in neither "conversion" from nor "rebellion" against the political perspectives of their fathers. A more supportable view suggests that the great majority of these students are attempting to fulfill and renew the political traditions of their families. However, data from our research which have not yet been analyzed as of this writing, will permit a more systematic analysis of the political orientations of the two generations.

Activism is related to a complex of values, not ostensibly political, shared by both the students and their parents. Data which we have just begun to analyze suggest that the political perspectives which differentiate the families of activists from other families at the same socioeconomic level are part of a more general clustering of values and orientations. Our findings and impressions on this point may be briefly summarized by saying that, whereas nonactivists and their parents tend to express conventional orientations toward achievement, material success, sexual morality and religion, the activists and their parents tend to place greater stress on involvement in intellectual and esthetic pursuits, humanitarian concerns, opportunity for self-expression, and tend to deemphasize or positively disvalue personal achievement, conventional morality and conventional religiosity.

When asked to rank order a list of "areas of life", nonactivist students and their parents typically indicate that marriage, career and religion are most important. Activists, on the other hand, typically rank these lower than the "world of ideas, art and music" and "work for national and international betterment"—and so, on the whole, do their parents (see also the relevant data presented by Trent and Craise, 1967).

When asked to indicate their vocational aspirations, nonactivist students are typically firmly decided on a career and typically mention orientations toward the professions, science and business. Activists, on the other hand, are very frequently undecided on a career; and most typically those who have decided mention college teaching, the arts or social work as aspirations.

These kinds of responses suggest, somewhat crudely, that student activists identify with life goals which are intellectual and "humanitarian" and that they reject conventional and "privatized" goals more frequently than do nonactivist students.

FOUR VALUE PATTERNS

More detailed analyses which we are just beginning to undertake support the view that the value-patterns expressed by activists are highly correlated with those of their parents. This analysis has involved the isolation of a number of value-patterns which emerged in the interview material, the development of systems of code categories related to each of these patterns, and the blind coding of all the interviews with respect to these categories. The kinds of data we are obtaining in this way may be illustrated by describing four of the value patterns we have observed:

Romanticism: Esthetic and Emotional Sensitivity

This variable is defined as: "sensitivity to beauty and art—appreciation of painting, literature and music, creativity in art forms—concern with esthetic experience and the development of capacities for esthetic expression—concern with emotions deriving from perception of beauty—attachment of great significance to esthetic experience. More broadly, it can be conceived of as involving explicit concern with experience as such, with feeling and passion, with immediate and inner experience; a concern for the realm of feeling rather than the rational, technological or instrumental side of life; preference for the realm of experience as against that of activity, doing or achieving." Thirteen items were coded in these terms: for each item a score of zero signified no mention of "romanticist" concerns, a score of one signified that such a concern appeared. Table 2 indicates the relationship between "romanticism" and Activism. Very few Activists received scores on Romanticism which placed them as "low"; conversely, there were very few high "romantics" among the Nonactivists.

Table 2
Scores on Selected Values by Activism (Percentages)

		Activists	Nonactivists
(a)	*Romanticism*		
	High	35	11
	Medium	47	49
	Low	18	40
(b)	*Intellectualism*		
	High	32	3
	Medium	65	57
	Low	3	40
(c)	*Humanitarianism*		
	High	35	0
	Medium	47	22
	Low	18	78
(d)	*Moralism*		
	High	6	54
	Medium	53	35
	Low	41	11
	N	34	37

Intellectualism

This variable is defined as: "Concern with ideas—desire to realize intellectual capacities—high valuation of intellectual creativities—appreciation of theory and knowledge—participation in intellectual activity (e.g., reading, studying, teaching, writing) —broad intellectual concerns." Ten items were scored for "intellectualism." Almost no Activists are low on this variable; almost no Nonactivists received a high score.

Humanitarianism

This variable is defined as: "Concern with plight of others in society; desire to help others—value on compassion and sympathy—desire to alleviate suffering; value on egalitarianism in the sense of opposing privilege based on social and economic distinction; particular sensitivity to the deprived position of the disadvantaged." This variable was coded for ten items; an attempt was made to exclude from this index all items referring directly to participation in social action. As might be expected, "humanitarianism" is strongly related to Activism, as evidenced in Table 2.

Moralism and Self-Control

This variable is defined as: "Concern about the importance of strictly controlling personal impulses—opposition to impulsive or spontaneous behavior—value on keeping tight control over emotions—adherence to conventional authority; adherence to conventional morality—a high degree of moralism about sex, drugs, alcohol, etc. reliance on a set of external and inflexible rules to govern moral behavior; emphasis on importance of hard work; concern with determination, "stick-to-itiveness"; antagonism toward idleness—value on diligence, entrepreneurship, task orientation, ambition." Twelve items were scored for this variable. As Table 2 suggests, "moralism" is also strongly related to activism; very few Activists score high on this variable, while the majority of Nonactivists are high scorers.

These values are strongly related to activism. They are also highly intercorrelated, and, most importantly, parent and student scores on these variables are strongly correlated.

These and other value patterns will be used as the basis for studying value transmission in families, generational similarities and differences and several other problems. Our data with respect to them provide further support for the view that the unconventionailty of activists flows out of and is supported by their family traditions.

Activists' parents are more "permissive" than parents of nonactivists. We have just begun to get some findings bearing on our hypothesis that parents of Activists will tend to have been more "permissive" in their child-rearing practices than parents of equivalent status whose children are not oriented toward activism.

One measure of parental permissiveness we have been using is a series of rating scales completed by each member of the family. A series of seven-point bipolar scales was presented in a format similar to that of the "Semantic Differential". Students were asked to indicate "how my mother (father) treated me as a child" on such scales as "warm-cold"; "stern-mild"; "hard-soft"—10 scales in all. Each parent, using the same scales, rated "how my child thinks I treated him".

Table 3 presents data on how sons and daughters rated each of their parents

Table 3
Sons and Daughters Ratings of Parents by Activism (Percentages)

Trait of Parent	Males		Females	
	Hi Act	Lo Act	Hi Act	Lo Act
mild-stern				
percent rating mother "mild"	63	44	59	47
percent rating father "mild"	48	33	48	32
soft-hard				
percent rating mother "soft"	69	61	60	57
percent rating father "soft"	50	50	62	51
lenient-severe				
percent rating mother "lenient"	94	61	66	63
percent rating father "lenient"	60	44	47	42
easy-strict				
percent rating mother "easy"	75	50	77	52
percent rating father "easy"	69	44	47	37
N	23	24	27	26

on each of four scales: "mild-stern"; "soft-hard"; "lenient-severe"; and "easy-strict". In general, this table shows that Activist sons and daughters tend to rate their parents as "milder", "more lenient", and "less severe" than do nonactivists. Similar data were obtained using the parents' ratings of themselves.

A different measure of permissiveness is based on the parents' response to a series of "hypothetical situations". Parents were asked, for example, what they would do if their son (daughter) "decided to drop out of school and doesn't know what he really wants to do". Responses to this open-ended question were coded as indicating "high intervention" or "low intervention". Data for fathers on this item are reported in Table 4. Another hypothetical situation presented to the parents was that their child was living with a member of the opposite sex. Responses to this item were coded as "strongly intervene, mildly intervene, not intervene". Data for this item for fathers appears in Table 5. Both tables show that fathers of Activists report themselves to be much less interventionist than fathers of nonactivists. Similar results were obtained with mothers, and for other hypothetical situations.

Table 4
Father's Intervention—"If Child Dropped Out of School"
(Percentages)

	Activism of Child	
Degree of Intervention	High	Low
Low	56	37
High	44	63
N	30	30

Clearly both types of measures just reported provide support for our hypothesis about the relationship between parental permissiveness and activism. We expect these relationships to be strengthened if "activism" is combined with certain of the value-patterns described earlier.

Table 5
Father's Intervention—"If Child Were Living
with Member of Opposite Sex"
(Percentages)

	Activism of Child	
Degree of Intervention	High	Low
None	20	14
Mild	50	28
Strong	30	58
N	30	30

A CONCLUDING NOTE

The data reported here constitute a small but representative sampling of the material we have collected in our studies of the student movement. In general, they provide support for the impressions and expectations we had when we undertook this work. Our view of the student movement as an expression of deep discontent felt by certain types of high status youth as they confront the incongruities between the values represented by the authority and occupational structure of the larger society and the values inculcated by their families and peer culture seems to fit well with the data we have obtained.

A variety of questions remain which, we hope, can be answered, at least in part, by further analyses of our data. Although it is clear that value differences between parents of Activists and Nonactivists are centrally relevant for understanding value, attitudinal and behavioral cleavages among types of students on the campus, it remains to be determined whether differences in family status, on the one hand, and childrearing practices, on the other, make an independent contribution to the variance. A second issue has to do with political ideology. First impressions of our data suggest that activists vary considerably with respect to their degree of politicization and their concern with ideological issues. The problem of isolating the key determinants of this variation is one we will be paying close attention to in further analysis of our interview material. Two factors are likely to be of importance here—first, the degree to which the student participates in radical student organizations; second, the political history of his parents.

At least two major issues are not confronted by the reasearch we have been doing. First, we have not examined in any detail the role of campus conditions as a determinant of student discontent (see Sampson, 1967 and Brown, 1967 for a further discussion of these institutional factors). The research reported here emphasizes family socialization and other antecedent experiences as determinants of student protest, and leads to the prediction that students experiencing other patterns of early socialization will be unlikely to be in revolt. This view needs to be counterbalanced by recalling instances of active student unrest on campuses where very few students are likely to have the backgrounds suggested here as critical. Is it possible that there are two components to the student protest movement—one generated to a great extent by early socialization; the second by grievances indigenous to the campus? At any rate, the interrelationships between personal dispositions and campus conditions need further detailed elucidation.

A second set of questions unanswerable by our research has to do with the future—what lies ahead for the movement as a whole and for the individual young people who participate in it? One direction for the student movement is toward institutionalization as an expression of youth discontent. This outcome, very typical of student movements in many countries, would represent a narrowing of the movement's political and social impact, a way of functionally integrating it into an otherwise stable society. Individual participants would be expected to pass through the movement on their way to eventual absorption, often at an elite level, into the established institutional order. An alternative direction would be toward the development of a full-fledged political "left", with the student movement serving, at least initially, as a nucleus. The potential for this latter development is apparent in recent events. It was the student movement which catalyzed professors and other adults into protest with respect to the Vietnam war. Students for a Democratic Society, the main organizational expression of the student movement, has had, for several years, a program for "community organizing", in which students and exstudents work full-time at the mobilization of constituencies for independent radical political and social action. This SDS program began in poverty areas; it is now beginning to spread to "middle class" communities. These efforts, and others like them, from Berkeley to New Haven, became particularly visible during the 1966 congressional elections, as a wave of "new left" candidates emerged across the country, often supported by large and sophisticated political organizations. Moreover, in addition to attempts at political organizations, SDS, through its "Radical Education Project" has begun to seek the involvement of faculty members, professionals and other intellectuals for a program of research and education designed to lay the foundations for an intellectually substantial and ideologically developed "new left".

At its convention in September, 1966, SDS approached, but did not finally decide, the question of whether to continue to maintain its character as a campus-based, student organization or to transform itself into a "Movement for a Democratic Society". Characteristically, the young people there assembled amended the organization's constitution so that anyone regardless of status or age could join, while simultaneously they affirmed the student character of the group by projecting a more vigorous program to organize uncommitted students.

The historical significance of the student movement of the Sixties remains to be determined. Its impact on the campus and on the larger society has already been substantial. It is clearly a product of deep discontent in certain significant and rapidly growing segments of the youth population. Whether it becomes an expression of generational discontent, or the forerunner of major political realignments—or simply disintegrates—cannot really be predicted by detached social scientists. The ultimate personal and political meaning of the student movement remains a matter to be determined by those who are involved with it—as participants, as allies, as critics, as enemies.

NOTES

[1] A more detailed report of the procedures and findings of these studies is available in Flacks (1966).

[2] For the purposes of this report, "activists" are those students who were in the top third on our Activism index; "nonactivists" are those students who were in the bottom third—this latter group reported virtually no participation in any activity associated with the student movement. The "activists" on the other hand had taken part in at least one activity indicating high commitment to the movement (e.g. going to jail, working full-time, serving in a leadership capacity).

REFERENCES

Aaron, Daniel. *Writers on the left.* New York: Avon, 1965.

Bell, Daniel. *The end of ideology.* New York: The Free Pree, 1962.

Braungart, R. G. Social stratification and political attitudes. Pennsylvania State University, 1966, (unpublished ms.).

Bronfenbrenner, U. The changing American child: A speculative analysis. *Merrill-Palmer Quarterly,* 1961, 7, 73–85.

Brown, Donald R. Student stress and the institutional environment. *Journal of Social Issues,* 1967, 23, 92–107.

Coser, Lewis. *Men of ideas.* New York: The Free Press, 1965.

Erikson, Erik. Identity and the life-cycle. *Psychological Issues,* 1959, 1, 1–171.

Erikson, Erik. *Childhood and society.* New York: Norton, 1963, 306–25.

Eisenstadt, Shmuel N. *From generation to generation.* Glencoe, Ill.: The Free Press, 1956.

Flacks, R. The liberated generation. University of Chicago, 1966. (mimeo)

Goldsen, Rose; Rosenberg, Morris; Williams, Robin; and Suchman, Edward. *What college students think,* Princeton, N.J.: Van Nostrand, 1960.

Jacob, Philip. *Changing values in college.* New York: Harper, 1957.

Keniston, Kenneth. *The uncommitted.* New York: Harcourt Brace, 1965a.

Keniston, Kenneth, Social change and youth in America. In E. Erikson (Ed.), *The challenge of youth.* Garden City, N. Y.: Doubleday Anchor, 1965b.

Keniston, Kenneth. The sources of student dissent. *Journal of Social Issues,* 1967, 23, 108–137.

Lasch, Christopher. *The new radicalism in America.* New York: Knopf, 1965.

Lipset, Seymour. *Political man, the social bases of politics.* Garden City, N.Y.: Doubleday Anchor, 1960.

Lipset, Seymour. University students and politics in underdeveloped countries. *Comparative Education Review,* 1966, 10, 132–62.

Lipset, Seymour and Altbach, P. Student politics and higher education in the United States. *Comparative Education Review,* 1966, 10, 320–49.

Miller, Daniel and Swanson, G. E. *The changing American parent.* New York: Wiley, 1958.

Newcomb, Theodore and Flacks, R. *Deviant subcultures on a college campus.* US Office of Education, 1963.

Parsons, Talcott. Youth in the context of American society. In E. Erikson (Ed.), *The challenge of youth.* Garden City, N.Y.: Doubleday Anchor, 1965.

Sampson, Edward E. Student activism and the decade of protest. *Journal of Social Issues,* 1967, 23, 1–33.

Shils, Edward. The intellectuals in the political development of new states. *World Politics,* 1960, 12, 329–68.

Stinchcombe, Arthur. *Rebellion in a high school.* Chicago: Quadrangle, 1964.

Trent, James W. and Craise, Judith L. Commitment and conformity in the American college. *Journal of Social Issues,* 1967, 23, 34–51.

Trow, Martin. Student cultures and administrative action. In Sutherland, R. et al. (Eds.), *Personality factors on the college campus.* Austin, Tex.: Hogg Foundation for Mental Health, 1962.

Veblen, Thorstein. The intellectual pre-eminence of Jews in modern Europe. In B. Rosenberg (Ed.), *Thorstein Veblen.* New York: Crowell, 1963.

PART FOUR

Aggregation: The Effects of Personality on the Functioning of Political Institutions

20

A General Conceptualization

In this contribution, Inkeles and Levinson present a conceptual framework for the analysis of the reciprocal impact of personality and the sociocultural systems of large organizations. The authors propose a conceptualization delineating four parallel areas in the "personal system" and in the organization. Individual psychophysical attributes are linked to the organizational "ecology"; the idea system of the individual is linked to the cultural properties of the organization; individual personality structure parallels organizational structure; and individual modes of adaptation parallel the social processes that describe the actual workings of the organization.

The conceptualization of organization and personality interaction presented here fits closely within the framework for analysis of role behavior presented by Levinson in "Role, Personality, and Social Structure in the Organizational Setting" (Selection four). At the level of macro-analysis, it also parallels the Smith map for analyzing individual behavior (selection two).

THE PERSONAL SYSTEM AND THE SOCIOCULTURAL SYSTEM IN LARGE-SCALE ORGANIZATIONS

Alex Inkeles and Daniel J. Levinson

A central problem in social psychology concerns the relevance of individual (and modal) personality for the functioning of sociocultural systems. This problem is of especial interest in the case of the large-scale organizations. However, little progress has been made despite the growing literature in this field. Empirical work is often overly narrow or conceptually sectarian. Greater attention should be given, we believe, to the development of a more comprehensive analytic scheme encompassing three major domains: (a) the individual personality; (b) the organization as a collective enterprise; and (c) the interrelations and reciprocal impact of individual and organization. We propose several areas of analysis (sets of variables) within each domain, and we cite two studies that indicate needed directions of further investigation.

Reprinted from *Sociometry*, 26 (1963), 217–29.

There is general agreement, we would suppose, that an individual's personality may exert some influence upon his role-performance. It has been more difficult to get social scientists to entertain the hypothesis that personality factors enter *systematically* as significant influences in the performance of whole sets of roles such as those of the occupational realm, the kinship system, or the political order. After the extensive, and often intense, post-war discussion of the relevant issues, however, many are now prepared to accept that idea, at least in principle, as a basis for further exploration. Those of us who hold strongly to this position have the responsibility to specify more precisely what we assume to be the relation of personality patterns to the functioning of social systems.

There is still a good deal of uncertainty as to which aspects of personality are most relevant for, and how they enter into, the functioning of institutions. This requires that we develop different, and broader, conceptions of personality than those which are now commonly used in organizational analysis. We will not pursue the interrelations of personality and social structure for long, however, before realizing that we must also adjust our thinking about social systems. We must treat these not only in the usual sociological terms of norms, statuses and roles, but also as characteristic milieus which confront individuals with demands, cross-pressures, dilemmas, stresses, opportunities, and supports which cannot be understood without reference to their psychological as well as their social meanings.

We shall deal here with the interrelations of personality and sociocultural system in the case of the large-scale organization (industrial firm, government agency, college, hospital, and the like).[1] Our chief purpose is to present the outlines of a systematic theoretical framework. We make no special claims for originality. Virtually all of the single components of this framework may be found at one place or another in the existing literature of organizational theory or of personality theory. However, very few attempts have previously been made to bring these diverse notions together into a reasonably comprehensive, integrated scheme.

The question guiding our inquiry may be stated as follows: if we wish to develop a genuine social psychology of organizational life, an understanding of the reciprocal impact of personality and organization, what theoretical domains must be taken into account? Three broad domains immediately suggest themselves, and they form the major rubrics of our scheme.

(a) A sociopsychological conception of the individual. Contemporary theories in psychology and sociology differ considerably in their emphasis upon, and their conceptualization of, different aspects of personality. Some focus primarily upon more central or underlying features such as unconscious fantasies and modes of ego defense, whereas others deal almost exclusively with more conscious values, attitudes, and self-concepts. Clearly, many aspects and levels of personality may influence, and be influenced by, the individual's participation in organizational life. A comprehensive sociopsychological analysis must therefore have room, theoretically and empirically, for diverse personal characteristics. We shall indicate below what seem to us the major analytic areas in this domain.

(b) A sociopsychological conception of the organization. Once again, different theoretical approaches in the social sciences emphasize different aspects of the organization as a collective enterprise. Technology, stratification, leadership, division of labor, informal structure—these and other aspects have claimed the attention of research workers. Most often, however, there is a focus on one or two and a neglect of the others. Our concern here is to designate the major analytic areas that merit inclusion in any attempt to characterize systematically an organization. In addition, from a sociopsychological point of view we wish to consider the organizational properties not merely in impersonal terms but rather in terms of their potential impact upon, and their influence by, the personalities of the individual members.

(c) A conception of the links and interrelation between person and organization. The forms of linkage are clearly numerous and complex. For illustrative purposes we have chosen one: the influence of modal personality on the functioning and the stability or change of the organization. Our question here is: in what sense does an organization "require" certain personality characteristics in its members, and what are the consequences for the organization if these characteristics do not obtain?

The approach taken here is, so to say, "antisectarian." We are trying to lay out, in a systematic fashion, the conceptual domains that must ultimately be utilized in a general theory of person-organization interrelations, and in the conduct of organizational research. We shall not take a sectarian stand—although we have our own preferences—regarding the relative merits of alternative theoretical conceptions within a domain, or regarding the causal importance of the various domains. It is not that we eschew theoretical controversy. Rather, we would suggest that controversy can be carried forward most fruitfully when it is placed within a broader intellectual framework.

Finally, we believe that current organizational research suffers greatly from the lack of an inclusive analytic scheme. Although there have been a number of excellent studies, the empirical work in this field has been generally haphazard and uncumulative. More systematic and comparative organizational research must be guided by a more broadly conceived analytic scheme. The following proposals concerning the study of the individual, the organization, and their interrelations, are offered as a first step toward that end.

THE PERSONAL SYSTEM

At the present time, there is no generally agreed upon set of categories for describing the personal properties of any individual. Two conceptions of the individual, commonly held by psychologists and sociologists, have led investigators to omit from systematic consideration aspects of the person which figure prominently in his organizational role. These have been characterized by Levinson as the "mirage" and the "sponge" theories.[2] The former, particularly characteristic of the psychoanalytic literature, regards unconscious motives and defenses as the essential features of personality; values, ideologies and behavior are treated explicitly or implicitly as mere epiphenomena or by-products. The "sponge" theory, more common among sociologists, treats the individual's ideas, values, goals and behavior as mere reflections of social structure, and by default leaves as the distinctly personal only those modes of reaction which are assumed to be unique or idiosyncratic. Both approaches fail to treat the person's values, ideas, role-conceptions, and role-behaviors as important phenomena in their own right, which cannot be understood merely by deduction from social norms nor by induction from unconscious fantasies and impulses.

This state of affairs is unfortunate. Clearly, very different conceptions of personality are involved here. When the psychoanalytically oriented psychologist uses the concept of personality almost exclusively to represent certain features of individual psychodynamics, the sociologist finds it too limited and lacking in social relevance. Similarly, when the sociologist conceives of personality solely in terms of the individual's orientations and values in regard to political and social issues the psychologist finds it too superficial and narrow.

We propose the adoption of a much broader and more neutral term, "the personal system," to represent the totality of the relatively enduring attributes which characterize an individual. For purposes of defining the personal system we do not care whether these attributes are widely shared with others or are distinctive for the given individual. It is of course important to know whether a given view is held by one man alone, by most men of his class, or by all men in his society. However, the meaning of such facts in any specific case cannot be determined without reference to a large number of other facts. Moreover, we include characteristics from all "levels" of personality: those which are, psychodynamically speaking, more peripheral, and those conceived to be more central or underlying. Those who wish may apply the term "personality" to any part of the personal system, and assign that part whatever role their theoretical orientation prescribes. Our concern here is with comprehensiveness. We wish to avoid prejudging questions of relevance, importance and the like. We leave for empirical exploration the relative "significance," however defined, of any particular element of the personal system.

The personal system may be encompassed analytically in four major areas. These areas are essentially heuristic; they are not yet adequately conceptualized and the boundaries between them are unclear at many points. Nonetheless, they have some utility in pointing up the wide variety of personal characteristics that must ultimately be taken into account.

1. Psychophysical and Psychosocial Attributes

This is an especially amorphous area. It contains a number of attributes that have been used frequently in empirical research by sociologists and psychologists; but their theoretrical status remains vague. We would include here such attributes as age, sex, body-type; general intelligence and specific skills (manual, artistic, mathematical, etc.); and temperamental qualities such as energy level, excitability, and the like.

We shall perhaps generate some controversy by including under this rubric various psychosocial attributes of the person, such as his income, occupation, political membership and reference groups, class of origin, and so on. A class and a political party are, of course, collective units and components of a broader social structure. However, membership in a class or party is an attribute of an individual, an element of his "personal system." A study of the relation between class level and child-rearing attitudes is concerned with two properties of the individual. It becomes a study of class as such only when it inquires into the sociocultural system encompassing all members of a given class and providing an environment within which certain kinds of child-rearing attitudes tend to evolve.

It is important to distinguish between the group membership or other "external" attributes and the more intrinsically psychological properties of the person (noted below). For example, "years of education" is a commonly used and empirically significant variable. While continuing to use it, we must go further and study independently such personal attributes as intellectual sophistication, values, and modes of cognitive functioning, which are imperfectly related to educational level. It is a persistent defect of sociological research that investigators assume too simple and direct a correlation between group-membership attributes of the person and other attributes falling in the areas noted below. The degree of relationship, and the causal context of the relationship, must be determined empirically and not taken for granted.

2. The Idea System

We are concerned here with the content and patterning of ideas in the individual. This area includes level and kind of factual information, technical knowledge, and empirical knowledge as culturally defined and validated. It includes, also, more general beliefs, attitudes, and values, and the patterning of these into broad conceptions of the cosmos, nature, society, and man. Within the organizational setting, it includes the person's ideology regarding the nature and the purposes of the organization and his conception of the various roles within it. A value, ideology or specific attitude is a part of the personal idea-system to the extent that it is held with some conviction and durability by the individual. Ideas do not qualify as part of the personal system merely because they are "widespread" in a given group or important in its culture. Ideologies, role-conceptions, values, and the like have their existence independently of any given individual, and have usually been studied by sociologists as properties of the sociocultural system. From a sociopsychological point of view, we are interested in them equally as components of the sociocultural system and as components of the personal system—and, ultimately, in the interrelations between the two.

3. Personality Structure: The Patterning of Psychodynamic Dispositions

The focus here is on the personal attributes most commonly emphasized in dynamic personality theories: character traits; core values and moral standards; unconscious motives, fantasies, conflicts and anxieties; modes of ego defense; ego ideal and life goals; and the like. To be included here, an attribute must be relatively enduring and difficult to change (though by no means unchangeable); it must play an important part in the internal functioning of personality and find manifold expression in a variety of life situations. A person will, we would suppose, find one organizational system more congenial than another to the extent that it more adequately meets his inner structural requirements—sustains his defenses, gratifies his wishes, permits fulfillment of his values, treads lightly on his vulnerabilities. When the organization makes demands that are initially stressful or otherwise incompatible with major dispositions of the person, this may lead in time to intrapsychic change, to efforts on his part toward inducing organizational change, to some form of accommodation or deviance, or to his leaving the organization. At any rate, the relevance of central personality dispositions for the person's functioning in the organization can be studied only if we conceptualize and measure these dispositions within the over-all framework of organizational analysis.

4. Modes of Adaptation and Behavioral Striving

We refer here to the personality in action, as it were, to the ways in which the individual comes to grips with the demands and opportunities of the external world. These aspects of the personal system are more "peripheral" than those in

(3) above, in the sense that they represent the ego's contact with the external world. They are accordingly subject to influence both from external sources and from "central" motives, defenses, and the like. To conceive of them as peripheral is not, however, to suggest that they are unimportant. Indeed, their position at the "outer face" of personality gives them a crucial significance for social psychology; they provide an essential link between depth psychology and sociology.

We include here the person's everyday modes of cognitive, affective, and conative functioning. What kinds of relationships does he tend to establish with other persons generally, and differentially with authorities, peers, subordinates, strangers, deviants? What kinds of feelings does he communicate to others; and what feelings does he evoke in others? What are the qualities of his cognitive functioning: diffuse, precisely analytic, hyper-intellectual, imaginative? What are his preferred modes of behavioral striving (conation)? Does he prefer a steady, even pace, or does he rather engage in bursts of furious activity which punctuate longer periods of relative quiescence or apathy? Is he firmly determined or capricious in his efforts; is he fiercely competitive, cooperative, solitary? These qualities are often regarded purely as matters of personal "style" having little social relevance. We would suggest, however, that they may have substantial consequences for the "fit" between individual and organization, and for organizational stability or change.

THE SOCIOCULTURAL SYSTEM OF THE ORGANIZATION

Since large scale organizations have been the focus of concerted research efforts in the past 10–15 years, it might be assumed that the task of structural analysis has been largely solved. Can one not go to any of the standard sources and find there a generally accepted scheme for the sociological analysis of the organization? Apparently not. The various studies use widely different schemes even at the descriptive level. The variations are due only in part to differences in general theory. They reflect even more, perhaps, the lack of a truly systematic comparative approach in empirical work: each investigator focuses on specific aspects of the organization studied, and his delineation of the organization's over-all system is largely idiosyncratic. In short, we have a number of organizational case studies but no generally applicable scheme that would provide a framework for comparative analysis.[3]

In formulating our own suggestions for a standard analytic scheme, we have been more concerned with inclusiveness than with taking one side or the other in current theoretical disputes. Our first goal is to develop the outlines of a truly comprehensive scheme embracing the major properties of any large-scale organization. A scheme of this kind would be useful as well in the analysis of other durable collectivities. We posit four sets of properties as comprising the "sociocultural system" of an organization. We shall briefly describe each of these in turn, giving a few illustrative examples.

1. Ecological Properties

These include, broadly speaking, the physical properties, technology, and resources of the organization. Technological change is coming increasingly to be recognized as a crucial aspect of organizational life, one that significantly influences and is influenced by other aspects. Additional ecological properties include architecture, size, density, or dispersion of population, life-span (duration), nature of the facilities and resources available for its work, and general degree of affluence or scarcity of rewards and conditions of work. Also relevant are the properties of the organization's external environment, and its relationships with various sectors of that environment. Is it competitive or monopolistic, revered or despised or taken for granted, free-acting or subject to scrutiny and control by outside agencies?

2. Cultural Properties

These include the guiding traditions, values, and "philosophy" as well as the major long-range goals and purposes of the organization. In the minds of its members, what is the organizational image, myth, or mystique? Is it conceived of as an extended family, controlled by an all-powerful, capriciously indulgent leader? Is it regarded primarily as a competitive, impersonal, profit-seeking machine, without moral obligation to anyone, or as a noble enterprise devoted selflessly to public service? It is trying merely to survive from year to year, or to expand and conquer, or to achieve and maintain an elite status, widely respected for the excellence of its work? The more explicitly stated goals are virtually always multiple and have to do with such things as production, profit, fostering of human health-education-welfare, social control, and the like. The organizational goals and myths may be consensually agreed upon. When they are defined differently by different groups (or by the same group at different times), the differences may become a source of internal strain.

3. Structural Properties

The study of social structure has, of course, been a major concern in sociology; indeed, at times the structural properties of organizations have been emphasized to the relative exclusion of all others. The organizational structure has at least the following components: a series of interrelated positions (offices, niches) providing for a division of labor; an ordering of positions into some form of status hierarchy providing for a distribution of authority and power, together with rules governing superordinate-subordinate relations; a system for the recruitment of new members; a system by which new members learn about the nature of the organization and the requirements and opportunities of their particular positions; a system of sanctions providing myriad forms of reward and punishment, presumably on the basis of the degree to which members fulfill or violate organizational values and norms; a system of communication providing for the transmission of ideas, information, and orders throughout various status-levels and sectors of the organization.

Systematic organizational analysis must take account of the above subsystems within the overall structure. How shall they be described? We sorely need a list of theoretically relevant dimensions or properties that can be used in the delineation of social structure in various types of organization.

4. Social Process Characteristics

The social structure provides a framework—a set of normative requirements, a form of patterning, and various devices for integrating and coordinating the members' activities. It is important, in addition, to describe the actual workings of the organization, which we refer to here as its "social process" characteristics. These are influenced in part, but only in part, by the structural arrangements. For the moment, the causal relations between these and other properties of the organization are not our primary concern. They can be interrelated only after they have been systematically distinguished and described.

Examples of social process characteristics are: rhythms of work (slow or fast, steady or pulsating); the degree of formality or informality in personal relationships; the formation of cliques and alliances (which in varying degrees foster or hinder organizational objectives); the emotional climate and types of emotional interchange (mutual support, subtle intimidation, periodic explosiveness, apathetic conformity, enthusiastic effort, ingratiation); qualities of mind such as bland or critical, inquiring or nonreflective, concrete or abstract.

It will be noted that the four areas used in the analysis of the sociocultural system closely parallel those of the personal system. There are conceptual similarities between the ecological properties of the organization and the psychophysical and psychosocial attributes of the individual; between the culture and the personal idea system; between the structural properties of the organization and of the individual; between the social process characteristics and the modes of individual adaptation. Although we are not committed to the maintenance of a complete isomorphism, we have found it useful thus far to proceed with this possibility in mind.

PERSONAL SYSTEM AND ORGANIZATIONAL FUNCTIONING

We turn now to our final question: What is the relevance of the personal system for the functioning and the stability or change of the organizational system? To illustrate our proposed mode of analysis, let us take "rhythm of work" as a property of the organization (Area 4).

Organizations differ markedly in the rhythms which the nature of the work permits or unrelentingly imposes. Factories with moving production lines experience a steady, unremitting pressure which demands evenness and continuity even though there can be substantial variation in the speed with which the line moves. Newspapers and magazines are also tied to a domineering schedule, but here time asserts itself in terms of a series of emergencies—the periodic and immutable deadlines. The content of certain kinds of magazines can, of course, be planned well ahead, but newspapers and news magazines cannot. Retail establishments reveal less regular rhythmic patterns. Saturdays are intensely busy, but shopping bursts are otherwise scattered throughout the year in connection with holidays and seasonal events. By contrast, many organizations work on an extremely smooth, regular or repetitive schedule which is traditionally established and involves few crises of any kind. This is true of schools (except perhaps at examination time) and to some extent libraries, many business offices such as insurance companies, some printing establishments, many small manufactories and large units producing standard items but not tied to a moving production line. Scheduling problems are again altogether different in organizations in which work involves a low level of standardization—for example shops fabricating special machines or parts, repair organizations, and the like.

Let us consider organizations characterized by a markedly uneven pattern in the rhythm of work. The functioning of these organizations will, we suggest, be significantly influenced by the conative patterns which are typical or modal among its personnel. In particular we would make the following hypotheses.

1. Recruitment will be more difficult for such organizations than for others lacking this characteristic.

2. Personnel in such organizations will display greater homogeneity in conative patterns than in other organizations, that is, there will be fewer modal categories and perhaps one really dominating mode.

3. Individuals having characteristics congruent with the required rhythms of work will, as a group, be relatively more "stable" members; they will have a lower rate of turnover than members having noncongruent characteristics.

4. Individuals whose conative style is incongruent with the required rhythms of work will show high rates of turnover; and those who remain longer with the firm will have shifted to positions largely free of the time pressures characteristic of the organization as a whole.

5. Comparing organizations in the same line of work, those having a higher proportion of members whose personal pattern of conative functioning is congruent with the rhythms of the organization will be more effective and efficient[4] in production.

We know of no standard test of conative patterns in the personality. If one exists, we doubt that it has been applied systematically to the personnel of any organization in a research design which would provide evidence to the hypotheses stated above. Our illustration thus remains for the moment little more than an academic exercise. Unfortunately, the situation is not greatly different even in the case of those features of the personal system, such as values, which have loomed larger in the attention of social scientists. A useful beginning has been made in a few studies which give some attention to the relevant dimensions. We cite two of them in order to suggest in broad outline the pattern which we hope will be set in future research.

In a study of unusually high quality Arthur Kornhauser and his associates explored the interrelations of personality and political participation as they affect a trade union organization, specifically the United Auto Workers' Union.[5] Their personal system measures included tests of authoritarianism, life satisfaction, social alienation and sense of futility in politics. These were related to measures of political interest, participation in Union affairs, pattern of voting, and the like. The research does not present truly independent measures of organizational functioning as influenced by personal system factors, but the authors make a number of interesting observations on this theme and point out the direction in which we should go.

Those high on authoritarianism tended to take extremist positions, either pro-union or anti-union, denying basic rights to those with whom they disagreed. For example, those who were extremely pro-union felt it was right for labor to support Stevenson, but would have denied business the right to support Eisenhower. Clearly such people could be a threat to democratic processes within their own organization. The authors comment: "Altogether our results show that these people (extremists, whether left or right) present a special challenge to political leadership both in the union and in the general society. . . . Their faith in powerful leaders, absolute obedience, and violence against deviates points to the danger of their being potential adherents of antidemocratic movements. . . ."[6] And again: "The problem of democracy in a large-scale society like ours, and more concretely in large-scale organizations like the union, is partly the problem of main-taining an adequate proportion of members who are capable of engaging in the market place of proposals and counter-proposals, immune from the feeling that 'the leader knows best' and from the temptation to condone, or to resort to, desperate measures of social and political crises." [7] The feared organizational outcome, the breakdown of union democracy, has not come about in this union. We can only speculate as to whether in those unions in which the breakdown of democracy is well advanced, the relative incidence of high authoritarianism and extremism is not greater than in the Auto Union. To suggest this possibility is, of course, not to minimize the role which the quality of leadership, the organizational structure, and the objective situation of any union may play in determining the outcome of the political process within it.

We may cite one other outstanding study relating elements of the personal system to organizational functioning, in this case a college. Stern, Stein, and Bloom [8] developed a broad synthetic characterization of two antipolar personality types. One type, the stereopaths, were more authoritarian and rigid, tending to depersonalize relations, to be exocathective and extraceptive. They were students in a college that stressed "abstract analysis, relativity of values and judgment rather than fixed standards, and an intraceptive rather than an impersonal orientation." In other words, the students having a stereopathic personality, sixteen percent of the total, constituted a modal group whose personality characteristics were markedly incongruent with the predominant values and mode of action of the college. Those at the opposite pole, the nonstereopaths, manifested qualities which were highly congruent with the values of the college and its typical class and study room procedures.

The stereopaths, although matched in intelligence to the nonstereopaths, performed less well on tests distinctive of this college, and were evaluated and graded lower by their instructors. Of those who withdrew at the end of the first year, 38 percent were stereopaths, 61 percent came from the middle range, and only 1 percent were nonstereopaths. In other words stereopaths contributed to withdrawals at twice the rate warranted by their weight in the student body, and nonstereopaths contributed only 1/16 of what they should have if all groups had contributed in proportion to their weight in the student body as a whole.

Clearly if the college wished to reduce the number withdrawing, it would be well advised to select its students from the nonstereopathic side of the distribution. If it did so, of course, other consequences perhaps not intended would follow. The student body would be more homogeneous in personality, and the challenge and stimulus of contrast and even conflict previously made possible by greater diversity would be lost.

In relating the person to the organization, both studies deal with members of only one position, namely, union member in the U.A.W. and student in the college. However, it cannot be assumed that the qualities, pressures, and needs of the organizations are exerted equally on all of its component parts; the general characteristics of an organizational setting may impinge quite differently on groups occupying different positions within the organization. Thus, the deadlines which dominate the occupational life of the reporter and editorial worker on a newspaper cannot be assumed to be terribly important pressures for the accountants and bookkeepers in the personnel or treasurer's office of the same organization. Also, members of these groups are deeply involved in other memberships which "cross-cut" that which is nominally their prime organizational involvement. Factory workers have their union, hospital doctors their medical association, and so on. The pressures created by these different organizational memberships are not necessarily wholly consistent or congruent. Thus, a further complication is introduced.

We cannot afford to neglect the ways in which the properties of the organization as a whole impinge upon its multiple component groups. At the same time, in studying the interaction of the personal system and the organizational system, we must consider the mediation of occupational and other subgroups within the organization. This will, of course, require that we develop a separate set of analytic categories adequate to the description of occupations. The task ultimately is to merge "occupational" and "organizational" perspectives in the analysis of "positions-in-organizations."

NOTES

[1] With appropriate modifications, the same general approach may be used in the analysis of smaller collective units, such as primary groups, and of larger structures and societies. For an earlier treatment of over-all societal analysis, and the problem of "national character," see Alex Inkeles and Daniel J. Levinson, "National character: The Study of Modal Personality and Sociocultural Systems," in Gardner Lindzey, ed., *Handbook of Social Psychology,* Cambridge, Mass.: Addison-Wesley, 1954.

[2] Daniel J. Levinson, "Idea Systems in the Individual and in Society," in George Zollschan and Walter Hirsch, ed., *Explorations in Social Change,* Boston: Houghton Mifflin, 1963.

[3] See, for example, the following organization studies: Alvin W. Gouldner, *Patterns of Industrial Bureaucracy,* Glencoe, Ill.: Free Press, 1954; Peter M. Blau, *The Dynamics of Bureaucracy: A Study of Interpersonal Relations in Two Government Agencies,* Chicago: University of Chicago Press, 1955; Philip Selznick, *TVA and the Grass Roots: A Study in the Sociology of Formal Organization,* Berkeley: University of California Press, 1949; Seymour M. Lipset, Martin Trow, and James Coleman, *Union Democracy: The Inside Politics of the International Typographical Union,* Glencoe Ill.: Free Press, 1956; Alfred H. Stanton and Morris S. Schwartz, *The Mental Hospital: A Study of Institutional Participation in Psychiatric Illness and Treatment,* New York: Basic Books, 1954; William A. Caudill, *The Psychiatric Hospital as a Small Society,* Cambridge, Mass.: Harvard University Press, 1958; Chris Argyris, *Personality and Organization: The Conflict Between System and the Individual,* New York: Harper Bros., 1957; Robert N. Rapoport (in collaboration with Rhona Rapoport and Irving Rosow), *Community as Doctor: New Perspectives on a Therapeutic Community,* London: Tavistock Publications, 1960; Temple Burling, Edith M. Lentz, and Robert N. Wilson, *The Give and Take in Hospitals: A Study of Human Organization in Hospitals,* New York: Putnam, 1956; Morris Janowitz, *The Professional Soldier: A Social and Political Portrait,* Glencoe, Ill.: Free Press, 1960.

For recent proposals in the direction of a more inclusive framework, see: Talcott Parsons, "The Mental Hospital as a Type of Organization," in Milton Greenblatt, Daniel J. Levinson, and Richard H. Williams, eds., *The Patient and the Mental Hospital,* Glencoe, Ill.: Free Press, 1957; Alvin W. Gouldner, "Organizational Analysis," in Robert K. Merton, et al., *Sociology Today: Problems and Prospects,* New York: Basic Books, 1959; Philip Selznick, *Leadership in Administration: A Sociological Interpretation,* Evanston, Ill.: Row, Peterson, 1959. However there is still a serious gap between general theory and empirical work in this field.

[4] By effectiveness we mean the extent to which the organization is able to meet the goals set for it or by it. We ask, is it a high or low producer, are its products outstanding or mediocre? Efficiency expresses the relation between output and the costs necessary to attain it. These costs include not only inputs expressed in terms of quality and quantity of resources consumed, but also a special category of outputs such as morale, rates of turnover and frequency of work stoppages or strikes which are obvious "costs" to the organization.

[5] Arthur Kornhouser, Harold I. Sheppard and Albert J. Mayer, *When Labor Votes,* New York: University Books, 1956.

[6] *Ibid.,* p. 176.

[7] *Ibid.,* pp. 249–50.

[8] George Stern, Morris I. Stein, and Benjamin S. Bloom, *Methods in Personality Assessment: Human Behavior in Complex Social Situations,* Glencoe, Ill.: The Free Press, 1956.

21

The Interaction Between Politicians' Personalities and Attributes of Their Roles and Political Systems

---

The findings of this study demonstrate what Inkeles and Levinson stressed as conceptually important in the preceding selection: the importance of identifying the properties of positions within an organization—as well as the properties of the whole organization—when investigating the personality traits of occupants of the positions. This study of politicians and businessmen in "Eastport" and politicians in two Louisiana parishes clarifies the need to locate political actors in their situational contexts in order to identify the linkage of personality traits to political behavior. As Greenstein has noted in reference to this investigation, "the most striking impressions left by their findings, when considered independently of situational factors, were (1) the lack of aggregate motivational difference between the politicians and the businessmen and (2) the extreme heterogeneity of the politicians on the McClelland measures. However, once controls were introduced for situational factors, particularly the actual (as opposed to formal) norms and expectations connected with various political offices in the three communities, distinct motivational profiles began to emerge." [1]

NOTES

[1] Fred I. Greenstein, *Personality and Politics: Problems of Evidence, Inference, and Conceptualization* (Chicago: Markham, 1969), p. 131.

POWER MOTIVATION AND
THE POLITICAL PERSONALITY

Rufus P. Browning and Herbert Jacob

How important is the desire for power in the quest for political office? To what extent does it dominate the acts of politicians, of political leaders? The common assumption, reflected in many political biographies and in popular writing, is that the quest for power propels many into politics and is a most likely explanation for much of the politician's activity. Political scientists—especially in recent years—have been a bit more cautious. Harold D. Lasswell wrote fifteen years ago that political man accentuates power, demands power for the self, accentuates expectations concerning power, and acquires at least a minimum proficiency in the skills of power.[1] Yet a few years later, speaking of democratic political man, Lasswell noted that the power-hungry individual may be too compulsive and rigid to win power; he is more likely to be found at the fringes of the political system than at its center.[2] In reviewing what little evidence existed on the motivations of politicians, Robert Lane suggested that "among the leaders of a democracy there is little tendency for a higher-than-average concentration of persons with needs to exercise power over others."[3]

Little empirical work has been done in the field, for valid measures of power motivation have not been available.[4] In recent years, however, psychologists have developed a projective test that taps power motivation as well as achievement and affiliative motivation. They have given the test to experimental groups, students, businessmen, and armed forces personnel, and to a nationwide sample. One of the developers of the test has used it to expound a unique psychological theory of economic development.[5] This paper applies the test for the first time to politicians. We examine the intensity of power motivation (as measured by the test) displayed by politicians in two widely separated locales. The questions we ask are: (1) How strongly are politicians motivated to seek power, achievement, and friendship (affiliation) as compared with nonpoliticians? (2) To what extent do characteristics of the political system—specifically, the kinds of positions available and the opportunity structure of the community—make a difference in the motivations of the individuals attracted to politics?

THE TEST OF MOTIVATION [6]

The test we used is an outgrowth of the Thematic Apperception Test. Like the TAT, it assumes that respondents will reveal deeply rooted impulses in their imaginative responses to pictures. The form we used consisted of six pictures: an older man talking to a younger one in a rather old-fashioned office; a man sitting at what is apparently a drafting table with a picture of a woman and children in front of him; seven younger men around a table; a man working at a desk in an otherwise dark office, hat and coat piled at the side; a man in city clothes talking to a boy

Reprinted from *Public Opinion Quarterly*, 28 (1964), 75–90.

sitting on a farm fence; and a man leaning back in what many people interpret as a seat in an airplane with papers or a book on his lap.

These pictures sometimes evoke stories with clear political content, such as this one:

> [This man] is organizing, no doubt, or joined an organization, giving his points or giving his political—giving out what he thinks is so, giving out his orders, or forming an organization. He's a leader. I have no doubt that he wants good government. If this is the same man in this picture, he has one thing in mind and that is to bring out the picture for generations to come. These people will go out, no doubt, this man is going out now to campaign. You've got four interested parties listening to him and they're going to bring charges against him.

The main character is an influential person, he is engaged in influencing activity, and he wants to be influential—all signs of concern about power. Power-oriented stories may also be present in an entirely nonpolitical context:

> It looks like a group of young fellows in a club. One is pointing up some decision, trying to get the others to go along. One is not interested at all, and one is undecided. The man sitting down, pointing, is the one who is very strong with his thoughts. He is going to win out and get his point across.

The scoring system does not depend on the context of the plot but rather on the actions or feelings depicted. When a story involves attempts to control others, it is scored for power motivation. Additional points are scored if someone in the story is actually influencing others, anticipates doing so, shows joy or anguish about influencing others, states a need to influence, or overcomes obstacles in influencing others. The stories are scored in a like manner for achievement motivation when stories concern individuals trying to do well in any activity and for affiliative motivation when stories involve attempts to win or maintain friendly relationships with others.

The scoring system has been standardized to allow self-training with the use of a manual, so that a novice can quickly score stories expertly.[7] Each story is scored separately for each of the motives. A maximum possible score on the six-story test is 60 for power and affiliative motivation and 66 for achievement, but these are never attained; almost all of our scores lie in the 0 to 20 range.

The test is well validated, in several ways.[8] Versions of it have been experimentally validated (mainly with students), in that the test has been shown to measure individual responses to experimental situations that are presumed to arouse motivation. For instance, men who were told the test was a measure of ability and might affect their career chances scored higher in achievement motivation than men who were told it was just a graduate student's experiment. Candidates for campus office had higher power motivation scores while waiting for ballots to be counted than other students showed during an ordinary classroom session. Students who had just been rated for popularity by their fraternity brothers scored higher in affiliative motivation than a fraternity group that took the test routinely along with a food-rating test.

More substantial and theoretically much more interesting validations than these, however, stem from dozens of studies exploring relationships between motivation, on the one hand, and features of behavior, role, status, upbringing, and other variables, on the other hand.[9] Studies have shown that men with strong achievement motivation perform well in a variety of tasks, tend to persist longer, choose moderate, realistic risks rather than very safe or very doubtful ones, and perform better as the chances of success drop, apparently stimulated by the challenge of a difficult task. Achievement motivation in men is the result of quite specific patterns of relationships with the boy's father and mother, and these characteristic child-raising practices are related to the socioeconomic class of the parents.

Somewhat fragmentary evidence indicates that men with strong power motivation are more argumentative and try to influence others more frequently.[10]

Studies of the behavioral correlates of affiliative motivation suggest that those who score high tend to seek approval more than others, but their peers rate them as relatively unpopular; they are also rated as overcautious and dependent on others for decisions. In contrast, men high in achievement motivation but low in affiliative motivation are rated as socially poised and adept, self-possessed, and consistent; this group is strong in such qualities as conversational facility and ability to communicate ideas effectively. Furthermore, this group (*low* in affiliative motivation) states a preference for working with people rather than with things.[11] Note that affiliative motivation—concern with warm, friendly relationships—is not necessarily an approach motive and apparently may often be a real barrier to dealing with people. It seems that strong concern for friendly personal relationships, perhaps accompanied by anxieties that interfere with attempts to relieve such concern, manifests itself in part in behavior that is usually not admired or liked—approval seeking, excessive caution, vacillation, etc. It is apparent that motive-generated acts may not lead to goal attainment and motive satisfaction. Affiliative motivation is not the same thing as sociability or liking to be with people. We should not expect the stereotype of the glad-handing politician to score high on this motive.

In short, these measures of motivation are associated with a large range of variables prominent in leadership recruitment and other behavior of leaders—e.g. risk taking, class background, dependence, consistency, sensivity to opportunities to influence others. For instance, it would be surprising if the ability to assess risks and a willingness to take moderate, realistic ones were not important ingredients in the rise to high office and in the making of public policy decisions. As another obvious example, we are very often concerned about the degree of dependence of political executives on the people with whom they deal. It seems plausible that motivational factors are important in cases like these.

ADMINISTRATION OF THE TEST

In the present application, the authors gave the test to politicians at the beginning of an hour-long interview on their political careers. It was introduced as a test of imagination, with no hint given that the purpose was to measure motivation. Stories respondents told were recorded in one case by shorthand (Browning) and in the other by tape recorder (Jacob), with respondents' consent. When the stories were scored, the identity of the respondent was effectively hidden.

We tested politicians in two places: a middle-sized Eastern city (Browning) and two parishes (counties) in Louisiana (Jacob). In Louisiana, the sample consisted of 50 elected local officials who represented 67 percent of all elected officials in their parishes.[12] In Eastern City, respondents were a random sample of 23 businessmen (not retired) who had been or were ward chairmen, had run for or held elective office (both local and state) in the city, or had held appointive patronage positions, usually only part-time in conjunction with political activity at the ward level.[13] In addition, the test was given in Eastern City to a sample of 18 politically inactive businessmen who matched 18 of the businessmen-politicians with respect to type and size of business, career level and specific occupation, religion, ethnic background, urban residence, average education, and age.

MOTIVATIONS OF POLITICIANS

In the literature of political science, one can find almost as many reasons for expecting politicians to exhibit moderate power motivation as high power motivation. Although politics is frequently concerned with power, blatantly power-hungry individuals are distrusted in a democratic system. It is common, nevertheless, to suppose that all politicians have at least some basic traits in common, among them concern for power.[14]

Our evidence does nothing to support this image. In Table 1, Eastern City

Table 1
Mean Motive Scores of Politically Active and
Inactive Businessmen in Eastern City
(18 Matched Pairs)

Motive*	Politicians	Nonpoliticians	Diff.	p of Diff.†
Power	6.5	5.2	1.3	.13‡
Affiliation	4.2	2.9	1.3	.28§
Achievement	7.4	6.1	1.3	.20‡

* Differences within groups between power, achievement, and affiliative motive scores do not signify that a group has, for instance, on the average "more" achievement than affiliative motivation; the evocation of motive-related imagery of various sorts is heavily dependent on the cues in the particular pictures used. Hence scores for each motive are comparable between individuals or groups, but not between motives in the same individual or group.

† From Wilcoxon matched-pairs signed-ranks test on ranked motive scores; hence the different p-values in spite of identical differences between means.

‡ One-tailed.

§ Two-tailed (difference not in predicted direction).

politicians have only slightly higher mean power motive scores than the matched nonpoliticians, and the variation within both groups is large. Indeed, in Louisiana, 12 of the 50 politicians scored zero on the test. In short, politicians we tested did not uniformly have any particular level of power motivation, and are not clearly different in power motivation from nonpoliticians of similar occupation and status.

The sociability of politicians has often been noted. The test permits us to assess concern for warm personal relationships. We hypothesized that politicians would score low on this trait, for much of politics is inimical to this kind of relationship. In contrast to sociability, i.e. a friendly manner, the real need for friendship and approval that characterize a high level of affiliative motivation is probably incompatible with political activity. Politicking often requires single-minded attention to winning over others or manipulating them; it may also entail hurting some friends and helping others if one tends to regard political acquaintances and associates as potential friends.

The data in Table 1 show that this line of reasoning is apparently wrong—in Eastern City, businessmen-politicians as a group are *more* concerned with friendship than businessmen who are not politicians. In Louisiana, the degree of dispersion on this measure was about the same as in Eastern City. As with power, politicians apparently do not possess a uniform level of affiliative motivation and are not clearly different from nonpoliticians.

Familiar characterizations of politics as involving risk taking and persistence led us to hypothesize that politicians would score high on achievement motivation. But the Eastern City politicians did not in any sense score significantly higher than nonpoliticians (Table 1). In Louisiana, 10 of the 50 had zero scores, while others scored quite high.

In sum, our data indicate that none of the three motives are peculiarly characteristic of the total samples of politicians tested. When compared with a control group, politicians did not differ markedly from nonpoliticians. Moreover, in both Eastern City and Louisiana, all three sets of motive scores showed considerable dispersion, indicating a lack of homogeneity in our samples with respect to motivation.

MOTIVATION IN THE CONTEXT OF POLITICAL SYSTEM

This variation in scores encourages us to look for factors that would lead individuals with different motives to enter or remain in politics. Two obvious sets of factors involve the characteristics of the political system, and within the system, the characteristics of the specific offices available. We believe that these characteristics engage the motivations of politicians in identifiable patterns that can help us explain the recruitment of certain individuals into politics.

Motivated behavior—for example, the choice of one activity over another less preferred—is the product of (1) the individual's underlying motivation, or need for a certain kind of satisfaction, and (2) his expectations or perception of motive satisfaction in the alternative activities.[15] A person highly motivated for power may choose to concentrate on business (or take it out on his wife) rather than get into politics. In some cases, this is the result of other motives—for instance, a desire to make a great deal of money, or a desire for prestige in a group in which business occupations are highly valued. But the choice is in part also the result of the individual's perceptions of business and politics. He may be quite ignorant of politics and expect opportunities for influence only in business. He may perceive opportunities in politics but expect, rightly or wrongly, that they are out of his reach. He may perceive political power but see politics as a dirty game in which one must deal with and accept as associates lower-class and perhaps even dishonest people. Choice depends on expectations or perceptions as well as on motives.

Many of the ingredients of the possible combinations of perceptions and motives are the consequence of the political system in which the individual finds himself. Is it easy or difficult to enter? Is accession to power closed to all outside a particular social, racial, or economic group? Are important decisions tightly controlled by a small, durable elite? Does political activity in the system involve considerable financial sacrifice? Is politics an arena where important decisions are in fact being made? Is politics a bitterly competitive activity in the community, or is it relaxed, easygoing, and friendly? The answers to this sort of question will help determine the kinds of satisfactions and dissatisfactions perceived in politics by individuals of varying socioeconomic status who are motivated in varying degrees for power, achievement, and affiliation. Men who are strongly power-motivated, for instance, are likely to be attracted only to certain kinds of political systems, and then only to certain offices or roles within the system. Men intensely motivated for achievement will get into politics and seek office only when they perceive opportunities for achieving, with effort, whatever it is they define as achievement—perhaps getting a new school or new streets built, or initiating a redevelopment program, or perhaps simply running a businesslike city government. Where such opportunities are seemingly not available, strongly achievement-motivated men are not likely to enter politics on their own initiative.[16]

We shall consider relationships, first, between motivation and kind of office held or run for and, second, between motivation and characteristics of the political systems.

Motivational Differences Among Offices

We made no systematic direct measurement of perceptions of power, achievement, and affiliative opportunities in the offices that appear in our samples, but we felt justified in dichotomizing the offices into positions with high and low potential for achievement and power (see Table 2). The division was carried out on the

Table 2
**Positions with High and Low Power and Achievement Potential
in Eastern City and in Casino and Christian Parishes, La.**

	Power Potential		Achievment Potential	
	High	Low	High	Low
Eastern City	City Council State Representative State Senator	City Clerk Registrars of Voters, Vital Statistics Patronage, sine-cure positions Ward chairmen	Same as for Power Potential	Same as for Power Potential
Casino Parish	Justice of the Peace Constable Parish Council Parish School Board State Representative Parish-wide (Sheriff, Assessor, etc.)	None	Parish Council Parish School Board State Representative Parish-wide	Justice of the Peace Constable
Christian Parish	Parish School Board Parish Council Parish-wide (Sheriff, Assessor, etc.)	Justice of the Peace Constable	Parish School Board Parish Council Parish-wide	Justice of the Peace Constable

basis of our own impressions and of the impressions of others, including some of the respondents intimately familiar with the communities. For this purpose, we defined positions with high power potential as those from which any occupant would be perceived to have relatively plentiful opportunities for advancement to more influential positions or for influence over matters of public policy, party affairs, or the enforcement of laws, where enforcement was in practice a matter of discretion for the office holder.[17] Not all occupants of these positions were influential, but the positions were generally regarded as ones from which one *could* exercise influence, and all the men who we knew were influential were occupants of positions of this sort.

To classify the offices according to achievement potential, we defined achievement potential as opportunity to attain policy objectives or to advance to higher offices. The definitions of achievement and power potential are largely overlapping, in practice—attaining policy objectives is, in our dictionary, equivalent to influencing matters of public policy. Consequently, positions high in achievement potential are also high in power potential. The converse is *not true,* however. Positions high in power potential may not be high in achievement potential. For example, if some of the ward chairmen in Eastern City had been party leaders who were influential with respect to party nominations but not with respect to public policy, they would have been classified high in power potential but low in achievement potential. Similarly in Christian Parish, where gambling is nonexistent and justices of the peace have little control over anything, they are rated as low in both respects; in Casino Parish, we have classified them as high in power but low in achievement potential, for they made decisions that affected gambling but could not hope to rise to higher office.

It must be understood that our categorizations depend not on formal characteristics of the offices but on an estimate of the prevailing expectations about the offices. Moreover, the distinctions were drawn without reference to the motive scores of the incumbents. The discussion and data which follow must be interpreted within the limitations of these operational definitions, but we believe that they are accurate both in terms of the meaning of the test of motivation and, roughly, in terms of perceptions of political offices in the communities studied.

Table 3
Mean Motive Scores of Non-School Board Politicians in Positions
with High and Low Power and Achievement Potential

Motive	Position Potential		Diff.	p of Diff.
	High (N)	Low (N)		
Eastern City:				
Power	7.9 ⎱	4.7 ⎱	3.2	.02
	⎰(10)	⎰(13)		
Achievement	8.3 ⎰	6.5 ⎰	1.8	.13
Louisiana parishes:				
Power	5.9 (26)	4.9 (10)	1.0	.26
Achievement	5.9 (14)	3.5 (22)	2.4	.06

Note: Combining Eastern City and Louisiana parishes and holding *place* constant, *p*-values of partial linear regression coefficients (*motive* on *position potential*) are: for power, .01; for achievement, .03. Other *p*-values from Mann-Whitney U test on ranked scores.

As Table 3 indicates, men in positions with high power and achievement potential in Eastern City had considerably higher power-motive scores and perhaps higher achievement-motive scores than those in low-potential positions. In Louisiana, the direction of differences in power and achievement motivation is the same as in Eastern City, but the difference in achievement motivation between high- and low-potential offices is relatively large, in power motivation, slight.

Since we have a nonpolitical control sample for the Eastern City politicians, we can check the implications of these data by comparing Eastern City politicians in high- and low-potential offices separately with their samples of matched political inactives. The hypothesis relating motivation of officeholders to the opportunities of the offices is strongly corroborated. Politicians in high-potential positions scored much higher in both achievement and power motivation than their matched sample (N = 9 pairs).[18] With each motive, only one nonpolitician scored higher than the politician he was matched to. In contrast, politicians in low-potential positions scored insignificantly lower in both motives than their matched inactives. In short, politicians in offices with high power and achievement potential are more strongly motivated for power and achievement than politically inactive men from the same occupational and socioeconomic strata. The implication is that high-potential offices attract men with relatively strong achievement and power motivation.

A role-theory explanation—that holders of high-potential offices have developed strong power and achievement motivation over a period of years because of long exposure to power and achievement opportunities—does not account for these results. In Eastern City, where data were gathered on candidates as well as on officeholders, candidates for high-potential positions have the same distinctive motivational characteristics as long-time officeholders. Moreover, politicians in high-potential positions in spite of weak power and achievement motivation are more likely to drop out of politics than strongly motivated officeholders, according to our data. Apparently, motivation affects entry into the political arena and willingness to remain in office, but officeholding does not determine underlying motivation (though it may serve to arouse existing motives). Some motive change may take place because of role learning, but these data do not support such a hypothesis.[19]

Fourteen school board members in the Louisiana parishes are excluded from Table 3 in order to make the data comparable to Eastern City figures, where school board members were not sampled. When school board members are examined separately, as in Table 4, we find that they score somewhat lower on power motivation

Table 4
Mean Motive Scores of Louisiana School Board Members and Other Louisiana Politicians in Positions with High Power and Achievement Potential

Motive	School Board (N = 14)	Other High Potential	(N)	Diff.	p of Diff.
Power	4.7	5.9	(26)	1.2	.13
Achievement	6.5	5.9	(14)	0.6	.34
Affiliation	3.0	1.7	(26)	1.3	.05

Note: Affiliative motive scores are for men in high-power-potential positions; *p*-values from Mann-Whitney U test.

and somewhat higher on achievement and affiliative motivation than other officials. The data are not conclusive, but they are suggestive. What might make school board members different from others who hold high-potential positions?

In many localities, school board elections are not considered to be part of the ordinary political game. Elections to the board are often nonpartisan. The board usually does not serve organization maintenance functions for local parties in the sense that mayoralty office or the city council often do through their control over patronage and over a range of policies. School board politics usually seems less "political" in the sense that there is (or appears to be) less open competition for leadership and less clearly power-oriented behavior. Serving on the school board has more of the flavor of civic duty, in which one is expected to do what is best for all, than of political career.

In Louisiana, only a few of these considerations hold true. The elections are as partisan as those for parish council; school boards control important sources of patronage through the dispensation of custodial and bus-driving positions, through the award of contracts, and through the purchase of land. It is true that there is more public comment when the school board is used for partisan purposes than when power politics are played on the parish council; candidates for the board make some effort to dissociate themselves from partisan politics, whereas other officials do not. Nevertheless, there are grounds for suspecting that motivational differences between school board members and other officials are smaller in the Louisiana parishes than in many other localities. In cities that have both vigorous party or factional politics and a nonpartisan school board, we expect motivational differences between the two sets of officeholders to be greater.

Motivational Differences Between Political Systems

Opportunities for exercising power and for achieving—hence for satisfying relevant motives—vary not only among offices within local political systems but also from one system to another. What are the distinctive features of the two political systems we studied? Eastern City's parties compete vigorously, and alternation between them occurs even though each has dominated the scene for several terms at a time in recent decades. At the same time, each party is tightly controlled by a small and only slowly changing set of leaders, so that mobility within the local party structure is somewhat limited. This is not necessarily a sharp restriction on achievement and power opportunities, however, since expectations are prevalent that it is possible to go on to state legislative office or higher from the position of councilman or mayor. Recent city administrations have been vigorous, initiating very important new policies, such as large-scale urban redevelopment. The city government is the focus of demands from diverse groups, and the consensus, in a relatively stagnant economy, is that the city's future depends heavily on the initiative and ability of its political leaders. Opportunity in the economic arena is further restricted by the exclusion of several immigrant minority groups from the highest positions in industry and finance.

The Louisiana parishes, in contrast, have witnessed immense growth and industrialization in recent years. There is no consensus that the most important decisions are to be made in the political process; rather, opportunities for power and achievement abound in the commercial and industrial life of the area. Parish politics is factional, fragmented, shifting, personal. There are no parties competing on the basis of issues, defining important public problems, and mobilizing support for their stands. Factions and individuals compete, but there is little focus on matters of general interest or on public problems that might appear as a challenge to men who otherwise would be attracted to business or professional careers. Furthermore, political mobility upward to state or national offices from a background of parish officeholding is practically unheard of.

In sum, opportunity for power and achievement in local politics is smaller in the parishes than in Eastern City; opportunity for movement up to higher office is much smaller; opportunity for power and achievement in the economic arena is relatively greater. These quite striking differences between Eastern City, on the one hand, and the two parishes, on the other, suggest that Eastern City politics will attract more strongly power- and achievement-motivated men than will the politics of Christian and Casino Parishes. If, as we suggested above in relation to school board politics, concern for policy is likely to stem from at least moderate levels of affiliative motivation, Eastern City politicians may also be somewhat more motivated in this direction.

The hypothesis is supported by data in Table 5, in which Eastern City business-

Table 5
Mean Motive Scores of Businessmen-Politicians in High- and
Low-Potential Positions in Louisiana and Eastern City*

Position Potential	La. Parishes	(N)	Eastern City	(N)	Diff.	p of Diff. Between Communities
Power motive:						
High	5.8	(13)	8.3	(10)	2.5	
						.04
Low	2.0	(2)	6.5	(13)	4.5	
Achievement motive:						
High	6.3	(9)	7.9	(10)	1.6	
						.04
Low	3.8	(6)	4.7	(13)	0.9	
Affiliation motive:						
High	1.5	(13)	3.0	(10)	1.5	
						.05
Low	3.5	(2)	4.3	(13)	0.8	

* School board men excluded.

Note: Affiliative motive scores are for men in high- and low-power-potential positions. The data in this table differ from those in Table 3 in that Louisiana politicians who are not businessmen are omitted to assure comparability with Eastern City data. All p-values are 1-tailed for partial linear regression coefficients for *motive* on *place* with *position potential* held constant as the second independent variable. Although 1-tailed significance levels of $\propto$ = .05 are reached or nearly reached for all six coefficients (*place* and *position potential* for each of three motives), it is of interest to note that these two variables together account for only between 7.5 and 20 percent of the variance in motive scores.

men-politicians are compared with those Louisiana politicians who are also businessmen, with power and achievement potential of their offices held constant. The Eastern City politicians show substantially higher power, achievement, and affiliative motivation than their counterparts in Louisiana.[20]

SUMMARY AND CONCLUSIONS

Simply being a politician does not entail a distinctive concern for power, or for achievement or affiliation. For the communities studied our data show that businessmen in local politics do not differ in motivation from politically inactive businessmen. However, patterns of political and nonpolitical opportunities in different communities, and the distribution of opportunities among political offices, are related to the motivational make-up of officeholders. The data for Eastern City and the Louisiana parishes are consistent with the propositions that relatively plentiful opportunities for power and achievement in the economic arena channel strongly motivated men into economic rather than political activity; that in communities where politics and political issues are at the center of attention and interest, men attracted to politics are likely to be more strongly power- and achievement-motivated than in communities where politics commands only peripheral interest; that political systems that offer upward political mobility attract men with relatively strong achievement and power motivation; and that concentration in a political system on matters of strictly party or factional organization and power, to the near exclusion of public policy concerns, tends to keep men with strong affiliative needs out of politics. Similar relationships hold for specific offices within the communities studied. Offices with high potential for power and achievement are occupied by men who are more strongly power- and achievement-motivated than politicians in low-potential offices.

The implications of data of this sort are not trivial, as a glance back to our summary of the behavioral correlates of these motives reminds. Groups of men who differ with respect to these traits will run a government in sharply different ways, we suspect. Furthermore, the pool of local politicians available for advancement to higher office is a major input to the pool of state and national leaders. Patterns of motivation in local politicians will determine in part what kinds of political leadership we experience in the future. What kind of political system is likely to recruit authoritarian leaders, men whose strong power motivation is untempered by affiliative concern? What sort of politics will produce leaders with high achievement motivation and the characteristics of high levels of performance, response to challenge, and a propensity for moderate risk that go with it?

It is here that the significance of data on personality is apparent, in the decisions of political leaders, in their yielding to certain pressures rather than to others, in their acceptance of some decision premises over others. Information on the motives of politicians provides us with links between complex social, economic, and political variables, on the one hand, and patterns of the recruitment and behavior of leaders, on the other.

NOTES

[1] Harold D. Lasswell, *Power and Personality,* New York, Norton, 1948, pp. 229–30.

[2] Harold D. Lasswell, "Effect of Personality on Political Participation," in R. Christie and M. Jahoda, editors, *Studies in the Scope and Method of "The Authoritarian Personality,"* Glencoe, Ill., Free Press, 1954.

[3] Robert E. Lane, *Political Life,* Glencoe, Ill., Free Press, 1959, p. 128.

[4] Still unique in its effort to test such hypotheses is J. B. McConaughy. "Certain Personality Factors of State Legislators in South Carolina," *American Political Science Review,* Vol. 44, 1950, pp. 897–903.

[5] David C. McClelland, *The Achieving Society,* Princeton, N.J., Princeton University Press, 1961.

[6] The main sources of information and theory about the test are David C. McClelland et al., *The Achievement Motive,* New York, Wiley, 1953; McClelland, *The Achieving Society*; and John W. Atkinson, editor, *Motives in Fantasy, Action and Society: A Method of Assessment and Study,* Princeton, N.J., Princeton University Press, 1958.

[7] See the scoring manuals in Atkinson, *op. cit.,* pp. 685–818. A score-rescore rank-order correlation of .90 indicates sufficient skill to use the results of the test for research purposes. Both authors attained this standard.

[8] See McClelland, *The Achievement Motive,* and Atkinson, *op. cit.,* Chaps. 3–6. The particular advantage of a validated psychological test in this research (in contrast, for example, to data from interviews) is that it provides an assurance that the same motives are being measured in many separate studies of a wide range of important dependent variables, ranging from class-related differences in child-raising practices to patterns of decision making. The network of theoretically meaningful empirical associations that attach to the test as the result of extensive research, and the repeated experimental validations, far outweigh in our opinion an unsuccessful attempt by Reitman to arouse achievement motivation in student subjects after the method of the original experimental validation studies. See Walter R. Reitman, "Motivational Induction and the Behavior Correlates of the Achievement and Affiliation Motives," *Journal of Abnormal and Social Psychology,* Vol. 60, 1960, pp. 8–13. In addition, it should be noted that projective measures of motivation are subject to special limitations vis-à-vis test-retest reliability. However, "it would not appear wise to insist on high test-retest reliability before using such measures because it is so hard to replicate testing conditions—to put the subject back in the condition he was in before he made the first response. Instead, one can rely

on other criteria, such as validity, for inferring stability of motivational dispositions indirectly" (McClelland, in Atkinson, *op. cit.,* p. 20). Test-retest checks have in fact yielded low correlations (about .4) (R. C. Birney, "The Reliability of the Achievement Motive," *Journal of Abnormal and Social Psychology,* Vol. 58, 1959, pp. 266–67).

[9] McClelland very briefly cites and summarizes conclusions from studies of the behavioral correlates of achievement motivation in "The Use of Measures of Human Motivation in the Study of Society," in Atkinson, *op. cit.,* p. 521, and much more extensively in *The Achieving Society,* Chaps. 6–8.

[10] J. Veroff, "Development and Validation of a Projective Measure of Power Motivation," in Atkinson, *op. cit.,* pp. 105–16, and "Power Motivation Related to Influence Attempts in a Two Person Group," Princeton, N.J., Princeton University, 1956, unpublished manuscript.

[11] T. E. Shipley, Jr., and J. Veroff, "A Projective Measure of Need for Affiliation," in Atkinson, *op. cit.,* pp. 83–94; J. W. Atkinson, R. W. Heyns, and J. Veroff, "The Effect of Experimental Arousal of the Affiliation Motive on Thematic Apperception," *ibid.,* pp. 95–104; and B. L. Groesbeck, "Toward Description of Personality in Terms of Configuration of Motives," *ibid.,* pp. 383–99.

[12] The remainder of the officials in the two parishes were accounted for as follows: 5.4 percent were located in remote fishing communities quite different from the rest of the parishes; 2.7 percent were women, for whom the test was not appropriate; 12.1 percent were respondents who took the test but for whom the tape recordings were defective; and 12.1 percent were officials who could not be contacted.

[13] Of a population of 32 businessmen-politicians, 27 were selected by a random process, 23 were interviewed. Of the 4 dropouts, 2 were out of town during the interviewing period, 2 refused to be interviewed.

[14] An earlier paper by one of the authors posited this view. H. Jacob, "Initial Recruitment of Elected Officials in the U.S.—A Model," *Journal of Politics,* Vol. 24, 1962, pp. 708–09.

[15] We are following here the suggestions of John W. Atkinson (*op. cit.,* Chap. 20).

[16] Inferring from high motive scores of certain officeholders that they sought office because of their motivation depends on the assumption that they initiated their own political activity rather than being recruited by their party. Our impression of the kind of men who are recruited by the parties for local and state offices is that they are likely to be less strongly power- and achievement-motivated than those who initiate their own activity; if so, motive scores of all those in office underestimate the role of motivation in self-recruitment.

[17] This last subcategory arises only in the case of some Louisiana justices of the peace and constables who exercised discretion over enforcement of gambling laws.

[18] These are the mean scores: power motive—politicians 8.3, nonpoliticians 4.2, $p = .03$; achievement motive—politicians 8.6, nonpoliticians 4.7, $p = .03$ (by Wilcoxon matched-pairs signed-ranks tests; see Sidney Siegel, *Nonparametric Statistics,* New York, McGraw-Hill, 1956).

[19] Still another explanation might attribute motive differences to differences in social class or class background: relatively high-status men are elected to high-potential offices, and their motivational characteristics are associated with their class rather than with the way they attain their political positions. In both localities, men in high-potential positions do come from somewhat higher-class families; they have somewhat more education (Louisiana only) and higher incomes. But those who rank highest with respect to these social characteristics do not account for the differences in motivation between men in high- and low-potential positions. Motivational differences remain when social class and class origin are held constant.

[20] We recognize that the data may also be interpreted as supporting either or both of two other hypotheses: (a) interviewer effects are responsible for the differences; (b) the relatively low motive scores of the Louisiana politicians simply mirror differences in the general populations of the two locales. Since there is no way of excluding these possibilities, our interpretation is only suggestive.

22

The Impact of a Leader's Personality
on His Political System

In this essay, Tucker marshals the evidence that points to a conception of the totalitarian dictator as a paranoid personality type. He then elucidates the crucial significance of the personality of the dictator in totalitarian decision-making. Tucker notes that research on "the authoritarian personality" was concerned with the psychic dynamics of followers rather than leaders. Nor did the literature on totalitarianism emphasize the personality of the leader: the leader was characteristically seen as fulfilling a function in the totalitarian system; less frequently was he considered to have much individual or systematic impact on the functioning of the system. More broadly, the theoretical literature on aggregate characteristics of political systems takes little note of what Tucker emphasizes—that critically placed single individuals can have a profound influence on the overall character of political systems.

Suggesting that Hitler and Stalin did, in fact, have systematic individual impact on the policies of their states, Tucker points to the relationship between policies of internal terror, policies of external aggression, the dictators' paranoid tendencies and the course of their leadership careers. Totalitarian terror was frequently explained in the political science literature in terms of the functional requisites of the totalitarian system; Tucker points out that in Soviet Russia some of the purges were obviously dysfunctional and, further, the terror effectively ended with Stalin's death.

The final section of Tucker's paper is an important critique of various objections to findings that emphasize the influence of a leader's personality on governmental decision-making. In particular, Tucker assays what he calls "the theory of organizational rejection of aberrant personalities from leadership positions." In connection with this discussion (and in connection with Tucker's demonstration that Hitler and Stalin functioned on the paranoid continuum), the reader might refer to selection 12.

THE DICTATOR AND TOTALITARIANISM

Robert C. Tucker

I

Significantly, we have few if any studies of the totalitarian dictator as a personality type. It may be that we are little closer to a working psychological model of him than Plato took us with his brilliant sketch of the ideal type of the "tyrant" in *The Republic*. The contemporary literature on totalitarianism does, of course, contain materials that are relevant to the problem of characterization of the totalitarian dictator.[1] Yet no frontal attack appears to have been made upon the problem. The purpose of the present article is to argue the need for one, and to do this in the context of a critical reexamination of the theory of totalitarianism. In the course of it I shall put forward some ideas of possible use in developing a conception of the dictator as a personality type.

First, a word on the use of the term "totalitarianism." Starting in the late 1930s and 1940s, a number of thinkers, mostly of European origin, evolved a theory of "totalitarianism" or the "total state" in an effort to account for the new type of dictatorship that had made its appearance in Germany under Hitler, Russia under Stalin, and perhaps also in Italy under Mussolini.[2] Hitler's Germany and Stalin's Russia were viewed as the two principal and indubitable manifestations of the novel political phenomenon. While the difficulty of precisely defining or describing this phenomenon was recognized, moreover, these writers felt that they were dealing with something qualitatively quite specific. It was not so much a form of political organization as a form of outlook and action, a peculiar mode of political life. Thus Hannah Arendt, whose *Origins of Totalitarianism* was in many ways a culminating synthesis of this entire trend of theory in the first stage, did not treat Lenin's Russia as genuinely totalitarian. She saw the original Bolshevik system as a "revolutionary dictatorship" rather than a totalitarian one, and 1929, the year of Stalin's advent to supreme power and the start of the great collectivization campaign, as "the first year of clear-cut totalitarian dictatorship in Russia."[3] Accordingly, Soviet totalitarianism was treated as preeminently a phenomenon of the Stalin era. Again, Mussolini's Italy was considered by some to be a totalitarian state. But others, including Arendt, did not feel that it fully merited this designation even though Mussolini himself had been the first, or among the first, to use the term "totalitarian" and had applied it to the Fascist conception of the state. The treatment of Hitler's Germany and Stalin's Russia as the prime representative expressions of totalitarian dictatorship has remained characteristic of this school of thought, at any rate until recently. I intend to follow this usage here, meaning by "totalitarianism" the special kind of dictatorship or political phenomenon that existed in Germany under Hitler, in Russia under Stalin and, though perhaps only marginally, in Italy under Mussolini. The possibility that this special political phenomenon may have existed or may yet come into existence elsewhere is not, however, meant to be excluded.

Reprinted from *World Politics,* 17, No. 4 (July, 1965), 555–83.

There is a large biographical literature on the totalitarian dictators. These works are typically political biographies that tell the story of the subject's life and career against the background of his time and the politics of his country. The biographies of Stalin by Souvarine, Deutscher, and Trotsky are representative examples. Although they contain frequently very penetrating passages of psychological characterization, these biographies and others like them generally avoid any attempt at a systematic analysis of the personality of the dictator under consideration. A notable exception to this rule is Alan Bullock's *Hitler: A Study in Tyranny,* which essays, in its well-known chapter on "The Dictator," an extended character portrait of the mature Hitler. Bullock depicts Hitler's obsessive hatred of the Jews, his craving to dominate, his need for adulation, his grandiose fantasies, and his extraordinary capacity for self-dramatization and self-deception (his *Wahnsystem,* as the British Ambassador, Sir Nevile Henderson, called it). But he also sees Hitler as an astute practical politician of very great ability, and suggests that the defining characteristic of his political personality lay in the "mixture of calculation and fanaticism." [4] Some elements of this characterization of Hitler may be of use in defining the totalitarian dictator as a personality type. But it is notable that the biographer does not view his subject in comparative perspective or note the broader implications of his analysis of Hitler's personality.

We should not underestimate either the difficulty of "typing" the totalitarian dictator or the resources available to us for dealing with this task. On the first point, it is clear that the dictators significantly differ from one another. Thus Hitler lacked Stalin's administrative talent and associated psychological traits, whereas Stalin was lacking in Hitler's remarkable oratorical powers and the qualities of personality that went along with them. A conception of the totalitarian dictator as a personality type would have to be sufficiently broad to transcend these differences and embrace only those decisively important characteristics that were shared. On the other hand, it would have to be sufficiently specific to enable us, in principle, to discriminate between the authentic totalitarian dictator on the order of Hitler or Stalin, and others, such as Lenin, Tito, Franco, and Perón, who may belong to different dictatorial classifications. The requisite combination of breadth and specificity will obviously not be easy to achieve. On the other hand, the present-day social scientist has impressive resources of data and ideas to draw upon in dealing with this problem. A rich store of factual information on the totalitarian dictators and others is available to us now. And work done in recent decades on personality and politics has yielded general concepts that may serve as useful tools of analysis. In his classic study of *Psychopathology and Politics,* to take the most important example, Harold Lasswell laid the groundwork for a "functional" politics that would focus prime attention not on political office as such but on political personality types, such as the "agitator," "theorist," and "administrator." Lasswell did not include the "dictator" among the original group of types, nor has he, to my knowledge, undertaken in later writings to define the totalitarian dictator as a personality type. But he has enunciated concepts and propositions that may be of great help in this enterprise. Notable among them is the proposition that "Political movements derive their vitality from the displacement of private affects upon public objects," and the closely related thesis that such displacement involves certain "processes of symbolization" whereby collective symbols are made proxy for self-symbols.[5] We shall have occasion in what follows to apply these ideas.

Also noteworthy in the present context is the literature that has developed around the theme of the "authoritarian personality." Having originated in Germany, this idea was introduced to the English-speaking public by Erich Fromm in his *Escape from Freedom* (1941). Fromm's thesis was that German National Socialism and other Fascist movements in Europe derived much of their mass appeal from the widespread incidence among the lower middle classes in these countries of a personality structure that he labeled "sado-masochistic" or the "authoritarian character." The authoritarian character combined a craving for power over others with a longing for submission to an overwhelmingly strong outside authority. Hitler himself, as revealed in *Mein Kampf,* was treated as an example, an "extreme form" of the authoritarian character. Continued research in this field led to the path-finding work by T. W. Adorno and his associates, *The Authoritarian Personality* (1950), which presented as a central theoretical construct the notion of an "F-syndrome" or potential fascism in the personality. A whole literature of criticism and discussion of this work has since arisen. The relevance of the theory and of research on the "authoritarian personality" (and related conceptions) to the study of totalitarian dictators as a personality type is obvious. On the other hand, it must be borne in mind that the conception of the authoritarian personality has grown out of efforts to improve our understanding of the psychology of authoritarian *followership,* and that the specific question of leader psychology has not been a conscious concern in much of this work. The researchers have primarily been interested in learning why large numbers of people in modern societies may be receptive to the appeals of authoritarian or totalitarian movements. The great importance of the problem is undeniable. But it cannot be taken for granted that the motives or personality traits that lead some persons to become followers of a totalitarian movement are the same as those which cause others to become its organizers and leaders. In this connection it appears to be a defect of Fromm's study mentioned above that it fails to reckon explicitly with the possibility that the personality needs which cause some people to want to lose their freedom are not the same as those which cause a Hitler, for example, to want to take it away from them. The relationship between the needs of the leader and the needs of the followers might well be one of complementarity rather than similarity.

II

Hardly less significant than the absence of a clear idea of the totalitarian dictator as a personality type is the absence of any resulting widespread sense that a need of political science is going unfulfilled. For evidence that this is so, and also for an explanation of why it is so, we may profitably turn to the literature of the recent past on the totalitarian dictatorship as a political system. Two overlapping stages may be distinguished in the growth of this literature. The first, extending from the late 1930s to the end of the 1940s, saw the emergence of the conception of the totalitarian state as a new, distinctively modern or nontraditional form of authoritarianism represented particularly in Nazi Germany and Soviet Russia. The second stage, coinciding with the growth of Soviet studies as an established branch of academic scholarship in postwar America, saw the detailed application of this conception to the Soviet system in its late Stalinist form, and also attempts at a kind of codification of the theory of totalitarianism.[6] It is only natural, of course, that in the late 1940s and early 1950s the attention of American scholars should have gravitated from the defunct Nazi case to the still very live totalitarianism of

Stalin's Russia, and that in their studies of the latter they should have relied heavily upon the model of a totalitarian polity that had already been worked out in the first stage.

It is no monolithic doctrine that we find reflected in the literature on totalitarianism. We are confronted, rather, with a variegated body of thought developed over an extended period by thinkers of diverse intellectual background and research interest among whom differences of emphasis and opinion exist. Still, there are certain recurring themes, certain basic ideas that tend to be shared by various representatives of the school and may be taken as typical.

First, the totalitarian dictatorship is viewed as being, unlike most traditional forms of authoritarian rule, a dictatorship with a mass social base and having a popular or pseudo-popular character. "The totalitarian state is the state of the masses," wrote Emil Lederer, and other theorists have followed him in taking modern "mass society" or "mass-men" as a foundation or recruiting ground of totalitarian movements that speak in the name of the masses and assert their affinity with them.[7] On the road to power, totalitarian parties strive to create mass movements that indoctrinate their followers with the party's ideology by propaganda and agitation. Once in power in the single-party state, however, the totalitarian elite imposes upon its mass social constituency an unprecedented tyranny, under which political power emanating from a single source penetrates every pore of the social organism and all the resources of modern technology are used for control purposes. Autonomous social groups are destroyed, giving way to the controlled mass organizations that serve as the elite's transmission belts to the now "atomized" masses of the population.

"Modern totalitarianism, unlike the more traditional dictatorships, is a highly bureaucratized system of power." [8] This sums up a second characteristic theme in the literature on the totalitarian dictatorship. In *Behemoth,* for example, Franz Neumann depicts the Nazi dictatorship as a system ruled, albeit chaotically and competitively, by four great bureaucratic machines—the ministerial bureaucracy and the bureaucratized leaderships of the Nazi party, the armed forces, and industry. The same basic theme receives a somewhat different emphasis from Arendt, who distinguishes "totalitarian bureaucracy" from bureaucracy of the traditional kind on the score of the former's "radical efficiency." [9] Both, however, share with other theorists of the school the view that totalitarianism carries the process of bureaucratization to its farthest extreme in modern society. There is, in fact, a tendency to regard the totalitarian state as a great bureaucratic monster functioning with machine-like impersonality in pursuit of its aims. Such an image is suggested, for example, by Arendt's later book, *Eichmann in Jerusalem,* which pictures the erstwhile director of operations in the Nazi "final solution" as a *kleiner Mann* of banal character who in supervising the murder of millions of Jews was dutifully carrying out his instructions as a higher functionary, a cogwheel in the totalitarian bureaucracy.

A third fundamental theme that has been both widely and heavily emphasized in the literature on totalitarianism has to do with systematic terror. Governmental use of terror is not itself held to be something distinctively new in the present age or peculiar to the totalitarian form of dictatorship. What distinguishes totalitarianism, according to the theorists, is rather the kind and degree of terror that is practiced, and also the characteristic predilection of totalitarian regimes for certain particular methods of spreading terror, such as the concentration camp and violent purges. Arendt, for example, differentiates "dictatorial terror," which is aimed against authentic opponents of the given regime, from an all-pervasive "totalitarian terror" that destroys not only actual political opponents but great numbers of wholly harmless people in purges, mass liquidations, and concentration camps; and she expresses the view that terror of the latter kind is "the very essence" of totalitarian government.[10] This view has found wide acceptance in the literature. Terror has variously been described, for example, as "the most universal characteristic of totalitarianism," [11] "the linchpin of modern totalitarianism," [12] and "the vital nerve of the totalitarian system." [13] So far as the question of the motivation of totalitarian terror is concerned, this is best considered under the next heading—the dynamics of totalitarianism.

The theorists of totalitarianism are in general and rather emphatic agreement that the totalitarian state is, in addition to its other characteristics, an extremely dynamic phenomenon. Sigmund Neumann, author of an outstanding work on the subject, saw the dynamics of the total state as revolutionary, and the political process in the totalitarian system as one of "permanent revolution." Others have used phrases like "permanent purge" and "permanent war" to describe essential aspects of the totalitarian dynamism in internal and external affairs. But why do totalitarian systems act in such ways? Whence their dynamics? The literature gives two kinds of answer to such questions. First, the characteristic behaviors of totalitarian regimes are explained by reference to postulated system-needs or functional requisites of totalitarianism itself as an operating socio-political system. A specimen of such reasoning is provided by Brzezinski when he writes, for example, that "The purge, arising as a combination of the rational motivations of the totalitarian leadership and the irrational stresses of the system, satisfies the need of the system for continued dynamism and energy," and further: "Totalitarianism is the system of the permanent purge. It promotes mobility and instability within totalitarianism. It necessitates constant reshuffling, and prevents the formation of too rigid lines of power demarcation within the system." [14]

A second and related line of explanation of the dynamics of totalitarianism stresses ideological motivation. The totalitarian ideology itself or the leaders' presumed obsession with it is treated as the source of the characteristic behavior of totalitarian regimes. Thus Friedrich describes Hitler's destruction of the Jews as "ideologically motivated." [15] On a higher plane of generality Arendt explains the action of totalitarian regimes by reference to a "supersense" that drives the leaders to demonstrate at all cost the validity of their ideological world-image. "The aggressiveness of totalitarianism," she goes on, "springs not from lust for power, and if it feverishly seeks to expand, it does so neither for expansion's sake nor for profit, but only for ideological reasons: to make the world consistent, to prove that its respective supersense has been right." [16] The postulate of an ideological fanaticism as the driving force of totalitarian conduct reappears in Inkeles' conception of the "totalitarian mystique," which he sees as the defining characteristic of the totalitarian leader himself. The "mystique" is pictured as a compulsion in the leader and his lieutenants to force reality into conformity with an ideologically given "higher law" or ideal plan for man and society: "One may fruitfully view the dictatorial leader as the man who sees himself as the essential *instrument* of the particular mystique to which he is addicted." [17] In an application of this mode of reasoning, Friedrich and Brzezinski seek to explain totalitarian terror by ideological fanaticism. Having said that the terror is the "vital nerve" of the totalitarian system, they write: "This system, because of the alleged ideological infallibility of its dogma, is propelled toward an increase of terror by a violent passion for unanimity." Such passion, they go on to suggest, is what makes the terror totalitarian: "It aims to fill everyone with fear and vents in full its passion for unanimity. Terror embraces the entire society, searching everywhere for actual or potential deviants from the totalitarian unity. . . . Total fear reigns." [18]

Turning to the question of the dictator, it cannot be said that the theorists of totalitarianism have overlooked his presence in the system. It is true that the dictator's role has, on occasion, been explicitly disparaged. Thus Franz Neumann argued that despite its proclamation of the *Führerprinzip* and cult of the ruler, the totalitarian state should not be seen as a *Führerstaat*. For the doctrine of one-man rule was "merely a device to prevent insight into the operation of the social-economic mechanism," and this mechanism, in turn, was one in which "The decisions of the Leader are merely the result of the compromises among the four leaderships." [19] Nor do we find the role of the dictator singled out in the various efforts to define what has been called the "totalitarian syndrome," the cluster of elements that characterizes the totalitarian system as a distinctive political formation.[20] Most of the theorists, however, recognize at some point the reality of dictatorial rule by a single individual in a fully totalitarian system. Friedrich and Brzezinski, for example, refer to the Nuremburg trials and Khrushchev's secret speech of 1956 as sources of evidence for the view that Mussolini, Hitler, and probably Stalin too were "the actual rulers of their respective countries," and they conclude that the totalitarian dictator "possesses more nearly absolute power than any previous type of political leader." [21] Much earlier Sigmund Neumann described the dictator as the "moving spirit" of the total state, and Arendt writes of "the absolute and unsurpassed concentration of power in the hands of a single man" who sits in the center of the movement "as the motor that swings it into motion." [22]

But "chief cogwheel" would have expressed more accurately the way in which she and others among the theorists actually seem to conceive the dictator's role. She ascribes to the Leader's lieutenants the view that he is "the simple consequence of this type of organization; he is needed, not as a person but as a function, and as such he is indispensable to the movement." [23] This also seems to be Arendt's own view, arising out of the general conception of the totalitarian system as a mechanistic leviathan operating under pressure of its own system-needs and the "supersense." Thus she depicts the all-powerful dictator as essentially a chief executive whose role is to bind the totalitarian system together into a unity and, by assuming blanket responsibility for everything done in the name of the regime, to relieve all the lesser functionaries of any sense of individual responsibility for their actions. Hitlers, as it were, are needed by totalitarian states in order to enable Eichmanns and others to perform their genocidal and like deeds in good conscience. The system-needs remain basic, according to this way of thinking; *Führers* are functional requisites of totalitarianism as a peculiar kind of system.

"Not as a person but as a function"—this phrase takes us to the heart of an issue that particularly needs pursuing. We cannot say that the dictator is missing from the model of the totalitarian state that has been elaborated. But he is present in it rather as a function than as a person. This helps to explain why the theorists, while taking cognizance of the dictator, accord him no more than secondary importance in the theory of totalitarianism. He is seen as fulfilling certain needs of the system, which of course he does. But the system, or its politics, is not in turn seen as fulfilling certain personal needs of his. Insofar as the theorists take a psychological view of him at all, they see him simply as sharing with the rest of the leadership the postulated supersense or totalitarian mystique. The assumption of a generalized ideological fanaticism takes the place of psychological analysis of the dictator as an individual personality. His political motivations consequently are not really appraised in psychological terms; his manner of displacing "private affects" upon "public objects" remains outside the purview of the theory of totalitarianism. And this, in my view, is a very great deficiency of the theory.

III

A sense of the theoretical inadequacy of the conception of totalitarianism seems to have been growing in American political science in the 1960s. Increasingly the complaint is heard that this construct is too narrow and limited to serve as a useful basic category for comparative analysis of contemporary one-party systems. It leaves out of view the nationalist single-party systems that share very many significant characteristics with the Fascist and Communist systems. It does not fare well in the face of the recent growth of diversity among Communist systems themselves. Furthermore, the politics of post-Stalin Russia have become more and more difficult to analyze in terms of the theory of totalitarianism, the fall of Khrushchev being only one in a long series of events that do not easily find places in the model of a totalitarian polity; and efforts to modify the model so that it will fit contemporary Soviet communism—e.g., by introducing the idea of a "rationalist totalitarianism"—seem of little avail. And owing to the tendency to see totalitarian systems as examples of what might be called government without politics, with a unitary elite controlling an atomized population by organization and terror, the theory of totalitarianism has obstructed rather than facilitated awareness of the intra-elite politics of factional conflict and policy debates that rage constantly behind the scenes of the Soviet and other Communist systems, despite their official pretensions to monolithic unity and their claims that factions are forbidden. For these and other reasons, some students of the comparative politics of modern authoritarianism have become dissatisfied with the concept of totalitarianism and have begun to formulate alternative basic categories, such as "movement-regimes," "mobilization systems," and the like.[24]

But are we now to discard the concept of totalitarianism as an obsolete or obsolescent category in modern political science? Considering it an essential part of our theoretical equipment, I for one would not like to see this happen. In order to prevent it from happening, however, it appears necessary to carry out a more radical critique of the theory of totalitarianism than has yet been made, rather as medicine may have to resort to a more radical form of treatment in order to save a patient. So far criticism has concentrated upon the deficiencies of the theory in application to systems or situations that were not in view or in existence at the time the theory was devised. The more radical critique must address itself to a different question: How valid was the theory as a representation of political reality in the two historical cases that it was particularly devised to explain—Hitler's Germany and Stalin's Russia? The time is now especially propitious for pursuing this question, since we have far more documentary and other information on the two cases than was available in earlier years. Here the question will be considered only in the aspect relating to the role of the dictator in the system.

When we confront the theoretical model of a totalitarian polity with what we now know about the factual situation in Hitler's Germany and Stalin's Russia, it appears that the model was seriously deficient in its omission of the personal factor from the dynamics of totalitarianism, its obliviousness to the impact of the dictator's personality upon the political system and process. For not only do Hitler and Stalin turn out to have been, as already indicated, autocrats who at many crucial points individually dominated the decision-making process and behavior of their governments, but the factual evidence likewise supports the further conclusions that (1) in both instances we have to do with individuals whose personalities would be classified somewhere on the continuum of psychiatric conditions designated as paranoid; and (2) in both instances the needs of the paranoidal personality were a powerful motivating factor in the dictatorial decision-making. The dictator did not, so to speak, confine the expression of his psychopathological needs to his private life while functioning "normally" in his public political capacity. Rather, he found a prime outlet for those needs in political ideology and political activity. In terms of Lasswell's formula, his psychopathological "private affects" were displaced onto "public objects." As a result, the dynamics of totalitarianism in Hitler's Germany and Stalin's Russia were profoundly influenced by the psychodynamics of the totalitarian dictator. The Soviet case is particularly instructive in this regard. For while our factual knowledge is less complete, we have here a system that survived the totalitarian dictator and thus some possibility of assessing the impact of his personality by studying the difference that his death made.

Before coming to power Hitler set forth in *Mein Kampf,* with its doctrine about a world-wide Jewish conspiracy to subvert the master race, a private vision of reality showing very strong parallels with psychiatric descriptions of a paranoid delusional system. Subsequently the vision began to be acted out inside Germany in the anti-Jewish terror, of which Hitler himself was the single most powerful driving force. Still later, when World War II was precipitated by the German invasion of Poland in 1939, it was Hitler's furiously insistent determination to (as he put it) "annihilate my enemies" that drove him, in the face of widespread apathy toward war in his own society and even in his own government, to push the world over the brink; and the story of his actions and reactions on the eve and in the uncertain early days of the conflict is like a page out a case history of paranoia, save that this was likewise a page of world history. During the war the internal terror continued, now on the scale of occupied Europe as a whole. It was Hitler's own will to genocide that generated the relentless pressure under which Himmler's terror machine proceeded during the war to carry out the murder of European Jewry: "Himmler organized the extermination of the Jews, but the man in whose mind so grotesque a plan had been conceived was Hitler. Without Hitler's authority, Himmler, a man solely of subordinate virtues, would never have dared to act on his own." [25]

Stalin's career differed from Hitler's, among other ways, in that he did not come to power as the recognized leader of his own movement but gradually took over from above a movement that had come to power much earlier under other leadership, mainly Lenin's. Certain other differences flowed from this. Whereas Hitler's personal dictatorship was established rather easily through the blood purge of June 1934, which took no more than a few hundred lives, Stalin's arose through the veritable conquest of the Communist party and Soviet state in the Great Purge of 1936–1938, in which an estimated five to nine million persons were arrested on charges of participation in an imaginary great anti-Soviet counterrevolutionary conspiracy. In this case the dictator's private vision of reality was not set forth in advance in a bible of the movement, but was woven into the preexisting Marxist-Leninist ideology during the show trials of 1936–1938, which for Stalin were a dramatization of his conspiracy view of Soviet and contemporary world history. The original party ideology was thus transformed according to Stalin's own dictates into the highly "personalized" new version of Soviet ideology that was expressed in the Moscow trials and in Stalin's *Short Course* of party history published in 1938. Contrary to the above-reviewed theory of totalitarianism, the Great Purge of 1936–1938 was not a product of the needs of Soviet totalitarianism as a system. Apart from the fact that it was only in the course of this purge that the Soviet state finally became a fully totalitarian one, especially in the sense of being the scene of permanent and pervasive terror, we have it now on highest Soviet authority that the purge was extremely dysfunctional for the Soviet state since it greatly weakened the ability of the country to withstand the coming test of total war. Not system-needs but the needs of Stalin, both political and psychopathological, underlay to a decisive degree the terror of 1936–1938.[26]

As in Hitler's case, we see in Stalin's the repetitive pattern, the subsequent reenactment in foreign relations of psychopathological themes and tendencies expressed earlier in the internal sphere. It was mainly in the postwar era of Soviet cold war against the West, against Tito, and so forth, that Stalin's psychological needs and drives found relatively uninhibited outlet in the field of external relations. Contributing factors included, on the one hand, the fact that an older and more deeply disordered Stalin was now less able to exercise restraint save in the face of very grave external danger, and, on the other hand, the capacity of a relatively more strong and less threatened Soviet Union to make its weight felt internationally with a large degree of impunity. We have the testimony of Khrushchev in the 1956 secret report that now "The willfulness of Stalin showed itself not only in decisions concerning the internal life of the country but also in the international relations of the Soviet Union," and that Stalin "demonstrated his suspicion and haughtiness not only in relation to individuals in the U.S.S.R., but in relation to whole parties and nations." The latter point is illustrated with a vivid recollection of Stalin in 1948 deciding on the break with Tito in a state of blind fury, exclaiming: "I will shake my little finger—and there will be no more Tito. He will fall."[27] Other postwar Soviet acts or policies that were influenced, if not directly caused, by Stalin's psychological needs include the imperious demands upon Turkey in 1945; the shutting down of cultural contacts and general isolationism of the 1947–1953 period; the extension of blood purges and show trials to Soviet-dominated Eastern Europe; the suspicion shown toward nationalist revolutions in Asia and elsewhere; and the unprecedentedly extreme Soviet psychological warfare of 1949–1953 against the West as manifested, in particular, in the savage propaganda campaign about alleged American germ warfare in Korea. There was, finally, the extraordinarily significant affair of the Kremlin doctors in January–February 1953, which had a vital bearing upon Soviet foreign policy as well as upon internal affairs. The way in which Stalin's psychopathology found expression in this final episode of his career will be discussed below.

In both Germany and Russia, then, the dictatorial personality exerted its impact originally in ideology and the internal life of the country, and later found a major field of expression in foreign relations as well. The internal impact was felt, among other ways, in the form of terror; the external, in a special sort of aggressiveness that may best be described, perhaps, as an externalization of the terror. In other words, domestic terror, which may be viewed under the aspect of "internal aggression" against elements of the population, was followed by foreign aggression, which may be viewed as a turning of the terror outward upon the world. Parenthetically, since this temporal order of priority was and generally would be conditioned by objective factors in the situation (e.g., the necessity for the dictator to capture control of his own society before he can channel his personality needs into foreign policy), there may be a basis for relatively early identification of a rising totalitarian dictator of the type of Stalin or Hitler. This suggests, moreover, that the international community might possibly develop a politics of prevention based on stopping the dictatorial personality at the stage of "internal aggression." However, this would necessitate a modification of the traditional doctrine of non-intervention insofar as it sanctions the unlimited right of a nation-state to deal with its own population as the ruler or regime sees fit, provided only that it continues to observe the accepted norms of international law in relations with other states. Upon the willingness and ability of the international community to recognize this problem, and to institute means of preventing individuals of paranoid tendency from gaining or long retaining control of states, may hang the human future. Were Hitler and Stalin, for example, dictators of their respective countries in the 1960s instead of the 1930s, the probability-coefficient of civilization's survival would be very low.[28]

The evidence disclosed by the Stalin and Hitler cases on the connection between dictatorial psychopathology and the politics of totalitarianism strongly suggests that the personal factor should be included in the theoretical model of a totalitarian system. On the basis of the factual record in these cases, as just summarized, the contribution of the dictator's personality to the dynamics of totalitarianism should be recognized as one of the regular and important components in the "syndrome." Such a conclusion appears all the more compelling in view of the extremely heavy emphasis that the theory has placed, as noted earlier, upon pervasive and permanent terror as the very essence of totalitarianism. For in the Soviet and Nazi cases, the dictators themselves, driven by pathological hatred and fear of what they perceived as insidiously conspiratorial enemy forces operating at home and abroad, were responsible to a very significant extent for the totalitarian terror that did in fact exist in Hitler's Germany and Stalin's Russia. The Soviet case is especially instructive since it reflects the relation of Stalin to the Stalinist terror, not only positively in the form of direct evidence of his determining role, but also negatively in the form of the decline of terror that began to be felt almost immediately after his death and has since continued. As late as January–February 1953, it may be said on the basis of the present writer's personal observations in Russia at that time, Soviet society was almost paralyzed with terror as preparations for another great purge developed to the accompaniment of ominous official charges that an anti-Soviet conspiracy, with threads leading to foreign intelligence services, was or had been abroad in the land. Stalin's death at that time not only cut short the purge operation but inaugurated the subsiding of the internal terror that had developed in a wavelike movement of advance and partial retreat ever since his rise to supreme power in 1929. Soviet citizens insistently refer to the subsiding of the terror as perhaps the most significant single expression of change they have experienced in post-Stalin Russia; and most foreign observers and scholars specializing in Soviet studies appear to agree with them on this point. Insofar as terror has continued to exist in post-Stalin Soviet society, it has become, to use Arendt's distinction, terror of the "dictatorial" rather than the "totalitarian" variety.

Given these facts and the premises of the theory of totalitarianism, certain conclusions concerning both Russia and totalitarianism would seem to follow.

First, if total terror is the essence of totalitarianism, then a Soviet political system in which such terror has ceased to exist and in which terror generally has greatly subsided over a substantial period of years should be pronounced, at least provisionally, post-totalitarian. Second, if the terror in Hitler's Germany was connected in considerable degree with Hitler as a personality, and that in Stalin's Russia with Stalin as a personality, then the explanations of totalitarian terror in terms of functional requisites of totalitarianism as a system or a general ideological fanaticism in the ruling elite would appear to have been basically erroneous—a conclusion which derives further strength from the fact that the ruling elite in post-Stalin Russia remains committed to the Communist ideology. Third, the theory of totalitarianism should not only bring the dictator and his personality into the "syndrome," but also should give specific recognition to the role of the dictatorial personality in the dynamics of totalitarian terror.

The theory of totalitarianism has not, however, moved in this direction. The indicated critical post-mortem on earlier interpretations of the dynamics of totalitarian terror has not appeared. The evidence from Hitler's Germany and Stalin's Russia on the relation of the dictator as a terroristic personality to the practice of totalitarian terror, and for such peculiarly totalitarian characteristics of it as its tendency to grow over time, has been generally disregarded. And instead of provisionally pronouncing post-Stalin Russia to be post-totalitarian on the ground that the terror has subsided, some theorists specializing in Soviet studies have taken the very different path of eliminating terror from the definition of totalitarianism. This leads to the thesis that what we see in Russia after Stalin is a system of "totalitarianism without terror." Thus Brzezinski, who had earlier viewed terror as the "most universal characteristic" of totalitarianism, writes that we seem to be witnessing the emergence in post-Stalin Russia of a "voluntarist totalitarian system" and that terror must now be seen not as something essential to a totalitarian system but only "as a manifestation of a particular stage in the development of the system." In explanation of this point he states further: "Terror and violence may be necessary to change a primitive, uneducated, and traditional society rapidly. Persuasion, indoctrination, and social control can work more effectively in relatively developed societies." [29]

But such a view of the causation of the terror is open both to the objections already leveled against explanations running in terms of system-needs, and to others in addition. It is debatable, and nowadays increasingly being debated, whether the terrorism of forced collectivization and industrialization in 1929–1933 was a necessity for Soviet communism in achieving its goals of modernization. Such a prominent Communist theorist and politician as Nikolai Bukharin was profoundly convinced that there was no such necessity, and many others in Russia at that time shared his view. Moreover, some western specialists on Russia and even, apparently, certain people in present-day Soviet Russia are increasingly of the opinion that his view was correct on the whole.[30] But even if we leave this question open, allowing for the possibility that terror and violence were in fact necessities of the modernization process in the Soviet case, the heightened terror by purge that was directed against the Communist party and Soviet managerial elite between 1934 and 1939 and was mounting again in 1949–1953 cannot be explained by the need to "change a primitive, uneducated, and traditional society rapidly." By 1934 collectivization was a *fait accompli* and generally accepted as such even by the peasantry, the pace and rigors of industrialization had slackened, and there was no serious resistance among the population or within the ruling Party to the continuing process of modernization. Certainly there was no opposition to it on such a scale that it required to be quelled by terroristic means. And just at this time, when any need for terror and violence for modernization purposes had subsided, a vast new intensification of it occurred on Stalin's initiative and under his personal direction. Moreover, terror rose again in a post-war Soviet Union which, despite the devastation visited upon it by the Second World War, was basically the urbanized and industrialized country that we know in our time. These facts do not square with the thesis that the terror was a manifestation of a particular stage in the development of the Soviet system connected with forced modernization. Nor does this thesis explain why the postulated stage in the development of the system should have lasted as long as Stalin lived and ended with his death or very soon after. In actuality, what this fact and other positive evidence indicate is that the Stalinist terror was in large part an expression of the needs of the dictatorial personality of Stalin, and that these needs continued to generate the terror as long as he lived. In my view, the instinct that originally led the theorists of totalitarianism to treat total terror as belonging to the very essence of this phenomenon was a sound one. But if their insight is to be salvaged, it will be necessary to reckon in a new way with the personal factor in the totalitarian terror and the dynamics of totalitarianism in general.

IV

We seem to be confronted with a resistance to the idea that the personality of the dictator may play a decisive part in the politics of totalitarianism. In conclusion it may be useful to explore its intellectual sources, examining both sides of some issues involved. Such an analysis of underlying issues is all the more pertinent in view of indications that the position taken by various theorists of totalitarianism reflects not simply the views of this school of theory but a rather broad spectrum of thinking among practitioners of contemporary social science. The thinking in question has to do with the influence of personality, and especially psychopathology, in decision-making and action in large-scale organizations, governments in particular.

Social scientists generally reject the "great man" theory of history as obsolete on the ground that historical phenomena are to be explained by social, political, and economic conditions and processes rather than by actions of individual leaders, who themselves are constrained by these conditions and involved in these processes. And many may be inclined to deny a major determining role to the dictatorial personality in totalitarian systems in part because of a feeling that to do otherwise would mean going back to an outmoded theory of the way in which history is made. However, no such implication follows. We do not face here a choice between explaining history by reference to leader-personalities or assigning them no importance at all. Historical explanation in the social sciences requires multiple approaches and a flexible willingness to vary them in accordance with the nature of the individual problems under consideration. To recognize that the influence of an individual personality on political events may be very great in certain special circumstances—most notably, those obtaining in a totalitarian dictatorship—is not to argue that this is a common phenomenon or that no other factors than the individual personality need be considered even in explaining events in this particular kind of case.

Secondly, some scholars are opposed to highlighting the dictator and his psychological motivations on the specific ground that to do so is to divert attention from the features of the totalitarian system that make it possible for him to act as he does. Objecting, for example, to the attempt to explain Stalin's Great Purge as resulting from the "aberrations of one man," Professor Leonard Schapiro writes, *inter alia,* that such an explanation fails to illuminate "the reasons which enabled one man to impose his will on so many millions." [31] It will hardly be disputed that an explanation of the behavior of a totalitarian dictator should take account of such situational factors as the structure of the political system within which he operates. But it does not follow that psychological explanations should be avoided. The investigator who finds in "aberrations of one man" a major determinant of the actions of a regime need not—and should not—concentrate exclusive attention upon this one determinant to the exclusion of other relevant factors. Nor does the location in the dictator himself of supreme personal responsibility for certain events absolve his associates and subordinates of their share of responsibility for carrying out the instructions that they received from him.

We come, finally, to a number of complex issues arising out of what I propose to call the theory of organizational rejection of aberrant personalities from leadership positions. It may be that nobody has ever advanced this theory as a whole. In any event, no formulation of it as a single connected argument has come to my attention, although individual elements of it appear here and there in the contemporary literature of political science. It begins with the proposition that modern society, owing to what has been called the "organizational revolution," has increasingly come to be dominated by large bureaucratic organizations, among which national governments themselves are of foremost importance. It may be recalled in this connection that totalitarian systems have been described as those in which the organizing of social life and the process of bureaucratization have gone farthest of all. Now it is held that the behavior of individuals, including leaders, in the structured social situations obtaining in large bureaucratic organizations is regulated to such a degree by the nature of the patterned roles that they play, the role expectations of others, and what may be called the rules of the game, that the influence of individual personality factors is, if not nullified, at any rate greatly circumscribed. As one political scientist expresses it, referring specifically to foreign policy elites, they operate in bureaucratic social situations and are subject to conditions that "tend to inhibit the impact of personality-oriented pressures." He infers that in dealing with the behavior of nation-states as actors within the international system, "non-logical explanations, while not completely irrelevant, are of little use." [32] Taking a similar position, and again with special reference to officials representing nation-states in international relations, another political scientist writes: "The individuals who represent these entities are constrained by colleagues, decision-making processes, and role expectations." [33]

If the effect of personality-oriented pressures is in general limited by constraints inherent in the structured social situations obtaining in organizations, a logical next step in the argument is to hold that individuals with serious emotional disorders will be even less likely than well-integrated personalities to express personality-oriented pressures in organization action. For such disorders will normally incapacitate individuals from successful leadership careers in the big bureaucratic organizations, since these persons will lack the stamina, the ability to work cooperatively with others, the trust in others, and so forth, which such leadership demands. And if, in the exceptional case, such an individual comes close to the pinnacle of decision-making power, counterpressures are generated within the organization that will greatly limit or even nullify his influence.[34] And such considerations may well seem applicable to totalitarian as well as other organizational settings. Moreover, it has been suggested that the peculiarly trying conditions of political life at the upper levels of a totalitarian state create an added obstacle to success of individuals with personality disorders. "So intense and continuous are the anxieties in a garrison-police state," writes Harold Lasswell, "that it is reasonable to suggest that only personalities who are basically integrated can endure. They must be in sufficient control of themselves to avoid over-suspiciousness, or they cannot identify confederates upon whom they can rely for common purposes."[35] Elsewhere Lasswell hypothesizes that while "anxiety-ridden persons" may be suitable for lower administrative niches in totalitarian systems, those in the top elite must have "relatively few internal conflicts" and be "comparatively free to make realistic appraisals of the environment," so that "It is probable that *a basically healthy personality is essential to survive the perpetual uncertainties of political life.*"[36]

The argumentation just outlined has merit; the question is, how much? Does it, in particular, warrant a conclusion that individuals with strong paranoid tendencies should not be expected to achieve and retain positions of supreme power in totalitarian movements and systems? I do not believe that it does. For the considerations that have been adduced here must be balanced against a series of countervailing considerations that appear to outweigh them. The countervailing considerations have to do with organizations, personality, and their interrelationships.

First, it seems inadvisable to discuss the problem on the plane of organization or bureaucracy in general. For distinctions between different sorts of organizations are quite important in assessing the likelihood that a given personality type or trait will be resisted, particularly if the type or trait falls in the category of psychopathology. We must distinguish, for example, between organizations that *are* bureaucracies, such as civil services, and organizations that merely *have* them, such as political parties. For psychological characteristics that might be a decided hindrance to success in the professional bureaucracy might be much less so, might in fact be a help, in a nonbureaucratic organizational milieu. Thus a Hitler would in all probability not have had a successful career in the *Reichsbank* under Hitler, who early in life rebelled against his father's wish that he become a civil servant and lacked many qualities requisite to success as one; but Hitler himself functioned in the very different organizational medium of the National Socialist movement and, later, of the higher Nazi leadership. Again, we must differentiate organizations in terms of their relative militance or nonmilitance, recognizing that at one extreme we find among political organizations some that are so militant in aim and outlook, so committed to political and psychological warfare as a mode of activity, that they may accurately be called "fighting organizations." Various revolutionary and extremist organizations would be cases in point—and cases that need to be considered because, as historical experience shows, under certain circumstances they achieve political power and furnish the leadership of modern states. Much of what has been said about organizational rejection of aberrant personalities is not applicable to organizations falling in this special category. Indeed, some of the very psychological characteristics that might tend to incapacitate an individual for a major role in other kinds of organizations may be potent qualifications for leadership of a fighting organization.

This organizational milieu is, in particular, favorable for the emergence in leadership positions of individuals of a type that may be called the "warfare personality." Hitler and Stalin were examples who also happened to be, in their respective ways, men of outstanding leadership ability. The warfare personality shows paranoid characteristics as psychiatrically defined,[37] but what is essential from the standpoint of this discussion is that it represents a *political* personality type. The characteristically paranoid perception of the world as an arena of deadly hostilities being conducted conspiratorially by an insidious and implacable enemy against the self finds highly systematized expression in terms of political and ideological symbols that are widely understood and accepted in the given social milieu. Through a special and radical form of displacement of private affects upon public objects, this world-image is politicized. In the resulting vision of reality, both attacker and intended victim are projected on the scale of large human collectivities. Consequently, in proclaiming the imperative need to fight back against an enveloping conspiratorial menace, the warfare personality identifies the enemy not as simply his own but as the society's and, in particular, the organization's. His particular vision of reality may therefore furnish potent ideological inspiration for a fighting organization, especially at at time of acute social malaise and crisis when conspiracy-centered outlooks show a certain plausibility and have an appeal to very many in the membership of the organization and in its wider social constituency. There is thus a possible close "fit" between the needs of a fighting organization *qua* organization for militant orientation and leadership, and the needs of a warfare personality *qua* personality for a leadership role and a life of unremitting struggle against enemies. Paradoxically, the very enemy-fixation that would help incapacitate the individual for leadership of most other organizations is here the key to the confluence of organization and personal needs.

There are other ways too in which psychopathological tendencies may prove highly "functional" for the warfare personality, both on the road to power in a fighting organization and also in his possible subsequent position as political ruler in a system of totalitarian character. Especially noteworthy is an extraordinary capacity for self-dramatization and self-deception. The presence of this quality in Hitler's personality has been mentioned above. We see it also in Stalin, and it appears to be a basic attribute of the warfare personality who is sufficiently gifted to qualify as a totalitarian dictator. He shows an outstanding ability, as it were, to project *mein Kampf* as *unser Kampf,* to pass himself off as merely the spearhead of the endangered group's resistance in a country-wide and ultimately world-wide struggle against the conspiratorial menace (however the latter is defined). What enables him to be so convincing in this capacity is self-dramatization, which in turn is serious rather than playful. He carries conviction because he has conviction. He is like an actor who lives his role while in the process of playing it, with the difference that he rarely if ever stops playing it. He is—if the cases of both Hitler and Stalin as subsequently documented are indicative—extremely egocentric as a personality, yet able to project himself with signal success as utterly group-centered, as a person for whom self is nothing and the organization or the movement or the system is all; and he can do this because he himself is so persuaded of the fact, being the first to believe in himself in his own role. He thus appears, but deceptively, as a peculiarly selfless prisoner of an abstract "ideological supersense" or "totalitarian mystique." The psychological reality is much more complex. We may, then, hypothesize that a capacity for what may be called sincere simulation, for effective masking of his own psychological needs as those of the organization or system, is a characteristic of the totalitarian dictator as a personality type. And it may be in part for this reason that scholarly students of totalitarianism have, as argued earlier here, unduly emphasized "system-needs" as motivating forces of totalitarianism and left out of account the impact of the needs of the dictatorial personality. They too have been deceived by him.

In the career of a totalitarian dictator a time may come, of course, when his vision of reality loses its persuasive power within the leadership of the movement, when he can no longer successfully project his psychological needs as needs of the system, when simulation fails. This is what appears to have happened toward the close of Stalin's life, and it is one of the reasons why his case is so extraordinarily instructive for theoretical analysis. Owing to his psychological rigidity on the one hand and postwar changes in objective conditions of the Soviet state on the other, a rift opened up in his last years between his policy views and those held by others in the inner circle of top leaders. By about 1949 the Soviet state could no longer really be said to exist in a hostile external environment, and even the world beyond the limits of the great new surrounding belt of Communist-dominated states remained dangerously hostile only insofar as Soviet acts and attitudes served to sustain the prevalent fear, suspicion, and unfriendliness. To some forces high in the leadership it appeared that these new circumstances permitted, and Soviet interests dictated, a diplomacy of international *détente* in the cold war. In presenting this view to Stalin, they apparently argued that the old "capitalist encirclement" was a thing of the past now that the USSR had a "socialist borderland" composed of friendly states.[38] However, Stalin, who for psychological reasons was obsessed with the omnipresence of "enemies" and convinced of the need to press the cold war in perpetuity, saw a diplomacy of *détente* as criminal folly, and relaxation of East-West tension, save on a momentary tactical basis, as out of the question.

In rejecting the *détente* policy, he put forward the psychologically very significant argument that the ideological postulate of a hostile capitalist encirclement must not be understood in "geographical" but rather in "political" terms, meaning that Soviet Russia must be seen as ringed with hatred and hostility even under the new circumstances when she had a "socialist borderland." And largely in order to demonstrate graphically that the hostile capitalist encirclement "still exists and operates," as the Soviet press put it at the time, he staged in the last year of his life the affair of the Kremlin doctors, which must be seen not simply as an "internal affair" but in its connection with Stalin's foreign policy. Analysis of this final (and probably fatal) episode in Stalin's political career shows that he was using the alleged Anglo-American-Jewish conspiracy for medical murder of Soviet leaders as a telling *riposte* against the high-level Soviet advocates of relaxation of international tension, and also as a basis for getting rid of these men and others with a new blood purge. The doctors' trial, which was apparently about to start at the very moment when Stalin providentially became "gravely ill," was to have dramatized—as the propaganda buildup for it in January–February 1953 showed—the continuing hostile machinations of what Stalin saw as a diabolical external enemy whose agents were operating internally in Russia, and even in the Kremlin, in the guise, for example, of Soviet doctors. All talk of a decrease of international tension, of improving relations with adversaries, would thus be exposed as a political absurdity. This interpretation of the affair is, incidentally, supported by Khrushchev's statement in the 1956 secret speech that Stalin, after distributing protocols of the doctors' confessions to members of the Politburo, told them: "You are blind like young kittens; what will happen without me? The country will perish because you do not know how to recognize enemies." [39] Stalin's politics of the "doctors' plot" were politics of paranoia. They represented the desperate effort of an aged warfare personality to continue acting out his private vision of reality and his bellicosity in the politics of his regime at a time when the vision had lost its credibility among the dictator's own entourage and the bellicosity endangered the system and all its beneficiaries.

If Stalin, as seems quite possible, was finally put out of the way so as to cut short the politics of paranoia on which he was engaged, this could be taken as evidence that even a totalitarian political organization has certain powers and a tendency to resist an aberrant personality in the role of dictator. But it would seem more reasonable to conclude that the developments toward the close of Stalin's life show how fearfully weak these powers and this tendency can be. If action was taken against him, this happened only at the eleventh hour when the very lives of those who took the action were immediately and unmistakably endangered by his further survival. It speaks against, rather than for, the theory of organizational rejection of aberrant personalities, in application to the totalitarian leader, that an aged dictator who had lost much of his erstwhile vigor and flexibility, who no longer (as was the case in the 1930s) had the advantage of being able to deceive likely victims as to his intentions, and whose psychopathological symptoms were flagrantly apparent to those around him, nevertheless managed to carry through to the final stage his preparations for a violent purge of—among others—close associates. From this viewpoint, the cases of both Stalin and Hitler emphasize a failure of the theory of organizational rejection to consider to what extent a totalitarian dictator may be able to emancipate himself from those very constraints, decision-making processes, structured situations, and role expectations that the theory treats as operative in governments generally. The point easily overlooked is that structured situations can be restructured, role expectations confounded, and roles themselves decisively remolded to fit the needs of the dictatorial personality.

By subordinating the terror machine directly to himself, as both Stalin and Hitler managed to do, by using it to terrorize associates as well as citizens at large, and by various other devices, a dictator, particularly if he is still sufficiently young and vigorous, may be able personally to dominate decisions and policy to an extraordinary degree in the organizational setting of totalitarianism. Not least among the means of nullifying institutional constraints is deliberate disorganization of higher decision-making bodies. In speaking, for example, of the personal character of Hitler's decision in August 1939 to attack Poland, Bullock points out that by then there was no longer in operation any supreme organ of government that might have organizationally constrained Hitler's power of making one-man decisions: "No Cabinet had now met for two years past, and anything that could be called a German Government had ceased to exist." [40] Stalin too, in his last years, disorganized the higher decision-making machinery of the Soviet Communist party as a means of keeping himself in a position to decide important questions on his own. Plenary sessions of the Party's Central Committee were no longer convened after 1947 or 1948, and the normal functioning of the Politburo appears to have terminated in early 1949. Policy problems were assigned to powerless ad hoc Politburo commissions variously called "quintets," "sextets," "septets," and so forth, with the result, according to Khrushchev, that the work of the Politburo itself was disorganized and some members were kept away from participation in reaching decisions on the most important state matters. One of the members, Voroshilov, was usually excluded from the occasional meetings of the Politburo that occurred because of Stalin's suspicion that he was a British agent.[41]

The foregoing considerations do not speak in favor of the theory of organizational rejection of aberrant personalities from leadership positions in totalitarian movements and systems. An individual who might be psychologically disqualified for successful leadership in very many large-scale oragnizations need not be so in the very special context of a fighting organization, in which his very psychopathology may be "functional" for leadership purposes. And insofar as the personality disorder would be in other ways be a serious handicap to the individual in the social role of supreme leader in a totalitarian system, this incapacitating effect would show up more strongly in his later years, when autocratic power may already be securely in his grasp, than in the critically important earlier years when he comes to power. We may recall in this connection that Stalin had emerged as Soviet supreme leader by 1929, when he entered his fiftieth year; that Hitler turned fifty as his power approached its zenith in 1938; and that Mussolini, much earlier, had become the head of the Italian government at the age of thirty-nine. Finally, we need to bear in mind that the bureaucratization of modern and especially of totalitarian society can foster as well as hinder the impact of personality. In particular, given a situation in which a warfare personality has managed, despite all obstacles, to climb to autocratic power in a totalitarian system, the very bureaucratic machinery that might resist personality-oriented pressures at lower levels may transmit them with terrifying results when they come from the very top. The bureaucratic organizations of the system then may become a conduit of the dictatorial psychopathology, so many machines for effectuating his will, serving his emotional needs, and acting out his private vision of reality.

For various reasons the repetition of this pattern, especially in modern states of major importance, may not be very likely at present. Organizational resistances are not, after all, negligible. Experience with totalitarian dictators is itself a force working against repetition, particularly in the countries that had the experience. Soviet leaders, for example, maintain that measures have been taken in the political system of the USSR to prevent a recurrence of uninhibited personal rule on the order of Stalin's and the kinds of "errors" associated with it; and the fall of Khrushchev is only the most convincing of a long series of indications that the Soviet dictatorship after Stalin has not again become an autocracy. Moreover, it may be that the combination of outstanding leadership talent with the full range of psychological characteristics that mark the potential totalitarian dictator as a personality type is an extreme rarity in modern societies. But even if it should follow from these and other considerations that the phenomenon with which we have been concerned here would only occur in the rare exceptional case, the conclusion would not be a very happy one. For we live in a time when even a single case may be one too many. One thing that political scientists can usefully do under these circumstances is to improve our understanding of the totalitarian dictator as a personality type, and of the personal element in the dynamics of totalitarianism.

NOTES

[1] See, for example, G. M. Gilbert, *The Psychology of Dictatorship* (New York 1950); Sigmund Neumann, *Permanent Revolution* (New York 1942), chap. 2; C. J. Friedrich and Z. Brzezinski, *Totalitarian Dictatorship and Autocracy* (Cambridge, Mass., 1956), chap. 2; and A. Inkeles, "The Totalitarian Mystique," in C. J. Friedrich, ed., *Totalitarianism* (Cambridge, Mass., 1954).

[2] The important earlier contributions include Sigmund Neumann, *Permanent Revolution*; Emil Lederer, *State of the Masses* (New York 1940); Franz Neumann, *Behemoth* (New York 1942); and Hannah Arendt, *The Origins of Totalitarianism* (New York 1951).

[3] *The Origins of Totalitarianism*, 391.

[4] *Hitler: A Study in Tyranny* (rev. edn., New York 1962), 375.

[5] *Psychopathology and Politics* (New York 1960), 173, 186.

[6] See, in particular, Merle Fainsod, *How Russia Is Ruled* (Cambridge, Mass., 1953); Z. Brzezinski, *The Permanent Purge* (Cambridge, Mass., 1956); Friedrich, ed., *Totalitarianism*; and Friedrich and Brzezinski, *Totalitarian Dictatorship and Autocracy*.

[7] *State of the Masses*, 45. See also Arendt, *The Origins of Totalitarinism*, chap. 10, and William Kornhauser, *The Politics of Mass Society* (Glencoe 1959). Franz Neumann, while agreeing that the transformation of men into "mass-men" is completed under totalitarianism, disagreed with the position of Lederer according to which the totalitarian state is a state *of* the masses. On this point, see *Behemoth*, 365–67.

[8] Friedrich and Brzezinski, *Totalitarian Dictatorship and Autocracy*, 19.

[9] *The Origins of Totalitarianism*, 245. For Franz Neumann's view, see *Behemoth*, 372–73. He writes there that "National Socialism must carry to an extreme the one process that characterizes the structure of modern society, bureaucratization." The thesis about the "radical efficiency" of totalitarian as distinguished from traditional bureaucracy appears to have been conclusively disproved in the light of what is now known about both the Nazi and the Stalinist bureaucracies. Bullock's investigations have led him to the conclusion, for example, that "The boasted totalitarian organization of the National Socialist State was in practice riddled with corruption and inefficiency under the patronage of the Nazi bosses. . . . At every level there were conflicts of authority, a fight for power and loot, and the familiar accompaniments of gangster rule, 'protection,' graft, and the 'rake-off' " (*Hitler: A Study in Tyranny*, 676). In *The German Occupation of Russia* (New York 1957), Alexander Dallin reaches a similar conclusion with regard to Nazi administration of the occupied territories. The speeches of Nikita Khrushchev and other official Soviet sources of the post-Stalin period provide a mass of illuminating detail on the inefficiency of the Stalinist totalitarian bureaucracy.

[10] *The Origins of Totalitarianism*, 315, 335. This distinction appears to be of use in explaining why Mussolini's Italy was only marginally a totalitarian state: the terror was of the "dictatorial" rather than of the "totalitarian" variety.

[11] Brzezinski, *The Permanent Purge*, 27. Brzezinski adds, in support of a view expressed by Arendt, that "terror within the totalitarian system actually must increase both in scope and in brutality with the growing stability of the regime," and further: "It is also a constant and pervading process of mass coercion, a continuum which persists throughout the totalitarian era" (*ibid.*).

[12] Fainsod, *How Russia Is Ruled*, 1st edn., 354.

[13] Friedrich and Brzezinski, *Totalitarian Dictatorship and Autocracy*, 132. They add: "The total scope and the pervasive and sustained character of totalitarian terror are . . . its unique qualities" (*ibid.*, 137).

[14] *The Permanent Purge*, 30, 36. Brzezinski's argument here appears to be, in part, an elaboration of the suggestion by Arendt that the Stalinist purge, as distinguished from earlier Bolshevik purges, was a means of maintaining a "permanent instability" in Soviet society, such instability being interpreted in turn as a functional requisite of totalitarianism as a system (*The Origins of Totalitarianism*, 376n.).

[15] *Totalitarianism*, 55.

[16] *The Origins of Totalitarianism*, 431–32.

[17] Friedrich, ed., *Totalitarianism*, 88, 91, 95–96. It may be noted that Inkeles views the "mystique" as a way of characterizing the totalitarian leader as a "psychological type." However, he seems to mean by "totalitarian leader" not solely the dictator but the whole higher leadership or ruling elite. And he explicitly discounts the need to penetrate beyond the ideological "mystique" into the psychology of the dictator as an individual. Indeed, he describes any attempt to trace the dictator's actions "to caprice, to paranoia, or some similar deviant personality manifestation" as a "residual category" type of explanation that can and should be avoided, e.g., by the "mystique" hypothesis (*ibid.*, 93).

[18] *Totalitarian Dictatorship and Autocracy*, 132, 137.

[19] *Behemoth*, 366, 469.

[20] In "Notes on the Theory of Dictatorship," Franz Neumann found five essential factors

in the modern totalitarian dictatorship: a police state, concentration of power, a monopolistic state party, totalitarian social controls, and reliance upon terror (*The Democratic and Authoritarian State* [Glencoe 1957], 244–45). In 1953 C. J. Friedrich proposed the following five features: an official ideology, a single mass party ("usually under a single leader"), a near-complete monopoly of control of all means of effective armed combat, similar control of all mass communication, and a system of terroristic police control (*Totalitarianism*, 52–53). In *Totalitarian Dictatorship and Autocracy* (pp. 9–10) a sixth feature—central control and direction of the economy—was added to the "syndrome."

[21] *Totalitarian Dictatorship and Autocracy*, 17, 18, 26.

[22] *Permanent Revolution*, 43; *The Origins of Totalitarianism*, 361, 392.

[23] *Ibid.*, 374. She writes further that "the Leader is irreplaceable because the whole complicated structure of the movement would lose its *raison d'être* without his commands" (*ibid.*, 362).

[24] For the concept of a "rationalist totalitarianism," see Z. Brzezinski, "Totalitarianism and Rationality," *American Political Science Review*, L (September 1956): 751–63. Examples of recent criticisms of the concept of totalitarianism are A. Z. Groth, "The 'Isms' in Totalitarianism," *ibid.*, LVIII (December 1964): 888–901; and this writer's "Towards a Comparative Politics of Movement-Regimes," *ibid.*, LV (June 1961): 281–89.

[25] Bullock, *Hitler: A Study in Tyranny*, 703. On Hitler's hysterical outburst on the eve of the war about annihilating his enemies, see Birger Dahlerus, *The Last Attempt* (London 1948), chap. 6; also Gilbert, *The Psychology of Dictatorship*, 301. For a full account of Hitler's actions and reactions during the entire crucial period of the war's beginning, see Bullock, chap. 9, esp. 536–39. Also of interest in this general connection is Ivone Kirkpatrick's account of the psychological motivations underlying Mussolini's decision to embark upon the Abyssinian war (*Mussolini: A Study in Power* [New York 1964], 320).

[26] For a detailed elaboration of this argument, along with an analysis of the ideology of the purge trials in terms of the analogy with a paranoid system, see the introduction to R. C. Tucker and S. F. Cohen, eds., *The Great Purge Trial* (New York 1965). It is significant that the conspiracy themes that Stalin incorporated into Marxist-Leninist ideology have largely lapsed or subsided in post-Stalin Russia.

[27] Nikita Khrushchev, *Crimes of the Stalin Era* (New York 1956), 48.

[28] The menace of the paranoid in the nuclear age has been strongly emphasized by Lasswell. Pointing out that "All mankind might be destroyed by a single paranoid in a position of power who could imagine no grander exit than using the globe as a gigantic funeral pyre," he goes on: "Even a modicum of security under present-day conditions calls for the discovery, neutralization and eventual prevention of the paranoid. And this calls for the overhauling of our whole inheritance of social institutions for the purpose of disclosing and eliminating the social factors that create these destructive types" (*Power and Personality* [New York 1948], 184). My own remarks above are meant to suggest that, pending the requisite systematic attack upon the problem, it may be possible to devise interim means of dealing with developing situations of this kind before it is too late.

[29] *Ideology and Power in Soviet Politics* (New York 1962), 80, 88–89. Fainsod, who in the 1953 first edition of his study of Soviet government had called terror the "linchpin of modern totalitarianism," in the 1963 edition revises this sentence to read: "Every totalitarian regime makes some place for terror in its system of controls" (*How Russia Is Ruled*, 2nd edn., 421). See also Allen Kassof, "The Administered Society: Totalitarianism Without Terror," *World Politics*, XVI (July 1964), 558–75.

[30] See, for example, "Was Stalin Really Necessary?" in Alec Nove's, *Economic Rationality and Soviet Politics* (New York 1964). Soviet second thoughts have been expressed, albeit very cautiously, in the form of criticism of unnecessary "excesses" in the implementation of the collectivization policy by Stalin.

[31] Leonard Schapiro, *The Communist Party of the Soviet Union* (New York 1959), 428–29. Marshall D. Shulman goes farther and questions "how far 'the system' can be absolved of responsibility for Stalinism, whatever may have been the condition of Stalin himself." He continues: "Perhaps 'the system' bore the main brunt of policy formation. It is reasonable to suppose that, even in a dictatorial society, much of what is done in the name of a leader is necessarily the product of a bureaucracy, and may imply any degree of responsibility from his active guidance to his inattention" (*Stalin's Foreign Policy Reconsidered* [Cambridge, Mass., 1963], 261). This is to disregard the factual evidence from post-Stalin Soviet sources, including Khrushchev's secret report, on the actualities of decision-making in Stalin's final years. The evidence may, of course, be incomplete and faulty, but it cannot simply be dismissed.

[32] Sidney Verba, "Assumptions of Rationality and Non-Rationality in Models of the International System," *World Politics*, XVI (October 1961): 105. "Non-logical explanations" are here defined as those referring to unconscious psychological pressures in the decision-making individuals.

[33] Morton A. Kaplan, "Old Realities and New Myths," *World Politics*, XVII (January 1965): 359.

[34] This is one of the themes, for example, of Arnold Rogow's important study of the career of James Forrestal as an instance of an emotionally disturbed personality rising close to the pinnacle of power. Rogow writes that beyond a certain point counter-pressures were generated inside the military establishment that Forrestal headed: "As Forrestal's behavior became more and more tense, he was consulted less by his associates and involved less in decisions." As part of the explanation for this, Rogow states: "Bureaucracies, whether governmental, corporate, or academic, do not welcome in their ranks those who are odd, deviant, or excessively nonconformist in behavior, and the military bureaucracy was no exception" (*James Forrestal: A Study of Personality, Politics, and Policy* [New York 1963], 350).

[35] "Political Constitution and Character," *Psychoanalysis and the Psychoanalytic Review*, XLVI, No. 4 (Winter 1960): 16.

[36] "The Selective Effect of Personality on Political Participation," in R. Christie and M. Jahoda, eds., *Studies in the Scope and Method of "The Authoritarian Personality"* (Glencoe 1964), 223. See also in this volume the essay by E. A. Shils, who argues that American "nativist leaders," generally characterized by "strong paranoid tendencies," are unable to develop "the flexible self-control required to build the administrative machinery in their organizations" and for this and other personality-associated reasons have had a "hard row to hoe" (*ibid.*, 46).

[37] The official handbook of the American Psychiatric Association describes paranoia as "characterized by an intricate, complex, and slowly developing paranoid system, often logically elaborated after a false interpretation of an actual occurrence," and adds: "The paranoid system is particularly isolated from much of the normal stream of consciousness, without hallucinations and with relative intactness and preservation of the remainder of the personality, in spite of a chronic and prolonged course" (*Mental Disorders* [Washington, D. C., 1952], 28).

[38] For a public formulation of reasoning to this effect, see, in particular, the beginning of Malenkov's address of November 6, 1949 (*Pravda*, November 7, 1949).

[39] *Crimes of the Stalin Era*, S49. The evidence for the interpretation that has been offered here of the division over foreign policy at the close of Stalin's lifetime, and of the political meaning of the affair of the Kremlin doctors, has been presented in greater detail and with documentation in my *Soviet Political Mind* (New York 1963), chap. 2.

[40] *Hitler: A Study in Tyranny*, 548. A similar view is presented by H. R. Trevor-Roper, who writes also that Nazi Germany's leading politicians "were not a government but a court —a court as negligible in its power of ruling, as incalculable in its capacity for intrigue, as any oriental sultanate" (*The Last Days of Hitler* [New York 1947], 1).

[41] This description of the situation under Stalin is based on Khrushchev, *Crimes of the Stalin Era*, S61–S62. See also the note by Boris Nicolaevsky, *ibid.*, S61.

23

An Experimental Approach
to Studying National Differences

Most of the "national character" literature has relied on inference—from cultural artifacts, institutions, or imperfectly validated clinical procedures—to study patterns of national personality and differences among national patterns. Milgram is one of the few investigators who has approached the question of national similarities and differences in behavior by making systematic, direct observations of individual behavior. In this study, he has selected, moreover, an issue with evident political significance: the response of individuals to group pressures. His method allows him to report actual behavior much more precisely than most investigators using quantitative methods are able.

The study is a self-explanatory model of clarity, but the following notes may provoke some further reflection. Milgram finds that his Norwegian subjects conform to group pressures against the evidence of the senses more than French subjects do. Milgram appears to infer tentatively that this willingness to conform is related to the superior Norwegian social welfare system. Second, Milgram's remarks on the reasons the French have such diverse political views should be compared (although there is no necessary contradiction) with the views of Converse and Dupeux, whose study of the French and American electorates is reprinted as Selection 24.

NATIONALITY AND CONFORMITY

Stanley Milgram

People who travel abroad seem to enjoy sending back reports on what people are like in various countries they visit. A variety of national stereotypes is part and parcel of popular knowledge. Italians are said to be "volatile," Germans "hard-working," the Dutch "clean," the Swiss "neat," the English "reserved," and so on. The habit of making generalizations about national groups is not a modern inven-

Scientific American, 205 (December, 1961), 45–51. Reprinted with permission. Copyright © 1961 by Scientific American, Inc. All rights reserved.

tion. Byzantine war manuals contain careful notes on the deportment of foreign populations, and Americans still recognize themselves in the brilliant national portrait drawn by Alexis de Tocqueville more than 100 years ago.

And yet the skeptical student must always come back to the question: "How do I know that what is said about a foreign group is true?" Prejudice and personal bias may color such accounts, and in the absence of objective evidence it is not easy to distinguish between fact and fiction. Thus the problem faced by the modern investigator who wishes to go beyond literary description is how to make an objective analysis of behavioral differences among national groups. By this he means simply an analysis that is not based on subjective judgment and that can be verified by any competent investigator who follows the same methods.

It is easy to show objectively that people in different countries often speak different languages, eat different foods and observe different social customs. But can one go further and show national differences in "character" or "personality"? When we turn to the more subtle dimensions of behavior, there is very little evidence to make a case for national differences. It is not that such differences are to be denied out of hand; it is just that we lack sufficient reliable information to make a clear judgment.

Before reporting the results of my own study let me refer briefly to some earlier efforts to achieve objectivity in studying this elusive problem. One approach has been to examine the literature and other cultural products of a nation in the hope of identifying underlying psychological characteristics. For example, Donald V. McGranahan of Harvard University studied successful stage plays performed in Germany and the U.S. and concluded that German stage characters were more devoted to principles and ideological notions, whereas the Americans were more concerned with the attainment of purely personal satisfactions. The obvious limitation of such a study is that the behavior and attitudes under examination are the synthetic ones of the stage and may bear little or no resemblance to those of real life.

Another indirect approach has relied on the tools of clinical psychology. This method was pioneered by anthropologists in the study of small, primitive societies and has only recently been applied to modern urban nations. These studies rely heavily on such tests as the Rorschach ink-blot test and the thematic apperception test (T.A.T.). In the latter the subject is shown a drawing of a situation that can be variously interpreted and is asked to make up a story about it. The major difficulty here is that the tests themselves have not been adequately validated and are basically impressionistic.

Finally, sample surveys of the type developed by Elmo Roper and George Gallup in this country have been applied to the problem. Geoffrey Gorer, an English social scientist, based his study *Exploring English Character* on a questionnaire distributed to 11,000 of his compatriots. The questions dealt with varied aspects of English life, such as courtship patterns, experiences in school and practices in the home. Unfortunately there are many reasons why an individual's answer may not correspond to the facts. He may deliberately distort his answers to produce a good impression, or he may have genuine misconceptions of his own behavior, attributable either to faulty memory or the blindness people often exhibit toward their own actions and motivations.

These methods should not be dismissed as unimportant in the study of national characteristics. Yet in principle if one wants to know whether the people of one nation behave differently from those of another, it would seem only reasonable to examine the relevant behavior directly, and to do so under conditions of controlled observations in order to reduce the effects of personal bias and to make measurement more precise.

An important step in this direction was reported in 1954 by an international team of psychologists who worked together as the Organization for Comparative Social Research. This team studied reactions to threat and rejection among school children in seven European nations, using hypotheses advanced by Stanley Schachter of Columbia University. The inquiry was not specifically designed to study national characteristics but chiefly to see if certain concepts regarding threat and rejection would hold up when tested in different countries. In the course of the study certain differences between countries did turn up, but the investigators felt they were not necessarily genuine. Conceivably they were due to defects in the experiment or to inadequacies in the theory behind it. Although its focus was on theory validation, this study is a landmark in crossnational research. Unfortunately the Organization for Comparative Social Research halted its research program when the study was completed.

My own investigation was begun in 1957. My objective was to see if experimental techniques could be applied to the study of national characteristics, and in particular to see if one could measure conformity in two European countries: Norway and France. Conformity was chosen for several reasons. First, a national culture can be said to exist only if men adhere, or conform, to common standards of behavior; this is the psychological mechanism underlying all cultural behavior. Second, conformity has become a burning issue in much of current social criticism; critics have argued that people have become too sensitive to the opinions of others, and that this represents an unhealthy development in modern society. Finally, good experimental methods have been developed for measuring conformity.

The chief tool of investigation was a modified form of the group-pressure experiment used by Solomon E. Asch and other social psychologists [see "Opinions and Social Pressure," by Solomon E. Asch, *Scientific American,* November, 1955] In Asch's original experiment a group of half a dozen subjects was shown a line of a certain length and asked to say which of three lines matched it. All but one of the subjects had been secretly instructed beforehand to select one of the "wrong" lines on each trial or in a certain percentage of the trials. The naive subject was so placed that he heard the answers of most of the group before he had to announce his own decision. Asch found that under this form of social pressure a large fraction of subjects went along with the group rather than accept the unmistakable evidence of their own eyes.

Our experiment is conducted with acoustic tones rather than with lines drawn on cards. Five of the subjects are confederates of the experimenter and conspire to put social pressure on the sixth subject. The subjects listen to two tones and are asked to say which is the longer. The five confederates answer first and their decisions are heard by the subject, who answers last. The confederates have been instructed to announce wrong answers on 16 of the 30 trials that constitute one experiment.

We elected to use tones rather than lines because they are better suited to an experimental method using "synthetic groups." Two psychologists working at Yale University, Robert Blake and Jack W. Brehm, had discovered that group-pressure experiments can be conducted without requiring the actual presence of confederates. It is sufficient if the subject thinks they are present and hears their voices through headphones. With tape recordings it is easy to create synthetic groups. Tapes do not have to be paid by the hour and they are always available.

When the test subject entered our laboratory, he saw several coats on hangers and immediately got the impression that others were present. He was taken to one of six closed booths, where he was provided with headphones and a microphone. As he listened to the instructions through the headphones he overheard the voices of the other "subjects" and assumed that all the booths were occupied. During the actual experiment he would hear five taped answers before he was asked to give his own.

Except when we made a technical slip the subject never caught on to the trick. Most subjects became deeply involved in the situation, and strong tensions were generated when they realized they must stand alone against five unanimous opponents. This situation created a genuine and deeply felt conflict that had to be resolved either through independence or conformity.

Once we had refined our techniques at Harvard University we were ready to experiment abroad with Norwegian and French subjects. In which of the two national environments would people go along with the group more and in which would there be greater independence?

Most of the subjects used in the Norwegian study were students attending the University of Oslo. Because this is the only full-fledged university in Norway, a good geographic representation was obtained. Our test sample included students from beyond the Arctic Circle, from the fiord country of western Norway and from Trondheim, the former Viking capital.

When the study moved to Paris, French students were selected who matched the Norwegians in age, level of education, fields of study, sex, marital status and— so far as possible—social class. Once again a good geographic distribution was obtained, because students from all parts of France came to study in Paris. A few of the French subjects came from French North African cities. Those used in the experiment were culturally as French as people living on the mainland; they were of French parentage and had been educated in French lycées.

In Norway the entire experiment was conducted by a native Norwegian and all the recorded voices were those of natives. In France the experiments were conducted by native Frenchmen. Much effort was made to match the tone and quality of the Norwegian and French groups. We made recordings until people who were sensitive to the nuances of both languages were satisfied that equivalent group atmospheres had been achieved.

Twenty Norwegian subjects and the same number of French subjects were studied in the first set of experiments. The Norwegian subjects conformed to the group on 62 percent of the critical trials (that is, trials in which the group deliberately voted wrong); the French subjects conformed to the group on 50 percent of the critical trials.

After each subject had taken part in the experiment he was told its true character and was asked to give his reactions. Almost all participants in both countries had accepted the experiment at face value and admitted feeling the strong pressure of the group. A Norwegian student from a farm in Nordland, above the Arctic Circle, said: "I think the experiment had a very ingenious arrangement. I had no idea about the setup until it was explained to me. Of course, it was a little embarrassing to be exposed in such a way." A self-critical student from Oslo remarked: "It was a real trick and I was stupid to have fallen into the trap. . . . It must be fun to study psychology." Similar reactions were obtained in France, where students were impressed with the idea of psychological experimentation. (In neither country is psychological research as widespread or as intensive as it is in the U.S., so that subjects are relatively unsophisticated about psychological deceptions.)

It would have been superficial, of course, to conduct just one experiment in Norway, another in France and then draw conclusions. In a second experiment we undertook to change the subject's attitude toward the importance of the experiment itself to see if this might alter the original findings. In this new series of trials (and in all subsequent ones) the subjects were told that the results of the experiments would be applied to the design of aircraft safety signals. In this way their performance was linked to a life-and-death issue. As one might have predicted, the subjects this time showed somewhat greater independence of the group, but once again the level of conformity was higher in Norway (56 percent) than it was in France (48 percent).

One possibility that had to be considered at the outset was that Norwegians and Frenchmen differ in their capacity for discriminating tonal lengths and that this led to the greater number of errors made by Norwegians in the group situation. We were able to show, however, by giving each subject a tone-discrimination test, that there was no difference in the level of discrimination of students in the two countries.

In both of the first two conformity experiments the subjects were required to do more than decide an issue in the face of unanimous opposition: they were also required to announce that decision openly for all to hear (or so the subject thought). Thus the act had the character of a public statement. We all recognize that the most obvious forms of conformity are the public ones. For example, when prevailing standards of dress or conduct are breached, the reaction is usually immediate and critical. So we decided we had better see if the Norwegians conformed more only under public conditions, when they had to declare their answers aloud. Accordingly, we undertook an experiment in both countries in which the subject was allowed to record his answers on paper rather than announce them to the group. The experiments were performed with a new group of 20 Norwegian and 20 French students.

When the requirement of a public response was eliminated, the amount of conformity dropped considerably in both countries. But for the third time the French subjects were more independent than the Norwegians. In Paris students went along with the group on 34 percent of the critical trials. In Oslo the figure was close to 50 percent. Therefore elimination of the requirement of a public response reduced conformity 14 percentage points in France but only 6 percentage points in Norway.

It is very puzzling that the Norwegians so often voted with the group, even when given a secret ballot. One possible interpretation is that the average Norwegian, for whatever reason, believes that his private action will ultimately become known to others. Interviews conducted among the Norwegians offer some indirect evidence for this conjecture. In spite of the assurances that the responses would be privately analyzed, one subject said he feared that because he had disagreed too often the experimenter would assemble the group and discuss the disagreements with them.

Another Norwegian subject, who had agreed with the group 12 out of 16 times, offered this explanation: "In the world now, you have to be not too much in opposition. In high school I was more independent than now. It's the modern way of life that you have to agree a little more. If you go around opposing, you might be looked upon as bad. Maybe this had an influence." He was then asked, "Even though you were answering in private?" and he replied, "Yes. I tried to put myself in a public situation, even though I was sitting in the booth in private."

A fourth experiment was designed to test the sensitivity of Norwegian and French subjects to a further aspect of group opinion. What would happen if subjects were exposed to overt and audible criticism from the conspiratorial group? It seemed reasonable to expect a higher degree of conformity under these conditions. On the other hand, active criticism might conceivably lead to a greater show of independence. Moreover, the Norwegians might react one way and the French another. Some of my associates speculated that audible criticism would merely serve to annoy the French subjects and make them stubborn and more resistant to the influence of the group.

To test these notions we recorded a number of appropriate reactions that we could switch on whenever the subject gave a response that contradicted the majority. The first sanction, in both Norway and France, was merely a slight snicker by a member of the majority. The other sanctions were more severe. In Norway they were based on the sentence "Skal du stikke deg ut?" which may be translated: "Are you trying to show off?" Roughly equivalent sentences were used with the French group. In Paris, when the subject opposed the group, he might hear through his headphones: "Voulez-vous vous faire remarquer?" ("Trying to be conspicuous?")

In both Norway and France this overt social criticism significantly increased conformity. In France subjects now went along with the majority on 59 percent of the critical trials. In Norway the percentage rose to 75 percent. But the reactions of subjects in the two countries was even more striking. In Norway subjects accepted the criticism impassively. In France, however, more than half the subjects made retaliatory response of their own when the group criticized them. Two French students, one from the Vosges mountain district and the other from the Department of Eure-et-Loire, became so enraged they directed a stream of abusive language at their taunters.

Even after we explained in the interview session that the entire experimental procedure had been recorded on tape, many of the subjects did not believe us. They could not understand how we could interject comments with such verisimilitude, particularly since we could not predict how they would respond at any given moment. This was achieved by making use of two tape recorders. One played the standard tape containing tones and the group judgments, with "dead" time for the subject; the other contained only the set of "criticisms" from members of the group. The two instruments could be controlled independently, allowing us to inject a remark whenever the subject's responses made it appropriate. The remarks followed the subject's independent responses immediately, creating a highly spontaneous effect.

Another series of experiments was designed to aid in the interpretation of the earlier findings. For example, many Norwegian subjects rationalized their behavior by stating in the interview that they went along with the others because they doubted their own judgment, and that if they had been given a chance to dispel this doubt they would have been more independent. An experiment was therefore carried out to test this notion. The subject was given a chance to reexamine the stimulus materials before giving his final judgment. He did this by sounding a bell in his booth whenever he wished to hear a pair of tones again. As before, the subject was openly censured by the group if he failed to conform, but he was not censured merely for asking to hear the tones repeated. It turned out that even the

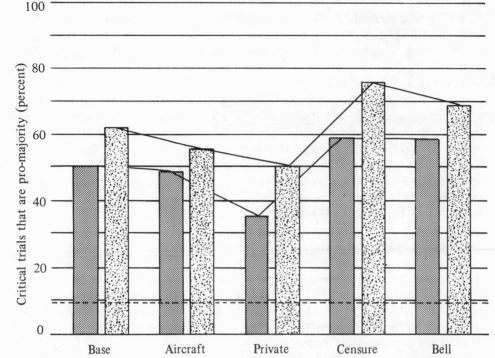

LEVEL OF CONFORMITY was higher for Norwegians (*speckled bars*) than French subjects (*gray bars*) in all five test situations, but fluctuated similarly for both. The broken black line indicates the error level of control groups of both nationalities in the absence of pressure. The first set of bars gives results for the basic experiment. In the next situation significance was increased by an announcement that the test results would affect aircraft safety. This "aircraft" factor was maintained in subsequent tests, in one of which the subjects recorded their answers privately instead of announcing them. In the "censure" situation critical comments (on tape) stepped up pressure on the subjects. In a final experiment censure continued and the subjects were allowed to request repetition of the test tones by sounding a bell; fewer Norwegians than Frenchmen proved "bold" enough to do so.

relatively simple act of requesting a repetition must be construed as an act of considerable independence. Only five of the Norwegians asked for a repetition of a tone on any trial, whereas 14 of the French subjects were "bold" enough to do so. And again the French showed more independence overall, voting with the group on 58 percent of the critical trials, compared with 69 percent for the Norwegians.

The study next moved out of the university and into the factory. When we tested 40 Norwegian industrial workers, we found that their level of conformity was about the same as that of the Norwegian students. There was, however, one important difference. Students were often tense and agitated during the experiment. The industrial workers took it all with good humor and frequently were amused when the true nature of the experiment was explained. We have not yet managed to study a comparable group of industrial workers in France.

No matter how the data are examined they point to greater independence among the French than among the Norwegians. Twelve percent of the Norwegian students conformed to the group on every one of the 16 critical trials, while only 1 percent of the French conformed on every occasion. Forty-one percent of the French students but only 25 percent of the Norwegians displayed strong independence. And in every one of the five experiments performed in both countries the French showed themselves to be the more resistant to group pressure.

These findings are by no means conclusive. Rather they must be regarded as the beginning of an inquiry that one would like to see extended. But incomplete as the findings are, they are likely to be far more reliable than armchair speculation on national character.

It is useful, nevertheless, to see if the experimental results are compatible with a nation's culture as one can observe it in daily life. If there were a conflict between the experimental findings and one's general impressions, further experiments and analysis would be called for until the conflict had been resolved. Conceivably the discrepancy might be due to viewing the culture through a screen of stereotypes and prejudices rather than seeing it with a clear eye. In any case, in our study experiment and observation seem to be in reasonable agreement. For whatever the evidence may be worth, I will offer my own impressions of the two countries under examination.

I found Norwegian society highly cohesive. Norwegians have a deep feeling of group identification, and they are strongly attuned to the needs and interests of those around them. Their sense of social responsibility finds expression in formidable institutions for the care and protection of Norwegian citizens. The heavy taxation required to support broad programs of social welfare is borne willingly. It would not be surprising to find that social cohesiveness of this sort goes hand in hand with a high degree of conformity.

Compared with the Norwegians, the French show far less consensus in both social and political life. The Norwegians have made do with a single constitution, drafted in 1814, while the French have not been able to achieve political stability within the framework of four republics. Though I hardly propose this as a general rule of social psychology, it seems true that the extreme diversity of opinion found in French national life asserts itself also on a more intimate scale. There is a tradition of dissent and critical argument that seeps down to the local *bistro*. The high value placed on critical judgment often seems to go beyond reasonable bounds; this in itself could account for the comparatively low degree of conformity we found in the French experiments. Furthermore, as Stanley Schachter has shown, the chronic existence of a wide range of opinion helps to free the individual from social pressure. Much the same point is made in recent studies of U.S. voting behavior. They reveal that the more a person is exposed to diverse viewpoints, the more likely he is to break away from the voting pattern of his native group. All these factors would help to explain the relatively independent judgments shown by French students.

The experiments demonstrate, in any case, that social conformity is not exclusively a U.S. phenomenon, as some critics would have us believe. Some amount of conformity would seem necessary to the functioning of any social system. The problem is to strike the right balance between individual initiative and social authority.

One may ask whether or not national borders really provide legitimate boundaries for the study of behavioral differences. My feeling is that boundaries are useful only to the extent to which they coincide with cultural, environmental or biological divisions. In many cases boundaries are themselves a historical recognition of common cultural practice. Furthermore, once boundaries are established they tend to set limits of their own on social communication.

For all this, a comparison of national cultures should not obscure the enor-

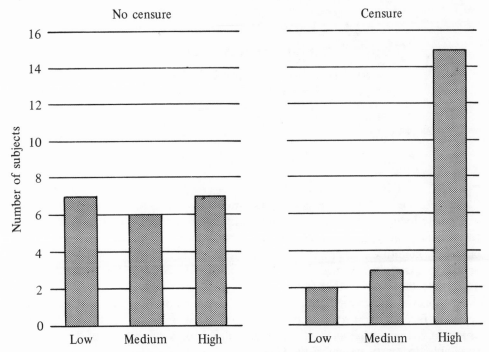

EFFECT OF CENSURE was to increase conformity. The charts show the degree of conformity among 20 Norwegians in the absence of censure (*left*) and when censure was
introduced in the form of criticism (*right*). The "low" conformity category includes
those who gave 6 or fewer promajority responses out of 16; "medium" is 7 to 11 and
"high" 12 or more.

mous variations in behavior within a single nation. Both the Norwegians and the
French displayed a full range of behavior from complete independence to complete
conformity. Probably there is no significant national comparison in which the extent of overlap does not approach or match the extent of differences. This should
not prevent us, however, from trying to establish norms and statistically valid
generalizations on behavior in different nations.

We are now planning further research in national characteristics. In a recent
seminar at Yale University students were given the task of trying to identify behavioral characteristics that might help to illuminate the Nazi epoch in German
history. The principal suggestions were that Germans might be found to be more
aggressive than Americans, to submit more readily to authority and to display
greater discipline. Whether these assumptions will hold up under experimental inquiry is an open question. A team of German and American investigators is plan-
nings a series of experiments designed to provide a comparative measure of behavior in the two countries.

24

A Sample Survey Approach
to Studying National Differences

The preceding selection is an empirical study of "national character" attributes as actually found in samples of individuals in different nations. It reports on actual respondents, analyzing them statistically, rather than following the earlier national character literature, which often extrapolated from case materials and cultural artifacts, or simply assumed a fit between individual personality and institutions. This study takes the further step of sampling national populations systematically, thus insuring the representativeness of the respondents. In addition, the present selection focuses on *specific institutional regularities* that may be related to some aspect of national character—the volatile "flash" political parties of France and the stable two-party system of the United States.

The fascinating finding of this inquiry is that differences in voting behavior in France and the United States appear to be associated with differences in childhood political socialization practices in the two nations: American children learn their parents' party identifications; French children for the most part, apparently do not. This, in turn, could be related to broader differences in family climate between the two nations.

The authors do not claim that the differences they find in childhood socialization experiences completely "explain" the difference in the French and American party systems. But they convincingly link socialization-related aggregate psychological attributes with system regularities. It can be argued that party loyalty is not a "personality" variable in the narrow sense and, hence, that this is not a study of personality and politics. Yet it is a demonstration that national differences in a psychological variable appear connected with national differences in the properties of political systems. And the procedure used here can be adapted to the study of other psychological variables. Further, identification variables, as Erikson's work stresses, may be among the key psychological forces linking individual ego development to social, cultural and political patterns.

POLITICIZATION OF THE ELECTORATE
IN FRANCE AND THE UNITED STATES

Philip E. Converse and Georges Dupeux

Since the revolutions in the latter part of the eighteenth century, France and the United States have followed quite different courses of political development. Nonetheless, a comparison of political institutions and the participation of citizens in these democracies should be of very special interest to social scientists in both countries, as well as elsewhere. Here is a thoroughgoing study of the relations of voters to parties in the two countries.

Philip E. Converse is Senior Study Director at the Survey Research Center and Assistant Professor of Sociology at the University of Michigan. He was one of the authors of The American Voter. *Georges Dupeux is Professor of History at the University of Bordeaux and the author of many articles on French political behavior.*

The turbulence of French politics has long fascinated observers, particularly when comparisons have been drawn with the stability or, according to one's point of view, the dull complacency of American political life. Profound ideological cleavages in France, the occasional threat of civil war, rather strong voter turnout, the instability of governments and republics, and the rise and fall of "flash" parties like the R.P.F. in 1951, the Poujadists in 1956, and the U.N.R. in 1958 have all contributed to the impression of a peculiar intensity in the tenor of French political life.

It is a sign of progress in the study of political behavior that such symptoms no longer seem to form a self-evident whole. We feel increasingly obliged, for example, to take note of the level in the society at which the symptoms are manifest. Most of our impressions of the French scene reflect only the behavior of French political leadership. Growing familiarity with survey data from broad publics has schooled us not to assume perfect continuity between the decision-making characteristics of a leadership and the predispositions of its rank and file. The extremism of the military elite in Algeria or ideological intransigence in the French National Assembly are in themselves poor proof that the shipyard worker in Nantes has political reflexes which differ from those of the shipyard worker in Norfolk.

We feel increasingly obliged, moreover, to discriminate between some of these well-known symptoms of turbulence, for they no longer point in a common direction as clearly as was once assumed. Two signs which unquestionably reflect mass electoral behavior in France provide a case in point. Turnout levels in France are indeed high relative to those in the United States,[1] suggesting that, in the politically indifferent strata of the electorate where nonvoting is considered, political motivations are more intense. On the other hand, we now doubt that the rise and fall of "flash" parties are parallel symptoms of intense involvement. Rather, it seems likely that such episodes represent spasms of political excitement in unusually

Public Opinion Quarterly, 26, No. 1 (Spring, 1962), 1–23. Reprinted as Chapter 14 of Angus Campbell *et al., Elections and the Political Order* (New York: Wiley, 1966), pp. 269–91.

hard times on the part of citizens whose year-in, year-out involvement in political affairs is abnormally weak.[2] Obviously, for France and the United States, the basic traditions of a two-party or a multiparty system affect the likelihood that the flash party phenomenon will occur. But other things being equal, it seems that such phenomena are hardly signals of long-term public involvement in politics but betray instead a normal weak involvement. The durably involved voter tends toward strong partisan commitments, and his behavior over time stabilizes party fortunes within a nation.

Other less direct indicators add doubt as to the high involvement of the broad French public. Demographically, French society differs from the American in its lesser urbanization and lower mean formal education. Intranational studies have persistently shown higher political involvement among urban residents and, more strongly still, among people of more advanced education. While cross-national extrapolation of such data may be precarious, it does leave further room to question our intuitive impressions.

We intend in this paper to examine comparative data on the French and American publics in an effort to determine more precisely the locus of Franco-American differences in these matters.[3] We shall consider the locus in qualitative terms, covering an extended series of political characteristics which run from expressions of involvement, acts of participation, and information seeking to orientations whereby the voter links party alternatives to the basic ideological issues in the society. We shall throughout maintain an interest as well in a vertical locus of differences. That is, we shall think of the two electorates as stratified from persistent nonvoters at the bottom, through the large middle mass of average voters, to citizens who engage in some further partisan activity, and thence by extrapolation to the higher leadership whose highly visible behavior is so frequently the source of our cross-national impressions. Such extrapolation is necessary, of course, because it is unlikely that the handful of "activists" whom we can distinguish at the top layer of both national samples include more than one or two persons who have ever had any direct hand in a leadership decision of even a parochial party organization or political interest group.

INVOLVEMENT, PARTICIPATION, AND INFORMATION SEEKING

While a relatively large number of comparisons may be drawn with regard to simple manifestations of political involvement in the two countries, these comparisons vary widely in quality. Broad differences in institutions and political practices in the two societies can serve to channel public interest in different directions. The French political poster, often a full-blown campaign document, is addressed to other goals than the American political billboard, and hence the reading of such posters in the two societies is in no sense comparable activity. Similarly, the national control of the domestic airwaves in France means that two media of communication are given a totally different cast than in the United States. This fact, coupled with reduced access to radio or television sets in France, renders the attention paid by the two publics to such political broadcasts fundamentally incomparable. Or, in a different vein, certain manifestations of involvement are known to vary widely in their frequency within a nation from one type of election to another, or for the same type of election between periods of crisis and troughs of routine politics. While an extended American time series has provided some useful norms, these were more difficult to find for the French data. In general, then, we shall elaborate upon only a few of the most solid comparisons, referring summarily to the flavor conveyed by other, looser comparisons.

Given the broad institutional differences between the two societies, it might seem useful to draw contrasts between self-estimates of psychological involvement between the two nations, however differently institutions might channel the ultimate behavorial expressions of such interest. While the data permit a number of matches between questions on political interest, posed at comparable times with comparable wording and with superficially comparable alternatives, one hesitates at comparisons which depend on crude "amount words" such as "very," "fairly," and the like. Cautiously, however, it may be observed that Americans gauge their interest in their elections at a higher level than do the French. Two to five times as many French respondents indicated that they were "not at all" interested in the 1958 elections as is the tendency for Americans with regard to their presidential elections; three to four times as many Americans say that they are "very" interested. Distributions from France in the more normal political year of 1953 show slightly higher levels of expressed interest, but even this distribution fails to approach the most unenthusiastic American distributions collected at the time of off-year congressional elections. For what it is worth, then, it is relatively hard to get French citizens to confess much interest in their elections.

Figure 1

Rates of several forms of political participation, France and the United States

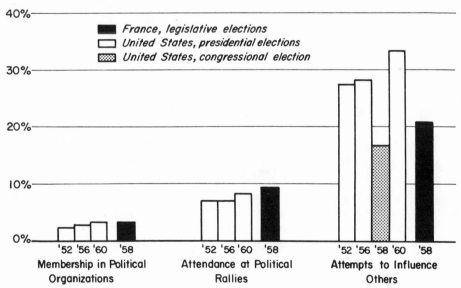

More solid are comparisons of reported acts of political participation selected as involving comparable motivation in the two systems: membership in political organizations, attendance at political rallies, and attempts to influence the political choice of others through informal communication.[4] As Figure 1 suggests, the cross-national similarities on these items are impressive. Furthermore, we can examine such additional points as the number of meetings attended by those French and Americans who do attend political gatherings. Graphs of the frequency of attendance by attender are almost indistinguishable between the two countries. The mean number of meetings attended among those who attend at all is in both cases a slight fraction over two. In sum, it is hard to imagine that any slight divergences in rates of attendance are crucial in any dramatic differences between the two systems.

Data were collected in both countries as well with regard to dependence on the mass media for political information. Here one of the most excellent bases for comparison which the data afford is provided by reports of the regularity with which political news about the elections was followed in daily newspapers. Although the structured alternatives again involve "amount words," there is a more tangible standard for responses implicit in the rhythm of newspaper production. "Regularly" or "never," when applied to readership of daily papers, has a common meaning in any language. Furthermore, we find empirically that responses to the newspaper questions show much higher stability for individuals over time than the direct interest questions. It is clear that we are dealing here with stable habits which are reliably reported.

Table 1
Frequency of Newspaper Reading for Political Information
(in per cent)

	France, 1958		United States, 1960	
	Post-referendum	Post-election	Post-election	
Regulièrement	19	18	44	Regularly
Souvent	12	10	12	Often
De temps en temps	25	29	16	From time to time
Très rarement	19	21	7	Just once in a great while
Jamais	25	22	21	Never
	100	100	100	

When we compare distributions from the two countries (Table 1), there seems little doubt of higher American devotion to newspapers as a source of political information. Furthermore, the French citizen appears also to monitor other media for political information less. Thus, for example, he is less likely to have a television or radio set than his American counterpart; but even among those French who possess sets, attention to political broadcasts is markedly less than for comparable Americans. As we have observed, these latter differences are not in themselves proof of lesser French motivation, since the choices offered through the airwaves are not comparable crossnationally. But such facts, along with further comparisons as to magazine reading, indicate that lower French attention to political material in the newspapers is not compensated for from other sources. Since elite political competition in France, even when reduced to simplest terms, is considerably more complex than two-party competition in the United States, it is ironic that the French voter exposes himself less faithfully to the flow of current political information.

Education being a strong determinant of all these information-seeking activities, it is of interest to control the substantial Franco-American differences in level of formal education. For Figure 2 we have applied a simple integer scoring to the five response categories of Table 1 and extracted means within education categories, the latter having been carefully tailored on the American side to match French intervals with regard to simple number of years of formal education. While the two curves do not match precisely, the main departures lie at the extremes, where case numbers are lowest, and hence where sampling error is bound to disperse results.[5] Where more than 200 cases are available from both sides, the estimates show a most remarkable convergence.

Figure 2

Frequency of newspaper reading for political information in France and the United States, by education.

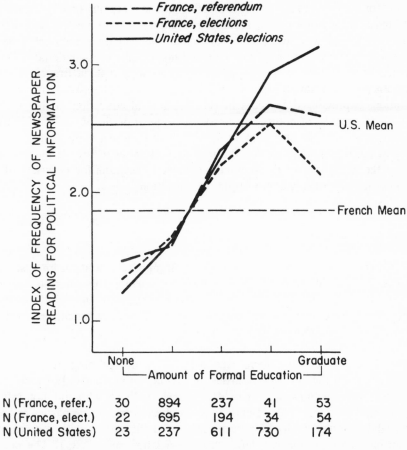

N (France, refer.)	30	894	237	41	53
N (France, elect.)	22	695	194	34	54
N (United States)	23	237	611	730	174

As we see, there are strong cross-national differences in total distribution of regularity of newspaper reading (as represented by the distance between the horizontal lines in Figure 2.) But these differences very nearly disappear (the general proximity of the two slopes, and their essential identity when case numbers are sufficient), with education controlled. The gap in total news reading for the two electorates comes about, then, simply because the American cases are loaded heavily to the right side of the graph, while the center of gravity of the French education distribution is to the left, or low, side. The capacity to move cross-national differences out to the marginals in this fashion not only strengthens presumption of common causal factors, but also is a reassuring anchor in the unknown waters of cross-national research, where the basic comparability of data must be held to special question. We shall see a more dramatic demonstration of this circuit of empirical reasoning below.

By way of summary, then, comparisons up to this point create a general sense of Franco-American similarity, with occasional mild divergences suggesting stronger American political involvement. The locus of these differences in the vertical sense is interesting. Let us bear in mind that most of these involvement actions in both societies stand in a scalar relationship to one another, in the Guttman sense. That is, the party member who passes the "hardest" of our items is very likely to have attended meetings, monitored the media, and so on. In this sense there is an underlying involvement dimension represented here. Furthermore, we have established cutting points on this dimension in quite different ranges of the continuum, at the high end for party membership and meeting attendance, but much deeper in the middle mass where information seeking and expressions of involvement are concerned. In a rough way, we may observe that the American data seem to show somewhat higher motivation in the middle ranges, with cross-national differences narrowing near the very top, and perhaps even showing a slight French advantage. Interestingly enough, this pattern would describe as well the cumulative frequency distributions expressing differences in years of formal education in the two countries. This identity is, of course, no proof that education accounts for the involvement divergences. But it does remind us that these patterns, if they differ cross-nationally at all, may partake of the sharper discontinuities in France between a tiny elite and the remainder of the population that one suspects for a variety of characteristics, and can readily demonstrate for education.[6]

PARTISAN ORIENTATIONS

The gross similarities between the two publics in apparent political interest do not, to be sure, remove the possibility that the Frenchman in his interested moments may respond to politics in much different terms than his American counterpart. Actually, when we consider the character of partisan ties felt by citizens in the two countries, we strike upon some contrasts of great magnitude.

If Americans are asked to locate themselves relative to the American party system, 75 percent classify themselves without further probing as psychological members of one of the two major parties, or of some minor party. In France, somewhat before the elections, less than 45 percent of those who did not refuse to answer the question were able to classify themselves in one of the parties or splinter groups, while another 10 to 15 percent associated themselves with a more or less recognizable broad *tendance* ("left," "right," a labor union, etc.). The cross-national differences of 20 to 30 percent are sufficiently large here to contribute to fundamental differences in the flavor of partisan processes in the two electorates. For a long time, we wrote off these differences as products of incomparable circumstances or of reticence on the part of the French concerning partisanship, most of which was being expressed not as refusal to answer the question, but as some other evasion. As we grew more familiar with the data, however, these differences took on vital new interest.

The hypothesis of concealed partisanship was very largely dispelled by a close reading of the actual interviews. It is undeniable that nearly 10 percent of the French sample explicitly refused to answer the question, as compared with a tiny fraction in the United States. However, we have already subtracted this group from the accounting. Beyond the explicit refusals, the remarks and explanations which often accompanied statements classified as "no party," or as "don't know which party," had a very genuine air about them which made them hard to read as hasty evasions. No few of these respondents were obviously embarrassed at their lack of a party; some confessed that they just hadn't been able to keep track of which party was which. The phrase "je n'y ai jamais pensé" was extremely common. Others indicated that they found it too hard to choose between so many parties; some indicated preferences for a specific political leader but admitted that they did not know which party he belonged to or, more often, had no interest in the identity of his party, whatever it might be. Others, forming a tiny minority of the nonparty people, rejected the notion of parties with some hostility.

It became clear, too, that people reporting no party attachments were distinct on other grounds from those who willingly classified themselves as close to a party. On our vertical involvement dimension, for example, they tended to fall in the bottom stratum of the least involved, just as the paper-thin stratum unable to choose a party in the United States consists heavily of the least involved. Demographically, these nonparty people were disproportionately housewives, poorly educated, young, and the other familiar statuses which tend to be uninformed and uninvolved.

Among actual party identifiers in France there was further interesting variation in the character of the party objects to which reference was made. A very few linked themselves with small new ideological splinter groups which had developed during the political crises of 1958. For these people, it was not enough to indicate that they felt closest to the Radical-Socialists, for example: they had to specify that they were Mendesists or anti-Mendesists, Valoisiens, and the like. Most identifiers suffered no difficulty in seeing themselves as "Radical-Socialists," completely shattered though the party was. Others, perceiving the system even more grossly, linked themselves only with a broad *tendance*. On involvement measures these groupings showed the expected differences: the grosser the discrimination, the lower the involvement.

In other ways as well it was clear that the extreme ideological fractionation of parties in France has few roots in the mass population, members of which simply pay too little attention to politics to follow the nicer discriminations involved. When asked whether the number of parties in France was too great, about right, or too few, 97 percent of those responding said there were too many parties, and less than 1 percent said there were too few. In response to an ensuing question as to the desirable number of parties, the mean of the number seen as optimal was 3.5 for the handful of adherents of the new ideological splinters, 3.0 for the partisans of the traditional mass parties, and less than 2.8 among those who had formed no party attachments. Perhaps the most apt expression of the problem of partisan fractionation and discrimination came from the naive respondent who opined that France should have two or three parties, "enough to express the differences in opinion."

The fact that large proportions of the French public have failed to form any very strong attachments to one of the political parties should not taken to mean that these people are totally disoriented in the French party system. In particular, a sensitivity to the gulf separating the Communist party from the remainder of French parties does pervade the mass public. There seems to be less confusion as to the identity of the Communist party than for any of the other parties; and for the bulk of non-Communists, the Communist party is a pariah. There are some nonidentifiers who appear to shift from Communist to non-Communist votes with abandon, and were all of these votes to fall to the Communists in the same election, the party would undoubtedly exceed its previous high-water mark in its proportion of the French popular vote. At the same time, however, one cannot help but be impressed by the number of respondents who, while indicating they were not really sure what they were in partisan terms, indicated as well at one point or another in the interview that they were not only non-Communist but anti-Communist. In other words, were the descriptions of party adherents to proceed simply in terms of a Communist, non-Communist division, the proportion of ready self-classifications would advance considerably toward the American figure, and would probably exceed that which could be attained by any other two-class division in France.

Nevertheless, the limited party attachments outside the Communist camp in France retain strong theoretical interest, as they seem so obviously linked to a symptom of turbulence which is clearly not an elite phenomenon alone—the flash party. With a very large proportion of the electorate feeling no anchoring loyalty, it is not surprising that a new party can attract a large vote "overnight," or that this base can be so rapidly dissolved. Furthermore, there is a problem here that is peculiarly French, in that the low proportion of expressed attachments cannot simply be seen as a necessary consequence of a multiparty system per se. Fairly comparable data from Norway, where six parties are prominent, show party attachments as widespread as those in the two-party United States.[7]

The French sample was asked further to recall the party or *tendance* which the respondent's father had supported at the polls. Here the departure from comparable American data became even more extreme (Table 2). Of those Americans

Table 2
Respondent's Characterization of Father's Political
Behavior, by Country, 1958
(in per cent)

	France	United States
Located father in party or broad *tendance*	25	76
Recalled father as "independent," "shifting around," or as apolitical, nonvoting	3	6
Total able to characterize father's political behavior	28	82
Unable to characterize father's political behavior	68	8
Father did not reside in country or was never a citizen		3
Did not know father; question not asked about father surrogate	4	6
Refused; other		1
	100	100
(N)	(1,166)	(1,795)

in 1958 having had a known father who had resided in the United States as an American citizen, thereby participating in American political life, 86 percent could characterize his partisanship, and another 5 percent knew enough of his political behavior to describe him as apolitical or independent. Among comparable French respondents, only 26 percent could link fathers with any party or with the vaguest of *tendances* (including such responses as "il a toujours voté pour la patrie"), and another 3 percent could describe the father's disposition as variable or apolitical. In other words, among those eligible to respond to the question, 91 percent of Americans could characterize their father's political behavior, as opposed to 29 percent of the French.

It goes without saying that differences of this magnitude rarely emerge from individual data in social research. And they occur at a point of prime theoretical interest. We have long been impressed in the United States by the degree to which partisan orientations appear to be passed hereditarily, from generation to generation, through families. It has seemed likely that such transmission is crucial in the stability of American partisan voting patterns. Therefore, we find it startling to encounter a situation in which huge discontinuities seem to appear in this transmission.

What do the French responses concerning paternal partisanship really mean? As best we can determine, they mean what they appear to mean: the French father is uncommunicative about his political behavior before his children, just as he is more reserved in the interviewing situation than Americans or Norwegians. It seems highly unlikely, for example, that Franco-American differences in recall represent French concealment: large numbers of the French willing to speak of their own party preference are unable to give the father's preference of a generation before, and explicit refusals to answer, while attaining 10 percent or more where own partisanship is at stake, are almost nonexistent for paternal partisanship.

Furthermore, we have come to reject the possibility that the bulk of the Franco-American difference is some simple consequence of the more fluid and complex French party system. Responses to a similar question in the Norwegian multiparty system look like our American results, and not like the French. Not is there reason to believe that the Frenchman has trouble finding comparable modern terms for the party groupings of a generation ago. As we have observed, the respondent was invited to give a rough equivalent of his father's position in terms of *tendance*. Moreover, where there are any elaborations of "I don't know" captured in the interview, the consistent theme seemed to be that the respondent did not feel he had ever known his father's position ("je n'ai jamais su"; "je ne lui ai jamais demandé"; "il ne disait rien à ses enfants"; "il n'en parlait jamais"). Finally, if special problems were occasioned on the French side by the changing party landscape over time, we should certainly expect that older French respondents would have greater difficulty locating their fathers politically than would younger respondents. They do not: the tabulation by age in France shows only the slightest of variations attributable to age, and these lend no support to the hypothesis (e.g., slightly less knowledge of father's position for children under thirty) and are variations which may be found in the comparable American table as well.

If we accept the proposition, then, that there are basic discontinuities in the familial transmission of party orientations in France, all of our theory would argue that weaker party attachments should result in the current generation. The data do indeed show a remarkable association between the two phenomena, once again involving differences of 30 percent or more. Both French and Americans who recall their father's partisanship are much more likely themselves to have developed party loyalties than are people who were not aware of their father's position. Of still greater importance are the more absolute Franco-American similarities. Setting aside those people whose fathers were noncitizens, dead, apolitical, or floaters, or who refused to answer the question, we can focus on the core of the comparison (in percent):

	Know Father's Party		Do Not Know Father's Party	
	France	U.S.	France	U.S.
Proportion having some partisan self-location (party or vague *tendance*)	79.4	81.6	47.7	50.7
Proportion that these are of total electorate	24	75	63	8

Where the socialization processes have been the same in the two societies, the results in current behavior appear to be the same, in rates of formation of identification. The strong cross-national differences lie in the socialization processes. In other words, we have come full circle again: we have encountered large national differences but have once again succeeded in moving them to the marginals of the table. This is our best assurance that our measurements are tapping comparable phenomena.

Partisan attachments appear therefore to be very weakly developed within the less politically involved half of the French electorate. While undoubtedly a large variety of factors, including the notoriety which the French parties had acquired in the later stages of the Fourth Republic, have helped to inhibit their development, more basic discontinuities of political socialization in the French family appear to be making some persisting contribution as well.[8] Of course, similar lack of party attachment does occur among people indifferent to politics in the American and Norwegian systems as well; but the strata of unidentified people are thinner in these systems and do not extend greatly above that layer of persistent nonvoters which is present in any system.

The link between an electorate heavily populated with voters feeling no continuing party attachments and a susceptibility to "flash" parties is an obvious one. It must be recognized at the outset, of course, that such phenomena arise only under the pressure of social, political, or economic dislocations occurring in some segment of the population, thereby generating an elite which wishes to organize a movement and a public which is restive. This means that even a system highly susceptible to such phenomena is not likely to experience them when it is functioning smoothly: their prevalence in postwar France cannot be divorced from the severe dislocations the society has been undergoing. Once misfortunes breed discontent, however, the proportions of partisans in an electorate is a datum of fundamental significance. One cannot fail to be impressed by the agility with which the strong partisan can blame the opposing party for almost any misfortune or deny the political relevance of the misfortune if some opposing party cannot conceivably be blamed. Hence, where partisans are concerned, misfortunes do relatively little to shift voting patterns. Independents, however, have no stake in such reinforcements and defenses and move more massively in response to grievances. In France, the institutions which conduce to a multiparty system make the organization of new party movements more feasible from an elite point of view than it is likely to be under two-party traditions. At the same time, the presence of a large number of French voters who have developed no continuing attachments to a particular party provides an "available" mass base for such movements. This available base is no necessary concomitant of a multiparty system, but is rather a peculiarity of the current French scene.

PARTIES AND POLICY CONTROVERSY

Whatever differences exist in partisan orientations, no assessment of politicization would be complete without consideration of the manner in which ideological conflict is worked out through the party system. If parties are recognized at all in the classical view of democratic process, they are relegated to a distinctly secondary position: they are means to policy ends, and should be judged by the citizen accordingly. In this light, the number of Americans with strong party loyalty and a poor sense of what either party stands for in policy terms represents a distinct perversion of the democratic process. In this light, too, weaker partisan orientations in the French populace might simply mean a relegation of party to second rank, with a primary focus on policy goals.

At an elite level, of course, there are distinct Franco-American differences in the phrasing of the means-end relation between party and policy, and these contrasts weigh heavily in our impressions of differences in quality of political process between the two systems. That is, while French political elites are not insensitive to party formations as instruments toward policy goals, the fact remains that parties are split and reshaped with relative freedom in order that the party may be the purest possible expression, not only of the politician's position on a single basic issue dimension, but of the total configuration of positions adopted on cross-cutting issue dimensions. On the American side, remarkable policy accommodations are made to preserve the semblance of party unity, and party competition for votes "in the middle" leads to a considerable blurring of interparty differences on policy. The crucial role of basic political institutions in stimulating either multipartite or bipartite trends has often been discussed, and whether French elite activities would survive long under American ground rules is a moot point. We may consider, however, whether the ideological clarity or intransigence associated with French political elites and the policy compromise or confusion which characterizes the American party system reflect properties of their mass publics.

Data have been collected in both countries concerning reactions to a variety of issues confronting the two systems. While both sets of items must be regarded as only the crudest samplings of hypothetical issue universes, selection on both sides was performed in an attempt to tap some of the most basic controversies of the period. In France, three items were devoted to the classic socioeconomic left and right, with one concerning the role of labor and the other two the relative roles of government and private enterprise in housing; two more involved the clerical question; a sixth item had to do with military expenditures and national prestige; a seventh concerned the freedom of the press to criticize the government. Of eight American questions, two dealt with social welfare legislation and a third with the relative role of government and private enterprise in housing and utilities, covering the classic right and left; two more dealt with the government's role in racial matters (FEPC and school desegregation); and three others were concerned with the internationalist or isolationist posture of the government in foreign affairs. All questions were in Likert scale form.

We shall focus upon three properties of these issues which we can more or less crudely measure in the two countries: (1) the degree to which public opinion is sharply crystallized on each issue; (2) the degree to which opinion within the two publics is polarized on each; and (3) for each issue, the degree to which individual opinion is associated with partisan preference.[9] Assuming the items do give fair coverage to most primary issue dimensions in the two nations, we are interested to see if opinion in France at a mass level appears more sharply crystallized or polarized, and to assess the manner in which policy concerns are linked with party preference. As before, we shall distinguish layers of both populations in terms of partisan involvement. At the top, we isolate as political "actives" those people who were either party members or reported attending two or more political rallies in the respective election campaigns, a group which amounts to 5 to 7 percent within each population and hence is sufficiently large for analysis. We also continue to distinguish between party identifiers (three-quarters of the American population, but half of the French) and nonidentifiers.

In both nations, the issue items were asked again of the same respondents after an interval of time. We take as a measure of crystallization of opinion the rank-order correlation between the two expressions of opinion. There is a good deal of internal evidence to suggest that "change" in opinion between the two readings is almost never a matter of true conversion, but rather represents haphazard reactions to items on which the respondent has never formed much opinion. With minor exceptions, there is no significant change in the marginal distributions of the tables, despite the high turnover of opinion. There is a persistent relation between the proportions of people who confess they have no opinion on any given issue and the amount of turnover shown by those who do attempt an opinion. As one might expect, too, there is a tendency for high crystallization, high polarization, and high party-relatedness to co-occur, despite intriguing exceptions. Clearly both publics are more likely to have arrived at stable prior opinions on some items than on others, and this degree of crystallization has an obvious bearing on the vitality of the role the issue dimension may play in partisan choice.

Unfortunately, the magnitude of these turnover coefficients may not be compared cross-nationally, since the interval between tests averaged little more than a month on the French side but ran twenty-six months on the American side.[10] Nevertheless, as Table 3 indicates, the level of these coefficients is by any standard remarkably low in both populations. Taken as test-retest reliability coefficients, they would send the psychologist in search of a better measuring instrument. After all, on an item where the stability seems relatively high (freedom of the press), less than eight Frenchmen in ten take the same side of the issue twice in a five-week period, when five out of ten would succeed in doing so by making entirely random choices. On the other hand, while more routine measurement error certainly imposes a rather constant ceiling on these coefficients which may not greatly exceed .8, the further incapacity of the two publics to respond reliably to these items must be considered a substantive datum of the first water. For if these items, reduced to an unusually simple vocabulary, fail to touch off well-formed opinions, the remoteness of both publics from most political and journalistic debate on such dimensions is obvious. It is not as though the items presented new controversies on which opinion had not yet had time to develop. With few exceptions, they have been the basic stuff of political disagreement for decades or generations. Opinions still unformed are unlikely to develop further.

In this light, then, it is interesting to compare the stability over time of reactions to parties with the stability of responses to these "basic" controversies shown in the first column of Table 3. This assessment is rather difficult on the French side in view of the frequent indeterminacy of party locations; however, it seems that, in a comparable period of time, affective reactions to the parties are more stable than issue reactions even in France. In the United States, we know that partisan reactions show dramatically greater stability than the issue responses. Most important, perhaps, is the failure of data in Table 3 to support an image of the mass French public as remaining aloof from party sentiments while hewing dogmatically to ideological goals. Beyond the political actives, stability of issue opinion seems unimpressive, and, for the majority of French voters without party attachments, the articulation of party choice with any of the issue dimensions covered here is slight indeed (Table 3, final column).

Table 3
Selected Issue Characteristics in France and the United States

	Crystallization		Polarization		Party-relatedness		
	Total Sample	Ac-tives	Total Sample	Ac-tives	Actives	Identi-fiers	Uniden-tified
France:							
State support of religious schools	.65	.74	1.54	1.62	.58	.39	.32
Strikes by government employees	.52	.69	1.60	1.70	.59	.31	.22
Current threat posed by clergy	.47	.80	1.32	1.64	.56	.34	.19
Freedom of press	.47	.68	1.50	1.60	.39	.22	.13
State responsibility for housing	.42	.34	1.39	1.45	.38	.13	.08
Level of military expenditures	.34	.46	1.36	1.56	.33	.18	.17
Private responsibility for housing	.28	.35	1.26	1.60	.37	.22	.04

					Total Sample Actives	Non-South		
						Ac-tives	Identi-fiers	Uniden-tified
United States:								
Federal school integration action	.42	.47	1.69	1.72	.00	.12	.07	− .06
Federal guarantees of employment	.35	.49	1.45	1.55	.16	.30	.19	.03
Federal FEPC	.34	.34	1.41	1.55	.00	.14	.06	.01
Federal aid to education	.34	.54	1.09	1.60	.16	.29	.21	.16
General isolationism-internationalism	.33	.25	1.48	1.48	.16	.06	.03	.04
Deployment of U.S. forces abroad	.28	.10	1.23	1.25	.07	.04	.05	− .02
Government vs. private enterprise in power and housing	.25	.41	1.37	1.45	.21	.27	.18	.21
Foreign aid	.24	.31	1.36	1.33	.11	.10	.02	− .05

While the instability of opinion in both nations is of primary interest in Table 3, several further comparisons may be summarized. The major cross-national contrast comes in the party-relatedness column, where French actives and partisans show much higher coefficients than their American counterparts. The most obvious American phenomenon which blunts interparty policy differences is the disparity between the southern and non-southern wings of the Democratic Party. While setting aside the southern Democratic rank and file does not remove the perceptual problem posed for northern Democrats who may find the top leaders of their party at odds on many issues, we complete this exercise in Table 3 to show that, even for actives, this regional limitation does not begin to bring the American coefficients up to the French level. While the higher French coefficients are no statistical necessity, it is likely that, in practice, closer party-relatedness is inevitable in the multiparty system. The interparty differences in opinion among French *partisans* appear to lie in about the same range as those found in Norway.[11] However, as we have seen, party attachments are more prevalent in Norway than in France; when the unidentified enter the French electorate in an actual vote, it is likely that individual issue opinions receive less clear expression across the electorate as a whole than is the case in Norway.

Beyond this primary contrast, Table 3 is impressive for its cross-national similarities. Actives in both countries show more highly crystallized opinions, and usually more polarized opinions as well, although American actives differ less sharply and consistently from their mass public than do French actives. In neither country do identifiers differ reliably from nonidentifiers with regard to crystallization or polarization of opinion. In both countries, however, there are quite reliable differences in party-relatedness, not only between actives and the remaining 95 percent of the population, but between identifiers and nonidentified. In other words, while the partisan manner of relating to the political process makes little difference in basic opinion formation save for the extremely active, the translation of these attitudes to some kind of party choice seems increasingly haphazard as party attachments become weaker.

Throughout these comparisons, however, we may remain struck by the fact that the "slope" is steeper on the French side: the differences between actives and mass are large relative to those in the United States. From the upper end of this steep slope, one might wish to extrapolate to the sharp and rigid cleavages on policy matters for which French elites are noted; for our purposes, it is sufficient to observe that these cleavages blur rapidly and lose their tone in the mass of the French electorate.

Finally, it should be observed that the issues seem to sort themselves into two rough categories in both nations: (1) emotional-symbol issues involving some of the more gross group conflicts within the two societies (racial in the United States, religious in France, along with items which touch in a direct way upon labor as an interest group), which show relatively high crystallization and polarization; and (2) more complex questions of relations between the state and private enterprise which, along with all foreign policy issues, tend to be less crystallized.

These differences in crystallization are scarcely surprising, as the objects and means involved in the second group of issues are clearly more remote from the common experience of the man-in-the-street. Yet the pattern is ironic, for the issues which show a stronger resonance in both mass publics tend to be those which both elites make some attempt to soft-pedal, in favor of direct debate over such more "ideological" matters as arrangements between state and private enterprise. The more resonant issues are not dead, of course, and are used for tactical advantage by elites in both countries. Calculations of vote gain are made in the United States on the basis of the religion of the nominee, and the clerical question in France has been resuscitated repeatedly as a handy crowbar to split apart government coalitions. At the same time, however, there is genuine elite effort to keep such cleavage issues in the background: the American public is told that religion is not a proper criterion for candidate choice, and the battleground for elite debate on the racial issue is usually displaced quite notably from race itself in the modern period. Similarly, much sophisticated French opinion has for some time argued that even the secondary role which the clerical question has been playing in elite debate exaggerates its importance.

Given this common background, the different manner in which the two types of controversy weave into partisan choices in the two countries is fascinating. In France, there is fair coincidence between the ordering of issues in terms of party-relatedness and the ordering on the other two properties. The clerical questions, for example, are highly crystallized and polarized, and show high levels of party-relatedness as well. The structure of party competition is such that, elite values notwithstanding, these emotional cleavages achieve prominent partisan expression. Such is not the case in the United States: there is little coincidence between the party-relatedness of issues and the other two properties. Indeed, the racial issue finds little clear party expression, while the "elite" issue concerning government and private enterprise, one of the least crystallized issues, is at the same time one of the most party-related across the full electorate.

Where mass or elite control of issue controversy is concerned, then, the two systems have rather paradoxical outcomes. By conception, the French party system is geared to elites, encouraging them to a multifaceted ideological expression which is too complex for most of the public to encompass. At the same time, the multi-dimensional clarity of party positions serves to return a measure of control to part of the public, for the more involved citizens can single out certain dimensions to reduce the system to manageable simplicity. These reductions are naturally made in terms of issues which are more resonant in the public, even if these are not the dimensions which the elites might wish to stress. The American system is less elite in conception; it is sufficiently simple in its gross characteristic that it is easier for the common citizen to follow it with only limited attention. But this simplification requires great blurring of party differences across most of the universe of possible issues, and the differences which are maintained are those which the competing elites select as battlegrounds. Hence, control of controversy which can be given partisan expression is, paradoxically, more nearly in elite hands.

CONCLUSIONS

We have attempted to sort through a number of those characteristics of French politics which add up to vague impressions of intense French politicization, in order to identify more precise loci for Franco-American differences. It appears likely that the more notable of these differences stem from the actions of elites and require study and explanation primarily at this level, rather than at the level of the mass electorate. While certain peculiarities reminiscent of French political elites are visible in the most politically active twentieth of the French population, these peculiarities fade out rapidly as one approaches the more "representative" portions of the broad French public.

It is unlikely that the common French citizen devotes any greater portion of his attention to politics than does his American counterpart, and he may well give less. His behavior is constrained within a much different set of political institutions, and these differences have important consequences for the character of his political behavior, including the opportunity of closer articulation between any crystallized opinions he may hold and an appropriate party instrument. However, the data give no striking reason to believe that the French citizen, either through the vagaries of national character, institutions, or history, is predisposed to form political opinions which are more sharply crystallized or which embrace a more comprehensive range of political issues than do comparable Americans. On both sides, opinion formation declines as objects and arrangements become more remote from the observer; and much of politics, for both French and Americans, is remote. Hence the proliferation of choices offered by the multi-party system is itself a mixed blessing: it is capitalized upon only by the more politically interested segments of the electorate, and appears to represent "too much" choice to be managed comfortably by citizens whose political involvement is average or less.

Over the range of characteristics surveyed, only one striking difference at the level of the mass public was encountered which seemed more uniquely French than the multiparty system itself. There is evidence of a widespread absence of party loyalties, a phenomenon which can be empirically associated with peculiarities in the French socialization process. This characteristic has obvious links with the major symptom of French political turbulence, which is based on the behavior of the mass population rather than that of elites—the current availability of a mass base for flash party movements under circumstances of distress.

NOTES

[1] They are not, of course, outstanding against the backdrop provided by other Western European nations.

[2] For a fuller discussion, see Angus Campbell, Philip E. Converse, Warren E. Miller, and Donald E. Stokes, *The American Voter*, New York, Wiley, 1960, Chap. 15.

[3] The French data were gathered in three waves of a national cross-section sample in the fall of 1958, during the constitutional referendum launching the Fifth Republic and the ensuing legislative elections. The study was jointly supported by the Consel Supérieur de la Recherche Scientifique, the Rockefeller Foundation, and the Fondation Nationale des Sciences Politiques. The American studies over six elections have been conducted by the Survey Research Center of the University of Michigan, under grants from the Rockefeller Foundation and the Carnegie Corporation. Informal cross-national collaboration prior to the 1958 French study led to a French interview schedule permitting more rigorous comparative analysis than unrelated studies usually offer.

[4] Of these three pairings, the first is technically the weakest. The American item asks about membership in "any political club or organization," while the French item focuses directly on political party membership, although the term "party" may be rather broadly construed in France. Furthermore, there were a substantial number of refusals to answer this membership item in France. These refusals have simply been removed from the calculations, since such treatment leaves the gross rate on the upper side of the range that informed estimates have suggested for total party membership in France, after realistic appraisal of the memberships claimed by the parties.

[5] The decline in reading among the most educated French citizens approaches statistical significance and is currently unaccounted for. We have been able to show that these people are not substituting political reviews and weekly magazines for daily news reading. The educated elite which follows the reviews also reads the newspapers faithfully; the remainder which fails to attend to the newspapers ignores political magazines as well.

[6] We shall not treat Franco-American differences in vote turnout, save to observe that they are probably more institutional than motivational. American registration requirements in many states are such that an American is persistently confronted by an institutional barrier which is rarely erected in France. It can be argued most strongly that the act of getting somewhere to register demands higher political motivation than getting to the polls on Election Day. Indeed, over half the Americans who fail to vote in major elections blame such registration barriers as change in residence, failure to renew on time, etc. If such reports are credited, the registration toll in the United States would easily make up the apparent Franco-American differences.

[7] Angus Campbell and Henry Valen, "Party Identification in Norway and the United States," *Public Opinion Quarterly*, Vol. 25, 1961, 505–525.

[8] Among other factors, an alleged paucity of voluntary associations acting vigorously to mediate between the mass of citizens and centralized authority in France has often been cited as a crucial differentium in the quality of the political process between France and the United States. See William Kornhauser, *The Politics of Mass Society*, Glencoe, Ill., Free Press, 1959. If such differences do exist, they may well have some bearing on the prevalence of partisan attachments, for it is clear intranationally, at least, that high rates of participation in nonpolitical voluntary associations and strong partisan attachments tend to co-occur at the

individual level (although it is much less clear whether this represents a causal progression or two aspects of the same stance toward community life). In other contexts, however, it has been argued that ostensibly nonpolitical associations of mass membership in France tend to play more vigorous roles as parapolitical agents than do comparable associations in the United States, which so often tend to regard political entanglement with horror. Both views have some appeal on the basis of loose impressions of the two societies, and are not in the strictest sense contradictory. However, their thrusts diverge sufficiently that a confrontation would seem worthwhile if either can be borne out by any systematic evidence. Where grassroots participation in expressly political associations is concerned, we have seen no notable differences between the nations in either membership rates or rates of attendance at political gatherings.

[9] Of these three properties, polarization is most dependent on question wording. It is measured by the standard deviation of the response distribution, after the five steps of the scale have been assigned simple integer scores. The statistic takes high values (e.g. over 1.50) only when the distribution of opinion is relatively U-shaped. Party-relatedness is measured by a rank-order correlation between the respondent's partisan position and his issue position. In the United States, the Democratic Party was presumed to be the more liberal on domestic issues and the more internationalist in foreign affairs, and respondents were arrayed from a Democratic to a Republican pole on the basis of party loyalty for identifiers, or patterns of 1956–1958 vote for nonidentifiers. In France, a panel of expert observers arranged the many parties or actions thereof on a socioeconomic left-right continuum and again on a continuum from clerical to anticlerical. The second was used to array respondents for the two religious issues; the first was used for the other five issues. Once again, nonidentifiers were located on the basis of reports of 1956 and 1958 votes. All rank-order correlations, including those used for the crystallization measure discussed in the text, are tau-betas, based on tables of equal rows and columns. See Hubert M. Blalock, *Social Statistics*, New York, McGraw-Hill, 1960, pp. 321ff.

[10] In American panel studies we are beginning to fill in a picture of the manner in which these coefficients erode over time. For example, coefficients after four years show almost no decline from their two-year levels, and it seems likely that, in the infrequent instances where opinions on these issues are truly crystallized, they are subject to little change. As the test-retest interval changes, we may suppose that the coefficient declines very rapidly in the brief period in which respondents forget their previous answers and hence are obliged to "guess again," and then stabilizes at a hard core of well-formed opinions. The French interval was so brief, however, that it is hard to imagine that the coefficients had yet dropped to their stabilized level. We would hazard the loose judgment that the French coefficients lie about where one would expect were they destined to decline to American levels in a comparable period of time.

[11] Campbell and Valen, *op. cit.*

25

Psychological Sources of International Conflict: An Ideal Typical Formulation

In this essay, Talcott Parsons analyzes the origins and patterns of aggression in western societies. Parsons argues that aggression is "the most important single factor in the dangerously disruptive potentialities of power relationships."

He views aggression less as a product of strength than of feelings of inadequacy and insecurity. He analyzes the contributions kinship and occupational systems make to the channeling of aggression into group hostilities. These group hostilities, Parsons argues, are inhibited by "the strong pressure to internal unity" in the nation state; thus, hostilities are further focused on "the potential conflict between nation-state units." One might, however, raise questions about whether the survey research literature on levels of political interest in western nations indicates that the "channeling" and "focusing" that Parsons postulates move aggression in the directions he suggests.

Parsons' analysis of who is responsible for group antagonisms is especially interesting. He points to the way in which rapid change disrupts symbolic continuities; at any point in this process, some groups are relatively "emancipated" while other groups are relatively "traditional." Some of the emancipated groups, notably "the best of the professions," become "relatively well institutionalized so that the dynamic process of which they are the agents is not so disturbing to them." But in the "fringe" elements of these emancipated groups "insecurity is expressed in compulsively distorted patterns of extreme emancipation which are highly provocative to the more traditionalized elements." This provocation leads to a "fundamentalist reaction," and thus to polarization.

Parsons' essay is a complex and ingenious attempt to link personal psychological processes with aggregate outcomes. Its conceptual clarity and balance compensate for what it lacks in empirical substantiation on the psychological versus systemic causation issues. But Parsons' sense of balance should not blind us to the biases of the analysis. "Compulsively distorted patterns of extreme emancipation" is not a convincing example of value-free application of social psychological diagnostic categories. It has often been said that a conservative mental set is entailed in the sorts of structural-functional analyses with which Parsons is identified, since innovation, whatever its merits or demerits, tends to be suspect a priori as "dysfunctional." The reader may judge for himself whether such strictures apply to this essay.

CERTAIN PRIMARY SOURCES AND PATTERNS OF AGGRESSION IN THE SOCIAL STRUCTURE OF THE WESTERN WORLD

Talcott Parsons

THE PROBLEM OF AGGRESSION

The problem of power and its control is not identical with that of aggression.[1] Without any conscious intent on the part of one individual or collectivity to gain at the expense of another, or even any unconscious disposition to do so, there would still be important sources of instability in the relations of individuals and social groups into which the use of power could and would play. There can, however, be little doubt that the widespread incidence of aggressive tendencies is the most important single factor in the dangerously disruptive potentialities of power relationships; and if these could be notably lessened, the prospects of effective control would be correspondingly enhanced.

Modern sociological and psychological analysis has greatly improved understanding of the factors and situations which produce aggressive dispositions. This understanding in turn carries with it the potentiality of devising and applying measures of deliberate control, although it is naive to suppose that control will follow automatically on knowledge of causes. Indeed the problem of utilizing what knowledge we have for control is so complex that no attempt will be made to deal with it in this brief paper, which will be confined to sketching a few of the diagnostic considerations on which any program of control would have to be based. This is not to depreciate the importance of an action program, but is merely an application of the principle of the division of labor. It is better to do one thing reasonably well than to attempt too many things and do none of them well.

All social behavior, including the "policies" of the most complex collectivities like nation-states, is ultimately the behavior of human beings, understandable in terms of the motivation of individuals, perhaps millions of them, *in the situations* in which they are placed. Therefore the psychological level of understanding of individual motivation is fundamental to even the most complex of mass phenomena. At the same time, however, the complications and modifications introduced by the facts of the organization of individuals in social systems are equally crucial. If it were possible to arrive at a statistically reliable estimate of the average strength of aggressive tendencies in the population of a nation, it would *by itself* be worthless as a basis of predicting the probability of that nation embarking on an aggressive war. The specific goals and objects to which these aggressive dispositions are attached, the ways in which they are depressed, deflected, projected, or can be directly expressed according to the forces which channel or oppose them, and the structure of situations into which they come—all these are equally important with any aggressive potential in general in determining concrete behavioral outcomes. Indeed they may be far more important to understand, since many of these factors in aggressive

Psychiatry, 10 (1947), 167–81. Reprinted by special permission of The William Alanson White Psychiatric Foundation, Inc.

behavior may be far more accessible to control than are the ultimate reservoirs of aggressive motivation themselves. The present analysis therefore will be largely concerned with the social structuring of aggression in Western society, rather taking for granted that there is an adequate reservoir to motivate the familiar types of aggressive behavior.

A few elementary facts about the psychology of aggression need, however, to be stated since they will underlie the analysis on the social level. There does not seem to be any very clear understanding of how far or in what sense aggressive dispositions in the sense here meant are inherited. It is, however, highly probable that there are very wide variations in hereditary constitution in this as in other respects and that the variations within any one ethnic population are far more significant than those between "races" or national groups. But whether on the individual or the group level, it is at least very doubtful how far anything like a human "beast of prey" by heredity exists. Ideas to that effect almost certainly contain far more projection and fantasy than solid empirical observation and analysis. Indeed there is much to be said for the hypothesis that aggression grows more out of weakness and handicap than out of biological strength.

Far more definite and clear is the relation between aggression on the one hand and insecurity and anxiety on the other. Whatever the hereditary potential, and whatever it may mean, there is an immense accumulation of evidence that in childhood aggressive patterns develop when security in some form, mostly in human relationships, is threatened, and when realistic fears shade over into anxiety of the neurotic type. This is a very complex field and only a few points can be brought out here.

Insecurity, as the term is used in psychology, certainly has a number of dimensions. One of the most important generalizations concerns the extent to which the specific patterning of reactions to insecurity is a function of the human relationships in which the child is placed rather than of its physical safety and welfare alone. One of the major human dimensions is unquestionably that of love or affection, which in most social systems centers on the relationship of mother and child. The absolute level of maternal affection is undoubtedly of fundamental significance, but equally so is its consistency. The withdrawal of love to which the child has become accustomed, or ambivalence, however deeply repressed, may have devastating effects. Similarly, relative distribution of affection between siblings is important. Frustration through withdrawal, if not absolutely low-level or absent, undoubtedly is normally reacted to with aggression. A common example is provided by the fantasies of children that they will die or commit suicide so the parents will be sorry for their maltreatment.

Another major dimension of security touches expectations of achievement and of conformity with behavioral standards. Here two contexts seem to be particularly important as sources of anxiety and aggression. The first is the sense of inadequacy, of being expected to do things which one is unable to achieve, and thus incurring punishment or the loss of rewards. The second is the sense of unfairness, of being unjustly punished or denied deserved rewards. In both cases the comparative context is fundamentally important. Inadequacy is highlighted by the superior achievements of others with whom one feels himself to be in competition, and unfairness almost always involves specific examples of what is felt to be unjust favoritism toward others. Again in both cases the consistency of the standards which are held up to the child and of adults in applying them is crucial. In this general context the sense of inadequacy or injustice may generate aggressive impulses, on the one hand toward those who are held to have imposed such unfair standards or applied them unfairly, and on the other hand toward more successful rivals or beneficiaries of unfair favoritism.

Two further facts about these structured patterns of aggression in childhood are particularly important. First, they are rooted in normal reactions to strain and frustration in human relations at the stages of development when the individual is particularly vulnerable, since he has not, as some psychologists say, yet attained a strong ego-development. But unless they are corrected by an adequate strengthening of security, these reactions readily embark on a cumulative vicious circle of "neurotic" fixation. The child who has reacted with anxiety and aggression to inadequate or ambivalent maternal love builds up defenses against re-exposure to such frustrating situations and becomes incapable of responding to genuine love. The child who has felt inadequate in the face of expectations beyond his capacity to fulfill becomes neurotically resistant to stimuli toward even the achievements he is capable of and aggressive toward all attempts to make him conform. Unless re-equilibration takes places in time, these defensive patterns persist and form rigid barriers to integration in a normal system of human relationships. The result is that the individual tends either to react aggressively, without being able to control himself, in situations which do not call for it at all, or to overreact far more violently than the situation calls for.

The second important fact is a result of the conflict of the aggressive impulses, thus generated and fixated, with the moral norms current in the family and society and the sentiments integrated with them. In childhood the persons in relation to whom such affects are developed are primarily the members of the child's own immediate family. But solidarity with them and affection toward them is a primary ethical imperative in the society. Indeed it is more than an ethical imperative, since these attitudes become "introjected" as part of the fundamental attitude system of the child himself. The hostile impulses therefore conflict both with his own standards and sentiments and with the realistic situation, and cannot be overtly expressed, except under strong emotional compulsion, or even tolerated as conscious thoughts. They tend therefore, to be dissociated from the positive, socially approved attitude system and "repressed." This repressed attitude system, however, persists and seeks indirect expression, especially in symbolic form. This may be purely in fantasy, but there is one particularly important phenomenon for the present context, namely displacement on a "scapegoat." If the father or mother or sibling cannot be overtly hated, a symbolically appropriate object outside the circle of persons who must be loved is chosen and gratification of the impulse indirectly secured. Precisely because his aggressive impulses are repressed, the person is unaware of the fact of displacement and by rationalization is convinced that this is a reasonable reaction to what the scapegoat has done or is likely to do if given a chance. There can be no doubt but what an enormously important component of group hostility has this psychological origin and character.

THE KINSHIP SYSTEM

"Western society" is a very complex entity with many different variations on national, regional, cultural, class, and other bases. There are, nevertheless, a small number of structurally distinctive features of it which, though unevenly distributed in different parts, are of such strategic significance for the whole that they can be singled out as presenting in the most accentuated form the problems which are crucial to the whole. These are, above all, those features associated with the development of the modern type of urban and industrial society, which is far more highly developed in the modern Western world than anywhere else or at any other period.[2]

In attempting to analyze the genesis and channeling of aggression in modern Western society, four aspects or structural-functional contexts appear to stand out as of paramount importance, and will be discussed in order. They are: First, the kinship system in its context in the larger society, since this is the environment in which the principal patterns in the individual personality become crystallized. Second, the occupational system, since this is the arena of the most important competitive process in which the individual must achieve his status. Third, the fundamental process of dynamic change by which traditional values and sentiments are exposed to a far more drastic and continuing disintegrating influence than in most societies. And fourth, the set of institutional structures through which aggression becomes organized in relation to a small number of structurally significant tensions, rather than diffused and dissipated in an indefinite variety of different channels without threatening the stability of the social system as a whole.[3]

The dominant feature of the kinship system of modern Western urban and industrial society is the relatively isolated conjugal family which is primarily dependent for its status and income on the occupational status of one member, the husband and father. This role, however, is segregated from the family structure itself, unlike the role of the peasant father. Work is normally done in separate premises, other members of the family do not cooperate in the work process and, above all, status is based on individual qualities and achievements which specifically cannot be shared by other members of the family unit.

It follows that sons on maturity must be emancipated from their families of orientation and "make their own way in the world" rather than fitting into a going concern organized around kinship. Determination of occupational status by family connections threatens the universalistic standards so important to the system as a whole. Daughters become overwhelmingly dependent on their marriage to the right individual man—not kinship group—for their status and security. In practice their parents cannot greatly help them—marriage becomes primarily a matter of individual responsibility and choice.

This kinship system in its larger setting involves a variety of influences on the child which favor high levels of insecurity structured in relatively definite and uniform ways and correspondingly a good deal of aggression. In the first place, the affective orientations of the child are concentrated on a very small number of persons, particularly since the family size is likely to be small. Of adult objects, particularly in the early years, the mother overwhelmingly predominates, because the care of household and children traditionally falls to her, and because the father is normally away from the household, at work most of the child's waking hours. This creates a very high degree of sensitivity to the emotional attitudes of the mother and of vulnerability to anything disturbing about them. To reinforce this, most associations outside the immediate family in the neighborhood play group and school are those in which the child cannot take security of love and status for granted but is placed in competition with others either directly or for adult approval by the teacher and parents. The fact that his mother loves him does not solve his problems; he must stand on his own feet. Furthermore doing well in such situations is highly valued in the society, and this attitude is apt to be shared by the mother, so that her own love and approval tend to become contingent on the child's objective performance rather than unconditional as it is in many societies.[4] This love is therefore more acutely needed than in most societies and more precarious. The situation is favorable to a high level of anxiety and hence of aggression. But because of the very acuteness of the need for affection and approval, direct expression of aggression is more than normally dangerous and hence likely to be repressed.

On top of this situation come factors which are differential between the sexes and not only intensify insecurity but have much to do with the direction aggressive tendencies take. Our kinship situation, it has been noted, throws children of both sexes overwhelmingly upon the mother as *the* emotionally significant adult. In such a situation "identification" in the sense that the adult becomes a "role model" is the normal result. For a girl this is normal and natural not only because she belongs to the same sex as the mother, but because the functions of housewife and mother are immediately before her eyes and are tangible and relatively easily understood by a child. Almost as soon as she is physically able, the girl begins a direct apprenticeship in the adult feminine role. It is very notable that girls' play consists in cooking, sewing, playing with dolls, and so on, activities which are a direct mimicry of their mothers'. But the boy does not have his father immediately available; in addition—especially in the middle classes, but increasingly perhaps in the lower— the things the father does are intangible and difficult for a child to understand, such as working in an office, or even running a complicated machine tool.

Thus the girl has a more favorable opportunity for emotional maturing through positive identification with an adult model, a fact which seems to have much to do with the well-known earlier maturity of girls. The boy on the other hand has a tendency to form a direct feminine identification, since his mother is the model most readily available and significant to him. But he is not destined to become an adult woman. Moreover he soon discovers that in certain vital respects women are considered inferior to men, that it would hence be shameful for him to grow up to be like a woman. Hence when boys emerge into what Freudians call the "latency period," their behavior tends to be marked by a kind of "compulsive masculinity." They refuse to have anything to do with girls. "Sissy" becomes the worst of all insults. They get interested in athletics and physical prowess, in the things in which men have the most primitive and obvious advantage over women. Furthermore they become allergic to all expression of tender emotion; they must be "taught." This universal pattern bears all the earmarks of a "reaction formation." It is so conspicuous, not because it is simply "masculine nature" but because it is a defense against a feminine identification. The commonness with which "mother fixation" is involved in all types of neurotic and psychotic disorders of Western men strongly confirms this. It may be inferred also that the ambivalence involved is an important source of anxiety—lest one not be able to prove his masculinity—and that aggression toward women who "after all are to blame," is an essential concomitant.

One particular aspect of this situation is worthy of special attention. In addition to the mother's being the object of love and identification, she is to the young boy the principal agent of socially significant discipline.[5] Not only does she administer the disciplines which make him a tolerable citizen of the family group, but she stimulates him to give a good account of himself outside the home and makes known her disappointment and disapproval if he fails to measure up to her expectations. She, above all, focuses in herself the symbols of what is "good" behavior, of conformity with the expectations of the respectable adult world. When he revolts against identification with his mother in the name of masculinity, it is not surprising that a boy unconsciously identifies "goodness" with femininity and that being a "bad boy" becomes a positive goal. It seems that the association of goodness with femininity, and therewith much of our Western ambivalence toward ethical values, has its roots in this situation. At any rate there is a strong tendency for boyish behavior to run in antisocial if not directly destructive directions, in striking contrast to that of preadolescent girls.

As would be expected if such a pattern is deep-seated and has continued for several generations, it becomes imbedded in the psychology of adults as well as children. The mother therefore secretly—usually unconsciously—admires such behavior and, particularly when it is combined with winning qualities in other respects, rewards it with her love—so the "bad" boy is enabled to have the best of both worlds. She may quite frequently treat such a "bad" son as her favorite as compared with a "sissy" brother who conforms with all her overt expectations much better.

It should be particularly noted that this is not the functionally dominant pattern of the adult masculine role. It combines an emphasis on physical prowess with a kind of irresponsibility. But the adult man predominantly gains his place by using his mind rather than his brawn and by accepting responsibility, not by repudiating it. There must therefore, in a large majority of boys, be a further transition as they grow to maturity; they must come to value other lines of achievement and accept responsibilities. It is to be presumed that this transition in turn is not accomplished without further repressions. At least this "bad boy" pattern did permit a direct outlet of aggression in physical terms, though to be sure this could not be directed against mothers. But the discipline of most adult masculine roles sharply limits that, although a sublimated form in competitive activities is still possible. It is however probable that this is one important source of a reservoir of latent aggression susceptible of mobilization in group antagonisms, and particularly war, because it legitimatizes physical aggression as such.

With girls the situation is different, but not intrinsically or necessarily more favorable. In childhood a girl has the opportunity to mature primarily through identification with the mother and hence introjection of the mother role pattern. But girls later face a situation of realistic insecurity which profoundly disturbs the continuity of transition to adulthood in this role. In many societies marriages are arranged by the older generation who are primarily concerned with providing good mothers for their grandchildren, and the qualities of this pattern are then a positive asset. But increasingly in Western society a girl must seek her fundamental adult security—which, inherently in the structure of the situation, depends overwhelmingly on her relation to the one particular man she marries—by direct appeal to the personal sentiments of men—and she must do so in competition with the other girls of her age group. Compared with the masculine problems of becoming established in a satisfactory occupational career line, it is a more severe type of competitive insecurity, because so much depends on the one step which is almost irrevocable and the average age of marriage is such that the occupational prospects of a suitor are necessarily still indefinite. In addition to this, she must compete for the personal favor of a young man who, in the nature of the influences to which he has been exposed, tends to be deeply ambivalent about the primary role his future wife is going to play, hence severely handicapped in making rational decisions on such matters.[6]

The undoubted predominant tendency in this situation is for the plane of competition in the process of selection of marriage partners to be deflected markedly from attraction to "good wives and mothers" (and husbands and fathers) toward an accent on "romantic love," certain rather immature types of sexuality, and "glamor" —the exploitation of certain specifically feminine assets of attraction.

Psychologically speaking, this situation implies two very fundamental sources of frustration for the growing girl. The first is the discovery of what is, in the relevant sense, "masculine superiority," the fact that her own security like that of other women is dependent on the favor—even "whim"—of a man, that she must compete for masculine favor and cannot stand on her own feet. This is a shock because in her early experience her mother was the center of the world and by identifying with her she expected to be in a similar position. Secondly, it turns out that the qualities and ideals which were the focus of her childhood identification and personality development are not the primary asset in solving her fundamental problem, are even to a degree a positive handicap. The severity and relative abruptness of this transition cannot but, in a large proportion of cases, be a source of much insecurity, hence the source of a high level of anxiety and of aggressive impulses. The primary source of this aggression is the sense of having been deceived, of being allowed to believe that a certain path was the way to security and success only to find that it does not seem to count. The aggression, it may be presumed, is directed both against men and against women: the latter because they are the primary "deceivers," they are not what they seem to be; the former because it is they who seem to have forced upon women this intolerable fate of having to be two or more incompatible things. This undoubtedly underlies the widespread ambivalence among women toward the role of motherhood, which is a primary factor in the declining birth rate, as well as toward sexual relations and the role of being a woman in any other fundamental respect.[7]

The upshot of the above analysis is in the first place that the typical Western individual—apart from any special constitutional predispositions—has been through an experience, in the process of growing to adulthood, which involved emotional strains of such severity as to produce an adult personality with a large reservoir of aggressive disposition. Secondly, the bulk of aggression generated from this source must in the nature of the case remain repressed. In spite of the disquieting amount of actual disruption of family solidarity, and quarreling and bickering even where families are not broken up, the social norms enjoining mutual affection among family members, especially respectful affection toward parents and love between spouses, are very powerful. Where such a large reservoir of repressed aggression exists but cannot be directly expressed, it tends to become "free-floating" and to be susceptible of mobilization against various kinds of scapegoats outside the immediate situation of its genesis.

In addition to establishing the basis for the existence of a large reservoir of repressed aggression, the above analysis tells us something of the directions which its indirect expression may be likely to take and the "themes" of grievance which are most likely to arouse aggressive reactions. In the first place, Western society is one in which most positions of large-scale responsibility are held by men. In this connection the cult of "compulsive masculinity" cannot but be of significance. Western men are peculiarly susceptible to the appeal of an adolescent type of assertively masculine behavior and attitude which may take various forms. They have in common a tendency to revolt against the routine aspects of the primarily institutionalized masculine role of sober responsibility, meticulous respect for the rights of others, and tender affection toward women. Assertion through physical prowess, with an endemic tendency toward violence and hence the military ideal, is inherent in the complex and the most dangerous potentiality.

It is, however, not only masculine psychology which is important in this respect. Through at least two channels the psychology of women may reinforce this tendency. First, there is undoubtedly widespread if repressed resentment on the part of women over being forced to accept their sex role and its contradictory components. This is expressed in an undercurrent of aggression toward the men with whom they are associated, which, given the latter's hypersensitiveness toward women's attitudes toward them, can be expected to accentuate the pattern of compulsive masculinity.

But this feminine resentment against men is only one side of an ambivalent structure of attitudes. The situation by virtue of which women have to acept an inferior position in crucial respects leads to an idealization of precisely the extreme type of aggressive masculinity. It is quite clear that Western men are peculiarly dependent emotionally on women and therefore feminine admiration of them will powerfully stimulate any pattern of behavior which can evoke it.[8]

The childhood situation of the Western world also provides the prototypes of what appear to be the two primarily significant themes or contexts of meaning in which it is easiest to evoke an aggressive reaction, since these are the contexts in which the people of the Western world have been oversensitized by the traumatic experiences of their childhood.

The first of these is the question of "adequacy," of living up to an acceptable standard of achievement or behavior. There is a tendency to be hypersensitive to any suggestion of inferiority or incapacity to achieve goals which have once been set. This in turn is manifested in two ways of primary significance for present purposes. On the one hand the peoples of Western society are highly susceptible to wishful and distorted beliefs in their own superiority to others, as individuals or in terms of any collectivity with which they are identified, since this belief, and its recognition by others, tends to allay anxiety about their own adequacy. On the other hand, since such a belief in superiority has compulsive characteristics, those who have to deal with such people find it "hard to take," even when the former have a highly realistic attitude. But it also stimulates a vicious circle of resentment on the part of those who, sharing the same hypersensitivity, are treated as inferior. It is, in other words, inordinately easy for either individual or group relationships in the Western world to become defined as relations of superiority and inferiority and to evoke aggressive responses, if the assumption of superiority is, even justly, questioned, or if, again even justly, there is any imputation of inferiority.

The second major context of meanings is that of loyalty, honesty, integrity, justice of dealing. Both in competition with others and in relation to expectations which he has been allowed to build up, the Western child has usually had the traumatic experience of disillusionment, of being "let down." The boy has not been allowed to emulate the ideal of his mother; when he has been "good," he has been punished rather than rewarded for it, and his "bad" brother has been preferred. The girl has found out both that her mother as a woman is an inferior being and that to be a "good woman," that is a mother, does not pay. These experiences are the prototype of a certain hypersensitivity to the question of whether others can be trusted either as individuals or collectivities. In sex relations there is a tendency to be compulsively preoccupied with the fidelity of the partner. In general there is an overreadiness to believe that the other fellow will attempt to deceive or injure one. Naturally, since this hypersensitivity is associated with repressed aggression, it is very easy for the aggressive impulse to be projected on the other party to the relation, producing the "paranoid" pattern of overreadiness to impute hostile intentions where they do not exist, or to exaggerate them grossly where they do. In its extreme form the rest of the world is apt to be seen as mainly preoccupied with plotting to destroy one or one's group. The Western tendency is to be "thin-skinned," unable to "take it," when frustrations must be faced and to place the blame on others when most of it belongs at home.

THE OCCUPATIONAL SYSTEM

The other most fundamental institutional structure of modern Western society, the occupational system, can for present purposes be dealt with much more briefly—especially since a good deal has been anticipated in dealing with kinship, the two being so closely interdependent. Its most essential feature is the primacy of functional achievement. This implies the selection of people on the basis of their capacities to perform the task, of innate ability and training, not of birth or any other antecedent element of status. It further implies the segregation of the technical role from other aspects of the incumbent's life, most of which are in the nature of the case governed by other types of standards. This takes the form in the type case of physical segregation and of segregation of personnel and activity, so that it involves a distinct system of relationships. Finally, it implies a peculiar type of discipline in that any type of personal feeling which might come in conflict with these relationships is subordinated to the requirements of the technical task, which are often highly exacting and often narrowly specialized.

There is an inherently competitive dimension of the occupational system. Even when competitive victory is not as such a major direct goal, but rather is subordinated to functional achievement as such, a selective process, which among other things governs access to opportunity for all the higher achievements, is inherent in the system. A man has to "win" the competition for selection, often repeatedly, in order to have an opportunity to prove his capacity for the higher achievements. The inevitable result of the competitive and selective processes is the distribution of the personnel of the system in a relatively elaborate hierarchy of prestige which is symbolized and expressed in manifold ways.

It is furthermore relevant that in the aggregate, particular roles, and still more organizations, undertake functions which are altogether unknown in simpler societies. Men are more frequently subjected to the discipline and strains of more exacting skills. But even more important are two other consequences. One is the involvement of people in systems of social relationship of very great complexity which, because of their newness and rapidly changing character, cannot be adequately governed by established and traditionalized norms. The other is the fact that explicit responsibility, in that great consequences hinge on the decisions and competence of individuals, is a far greater factor than in simpler societies. In view of what we know of the deep-seated tendencies to dependency and the psychological difficulties involved in assuming responsibility, this is a fact of prime importance.

When these features of the occupational system are brought into relation to the personality structure discussed above, two classes of conclusions touching the problem of aggression appear to follow. The first set concerns the relation to the general levels of aggression in the society, the second the channeling of what exists into different actual and potential types and directions of expression.

Though it is difficult to arrive at more than a very rough judgment, it seems clear that the balance is rather heavily on the side of increasing rather than reducing the levels of insecurity and hence of anxiety and aggression—the foundations of which are laid in the process of socialization in the family. It is true that the wide field for competitive activity provides some outlets which are constructive for sublimating aggression by harnessing it to the motivation of constructive achievement, and at the same time "winning." But the other side of the medal is the condemnation of probably a considerably larger number to being "losers"—since success in such a system is to a considerable degree inherently relative—and thereby feeding any tendency to feel unduly inadequate or unjustly treated. At the same time, participation in the occupational system means subjection to a severe discipline. It means continual control of emotions so that repression and dissociation are favored rather than counteracted.[9] Perhaps most important of all, however, the competitive process is governed by a rather strict code which is very often in conflict with immediate impulses. In particular it is essential to be a "good loser" and take one's misfortunes and disappointments with outward equanimity. This reinforces the need to repress feelings of resentment against unfair treatment, whether the feelings are realistically justified or not, and hence their availability for mobilization in indirect channels of expression.

The above considerations apply primarily to men since they are the primary carriers of the occupational system. Conversely, however, by the segregation of occupational from familial roles, most women are denied a sense of participation with *their men* in a common enterprise. Moreover, it is in the occupational sphere that the "big things" are done, and this drastic exclusion must herve to increase the inferiority feelings of women and hence their resentment at their condemnation by the accident of sex to an inferior role.

In respect to the channeling of aggression as distinguished from its absolute level, two things are of primary importance. First, if there are no reasons to suppose that, on the average, absolute levels are lowered, at the same time few direct outlets are provided for most types of aggressive impulse. Hence the general need for indirect channels of expression, particularly by displacement on scapegoats, is reinforced by experience in this sphere of life.

Secondly, it is above all in the occupational sphere that the primary institutionalization of the basic themes of the above discussion takes place—childhood is an apprenticeship for the final test which the adult world imposes on man. Ability to perform well and hold one's own or excel in competition is the primary realistic test of adult adequacy, but many, probably the considerable majority, are condemned to what, especially if they are oversensitive, they must feel to be an unsatisfactory experience. Many also will inevitably feel they have been unjustly treated, because there is in fact much injustice, much of which is very deeply rooted in the nature of the society, and because many are disposed to be paranoid and see more injustice than actually exists. To feel unjustly treated is moreover not only a balm to one's sense of resentment, it is an alibi for failure, since how could one succeed if he is not given a chance?

Thus the kinship and the occupational systems constitute from the present point of view a mutually reinforcing system of forces acting on the individual to generate large quantities of aggressive impulse, to repress the greater part of it, and to channel it in the direction of finding agencies which can be symbolically held responsible for failure and for deception and injustice to the individual and to those with whom he is identified.[10] Perhaps the most important mitigation of the general situation which the working of the occupational system brings about is that occupational success may do much to reduce the pressure toward compulsive masculinity. But the difficulty here is that sufficient success to have this effect is attainable only to a minority of the masculine population. Lack of it would seem to have the opposite effect, and this is just as much a consequence of the system as the other.

THE STRUCTURE OF GROUP HOSTILITY

The occupational system of the Western world is probably the most important institutional "precipitate" of a fundamental dynamic process which Max Weber has called the "process of rationalization." Through it, as well as other channels, this process has had a fundamental part in structuring attitudes in the Western world which is relevant to the problem of aggression and hence calls for a brief discussion.

The progress of science and related elements of rational thought is the core and fundamental prototype of the process. Science is an inherently dynamic thing. Unless prevented by influences extraneous to it, it will continually evolve. Moreover, unless science is hermetically insulated from the rest of social life, which is manifestly impossible, this dynamic process of change will be extended into neighboring realms of thought, for example, philosophical and religious thought, and in the direction of practical application wherever rational norms play a significant role in the determination of action. Hence through this dynamic factor, a continuing process of change is introduced, both into the primary symbolic systems which help to integrate the life of a society, and into the structure of the situations in which a large part of the population must carry on their activities.

The significance of this arises in the first place from the fact that there is much evidence that security in the sense relevant to this analysis is to a high degree a function of the stability of certain elements of the socio-cultural situation. This is true especially because certain aspects of the situations people face are involved in the actual and, as they feel it, prospective fulfillment of their "legitimate expectations." These expectations are, even apart from any neurotic distortions, apt to be highly concrete so that any change, even if it is not intrinsically unfavorable, is apt to be disturbing and arouse a reaction of anxiety. It should above all be noted that technological change inevitably disrupts the informal human relationships of the members of working groups—relationships which have been shown to be highly important to the stability and working efficiency of the participants.[11] On the other hand, the corresponding process of change on the level of ideas and symbols tends to disrupt established symbolic systems which are exceedingly important to the security and stability of the orientation of people.

The weight of evidence seems to be that the amount of such change to which even the best-integrated personalities can adapt without the possibility of upsetting the smooth functioning of personality is rather limited; but in proportion as there is a neurotic type of insecurity, there tends to be a compulsive need for stability in these respects. The capacity to adapt to both types of change is a function of "emotional maturity," and the above analysis has shown that there must be serious limitations on the levels of emotional maturity which most members of Western society can have attained. There seems, therefore, to be no doubt that the continuing incidence of dynamic change through the process of rationalization is one major source of the generalized insecurity which characterizes our society. As such it should also be a major factor in maintaining the reservoir of aggressive impulses at a high level. It is a factor so deep-seated in our society that it must be expected to continue to operate on a major scale for the foreseeable future; only profound changes in the whole social situation which would invalidate the greater part of this analysis would produce a situation where this would not be true.

It is not, however, the significance of the process of rationalization, as a source of quantitative addition to the reservoir of aggression, which is most important, but rather the way it operates to structure the direction of its actual and potential expression. It is a major factor in the polarization of attitudes in the society, especially as they are distributed between different groups in the population in such a way as to focus anxiety and aggression on a single structured line of tension.

It must be remembered that the incidence of the process of rationalization is highly uneven in the social structure. With respect to any given level of traditionalized values, symbols, and structuring of situations, there are always relatively "emancipated" and relatively traditional groups and sectors of the society. Certain of the emancipated groups, like the best of the professions for instance, become relatively well institutionalized so that the dynamic process of which they are agents is not so disturbing to them. They always, however, contain at least a fringe, if not more, where insecurity is expressed in compulsively distorted patterns of extreme emancipation which are highly provocative to the more traditionalized elements, which lead into a vicious circle in proportion as elements of both groups are compulsively motivated.

The process is, however, always tending to spread into the relatively traditionalized areas of the society and thereby tending to threaten the security of the population elements most dependent on traditionalized patterns. Partly these elements already have serious insecurities and are compulsively dependent on traditionalism; partly change introduces new insecurities. In either case, the result is to stimulate what has elsewhere been called a "fundamentalist reaction," a compulsively distorted exaggeration of traditional values and other related patterns.[12] This above all attaches to those elements of culture and society which are not so readily and in the same sense susceptible of rationalization as are the areas of science, technology, and administrative organization—namely, religion, family, class attitudes, the informal traditions of ethnic culture, and the like, where non-logical symbolic systems are heavily involved.

The reverse side of the exaggerated assertion of these traditional patterns is the aggressive attack on the symbols which appear to threaten them, science as such, atheism and other antireligious aspects of liberal rationalism, the relaxation of traditional sex morality—especially in the larger urban communities and in "bohemian" circles—political and economic radicalism, and the like. The compulsive adherents of emancipated values on the other hand tend to brand all traditional values as "stupid," reactionary, unenlightened, and thus a vicious circle of mounting antagonism readily gets started. This polarization in fact corresponds roughly to structured differentiations of the society, with latent or more or less actual conflicts of interest as between rural and urban elements, capital and labor, upper and lower class groups, and the like, which feed fuel to the flames.

It is above all important that the values about which the fundamentalist pattern of reaction tends to cluster are those particularly important in the constitution and symbolization of informal group solidarities—those of families, social class, socioreligious groups, ethnic groups, and nations. Many of these solidarities are seriously in conflict with the explicit values of the Western world which largely stem from the rationalistic traditions of the Enlightenment.[13] They are hence particularly difficult to defend against rationalistic attack. Since, however, they are of fundamental emotional importance, the consequence more frequently than not is their "defensive" assertion rather than their abandonment. This very difficulty of rational defense when rational values are in fact accepted, favors this context as a field for the mobilization of repressed aggression, since it is in a state of bafflement that people are most likely to react with "unreasonable" aggression.

These circumstances seem to go far toward explaining the striking fact that aggression in the Western world tends to focus so much on antagonisms between solidary groups. Some of these groups are, to be sure, those growing out of the formal and utilitarian structure of modern society, like the conflict of business and the labor unions. Probably more important, however, are the lines of conflict which cut across these groups, particularly those between religious and ethnic groups within nations and, above all, the conflict of nationalisms. Group conflict seems to be particularly significant because on the one hand solidarity with an informal group, the appeal of which is to "infrarational" sentiments, is a peculiarly potent measure for allaying the neurotic types of anxiety which are so common; on the other hand an antagonistic group is a peculiarly appropriate symbolic object on which to displace the emotional reactions which cannot be openly expressed within one's own group lest they threaten its solidarity. In this whole context, it is peculiarly appropriate that groups be available in regard to which the ambivalent structure of emotions in relation to the two dominant themes discussed above can be expressed. The "out-group" should, that is, be a group in relation to which one's own group can feel a comfortably self-righteous sense of superiority and at the same time a group which can be plausibly accused of arrogating to itself an illegitimate superiority of its own. Correspondingly it should be a group with strong claims to a position of high ethical standing of its own which, however, can plausibly be made out to be essentially specious and to conceal a subtle deception. The Jews have in both these connections furnished almost the ideal scapegoat throughout the Western world.

Latent aggression has thus been channeled into internal group conflicts of various sorts throughout the Western world: anti-Semitism and anti-laborism, and anti-Negro, anti-Catholic, and antiforeigner feelings are found in this country. There are, however, potent reasons why nationalism should be the most important and serious focus of these tendencies. The first is the realistic basis of it. The organization of our civilization into nation-states which are the dominant power units has been a crucial realistic fact of the situation. Above all, in the chronic tendency to resort to war in crisis situations the loyalty to one's government has been to be in one sense the ultimate residual loyalty, the one which could claim any sacrifice no matter how great if need be.

At the same time it is highly significant that as between the fundamentalist and the emancipated poles of modern attitude structure, nationalistic loyalty as such is largely neutral. It is, however, a particularly suitable focus for fundamentalist sentiments in accusing their opponents of a specious sincerity since it does tend to be an ultimate test of altruism and sincerity. The "foreigner" is, moreover, outside the principal immediate system of law and order; hence aggression toward him does not carry the same opprobrium or immediate danger of reprisal that it does toward one's "fellow-citizen." Hostility to the foreigner has thus furnished a means of transcending the principal, immediately threatening group conflicts, of achieving "unity"—but at the expense of a less immediate but in fact more dangerous threat to security, since national states now command such destructive weapons that war between them is approaching suicidal significance.

Thus the immense reservoir of aggression in Western society is sharply inhibited from direct expression within the smaller groups in which it is primarily generated. The structure of the society in which it is produced contains a strong predisposition for it to be channeled into group antagonisms. The significance of the nation-state is, however, such that there is a strong pressure to internal unity within each such unit and therefore a tendency to focus aggression on the potential conflicts between nation-state units. In addition to the existence of a plurality of such units, each a potential target of the focused aggression from all the others, the situation is particularly unstable because of the endemic tendency to define their relations in the manner least calculated to build an effectively solidary international order. Each state is, namely, highly ambivalent about the superiority-inferiority question. Each tends to have a deep-seated presumption of its own superiority and a corresponding resentment against any other's corresponding presumption. Each at the same time tends to feel that it has been unfairly treated in the past and is ready on the slightest provocation to assume that the others are ready to plot new outrages in the immediate future. Each tends to be easily convinced of the righteousness of its own policy while at the same time it is overready to suspect the motives of all others. In short, the "jungle philosophy"—which corresponds to a larger element in the real sentiments of all of us than can readily be admitted, even to ourselves—tends to be projected onto the relations of nation-states at precisely the point where, under the technological and organizational situation of the modern world, it can do the most harm.

CONCLUSION

In conclusion, to forestall misunderstanding, it is well to call explicit attention to some of the limitations of the analysis just developed. That it is specifically limited to analyzing sources of aggression and their channeling has already been stated. It needs, however, to be repeated that the more positive sides are deliberately omitted. It is thus not in any sense a complete or balanced picture of the dynamic psychological balance of Western society, even so far as such a picture could be drawn in the light of present knowledge and on a comparable level of generality and abstraction. Above all, it should not by itself be taken as an adequate basis for any suggestions of remedial action. By omitting consideration of the positive aspects, it has precisely neglected the principal assets on which any such program would have to rely. It is confined to a specifically limited diagnostic function. Its results must be combined with those of other studies before they have any practical value beyond this.

This analysis has been couched in terms of a very high level of "ideal-typical" abstraction. It has presumed to deal with the social structure and psychological dynamics of the Western world as a whole, in full consciousness of the fact that there are and have been innumerable ranges of variation within this enormously complicated sociocultural system, many of which are of prime significance to any practical purpose.

In the first place, within any one national society this analysis applies unequally to different elements of its population. In fact it applies most completely and directly to the urban, middle-class elements, those which have been most heavily involved in the consequences of the industrial revolution. Substantial modifications need to be made in dealing with rural populations. The same is true of the highest elite groups, particularly those whose position was firmly institutionalized before the major social changes of the industrial era took place. This is especially true of the older European hereditary aristocracies. It is even necessary to make substantial modifications for the case of social groups which have so low a status that their being in the major competition for places on the general scale of prestige cannot be realistically supposed, thus for large parts, at least, of the "proletarian" elements. These are only among the most conspicuous of the qualifications, each of which would have important consequences for the psychological reaction patterns of the relevant groups.

Similarly, most of the "secondary" complications of the system of dynamic relationships under consideration have perforce been neglected. It is a fact of the first importance that, for instance, in American adult culture there is a fundamentally important institutionalization of "adolescent" values which is in continual competition with the main system.

Finally, it is quite clear that there are extremely important national variations in the relevant patterns. To a considerable degree the analysis has been focused on American conditions. Their greater familiarity favors this. But it is not necessarily a source of serious bias, since in certain respects the United States represents a closer approach to the "ideal type" of structure which is of prime strategic significance for the whole Western world—significant because the fundamental patterns of industrial society have been less modified by powerful institutional complexes which were present in the preexisting society.

France, for instance, has developed less far along these lines than most Western countries, and has integrated more of the older society with the new tendencies. There seems, for instance, to have been far less isolation of the immediate conjugal family there than in this country.

Certain of the consequences most important to the practical situation have appeared most highly developed in Germany and greatly accentuated under the Nazi regime.[14] The peculiarly virulent nationalistic aggressiveness of Nazi Germany certainly cannot be adequately explained in terms of the factors analyzed in the present paper. It depended on other elements which were either peculiar to Germany, or relatively far more important there than for instance in this country. This is true of the strongly authoritarian character of the father-son relationship, and of the much more sharply subordinated position of women in Germany. There was also a much more rigidly formalistic and hierarchical occupational system there, and conditions were much more favorable to the development of a strongly militaristic variety of nationalism.

Nevertheless, differences of this sort do not invalidate the analysis presented here. They are, however extremely deviant, variations on the same fundamental themes. Much of the general foundation of the situation has been in fact common to all the major nations of the Western world where the process of industrialization and rationalization has taken strong hold. It is a question, not of a right and a wrong analysis, but of the appropriate adaptation of one which is in the nature of the case general and abstract, to the concretely variable circumstances of different particular situations. This adaptation is achieved, not by substituting a new "correct" for an incorrect explanation, but by introducing an analysis of the effect of specific modifications of the generalized structure presented here, and by taking account of additional factors which the generality of this analysis has not permitted to be treated.

NOTES

[1] "Aggression" will here be defined as the disposition on the part of an individual or a collectivity to orient its action to goals which include a conscious or unconscious intention illegitimately to injure the interests of other individuals or collectivities in the same system. The term *illegitimately* deliberately implies that the individual or collectivity in question is integrated, however imperfectly, in a moral order which defines reciprocal rights and obligations. The universality of the existence of a moral order in this sense is a cardinal thesis of modern social science. This is not to say that world society constitutes one integrated moral order in this sense; on the contrary, the diversity of such orders is a primary problem of integration, but it is *not* as such the problem of aggression. Thus friction and hostility arising from lack of mutual understanding or mere thoughtlessness or insensitiveness to the position of the other party are not as such acts of aggression, although aggressive dispositions become attracted to these situations as fields of expression perhaps more readily than any others, because they are easier to rationalize.

The use of the term aggression here is thus narrower than in some psychological, particularly psychoanalytic, discussions. In particular "self-assertion" the "drive to mastery"—for example, of a technical skill—without meaningful hostility to others, will not be treated as aggression. It will not be an issue in the present analysis to decide as to whether, on deeper psychological levels, aggression in the sense here meant, and nonaggressive self-assertion, or mastery, are fundamentally different or whether they derive from the same roots. On the level of *social behavior* the difference is fundamental, and that is what matters in the present context.

[2] Modern Japan and the Early Roman Empire are the two cases outside this sphere which have gone farthest in approaching the modern Western situation.

[3] The study which comes closest to the present attempt in approach and analytical method is Clyde Kluckhohn's *Navaho Witchcraft,* Papers of the Peabody Museum of American Archaeology and Ethnology, Harvard University (1944), 22: no. 2 (see also the author's review, *American Journal of Sociology* [1946] 51:566–569). Naturally because of the vast extent of Western society, the facts must be determined on a basis of broad general impressions rather than on specific field observation. This does not, however, invalidate the comparability of the two analyses. There is a very important sense in which nationalism in the Western world is the functional equivalent of Navaho witchcraft.

[4] See Mead, Margaret, *And Keep Your Powder Dry,* N. Y., William Morrow, 1942, for a discussion of the pattern of "conditional love" and its consequences.

[5] In this she is followed by a teacher who in the United States is almost always a woman until quite a late stage in the process of schooling.

[6] An additional feature of this ambivalence not touched above concerns attitudes toward sex. The fact of the incest taboo plus the intensity of emotional concentration on the mother makes for strong inhibitions against sexual attachments, since the sexual relation to the mother becomes the ideal of love. The revolt against this attachment in the "bad boy" pattern thus very readily draws the attitude toward sex into the polarity, and sexual interests become "bad" but attractive. Indeed frequently the hedonic aspect of sex becomes tinged with aggression; sexuality is, so to speak, a means of taking revenge on women for their maltreatment of boys as children. It is notable that the sentimentally idealized stereotype of the "good" woman is strikingly asexual. It may be presumed that this stereotype is largely the product of masculine fantasies.

[7] In this and other previous discussions emphasis has been deliberately placed on the negative aspect of the situation, the strains and their disruptive consequences. This is because present interest is in sources of aggression. The positive side is not evaluated; hence the reader should exercise great care not to take this discussion as a general appraisal of the emotional qualities of the Western kinship system. Furthermore it should go without saying that these patterns have a very unequal incidence in the population, ranging from virtual negligibility to pathological intensity.

[8] The indications are that this feminine admiration, not to say adulation, of the "heroic" "He-man" pattern played a major role in the spread of the Nazi movement in Germany.

[9] This discipline includes adherence to sharply objective standards in the face of the strains growing out of the emotional complexity of the system of social relationships of the work situation, and the additional strains imposed by high levels of responsibility for those who have to assume it. In addition, the mobility which is inherent in such a system has two further significant consequences. Status is inherently insecure, in that it cannot be guaranteed independently of performance—to say nothing of the results of economic fluctuations in causing unemployment and the like. Then technological and organizational change, as well as promotion and job change of the individual, are also inherent and make it difficult to "settle down" to a complete emotional adjustment to any one stable situation; it is necessary to make continual new adjustments with all the attendant emotional difficulty.

[10] If anything, probably the kinship system has to absorb more strains originating in the occupational system than vice versa. In any case the effect of these strains is to accentuate the sources of aggression inherent in the kinship system rather than to mitigate them. This would appear to operate above all through the influence on children of parents who themselves are showing the effect of tension. In so far as a man "takes out" the frustrations of his occupational situation on his wife she may in turn "take it out" on the children.

[11] Cf. Roethlisberger, F. J., and Dickson, William J., *Management and the Worker*; Cambridge: Harvard University Press, 1941.

[12] Cf. Parsons, Talcott, "Some Sociological Aspects of the Fascist Movements," *Social Forces*, Nov. 1942, reprinted as Chapter VII above. Also: "The Sociology of Modern Anti-Semitism" in *Jews in a Gentile World*, Graeber & Britt (eds.); N. Y.: Macmillan 1942.

[13] Cf. Gunnar Myrdal's discussion of "The American Creed" in *An American Dilemma;* N. Y.: Harpers 1944 (2 vols.).

[14] Cf. Parsons, T., "Democracy and Social Structure in Pre-Nazi Germany," *Journal of Legal and Political Sociology,* Nov. 1942, and "The Problem of Controlled Institutional Change," *Psychiatry* (1945) 8:79–101. See also Erikson, Eric Homburger, "Hitler's Imagery and the Dream of German Youth," *Psychiatry* (1942) 5:475–493.

26

A Critique of Clinical Psychological Approaches to the Explanation of International Conflict

The following remarks by a political scientist who specializes in the study of international politics are a response to assertions concerning the roots of international conflict such as those made in the previous essay by Parsons—including many that have been much less qualified than Parsons' sophisticated discussion. In particular, the reader should reflect on Osgood's sharp querying of the premise that international conflict necessarily results from, or is even related to, the types of inner tensions that concern clinicians. Arguments such as that of Osgood's seek to replace hypotheses about ego-defensive motivational sources of behavior with alternative hypotheses suggesting that the same behavior may in fact—to use the terminology introduced by Smith in selection two—have its roots in realistic object appraisal. It is not fully clear how one might set such alternative views to an empirical test.

OBSERVATIONS ON THE CLINICAL APPROACH TO INTERNATIONAL TENSIONS

Robert E. Osgood

Some recent studies of international tensions purport to contain special insights into the cause and cure of international conflicts that lead to war. They are based upon a distinct conceptual framework and methodology derived from sociological and psychological premises about international behavior. Other tensions studies are distinguished from the orthodox text book approaches to international harmony and disharmony chiefly by their assiduous refinement of prosaic insights and concepts and by their special vocabulary for translating common sense into "scientific" terms. It is the former group of studies toward which my observations are directed.

These observations are not based on an exhaustive investigation of the entire field of tensions research; so it is not sure how many sociological feet the shoes described here actually fit. However, it does seem that a great deal of the postwar

Reprinted from *Social Problems*, 2, No. 3 (1955), 176–80.

sociological analysis of international tensions is based upon misleading assumptions about the fundamental nature of international society, the ideal state of international relations, and the method of achieving this ideal. Together, these assumptions compose what one might call the clinical approach. This approach regards international tensions—at least those that lead to conflict—as a sickness of the world community. Its chief aim is to eliminate or relieve these tensions so as to restore the community to its normal state of harmonious health. It seeks to do this by direct treatment of alleged deficiencies of behavior and knowledge, which are presumed to cause the tensions. Each of these three assumptions will be analyzed briefly in order to explain in what sense the clinical approach is misleading. The following assumptions are by no means always set forth in such explicit and naked form; nor do all of them necessarily appear in every study. Nevertheless, they are all closely and logically related and seem to underlie much of the analysis of international tensions by social psychologists, whether or not it deals with tensions as such.

FIRST ASSUMPTION

It is misleading to equate the normal state of international relations with the absence of tensions and to regard deviations from this state as unnatural or abnormal; for the analogy implies that there is a natural harmony of interests, aims, and desires among nations—like the harmonious relations of the parts of a healthy body—and that tensions are inconsistent with the inherent nature of international society—like diseases or functional disorders in a sick body. In reality, the "normal" state of international relations for the foreseeable future is as much disharmony as harmony of national interests, aims, and desires. This disharmony arises, fundamentally, from the intimate and intense personal identification of the individual with the national group, which, in turn, produces that profound and compelling emotional coalescence of individual altruism and group egoism that characterizes modern national allegiances.

Given the fundamental fact of personal identification, tensions and conflicts among different nations' interests, aims, and desires, inevitably arise from the diversity of political, social, and cultural conditions which shape national ends. Since the force of national egoism precludes the orderly procedures of law and government, as well as most of the restraints of conscience and custom, which mitigate and control conflicts among lesser groups within the nation, international relations is more accurately characterized as a struggle for power than as a harmony of interests. A conceptual framework of international relations that minimizes the force of national egoism, the incompatibility of national ends, and the struggle for power by transmuting the ideal of international harmony into the concept of a natural harmony of interests, must lead to faulty analysis of the cause of tensions and to unrealistic expectations concerning the mitigation of tensions.

SECOND ASSUMPTION

The assumption that international relations are normally and naturally harmonious is obviously congenial with the normative assumption that international relations ought to be free of tensions—except, perhaps, for an undefined minimum necessary to human vitality. This normative assumption seems to be inspired by the laudable zeal of the social reformer, who, believing that men are naturally good and rational, strives to abolish the defects in their environment and training that prevent them from acting that way. He hopes that in this manner his scientific knowledge of society will point out the way in which all people, without regard for national or other distinctions, may live together in a spirit of tolerant understanding and settle their disputes by impartial reference to reason, law, and morality rather than by resort to coercion.

Obviously, in terms of this abstract ideal, international tensions that lead to conflicts are bad things and ought to be curbed; and this is, in fact, the guiding aim of the clinical approach. However, I think it is misleading to erect the relief of tensions into a primary value by approaching tensions in the context of an ideal state of affairs, abstracted from the actual political circumstances in which they occur. For, given the actual disharmony and incompatibility of national in-terests, aims, and desires—for which there is ample empirical evidence throughout the age of nationalism and down to the present time—the relief of tensions can be a good thing only if there is no moral basis for preferring one nation's ends to another's. If, on the other hand, there is a valid moral distinction among incom-patible national ends, then the absence of tensions should be taken as a sign of moral blindness or cowardice; and what is really required is an increase of tension, not a decrease.

Actually, of course, the clinical approach is neither morally blind nor cowardly. It simply avoids the moral problem by assuming that the desired absence of tensions and the assumed compatibility of national ends will occur in an ideal world in which all nations subordinate their particular interests, aims, and desires to transcendent moral principles. However, by abstracting tensions from their real political context and, in effect, elevating the elimination of tensions into an absolute value, the clinical approach obscures the real moral problem in international society. That problem is how to maximize liberal and humane values in a world of incompatible and even irreconcilable national ends—ends which are inevitably corrupted with national self-interest but among which moral choice is imperative.

THIRD ASSUMPTION

Consistent with its aversion to power politics and its abstraction of tensions from their actual political context, the clinical approach looks upon conflicts of national interest and power as merely the superficial symptoms of some socio-psychological malady and not as anything fundamentally inherent in the existing conditions of international society. The underlying assumption seems to be that, since inter-national conflicts result from tensions and since tensions occur within the mind, therefore if one can find the psychological roots of tensions, one may be able to modify or eliminate them and, accordingly, get rid of the international conflicts that can lead to war. Since international society is assumed to embody a naturally rational and harmonious relationship among its parts, it follows that deviations from this norm spring from some sort of remediable misbehavior or misunderstanding. There-fore, the clinical approach looks for the psychological roots of tensions in frustrations and maladjustments that interfere with rational behavior among nations and in biases and stereotypes that interfere with mutual understanding. It seeks to relieve tensions by ameliorating the offending frustrations and maladjustments and by correcting prejudices and stereotypes.

One cannot deny that frustrations and maladjustments may contribute in some measure toward creating unwarranted international tensions, but it is highly misleading to assume that the most important or profound source of tensions is the individual's immediate social and psychological environment rather than the international political environment itself. For it is quite impossible to explain actual situations of international tension or harmony by reference to the social and psychological environment alone but quite reasonable and necessary to explain them primarily by reference to the international environment, to its conflicts and incompatibilities of national purpose and power.

An obvious historical generalization illustrates this point: Between the same nations, harmony has often changed to animosity and tension, and animosity and tensions to harmony, in a manner which cannot be explained by any transformation of social or psychological influence not derived from political circumstances. Consider, for example, the change from harmony to tension in the United States' relations with Japan and Germany after the turn of the twentieth century or the change from tension to relative harmony between the United States and Great Britain in the same period.

It is similarly unrealistic to explain situations of international tension or harmony primarily by reference to ignorance, bias, or misunderstanding. Great powers with little knowledge or understanding of one another have enjoyed relations virtually free from tension, as in the case of the United States and Russia before the First World War. Some of the most serious tensions have occurred between nations which understood each other very well and even between nations which shared a similar cultural background and outlook. Thus the shifts in Anglo-American tension during the nineteenth century cannot reasonably be explained by shifts in cultural compatibility or in the level of knowledge and understanding between the two peoples. Mutual understanding may, in fact, be a major stimulus to animosity—among nations as among individuals. I believe that the present tension between the United States and the Soviet Union arises in large measure from a rational understanding on the part of both nations of the profound incompatibility of their aims, interests, and principles. As for national stereotypes and biases, I think that a careful historical investigation of the changes in one nation's attitude toward another nation would show that it is primarily political relations that determine the stereotypes and biases and not the other way around; and that, insofar as the stereotypes and biases cause international tension, it is largely because they coincide with genuine political incompatibilities.

If these historical generalizations are true, then it is quite misleading to assume that international tensions can be eliminated or curbed by direct treatment of alleged emotional or intellectual maladies presumed to hinder the normal, healthy functioning of the international order. Negative historical evidence is reinforced by sociological and psychological studies themselves, many of which strongly indicate, whether explicitly or not, that the circumstances responsible for relevant individual frustrations and maladjustments, biases and stereotypes, are so deeply embedded in the individual's whole social and cultural environment that it would be prohibitively difficult to alter or manipulate them even if this were otherwise an effective way of relieving international tensions.

Moreover, even if alteration and manipulation were easy, the chances of producing significant changes in international tensions by direct operation upon the social and psychological environment without operating upon the international political environment as well would seem to be extremely unpromising; for there is certainly a two-way relationship here, and, as has already been indicated, the international political environment is the decisive influence. For example, let us concede that international tensions result from a frustration-aggression process. Nevertheless, the direction of aggressiveness toward a particular nation in a particular form under particular circumstances derives primarily from the political relations among sovereign nations.

All these difficulties in altering tensions by direct, clinical treatment are quite apart from the virtually insurmountable practical obstacles in the way of tampering with the social and psychological environment of sovereign, independent nations, even if some impartial body of experts knew what to tamper with and had the technical ability to tamper with it.

Then does all this mean that sociological investigation of international tensions is a blind alley? I think it need not be. If the examination of the social and psychological roots of national behavior in a political vacuum has its limitations, so does the orthodox analysis of purely political relations between national governments. One of the virtues of the sociological approach to tensions is that it goes beneath the legal and institutional arrangements and the formal relations among governments and examines the attitudes, values, and motives which underlies them. Thus it serves to remind us that the study of international politics is a branch of the study of human nature.

An integrated sociological, psychological, and political approach to international tensions might explore fruitful and relatively unexploited fields of research. But an integrated approach requires more than an eclectic methodology. It requires a realistic conceptual framework of international relations, one that takes adequate account of the force of national egoism, the incompatibility of national ends, and the decisive influence of the political environment in which tensions occur. If this requirement were met, I think that sociologists might tell us a great deal more about how to live with international tensions than about how to get rid of them.

REFERENCES

Representative expressions of the clinical approach can be found in studies made in conjunction with UNESCO Tensions Project, which are surveyed by Otto Klineberg in the *International Social Science Bulletin* 1 (1949), nos. 1–2, 11–21, and Robert Angell in the *American Sociological Review* 15 (April, 1950), 282–87. See also, Hadley Cantril, ed., *Tensions That Cause Wars*, Urbana: University of Illinois, 1950; George W. Kisker, ed., *World Tension*, N. Y.: Prentice-Hall, 1951; Otto Klineberg, *Tensions Affecting International Understanding*, N. Y.: Social Science Research Council, 1950; Clyde Kluckhohn, *Mirror for Man*, N. Y.: Whittlesey House, 1949; David Krech and Richard S. Crutchfield, *Theory and Problems of Social Psychology*, N. Y.: McGraw-Hill, 1948.

27

A Model Building Approach to Searching for the Psychological Prerequisites of System Functioning

The following essay consists largely of an effort to describe and briefly suggest the empirical implications of a particularly comprehensive formulation for studying the relationship between a social structure and the psychological characteristics of the individuals who comprise it.

HAROLD D. LASSWELL'S CONCEPT OF DEMOCRATIC CHARACTER

Fred I. Greenstein

"Adequate assessment of the functioning of any social system," Inkeles comments, "or of the maintenance and change of particular patterns within it, may in important degree depend on knowledge of the particular personality traits, needs, structures, and adjustments of the participants in the system. . . . In the degree and quality of the fit between the modal personality patterns prevalent in the population and the role demands characteristic of the social system lies one of the keys to the system's functioning and one of the central points for the articulation of psychological and sociological theory." [1] Inkeles' statement appears in an essay which represents one of a number of recent efforts to reconceptualize the field of inquiry that hitherto has been known as "culture-and-personality" (or "national character") on a sufficiently clear basis to permit rigorous, systematic research. [2]

My purpose here is to provide a simple, clear exposition of one attempt to grapple with the problem of analyzing the connections between personality and social system—Harold D. Lasswell's delineation of the "democratic character." [3] This foray into exegesis may be justified on several grounds. Lasswell's thought is at once conceptually precise and comprehensive in scope. Therefore, his specific

This is a slightly edited version of an article that appeared in Italian as "Il concetto di carattere democratico in H. D. Lasswell," in *Quaderni di Sociologia,* 15 (1966), 185–95 and in English in *Journal of Politics,* 30 (1968), 696–709.

discussion of personality and democracy can be generalized to suggest a broad formula for analyzing interrelations between the distribution of individual psychological characteristics in societies and forms of societal organization. Second, the specific substantive hypotheses offered by Lasswell about democratic character are of interest. Indeed, Lasswell's substantive hypotheses, as well as his broader framework for thinking about personality and social structure, offer suggestions for bridging two bodies of writing between which there has been little fruitful interchange—writings on the social prerequisites of democracy (and non-democracy) and writings on the psychological prerequisites of these phenomena. Finally, this essay of Lasswell's, like many other of his writings, cries out for popularization. As presently stated, the argument is exceptionally elliptical, taking for granted or presenting in abbreviated form many points which must be expanded upon if they are to be clear to readers who are not familiar with Lasswell's rhetorical idiosyncracies and who are not steeped in the specialized terminology he has spun out over the years.

The exposition that follows fails to do justice to all of the subtleties of Lasswell's formulation. I also avoid placing Lasswell's discussion of the democratic character in the larger context of his work, except so far as it becomes necessary. And where possible, I paraphrase his special terminology with terms in more general usage.

The portions of Lasswell's discussion we shall be concerned with fall into four subdivisions, as do my remarks:

1. A model (that is, an analytic discussion in ideal-typical terms) of the key components of "the democratic community"—the social system in which the "democratic character" (which also is a model or ideal type) functions. (*Democratic Character,* pp. 473–80).

2. A definitional discussion of the concepts "personality" and "character," elucidating the various subcomponents of personality and the way they combine to form character. The definition of character, which makes it possible to use this term roughly as the layman does when he speaks of "strength" or "weakness" of character, provides the connection between the psychological and the social aspects of Lasswell's analysis. (*Democratic Character,* pp. 480–83).

3. A model of *democratic* character which, in effect, takes the empty boxes supplied by the definitional discussion of personality and character, filling them with hypothetical formulations about the psychological characteristics consistent with the behavioral requirements of the model of democracy. This filling of boxes, it should be added, is not merely the tautological linking of a model of a social system with a parallel model of the character structure consistent with the functioning of the system. In part, Lasswell's model of democratic character stems from sources independent of his conceptualization of the democratic community—*viz.,* general psychoanalytic theory and the psychoanalytically derived corpus of research on "authoritarianism." (*Democratic Character,* pp. 495–514).

4. Finally, in an abbreviated form upon which I shall expand somewhat, Lasswell states a number of hypotheses and general questions about the degree to which social actors who possess democratic characters are in fact necessary for the formation and maintenance of democratic communities.

A further and unquestionably integral aspect of Lasswell's essay, which I shall touch upon only briefly, stems from the unique marriage of theory and practice implied in his notion that the social sciences be thought of as "policy sciences." The policy science approach entails tying research on democratic character in with experimental social reform programs designed to achieve the state of affairs described in the model of the democratic community. (*Democratic Character,* pp. 514–25).

I. CHARACTERIZATION OF THE SOCIAL SYSTEM—THE "DEMOCRATIC COMMUNITY"

In his discussion of the "democratic community" Lasswell works with a conception of democracy which is far more comprehensive than that customarily used in political analysis—in effect, it is a broadly social conception of democracy, applying to all significant spheres of life, including, but not restricted to, the processes connected with government. Many political scientists[4] have argued, partly on grounds of analytic clarity, for confining the term "democracy" to the political. We, however, may pass over the question of whether Lasswell's conception of democracy is "useful," since our concern is more with his intellectual strategy than with the substance of his argument. The strategy is to make explicit the dimensions of the social system, as a necessary first step to determining what, if any, member personalities the system may demand in order to maintain itself. Further, the strategy calls for specifying the dimensions of the system in some operational detail, describing it in terms of the aspects of its members' behavior (including their patterns of belief) which form the system's defining characteristics.

Lasswell's democratic community, in overly brief summary, is a community in which values (a term broadly conceived to include all of the human desiderata) are widely shared among the citizenry rather than monopolized by a portion of the community. Furthermore, the members of the community believe that this *should* be the state of affairs. In much of his work, Lasswell makes use of the analytic convention of classifying the values sought by social actors into a limited number of categories, which for some purposes may be treated as exhaustive and mutually exclusive—categories such as power, rectitude, respect, well-being, and skill. His model of the democratic community employs this convention. For each of the values in Lasswell's classification a series of behavioral specifications are made; these serve as operational indicators of democracy. Thus, for example, the following considerations apply to the value of power in Lasswell's model of the democratic community: (1) citizens believe that there should be general participation in the making of decisions; (2) there in fact *is* widespread participation in decision-making; (3) officeholders may be criticized without fear of retaliation; (4) access to the resources which enable one to make political decisions is on the basis of merit; etc. Similar specifications are made for the other values.

While there is much more to be said in connection with Lasswell's model of democracy, and (as Lasswell makes clear) the model itself would require further specification and elaboration if it were to be used as a guide for research or action, the point to be made here is simply that an explicit model of role behavior in the social system is central in Lasswell's intellectual strategy.

II. DEFINITIONAL DISCUSSION OF PERSONALITY AND CHARACTER

Lasswell conceives of "personality" as a comprehensive term describing all the "enduring traits of the individual which are manifested in interpersonal relations."

"Character" is a more restricted term, referring to certain aspects of personality. Personality consists of three major systems, paralleling (though imperfectly) the structural view of personality that emerged in Freud's later works:

1. *Conscious processes,* including the aptitudes, skills and knowledge of the individual (ego).

2. *Unconscious drives* (id).

3. "The automatic and *unconscious restrictions and compulsions* modify the expression of basic drives" (superego, including "defenses" and "ego-ideals").

Underlying this threefold division is the familiar psychoanalytic conception of the tasks of the acting ego: the executive agency of the psyche deals simultaneously with primitive, unsocialized impulses of the id that seek expression, with super ego admonitions that these impulses not be expressed, and with the requirements of external reality.

The conscious ego processes include the *self-system,* which itself consists of three subsystems:

a. *Identifications.* The individual's conceptions of who he is and what larger collectivities (family, ethnic group, class, political party, nation) he is a part of.

b. *Preferences* (Lasswell's term is "demands"). The sum total of the individual's goals, moral judgments, and beliefs about what is desirable.

c. *Cognitive understandings.* Lasswell's term here is "expectations," but by this he refers to all "factual" assumptions about reality—assumptions about the past and present, as well as about the future. This term "character" is a crucial term in Lasswell's analysis and it refers to the self-system *along with* those aspects of the unconscious systems which serve to support or to undermine the conscious purposes of the self-system. In a strong character, the unconscious energies are in harmony with the individual's conscious purposes and serve to advance them. Unconscious aspects of the personality may, on the other hand, be at war with the conscious purposes of the self-system, in which case the individual is unintentionally hypocritical—his actions belie his protestations. Or the conflict between contradictory conscious and unconscious goals may be so energy-consuming that the individual is unable to muster sufficient effort to accomplish his purposes.

The nexus between character and social system is provided by the (by no means novel) formulation that the individual's behavioral response is determined by his inner predispositions and the external cues (rewards and punishments) of his environment. The external forces on the individual and his strength of character stand in a kind of a tug-of-war relationship to each other. Where environmental pressure toward a course of action is low (or where the environmental cues are ambiguous) even an individual of weak character may act in a way consistent with his conscious goals. Where the environment actually sanctions goal-consistent behavior, such behavior is likely *a fortiori.* Finally, and most important for the theory of democratic character, a strong character permits action consistent with one's goals *under adverse environmental circumstances.*

III. THE DEMOCRATIC CHARACTER

As I have already indicated, the formulation of democratic character brings together Lasswell's constructs of "character" and "democratic community," as well as drawing independently upon certain results of psychoanalytically oriented personality research. First we may consider the content of the three major components of the self-system in the democratic character.

1. Identifications

The democratic community, Lasswell hypothesizes, calls for participants who have the capacity to identify broadly and positively with others. Lasswell speaks of the ego which has this capacity as "open"—it is warm, expansive, and capable of transcending the cultural categories (e.g., class, caste, nationality) which divide men. Certain "saints" who were able to withstand the most extreme adversities of the jungle society of Nazi concentration camps without succumbing to hate of their captors provide an extreme illustration of how this particular personality feature might be so thoroughly grounded in character as to resist the most antithetical environment.

2. Preferences

It is at this point that Lasswell reaches back most explicitly to his model of the democratic community. This model, it will be remembered, specifies the values pursued by men in such a community and notes in some detail the pattern of social behavior involved in insuring that these values are shared widely in the community. The individual whose character is democratic *wants* to share values[5] —he wants to behave in the pattern specified by the model of democratic community. (The resemblances are considerable here to Fromm's conception of social character: that which makes us want to do what society requires us to do). Further, the democratic character is multivalued rather than obsessed with a single end to the exclusion of others. Lasswell illustrates the reason for making this stipulation with a series of sketches, after the manner of Theophrastus' *Characters,* of the social and psychological effects of *idées fixés*—exclusive value preoccupations. He describes, *inter alia,* the authoritarian power-seeker, the greedy wealth-seeker, the vain respect-seeker, etc. In each case the resulting behavior is inconsistent with maintenance of the democratic community. Fixation on coercive power —on imposing one's will on others—as an end in itself ("scope value," in Lasswell's terminology) is especially corrosive of democracy.[6]

3. Cognitive Understandings

In addition to the capacities discussed so far (expansiveness in identifications and democratic preferences) the conscious self of the democratic character also has a variety of cognitive requirements. The democrat's map of the factual landscape must be consistent with democratic behavior. The cognitive pattern Lasswell emphasizes is belief in the benevolent potentialities of mankind. If not in his conception of man's present behavior, at least in his notion of man's potential capacities, the democrat acts on assumptions that are more Rousseauesque than Hobbesian.

All of the foregoing attributes of the democratic self-system are, of course, to varying degrees fostered or impeded by the childhood and post-childhood socialization processes. As Lasswell notes, there evidently are some societies (e.g., the Dobu, as described by Fortune and Benedict)[7] in which the expectation is formed by quite early in childhood that man has quite the opposite of benevolent potentialities. There also are variations in child rearing practices (within as well as between societies) which preclude or foster expansive identifications and multi-valued preferences.

4. The Working of the Unconscious in the Democratic Character

Once the self-system has been indicated, the remaining element in Lasswell's definitional formulation of "character" is the degree of support or nonsupport received by the self-system from the unconscious components of the personality (the energy system). In the democratic character, not only are the conscious portions of the personality congruent with the behavioral requirements of the democratic community, but so also are the unconscious components. Here are some of the ways in which the disruptive effects of unconscious forces might produce deviation from this ideal.

Energies may be so divided—because, say, of id-superego conflict—that the ego is weakened and the individual fails to contribute to the democratic social system, or to resist anti-democratic encroachments.

The unconscious may betray the consciously democratic self-system by producing eruptions of undemocratic behavior, as in the vocal democrat who sabotages his ostensible goals by behaving in an authoritarian manner.[8]

The unconscious may subvert the democratic self-system by generating ego-defensive hostility, which demands some behavioral outlet. That is to say, the ostensible democrat may be benign in his conscious orientations to others, but at unconscious levels of psychic functioning, he may have aggressive and destructive impulses that tend to find their way indirectly into his interpersonal relations, thus sabotaging his conscious purposes.

One interesting question raised by Lasswell (and relevant to our discussion below about the diversity of personality types which can be utilized by a social system) is whether a character divided against itself may in fact contribute positively to the functioning of a democratic social system. In other words, can non-democratic or undemocratic characters serve democracy? In the simplest instance, cannot the destructive impulses generated by inner conflict be turned against the enemies of democracy? What about consciously democratic self-systems which have been formed in reaction to undemocratic impulses at the unconscious level— for example, the rebellious child of authoritarian parents? Lasswell advances two hypotheses: such personalities will have low capacities for constructive action because of the energy loss suffered by defensive personality operations; such compensatory personality formations will be less enduring than more direct ones (e.g., the apostate radical may later turn to religious orthodoxy).[9]

IV. HYPOTHESES ABOUT THE INTERCONNECTIONS OF CHARACTER AND SOCIAL COMMUNITY

Up to this point, largely as a result of the ideal-typical nature of his formulations, Lasswell's discussion of character and community has a beguilingly (or perhaps disturbingly) simple, bolt-in-nut quality. The community presents certain behavioral requirements; we insert the personality type most congruent with them. Then, briefly and tersely, Lasswell gives an indication of the complexity of analyzing personality and social structure in the "real world" (rather than the world of analytical models) and of his own agnosticism toward the particular hypotheses he has advanced (often in the deceptively pontifical form of declarative sentences):

When we study the equilibrium of factors sustaining or undermining the equilibrium of democratic activity in a specific community, or on the part of a person, during a selected period, it may sometimes appear that democratic conduct does not depend, to a significant degree, upon democratic character. It may seem, for example, that the giving of immediate indulgence to democratic responses, and the inflicting of immediate deprivation upon anti-democratic acts, will outweigh the factors making against democratic conduct. . . . The following questions are among those whose relevance will not diminish: To what extent is it possible to achieve democratic conduct in adult life without forming democratic character in early life? To what extent can democratic character formed in early life persist against anti-democratic environments in later life? In what measure can democratic conduct in later life form democratic character among adults (and the preadults influenced by them)? [10]

This condensed set of assertions and questions is sweeping in its implications for research. Lasswell, in effect, is making it clear that all of the analytic operations he has performed in delineating the democratic character and the democratic community are preliminaries to mounting a rich variety of investigations into processes of personality development and the interplay of personality and environmental situation. We might briefly sketch some of these research implications, especially as they apply to the second set of problems: to what degree does "democratic conduct . . . depend . . . upon democratic character?"

Very schematically, we can indicate in the illustrative figure that follows several further operations which could constitute the initial steps in a systematic attempt to ground Lasswell's formulation in a program of inquiry: first, a series of analyses of existing "real world" communities (box 1 in the figure) would be conducted, paralleling the distinctions made in Lasswell's model of the democratic community (box 1a of the figure). Secondly, there would be a series of analyses of the distribution of personality types in existing communities (box 2), paralleling the elements in the model of the democratic character (box 2a). The crucial problem then would be to fill in the shaded area from the analytic models of community and character, represented by the unshaded areas in the figure, on to the empirical considerations that arise in the shaded boxes in the figure, including still one more box, which I have numbered (3) and which consists of propositions about the relationship between community structure and character structure.

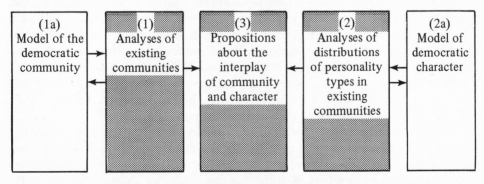

These, of course, are tasks of enormous proportions, and from what has been said so far (in Lasswell's essay and my gloss upon it) we can only dimly perceive what might be involved both in further conceptualization of the problem and in the development of appropriate research technology. Certain general clues to how we might proceed are contained in Inkeles' suggestion that social institutions can be usefully analyzed in terms of the psychological demands posed by the various roles which are central to their functioning and his suggestion that personality censuses be assembled of the distribution of psychological characteristics among role incumbents.[11] As I have tried to indicate, this also is the implication of Lasswell's own ideal typical formulation—his model of community is in terms of behavioral requirements and his model of character is so set up as to direct attention to the aspects of individual predisposition which would seem to be relevant to meeting or failing to meet the behavioral requirements.

At this point, we may profitably ask how necessary Lasswell's two models (or their equivalents) are to the entire enterprise of studying character and democracy, or, more generally, personality and society. Could we not, in the schematic summary above, dispense with (1a) and (2a)? This is a difficult question to answer, since we are dealing with a matter of research strategy rather than a hypothesis which might straightforwardly be tested by empirical means. My own impression is that the two models are, if not essential, at least highly productive and suggestive. They serve to make explicit the variables and potential relationships likely to be of interest in analyzing the "real world" interplay of personality and society ((1) and (2)). By clarifying the elements of analysis they serve to stimulate hypotheses. In terms of a further feature of Lasswell's own purposes, they are essential. Lasswell has long been concerned with the explicit articulation of social inquiry and social planning—i.e., with expanding the social scientist's role to include the tasks of clarifying policy alternatives and assisting in policy making by investigating the likely consequences of alternative courses of action. From this standpoint, it is absolutely essential to have models of the democratic community and character, because the models (subject, of course, to revision in the light of mature consideration based on reflection and inquiry) provide not only analytic clarity, but also tentative statements of the goals for social action. Thus, for Lasswell as a policy scientist, points (1a) and (2a) on our sketch serve as heuristic devices for examining (1) and (2). But the further significance of (1a) and (2a) is as directions in which existing arrangements (1) and (2) may move.

As I have said, an enormous program of conceptualization and inquiry is entailed in the central area of our chart. My purpose here is not to outline that program, but to suggest that it may be desirable. I shall, however, in conclusion, indicate a number of closely related questions that commonly are raised concerning any attempt to make general observations about the connections between distributions of individual psychological characteristics in a social system and system functioning. These are questions which would have to be dealt with in any satisfactory attempt to put Lasswell's formulation (or a modification thereof) into use. These questions cannot be answered here, but it is possible to note briefly some of the directions which efforts to answer them might take.

Critics of the existing literature on national character, culture and personality, modal personality and similar topics commonly point out that such writings presuppose a far too simple conception between the workings of social systems and the personalities of members of social systems. Shils, for example, in noting the lack of one-to-one correspondence between personality and social system, points out that all existing societies draw upon a diversity of personality types.[12] In an observation which has some bearing upon Lasswell's discussion of whether reaction formation is a sound basis for democratic character, Shils argues that non-democratic personalities may serve essential functions in democracies. Democracies presumably need dutiful subordinate bureaucrats. In addition, Shils, like Lasswell, notes that there are situational, as well as personality determinants of behavior. In particular, he points to the importance of social roles, noting that individuals of quite varying personal characteristics will often behave similarly (if not identically) in common roles. Personality has a significant effect on institutional functioning, Shils argues, mainly through the behavior of leaders who are relatively unrestricted by clear-cut role requirements, and in unstructured situations, where the roles of individual actors are ill-defined. Shils' implication that studying the psychological characteristics of leaders is more important than studying the psychological characteristics of followers parallels Dahl's discussion of consensus on the rules of the game of politics as a prerequisite for democratic political behavior. Confronted with the finding that such consensus evidently is not present in the electorate, Dahl concludes that it is among the politically active segments of the population—especially the politicians themselves—that consensus is necessary.[13]

These and related points are sometimes construed as obstacles to the study of personality and society. It is more useful to draw on such caveats and qualifications positively in order to conduct the study of personality and society at an appropriate level of sophistication. In terms of our operations (1a) and (2a)— the construction of ideal typical models of the democratic community and the democratic character—must be conducted in ways that accommodate the complexity of reality. Our models must seek to identify interaction of the sort Shils refers to: e.g., between the kind of role a political actor fills and the degree to which his personal proclivities come into play in his role behavior.

We might conceive, for example, of detailed structural analyses of entire societies—or, more practically, of key segments of societies, such as legislatures, private and public bureaucracies, and local communities. These analyses would carefully trace out the patterns of decision-making that are central to the functioning of such social organizations. Each role (or the major roles) in such decision-making structures would be analyzed in terms of the patterns of behavior which are consistent with varying states of the structure. Psychological consensus would be made of the types of individuals in the various roles and of the interaction of situational and personal factors in behavior. For any structure it might be found, for example, that a substantial range of personal characteristics is consistent with the effective performance of some roles (although certain personality characteristics might be inconsistent with these roles); other roles might demand a rather restricted range of personality characteristics.

We may briefly note the place in such an analysis of Lasswell's formulation of "character" as the self-system and its capacity to channel unconscious energies effectively. An illustration of the uses of this formulation can be taken from Lipset's argument that democracies are likely to be stable when competing political forces have independent bases of political power *and* there is widespread agreement on the legitimacy of opposition.[14] Both are necessary and neither sufficient, Lipset asserts, basing his reasoning on the experiences of trade unions and other groups in maintaining internal democracy. If an organization has competing groups, but competition is considered illegitimate, each group will attempt totally to eliminate the other, and the intensity of political conflict will preclude stable democracy. If, on the other hand, the political actors are ideologically devoted to democracy (that is, if they believe that competition is legitimate), they may nevertheless succumb to the temptation to eliminate the opposition, if certain structural requirements of democracy—i.e., independent bases of opposition power —are not present. Lasswell's notion of character makes it possible to expand upon Lipset's formulation, by predicting that *the more deeply rooted in character is the democratic commitment, the less necessary are the structural prerequisites of democracy.*[15]

V. SUMMARY AND CONCLUSION

At this point, a very rough sense may have been conveyed of how the formulation in Lasswell's "Democratic Character" can be extended to encompass and bridge the two largely unrelated bodies of writing on social prerequistes and psychological prerequistes of democracy, and it should also be evident that Lasswell's formulations are more generally relevant to the knotty problem of studying the connections between personality and society. One may, of course, be skeptical about the feasibility of global inquiries of the sort Lasswell's formulation suggests. Yet it should be emphasized that this does not eliminate the usefulness of the formulation. Such an overall conceptualization need not be thought of as the prospectus for a mammoth foundation grant in support of a long-term interdisciplinary investigation. Instead, we can consider the formulation as one of a number of possible overviews which enable us to organize existing knowledge and generate hypotheses, thus increasing the capacity of individual investigators to choose strategically among future topics of research.

In summary, the Lasswell formula for study of personality and society (as selectively described here) is: First, construct an ideal typical conception of the society in terms of behavioral requirements. Second, using an explicit conception of the major dimensions of personality and character, set up an additional ideal typical formulation (drawing on current knowledge of personality) of the psychological characteristics that would enable actors to operate such a social system. Then perform similar, but more complicated, empirical operations on the structure of whatever existing society or societies you propose to study, and on the psychological characteristics of its members. The notion of character as capacity to maintain a behavior pattern under adverse circumstances provides the connecting link between personality and society.

NOTES

[1] Alex Inkeles, "Sociology and Psychology," in Sigmund Koch, ed., *Psychology: A Study of a Science,* Vol. 6 (New York: McGraw-Hill, 1963), p. 320.

[2] For references to other attempts, see Robert A. LeVine, "Culture and Personality," in Bernard J. Siegel, ed., *Biennial Review of Anthropology: 1963* (Stanford: Stanford University Press, 1963), pp. 109–11. Also see Herbert Phillips, "The Relationship between Personality and Social Structure in a Siamese Peasant Community," *Human Organization,* Vol. 22 (1963), pp. 105–108.

[3] Harold D. Lasswell, "Democratic Character," in *Political Writings of Harold D. Lasswell* (Glencoe, Illinois: Free Press, 1951). Hereafter cited as "Democratic Character."

⁴ For example, Austin Ranney and Willmoore Kendall in their *Democracy and the American Party System* (New York: Harcourt, Brace, 1956).

⁵ I should repeat that to Lasswell the term "values" refers to any and all of the desired objects sought by men—to "that which is valued." This, of course, jars with much common usage in which the term has a subjective reference (in common usage one's values are, as it were, in one's head).

⁶ This portion of his argument is expanded at length in Lasswell's *Power and Personality* (New York: Norton, 1948).

⁷ Reo Fortune, *The Sorcerers of Dobu* (London: Routledge, 1932); Ruth Benedict, *Patterns of Culture* (Boston: Houghton Mifflin, 1934).

⁸ See the interpretation of Woodrow Wilson's personality in Alexander George and Julliette George, *Woodrow Wilson and Colonel House: A Personality Study* (New York: John Day, 1956).

⁹ We may assume that this, like other of Lasswell's suggestions, is capable of an accordian-like expansion. One might, for example, predict that some democrats-by-reaction formation would be hyperactive, rather than inactive, as a result of personality conflict. Moreover, a fuller elaboration of hypotheses on the democrat whose unconscious impulses are antidemocratic would deal with the sort of self-betrayal analyzed in the work cited in note 8.

¹⁰ "Democratic Character," p. 523.

¹¹ Inkeles, "Sociology and Psychology," p. 320.

¹² Edward Shils, "Authoritarianism: 'Right' and 'Left,'" in Richard Christie and Marie Jahoda, eds., *Studies in the Scope and Method of "The Authoritarian Personality"* (Glencoe, Illinois: The Free Press, 1954), pp. 24–49.

¹³ Robert A. Dahl, *Who Governs?* (New Haven: Yale University Press, 1961), chapters 27 and 28.

¹⁴ Seymour M. Lipset, et al., *Union Democracy* (Glencoe: Free Press, 1956).

¹⁵ Including various other of the structural prerequisites referred to in the literature— e.g., the "requirement" of a high level of economic development.

28

The Effects of Political Systems on Personality

In this brilliant chapter of *Psychopathology and Politics* (the single exception to our policy of not publishing chapters out of larger works), Lasswell generalizes his famous hypothesis that political movements "derive their vitality from the displacement of private affects upon public objects." He then discusses the probable modal tendencies in this displacement: "Political crises are complicated by the reactivation of specific primitive motives which were organized in the early experience of the individuals concerned." He goes on to give an explanation of the special reasons for the appeal of political symbols as objects for displaced affects, analyzing the process of political symbolization.

These connected descriptive sections of the chapter lead Lasswell into consideration of the efficacy of discussion as the technique for relieving the political tensions on which the politics of democratic states are based. Lasswell argues that discussion often "arouses a psychology of conflict which produces obstructive, fictitious, and irrelevant values." This exacerbates rather than relieves tensions. He goes on to contend:

The problem of politics is less to solve conflicts than to prevent them; less to serve as a safety valve for social protest than to apply social energy to the abolition of recurrent sources of strain in society. This redefinition of the problem of politics may be called the idea of preventive politics.

Lasswell's sketchy but daring proposal of how "the politics of prevention" is to be conducted anticipates his later writings proposing that social science knowledge be channelled into systematic efforts at social change—that the social sciences become "policy sciences." Lasswell presents a detailed sketch of the varied training appropriate for a practitioner of preventive politics—in anthropology, child development and psychoanalysis, for example. Finally, he suggests that inquiry into the roots of social problems should include an audit of the human consequences of existing social and political processes. In terms of the categories that organize this reader, his proposed audit reverses the logic of aggregation, asking, in effect, not only what consequences individual psychological orientations have for the aggregate, but how institutions affect the individuals who are aggregated into them. Lasswell's assumption is that such audits will be of profound normative significance, helping the members of societies to arrive at desired and desirable social policies.

This is the bare outline of a chapter rich in implications and in psycho-political simplifications. Lasswell's observations on familial and political authority, the psychic risks of radicalism, the dynamics of youth movements, war, riots, social panic at unpunished crime, and the sublimation of homosexual trends in politics are, in the hindsight of more than four decades of later theorizing and research, partly drastic oversimplifications of the sort that abounded in the days of pre-ego psychology writings on those topics. But even his oversimplifications suggest challenging hypotheses that have not been sufficiently explored. His reflections on the transfer of emotions about familial authority to political authority provide the most obvious example of a problem that has been insufficiently studied to this day.

THE POLITICS OF PREVENTION

Harold D. Lasswell

Political movements derive their vitality from the displacement of private affects upon public objects. The intensive scrutiny of the individual by psychopathological methods discloses the prime importance of hitherto neglected motives in the determination of political traits and beliefs. The adult who is studied at any given cross-section of his career is the product of a long and gradual development in the course of which many of his motivations fail to modify according to the demands of unfolding reality. The adult is left with an impulse life which is but partially integrated to adulthood. Primitive psychological structures continue in more or less disguised form to control his thought and effort.

The state is a symbol of authority, and as such is the legatee of attitudes which have been organized in the life of the individual within the intimate interpersonal sphere of the home and friendship group. At one phase of childhood development the wisdom and might of the physical symbol of authority, typically the father, is enormously exaggerated by the child. Eder traces the significance of this for the state in the following words:

> What occurs as we come more in touch with the external world, when the principle of reality develops, is the finding of surrogates for this ideal father. We discover that the parent is not all-wise, all-powerful, all-good, but we still need to find persons or abstractions upon which we can distribute these and similar attributes. By a process of fission these feelings are displaced on to and may be distributed among a number of surrogates. The surrogates may be persons, animals, things or abstract ideas; the headmaster, the dog, the rabbit, the Empire, the Aryan race, or any particular "ism."

He comments that it is upon this self-ideal that is formed the possibility of leadership, of leaders, and of the supreme leader, who is the one capable of doing all that the child once thought the physical father could do. The unconscious motivation is reflected in the sober formula of Blackstone, "The sovereign is not only incapable of doing wrong, but even of thinking wrong: he can never mean to do an improper thing; in him is no folly or weakness." [1]

There is very deep meaning in the phrase of Paley's that "a family contains the

Harold D. Lasswell, *Psychopathology and Politics* (Chicago: University of Chicago Press, 1930); reprinted in *Political Writings of Harold D. Lasswell* (Glencoe, Ill.: Free Press, 1951); and paperback edition of *Psychopathology and Politics,* with "Afterthoughts: Thirty Years Later" (New York: Viking Press, 1960). The paperback edition omits a bibliographical appendix.

rudiments of an empire." The family experience organizes very powerful drives in successive levels of integration, and these primitive attitudes are often called into play as the unobserved partners of rational reactions. To chose another extract from Eder:

> The behaviour of the elected or representative politician betrays many charac-teristics derived from the family. For example, during the time I filled a political job in Palestine I noticed in myself (and in my colleagues) the satisfaction it gave me to have secret information, knowledge which must on no account be imparted to others. Of course good reasons were always to be found: the people would misuse the informa-tion or it would depress them unduly and so on—pretty exactly the parent's atti-tude about imparting information, especially of a sexual nature, to the children. . . .
> At the back of secret diplomacy, and indeed the whole relationship of the official to the non-official, there rests this father-child affect. This also serves to explain the passion aroused in former days by any proposed extension of the franchise.

In the sphere of political dogma, unconscious conflicts play the same role which Theodore Reik discussed when he drew a parallel between religious dogma and obsessive ideas.[2] Dogma is a defensive reaction against doubt in the mind of the theorist, but against doubt of which he is unaware. The unconscious hatred of author-ity discloses itself in the endless capacity of the theorist to imagine new reasons for disbelief, and in his capacity to labor over trivialities, and to reduce his whole intel-lectual scheme to a logical absurdity. Sometimes this appears in a cryptic formula to which some sort of mysterious potency is ascribed, but which is hopelessly con-tradictory in so far as it possesses any manifest meaning. The celebrated doctrine of the unity of the trinity is an instance of such culminating nonsense. Words lose their rational reference points and become packed with unconscious symbolism of the ambivalent variety. The description of sovereignty found in Blackstone refers to nothing palpable, and functions principally as an incantation. Much solemn juridi-cal speculation, since so much of it is elaborated by obsessive thinkers, ends thus. Deep doubts about the self are displaced on to doubts about the world outside, and these doubts are sought to be allayed by ostentatious preoccupation with truth.

Defiance of authority is defiance of the introjected conscience, and involves a measure of self-punishment. We have seen how a powerful need for self-punish-ment is the stuff out of which martyrs and sensational failures are made; but of more general importance is the role of the sense of guilt in supporting the *status quo*. Deviation from accepted patterns becomes equivalent to sin, and the conscience visits discomforts upon those who dare to innovate. Radical ideas become "sacrile-gious" and "disloyal" in the view of the primitive conscience, for they tend to repre-sent more than a limited defiance of authority. They put the whole structure of the personality under strain. The childish conscience is easily intimidated into preserving order on slight provocation; it knows little of the capacity to consider the piecemeal reconstruction of values. "Radicalism" is felt as a challenge to the whole system of resistances which are binding down the illicit impulses of the personality, rather than as an opportunity for detached consideration of the relation of the self to the rest of reality. There is little boldness in political thinking which is not accompanied by an overdose of defiance, for even those who succeed in breaking through the intimidations of their infantile consciences must often succumb in some measure and "pay out." Much of the struggle, the fearful *Sturm und Drang* of the eman-cipated thinker, is his unconscious tribute to the exactions of the tribunal which he erected within himself at an early age, and which continues to treat innovation as *ipso facto* dangerous. The nonobsessive thinker is one who can coolly contemplate revisions in the relations of man to reality unperturbed by his antiquated conscience. Often readjustments of human affairs which are proposed are driven to absurdity because the original mind is compelled to transform his mere departure from the conventional into a defiance of conventionality. When one perceives the operation of this powerful self-punishment drive, and the secondary efforts to free one's self from feelings of guilt for defying the authorized order, it is possible to remain understandingly tolerant of the eccentricities of creative minds. To put the point a bit sharply, it is safe to say that the adult mind is only partly adult; the conscience may be four years old. The conscience, the introjected nursemaid, reacts undiscriminatingly to change, and construes it as rebellion.

The organization of motives which occurs in adolescence possesses direct significance for the interpretation of political interests.

The physical and mental storm of puberty and adolescence often culminates in the displacement of loves upon all humanity or a selected part of it, and in acts of devotion to the whole. It is here that the fundamental processes of loyalty are most clearly evident as they relate to public life. S. Bernfeld has written extensively on the psychology of the German youth movement. He comments on the very different lengths of puberty, and distinguishes between the physical and the psychological processes. When the psychological processes outlive the physical ones, certain characteristic reaction types arise. Dr. Bernfeld believes that the discrepant type prevails most characteristically in the youth movement, and he enumerates its characteristics. The interests of this group are turned toward "ideal" objects like politics, humanity, and art. The relation to these objects is productive, since the youth tries to produce a new form of politics or art. There is always a great deal of self-confidence present, or many symptoms of a repression that has failed. This is expressed in the high opinion of one's self and the low opinion one holds of his companions. An outstanding individual, the friend or master, is loved and revered. Often this love for a friend is extended to the whole group. The sexual components of the personality do not concentrate on finding objects, but in creating a new narcissistic situation. Bernfeld distinguishes this secondary narcissism from infantile narcissism on the ground that it is accompanied by deep depression reminiscent of melancholia. The reason lies in the formation of an ideal self that attracts a great part of the libido and enters into contrast with the real ego, a process which is particularly characteristic of the complex or discrepant type which he found in the youth movement.[3]

Political life seems to sublimate many homosexual trends. Politicians characteristically work together in little cliques and clubs, and many of them show marked difficulties in reaching a stable heterosexual adjustment. In military life, when men are thrown together under intimate conditions, the sublimations often break down and the homosexual drives find direct expression. A German general has gone so far as to declare that one reason why Germany lost the war was that the command was shot through with jealousies growing out of homosexual rivalry. Dr. K. G. Heimsoth has prepared a manuscript describing the role of homosexuality in the volunteer forces which continued to operate against the Poles and the communists after the war. In the case of certain leaders, at least, the reputation for overt homosexuality was no handicap; indeed, the reverse seemed to be true. Franz Alexander has suggested that one reason why homosexuality is viewed with contempt in modern life is the vague sense that complex cultural achievement depends on an inhibited sexuality, and that direct gratification tends to dissolve society into self-satisfied pairs and cliques. The observations of Heimsoth throw some doubt on the wisdom of this "vague sense." [4] The prominence of alcoholism and promiscuity among like-sex groups has often been observed, and both indulgences appear to be closely connected with homosexual impulses.[5]

Political crises are complicated by the concurrent reactivation of specific primitive impulses. War is the classical situation in which the elementary psychological structures are no longer held in subordination to complex reactions. The acts of cruelty and lust which are inseparably connected with war have disclosed vividly to all who care to see the narrow margin which separates the social from the asocial nature of man. The excesses of heroism and abnegation are alike primitive in their manifestations, and show that all the primitive psychological structures are not anti-social, but asocial, and may often function on behalf of human solidarity.[6]

Why does society become demoralized in the process of revolution? Why should a change in the political procedures of the community unleash such excesses in behavior? Reflection might lead one to suppose that since important decisions are in process of being made, calm deliberation would characterize society. Evidently a reactivating process is at work here; there is a regressive tendency to reawaken primitive sadism and lust. The conspicuous disproportionality between the problem and the behavior necessitates an explanation in such terms. Federn published a sketch of the psychology of revolution in his pamphlet *Die vaterlose Gesellschaft* in 1919. When the ruler falls, the unconscious triumphantly interprets this as a release from all constraint, and the individuals in the community who possess the least solidified personality structures are compulsively driven to acts of theft and violence. An interview which Federn gave to Edgar Ansel Mowrer in 1927 on the occasion of the Vienna riots reviews in somewhat popular form some of his conceptions.

Vienna, Austria, July 20.—"Distrust of father was the chief cause of the Vienna riot," said Paul Federn, onetime president of the Psychoanalytical Society. From a psychoanalytical standpoint all authority is the father, and this formerly for Austria was incorporated in the imposing figure of Emperor Franz Josef. But during the war the father deceived and maltreated his children, and only the material preoccupations of life and the joyous outburst when at the close of the war the old authority broke asunder prevented Austria from having a revolution then.

The state again built up the old ruling caste and began to hope for restoration, and therefore an abyss opened between Vienna, which under socialist leadership is trying to replace the traditional father principle by a new brotherhood, and the Austrian federal state, which had returned to a modified father idea. Trust in father is the child's deepest instinct. Vienna first respected the Austrian republic, but gradually this belief was undermined by the continual misery, by newspapers preaching fanaticism and by legal decisions which virtually destroyed the people's belief in the new father's justice.

Accordingly there occurred a spontaneous manifestation which unconsciously drove the disillusioned and furious children to destroy precisely those things on which the paternal authority seems to rest—namely, records and legal documents.

Why the peaceful Viennese should suddenly be transformed temporarily into mad beasts is also clear to the psychoanalysts. Had the police offered no resistance the crowd would soon have dispersed and no harm would have been done. But once the police fired blood flowed and the mob reacted savagely, responding to the ancient fear of castration by the father which is present in all of us unconsciously in the face of the punishing authority. Therefore, fear grew along with the violence, each increase leading to new violence and greater fear, as appeasement can only follow a complete outbreak and as the inhabitants were widely scattered in their houses it took three days before the last hatred could fully get out.

One further point can only be explained by psychoanalysis. The social democratic leaders are at heart revolutionary, but they did not wish this demonstration. They realized that revolution in little Austria today would be suicidal, and, therefore, at a given moment called out the republican guard with orders to interfere and prevent violence. The guard arrived much too late.

Why did not the leaders send out the guard at 6 a.m. when they knew the demonstration was beginning? They say they "forgot." This is a flagrant example of unconscious forgetfulness. The socialists forgot to take the only step which could have prevented something which they consciously disapproved, but unconsciously desired.

The Vienna riots were in the deepest sense a family row.[7]

Eder speculates about the unconscious factors in the well-known tendency of certain political alternatives to succeed one another in crude pendulum fashion.

I think it was Mr. Zangwill who once said that it is a principle of the British Constitution that the King can do no wrong and his ministers no right. That is to say, the ambivalency originally experienced toward the father is now split; the sentiment of disloyalty, etc., is displaced on to the King's ministers, or on to some of them, or on to the opposition. . . . Modern society has discovered the principle of election, and the vote to give expression to the hostile feelings toward their rulers. Psychoanalytically an election may be regarded as the sublimation of regicide (primary parricide) with the object of placing oneself on the throne; the vote is like a repeating decimal; the father is killed but never dies. The ministers are our substitutes for ourselves. Hence the political maxim of the swing of the pendulum.

Alexander and Staub have undertaken to explain the unconscious basis of the crisis which is produced in the community when criminals are permitted to go with no punishment or with light punishment. The study of personality genesis shows that the sublimation of primitive impulses is possible on the basis of a kind of primitive "social contract." The individual foregoes direct indulgences (which have the disadvantage of bringing him into conflict with authority), and substitutes more complex patterns of behavior on the tacit understanding that love and safety will thereby be insured. When another individual breaks over and gratifies his illicit impulses directly on a primitive level, the equilibrium of every personality is threatened. The conscious self perceives that it is possible to "get by," and this threatens the whole structure of sublimation. The superego tries to maintain order by directing energy against the ego, perhaps subjecting it to "pricks of conscience," for so much as entertaining the possibility of illicit gratification, and seeks to turn the ego toward activities which reduce temptation. This may involve the reconstruction of the environment by seeking to eliminate the "non-ideal" elements in it, and may be exemplified in the panicky demand for the annihilation of the outsider (who is a criminal) for the sake of keeping the chains on the insider (who is a criminal). Every criminal is a threat to the whole social order since he reinstates with more or less success an acute conflict within the lives of all members of society. The success of the superego depends upon imposing certain ways of interpreting reality upon the self. When reality grossly refuses to conform to the "ideal," the energies of the self are divided, and an acute crisis supervenes. The superego undertakes to reinforce its side of the contradictory ego trends by punishing the ego and by forcing the projection of this situation upon the outer world. Certain aspects of the outer world become "bad" because they are connected in private experience with the pangs inflicted by the taskmaster within, the conscience. A strong conscience may enforce this "distortion" of reality upon the self to such a degree that the self acts on quite fantastic assumptions about reality. These are most acutely manifested in such phenomena as confusion states, hallucinations, and delusions, all of which are forms of deformed reality. When reality becomes "ominous," violent efforts to change may appear futile, and safety is sought in physical flight, or in physical passivity and autistic preoccupation. Since our conceptions of reality are based upon little "first-hand" experience of the world about us, the superego usually has a rather easy time of it.

Political movements, then, derive their vitality from the displacement of private affects upon public objects, and political crises are complicated by the concurrent reactivation of specific primitive motives. Just how does it happen that the private and primitive drives find their way to political symbols? What are the circumstances which favor the selection of political targets of displacement?

Political life is carried on with symbols of the whole. Politics has to do with collective processes and public acts, and so intricate are these processes that with the best of intentions, it is extremely difficult to establish an unambiguous relationship between the symbols of the whole and the processes which they are presumed to designate. To the common run of mankind, the reference points of political symbols are remote from daily experience, though they are rendered familiar through constant reiteration. This ambiguity of reference, combined with universality of use, renders the words which signify parties, classes, nations, institutions, policies, and modes of political participation readily available for the displacement of private affects. The manifest, rational differences of opinion become complicated by the play of private motives until the symbol is nothing but a focus for the cumulation of irrelevancies. Since the dialectic of politics is conducted in terms of the whole, the private motives are readily rationalized in terms of collective advantage.

Politics, moreover, is the sphere of conflict, and brings out all the vanity and venom, the narcissism and aggression, of the contending parties. It is becoming something of a commonplace that politics is the arena of the irrational. But a more accurate description would be that politics is the process by which the irrational bases of society are brought out into the open. So long as the moral order functions with spontaneous smoothness, there is no questioning the justification of prevailing values. But when the moral order has been devalued and called into question, a sincere and general effort may be made to find a reflectively defensible solution of the resulting conflict. Politics seems to be irrational because it is the only phase of collective life in which society tries to be rational. Its very existence shows that the moral order, with all its irrational and non-rational sanctions, is no longer accepted without a challenge. A political difference is the outcome of a moral crisis, and it terminates in a new moral consensus. Politics is the transition between one unchallenged consensus and the next. It begins in conflict and eventuates in a solution. But the solution is not the "rationally best" solution, but the emotionally satisfactory one. The rational and dialectical phases of politics are subsidiary to the process of redefining an emotional consensus.

Although the dynamic of politics is to be sought in the tension level of the individuals in society, it is to be taken for granted that all individual tensions are not removed by political symbolization and exertion. When Y hits a foreman in the jaw whom he imagines has insulted him, Y is relieving his tensions. But if the act is construed by him as a personal affair with the foreman, the act is not political. Political acts are joint acts; they depend upon emotional bonds.

Now people who act together get emotionally bound together. This process of becoming emotionally bound is dependent on no conscious process. Freud said that he was made clearly aware of the emotional factor in human relations by observing that those who work together extend their contact to dining and relaxing together. Those with whom we work are endowed with rich meanings on the basis of our past experience with human beings. Since all of our motives are going concerns within the personality, our libido is more or less concentrated upon those with whom we come in touch. This reinforces the perception of similarities and supplies the dynamic for the identification process. Even the negative identification is a tribute to the extent to which the affective resources of the personality become mobilized in human contact.

People who are emotionally bound together are not yet involved in a political movement. Politics begins when they achieve a symbolic definition of themselves in relation to demands upon the world. The pre-political phase of the labor movement as sketched by Nexo in his *Pelle the Conqueror* is an able characterization of what the facts may be. The workers had plenty of grievances against their employers, but individuals took it out in sporadic acts of violence and in frequent debauchery. It was not until a new "set" of mind was achieved with the appearance of socialist symbols, and their adoption, that the tension found an outlet in political form. When J hits a foreman on the jaw because the foreman swore at him, J is not acting for the working classes; but after J becomes a socialist, his acts are symbolically significant of the expanded personality which he possesses. Acts cease to be merely private acts; they have become related to remote social objects. The conception of the self has new points of reference and points of reference which interlock with those of others.

It is of the utmost importance to political science to examine in detail, not only the factors which contribute to the raising and lowering of the tension level, but the processes of symbolization. In regard to the former aspect of the problem, data will have to be taken from specialists of many kinds, but in regard to the latter problem, the student can come into ready contact with the raw material. The stock in trade of realistic politics is the analysis of the history of "pressure groups," ranging from such associations as the Fabian Society through political parties to conspirative organizations. What are the conditions under which the idea is itself invented, and what are the conditions of its propagation? That is to say: What are the laws of symbolization in political activity?

I wish to call attention to certain possibilities. Several social movements will be found which represent a desire on the part of an intimate circle to perpetuate their relationship at the expense of society. It is worth remembering that Loyola and the other young men who founded the Jesuits were in long friendly relationship before they hit upon their famous project. Not only that: they were anxious to remain in some sort of personal relation through life, and they invented many expedients before they hit on the final one. What we had here was a friendly group which desired to preserve their personal connections before they knew how they could actually do it. It is less true to say that institutions are the lengthened shadow of a great man than that they are the residue of a friendly few.

Other social movements will be found to have adopted their project from a lone thinker with whom they have no direct connection. The process here is that one member of the group, with whom the others are identified, is impressed by the scheme and interprets and defends it to the others. He gets a hearing because of his emotional claim on the others, and he may whip the doubters and waverers into line by wheedling or by threatening to withdraw affection.

The formation of a radiating nucleus for an idea is especially common among adolescents, and among those who function best in single-sex groups. Thrasher has described gangs which had a mission in his book on *The Gang,* and the literature of youth study is full of instances of two's, three's and quartettes which have sworn undying fealty to one another, and to a project of social reform. When the idea is embraced later in life it not infrequently appears among those who have shown pronounced evidence of emotional maladjustment. Much social and political life is a symptom of the delayed adolescence of its propagators, which is, of course, no necessary criticism of its content.

The psychology of personal, oratorical, and printed persuasion by means of which support is won for particular symbols has yet to be written. William I. Thomas long ago commented on the quasi-sexual approach of the revivalist to the audience. Some orators are of an intimate, sympathetic, pleading type, and resemble the attempts made by some males to overcome the shyness of the female. Other orators fit into the feared yet revered father pattern; others are clowns who amuse by releasing much repressed material; others address the socially adjusted and disciplined level of the personality. Thus the relationship between the speaker and the audience has its powerful emotional aspects, which are not yet adequately explored. There are some who excel in face-to-face relations, but who make a poor showing out on the platform.

The processes of symbolization can be studied with particular ease when widespread and disturbing changes occur in the life situation of many members of society. Famine, pestilence, unemployment, high living costs, and a catalogue of other disturbances may simultaneously produce adjustment problems for many people. One of the first results is to release affects from their previous objects and to create a state of susceptibility to proposals. All sorts of symbols are ready, or readily invented, to refix the mobile affects. "Take it to the Lord in prayer," "Vote socialist," "Down with the Jews," "Restore pep with pepsin," "Try your luck on the horses"—all sorts of alternatives become available. The prescriptions are tied up with diagnoses, and the diagnoses in turn imply prescriptions. "A sinful world," "Wall Street," "a collapse in the foreign market"—all sorts of diagnoses float about, steadily defining and redefining the situation for the individuals affected. Political symbols must compete with symbols from every sphere of life, and an interesting inquiry could be made into the relative polarizing power of political and other forms of social symbolism. Certainly the modern world expects to fire the health commissioner rather than burn a witch when the plague breaks out.

The competition among symbols to serve as foci of concentration for the aroused emotions of the community leads to the survival of a small number of master-symbols. The mobilization of the community for action demands economy in the terms in which objectives are put. The agitation for the control of the liquor traffic passed through many phases in America until finally legal prohibition became the chief dividing line. To prohibit or not to prohibit grew into the overmastering dichotomy of public thought.

Symbolization thus necessitates dichotomization. The program of social action must be couched in "yes" and "no" form if decision is to be possible. The problem of he who would manipulate the concentration of affect about a particular symbol is to reinforce its competitive power by leading as many elements as possible in society to read their private meanings into it. This reinforcement and facilitation of the symbol involves the use of men of prestige in its advocacy, the assimilation of special economic and other group aims, and the invention of appeals to unconscious drives. Propaganda on behalf of a symbol can become a powerful factor in social development because of the flexibility in the displacement of emotion from one set of symbols to another. There is always a rather considerable reservoir of unrest and discontent in society, and there is nothing absolutely fixed and predestined about the particular symbol which will have attracting power.

The analysis of motives which are unconscious for most people, though widespread, gives the propagandist a clue to certain nearly universal forms of appeal. The moving pictures which have been produced by the communist government in Russia are often remarkable examples of the use of symbols which not only have their conscious affective dimension, but which mobilize deep unconscious impulses. In one film, for instance, it is the mother who suffers under tsarism and fans the flames of revolt. Analysis has disclosed the general, and presumably universal, meaning of the attachment to the land. The boy child's wish for union with the mother, for all-embracing care and protection, undergoes some measure of sublimation in social life. Eder remarks that it finds expression in attachment to the earth, the land, the mother country, home. The *Heimweh* of the Swiss, the pious Jew's desire for burial in Palestine, and a host of similar manifestations are instances of this emotional tie whose significance for state loyalty is large.

At first sight it might appear questionable that political science can ever profit from the disclosure of motives which are supposed to operate in the unconscious of every human being. If these motives are equally operative, how can they throw any light on differences in political behavior? And are we not able to point to conditions of a more localized and definite nature which suitably explain why the Republican party loses out when the farmer loses his crops? Or why there is revolution in 1918 and not in 1925?

The mere fact that motives are more or less universal does not mean that they are always activated with the same intensity. They may block one another, until some exciting condition disturbs the adjustment and releases stores of energy. Indeed, the exploration of unconscious motivation lays the basis for the understanding of the well-known disproportionality between responses and immediate stimuli, a disproportionality which has been the subject of much puzzled and satiric comment. Farmers do vote against the Republicans when the crops fail through adverse weather conditions, although reflection would tend to minimize the possibility that the party in power exercises much authority over the weather. Oversights in personal relations which seem very slight do actually give rise to huge affective reactions. The clue to the magnitude of this notorious disproportionality is to be found in the nature of the deeper (earlier) psychological structures of the individual. By the intensive analysis of representative people, it is possible to obtain clues to the nature of these "unseen forces," and to devise ways and means of dealing with them for the accomplishment of social purposes.

Modern democratic society is accustomed to the settlement of differences in discussion and in voting. This is a special form of politics, for differences may also be settled with a minimum of discussion and a maximum of coercion. In its modern manifestation, democracy and representative government have enthroned "government by discussion," that is, "government by public opinion." President Lowell some time ago pointed out that public opinion could only be said to exist where constitutional principles were agreed upon. Differences must be treated as defined within an area of agreement. Democratic and representative institutions presuppose the existence of the public which is made up of all those who follow affairs and expect to determine policy in discussion and by measures short of coercion. The public has a common focus of attention, a consensus on constitutional principles, and a zone of tolerance for conflicting demands respecting social policy.

When debate is admissible, some standards of right are tacitly admitted to be uncertain. The zone of the debatable is not fixed and immutable, but flexible and shifting. Questions rise and debate proceeds; and presently the resulting solution is no longer discussible. It has become sanctified by all the sentiments which buttress the moral order, and any challenge is met by the unanimous and spontaneous action of the community in its defense. In the presence of a challenge, the public may be dissolved into a crowd, by which is meant a group whose members are emotionally aroused and intolerant of dissent.

What light does the study of the genesis of personality throw on the factors which determine which symbols are debatable? What is the mechanism of the process by which the moral patterns are broken up, discussed, and eventually reincorporated in more or less modified form into the moral consensus of the community?

The growth of emotional bonds among individuals of diverse cultural and personal traits is the most powerful solvent of the moral order. A valuable treatise could be constructed on the theme, "Friendship versus Morality." It is well known that governments are continually handicapped in the impersonal application of a rule by the play of personal loyalties. Robert E. Park has stressed the importance of curiosity in the field of interracial relations. In no small measure this is very primitive curiosity about the sexual structure and behavior of odd-looking folks. When personal ties are built up, exceptions are made in favor of the friend; what, indeed, is the constitution among friends?

The mechanism is clear by which issues once settled are presently nondebatable. Growing individuals incorporate the end result into their own personalities through the process of identification and introjection. Once a part of the superego of the rising generation, the moral consensus is complete. Where no dissent is tolerated and dialectic is impossible, we are dealing with a superego phenomenon. Certain symbols are sacrosanct, and aspersions upon them produce the crowd mind and not the public.[8]

Even this brief sketch of political symbolization has shown ample grounds for concluding that political demands probably bear but a limited relevance to social needs. The political symbol becomes ladened with the residue of successive positive and negative identifications, and with the emotional charge of displaced private motives. This accumulation of irrelevancy usually signifies that tension exists in the lives of many people, and it may possess a diagnostic value to the objective investigator. The individual who is sorely divided against himself may seek peace by unifying himself against an outsider. This is the well-known "peacefulness of being at war." But the permanent removal of the tensions of the personality may depend upon the reconstruction of the individual's view of the world, and not upon belligerent crusades to change the world.

The democratic state depends upon the technique of discussion to relieve the strains of adjustment to a changing world. If the analysis of the individual discloses the probable irrelevance of what the person demands to what he needs (i.e., to that which will produce a permanent relief of strain), serious doubt is cast upon the efficacy of the technique of discussion as a means of handling social problems.

The premise of democracy is that each man is the best judge of his own interest, and that all whose interests are affected should be consulted in the determination of policy. Thus the procedure of a democratic society is to clear the way to the presentation of various demands by interested parties, leaving the coast clear for bargain and compromise, or for creative invention and integration.

The findings of personality research show that the individual is a poor judge of his own interest. The individual who chooses a political policy as a symbol of his wants is usually trying to relieve his own disorders by irrelevant palliatives. An examination of the total state of the person will frequently show that his theory of his own interests is far removed from the course of procedure which will give him a happy and well-adjusted life. Human behavior toward remote social objects, familiarity with which is beyond the personal experience of but a few, is especially likely to be a symptomatic rather than a healthy and reflective adjustment.

In a sense, politics proceeds by the creation of fictitious values. The person who is solicited to testify to his own interest is stimulated by the problem put to him to commit himself. The terms in which he couches his own interest vary according to a multitude of factors, but whatever the conditioning influences may be, the resulting theory of his interest becomes invested with his own narcissism. The political symbol is presumably an instrumental makeshift toward the advancement of the other values of the personality; but it very quickly ceases to be an instrumental value, and becomes a terminal value, no longer the servant but the coequal, or indeed the master. Thus the human animal distinguishes himself by his infinite capacity for making ends of his means.

It should not be hastily assumed that because a particular set of controversies passes out of the public mind that the implied problems were solved in any fundamental sense. Quite often, the solution is a magical solution which changes nothing in the conditions affecting the tension level of the community, and which merely permits the community to distract its attention to another set of equally irrelevant symbols. The number of statutes which pass the legislature, or the number of decrees which are handed down by the executive, but which change nothing in the permanent practices of society, is a rough index of the role of magic in politics.

In some measure, of course, discontent is relieved in the very process of agitating, discussing, and legislating about social changes which in the end are not substantially affected. Political symbolization has its catharsis function, and consumes the energies which are released by the maladaptations of individuals to one another.

But discussion often leads to modifications in social practice which complicate social problems. About all that can be said for various punitive measures resorted to by the community is that they have presently broken down and ceased to continue the damage which they began to inflict on society.

Generalizing broadly, political methods have involved the manipulation of symbols, goods, and violence, as in propaganda, bribery, and assassination. It is common to act on the assumption that they are to be applied in the settlement of conflicting demands, and not in the obviation of conflict. In so far as they rest upon a philosophy, they identify the problem of politics with the problem of coping with differences which are sharply drawn.

The identification of the field of politics with the field of battle, whether the theater be the frontier or the forum, has produced an unfortunate warp in the minds of those who manage affairs, or those who simply think about the management of affairs. The contribution of politics has been thought to be in the elaboration of the methods by which conflicts are resolved. This has produced a vast diversion of energy toward the study of the formal etiquette of government. In some vague way, the problem of politics is the advancement of the good life, but this is at once assumed to depend upon the modification of the mechanisms of government. Democratic theorists in particular have hastily assumed that social harmony depends upon discussion, and that discussion depends upon the formal consultation of all those affected by social policies.

The time has come to abandon the assumption that the problem of politics is the problem of promoting discussion among all the interests concerned in a given problem. Discussion frequently complicates social difficulties, for the discussion by far-flung interests arouses a psychology of conflict which produces obstructive, fictitious, and irrelevant values. The problem of politics is less to solve conflicts than to prevent them; less to serve as a safety valve for social protest than to apply social energy to the abolition of recurrent sources of strain in society.

This redefinition of the problem of politics may be called the idea of preventive politics. The politics of prevention draws attention squarely to the central problem of reducing the level of strain and maladaptation in society. In some measure, it will proceed by encouraging discussion among all those who are affected by social policy, but this will be no iron-clad rule. In some measure, it will proceed by improving the machinery of settling disputes, but this will be subordinated to a comprehensive program, and no longer treated as an especially desirable mode of handling the situation.

The recognition that people are poor judges of their own interest is often supposed to lead to the conclusion that a dictator is essential. But no student of individual psychology can fail to share the conviction of Kempf that "Society is *not* safe . . . when it is forced to follow the dictations of one individual, of one autonomic apparatus, no matter how splendidly and altruistically it may be conditioned." Our thinking has too long been misled by the threadbare terminology of democracy versus dictatorship, of democracy versus aristocracy. Our problem is to be ruled by the truth about the conditions of harmonious human relations, and the discovery of the truth is an object of specialized research; it is no monopoly of people as people, or of the ruler as ruler. As our devices of accurate ascertainment are invented and spread, they are explained and applied by many individuals inside the social order. Knowledge of this kind is a slow and laborious accumulation.

The politics of prevention does not depend upon a series of changes in the organization of government. It depends upon a reorientation in the minds of those who think about society around the central problems: What are the principal factors which modify the tension level of the community? What is the specific relevance of a proposed line of action to the temporary and permanent modification of the tension level?

The politics of prevention will insist upon a rigorous audit of the human consequences of prevailing political practices. How does politics affect politicians? One way to consider the human value of social action is to see what that form of social action does to the actors. When a judge has been on the bench thirty years, what manner of man has he become? When an agitator has been agitating for thirty years, what has happened to him? How do different kinds of political administrators compare with doctors, musicians, and scientists? Such a set of inquiries would presuppose that we were able to ascertain the traits with which the various individuals began to practice their role in society. Were we able to show what certain lines of human endeavor did to the same reactive type, we would lay the foundation for a profound change in society's esteem for various occupations.

Any audit of the human significance of politics would have to press far beyond the narrow circle of professional politicians. Crises like wars, revolutions, and elections enter the lives of people in far reaching ways. The effect of crises on mental attitude is an important and uncertain field. Thus it is reported that during the rebellion of 1745–46 in Scotland there was little hysteria (in the technical pathological sense). The same was true of the French Revolution and of the Irish Rebellion. Rush reported on his book *On the Influence of the American Revolution on the Human Body* that many hysterical women were "restored to perfect health by the events of the time." Havelock Ellis, who cites these instances, comments that "in such cases the emotional tension is given an opportunity for explosion in new and impersonal channels, and the chain of morbid personal emotions is broken." [9]

The physical consequences of political symbolism may be made the topic of investigation from this point of view:

> When the affect can not acquire what it needs, uncomfortable tensions or anxiety (fear) are felt, and the use of the symbol or fetish, relieving this anxiety, has a marked physiological value in that it prevents the adrenal, thyroid, circulatory, hepatic and pulmonic compensatory strivings from becoming excessive. [10]

Political programs will continually demand reconsideration in the light of the factors which current research discloses as bearing upon the tension level. Franz Alexander recently drew attention to the strains produced in modern civilization by the growing sphere of purposive action. He summed up the facts in the process of civilized development in the following way: "Human expressions of instinct are subject to a continual tendency to rationalization, that is, they develop more and more from playful, uncoordinated, purely pleasure efforts into purposive actions." The "discomfort of civilization" of which Freud recently wrote in the *Unbehagen der Kultur* is characteristic of the rationalized cultures with which we are acquainted. Life is poor in libidinal gratifications of the primitive kind which the peasant, who is in close touch with elementary things, is in a position to enjoy. [11] Modern life furnishes irrational outlets in the moving picture and in sensational crime news. But it may be that other means of relieving the strain of modern living can be invented which will have fewer drawbacks.

Preventive politics will search for the definite assessment, then, of cultural patterns in terms of their human consequences. Some of these human results will be deplored as "pathological," while others will be welcomed as "healthy." One complicating factor is that valuable contributions to culture are often made by men who are in other respects pathological. Many pathological persons are constrained by their personal difficulties to displace more or less successfully upon remote problems, and to achieve valuable contributions to knowledge and social policy. [12] Of course the notion of the pathological is itself full of ambiguities. The individual who is subject to epileptic seizures may be considered in one culture not a subnormal and diseased person, but a supernormal person. Indeed, it may be said that society depends upon a certain amount of pathology, in the sense that society does not encourage the free criticism of social life, but establishes taboos upon reflective thinking about its own presuppositions. If the individual is pathological to the extent that he is unable to contemplate any fact with equanimity, and to elaborate impulse through the processes of thought, it is obvious that society does much to nurture disease. This leads to the apparent paradox that successful social adjustment consists in contracting the current diseases. If "health" merely means a statistical report upon the "average," the scrutiny of the individual ceases to carry much meaning for the modification of social patterns. But if "health" means something more than "average," the intensive study of individuals gives us a vantage ground for the revaluation of the human consequences of cultural patterns, and the criticism of these patterns. [13]

If the politics of prevention spreads in society, a different type of education will become necessary for those who administer society or think about it. This education will start from the proposition that it takes longer to train a good social scientists than it takes to train a good physical scientist.[14] The social administrator and social scientist must be brought into direct contact with his material in its most varied manifestations. He must mix with rich and poor, with savage and civilized, with sick and well, with old and young. His contacts must be primary and not exclusively secondary. He must have an opportunity for prolonged self-scrutiny by the best-developed methods of personality study, and he must laboriously achieve a capacity to deal objectively with himself and with all others in human society.

This complicated experience is necessary since our scale of values is less the outcome of our dialectical than of our other experiences in life. Values change more by the unconscious redefinition of meaning than by rational analysis. Every contact and every procedure which discloses new facts has its repercussions upon the matrix of partially verbalized experience, which is the seeding ground of conscious ideas.

One peculiarity of the problem of the social scientist is that he must establish personal contact with his material. The physical scientist who works in a laboratory spends more time adjusting his machinery than in making his observations, and the social scientist who works in the field must spend more time establishing contacts than in noting and reporting observations. What the instrumentation technique is to the physicist, the cultivation of favorable human points of vantage is for most social scientists. This means that the student of society, as well as the manager of social relations, must acquire the technique of social intercourse in unusual degree, unless he is to suffer from serious handicaps, and his training must be directed with this in mind.

The experience of the administrator-investigator must include some definite familiarity with all the elements which bear importantly upon the traits and interests of the individual. This means that he must have the most relevant material brought to his attention from the fields of psychology, psychopathology, physiology, medicine, and social science. Since our institutions of higher learning are poorly organized at the present time to handle this program, thorough curricular reconstructions will be indispensable.[15]

What has been said in this chapter may be passed in brief review. Political movements derive their vitality from the displacement of private affects upon public objects. Political crises are complicated by the concurrent reactivation of specific primitive motives which were organized in the early experience of the individuals concerned. Political symbols are particularly adapted to serve as targets for displaced affect because of their ambiguity of reference, in relation to individual experience, and because of their general circulation. Although the dynamic of politics is the tension level of individuals, all tension does not produce political acts. Nor do all emotional bonds lead to political action. Political acts depend upon the symbolization of the discontent of the individual in terms of a more inclusive self which champions a set of demands for social action.

Political demands are of limited relevance to the changes which will produce permanent reductions in the tension level of society. The political methods of coercion, exhortation, and discussion assume that the role of politics is to solve conflicts when they have happened. The ideal of a politics of prevention is to obviate conflict by the definite reduction of the tension level of society by effective methods, of which discussion will be but one. The preventive point of view insists upon a continuing audit of the human consequences of social acts, and especially of political acts. The achievement of the ideal of preventive politics depends less upon changes in social organization than upon improving the methods and the education of social administrators and social scientists.

The preventive politics of the future will be intimately allied to general medicine, psychopathology, physiological psychology, and related disciplines. Its practitioners will gradually win respect in society among puzzled people who feel their responsibilities and who respect objective findings. A comprehensive functional conception of political life will state problems of investigation, and keep receptive the minds of those who reflect at length upon the state.

NOTES

[1] See the chapter on "Psycho-analysis in Relation to Politics" in *Social Aspects of Psycho-Analysis* (London, 1924).

[2] "Dogma und Zwangsidee," *Imago* XIII (1927), 247–382.

[3] Succinctly described in "Über eine typische Form der männlichen pubertät," *Imago* IX (1923), 169 ff. On the homoerotic elements, see Hans Blüher, *Die deutsche Wandervogelbewegung als erotisches Phänomen,* and his more elaborate volume cited in the Bibliography.

[4] I was kindly permitted to see this manuscript which is not yet published.

[5] See Sandor Rado, "Die psychischen Wirkungen der Rauschgifte," *Internationale Zeitscrift für Psychoanalyse* XII (1926), 540–56; A. Keilholz, "Analyseversuch bei Delirium Tremens," *ibid.,* pp. 478–92; and Stekel's volumes.

[6] For a sketch of the unconscious processes involved in warfare, see S. Freud, "Zeitgemässes über Krieg und Tod," *Imago* IV (1915–16), 1–21; Ernest Jones, *Essays in Psycho-Analysis*; William A. White, *Thoughts of a Psychiatrist on the War and After.*

[7] *Chicago Daily News,* July 20, 1927.

[8] The distinction between the crowd and the public is best developed in the writings of Robert E. Park. Freud undertook to explain the crowd on the theory that an emotional bond was forged by identification of the individual with a leader, and by a process of partial identification through the perception of this similar relationship to the leader. He set out from the observation that when people are interacting upon one another they behave differently than when they are alone. The loss of individuality represents a relinquishment of narcissistic gratification which can only come when libido is directed outward toward objects. Freud's theory applies strictly to a special case of crowd behavior only. Crowd states may also arise when interlocking partial identifications occur on the perception of a common threat. Crowd behavior often arises before anybody assumes a "leading" role, and rival leaders are "selected" by the crowd.

[9] *Studies in the Psychology of Sex* I, 231.

[10] Kempf, *Psychopathology,* p. 704.

[11] Franz Alexander, "Mental Hygiene and Criminology," *First International Congress on Mental Hygiene.*

[12] For an appreciation of the role of the pathological person in society see Wilhelm Lange-Eichbaum, *Genie-Irrsinn, und Ruhm,* and Karl Birnbaum, *Grundzüge der Kulturpsychopathologie.*

[13] Something like this is no doubt the thought in Trigant Burrow's very obscure book on *The Social Basis of Consciousness.*

[14] This point was forcibly made by Beardsley Ruml in his speech at the dedication of the Social Science Research Building at the University of Chicago. See *The New Social Science,* edited by Leonard D. White, pp. 99–111.

[15] I have suggested that those who write human biography should be included among those who require this comprehensive training. See "The Scientific Study of Human Biography," *Scientific Monthly,* January, 1930.

Author Index

Subject Index